ALSO BY TAYLOR BRANCH

At Canaan's Edge: America in the King Years, 1965–68

Pillar of Fire: America in the King Years, 1963–65

Parting the Waters: America in the King Years, 1954–63

Labyrinth (with Eugene M. Propper)

The Empire Blues

Second Wind (with Bill Russell)

Blowing the Whistle: Dissent in the Public Interest
(with Charles Peters)

TAYLOR
BRANCH

THE

CLINTON
TAPES

★

Wrestling History

with the

President

Simon & Schuster

New York   London   Toronto   Sydney

 Simon & Schuster
1230 Avenue of the Americas
New York, NY 10020

First Simon & Schuster hardcover edition September 2009

SIMON & SCHUSTER and colophon are registered
trademarks of Simon & Schuster, Inc.

For information about special discounts for bulk purchases,
please contact Simon & Schuster Special Sales at
1-866-506-1949 or business@simonandschuster.com.

The Simon & Schuster Speakers Bureau can bring authors
to your live event. For more information or to book an event,
contact the Simon & Schuster Speakers Bureau at
1-866-248-3049 or visit our website at www.simonspeakers.com.

Designed by Nancy Singer

Manufactured in the United States of America

10   9   8   7   6   5   4   3   2   1

Library of Congress Cataloging-in-Publication Data is available.

ISBN 978-1-4165-4333-6
ISBN 978-1-4165-9434-5 (ebook)

PHOTO CREDITS:
Official White House Photograph: 1, 2, 3, 11, 13, 14, 15, 16, 17
William J. Clinton Presidential Library: 4, 8, 9
Illustration by Jason Snyder: 5
Taylor Branch: 6, 10, 12
The White House Historical Association: 7

For my mother, Jane Branch

And for five inspirations to write history:

*Hannah Arendt, Shelby Foote, John Hope Franklin,
Garry Wills, and Emmett Wright Jr.*

CONTENTS

THE
CLINTON
TAPES

CHAPTER ONE

TWIN
RECORDERS

Session One
Thursday, October 14, 1993

President Clinton found me waiting alone in his upstairs office called the Treaty Room, testing my tiny twin recorders on one corner of a massive but graceful Victorian desk. It contained a drawer for each cabinet department under Ulysses Grant, he observed, when Washington could be run from a single piece of furniture. The president invited me to begin our work in another room, and I gave him sample historical transcripts to look over while I repacked my briefcase. He scanned to lively passages. An anguished Lyndon Johnson was telling Georgia senator Richard Russell in 1964 that the idea of sending combat soldiers to Vietnam "makes the chills run up my back." A flirtatious LBJ was pleading with publisher Katharine Graham for kinder coverage in her *Washington Post*. Clinton asked about Johnson's telephone taping system. How did it work? How did he keep it secret? For a moment, he seemed to dare the unthinkable. White House recordings have been taboo since their raw authenticity drove Richard Nixon from office in 1974. Most tapes of the Cold War presidents still lay unknown or neglected. By the time scholars and future readers realize their incomparable value for history, these unfiltered ears to a people's government will be long since extinct. To compensate for that loss, Clinton had resolved to tape a periodic diary with my help.

The president led west through his official residence. Its stately decor would become familiar and often comforting, but for now my nerves reduced the Treaty Room to a blurry mass of burgundy around tall bookcases and a giant Heriz rug. Ahead, walls of rich yellow enveloped a long central hall of movie-set patriotism that clashed for me with Clinton's solitary ease. He wore casual slacks and carried a book about President Kennedy under an arm. His manner betrayed no pomp, and his speech retained the colloquial Southernism we had shared as youthful campaign partners in 1972, before the twenty-year gap in our acquaintance. I suffered flashes of Rip van Winkle disorientation that a lost roommate had turned up President of the United States. Now, instead of rehashing the day's crises with co-workers at Scholz's beer garden in Austin, Texas, I followed Clinton into a family parlor next to the bedroom he shared with Hillary. The plump sofas and console television could have belonged to a cozy hotel suite. Red folders identified classified night reading, marked for action or information. Crossword puzzles and playing cards mingled with books. On one wall, there was a stylized painting of their precocious daughter Chelsea, then thirteen, dressed up like a cross between Bo Peep and Bette Midler.

We sat down at his card table. I retrieved two items to help me prompt him with questions: a daily log of major political events, compiled mostly from newspapers, and a stenographer's notepad listing priority topics for this trial session. With the microcassette recorders placed between us, I noted the time and occasion for the record. From the start, Clinton's history project adapted to obstacles beyond the lack of precedent or guidance. We raced to catch up with a daunting backlog from his first nine tumultuous months in office. He sought to recall a president's firsthand experience, but the job intruded within minutes in a call from his chief congressional liaison, Howard Paster. When I started to leave for his privacy, the president beckoned me to stay. He jotted down the names of five senators, asked an operator to find them, and told me the Senate was voting late that night on Arizona Republican John McCain's amendment requiring the immediate withdrawal of U.S. troops from Somalia.* Only eleven days ago, forces loyal to Somali warlord Mo-

---

* President Bush had dispatched 25,000 U.S. soldiers the previous year in a U.N. humanitarian mission, Operation Restore Hope, designed to relieve famine in strife-torn Somalia.

hamed Farah Aidid had shot down two Black Hawk helicopters, killed nineteen Rangers, and dragged American corpses through the streets of Mogadishu in a searing disaster that Clinton likened to JFK's Bay of Pigs. Now the president said he must convince five swing senators or suffer a political defeat that he believed would injure the country.

I turned off the recorders to weigh unforeseen questions. Why not tape the president's side of these conversations? That would preserve his actual performance—lobbying, cajoling, *being* president—in addition to his private memories. After all, Clinton had just contemplated the treasure of predecessors who taped both sides of their business calls. To record only his words would avoid the ethical drawbacks of taping others without their knowledge or consent. On the other hand, posterity would get only half the exchange—what I was hearing, without the senators' interaction—which would be hard to decipher. Also, could the president himself be sure that recording would not inhibit him? How could we secure a vivid, accurate past without harming the present?

It seemed prudent on balance to tape, but there was precious little time to analyze such judgments. No sooner did Clinton finish with one senator than a White House operator buzzed with another on the line. He was on the phone before I could confirm my rationale with him, and I merely pointed to the little red lights on the recorders when I turned them back on. He nodded. I did not emphasize the gesture for fear of breaking his concentration, or of signaling alarm when I meant to convey assurance. The president worked his way through the list for more than half an hour. "Harry Reid [Democrat of Nevada] is the most underrated man in the Senate," he remarked between calls, then plunged again to solicit support. "Can you help me out on this?" he asked. He told them he had "bent over backward" to forge a compromise with Senator Robert Byrd, Democrat of West Virginia, who also favored immediate withdrawal, binding the administration to leave Somalia within six months unless Congress agreed otherwise.

Clinton said he hoped to be out sooner, but he advanced two main reasons for the flexible grace period. First, he wanted to restore some balance in fragile, starving Somalia. U.S. reinforcements this week had convinced General Aidid that he would "pay very dearly" for attacks, Clinton told the senators. He said his commanders just that day had secured the release of a Black Hawk pilot without making concessions. Killing Americans had enhanced Aidid's local prestige, even though his own forces suffered nearly a thousand casualties, and too precipitous an exit by the United States would oblige the rival Somali clans to fight for gangland parity. Second, Clinton argued that McCain's mandated retreat would undermine potential for international missions around the world. Japan, he told the senators, very reluctantly had supplied troops to a U.N. force that persevered through losses to help Cambodia establish a historic, underappreciated stability in the wake of Khmer Rouge atrocities. He said other nations closely watched our example. If the United States fled Somalia, it would become still harder to forge peace-keeping coalitions for Bosnia or the Middle East.

The Byrd compromise would narrowly prevail over McCain's withdrawal amendment. With the senators, and on tape with me, President Clinton sifted the lessons from Somalia. He said he had allowed the United States to get caught up in a vengeful obsession. U.N. secretary-general Boutros Boutros-Ghali "had a hard-on for Aidid," he said, because a June attack that killed twenty-four Pakistanis was the worst single outrage yet inflicted on U.N. peacekeepers. Boutros-Ghali had secured an international arrest warrant, then called for participant nations in the Somali crisis to capture Aidid for trial. Against such pressure, Italian prime minister Carlo Ciampi had objected that a "sheriff's job" would ruin the U.N.'s stated mission of humanitarian and political assistance. Ciampi proved wise, the president said with a sigh, but nobody paid much attention to Italian politicians.

Clinton recalled similar warnings from General Colin Powell, the outgoing chairman of his Joint Chiefs of Staff, that a targeted pursuit of Aidid would dominate and eventually displace key political efforts to reconcile factions throughout Somalia. Moreover, Powell had been skeptical of proposals for pinpoint operations in the sunbaked chaos of Mogadishu. He had predicted slim chances for an intelligence-driven "snatch" by elite units, but the president had given in to wishful optimism, despite hearing more than enough doubt to justify caution. He said Powell himself, in one of his last acts before retiring from the Army, had endorsed the confidence of U.S. generals that they could track down Aidid.

• • •

THE PRESIDENT DESCRIBED Powell as a skillful, well-spoken political manager who muffled his own opinions to broker consensus among diverse interests and personalities. This was a role Clinton admired, though in time he would perceive its limitations in Powell as a potential rival for the White House. After the phone calls on Somalia, he projected his characterization of Powell back to the controversy that engulfed his presidency from its first day, over a campaign promise to lift the ban on gay and lesbian soldiers. When the Joint Chiefs came to the Oval Office on the night of January 25, he recalled, Powell had deferred to his four service chiefs. The president sketched each vehement presentation, saying they objected to homosexual soldiers variously as immoral, inflammatory, and dangerous. He said Powell confined himself to more neutral observations about maintaining morale and cohesion, along with a formal pledge that the chiefs would obey the commander in chief in spite of their personal views. Privately, Clinton added, Powell advised him to discount the pledge because all the chiefs would communicate these views strongly to Congress, which could and would overturn any presidential order.

Powell was correct, said Clinton. Congress held sway. If he had issued an executive order, a super-majority stood poised not only to reinstate the ban on homosexual soldiers but to override any presidential veto. Support for ending the ban fell below 25 percent in Congress, he added. The president engaged a question about the introductory meeting with Democratic senators on the night of January 28. Pleasantries about the inauguration had mixed with worries over gay soldiers, he said, until elder statesman Robert Byrd changed the tone with his first words. "Suetonius, the Roman historian," Clinton quoted Byrd, "lived into the reign of Emperor Hadrian during the second century." According to Suetonius, Julius Caesar never lived down reports of a youthful affair with King Nicomedes of Bithynia (in modern Turkey), such that wags dared to mock the mighty emperor as "every woman's man and every man's woman." Byrd told his colleagues and Clinton that for one senator, at least, this homosexual seed had something to do with the fall of the world's greatest military empire.

On our tape, Clinton re-created Byrd's speech with feeling. Byrd said homosexuality was a sin. It was unnatural. God didn't like it. The

Army shouldn't want it, and Byrd could never accept such a bargain with the devil. Clinton said this classical foray rocked everyone back in their seats, and touched off discussions ranging from ancient Greece to cyberspace. Some senators noted that the Roman emperors won brutal wars for centuries while indulging every imaginable vice. (Augustus Caesar ravaged both sexes, wrote the gossipy Suetonius, and softened the hair on his legs with red-hot walnut shells.) Byrd invoked Bible passages. The president said, well, those verses may be so, but in the same Bible "homosexuality did not make the top-ten list of sins." By contrast, he told the senators, the Ten Commandments did ban false witness and adultery, and they all knew that plenty of liars and philanderers were good soldiers. He said there were sharp stabs of tension in the Oval Office, leavened with astonishment at such a debate between senators and a brand-new president. "I couldn't tell," said Clinton, "whether [Massachusetts Democrat] Teddy Kennedy was going to start giggling or jump out the window."

Sam Nunn of Georgia had interjected that adultery was in fact a punishable crime under the Uniform Code of Military Justice. Yes, Clinton said he replied, but military investigators did not launch dragnets for unfaithful spouses or make recruits swear that they are not adulterers. From the start, he told them, his primary goal was ending the requirement that gay and lesbian citizens must affirmatively lie to serve in the armed forces. He wanted standards to rest on conduct rather than identity. If homosexual soldiers followed military discipline, and steered clear of infractions equivalent to harassment by heterosexuals, or unseemly displays, he felt their private behavior should stay private. The president said fellow Democrat Charles Robb had spoken up to agree, despite the political problems it would cause him in conservative Virginia. Robb, a Marine veteran, endorsed Clinton's position as honorable and consistent. The Joint Chiefs, said the president, took almost the opposite view. They needed hypocrisy and demanded inconsistency. They tolerated homosexual troops by the tens of thousands so long as those troops stayed closeted and vulnerable. "It was a soldier *saying* he was gay that offended them more than the lies," Clinton recalled, "and really more than the private behavior." If homosexual soldiers were allowed to be truthful, he explained, military commanders feared disruption or worse from a viscerally anti-gay core of their troops, which they estimated to run about 30 percent.

I asked whether the president thought political posturing on gay soldiers was more blatant than usual. Pentagon officials had floated the notion of "segregated" homosexual units. Critics sidestepped the essential choices by alleging that Clinton mishandled some unspecified solution, and, with photographers in tow, Senator Nunn and others toured the bowels of a Navy ship to shiver at the prospect of gay sailors in close quarters. On the tapes, Clinton came to Nunn's defense. He deplored his White House staff, and Nunn's own Senate staff, for leaking stories that Nunn was bitter about not being president, or secretary of defense. The president, however, said he accepted Nunn as a genuine social conservative in step with his constituencies in Georgia and the military. Beyond that, Clinton said he respected Nunn as a professional who cooperated across shifting lines of division. It was Nunn, he disclosed, who first proposed to him the six-month delay to fashion a suitable compromise, suggesting that only a public detour would get gay soldiers out of the headlines so Clinton could begin his chosen agenda.

The president was philosophical about the "don't ask, don't tell" policy that had emerged in July. To his regret, it enshrined the double standard he sought to remove. He quoted Hillary, who in turn was citing Oscar Wilde, that "hypocrisy is the homage vice pays to virtue." Over time, the president said, Americans would grow more comfortable with gay soldiers than with an official policy of winks and deceit. Public discourse about homosexuality, like its modern connotation for the word "gay" itself, was barely twenty years old. By historical timetables, a previously unmentionable taboo was gaining legitimacy at a rapid pace. Still, Clinton would be disappointed that military authorities kept finding ways around their promise not to ferret out homosexual soldiers for expulsion.

The president treated posturing as a natural element. He remarked, for instance, that he had no idea what Senate Republican leader Bob Dole of Kansas thought about the merits of gays in the military. "He may genuinely be for it or against it," said Clinton. "All our discussions have been about the politics." He said Dole advised him quite candidly that he intended to keep the issue alive as long as he could to trap Clinton on weak ground, where he would "take a pretty good beating." Similarly, the president said Dole consistently advised that budgets were the most partisan matters between Congress and the White House, and that Clinton could expect to get few if any Republican votes for his omnibus bill on taxes and spending. Clinton said Dole spoke of the opposition's job not as making deals but rather making the president fail, so he could be replaced as quickly as possible. In fact, he said Dole himself started running for president within ten days of Clinton's inauguration. "Every time he goes to Kansas," remarked the president, "he stops off in New Hampshire on the way."

This was the first of many times that President Clinton spoke matter-of-factly about political warfare. He never begrudged survival and ambition in politicians, whether friend or foe. Indeed, he reveled in calculations from opposing points of view. These human assessments were among many intersecting factors that made politics so enthralling to him—including trends, accidents, strategy, communication, and precise election returns by district. He loved politics so much that he could speak almost fondly of his own defeats, seemingly because he had a prime seat to examine them in retrospect.

AT OUR FIRST session, he volunteered without a question that the two biggest failures of his presidency so far were the defeat of his economic stimulus package and his inability to lift the arms embargo in Bosnia. He said the stimulus package would have been a symbolically important public investment in jobs and economic growth, especially after worse-than-projected budget numbers had forced him to defer his campaign promise for a broad middle-class tax cut. His first mistake, said Clinton, was proposing the stimulus package first rather than together with his budget bill. The latter course would have emphasized how small the stimulus was relative to the overall deficit, but Clinton's approach opened him to attack as another Democratic spendthrift. His second and bigger mistake, he added, was rejecting advice from his chief of staff, Mack McLarty, to bargain for the necessary votes by agreeing to trim the stimulus bill in Congress. Instead, said the president, he went for broke at the urging of Senator Byrd, chair of the Appropriations Committee, who predicted wrongly that enough opposing senators would give way in the end. The result was no stimulus bill at all. I asked whether Byrd may have gotten greedy from long years steering appropriations into his home state of West Virginia. There could be something to that, Clinton replied, but he said the bigger lesson was that reputations don't count votes. In this case, his rookie chief of staff had proved more accurate than the venerated master of Senate history and procedure.

On Bosnia, the president said his government first had been divided over proposals for direct intervention to stop the infamous spasms of violence, the ethnic cleansing, that had plagued the former Yugoslavia since the end of the Cold War.* He said General Powell and others had recommended against various military options, arguing that air attacks were tempting and safe but could not compel a truce, and that ground troops would be exposed among hostile foreigners in difficult terrain. Within weeks, the new administration had explored ideas to relax the international embargo on arms shipments to the region, reasoning that the embargo penalized the weakest, most victimized nation of Bosnia-Herzegovina. Unlike its neighbors in Serbia and Croatia, the heavily Muslim population of Bosnia was isolated without access to arms smuggled across the borders. The Bosnian government wanted the embargo lifted so its people could defend themselves, thereby opening a chance for military balance among the antagonists that could lead to a political settlement.

Clinton said U.S. allies in Europe blocked proposals to adjust or remove the embargo. They justified their opposition on plausible humanitarian grounds, arguing that more arms would only fuel the bloodshed, but privately, said the president, key allies objected that an independent Bosnia would be "unnatural" as the only Muslim nation in Europe. He said they favored the embargo precisely because it locked in Bosnia's disadvantage. Worse, he added, they parried numerous alternatives as a danger to the some eight thousand European peacekeepers

---

* Beginning in 1992, four of the six provinces gained international recognition as independent countries: Slovenia, Macedonia, Croatia, and Bosnia-Herzegovina. The remaining Yugoslav Republic consisted of Serbia and Montenegro, with a capital in Belgrade. Its president, Slobodan Milosevic, led protracted, irredentist wars to consolidate with ethnic Serbs elsewhere, meeting resistance especially in Croatia and Bosnia-Herzegovina.

deployed in Bosnia to safeguard emergency shipments of food and medical supplies. They challenged U.S. standing to propose shifts in policy with no American soldiers at risk. While upholding their peacekeepers as a badge of commitment, they turned these troops effectively into a shield for the steady dismemberment of Bosnia by Serb forces. When I expressed shock at such cynicism, reminiscent of the blind-eye diplomacy regarding the plight of Europe's Jews during World War II, President Clinton only shrugged. He said President François Mitterrand of France had been especially blunt in saying that Bosnia did not belong, and that British officials also spoke of a painful but realistic restoration of Christian Europe. Against Britain and France, he said, German chancellor Helmut Kohl among others had supported moves to reconsider the United Nations arms embargo, failing in part because Germany did not hold a seat on the U.N. Security Council. Clinton sounded as though he were obliged to start over. He groped amid these chastening constraints for new leadership options to stop Bosnia's mass sectarian violence.

In a less chilling tone, the president analyzed his administration's early penchant for leaking stories to the press. He attributed nearly all the troublesome episodes to his own White House staff, as opposed to cabinet officers or bureaucrats, and he distinguished the leakers by motive and character. Whereas officials in most governments planted stories in order to influence policy, or to jockey for position against rivals, Clinton diagnosed his leaks as the product of youthful exuberance. He said they seemed to be ego-driven, from staff members eager to see their words in the news or prove they were the first to know something. Such leaks often were frivolous, whimsical, and inaccurate, he said. By playing to the swagger in his young aides, reporters elicited stories of froth that gave fodder to his political opposition. Clinton cited the uproar over one fictional report that he planned a luxury tax to keep rich people from buying supplementary health insurance. And by press fiat, before his first organizational meeting in the White House, a mischievous leak had vaulted gays in the military to the top of the national agenda.[*] The

---

[*] Eric Schmitt, "The Inauguration/Clinton Set to End Ban on Gay Troops," *New York Times,* January 21, 1993, p. 1.

president complained that he had never really had a "honeymoon" in the press. Not for the last time, he said it was nettlesome to deal with sensational leaks rather than substantive politics, but he thought things were getting better.

In reviewing his early failures to secure an attorney general, the president stressed the vagaries of political culture. He said he still admired the first choice, Zoë Baird, whose vetting for the post was all but complete when someone noticed that she had just paid her overdue employer's share of Social Security taxes for two illegal immigrants working in her home. The tardy payment raised a fresh issue of fitness for the office, since the attorney general was responsible for the fair enforcement of immigration laws. Clinton said the climate turned so swiftly that her Senate confirmation was doomed before their first meeting, which became a poignant farewell instead of a potential clash. Baird spoke graciously, and behaved nobly, from his point of view. She went out before the press to "fall on her sword," withdrawing her nomination

His mood soured with first mention of the next choice, U.S. District Court Judge Kimba Wood. He had not yet asked her to become attorney general, Clinton insisted, or even agreed to do so. Instead, a staff member leaked her name, which hyped the nomination into a controlling reality. Then, when news emerged that Judge Wood had "nanny tax" problems, too, the president said she raised distinctions between her case and Zoë Baird's to defend her prior assurances on this now very sore point. Clinton used the word "livid" several times to describe his reaction. He said her obtuseness about politics and public perception made him glad to pull the plug on a nomination he never made.

There was relief tinged with misgiving about his final selection, Janet Reno. Clinton's close friend from Little Rock, political science professor Diane Blair, remembered Reno as a schoolmate of inspirational talent at Cornell. When he called to take soundings, Florida Democratic senator Bob Graham had described Reno, a Floridian, as a model prosecutor of intelligence, integrity, and drive. Clinton agreed with these assessments. He said Reno considered her opinions carefully, expressed them cogently, and fought for them very hard. Yet he also said there was "something about her approach" to the job that troubled him. He mentioned that when he asked her to replace the much criticized FBI director William Sessions, to get a fresh start as provided by law, Reno had demanded several months to make her own independent assessment before she concurred. He said she tended to remove herself from consultation like a judge, as sometimes required, and that she was not very good at reading her colleagues in government or providing overall direction. For Clinton, this impeded her management of the Justice Department's many functions, from drug enforcement and prison policy to antitrust. Her aloofness weakened executive control vested in the president. More personally, it seemed to me, he was complaining that her astringent outlook on politics left them a mismatched, conversational dud.

Two aspects of his bumpy ride at the Justice Department carried over into Clinton's choice for the Supreme Court. First, he said he had hoped to select a "political" justice, if possible, with a background and reputation in holding elective office. His goal was to restore appreciation for the Court as an integral branch of balanced government, rather than a technical specialty for lawyers and judges, and to redress decades of corrosive cynicism about politics. Second, when circumstances derailed his top political choices, Clinton said he ran into yet another snarl on the treatment of household employees. A review had revealed minor tax deficiencies for Judge Stephen Breyer, which he corrected. Then the president had read Breyer's judicial opinions, and interviewed him personally among several finalists, before the "nanny tax" question reemerged in subtler form. Judge Breyer had put two dates on his check to satisfy the amount due. The earlier one, written shortly after the resignation of Justice Byron "Whizzer" White in March, was scratched out in favor of a second date, weeks later, when Democratic governor Mario Cuomo of New York had publicly withdrawn from consideration. Taken together, said the president, the two dates could suggest that Judge Breyer was willing to pay this small, obscure tax only if necessary to secure a seat on the Supreme Court. He could be portrayed as both scofflaw and skinflint. The evidence was far from conclusive, but Clinton said it was enough to result in a petty public squabble, which might overshadow Breyer's qualifications to become a fine justice.

IT WAS MIDNIGHT. President Clinton said he was too tired to finish describing his Supreme Court selection—a big subject—but he kept talking as though on automatic pilot. He mentioned numerous controversies including the disastrous, lethal FBI raid on sect leader David Koresh's armed compound in Waco, Texas. I left the recorders running for a time to capture his unguarded reminiscence, then turned them off to rewind, fearing that Clinton might judge these sessions too meandering or exhausting. We were just beginning to establish a routine for our off-the-books history project, with only four or five people witting of its logistics. The president's sole commitment was to send for me again if and when he found time.

I labeled each of the rewound microcassettes in ink, and gave them both to Clinton with a reminder of our talks on custody of the tapes. We had discussed several options for splitting up the duplicates in order to safeguard a backup if one set were lost, seized, or subpoenaed, but he accepted my recommendation that he keep all the tapes, personally, at least for now. In my view, no extra security from legal privilege or a separate custodian, including myself, outweighed the value of building up the president's confidence that he could speak candidly for a unique, verbatim record under his control. I had promised to do everything I could to keep the project itself a secret. He said he had a good hiding place for the tapes. He planned to make first use of them for his memoirs, then eventually to release the transcripts at his presidential library.

Down through the Usher's Office, on past an occasional Secret Service agent in the deserted White House corridors, my footsteps echoed as my mind raced. Had I asked the right questions? Too many or not enough? There were so many topics. My instinct was to intervene as little as possible by dangling neutral subjects for the president to engage or not, but he seemed to respond more vigorously to questions with a point of view. He asked what kind of information I thought future historians would find most useful, knowing that my own work for years had been sifting presidential clues from the civil rights era. Who could predict what posterity would care about, or judge to be right and wrong? In one sense, Clinton's perspective seemed unremarkable, like a bull session between friends. However, it was also true that revelations lay hidden everywhere for specialists and regular citizens alike. A U.S. president was framing issues, telling stories, and thinking out loud. Inescapably, he let on what he did and did not notice inside the nation's central bunker—what penetrated the walls of government and the clatter of opinion, and how he shaped and responded to what penetrated.

Here by design was raw material for future history, which filled me with excitement to preserve my own fresh but fleeting witness. I popped a blank microcassette into one of the recorders. For more than an hour on the drive home to Baltimore, finishing in the dark stillness of our driveway, I dictated every impression and detail I could remember. These instant recollections would become a habit, forming the basis for this book.

CHAPTER TWO

REUNION

First Encounter
Katharine Graham Dinner
Monday, December 7, 1992

First Inauguration
Wednesday, January 20, 1993

Hearts and a Bargain
Two Families in the White House
Tuesday, September 28, 1993

Our new venture had started with convenience and a dusty friendship. From the first exploratory talks, Bill Clinton and I reconnected in shorthand reminiscence about our background as white Southerners who had come of age during the civil rights movement. Born into nonpolitical families, each of us was successively unmoored, inspired, and captivated by the reverberations of a democracy so profoundly enlarged. We had not seen each other since 1972, having drifted apart in the turmoil of that era, but we yearned for its core optimism. Twenty years later, we found ourselves using similar words, such as "heal" and "repair." We thought history and modern politics were out of balance. His White House tapes project emerged from a fitful reunion of two graying baby boomers, one of whom was about to become President of the United States.

The first harbinger landed on our doorstep six days after the 1992 election. Like most newspapers, my hometown *Baltimore Sun* described the president-elect in a whirl—still resting but giddy, his voice recovered, jogging around Little Rock in a phalanx of security agents with occasional stops at Doe's Eat Place or McDonald's, charming old first-grade classmates and chatting about everything from his favorite cemetery to the $1.4 trillion federal budget. According to a front-page feature, Clinton assured a concerned friend on the street that he did not light his cigars, and he confessed finishing only one new mystery book, *Private Eyes* by Jonathan Kellerman, above a crush of reading for the transition. Clinton greeted well-wishers visiting Little Rock from many states including Maryland, said the *Sun*, emphasizing a local news angle. He was sad that thousands of election night celebrants had left town without his knowledge. "He said, for instance, that Baltimore novelist Taylor Branch, a long-time friend, had come and gone 'and I never saw him,' " the story concluded on an inside page. " 'I'm just sick about it. I'll call him this week some time.' "

The telephone started ringing. Friends teased me about getting promoted to "novelist," especially those few who knew of my one forgettable experiment in published fiction. Strangers boldly forwarded messages and manifestos for the incoming president. A local charity booster tasked me to secure an old pair of Clinton's running shoes for an HIV/AIDS benefit auction. Eager inquiries about whether the president-elect had called grew embarrassing. Traces of skepticism mingled with disappointment in people's reactions, both to my denial of any word from Clinton and to the truthful story that my wife, Christy, and I made our only Little Rock trip spontaneously, without invitation or prior involvement in the presidential campaign of Clinton and Al Gore.

Some fifty thousand fellow pilgrims had gathered on election night near the Old State House in Little Rock, where, to control unprecedented crowds, the city lined the streets with Mardi Gras barricades borrowed from New Orleans. During the climactic vote count, we did not even try to find the campaign's genial chief of staff, Eli Segal, with whom Christy and I each had worked independently as political reformers straight out of school, before we met each other. We did locate Judy Green, who had been a kind of surrogate mother in Washington to many activists against the Vietnam War. A generation later, she retained that presence in a full-time job as office manager for the Clinton-Gore headquarters in Little Rock, where her college-age daughter worked in James Carville's much publicized "War Room." Judy directed us through the chaos to mutual friends prowling the corridors of the Excelsior Hotel (now the Peabody), talking their way into celebrity suites on the rationale that high-powered people would have inside information on the presidential results. We tagged along, reminded of an unpleasant status frenzy in campaign politics, until I was pulled forward to introduce our roving intruders to Democratic fund-raiser Patricia Medavoy, whom I knew from a recent celebration lunch when her then husband, Mike, had acquired movie rights to *Parting the Waters,* my first Martin Luther King book, for his Hollywood studio, Columbia-TriStar Pictures. I had no apprehension yet that the film project would fail, but the option funds had made possible our Little Rock splurge.

We found the crowd downstairs backed up solid to the Excelsior Hotel entrance, pulsing with rumors that Clinton would make an appearance in front of the Old State House. Buyers snapped up victory T-shirts. It was cold, but an ice sculpture of the White House melted in the antiquated hotel lobby, where scattered enthusiasts let loose the Arkansas hog call. People outside climbed trees and stood on balconies draped in bunting, perched for a distant glimpse of Clinton across the way. We were blocked until a local guide led us sideways more than a hundred yards and down into a basement near the Arkansas River, where we followed at a trot through underground utility rooms, perhaps between buildings, fearing a dead end or worse but caught up by a wild itch to get ahead. Finally darting up through an alley door, trying to look like we belonged, we discovered ourselves in a sparser crowd off a corner of the Old State House. We shivered under big trees, still several security zones away, but we could see better in person than on the giant television monitors when the three Clintons stepped forth into the bedlam. They walked separately back and forth under the portico, waving. The president-elect was ebullient, if hoarse. He pledged to remember campaign stories from people of every kind, including those who had given up hope or had never before voted. "This election," he declared, "is a clarion call for our country to face the challenges of the end of the Cold War and the beginning of the next century."

Friends back home mercifully stopped asking whether Clinton ever followed through on his stated intention to call. This was a relief, because the questions had acquired an edge. Did he frequently break promises? Did I think his reported comment about me was generous or calculated? Even a tiny incident showed how hard it was to be neutral about a president, and the baffling newspaper quote folded into my larger ambivalence about politics. Personal observation on election night brought home many familiar, positive mannerisms in Bill Clinton—and for that matter, in Hillary—from our shared apartment long ago, but a nonstop career in Arkansas elections must have added layers of control. His "Forgotten Middle Class" campaign slogan made me wince at its resemblance to Richard Nixon's "Silent Majority." Clinton and politics had processed each other for the world stage, but how much did that make him a new creature? While I pulled for the best, and thrilled with hope from the election, our truncated friendship turned Bill Clinton into a greater mystery for me than if I had never known him.

THEN, SHORTLY AFTER Thanksgiving, someone from the transition office sent word that he wanted to see me. Christy and I drove to Washington on December 7, remembering the gated exterior of the Georgetown mansion owned by *Washington Post* publisher Katharine Graham from many trips with our two children to the public gardens and playground across the street. Full of puzzled anticipation, we knew only that fellow attendees would include Baltimore mayor Kurt Schmoke, for whom Christy worked as a speechwriter, and his wife, Patricia. It seemed silly to think a president-elect would initiate any business with mayors and amateurs at a dinner party, but if the invitation was purely social, we figured to be the stalest of FOB (Friend of Bill) guests. Christy had never met either Clinton, and my last contact—other than a passing wave in 1977—was packing up from a somber defeat as Texas coordinators in the 1972 presidential campaign of George McGovern, with the fresh sweethearts Bill and Hillary rushing back for makeup exams at Yale Law School.

This was different, with an atmosphere more imposing than the venue. Flashing police cruisers and ominous black SUVs dotted the approach. Many people arrived in their "most sincere automobile," quipped an observer, anticipating a humbler Democratic fashion after twelve years of limousine Republicans, but a Rolls-Royce pulled up with the British ambassador. Clumps of people waited along the fence for a sighting of Clinton, and journalists screened the entrance because Mrs. Graham had declined to release the guest list. "I just have to say it's a private dinner," she told her own reporters before receiving newcomers sprinkled among potentates inside. I had met her once or twice through my early mentor, Charlie Peters, editor of *The Washington Monthly*. Vernon Jordan, chair of the Clinton transition team, introduced me as a frightened young graduate student he had hired to register black voters in the summer of 1969. Vernon enjoyed yarns from his background in civil rights, before success in corporate law, and I knew him well enough to joke that we all could have survived back then on his current tailoring budget for British and Italian dress shirts. My association was peripheral or less with the other guests, many of whom populated the news. Christy and I searched place cards carefully arranged through the rooms downstairs, finding hers at Vice President–elect Al Gore's table of eight, seated between *New York Times* columnist William Safire and Democratic National Committee chair Ron Brown. Christy calmed herself as we moved on to remote areas. Under a tent outside, we inspected another dozen or so round caterer's tables to the far end of the lawn, where my name turned up beside economist Alice Rivlin next to place cards waiting for Mrs. Graham and President-elect Clinton himself.

How could two virtual tourists be assigned such choice spots? A simple explanation seemed likely, but, being clueless, Christy and I told each other to enjoy the moment with no jobs or political appointments at stake. Muffled commotion at the gate announced the Clintons, who made their way slowly through the house. When they came near, and made introductions around, he announced brightly that he hadn't seen me in years. He drew me deftly aside, whereupon two Secret Service agents stepped behind us to create a small barrier at the edge of the tent. It was like a dance step.

"Can you believe all this?" he confided with boyish delight. I said it was a lot to take in, and extended my congratulations. He mentioned recent contact with a couple of people we had known together in Texas. I could only smile at the memory of these vivid characters and regret losing track of them. He said he was proud of me for the years of effort it took to write *Parting the Waters*. "It's good," he said, emphasizing that he had read more than the long narrative text. A lot of the footnotes came from presidential libraries, Clinton observed. His tone changed. He said the book made him think of two questions, or favors. First, did I think historians fifty years from now would find good enough raw material in his own library to recapture the inner dynamics of his presidency, as I was trying to do for the John Kennedy and Lyndon Johnson years? Second, would I outline some thoughts for him on themes of generational change? Not only the upcoming millennium and the end of the Cold War, he suggested, but also what it meant for two Southerners to head the winning presidential ticket so soon after the stigma of segregation.

Promising of course to send some thoughts on the generations, I jumped to his question about presidential libraries. I told him the preservation of White House records was a vital but obscure field, changing rapidly. Whole new windows were opening on the past but closing for the future. Ironically, it was getting harder in the information age to preserve accurate minutes of high-level government meetings. I started to explain how we were oddly indebted to Oliver Stone's conspiracy film on the Kennedy assassination for prying open the first release of actual LBJ telephone recordings in what seemed to be an enormous secret trove.

By then Clinton was nodding. The small dam of people waiting to meet him was about to break. When he moved on, I tried to absorb the surprises from the two-minute reunion. By reconnecting across barriers of time and reserve, not to mention the distraction of Secret Service agents, he triggered awareness of the rare person with whom you can pick right up again no matter how or when you left off. Whatever divided us, the bonded foundation of twenty-five-year-old dreamers was still there. At the opposite extreme, Clinton sent an impersonal and cerebral message of equal intensity. He was preparing for history even before taking office. No doubt he yearned to build a shining record from the seat of Abraham Lincoln and Franklin Roosevelt, but he inquired about historical tools and sensors that could amplify his legacy either way, good or bad. In reaching out to me and my footnotes, Clinton sent a laserlike message about the relationship between his profession and mine. Could he know that he was touching on some of the most difficult issues in presidential historiography? He raised farsighted questions from a premise that politics and history shape each other through the political culture, where the national heritage and prevailing sensibilities intersect with everyday life.

Mrs. Graham led an exchange of toasts after dinner. They were pleasant but scripted until Clinton stood to reply. Speaking without notes, he confronted a gaping fissure between voters and their national government. He said candidates had won power all his adult life by running against Washington, which over time distorted and degraded the American experiment. Clinton challenged the establishment figures before him to restore balance. They should shift from internal feuds and intrigues to the substantive goals that had inspired a distinctive national politics in the first place. "Washington is a better place than most people think it is," he declared. He gave personal thanks to one of the most iconic guests, revealing that Robert McNamara, both Kennedy's and Johnson's secretary of defense and a chief architect of the Vietnam War, had written him a letter of wrenching belief that a Clinton presidency could help those still scarred by the Vietnam War find a higher patriotism in the strength of their disagreements.* "I hope to bring more of the country to the capital," Clinton concluded, "and more of the capital to the country." His toast moved skeptics to their feet. William Safire conceded that only a masterful tone could win over the "high-tension" crowd. Opponents and insiders buzzed with approval.

THE GRAHAM DINNER was a fleeting triumph for Clinton, who would be estranged from Washington's permanent leaders. Its effect lasted longer

---

* Clinton only paraphrased the letter at the Graham dinner. What moved McNamara to write was a news story about the ordeal of Clinton's friendship with his Oxford University housemate, Frank Aller, who had resisted conscription for the Vietnam War and committed suicide in 1971. Clinton would quote from McNamara's letter in his 2004 autobiography, *My Life:* "For me—and I believe for the nation as well—the Vietnam War finally ended the day you were elected president. By their votes, the American people, at long last, recognized that the Allers and the Clintons, when they questioned the wisdom and morality of their government's decisions relating to Vietnam, were no less patriotic than those who served in uniform."

on me. For years, my goal had been bringing presidents and other historical figures to life on the page by penetrating the myths that encase
them. Yet my own political culture led me to project a coating of wax
and mechanized motives onto someone I actually knew—only now to
feel a jolting revelation that he was essentially the same person. Should
this have been obvious, or should it put me all the more on guard against
being snookered? Both thoughts were disconcerting. My instinctive resolve was to keep revising personal judgments about a friend while giving the president-elect all the civic respect due his office.

The fax machine transmitted my reflections on generational change,
as requested. ("Should you want to kick any of this around, or have me
work on some language, send the word," I wrote Clinton. "Christy and
I are bursting with hope and prayers for you.") No further word came, as
the president-elect disappeared into headlines about cabinet appointments and his two-day economic summit in Little Rock. Silence on generational change was almost a relief, as I had little to add on a vague
topic that invited pontification, but his question about footnotes and
future libraries still fascinated me with the range of Clinton's mind.
Could he really be making decisions now on that specialized, low-
priority item? I suppressed an urge to volunteer advice, thinking the
initiative properly belonged to him.

My friend and former book editor, Dan Okrent, called to say the
Clinton people accepted a last-minute, long-shot proposal for a *Life*
magazine photo essay at Clinton's elbow on inauguration day, only two
days hence. They had selected my name from a list of possible writers for
the text, if I would agree. Dan assured me that *Life* wanted neither objective criticism nor a friend's personal story, and that Clinton apparently
trusted me to write an accurate but descriptive account. This temporary
assignment put me into quite an uproar, shifting me back into the rush
of journalism after years of work in history, then back again when another caller urgently invited me to a private rehearsal for the inaugural
address, saying the president-elect wanted my historical opinion.

At Blair House, the official guest residence across from the White
House, speechwriters David Kusnet and Michael Waldman gave me a
draft headed "1/19/93, 4am, 1899 words." It was then ten o'clock, six
hours later, and they had beaten by one word their mandate to get the

address as short as JFK's famous "Ask not" speech of 1961. Tommy Caplan arrived shortly with a large lipstick stain on his collar and a single-spaced memo of suggested insertions for the address. I thought Caplan, whom I barely knew as a fellow writer from Baltimore, sweet-tempered and eccentric, had misconstrued our role in a review panel for the finished product, but it quickly turned out that he had a far clearer idea of Clinton's work habits, having remained a steadfast friend since college. The president-elect was rewriting the first half of the address in the master suite. When he joined us in its sitting room, aides who could decipher his handwriting pitched into transcribing what he had written while Clinton polled the group. He seconded a general call for better tempo and refrain, saying he wanted more spiritual lift. George Stephanopoulos, Clinton's chief adviser for this meeting, introduced himself in my direction with a sheepish announcement: "Taylor, I hate to say it, but this session is off the record." I said fine, as my *Life* assignment was only for the next day, and this seemed to clear me for work on an ad hoc team revising what we named the "Thomas Jefferson section."

More than twelve hours later, we reconvened in the elegant second-floor library at Blair House. My note to myself from one of several short breaks minimized our contributions so far: "I think a fair summary is that while everyone seems to be pleasant, they are adapted to the notion that the inaugural address will be written largely by Bill himself at the last minute." The Clintons and Gores returned well after midnight from a black-tie concert. Hillary kicked off her shoes and stood at the lectern to read my copy of the latest draft, headed "1/20/93, 12:05 AM, 1609 words." She said it was fine and went off sensibly to bed. The rest of us offered comments as Clinton read out loud from the lectern. Speech coach Michael Sheehan timed successive versions with a stopwatch, but seldom got through a whole draft because Clinton stopped frequently to invite debate over phrases and individual words, asking, "How does *this* sound?" He trimmed programmatic lists for political reasons, saying every list left you vulnerable to those not included. The speech got shorter, as suggested additions still fared poorly. About four o'clock, Al Gore recommended sleep for the long day about to dawn, and Clinton yielded. He remarked wryly that he could not miss work the first moment he would earn more than Hillary, on a big raise from his governor's salary of $35,000. As we disbanded, a weary young Army technician rolled his eyes when I asked if his TelePrompTer duty often lasted so late. Speech rehearsals with Clinton's predecessor, George H. W. Bush, were scheduled for brief intervals, he said, and never went past five in the afternoon.

The Blair House foyer crackled with adrenaline less than four hours later. From a national security briefing, Clinton went by motorcade to Metropolitan AME Church for an inaugural prayer service that woke me up with the joyful music and ecumenical hope characteristic of a mass meeting in the heyday of the civil rights movement. Among the speakers came Imam Wallace D. Muhammad, reciting Quranic verses of peace in Arabic and English. An ally of Malcolm X in his youth, Muhammad had gone on to reform his own father's sectarian Nation of Islam. In a book interview, he once had expressed to me his long-term ambition for American Muslims to help reconcile world Islam with democracy. I considered Muhammad the nation's most underappreciated religious figure in the twentieth century, but here he was preaching unnoticed to the incoming Clintons, soon followed by Martin Luther King's former colleague Gardner Taylor. "It is as if we have come again to Camelot," Taylor began merrily, "but this time with the atmosphere of the Ozarks." His jokes elicited peals of laughter, and he preached earnestly from the tenth chapter of Luke. In between, Reverend Taylor's precise diction achieved a thunderous rhythm about politics. "We are here to establish before the world that people can be brought together," he declared, "in the highest and most difficult undertaking known to the unity of men and women. That people can govern themselves. This is the American proposition in history."

On the front row, Clinton nodded his head to agree as the packed congregation burbled with cries of amen. He turned especially to Gore, and was on the same theme when he pulled me through to a huddle on the sidewalk back at Blair House. "Were they giving my speech in there or what?" he exclaimed above the noise. People lined the other side of Pennsylvania Avenue, some of them shouting and dancing, oblivious to one severe-looking woman with a crude poster: MR. CLINTON DO NOT MOCK GOD. Nearly a hundred press photographers toed a yellow line in the street like a firing squad. Clinton said he had just been telling Al and

Tipper Gore how he had met the participants in the service. Gardner Taylor was Vernon Jordan's idea to avoid picking a main speaker from the contending bishops and major denominations. "Vernon said bring Gardner down here and he will get you ahead of all the church politics," Clinton told us, adding that he must mean a lot to me. I said yes, and ventured that Reverend Taylor made me think of a line from Martin Luther King for the very end of the inaugural address, just before Clinton was to invoke trumpets and changing the guard: "From this mountaintop of celebration, we hear a call to service in the valley." Clinton mulled this over as people jostled from behind. Stephanopoulos said, "We have room to let go if you want." I said the quote marked King's defining course against comfort and his own advisers, straight down from the Nobel Prize ceremony to begin his perilous crusade for voting rights in Selma. "Yeah," Clinton said tentatively. "Let's write that down."

He paused to introduce Tommy Caplan's father, but held back our sidewalk huddle to tell us that the sermon made him think we should add a clause about never taking democratic ideals for granted. We agreed on a section where it would belong, then traded wording as we pushed through the Blair House entrance up the stairs to sanctuary. With his speech team reassembled from various nap spots, Clinton announced that both Hillary and Chelsea adamantly opposed the sentence "we must love one another" in his summons to civic engagement. They preferred "care for one another." Stephanopoulos made what he called "one last argument for love," but Clinton said the women thought the word would be interpreted not so much as soft but flaky, the way many people had thought of Jimmy Carter. "Okay, no love," Stephanopoulos conceded, moving to make the correction at the TelePrompTer machine. I joined him there with trepidation when Clinton pointed for me to supply the exact wording of the two sidewalk changes, including a new clause in the foreign policy summation: "But our greatest strength is the power of our ideas, which are still new in many lands." Aides clamored to emend texts being held for worldwide release, while others crowded around the lectern where Clinton was comparing three renditions of a Bible verse in the speech.

"With all due respect!" a big voice rang out. "Can we get to work?" It was Al Gore from his center chair in the library. He voted for the King

James translation, which carried, and the cacophony died to a whisper. Speech coach Sheehan warned Clinton not to expect any of the usual audience response to help him gauge pace in the address, because his outdoor crowd would seem miles below the West Capitol platform. Gore seconded the pointers on delivery, telling Clinton that Sheehan "needs your full attention on this." The president should pause briefly and then relaunch after each applause line, as though lifted to a higher plane. When Gore blessed the final rehearsal–"This is a winner"–the room evacuated behind Clinton, who was late to meet outgoing President Bush for their joint ride to Capitol Hill. Stephanopoulos had a Marine driver waiting to rush us with the first printed copies along empty streets blocked off for the inaugural parade. We split up in the Rotunda. He went to find the leadership chamber, telling guards that Clinton "will go crazy any minute" without a speech to study during the ceremony. I waited with a backup copy at the top of the stairs, and the inaugural procession swept me down to the front rows overlooking the Mall.

Circumstance thus placed me among Supreme Court justices and other prime dignitaries of the United States for the transfer of power, uniquely without a seat. Calls to stand for prayer and observance were a welcome relief, as I was otherwise obliged to squat at length beside two fire extinguishers just off the aisle, pretending to have a chair. In that state, ripples of the absurd tempered my awe and fatigue. As Sheehan predicted, the address did seem to vanish into the cavernous sky above the multitude. There was little resonance, let alone the emotional wallop of the toast at Katharine Graham's dinner. After Clinton's smiling exit, now officially president, the senators and diplomats around me talked mostly of themselves, and the response to the speech seemed muted at best. Perhaps a letdown was inevitable for someone so invested in the content, especially when my stark isolation registered. Exposed like a waif, having secured neither a press badge for *Life* nor any of the flashy inauguration credentials around everyone else's neck, I sneaked off the Capitol grounds.

IT TOOK MORE than four hours to get inside the White House. In the first moments of the Clinton administration, the few employees who could work the telephones could not yet find those in authority, and vice versa. Several operators barely humored the claim that a stranger was overdue to join the Clintons, but one beleaguered young assistant left her post to help clear me through a gate toward the West Wing communications area, figuring someone there could help. She escorted me through security checkpoints in corridors crammed with boxes and furniture dollies. Computer installers marched everywhere in quartets. We passed the Oval Office, whose doors stood wide open. I had visited the sanctum only once, as a ten-year-old on tour with the Atlanta Boy Choir to sing for President Dwight Eisenhower and Mamie in 1957, but those dim memories held nothing like this beehive of workers with stepladders, vacuum cleaners, and scattered bottles of Windex. Much of the afternoon marooned me in a chaotic press room. A junior speechwriter kindly ran interference toward the parade outside, only to be repulsed because my temporary pass was pink instead of brown. Finally, a nightingale who recognized me from Blair House managed to cow the military guards simply by announcing that she worked in the Social Office.

President Clinton stood to applaud an Air Force marching band. "I'm getting a second wind," he said, blithely accommodating politicians who stopped by to have photographs made with him during the parade. Visitors were thinning out in the presidential reviewing stand, which featured a covered roof, an open-air vista of Pennsylvania Avenue, and adjustable warmers for each seat on the front row. Colin Powell and the Joint Chiefs still rose dutifully every minute or less to salute the flags passing with a platoon of Boy Scouts, then with Elvis impersonators in a statuary of penguins, the 1776 Society of Concord, Massachusetts, and a solemn procession of the block-long AIDS memorial quilt. Both Clintons sadly called out the names on AIDS patches dedicated to friends, and Vice President Gore said one victim had been his neighbor. Last came a float with Miss Arkansas, and then the president departed. "Great job," he told three startled butlers in the temporary kitchen to the rear. "I hope you didn't freeze to death." He hurried along a bright blue protective plank-way over the lawn toward the White House, calling, "Hey, Hillary, wait." He caught up and took her hand.

Chief Usher Gary Walters opened the front door like a real-estate agent on the fantasy home tour. "Thank you," said Clinton. "Is it ready?"

With two aides, Walters led the three of us through the darkened grand entrance, our footsteps echoing, around three right turns into the president's private elevator, which stalled. There was an awkward silence. "We should have walked up," said the president. "If I am ever on an elevator trying to get special treatment, there is a better than 50-50 chance the elevator won't work." The ushers tried not to laugh, but seemed relieved by his levity, and the gilded box eventually rose to the second floor.

We crossed the yellow central hall into the master bedroom for the first time, taking it in. Two small men bowed politely. "Sir, I'm Angelito," said one steward. His colleague, Antonio, introduced himself as we looked at curved indentations on the north inside wall. Angelito said carpenters would adjust missing shelves to fit the size of new books, and Hillary nodded. "That's one of our major deals, bookshelves," she said, turning around, looking for her things to get ready for the evening's twelve inaugural balls. "I don't even know how to start." She excused herself to find her parents and Chelsea, who was running around in curlers and a white robe with four friends sleeping over from Arkansas. We followed Angelito to a large closet, where two valets were busily arranging racks of hats, boots, moccasins, sneakers, dress shoes, and neckties. On discovering that the valets came from the Philippines, the president told them his Arkansas director of international marketing also came from there, prompting some discussion of Philippine geography and travel. Then he led me into the parlor, saying, "Let me show you our sort of living room here," and continued eastward down the hall. Among many boxes stacked in the Treaty Room, he found several bags of golf clubs and a special rocking chair he had owned since childhood, with oak leaves carved around an elaborate moon face. He confirmed that he had just taken the oath of office on one of three Bibles already stacked on the big desk. "Yes, my grandmother gave it to me," said Clinton, looking pensive when I complimented his choice of Galatians 6:9 in the speech. "It sounded all right, didn't it?" he asked, pausing. "When we finally got there."

The president said he wanted to figure out which guest chamber was the Lincoln Bedroom. On the way, he remarked that while Lincoln did not actually sleep there, he thought the name originated from Mrs. Lincoln's purchase of its rosewood bed, in which their son Willie later died.

Turning as we walked, he said abruptly, "I can't tell you how glad it made me to be back together with you." My reply was trite but true: "Well, I will never forget it." He thanked me for jumping into the whirlwind on short notice, and mentioned the collaboration again when we crossed from the Lincoln Bedroom to the other stately guest room on the second floor. "Did you enjoy working with those guys?" he asked. We were standing at a front window of the Queens' Bedroom, looking toward Lafayette Park. I told him everyone on the team seemed sharp, and we all cooperated well on the editing, but that Clinton himself did much of the original composition. "Not many speechwriters," I added, "could have been as egoless as David and Michael with all those outsiders barging in late on their work."

I waited. The president was weighing something, perhaps a judgment or request, but I decided not to speculate. He moved on instead to a sitting room at the east end of the central hall, where visitors once had waited to see Lincoln, and nearly bumped into a housekeeper leaving a closet. The president coaxed out some of her biography. "Nice to meet you," he said. "Nice to meet *you*," Annie Barrett replied, flustered. He asked her to help him out by repeating names for a while. We went up to a furnished landing off the double stairwell halfway to the third floor, with a large window facing the Treasury. Clinton turned in circles, asking himself out loud if this was where President Ronald Reagan had convalesced after being shot.

"No, sir," a voice called from above. "You're in the wrong room. You want the Solarium." It was James Selmon, one of the butlers from the reviewing stand. He led us down a smaller hall that connected some twenty third-floor rooms, including seven guest bedrooms fashioned from the old attic quarters for Zachary Taylor's slaves. White House Photographer Bob McNeely scurried ahead to shoot the president's walk up an inclined corridor lined with engraved prints from *Harper's Weekly* and *Frank Leslie's Illustrated,* past a kitchen nook, to the window-wrapped sunroom facing south above the Truman Balcony. Clinton plopped in a familiar chair. "This is another one of my rockers," he said, and everyone else withdrew to let us talk.

He asked how long I had lived in Baltimore and whether I ever saw my ex-wife. He reminisced about Texas politicians we had recruited for

the statewide McGovern campaign in 1972. "What was weird was that I
had kept in touch with [former Texas agriculture commissioner] John
White for years, but he was pretty mean to me in the campaign," said the
president. "At first I thought he was trying to get his man Lloyd Bentsen
into the race, but he just kept on doing it and I never figured out why."
For the readers of *Life*, Clinton acknowledged no pinch-me moment
since taking office.* His answers tended to blend personality sketches
with lessons or questions on his mind. He portrayed the remarkably
cordial relationship with President Bush, for instance, as a by-product of
Bush's tendency to "offload" electoral politics to ideologues and professionals. Clinton thought Bush had kept a genial but costly distance from
his own nasty campaign. "You must try to integrate what you do—who
you are as a person, as a public servant, and as a candidate," said the new
president. "Everybody's always hedging a bit, but at least there needs to
be some sort of internal consistency. If it's not there, it can get you into
a lot of trouble."

Downstairs, Hillary stood with arms outstretched in a long-sleeved
formal gown of deep blue, surrounded by three dress designers, an acces-
sory expert, and a hairdresser named Christophe. She escaped the fuss of
being photographed to take a quiet walk with me down the long central
hall. We caught up mostly in small talk as fellow parents. The common
memory that stood out from our earlier years was a lunch in Washington
not long after Texas, about politics and love troubles, culminating for
me with her plaintive question: "Have you ever *been* to Little Rock?" The
first lady smiled but winced at my recollection. Thinking she might
worry about a potential slur on her adopted state, I told her I still considered the question intensely and legitimately personal. Had she loved
Clinton enough to leave home in the big-city lights, and her dream job
on the Nixon impeachment committee, for a new life hitched to Arkansas politics?

Emerging from the bedroom in his inaugural tuxedo, President
Clinton beamed at the sight of his daughter being photographed with
her friends. "I want to get in on this," he said. Neither he nor Hillary
could talk Chelsea out of wearing oversized emerald green earrings.

---

* "Backstage: January 20, 1993," *Life*, March 1993, pp. 33–43.

Aides herded everyone including grandparents and stylists down to complete the immense motorcade that was behind schedule. Someone threw me into the second "control car" with photographer McNeely and a skinny Navy commander carrying the nuclear launch codes in the ever-present satchel called "the football," with a thick antenna protruding from its top. Sirens and strobe lights bathed a short ride into passageways beneath the Capital Hilton Hotel, where the president shook hands with employees all the way into his holding room. Vice President Gore quarterbacked the two couples from there, suggesting that it would be more dramatic to remove the ladies' winter capes in full view of the crowd, and they plunged into the bracing welcome of "Ruffles and Flourishes/Hail to the Chief." I lasted only two more stops—the Medal of Honor Ball and the Arkansas Ball. Clinton waltzed on through another long night, until shortly before a morning reception to begin his first full day in the White House.

LIFE RESUMED OUTSIDE the bubble, and Clinton's salvo about preserving history was lost but not forgotten. To regain equilibrium, I dropped my own guarded pose about the long lapse of friendship, while resolving to curtail any burden of expectation on all sides. "I will never push myself on you or your staff," pledged my letter of thanks for sharing the inauguration, which invited either Clinton to call if they needed "an ad hoc sounding board and personal refuge." On a featured subject from the few private moments with each of them—our children—I updated my nine-year-old son, Franklin's, struggle to overcome a rare, degenerative hip disease called Legg-Perthes, which had knocked him abruptly from Little League to crutches. "He has taken up chess and swimming," I wrote, "and his child's courage has inspired his anxiety-ridden parents." Hillary's reply concluded, "Know that we will be remembering your family as well, especially Franklin," with a handwritten postscript: "Hope to see you soon!" I could only guess the volume of such correspondence, and wonder how much her staff helped her keep up with it.

In March, I sent the president two paragraphs about his announced schedule. One expressed eagerness for him to throw out the first pitch for baseball's opening day at Baltimore's exquisite new park in Camden Yards. Only half in jest, I offered him warm-up assistance from Franklin, whose recovery was spawning hopes that he would walk normally again and even run. "He has spent ten months now in his awkward leg brace," I reported as a lump-throated father and insufferable coach, "but he can still throw and catch like a pro." More to business, I passed along a short notice of an evening just spent with the exiled President Jean-Bertrand Aristide of Haiti, who was due to meet Clinton a few days later. For me, a lifelong stranger to heads of state, it seemed a bizarre coincidence to be thrown together with two of them now, spanning such extremes, from global superpower to the poorest country in the hemisphere. Film director Jonathan Demme, a new partner heading the cinema project for *Parting the Waters,* and a devotee of Haitian culture, had arranged the latter introduction. I decided not to impinge on Clinton's first impressions of Aristide with any details. "I think you will like him," my note predicted simply. "Together, the two of you have a chance to accomplish something truly historic."

Pleasantries came sporadically in return. On baseball's opening day, emissaries somehow located us in the stands with a confidential invitation for the whole family to join the president upstairs. The four of us followed sheepishly to the owner's box, where Clinton as always made instant contact with everyone. My lasting image is of him and Franklin standing almost back-to-back, mutually oblivious—Franklin in the A-frame brace with its metal bar holding his knees far apart, riveted by his Orioles on the field below, while Clinton received a densely revolving throng.

Some weeks later, the White House Social Office began a ritual new to Christy and me for a large dinner in June, moving from dress requirements and security procedures to formal escorts and calligraphic nameplates for everyone seated in the Blue, Green, and Red Rooms, where the U.S. Marine Chamber Orchestra fanned out among tables to perform before the toasts. When an usher whispered that the Clintons wanted us to join them after dinner upstairs, I assumed they had selected us for a smaller reception like the reviewing stand or the owner's box, which pleased me for a chance to show Christy the storied rooms of the second-floor residence. No other guests appeared, however, and the president wasted no time when he got me alone. He said he needed "an Arthur Schlesinger" to handle the historical problems we had discussed.

He wanted to put an in-house scholar on his staff who could become the chronicler of record, like Schlesinger for JFK. What did I think?

Reeling, I played for time by complimenting the president for his quest to devise a practical solution. Schlesinger's books on John and Robert Kennedy were enormously influential, I said, but they may not be good models for political history. Much of their impact came from martyred subjects in watershed times, and the books were considered works of advocacy even in a more innocent media era. This may not have disqualified Schlesinger as an objective historian, but he had functioned more as a pundit ever since. While making these points, I tried to imagine myself setting aside the commitment to finish my Martin Luther King histories, which I could not do, and I scrambled for a suitable reply to the president right in front of me. Clinton had not offered me this historian's post explicitly. There would be no shortage of willing scholars, I said, but both sides would face severe constraints. A would-be historian first must take leave to spend up to seven years in a Clinton White House, contending for access to the president, becoming more or less a target both inside and outside the administration. Even so, privileged access inevitably would discount the future work of any biographer, like Edmund Morris for Reagan. Rightly, from the start, I would be considered partial to Clinton as his political colleague from long ago, and no "court history" by me could earn much credit for either of us.

We debated briefly. He said surely there was value in authorized history, depending on its quality—if only to present an alternative set of facts. His disappointment sharpened into complaints about the distorted press coverage in a recent string of what he called bogus scandals such as his airport haircut. The president said he wanted to answer his critics, and to me his intensity on the point seemed misguided. While I was relieved that his goal seemed bigger than recruiting me, I groped for a way to warn him. I said he would do well to distinguish between short-term and long-term problems. He should concentrate on making the best history he could. No president can script the future by controlling its writers or themes, but every president can govern with an eye on tomorrow. That means navigating politics, including relations with the press, and it recommends gathering detailed records vibrant enough to help posterity establish truth over myth.

President Clinton did not appear to be convinced, but he tried another tack. Would I meet with a small group that he and Hillary had formed to consider these record-keeping options? Of course I would. The question left me chastened for thinking his "in-house historian" idea was a lone, quick-fix solution. The creation of such a group hinted of past efforts and internal resistance, which made me realize how little I knew of the competing pressures even in this little corner of the presidency. Some of them surfaced only a few days later at the meeting at the Williams & Connolly law firm. Maggie Williams was there as Hillary's chief of staff, and George Stephanopoulos represented the president. Unexpectedly, I found myself in the role of salesman pitching wares to skeptical buyers. I distributed file samples of my own research on the 1960s, ranging from the temporary bonanza of telephone transcripts down to personal tidbits scribbled by LBJ's secretaries on his daily calendar. There were also diaries and oral histories, plus detailed notes from dramatic meetings on the Vietnam War—some taken by high-level aides such as Jack Valenti, others by Tom Johnson, a young scribe who later became president of CNN.

The samples met a chilly reception. It was objected that note takers would inhibit debate, robbing the president of candid advice, and I made little headway by doubting the value of any advisers or advice that could be stifled for fear of public disclosure. Given that presidents had not been afraid to gather these records all through the Cold War, when the U.S.-Soviet standoff menaced the whole earth, I asked how we could justify hiding our deliberations now. The claims of secrecy provided no excuse. In addition to detailed written minutes, there were actual recordings of many crucial debates within the Kennedy, Johnson, and Nixon administrations that were *still* secret, unnecessarily, but at least they existed. Only disrespect for the public record, or for current deliberations themselves, could explain the willful trend to preserve less. As a fifth possibility on my list, I proposed that the Clinton administration reconstitute taping procedures for selected White House meetings.

"This suggestion was rejected," Bob Barnett recorded tersely in his July 6 report. A Washington lawyer who specialized in media relations, Barnett was looking ahead to represent both Clintons on book contracts, and the president had asked him to chair our task force with a dual pur-

pose. By improving records now, we sought to enhance the available recall
for future Clinton memoirs as well as the research base destined for public
access through the presidential library system. Barnett convened the group
several times into August, occasionally inviting expert colleagues from
Williams & Connolly, but attendance dropped off for lack of momentum.
The lawyers were trained to worry about risks—subpoenas, liability, privacy
disputes—and government officials tended to fret about turf boundaries or
control. These barriers gave me second thoughts about Clinton's proposal
for an in-house historian. Perhaps it was the only viable upgrade. As he
had directed, I called Nancy Hernreich with word that our group had
pretty much finished. She was a stranger to me then, having come up from
Arkansas to manage the Oval Office, but there seemed to be a note of
sympathy in her spare reply that the president had received Barnett's reports and would take appropriate steps. Hernreich was steely warm, and in
subsequent years she would remain the soul of discretion long after en-
dearing herself as a staunch friend to the history initiative. She betrayed
no agenda when asking me to bring Christy and the children for a White
House dinner on September 28.

MACY, OUR TWELVE-YEAR-OLD, reserved nearly all her bursting enthusiasm for
the teen band New Kids on the Block. Franklin, who was finally out of
his brace, went bug-eyed with admiration for the bomb-sniffing dog that
searched our car at the gate, but then he recovered his sister's pained
indifference to the White House, as though anticipating another loud
scrum of adults who did not know how many outs there were. They
endured our fascination with the historic dinnerware on display in the
China Room, until President Clinton culled me from the preliminary
tour for a walk around the spongy exercise track on the South Lawn. He
carried a mug of coffee. His brisk pace summoned up images of reporters trotting along behind LBJ's marathon press briefings in the 1960s,
and my heart sank with his opening references to a new book on President Kennedy by Richard Reeves. Citing its introductory statement that
the eyewitness accounts of Schlesinger and Ted Sorensen held up as essential biography "after all these years," the president still wanted someone placed inside the White House "to take care of the history." Would
I reconsider my objections?

That would not be my preference, I said, but I would help him find someone else. The role felt compromised to me. It would not seem right to draw a salary from the taxpayers as a historian-in-writing, affecting a neutral pose rather than pitching in to help now. My motivation did not fit the job. "Honestly, I feel more like a staff person," I told the president, adding that a political post for me was strictly hypothetical. Clinton did a slight double take and smiled. "That would be good," he replied, seeming to take my gesture as a sugarcoated sign of discomfort. Well then, he asked, should he plan to handle the history in his own memoirs? If he did not bring a writer into the White House, what should he do now? I said two things stood out: he should get note takers into all his meetings, and begin a systematic diary or oral history. Neither step would be easy. The president said maybe Stephanopoulos would take notes, but I said the Barnett group had convinced me that no member of the senior staff would take on the job. He asked why—because they didn't think they could be accurate enough? No, I replied gently— because they considered the task demeaning, and because all the principals would resist notes as a potential threat.

The president frowned. He said he had a good memory but precious little time for dictation. Also, his one trial effort had produced a sobering discovery. "I can't just sit down and talk into a tape recorder," he said. "I need questions. I need somebody responding to me." This was not uncommon, I replied, and oral history dialogue had developed since World War II to replace letters as a source for personal memory. One advantage of a prompted diary was that Clinton could initiate the project virtually alone, which would help safeguard the results. He needed only a trusted interviewer and some confidential logistics. From my own experience, I could get him started until someone on his staff picked up the relatively simple arts. The president seized on the notion. "Oh, that's even better," he said brightly. I wasn't sure whether he meant better than the in-house historian's job, or better than relying on an aide, but he said we should get going right away.

We were finishing our second lap on the exercise track when Chelsea arrived in a chauffeured plain sedan. She was positive in her report on school and ballet practice until the president said she was expected to join us all for dinner. Chelsea looked stricken. She said dinner was out of the question because she was so stressed, and he would not believe how much homework she faced. The stalemate required discussion a few paces away from me, and Chelsea wound up chafing in good grace through an abbreviated meal—not with scores or hundreds but only two families in a second-floor dining room across the central hall from the family parlor. Hillary came in late, and sighed when no one would join her in a glass of wine after her opening day of testimony before two House committees. The president congratulated her on glowing reviews. Even opponents said she spoke on health care flawlessly for hours without notes or aides to consult. Maureen Dowd of the *New York Times* was reporting that her "feminine imprint" ended an era on Capitol Hill, where she was only the third first lady to testify and the first to present a major piece of legislation. Speaking almost in shorthand, Hillary traded the day's inside stories with Clinton on health care and world crises from Bosnia to Somalia.

Chelsea answered questions about her first year in high school, and about being a Cubs fan. Our children disclosed what bribes from me it had taken for them to memorize the Gettysburg Address in tribute to the excellent book *Lincoln at Gettysburg,* which reminded Hillary that she had spent long interview sessions for a profile by its author, Garry Wills, only to have editors at *Time* magazine disappoint her by canceling the article on the claim that Wills wrote over the heads of their readers. When the president asked Christy why her boss, Mayor Schmoke of Baltimore, did not run for governor of Maryland, she said he had "cleared the decks" to run, politically and with his family, but decided in the end that he felt no agenda strongly enough to carry him through a race for governor. Clinton found such reasoning parallel to his own instincts to run for president in 1992 instead of 1988, both times against prevailing advice about openings in the political cycle. He relieved weighty topics with a lighthearted protest over the dual menu: whole artichokes followed by seafood broth for us, as opposed to the youth fare of celebrated waffle fries from the White House chef. Hillary invited us to guess our dinnerware's honored state by the individual flowers and birds artfully depicted on Lady Bird Johnson's set of china. The answer was inscribed on the bottom of each plate.

Chelsea soon escaped to do her homework. Hillary broke away to a night briefing for tomorrow's continued testimony, taking Christy with her. The president escorted Macy and Franklin to see the handwritten draft of the Gettysburg Address in the Lincoln Bedroom, dispensing stories he had absorbed since January about historic paintings and artifacts. Then he instigated a game of cards in the family parlor, and explained the rules for five-handed hearts when Christy returned. A number of rounds ensued, one of them ending in good-natured confusion over cards dropped with only two tricks left. Franklin would have played them in the correct order to foil Clinton's daring attempt to shoot the moon, the president insisted, a stickler to accept his own downfall. Later, he took me aside to discuss exactly how our collaboration would work. We quickly reached an understanding on the need for secrecy and careful custody. I said his confident control now was the key to building a candid public record for later, and pledged to step silently aside whenever he wished. He asked me to send a memo on procedures to Nancy Hernreich, who would schedule our first session. In the meantime, I would think about how to prepare and organize questions. My notes that night summarized the plan: "I'm going to help him get an oral history project started, and see how much we can cover, and how much time he has for it, and try to institute it regularly."

It was easy but pointless to say we should have started earlier in his term. We were improvising a routine in confidence, with whatever time and candor Clinton wanted to carve from his presidency. Initiative and control rightly belonged to the president, and while I believed he trusted my assurances—including a pledge not to disclose this delicious, newsworthy secret project, even to my extended family—he did not need my advance promise to stand aside at his wish. All he had to do was stop sending for me. Commitment was not strictly personal on either side. He knew I would recommend a systematic diary to any president.

Driving home, I asked my family for their impressions of the White House. Macy noticed that Chelsea had followed all the grown-up conversation and yet still worried about her homework. "That scared me about high school," she said. Franklin popped up suspiciously from the backseat: "Dad, are you recording this?" I confessed bringing my little machine for the special occasion. Christy recalled Hillary's staff briefing, and complimented the glorious fresh roses in the family quarters, then asked what the president had discussed in private. Macy interrupted as our future finance whiz: "Daddy, if you help him with this thing, um, would you get paid?" She scrunched up her nose when I said it would be a wonderful experience. Franklin allowed that President Clinton played hearts with grave concentration, holding his head a lot. Macy said his hands shook. "He made me nervous," said Franklin, "but he was really good."

CHAPTER THREE

THE TRUMAN BALCONY

Sunday, October 17, 1993

The next call came only three days after our first session. Nancy Hernreich's assistant said the president had a window in his schedule if I could arrange to drive down within the next few hours, and this spontaneous invitation struck me as a favorable sign. I did not anticipate any special hazards for a daytime rendezvous until a uniformed guard blocked me at the Southwest Gate to the White House compound. Anyone with my name who may have an appointment, he said carefully, was cleared to enter in a Ford Bronco. He studied my Ranger pickup with a dubious eye. When I asked him to call the Usher's Office to clear up the discrepancy, he replied that the South Grounds were closed to parking, anyway. His colleagues grew suddenly more agitated. The guard instructed me to circle back through a north gate instead, with an urgency that made me turn around before I knew where to go. Agents in suits pointed and converged, shouting that each direction was the wrong one until they wedged my truck off near a fence under trees. Only then did the first flashing lights of a long motorcade glide through the gate behind me. Much relieved, but still blocked from the South Grounds, I made my way all around the White House to park on the street and presented myself at the Northwest Gate. This led to security checks, inspections of my briefcase, a temporary badge, and escorted passage to several stops at offices in the West Wing, each time relayed as a residence-bound curiosity until the ushers finally welcomed me like a prodigal cousin.

They sent me upstairs with a tuxedoed White House Doorman, John Fanning, who parked me again in the Treaty Room.

President Clinton arrived in sneakers and warm-ups. He said he had just returned from a run along the Potomac River, which accounted for the motorcade, and proposed that we talk outside on the Truman Balcony. It was a beautiful day, he said, and we could escape there from an ongoing mobilization to attend a late afternoon performance by the acrobatic troupe Cirque du Soleil. After his shower, Clinton returned in blue jeans and a Yale sweatshirt. He led me on a detour into the small family kitchen, across the central hall from his bedroom, where he retrieved two bowls from the refrigerator. There was something deftly casual, yet furtive, about the way he heated one of them in the microwave, as if to suggest that he had just earned this treat with exercise and fixed it himself, but was not advertising it to Hillary or the butlers. My own weakness for snacks made me grateful that the thick, heated bean dip looked unappetizing. We carried it along with a bowl of salsa and a large bag of tostada chips through the oval sitting room of the residence, between the Treaty Room and the family parlor. A hidden door on the south wall opened to the Truman Balcony. The two of us set up shop on a glass-top table just around its eastern curve toward the Treasury Department. Beyond the manicured South Grounds stretched a magnificent vista of the Ellipse and the Washington Monument, with the cupola of the Jefferson Memorial in the distance.

On the tapes, President Clinton confirmed that he had favored Governor Mario Cuomo for the Supreme Court. He said he had broached the idea to Cuomo months before there was a vacancy, and that Cuomo had asked him for as much warning as possible to consider a major life decision. Accordingly, he had placed a call to Cuomo even before the public announcement that Justice White would retire, but he said Cuomo would not return his call for several days into a news tempest over the pending appointment. "I couldn't believe it," said Clinton. If publicized, such a rebuff itself could injure a sitting president, but he confessed how and why he pursued his coy champion nonetheless. Cuomo combined intellectual depth with a passion for difficult issues, he said, and when they did talk, he extolled this potential for greatness along with Cuomo's capacity to elevate themes of public service within the law. Still, the governor pulled back. There were Hamlet-like flurries of reversal, but Cuomo always declined again with reasons that struck Clinton more like a slogan—that he had started in New York politics and wanted to finish there. The president said he was perplexed. He seemed wounded, with an edge. "I felt like Diogenes wandering in Athens," he said, "asking, Where is an honest man I can give this job to?"

Clinton said his next choice was Bruce Babbitt of Arizona, another colleague from their years together in the National Governors Association. Like Cuomo, Babbitt would have fulfilled Clinton's desire to appoint a political justice who had never served as a judge. The president had no doubts about Babbitt's qualifications or his willingness to take the job. Here the indecision was all his own, Clinton disclosed, and frankly political. He said the crux of his problem was that the 1992 election had opened shaky inroads for a Democratic ticket in the West. Clinton reeled off the results from memory, state by state. He and Gore had carried Colorado, Nevada, New Mexico, and Montana. They lost South Dakota by twelve thousand votes, Arizona by less than two percentage points. He acknowledged finishing third to Bush and independent candidate Ross Perot in Utah, but said the only other Western state he lost badly was Idaho, where he did not even campaign. Having installed Babbitt at the Interior Department on a difficult political mission, the president said, he had scoured the landscape for a replacement who might pull off vital reforms in that distinctive regional culture—devoted to below-market grazing fees on public lands, and to freewheeling exploitation of timber and mineral resources—without forfeiting the Democratic gains at the polls. When the search proved fruitless, the president said he had resolved to keep Babbitt at Interior, sacrificing a subordinate's ambition to his own. "Bruce, I just can't put you on this Court," he recalled telling him directly. "I can't take the risk and absorb the hit myself, personally and politically." Clinton consoled himself that Babbitt understood his difficult choice, and never complained.

Hard experience with Cuomo and Babbitt underscored why presidents had appointed so few nonjudges to the Supreme Court. In describing the finalists, President Clinton said that after reading many reviews and judicial opinions, it was the personal interview that drew him to Judge Ruth Bader Ginsburg. I asked what impressed him most, whether it was her creativity or a particular idea or some other quality, and he highlighted the presentation of her family background leading into a legal career. He said she had a great life story. He had a special feeling that she could become a distinguished justice. My questions elicited little beyond that. He seemed to find in her a kindred approach that blended human touches with abstract analysis, recognizing personal struggle beneath every big issue in law and politics.

THERE WAS STIRRING around the motorcade parked along the driveway forty feet below. Butlers came out on the Truman Balcony to serve fresh Diet Cokes, and aides followed with word that they needed to leave for the circus half an hour early. Such entrances in a bunch came to telegraph the insistent rhythm of the president's schedule. We shifted forward in our reprise of 1993 for the remaining time, because Clinton wanted to focus on the historic Israeli-Palestinian signing ceremony at the White House on September 13. He claimed no influence on the secret negotiations leading up to the surprise agreement, nor much knowledge. During the transition, he had been briefed as president-elect on new back-channel talks brokered by Norwegian officials. He had approved the talks in general, said Clinton, with modest hope and no instructions. The process had originated through academics and other intermediaries almost as a private exercise, since the Israeli government and the PLO, the Palestine Liberation Organization, still denied each other standing for dialogue even as belligerents. Not until breakthroughs in the summer did high officials engage each other directly, if secretly, dropping their careful pose that the Oslo talks were a phantom that could be disowned.

The president's optimism had been misplaced on Syria. "I was wrong," he said. Of the many aging leaders in the Middle East, who had been fighting wars much of their lives, Clinton thought Syria's President Hafez al-Asad was most ready and able to initiate peace with Israel, so that he could recover the Golan Heights, lost in the 1967 war, for his nation before he died. The president also thought the necessary elements of a comprehensive settlement between Israel and Syria were less difficult than potential Israeli agreements with Jordan, Lebanon, or the Palestinians. Accordingly, he had nurtured his hunch about likely progress on the Syrian front in several private conversations, including his first White House meeting with Israeli prime minister Yitzhak Rabin, on March 15. When the September breakthrough came on the Palestinian front instead, leaping all the way from unknown Oslo talks to an interim peace agreement, Clinton said he learned only days in advance and was hardly less stunned than others. He remembered a phone call about the news aboard Air Force One, in flight from Cleveland, telling Rabin he was thrilled precisely because the Palestinian impasses were so wrenching and complex—Jerusalem, refugees, Israeli settlements on the West Bank. And he knew how hard it was for a soldier like Rabin to countenance the PLO leader Yasir Arafat after so many decades burying friends killed by Palestinians. "Yes, it's very hard, Mr. President," Clinton quoted Rabin's reply, "but, after all, we don't need to make peace with our friends."

This statement from Rabin entered public lore. Because the September 13 ceremony was in the world's spotlight, much of Clinton's account would emerge in news stories and memoirs, including his own, to answer the hunger for details about the backstage diplomacy. For instance, it took rehearsals and crisis managers to orchestrate the drama culminating in "the handshake" between grizzled enemies Arafat and Rabin, and there were comically elaborate precautions to ward off subsequent kissing on camera, especially by Arafat. Clinton said his national security adviser, Anthony Lake, had drilled the participants to place their left hand on the right shoulder of their handshake partners in a gesture of friendship that, without giving visible offense, also served to block any advances toward the customary Arab buss and embrace.

Protocol experts compressed nearly all the arrangements into a few days before the ceremony. What Clinton left on the tapes mostly are nuances about his few interventions. He said his own government first had been divided about whether he should host the event, as requested by all parties including the Norwegian government. Foreigners wanted to advertise U.S. support for the peace process, but dissenters within the administration warned of terrorist reprisals and of political damage from association with a likely failure. When he sided firmly behind the White House site, Clinton said he received a strong tide of internal advice to limit exposure by confining the ceremony at the level of the foreign ministers who were actually to sign the agreement (called the Declaration of Principles). This would achieve the written commitment without the public spectacle of Arafat and Rabin, but Clinton considered the symbolism of top leaders crucial. He finessed the issue by announcing that all sides were welcome to send any representative they wished.

"That gave Arafat a hole big enough to drive a truck through," said the president. Arafat quickly declared that he would come, seizing the chance to elevate his stature among the leaders of established governments. Arafat's statement in turn put enormous pressure on Rabin to be there for balance, despite his heartfelt desire to be anywhere else. President Clinton said that Israeli politics also pushed Rabin to join Foreign Minister Shimon Peres, his rival in the Labor Party, lest the separation appear to weaken both their government and the peace process. "If Rabin didn't come," said Clinton, "it would look like the military hero was just acquiescing in something engineered by Peres the dreamer." Even so, he recalled, Rabin's attendance remained uncertain in the midst of the furious political maneuvering. The Israeli government sent signals that Clinton was obliged to invite Rabin but did not really mean it, secretly hoping he would stay away, and rumors flew that Jewish voters in the United States would never forgive Clinton for subjecting Rabin to the public humiliation of standing next to Yasir Arafat. There was talk of prominent Americans boycotting the White House ceremony because Israeli law and U.S. policy still banned contact with PLO representatives as terrorists. The president said he called Israel at least twice to cut through the confusion. "My public position and my private position are the same," he told Rabin. "I want you to come if you want to come. If you do, I'll handle all the problems it might cause here among American Jews and American Arabs." Still, Clinton received maddening reports through the State Department that Rabin did not believe he was welcome. So he issued specific midnight instructions for a call to Israel's ambassador in the United States, Itamar Rabinovich. "I want you to wait at least an hour," Clinton said he told Tony Lake. "Late enough to be sure you'll wake him up, because then he'll know it's important. Tell Rabinovich the president is disturbed by reports that the prime minister doesn't feel welcome. Tell him in the strongest possible terms that he will be most welcome, and that I think it's a good idea for him to be here."

Finally, the president said he had to plead with Syrian president Asad to let his ambassador in Washington attend the ceremony. Asad fretted that he would be left out if Israel made peace with Syria's neighbors, and was determined not to accept weaker terms as a latecomer. Although Clinton knew this, the degree and detail of new anxiety caught him off guard. "Mr. President, is this your idea," Asad had asked him, "or is it Rabin's idea, that we have to be represented?" Clinton responded that he could not speak for Rabin, and could only assume the prime minister wanted Syria to be present. "But let's not put this in the context of politics between Israel and Syria," he added to Asad. "I want you to come as a favor to me, because it will be a big story if the Syrian ambassador is not here, and it will detract from the overall event." He said Asad had paused and then replied, "Okay, I will come as a favor to you."

Before the White House ceremony itself, there was a famously awkward standoff when the Israelis and Palestinians gathered for the first time. They clumped on opposite sides of the formal Blue Room, beneath the matching Yellow Oval Room in the president's residence. No one mingled, and all the delegations including the Americans whispered among themselves until Clinton dispatched Vice President Gore with a hastily contrived proposal to send away the White House photographer, Bob McNeely, so the leaders could greet each other informally without fear that some unflattering image might encircle the globe. Clinton said Gore returned quickly, looking miserable and abused, to report that Rabin "stiffed me." The president and vice president stood beside Hillary and Tipper, along with Secretary of State Warren Christopher, and eventually the president himself crossed the divide. When he beckoned Rabin and Arafat to a preliminary introduction, Rabin clasped his arms firmly behind him, shook his head, and uttered his first terse words to the assembly, "At the ceremony, at the ceremony." Then Arafat folded his arms on his chest and replied, "Fine, at the ceremony."

This social freeze among principals reflected the Middle East, while their seconds haggled over political details until the last minute. Israeli diplomats threatened to bolt if Arafat decorated his tunic with any military insignia, let alone a pistol, and the Palestinians refused to accept the final version of the agreement because the signature spot for Mahmoud Abbas, Arafat's foreign deputy, was marked "Palestinian team" instead of

"Palestine Liberation Organization." With no time to type a new original, the staff inserted a handwritten "For the PLO" to grant some form
of recognition. The document made its way over from the West Wing,
and escorts moved the dignitaries outside to take seats among a host
gathered on the South Lawn. Only Clinton, Arafat, and Rabin lagged
behind to make their grand entrance from the Diplomatic Reception
Room, directly beneath the Blue Room and two floors below the balcony where the president was recording his memories a month later. He
recalled telling them on the way downstairs that they had a long way to
go, that they were about to walk alone through the door ahead and he
wanted things to go smoothly for them both. At last came a few thawing
words in response, which the president would release as a sign of hope.
"We have a lot of work to do," said Rabin. Arafat replied, "Yes, we do,
Mr. Prime Minister, and I'm willing to do my part."

Pictures from the televised ceremony became instant icons. Clinton
stood between Arafat and Rabin during the unrehearsed handshake, his
own hands outstretched behind them on either side. On the tapes, he
warned against concluding from visual evidence that Arafat relished the
contact whereas Rabin abhorred it. He said their words conveyed something quite different. Rabin spoke like an anguished prophet filled with
determination for peace, saying "enough of blood and tears, enough."
By contrast, Arafat, who spoke excellent English, gave a speech in Arabic
that said little and inspired less. It did not even affirm his recent letter of
peace, while seeming to begrudge concessions already made. Clinton
said Arafat was consumed with worry about how his words would play
back home. He liked being on television but doubted his course. Rabin
was almost the reverse.

Their combined reality made the agreement a fragile miracle. Under
the Declaration of Principles, the two sides not only granted each other
coexistence for the first time but they also adopted a common agenda.
The Israeli government pledged to let the PLO develop many autono-
mous functions of government, including the election of popular representatives, in territories occupied by Israel since the Six Day War of 1967.
The PLO agreed to secure public order in the territories, including protection against violent attacks upon Israel. Upon these hopes, the two
sides framed the difficult issues for "final status" peace negotiations over

a five-year timetable, aimed toward mutual recognition between Israel and a newly established nation of Palestine.

THE ISRAELI–PLO CEREMONY of September 13 set in motion a high-stakes international drama that would consume Clinton intermittently until his last hours in office. Not knowing the outcome, he shifted on the tapes to another precarious crusade launched the very next morning at the White House with former presidents Gerald Ford, Jimmy Carter, and George Bush. If Ronald Reagan were well enough, and Richard Nixon had not been grieving the recent death of his wife, Clinton said all five living ex-presidents would have joined in unprecedented unity to seek congressional approval for the North American Free Trade Agreement. He described NAFTA as a mixed issue of good policy and bad politics. While good for the country, he asserted, NAFTA cost him the passionate opposition of traditional Democratic allies from labor unions and environmental groups.

The president outlined the theoretical arguments for free trade, and trotted out the endorsements of Nobel Prize economists overwhelmingly behind NAFTA, but his analysis focused on two members of the House leadership. David Bonior of Michigan, the Democratic whip, represented a Detroit economy decimated by two decades of foreign competition in the automobile industry. Clinton saw in Bonior an articulate foe who believed NAFTA would skew benefits to corporate executives at the expense of displaced working families. Bonior did engage Clinton in a running, substantive debate on his counterargument that Michigan could be a net beneficiary under NAFTA. Clinton said Michigan had suffered the worst already, and had begun to retool for new industries. Wage competition risked the continued export of certain jobs to cheaper countries, but Clinton argued that a shrinking world made such risk inevitable with or without NAFTA. He said Bonior conceded his point that NAFTA at least would open foreign markets to U.S. exports, while creating higher environmental and fair-labor standards in overseas factories, but Bonior's labor constituents did not trust rosy projections from politicians or corporations. They felt sucker punched, said Clinton. They were "beyond rational" on free trade, and demanded protectionism to the point that they evaluated political candidates solely on that issue. The president thought many labor leaders, like some environ-mentalists, were prone to drag their feet ineffectually and let the perfect become an enemy of the good. He considered Bonior's vote lost. More-over, he expected Bonior's leadership of opposing forces to be energetic and effective. Yet he spoke warmly of him. Whatever NAFTA's outcome in Congress, he said, Bonior would move on without rancor to support the president again whenever he could. Clinton appreciated his ap-proach to public service. He lamented that Bonior's controlled ardor was becoming rare in a political culture given to indulge rather than overcome personal grievances.

President Clinton sketched a more calculating figure in Richard Gephardt, the House majority leader from Missouri. Being close to trade unions, Gephardt spoke earnestly against unfairness to working families, but he also perceived larger benefits from NAFTA over time. According to Clinton, Gephardt's mind was divided on the merits, which elevated two political factors in the NAFTA alignment. First, Gephardt was plan-ning to run for president, and he would depend heavily on organized labor to campaign against Clinton or Gore. Second, he knew that if he stood with Clinton on NAFTA, it would practically force Bonior to mount a leadership challenge against him or Speaker Tom Foley of Washington. Therefore, Gephardt would stick with Bonior against NAFTA, Clinton figured, if only to contain a potential split among House Democrats.

Predicting safe passage in the Senate, President Clinton said the fate of NAFTA would rest on his temporary alliance with House Republicans plus a concerted effort to pick off enough Democrats from their own united leadership. Although the partisan lines were blurred, he said, it would come down to an old-fashioned struggle for votes, district by district. He estimated that he was starting at least twenty short of victory, but singled out no targets or strategies. Instead, he shifted back to presi-dential chemistry at the kickoff event for NAFTA. Carter and Bush had stayed with him overnight, and Clinton said he was amazed that Bush accepted a guest invitation at his former home so soon after being evicted. He noted that Barbara Bush stayed away. He said Gerald Ford joined them for dinner on the night of the Middle East ceremony, then again for a private breakfast before the NAFTA presentation. Clinton's

staff had found no prior record of so many presidents eating meals together at the White House.

The four of them had reminisced about Middle East history at dinner, Clinton added, but they suffered a conversational lull the next morning until they discovered a shared distaste for Texas multimillionaire Ross
Perot. He said Ford pronounced Perot a phony who had wheedled his
fortune from taxpayers in sole-source government contracts but masquer-
aded as a showcase of free market discipline. Carter resented Perot's cowboy machismo for goading his administration into the disastrous 1980
commando raid to rescue American diplomats held hostage by Iran.
Bush, of course, smarted from Perot's spoiler role as a third-party candidate in 1992, which he believed may have cost him reelection, but Clinton recalled greater animus from Bush over insinuations that Perot was
the real, rough-and-tumble Texan whereas Bush was only a country club
transplant. Clinton still seemed startled that the combined presidents
had stomped on Perot all through breakfast. His own complaints were
relatively mild. Until recently, he saw Perot mostly as a maverick with a
knack for sound bites, but then Clinton had tried a courtesy call to explain how the hard-won budget package answered Perot's central theme
and purpose by setting a course to eliminate the nation's chronic budget
deficit. In response, Perot dismissed the package as a fraud and refused to
discuss its components. Although this episode gave the president a story
to tell his three colleagues—that Perot was all about political poses, not
substance—Clinton fell behind in competitive rounds of biting recollection. He said Bush, in a surprising departure from his gracious aplomb
about the election result, sustained the wittiest vitriol about Perot.

WE DISCUSSED NO more topics at length. Already late, the president pulled
away to check on the circus and other matters, promising to return for
the rewound cassettes. He made glancing comments on and off the
tapes, sometimes asking me to remind him of some subject or event at
the next session. He said insomnia had made him read the book of
Joshua before the Middle East ceremony, for instance, and he gave credit
to National Security Council assistant Jeremy Rosner for drafting his
lyrical remarks. He offered a few sentences on health care, including a
remarkably calm description of finding himself without a text when he

began his televised address to Congress two days ago, and being obliged to ad-lib for nearly ten minutes until aides inserted the correct speech in the TelePrompTer. He said health costs were rising at five times the rate of inflation and would "eat this government alive" if not checked. He said there was talk of an international tribunal for Somali warlord General Aidid if they could ever catch him. He said members of Congress were "all upset" that Al Gore's initiatives to streamline government would impact the subcommittee system, disturbing their established relations with the bureaucracy.

There was a haphazard quality about our talks. The president sank deeply into some stories but skimmed over others. His emphasis varied widely from personal insight or grand analysis to minute statistical detail. The overall approach seemed to reflect innate curiosity harnessed to a puzzle worker's compulsion. Clinton reveled in big puzzles with a human factor. Perhaps such a trait explained why he said so much about the two justices he did not appoint and so little about the one he did. Cuomo and Babbitt preoccupied him as a mystery, or mistake, whereas Ginsburg was a settled choice.

That afternoon I pushed several such theories from my mind. They were fun but premature, and I concentrated on preserving firsthand memories to supplement the record being stowed away in Clinton's possession. Interpretation could wait, to be carried on by future students of the presidency or the Clinton years. I made a note that we had not yet mentioned post-Soviet Russia in our review of 1993. In the five minutes or so that it took to rewind the tapes, I marveled at the views from the Truman Balcony. Stark contrasts occurred. The White House was a fortress, as my own flyspeck woes getting past security had demonstrated, but the president had been sitting in plain view for more than an hour. I studied distant figures walking along the Ellipse, wondering if they could distinguish Clinton from me. On weekdays, citizens lined up all the way out there to tour the White House, while Secret Service professionals must have weighed the risk that a president could be shot here on its porch. I felt a passing flick of exposure myself, but no one seemed to notice the balcony at all.

CHAPTER FOUR

CULTURE CLASHES: FROM BOSNIA TO A HAIRCUT

Wednesday, October 20, 1993

Monday, November 1, 1993

Thursday, November 4, 1993

A third session in the span of six days allowed a personal introduction to Nancy Hernreich, who secluded me in her decorated cubbyhole just outside the Oval Office. It was an old stationery closet, which provided a more discreet place to wait than the main reception area. The whole West Wing was a fishbowl, she explained, especially in the daytime, and anyone who saw me would ask or wonder what business I had so near the president. My long interview would have drawn competitive scrutiny if listed on the president's public calendar, but the disguised alternative—an open time slot—invited interruption by those with urgent claims to a presidential moment. Nancy gave me tips on how to deflect their curiosity, and warned that my allotted hour could be compressed or scrubbed by anything from a crisis to a presidential whim. She said feedback from the president had overcome her reluctance to schedule me during business hours. He was pushing hard to catch up with the backlog of major events in 1993, which was a positive sign for the re-corded history project, and she had squeezed in today's risky experiment because all his nights through October were committed already to din-ner events or travel.

Staff secretary John Podesta dropped by shortly with a sheaf of pa-pers for President Clinton's signature. He asked what I was doing there, and remarked with a knowing wink that it must be pretty secret for Nancy to hide me beforehand in her little office. Podesta's incisive wit seemed to divine everything she just told me. As smoothly as possible, I said the president was consulting me about the preservation of historical materials for his future library. This did not surprise Podesta, who had been included in some of our communications with the National Ar-chives about creating a White House office on history. I added that it was a happy coincidence to see the staff secretary, who managed the flow of documents, because we were looking for the human factor in White House records. Would his files hold many clues to the personal dynamics behind government decisions? Podesta smiled incredulously. His reply—you mean, what really happened?—suggested that files were supposed to bury decisions rather than expose them, and he confirmed my reports that no one was taking notes in presidential meetings.

When I asked Podesta to suggest potential note takers, he listed Syl-via Mathews of the Domestic Policy Council, and Bruce Lindsey, the president's adviser from Arkansas. He said they were trusted and thor-ough, but that neither may want the job. Before he could ask me an-other question, I nodded at Senator John Breaux of Louisiana to wonder out loud whether he reminded Podesta of the comic actor Dabney Cole-man. Breaux was leaning against a table in the reception area, chewing gum, and Podesta studied him with an impish gravity I took as a friendly signal that he would not press for details of my work with the president. He asked if I meant only in appearance or also in behavior, like the mis-chievous villain Coleman played in the film *Nine to Five*. Before I could answer, he deadpanned, "A little of both."

In the Oval Office, which was airy and quiet, I proposed to President Clinton that since our time might be cut short by the bustling petition-ers outside, perhaps we should tackle a single theme by recording his impressions of individual foreign leaders. He agreed to begin with U.N.

secretary-general Boutros Boutros-Ghali, who had visited him in February for private talks about the besieged Bosnian capital of Sarajevo. The president portrayed Boutros-Ghali as a garrulous man of energy and ambition, who eagerly described U.N. missions all over the world— including those with no policy disputes to be resolved, on which Clinton had been briefed already. His enthusiasm could be infectious, said the president, but at times it conveyed an annoying sense that all national leaders worked for Boutros-Ghali and should rise above their parochial concerns. Clinton said he had made an effort to respond in balanced language, that he would work with Congress to make up the shameful arrears in U.S. dues to the United Nations, for instance, because it was a responsible course apart from any duty to Boutros-Ghali himself.

On only one issue did Boutros-Ghali surprise him: the secretary-general was lukewarm at best about the U.N.'s humanitarian airlift to prevent starvation in besieged Bosnian cities. Clinton said the airlift, though overshadowed by atrocities, had saved many thousands of lives since February, but that Boutros-Ghali discounted the effort. He said the secretary-general insisted that Muslim enclaves in the Balkans were doomed as illegitimate, and that the United Nations should do no more than support halfheartedly a proposal for stopgap ethnic "cantons," which could not survive. Boutros-Ghali told him that it had required "the iron hand of Tito," Yugoslavia's former strongman, to protect multiethnic cities like Sarajevo, Clinton recalled. Not only did this notion ignore long periods of stable coexistence before Tito, but it was a striking departure from the secretary-general's global perspective. Privately, on Bosnia, the president found that Boutros-Ghali of Egypt shared the cold-blooded realpolitik of some European leaders.

Strains of authoritarian nationalism also menaced President Boris Yeltsin in Russia, where powerful elements in the new Duma, or parliament, agitated to reconstitute the recently dissolved Soviet empire. Clinton outlined heated debates within his government about the policy toward Russia. Many advisers argued that President Bush had hurt U.S. interests by aligning himself too closely with Mikhail Gorbachev, and urged Clinton not to make the same mistake with Yeltsin. They warned him to hedge support for the fledgling Russian government in case Yeltsin lost power or turned into a tyrant himself, but Clinton said he felt no choice going in but to treat Yeltsin as the only recognized hope for democratic reform. He said the collapse of Communist society left Yeltsin vulnerable in the Kremlin and a proud beggar among the great nations. On balance, Clinton still believed that Yeltsin would resist powerful movements to lash out at enemies and scapegoats, or go back to Communism, and would stick with the daunting task to create a Russian network of free institutions: markets, elections, infrastructure, credit, public justice.

Much of what Clinton recorded about Yeltsin has seeped into accounts of their first summit, in April in Vancouver, Canada. They had much in common as earthy politicians of humble origin and resilient charm. Yeltsin famously told reporters that although he enjoyed meeting President Clinton, "to have a really good time one must be in the presence of a beautiful woman." Clinton told me Yeltsin was missing two fingers on his left hand from a factory accident in his youth. He said Yeltsin had given advance notice in Vancouver that he would publicly chastise Clinton in order to inoculate himself from the nationalist backlash in Russia, and, sure enough, Yeltsin had flogged him for belittling Russia. Clinton said he cut Yeltsin slack because both he and his country were a teetering mess. A dinner in Vancouver had convinced him that alcohol was more than a sporting problem, as Yeltsin drank through the meal without touching his food. That same evening, Yeltsin solicited reams of advice about how to acquire economic assistance from other nations, beyond Clinton's U.S. aid package of $2.5 billion, and Clinton confessed that he probably did say what the Canadian reporters found afterward in a crumpled note discarded by Yeltsin's translator: "Sometimes the Japanese say yes when they mean no." This touched off a storm of indignation in Japan, which the president said he was obliged to calm. He did better in a briefing restricted to the Russian press corps, expounding on his youthful immersion in their nation's classical arts, including the novels of Tolstoy and Dostoyevsky. When he praised the difficult last movement of Shostakovich's Fifth Symphony, recalling that Leonard Bernstein once had conducted it in Moscow at a faster tempo than anyone else dared, the president said the Russian reporters told him he was full of surprises, like Yeltsin. After Vancouver, Clinton said, he worked hard to get Yeltsin invited to the G-7 economic summit in Tokyo and to secure for Russia an international aid package from the G-7 nations—only to be ambushed by new reports that Russia was dumping nuclear waste into the Sea of Japan. He said life with Yeltsin was a constant adventure.

Kiichi Miyazawa, the Japanese prime minister, had come to Washington before hosting the G-7 meetings in July. President Clinton described him as a likable figure, whose fluency in English extended to nuanced humor and even Arkansas slang. Conversational ease made more palatable their difficult talks about the looming end of Japan's economic miracle, which would impede growth in many countries. Miyazawa had agreed with Clinton's diagnosis of the Japanese economy being constricted by trade and credit barriers, an artificially high savings rate, and government protection for cartels, but the prime minister faced political obstacles to every reform. Clinton pointed to a small copy of Rodin's sculpture *The Thinker,* and said his photographer had captured Miyazawa there in a tandem pose that unconsciously mimicked its befuddled gaze. Miyazawa's government was on the brink of collapse from chronic, large-scale corruption that reinforced Japan's structural paralysis. One official had been caught with $50 million in gold bullion under his bed. At home, Clinton mused, Illinois's Dan Rostenkowski, the powerful Democratic chair of the House Ways and Means Committee, was being engulfed by comparatively trifling charges that he had cashed in $21,000 from his congressional stamp allowance, whereas in Japan it took a fortune under your bed to ignite a scandal.

The president said the G-7 summit had become a surprise triumph in part by exceeding low expectations. For all his own image problems, from gays in the military to the tempest over his haircut on a Los Angeles runway, Clinton found himself politically stronger than his fellow world leaders. He said Mitterrand of France was in trouble and so was the British prime minister, John Major. China's Jiang Zemin behaved cautiously in the wake of his powerful predecessor, Deng Xiaoping, while Prime Minister Kim Campbell of Canada was even newer and already under fire. Accordingly, the major powers deferred to Clinton's initiatives on economic cooperation, and his trade team hammered out three significant bilateral agreements. In addition, the president thought he made important symbolic connections to the Japanese people at public events, such as his question-and-answer session with students at Waseda University. He said he and Hillary could feel the positive response when they stepped out of their motorcade to walk through the streets of Tokyo for talks with small business groups. The international press had relayed glowing reports to foreign citizens, said the president, but even the more skeptical domestic reporters had noted promise in Tokyo beyond the usual bland summit.

Not for the last time, Clinton described Germany's chancellor, Helmut Kohl, as his best new friend among heads of state. Conservative and durable—holding national office since 1982—Kohl was a lone exception among the new or tentative leaders at the G-7 meetings. In Clinton's portrayal, their differences produced a bonding rather than friction or estrangement. They both regarded politics as a vehicle for major improvements in everyday life. At great political risk, Kohl had led the efforts to reunify Germany after the Cold War, and he was moving ahead with even larger plans to integrate the economies of Europe. His experience in practical dreams was a natural fit for Clinton's foreign policy hopes to expand NATO, promote global trade, and forge regional peace agreements. Kohl was the only politician Clinton repeatedly labeled smart in our sessions, sometimes with an admiring shake of his head. The chancellor lacked the personal chemistry to improvise or excel at public events, such as Clinton's town-hall meetings with foreign students, but Clinton said Kohl found other ways to fold public relations into his gift for strategic politics. Before the Tokyo summit, the president remarked, he had called Germany so often that Kohl jokingly likened himself to Clinton's "old Dutch uncle," dispensing advice and reassurance.

A question about South Africa yielded a stream of memory about the two transformational leaders who had visited the White House together in July. F. W. de Klerk, the last president of the apartheid regime, had released in 1990 the world's most famous prisoner, Nelson Mandela. For their ensuing negotiations, which peacefully dismantled apartheid with a new constitution, Mandela and de Klerk were about to receive the Nobel Peace Prize jointly, and they had traveled with Clinton to Fourth of July celebrations in Philadelphia. Earlier, I tested our frankness by commenting that Clinton's address on that auspicious occasion—standing at the birthplace of American freedom with the founders of miraculous new hope in South Africa—had fallen well short of his eloquence at the Rabin-Arafat ceremony. The president only shrugged, saying he gave too many speeches to work on them all himself. He was much more interested in the complexity of South Africa's emerging order, with Mandela expected to displace de Klerk in elections next year. They had less trouble with each other than with supporters in their own camps, Clinton observed. He said white supremacy groups flanked de Klerk on the right, threatening terrorism to conceal their political weakness, and he analyzed Mandela's efforts to contain Chief Mangosuthu Buthelezi's threat of a separatist boycott by the seven million members of his Zulu tribe. Mandela exuded a serene charisma in public, he said, while privately keeping up such a stream of banter and personal inquiry that admiring White House aides called him downright chatty. Anyone who endured twenty-seven years in prison could talk all he wanted, Clinton quipped. He quoted de Klerk to illustrate a promising sense of comfort between the rival partners: "Nelson, you may beat me in the election, but I may do better than you think. I will have the only multiracial campaign, and I intend to keep it." The president hoped de Klerk could survive the upheaval ahead to lead a constructive opposition.

Clinton skimmed through his introductions to other peers. He had taken pains to see President Carlos Menem of Argentina before the Tokyo summit in order to signal resolve on NAFTA with attention to a frequently neglected area in U.S. foreign policy. Apart from the Asian Rim, said the president, South America was the most rapidly growing regional economy. He described Menem as a dashing figure who rode horses, held court with movie stars, idolized former strongman Juan Perón, and offered a shrewd promise for reform mixed with a suspect commitment to democratic methods. Clinton mentioned to me his visit to South Korea, which he called the last hostile trip wire from the Cold War, but his interest seemed to drift from President Kim Young-sam, who was distracted by his own political battles, to the U.S. troops stationed below the bleak DMZ. He recalled conversations with individual soldiers, some by name, and told of wheedling from the commander's modest wife that she herself was a former paratrooper. "I love those people," said Clinton.

• • •

THE PRESIDENT EXCUSED himself to the bathroom. No sooner did he leave the Oval Office by a side door than Nancy Hernreich entered to say the president must depart with Mack McLarty for a NAFTA event. McLarty himself came just behind her, followed by photographer Bob McNeely and Clinton's young personal aide Andrew Friendly. I tried to conceal my recorders casually. Andrew, whom I had met during the inauguration, approached me quietly to say he thought our new project was very important. I thanked him vaguely, not knowing what details had been disclosed, and told him the president may want him to sit in on future sessions as a natural choice to take over my role. When the president returned, he told McLarty that he had discussed NAFTA with the first legislator he did not believe he could convince on the merits. McLarty commented that Clinton indeed had seemed discouraged after the call. "We're nip and tuck right now with [Representative] Joe Kennedy," he added. The president agreed that the substance of NAFTA consistently lost to raw politics, with heavy pressure especially from trade unions. He speculated that NAFTA would be at least thirty votes closer to a majority if Congress voted by secret ballot. Sending the others ahead, he told me to bring the tapes back next time because he couldn't wait for me to rewind and label them now. On the way out, he reacted favorably to John Podesta's suggestions for a note taker on domestic policy, and he welcomed my offer to sound out Tony Lake about securing regular notes from the presidential meetings on national security. Such recommendations would require follow-up with lawyers, the president observed, but at least we were getting a start on the diary. Then he was gone.

I returned to retrieve my tape materials from an Oval Office that seemed eerily quiet, drained of the energy around a president. The emptiness spawed a reverie from my daily work. I was writing about the 1964 Freedom Summer, the height of the civil rights era, when young people had raised simple democratic witness from Mississippi to rattle and move officials in this same room. Together, citizens and politicians had erected landmarks of freedom, and thoughts of their combined legacy enhanced my splendid view of the Rose Garden until Nancy Hernreich snapped me back to reality. She provided an escort through the West Wing down to the national security enclave. I waited there quite a while before Tony Lake emerged to say sheepishly that an unexpected crisis prevented him from inviting me into his office. He had sent for me, he explained, because of a tip from Vernon Jordan that I may be concealing a matter of grave national importance involving a veteran reporter at *The Wall Street Journal.*

I sighed. At least that bizarre tale gave me a chance to say hello, I replied, then handed over a letter from the reporter, who had been pestering me since my *Life* magazine article to arrange a private audience with Clinton, claiming to know from spy sources in Moscow and Israel of a super-secret new weapon that endangered all human life. The reporter had rebuffed my suggestions that he write a story to alert the public, or submit his information through government channels, by insisting that officials beneath Clinton himself were conspirators in a cover-up. He said the stakes were too high. "It's as if I'd discovered the atom bomb had been stolen," his note warned me, "before anyone else knew it had been invented." I told Lake I could not burden the president with what seemed to be a lunatic, who probably needed help, but I was glad to be rid of it.

The national security adviser pocketed the letter as a familiar sort of nuisance. "There are a lot of loony people in Washington," said Lake. "Sometimes I think I'm loony myself." He nodded toward his office door and confided that CIA director James Woolsey was inside with several deputies so secret he could not let me see them. He could speak generally, since the news was leaking already to media outlets, of Woolsey's day on Capitol Hill spreading unsubstantiated reports that the exiled Aristide of Haiti was a psychotic and drug addict, unfit to hold office. He said lurid publicity inevitably would undermine the administration's avowed goal of restoring Aristide as the elected president, but Clinton could not easily fire or restrain Woolsey for giving classified testimony to Congress, even if it was unverified and nutty. I tried to absorb Lake's predicament, but could only convey to him my own contrary experience with Aristide. Did anyone know that he had learned Hebrew in Jerusalem as a young priest? Our introduction to each other had slipped into an enthralled discussion of Martin Luther King's friendship with the learned rabbi Abraham Heschel, how it was grounded in a common conviction that bold doctrines of prophetic justice—equal souls before God—had laid an ancient foundation for the democratic concept of equal votes. This was rarefied stuff for a poor Haitian priest. Subsequent evenings had revealed Aristide's committed grasp of nonviolent politics and theology, which chastened me for my worries about associating with him. In the press, his name commonly evoked ominous images of a witch doctor combined with Robespierre, the evil genius of the French Revolution.

Lake shifted and stared. So I knew Aristide? Whether saint or devil, the conflicting images made Haiti policy a vexing snare. He said he had to get back to Woolsey. His deputy, Sandy Berger, came out in some distress to survey my impressions of Aristide's practical mind. Just last week, the administration had pulled back its first shipload of U.S. peacekeepers to Haiti because of dockside rioting by thugs, and Clinton was getting hammered both for weakness and misplaced sympathy. The *Washington Post* cited Haiti as proof that the administration lacked a "coherent" foreign policy. I agreed to outline possible steps concerning Aristide the administration could take to rise above the impasse.

Before Lake departed, I took him aside to inquire on the president's behalf about note takers in his national security meetings. There were none, he replied, and he would have to think very hard before having any. Lake made his predilections clear by quoting seminal advice from the legendary counselor for presidents, Clark Clifford: "Never write anything down." He waved aside my pitch for mutual reinforcement between good history and public service, noting that his mentor, Averell Harriman, the "crocodile" of Cold War diplomacy, had conducted his government business on the telephone to avoid leaving a dangerous trail. Lake was playful but brusque, which reminded me that we had dubbed him a cutthroat hippie in graduate school. In the late 1960s, already back from a harsh Foreign Service tour in Vietnam, Tony had concocted ferocious competitions even when tossing a Frisbee on the campus lawn of the Woodrow Wilson School at Princeton. Now his secretive shield posed more bureaucratic obstacles to the collection of White House records, and I left the White House with dampened prospects in my assigned field of competence. Keeping accurate notes for history seemed taboo at least in the foreign policy shop, where I sensed a great need for a kibitzer on Haiti.

• • •

THE FOURTH AND fifth catch-up sessions fell in the week of November 1. On Monday, I waited nearly an hour, engrossed in the Treaty Room's art and artifacts. An oil painting by George Healy hung on the north wall, showing Lincoln at his last military council with Civil War commanders Ulysses S. Grant, William Tecumseh Sherman, and Adm. David Porter, in a ship's cabin. General Sherman is wagging a finger with characteristic emphasis, but Lincoln dominates the scene by listening with his chin rested in one hand. The room draws its name from Theobald Chartran's larger canvas on the west wall—a classically heroic portrait of President William McKinley in this chamber, presiding over treaty ceremonies to end the 1898 Spanish-American War. Its background depicts the South Lawn landscape through a window with a detailed casement to match the actual structure to the left. At least a dozen golf clubs stood loose in the southwest corner, including several antiques with wooden shafts. A biography of Mark Twain lay askew on the pin-neat desk. I browsed through several books from the shelves, and had opened Senator Daniel Patrick Moynihan's startling but academic proposal to abolish the CIA when President Clinton swept in shortly after ten o'clock that night.

He said he was mad at Moynihan for carping in public against the finished proposal on health care reform. Going down the central hall, he apologized for the delay and volunteered that he had been talking about the Haiti dilemma with our mutual friend Deputy Secretary of State Strobe Talbott of the State Department. We stopped by the kitchen to pick up Diet Cokes. The president carried an expensive cigar, which he unwrapped and trimmed in the parlor room. As we talked, he twirled, clenched, and chewed the unlit tobacco, periodically rearranging its disintegrated bits on the card table. He sniffled a lot, fighting a cold. My questions drew cursory replies on topics ranging from the Brady Bill on gun control to the New York mayoral race and Clinton's visit to the JFK Museum in Boston, where he said Jacqueline Onassis had dropped out early from a silent, uncomfortable public remembrance of her role as first lady.

His answers kept skipping to the unpleasant reception for his health care bill, which he and Hillary had delivered to Congress on October 27. He said it had been picked apart—lampooned for its massive 1,342 pages and caricatured as a power grab for liberals hooked on big government. The president chafed already against political disadvantage. "Criticism works," he lamented. "Being responsible and comprehensive doesn't work, because it doesn't sell or create controversy." He did not begrudge his political opponents so much—saying he would use similar tactics if he were on the other side—but he chafed against the press's shortcomings. He invoked a private analysis by Helmut Kohl. Across his long career in governance, the German chancellor had told him, the biggest change was a qualitative shift in Western press coverage from substance to entertainment. Clinton said Kohl thought reporters were detached from the stakes of politics for their readers, to the point that many no longer took pride in their journalism.

This was not the president's first discourse on the press. He tended to mix complaints with speculations about why the media was sour on him, and I tried to strike a balance between steering him to other topics and giving future historians the natural flow of his thought. My questions nudged him back to the end of April, when press evaluations of his first hundred days seemed to concur with his own statement that the administration was "out of focus." Clinton quickly made distinctions. "Well, that's different from what Friedman wrote," he said, citing phrases from a *New York Times* article written jointly by Thomas Friedman and Maureen Dowd, as well as a similar appraisal in the *Washington Post* by Ann Devroy. He meant he had not yet learned how to establish a clear public focus on his ambitious agenda, which he ticked off on the fingers of both hands. What they wrote, he charged, was that he dithered because he lacked conviction and wanted to please all sides. They focused the news on their presumptions about his character and motives.

Lingering resentment spilled forth when he described the furor over his haircut in May. The basic accusation was a lie, he fumed, and reporters knew it was a lie. Clinton sketched his version of the trip to Los Angeles. His barber remained Hillary's stylist Christophe, who lived there. Protocol did not allow the release of the presidential motorcade until Clinton boarded Air Force One, which made the plane the only site for a haircut without prolonged tie-ups by and for the massive armada. He had called the FAA personally about potential inconvenience to air traffic, said the president, but only two newspapers—months later—bothered to verify that his pause on the runway caused no delay to other flights. All the others discarded truth and proportion to launch sensational headlines: "Man of the People or Just Another Elitist?" Heaping scorn on both images of Clinton, reporters wrote stories about the press frenzy itself as a political force. *New York Times* columnist Anthony Lewis wondered in print whether Clinton could save his presidency from the haircut metaphor: "Or are we headed for another failure that will further erode public faith in the political system?"

The president's annoyance subsided into reflection. Justified or not, he said, he should have anticipated trouble from a runway haircut by Christophe. Chronic flaps had prompted him to hire political adviser David Gergen, at the suggestion of Mack McLarty, and Clinton defended the choice against internal grumbling that Gergen had served three Republican presidents. Gergen reciprocated across partisan lines to accept the job, he noted, and no Clinton deputy before Gergen had any prior experience at the White House. In retrospect, Clinton believed he had devoted too much transition time and energy to the selection of cabinet and sub-cabinet appointments, and too little to the White House staff. He said George Stephanopoulos was adapting fairly well to his reduced role in public relations, which was not his strong suit.

Chelsea dropped by to say good night, followed soon by Hillary in her bathrobe. I needled her again that she should be dictating her own oral history, especially now that she was managing the health care bill. Joking coyly, Hillary said she feared Bob Packwood would get hold of her diary if she kept one. Republican senator Packwood of Oregon was embroiled in a career-ending scandal over his diary references to his own boorish groping of female employees. The president jumped in to say that Hillary would deserve to get in trouble if she recorded the sort of behavior Packwood did. I argued that Packwood's diary was at issue only because he had disclosed it himself in a misguided attempt to rebut similar accusations. Clinton agreed that Packwood's defense had compounded the damage, but he insisted the senator should have known better than to write down those details in the first place. He and Hillary shared dismay that the Senate was debating a subpoena of Packwood instead of the Clinton crime bill. After Hillary left, the president said she had greater misgivings than he did about a diary. It was hard for her to open up, and harder to trust the value of future scrutiny, but he said I could keep urging her along.

IT WAS LATE. I told Clinton that if he had the strength to resume taping, we should switch from media diversions to one of his major initiatives for the first year, such as Bosnia or the anti-deficit budget resolution. The latter subject seemed to revive him. He said the budget package was key to everything he hoped to achieve in both politics and the economy. Chronic deficits not only drove up interest rates, sucking investment money out of the private economy, but they also fostered cynicism. Public discourse was stunted by belief that government was inherently bankrupt. Beyond labels of liberal and conservative, a resignation to deficits corroded democracy's core proposition that people can govern themselves. For that reason, Clinton had dramatized the budget challenge through the campaign and in his public seminars on the economy during the transition. He reviewed his painful decision to postpone middle-class tax cuts because of worsening projections for the deficit. He sketched the contentious debates to shape the five-year omnibus resolution: $500 billion in deficit reduction, almost evenly divided between spending cuts and tax increases. As always, he emphasized that 80 percent of new taxes would fall on citizens with yearly incomes above $200,000.

On future tapes, the president would circle back often to different aspects of the budget decision, but he concentrated first on the swing votes among members of Congress. In the Senate, where the measure twice surmounted cliffhanger ties on Vice President Gore's deciding votes, Clinton expressed irritation with Democrat Sam Nunn of Georgia. He said Nunn voted no even though he understood the economics, favored the overall package, and enjoyed a seat safe from political retaliation—only because he was miffed that the bill did not include his pet amendment on Medicaid cuts. The amendment was tiny, said the president, and Nunn could not mobilize even twenty senators behind it. His description of their private bargaining made Nunn sound petulant but consistent and discreet, leaving room for sharper complaints against Democratic senator David Boren of Oklahoma. Boren voted yes, then no, and the president said Boren's reversal frosted him all over again when two Oklahomans in the House followed suit because they felt too exposed without political cover from their senator. Boren could not explain his votes in principle or political necessity, asserted Clinton. The senator seemed to relish a spoiler's whimsy that violated Clinton's code of honorable warfare. He said the closest thing Boren offered to rational objection was a straight-faced wish that the landmark bill could be more bipartisan, which made the president groan with amazement. He would have *loved* a few Republican votes, if only to secure victory, but that was the whole point. Boren was fully aware of Republican leader Bob Dole's frank dictum that there was no such thing as a bipartisan budget. Dole still invoked his searing memory of Republicans losing control of the Senate in 1986 because his party helped pass a minimal COLA (cost of living adjustment) reduction to shore up Social Security. Until now, both parties had hidden behind posturing rather than finding solutions on the deficit, and Dole still marshaled party discipline against any tax increases or significant spending cuts.

Clinton reviewed the clashes and drawbacks behind his decision to pursue the anti-deficit budget package without a single Republican vote in either chamber of Congress. He pointed out one obscure advantage—that spending cuts were slightly easier when legislation had to accommodate only one party's earmarked projects—but the political risks and difficulties were legion. A surprise gift determined the struggle. Privately, Senator Dennis DeConcini of Arizona reminded Clinton why the proposed 4.5-cent gasoline tax increase alone made this a "tough vote" in a Western state, which was a euphemism for suicidal, but said he could not bear to let fail this pivotal step toward fiscal responsibility. DeConcini told the president he wanted nothing specific for his vote, except that he be considered for "some place in public life" if he lost his seat* and the budget resolution collapsed. The president said Democratic senator Bob Kerrey of Nebraska equivocated to the end by milking his temptation to switch like Boren, which would have reversed the result in contradictory speeches that faulted Clinton for demanding too much

---

* DeConcini did not run for a fourth term in 1994. He retired to law practice, and President Clinton appointed him to the board of the Federal Home Loan Mortgage Corporation.

public sacrifice and not enough. There was something a little screwy about Kerrey, Clinton observed. They had been allies as fellow governors, then friendly rivals for president, but Clinton thought Kerrey might be carried away on the zeal of his Navy SEAL training to finish every battle.

Final passage in the House also teetered with only a handful of members left to vote. The president dissected the politics and personalities behind choices both ways, emphasizing his disappointment with fellow Arkansan and Democrat Ray Thornton for casting the last "no" even though he had a safe seat, built on his record of distinguished service, and enjoyed political cover from both Arkansas senators. In Clinton's view, a craven retreat by Thornton extracted the ultimate political heroism from Representative Marjorie Margolies-Mezvinsky, a Democrat whose district in suburban Philadelphia contained a high proportion of wealthy citizens who would resent tax increases. On the House floor, gleeful Republicans broke into a derisive chorus of "Bye, bye Margie" as she cast the decisive "yes" to seal approval for the bill, 218–216, at the certain cost of her own political career. This was cruel but instructive, the president concluded, signaling that he wanted to stop our session.

It was after midnight, some ten weeks since he signed the Omnibus Budget Reconciliation Act into law on August 10. Clinton had survived a great political contest, which receded quickly, but the issue would return. No one could be certain of the actual impact in future years. Republican leaders predicted disaster—and *higher* deficits, not lower ones—from what Representative Bill Archer of Texas called "a job-killing poison for the economy," and they also bet that voters cared more about political labels than mind-numbing budget arguments over perennial debt. House minority leader Newt Gingrich of Georgia announced plans to challenge every legislator who had supported the bill, arguing that any one of those Democrats could have stopped Clinton's "massive tax increase." The president declined to forecast a political outcome as he walked me to his private elevator. Somewhat to my surprise, he waited politely with me until the door opened. His nose was red, and he still sniffled miserably, but he was benign about the tests of presidential strength. They came rapidly, on many fronts, and it was wise not to worry too far ahead. November would be NAFTA month, he said, and he did not yet have the votes to prevail.

THREE NIGHTS LATER, the fifth session lasted only an hour. I found the president behind his desk in the Treaty Room, sifting through papers stacked in a dozen color-coded folders. His cold was much better. He said Chelsea was waiting for help with her homework in ninth-grade math, which was much more difficult than he remembered, but first he had to finish at least the red folders. Podesta gave him too much night work, he complained, and nobody had told him I was coming. He said he didn't blame me, knowing that I had just been called down from Baltimore on short notice, but we needed to work fast. I followed his darting commentary down the hall into the parlor room. He seemed harried, alternately pleasant and out of sorts, mostly with his staff. His mood seemed to fit most of the topics we covered on tape.

On the Lani Guinier controversy, for instance, the president said he did not feel very well-served by the vetting personnel for Justice Department nominees. He thought officials must have assumed that he knew everything about Guinier, and would vouch for her, because she was his personal choice to head the Civil Rights Division. He and Guinier had known each other since law school. They were friends. He admired her brains and dedication, but he did not read her old law review articles until critics accused his new nominee of reverse racism. Clinton summarized the thorny academic question beneath the dispute: could the courts provide a remedy when racial majorities stacked parliamentary rules against a minority? Guinier once argued for a rare legal decision requiring super-majority approval where the courts found that minority representation had been denied consistently. The president said he could not support her position, but he did not believe the article alone disqualified Guinier. After all, her prior opinions were not government policy. He would have defended the nomination and Guinier had it not been for the bruising Senate politics. Clinton said she did not do well in her early interviews for confirmation. Even before the adverse publicity, key senators had warned of coolness among her own supporters, including Democrats Barbara Mikulski, Ted Kennedy, and Illinois's Carol Moseley Braun. Worse, Joe Biden of Delaware doubted that he could move the nomination favorably through his Judiciary Committee. When the White House staff scoffed at these reports, confident that Senate liberals eventually would support Guinier, the president had checked directly with the majority leader, George Mitchell of Maine, who strongly advised him not to mount a fight, said Clinton, because the nominee had made a bad impression on the senators who should have been her staunchest advocates. Next the president called Vernon Jordan, who had known the Guinier family for many years. ("Vernon knows everybody," said Clinton.) Jordan confided that Guinier was "just like her dad," and would take offense under pressure. She would behave regally, as though the nomination were hers by birthright.

Sure enough, said Clinton, Guinier had come to the Oval Office in June determined to justify herself. She emphasized her opinions rather than her willingness to represent the administration, arguing that she could convince the senators. Attorney General Reno had agreed that Guinier deserved at least a chance to win confirmation, said the president, but he overruled them both. Regardless of the outcome, her hearings would guarantee several weeks of bad publicity when the administration already was "bleeding in the water." Her chance was not worth the larger cost. He asked Guinier to withdraw her nomination, but she refused. "Then I will have to pull you down," Clinton told her, meaning he would retract her name, and his stance heated the awkward showdown. She told the president he owed her the right to defend herself, lest he ruin her reputation by prejudgment and defeat. On the contrary, Clinton replied, this public sacrifice would magnify her reputation, not ruin it. "I'll be the asshole," he told her, "and you can be the hero." Clinton said this was more or less how the conflict played out. He thought he had cut his losses prudently, but vetting mistakes continued to haunt this sensitive job. Having delegated the selection of Guinier's replacement to Reno and the civil rights community, Clinton learned belatedly that his second nominee, John Payton, who would be tasked with safeguarding rights including that of the vote, had not bothered to vote himself in at least ten years.

The president's pique carried over to his description of an ongoing scandal at the White House Travel Office, whose primary task was to handle logistics for the traveling press corps. An internal audit had revealed cash stuffed into drawers, and many thousands of dollars were missing from reimbursement accounts owed to the government by news organizations. Clinton said he learned belatedly of these results, which accented rumors that the Travel Office had become a "sweetheart deal" for the reporters, giving them discounts and favors. To defend the dismissal of all seven employees in May, he remarked that they were White House appointees who served "at the pleasure of the president," not protected civil servants, and he argued that a fresh team might have restored fair balance for the taxpayers. However, the news media raised a great howl of protest, and Clinton complained that none of the stories acknowledged a blatant conflict for the press in an otherwise minor administrative decision. Reporters ignored or downplayed the alleged irregularities in the Travel Office, without disclosing that the employees there often were friends who adjusted their bills and expedited their luggage through Customs. He said journalism reveled in everyone's selfish interests but its own. Worse, he fumed, the administration had lost any hope to gain balance in the public debate, because some White House official leaked word that the FBI had been called in to mount a criminal investigation of the fired employees. The investigation itself was proper, Clinton observed, but the leak was prejudicial and vindictive. It helped establish suspicion that the White House must be covering up some corrupt motive for a baffling purge at the Travel Office. "I should have fired somebody for that," said the president, more than once.

In a recurring theme, President Clinton was uniquely passive about the press. He treated bad publicity as a scourge to be endured rather than a problem to be dissected, managed, even positively transformed—the way he routinely approached world crises and political adversaries. Unlike President Kennedy, who studiously had charmed reporters, and enjoyed feeding them stories, Clinton usually recoiled. He dwelled instead on in-house errors, and returned to them minutes later when describing the July 20 suicide of the deputy White House counsel, Vincent Foster. The president said the Travel Office furor had contributed to a mysterious depression, because Foster thought their mutual friend from Arkansas, Mack McLarty, had mismanaged White House reaction—in particular by allowing the press leak about an FBI criminal investigation. Separately, said Clinton, Foster was already stunned by personal criticism from *The Wall Street Journal*. One editorial, "Who Is Vincent Foster?" had demanded his photograph to illustrate forthcoming attacks on the new administration's "carelessness about following the law." The president said Foster was known in Arkansas for professional strength through many tough lawsuits, and was often called "Mister Integrity." All his life, Foster was accustomed to fierce disagreements but never to barbed presumptions of dishonor. In a suicide note reconstituted from torn bits, he had confessed himself unprepared for "the spotlight of public life in Washington. Here ruining people is considered sport . . ." Clinton regretted that he did not counsel him to ignore these editorials. "*The Wall Street Journal* is a great newspaper with an editorial board that is kind of whacko and irresponsible," he said. "Nobody reads their opinions very much."

The president reviewed his own shock. McLarty had pulled him out of a Larry King interview on CNN with news that Foster, after leaving the White House alone that day, had been discovered in a Civil War park overlooking the Potomac River, his body leaning against a cannon with an heirloom family pistol still in his hand. He left a wife and three small children, and the president used first names for them all. Clinton said he and Vince had lived next door to each other in Hope, attending Miss Mary's kindergarten class together with McLarty. In many ways he had always looked up to Foster, who became Hillary's mentor and best friend among the partners of the prestigious Rose Law Firm in Little Rock. The president said he would carry an unfathomable grief the way he did for Frank Aller, his fellow Rhodes Scholar who had plumbed conflicting loyalties over the Vietnam War. "My housemate committed suicide in September of 1971," said Clinton, "and I remember it as vividly as if it happened yesterday." Groping for causes, he talked of chemical imbalances and genetic predispositions. He had learned that Foster's mother's sister had committed suicide. A few minutes later, he noted from intelligence reports that both parents of the Serbian war leader Slobodan Milosevic had killed themselves long after their divorce, while living in separate households.

THE PRESIDENT PAUSED to take a phone call from William Natcher of Kentucky, who chaired the House Appropriations Committee. Clinton's end of the conversation mingled folksy good wishes with technical forecasts on the possible effects of NAFTA under different assumptions, jobs lost versus jobs gained. His mood brightened steadily until he hung up. "Hot damn!" said Clinton. He introduced his recap with an affectionate profile of Natcher as a grand old gentleman who had kept a daily journal for forty years in Congress, never missing a vote. You would find fascinating stories recorded there, he bet, without prurience or self-aggrandizement "like Packwood." Natcher had made himself an expert on the Appropriations Committee for decades, serving patiently until his colleagues bucked the seniority system to oust the enfeebled but irascible chairman, Democrat Jamie Whitten of Mississippi. ("Nobody liked him very much anyway," said Clinton.) Now Whitten was an odd relic in the House, stripped of internal leverage, and Natcher finally headed the appropriations process. He had just passed the eleventh of thirteen annual spending bills required to run the government, said the president, and Natcher's main purpose for the call was to explain why it would not be wise for him to take a position on NAFTA before shepherding the last two spending bills through the House. Then, Natcher promised, he would see if he could find a way to support NAFTA.

The message seemed noncommittal, but Clinton discerned good news on several fronts. Natcher's shrewdness boded well for a vital budget cycle under the new anti-deficit regime, and the chairman clearly did not think NAFTA was doomed in the House, as many believed. His promise—while not a commitment—would make it harder for him to justify a vote the other way. Clinton interpreted Natcher as a provisional volunteer on NAFTA, especially if his vote was sorely needed. On the pitfalls of political communication, the president confirmed and complimented an investigative report in the *Washington Post* about how the administration had made several changes in prospective NAFTA rules to satisfy Hispanic legislators—only to have those legislators turn around and say they would vote against the bill regardless, leaving Clinton stuck with the changes for nothing.

Poor deal making also aggravated recent conflicts over the grazing policy for cattle and sheep on public lands. The government's rates were scandalously low, said the president—so much so that his original anti-deficit bill included a provision to raise fees toward the market levels charged by private landowners. When four or five Western senators

threatened to vote against the whole package unless the increase was removed, McLarty backed down in what Clinton called one of his few
mistakes so far—not the retreat itself but McLarty's failure to bargain
with the senators. "He should have gotten something for taking it out,"
the president complained. Not long after that, he added with dismay,
Interior Secretary Babbitt had announced plans to double federal grazing fees by administrative fiat, without consulting Western governors or
legislators in advance. This "ham-handed approach" vexed Clinton. He
said bipartisan revolt simmered in the grazing states where unsettled fees
enraged the few elected Democrats. Senator Ben Nighthorse Campbell
of Colorado, a Democrat, already was vowing privately to switch parties,*
the president disclosed, and gnarled disputes made the Interior Department one of chairman Natcher's two unfinished appropriations bills.
Outsiders found it hard to understand the regional passion behind a
subsidy for only 2 percent of the population, said Clinton, but Westerners insist that their whole way of life rests on cheap access to public land.
He likened their attachment to Southern attitudes about federal crop
payments, or segregation in the old days. Clinton said Babbitt was still
coping gamely, and remained his best choice for the Interior Department. In a wry aside, though, he said the episode made hash of his arduous spring calculations that Babbitt could not be spared for the Supreme
Court because of his indispensable political skills on Western issues.

Grazing politics filtered into the upcoming vote on NAFTA, which
Clinton referred to as another milestone like the budget package. Fretting that defeat would make it difficult to accomplish anything in foreign policy, he explained his decision today to let Vice President Gore
debate Ross Perot on television. Perot was jockeying to hold the event
before a stacked crowd at one of his anti-NAFTA rallies, but Clinton
thought Gore would hold his own in a neutral forum. He asked to stop
soon because he still wanted to see Chelsea about her math homework.
I told him we had caught up with most of the major events of 1993—
except for the June 28 missile strike he had ordered on the Iraqi intelligence headquarters in Baghdad, retaliating for Saddam Hussein's foiled

* Campbell indeed switched to the Republican Party fifteen months later, on
March 3, 1995, and served in the Senate until 2005.

plot to assassinate ex-President Bush. Clinton said good, let's do Iraq next time.

The president was tired, and remarked that he had more NAFTA calls to make before bed. I hurried to rewind and label the duplicate tapes. While making small talk about his family adjustments for Chelsea in the White House, I explained why I was uncomfortable for us both about the two tapes he had left behind after our session in the Oval Office. I had brought them back so that he could exercise sole control, as we had carefully agreed. Within a year, we would develop routines to manage secure storage in light of his hasty exits, but now Clinton silently retrieved the other tapes from a closet off the family bathroom. I decided not to ask whether he had a personal safe in there. Instead, I consolidated a duplicate set of the five cassettes from our sessions into each of two cardboard boxes, handed them over, and took my leave, but the president walked with me into the central hall.

He said he and Hillary were grateful for general cooperation in their quest to provide Chelsea a relatively normal life. One *New York Times* article had collected snide comments about unruly hair in her gangly teenage phase, but the *Times* subsequently published a scalding rebuke of its "child abuse" journalism by Harry Truman's daughter, Margaret. Since then, Clinton said, a mannerly restraint had prevailed across the media except for Rush Limbaugh. On the positive side, one magazine article reported a murmur of student approval that Chelsea, dressed as a fortune-teller, had stepped away from her overfull line at a Sidwell Friends School carnival until some customers drifted into a classmate's empty line. The president and Hillary, while grateful for the kindly news item, had decided after some debate not to draw Chelsea's attention to it for fear of raising her sensitivity about being watched by new peers at school. He said you could get all wound up in such parental judgments.

At the elevator, Clinton asked me to add an unknown event to my list of future topics. He said he had recently completed a traumatic interview for *Rolling Stone* magazine. I promised to make a note of it—being anxious not to impose further upon his evening—but he stepped into the elevator doorway with something clearly on his mind. He said *Rolling Stone*'s founder, Jann Wenner, had come to the White House with author William Greider, a former *Washington Post* editor whose books included a populist critique of the Federal Reserve banking system. They had agreed not to discuss NAFTA because of Greider's implacable opposition, and the president said all went fine until Greider brandished a photograph of a destitute-looking American to mount a sudden, dramatic attack. Clinton quoted him eloquently in an accelerating rhythm I could only paraphrase minutes later on the way home. Greider confronted him, saying here is one of the countless poor people who looked to you for leadership—you were their last hope. Now they feel utterly disillusioned and abandoned. Can you look into this face and name one thing you have done to help? Or one principle you won't compromise? One cause you will uphold? One belief you would die for?

The president said he had replied in kind. "I kind of went off on him," he recalled. He told Greider he had done things already that no other president would do. He had raised taxes on the rich and lowered them for the working poor. He had introduced the AmeriCorps national service program, which *Rolling Stone* campaigned for, and established it in law. He was taking on the gun lobby and the tobacco industry. He had proposed fair treatment for gay soldiers. He was fighting for national health care coverage, and more, but liberals paid very little attention to any of these things because they were bitchy and cynical about politics. They resented Clinton for respecting the votes of conservatives or the opinions of moderates. They wanted him to behave like a dictator because they didn't really care about results in the world. By now the president was quite worked up, waving hands that again seemed strikingly long and bony but graceful. Pointing at me, he said he had pointed at Greider to tell him the problem is you, Bill Greider. You are a faulty citizen. You don't mobilize or persuade, because you only worry about being doctrinaire and proud. You are betraying your own principles with self-righteousness.

Clinton took a breath. "I did everything but fart in his face," he concluded, adding ruefully that the outburst was a mistake that would come back to plague him. To be consoling, I said it might turn out well for him to express some honest frustration in public. He looked worried. Maybe so, he replied, but he thought he had cussed a lot in words a president shouldn't use on the record. I asked whether the White House press office had made its own recording to ensure accuracy in the *Rolling*

Stone version, and Clinton said no. He hoped Jann Wenner might stick up for him a little, and perhaps even find the interview too vituperative to publish at all. I said he must be kidding. Not publish a presidential interview full of passion and controversy? I thought it more likely to wind up on the cover, which made Clinton wince. He let my elevator go.

It was nearly midnight. The monuments and fountains were bathed in soothing light, oblivious to the turmoil inside the White House. I had a fleeting thought that Clinton's bothersome secret might explain his undertone of grievance through our session, but it seemed that he routinely compartmentalized far bigger troubles than a press interview.

CHAPTER FIVE

PASSAGES: NAFTA, CHINA, WHITEWATER

Monday, November 22, 1993

Monday, December 6, 1993

The upstairs parlor seemed vacant shortly before ten o'clock at night, but President Clinton's voice called out for me to join him in one of the closets. Rummaging among cardboard boxes, he held up various "Save the Children" neckties to solicit my vote on thank-you gifts for church leaders who had hosted him the day before, in the fire- and recession-ravaged areas of Southern California. He said two of them—a Presbyterian minister in Pasadena and a Mexican-American priest in East L.A.—had preached whole sermons on Clinton's extemporaneous remarks in Memphis only the week before. Did I know about that event? I told him I had seen only passing news stories, and would add Memphis to our list of topics. He said it somehow hit a nerve, reminding him that a president's words can acquire lasting symbolic force. He wanted to keep up experiments with language and venue, because you can never be sure what might bring your message to life. When I told him I still found promise in some of his "New Covenant" phrases about building the bonds of public trust among citizens, he replied gently that such vocabulary had not caught on very well during the campaign. It might work better for him now, he added, because voters were open to more lyrical expression from a president *if* they approved the political context. Clinton said he was looking for themes to help people gather strength and security for bold changes.

Hillary came in to say good night, wearing her nightgown and bathrobe, offering a reprise of her day at a health care conference in Atlanta. Physicians there had received her politely until she explained a task force conclusion that government policy was tilting the balance of medical personnel too heavily toward specialists, away from general care. She said an indignant questioner then popped up from the audience: "Are you trying to tell me that the *government* decided I should become a thoracic surgeon?" No, she replied, but government support did encourage specialists through the teaching hospitals and the fee schedules for Medicare and Medicaid. Whereupon the surgeon asserted that government had nothing to do with Medicare, and her speech had dissolved in a flood of objections. Hillary sighed that she paddled upstream as usual, which touched off a witty exchange. She and the president completed each other's sentences in a chortling spoof of doctrinaire contradictions in medical policy. Doctors were models of free enterprise who professed not to care about money. Even the government may be less bureaucratic than insurance companies, which were efficient only when they denied coverage or told doctors what to do. No American could be denied quality health care, but no one was required to pay for it. Thus updated by their familiar shorthand, the president urged her to soldier on for reform.

As we began to record, the president explained why the parlor furniture had been rearranged. The Secret Service had just installed bulletproof glass, he said, so that he could move our table next to the south window and look outside while he played cards. Puzzled, I asked him whether the Secret Service minded that he sat in the open for hours on the Truman Balcony, protected by no glass at all. No, they don't seem to worry about the balcony so much, he replied, but they get upset when he sits inside a regular window. The president shrugged. It seemed a relief for him to let one case of tangled logic slide when so many others demanded attention.

One of my final questions evoked detailed memories about the death of Hillary's father. Clinton said Hugh Rodham's massive stroke

on March 19 had turned into a prolonged and terrible ordeal for everyone involved. Doctors brought in charts showing negligible brain activity, and reported no hope for recovery, but the comatose patient could
squeeze your finger at times. "He was still there," said the president. Yet
the eighty-one-year-old man did not otherwise move or speak as the
family kept vigil around his hospital bed in Little Rock. In the first week,
there was desperate friction over two or three claims that his eyes briefly
fluttered. (Hillary later revealed that her two brothers even tried to rouse
him by singing the *Flintstones* theme song, a television jingle he had despised since their childhood.) The president said he did not say much
himself through the agonized debate about keeping the elder Rodham
alive by artificial life support. Occasionally, he marveled that he had just
put Hillary in charge of health care reform for the whole country, and
here they were paralyzed like most families over mortal choices, clinging
to options and miracles, torn apart over who should decide what for
whom, while spending a whole lot of somebody else's money that was
basically not going to do anyone any good. Clinton said they felt acutely
why health care decisions were so hard.

After nine days, the exhausted Rodham siblings signed consent
forms to disconnect the respirator while continuing intravenous food
and natural care, but their father did not die within hours as predicted.
"He just kept breathing on his own," said Clinton. "He was a very tough
old geezer." The family vigil extended more than another week, with
Chelsea out of school to sit with her grandfather, and the president
breaking away to some official obligations—the Boris Yeltsin summit in
Vancouver, talks with Egypt's president, Hosni Mubarak, at the White
House. When Hugh Rodham finally succumbed on April 7, Clinton
said he returned first for the funeral at Hillary's Methodist church in
Little Rock, then for the burial in Scranton, Pennsylvania. "That's where
his people were from," said Clinton, adding that his father-in-law had
kept ties there since moving to Chicago. Beneath its modern development, Scranton remained what the president called a "bar culture" divided between working Catholics and Protestants, and survivors came
together across cultural lines to memorialize Hugh Rodham in colorful
yarns. A friend told of young Rodham once roller-skating into church
with a loud offer to play organ hymns for the service, though he knew

nothing of the instrument. Gruff and clannish, Rodham had molded his daughter into a Republican "Goldwater girl," then doted on Hillary's self-made gumption even as he fulminated against her defection to the mushy bra-burning Democrats. Humor and truce zones tempered their political conflict. "Hillary really loved her dad," Clinton emphasized, "and I did, too."

The president became quite animated when reminded of his wish to record something about the previous week's Memphis speech of November 13. He said the circumstances overwhelmed him. It was a convention of the Church of God in Christ—which he called the most rapidly growing U.S. denomination of any kind, black or white—at the cavernous Mason Temple where Martin Luther King had given a last prophetic sermon on the night before his assassination in 1968. Clinton arrived there in time to spend forty minutes on the stage, reflecting on the historic site as he listened to the powerful sermons and uplifting choirs. He said it struck him that before these people helped him win the presidency, their forebears had changed his life to make him want to run. He repeated his theory that a simple line still divided most American voters between those who considered King's 1960s on balance a good thing or a bad thing. So far, among white Southerners of our generation, the political numbers still ran heavily toward resentment of that era, but Clinton felt determined to advance a common legacy. "It just welled up," he said. "I gave that speech from the heart, more or less off-the-cuff."

The president did not recite extensively from his speech on tape, saying he would get me a copy. He called it a hardheaded tribute to Martin Luther King's public philosophy. Presuming to imagine how King might look upon the world since his death, Clinton had praised great swaths of freedom for groups, beyond the core movement of African-Americans, overlooked or taken for granted. He lamented an urban despair so pervasive that he said juvenile drug lords were killing each other and preteen girls were routinely planning their own funerals. Clinton called for a renewal of King's concept of public service, which provided leadership for the whole country. He said it blended goals of external political reform with internal change to meet the nation's spiritual crisis. The president plainly relished the King-like acclaim for spontaneous oratory, but he found significance well beyond his candid communion with largely black audiences. He said Memphis was his best presidential speech to date "bar none." I thought his enthusiasm might fade with time, especially because of the scant press coverage, but Clinton reiterated that its content and wording were more significant than other messages broadcast to millions, including the State of the Union Address. A decade later, he would quote nearly five hundred words from the Memphis speech in his autobiography.

The president needed very few questions to compose his own narrative about the final battles in Congress over the North American Free Trade Agreement. He said with a big smile that House Speaker Tom Foley called NAFTA "the Lazarus Act," because it was raised miraculously from the dead. Less than two weeks ago, he added, House leaders David Bonior and Dick Gephardt had come to the White House proposing to delay the final vote scheduled for November 17 because they did not want to humiliate their own president just before his summit with Asian heads of state. Clinton said he appreciated the gesture, but had declined, and the bill was still forty votes behind on November 14 when he hosted a dinner for that many undecided House members in the great flurry of last-minute jawboning and deal making.

Clinton talked personally with nearly two hundred representatives about NAFTA, and he told stories from many angles. Connecticut went against him almost unanimously, but Democrat Steny Hoyer helped secure Maryland. He said Charles Rangel of Harlem, another Democrat, was typical of many who told him finally that NAFTA was probably good for the country but not for his district. One representative from rural Louisiana voted no when a major new employer refused to state publicly that he would never move his business to Mexico if NAFTA passed. ("He probably did the right thing," Clinton said with a sigh of the lost vote, citing Louisiana politics and the caution of corporate lawyers.) The president described how his negotiators averted disaster in Florida, where twenty-one of twenty-three Democrats were against NAFTA until changes placated citrus growers. He talked about complicated "inner-thread agreements" on textile imports, modified trade rules for fresh-cut flowers to win over California Democrat Norman Mineta, and even technical adjustments at Customs to detect phony "Made in

Madagascar" labels in goods transshipped through intermediate ports. Clinton defended the horse trading among politicians. "It's not like we were giving them backrubs or whorehouses or money, or things like that," he said. "We were trying to make policy accommodations in exchange for enough votes, and they were trying to look out for the folks back home. That's what the voters hired us to do."

On the public front, the president said Al Gore conducted his own preparations for the televised debate on NAFTA with Ross Perot. Clinton had requested only that the vice president dispute Perot's folksy claim to identify uniquely with American workers, and Gore went after that emotional connection by pointing out that trade was not just a wonkish issue for Nobel Prize economists. NAFTA was also the tough choice of people who had spent their careers fighting for people threatened by job loss—that you cannot hide from the global economy, but must adapt to its larger opportunities. In the debate, Clinton said Gore exceeded his hopes by revealing that Perot had created his own free trade tax shelter along the Mexican border, to ensure profits for him whether NAFTA passed or not, and by debunking Perot's grand pronouncements. Gore shrewdly needled Perot for predicting that forty thousand U.S. soldiers would be killed in the Gulf War of 1991, and that one hundred banks would fail within a month if Clinton became president. Clinton thought these jabs irritated Perot enough to make him forget his funny one-liners until the end of the debate, which Gore clearly won. On the tapes, the president distributed praise to all his NAFTA vote counters, including White House aides Mickey Kantor and Bill Daley, but he lamented a last-minute visit from Representative Cynthia McKinney, a Georgia Democrat. She had collected presidential photos and souvenirs while setting forth why it would be a mistake to support NAFTA in her district. Clinton said McKinney behaved admirably, and he accepted her analysis, but he reproached his schedulers for wasting a precious half-hour in the Oval Office with someone whose vote was locked up the other way.

NAFTA's decisive victory in the House, by a tally of 234–200, shocked supporters and opponents alike. Critics who had predicted failure amended their complaints about the administration's pell-mell style to insist that the president should have submitted NAFTA earlier in the year. Clinton rejected the notion as face-saving froth. NAFTA and his anti-deficit package were a bad legislative mix, he said, and overlapping them in Congress very likely would have doomed them both. As it was, having sequenced these hurdles properly around the Rabin-Arafat ceremonies in September, Clinton thought he could recover political momentum for his other major initiatives such as health care and the Brady Bill on handgun safety. He already had called AFL-CIO president Lane Kirkland to begin healing his split over NAFTA with many traditional allies. "I'll have to let them jump on me for a while," he said, and it was always easier for a president to reconcile from a position of strength.

Clinton said his whole team was "sky high" from the NAFTA vote on leaving the next day for a foreign policy summit in Seattle. The Asia-Pacific Economic Cooperation (APEC) group was only a few years old but full of promise. Its member nations, which bordered on the Pacific Ocean, accounted for more than half of the world's economic production, and Clinton was no longer the untested newcomer among the national leaders. Since his introductions at a similar meeting in Vancouver, new prime ministers had come to power already in Japan and Canada. The incoming Morihiro Hosokawa was so buffeted over Japan's stagnation that Clinton said they agreed to postpone their talks. He spent more time with Jean Chrétien of Canada, who, like Clinton, had narrowly defeated an incumbent conservative, falling short of a popular majority. Chrétien spoke Clinton's language in politics—of leaders understanding each other's political constraints, finding ways to get things done. The prime minister confided that he must act—or at least speak—more independently of the United States than his predecessors, who had been ousted in part because Canadian voters disliked their subservience to Reagan and Bush. Clinton and Chrétien held preliminary talks on numerous subjects including the restoration of Haiti's elected government. The president said Canada was one of the few governments in our hemisphere that favored a more aggressive international cooperation toward that goal.

Clinton said he had been spending a lot of time on Haiti, which was a new focus for him. In the cold light of public opinion, he said few Americans cared unless Haitians washed up on our shores. Even lately, as desperate thousands of refugees floated toward Florida on overloaded

boats, or drowned on the way, most of his advisers recoiled from engagement. Senator Sam Nunn had just volunteered a few ideas about how to
move the diplomacy along, but Nunn wanted to circumvent Haiti's recent election results because he did not think Aristide could run the
country. Clinton said General Colin Powell had offered similar advice
before his recent retirement from the Joint Chiefs. Powell, like many
descendants of British colonies in the Caribbean, considered Haiti an
unruly French culture that must be governed by a strong hand. He judged
democracy there a tenuous hope at best, especially under Aristide, whom
Powell regarded as something of a "voodoo visionary." Clinton said Powell adamantly opposed any military intervention in Haiti, pointing out
that the last U.S. expedition, in 1915, to land there had stayed on twenty
years. It would be easy to topple the coup regime, Powell advised, but
then impossible to leave any success behind. He said Clinton would face
a devil's choice: occupy a seething cauldron indefinitely—trapped—or exit
and watch Haiti revert to its authoritarian past.

The president said he was not wholly convinced by Powell, and that
the new chairman of the Joint Chiefs, Army general John Shalikashvili,
had not yet formed a recommendation. Clinton thought he might conceivably devise a mission of limited risk and duration to give Haitian
democracy a chance. He said Aristide did retain unprecedented, overwhelming public support among Haitians, and even detractors conceded that he had a quick mind. Former president Jimmy Carter, who
had his own doubts about Haiti, once told Clinton of seeing Aristide
hold a diverse crowd spellbound in no fewer than five languages. Now
exiled in Washington, becoming fluent in English, Aristide had first
struck the president as a soft-spoken ascetic (which Clinton pronounced
"a-*seed*-ic"), yet sensible about politics. Clinton said he shared Aristide's
reservations about this past summer's international agreement, brokered
on Governors Island in New York Harbor, because the timing was backward. It allowed Haiti's coup leaders to vacate their military commands
after, rather than before, Aristide returned from exile to resume the presidency. In the past two months, soldiers had dragged Aristide's chief
business supporter from his church pew to public assassination, and had
gunned down Aristide's justice minister on the streets of Port-au-Prince.
Clinton pondered whether any elected president could govern Haiti

under such circumstances. "I couldn't run *this* country," he said, "if I was fighting the Pentagon and the police forces in every city."

From briefings, he concluded that Haiti's coup leaders had accepted the Governors Island agreement in principle only because they did not believe Aristide would issue its stipulated grants of amnesty to them for crimes known and unknown. Once Aristide did so, sacrificing justice for change, Clinton said the top military officers went into a stall. No longer mere hirelings of wealthy Haitians, they had assumed personal control of the large state enterprises, which they would relinquish only if some external force threw them out. This was the daunting task the president said he discussed with Prime Minister Chrétien. They faced inertia within and between Western governments, fueled by grim predictions, widespread indifference, and crippling opposition. Senator Dole had announced that restoring Aristide to Haiti was not worth the life of a single American soldier. "So how do you get around that?" asked Clinton, stumped, but he said he was not yet resigned, either.

I resolved not to ask further about Haiti, sensing that the president had expounded already for my benefit. From our informal moments off the tape, he knew of my occasional contacts with Aristide and his tiny group of supporters in Washington. Clinton's review of Haiti did not seem forced, nor his future course clear, but I hoped to avoid distorting his private record of deliberations. My questions shifted back to the Seattle summit, and the president first emphasized the pariah nation absent from APEC. "Everybody is upset over North Korea," he said, sketching reports of enriched uranium and other ominous signs of a nuclear bomb program. It may surprise some people that China was especially worried, he added, but China enjoyed some eight times more economic exchange with South Korea than with North Korea, China's ally and South Korea's mortal enemy. This unspoken reality further snarled diplomacy over the bomb, which Clinton said he wanted to save for a later session because he was meeting about it tomorrow with Kim Young-sam, South Korea's new president.

What stuck with him from Seattle was a tough private talk with the Chinese president, Jiang Zemin. Clinton said he and Jiang had sat across from each other at a small table about the size of the card table between us now, with only a translator on each side, as Jiang read a speech to him about the glorious history of China and the folly of attempts to influence her internal affairs. It went on so long that Clinton said he finally felt obliged to interrupt. Speaking in direct sentences, with all the charm he could muster, he invited the Chinese leader to get down to business. He told Jiang he didn't want to change China's political institutions. Nor did he object to prisons. In fact, America had lots of people in prison, and Clinton wanted to put away even more. But he did care about basic human rights, and, even if he didn't, he had a Congress that did. To improve relations, Jiang needed only to do a few things already permissible within Chinese standards and law. Clinton named four, including an effective ban on export goods made by prison labor. When he finished, however, Jiang simply resumed his speech.

The president said he and Jiang talked persistently past one another in disconnected monologues, and stiff formality further inhibited conversation. Protocol officers had coached Clinton never to smile in Jiang's presence, for instance, lest word leak that he had insulted China with improper familiarity. The long, fruitless encounter neutralized what the president called his instinctive approach with counterparts, to break down rhetorical positions toward some personal tie for joint solutions. He said outright that Jiang had frustrated him. I asked several questions about the nature of Jiang's declarations, including whether he had couched them at all in the Marxist language of the ruling Communist Party. The president replied no—never. Indeed, he frowned at such a quaint thought, confirming that China's official ideology, while not overtly renounced, was passé even in its formalized demands. Clinton said Jiang touted instead the power of mother China, like a successor to one of the ancient dynasties.

His memories of the China summit reached a subdued impasse. I switched to smaller subjects and got breezy answers about scandals simmering in the press, such as a retracted boast by Republican consultant Ed Rollins of having paid preachers to suppress the black vote this year in New Jersey. Clinton shrugged off newspaper stories recurring lately about a 1978 land deal in Arkansas. He said the issue had been covered extensively during the 1992 primaries. In a quick summary, he said he and Hillary had lost money as passive investors in a proposed subdivision called Whitewater, and that Jim McDougal, its principal developer, later got into serious legal trouble as the owner of a failed savings and loan. Various alleged improprieties had been advanced and disproved, including charges that Clinton as governor had favored his partner's S&L. Now there were allegations that McDougal had gathered up checks for Clinton's gubernatorial campaigns and then illegally reimbursed the original donors. The president said he didn't believe the reimbursements took place, and, whether they did or not, he and Hillary knew nothing of such a scheme—they took the donations in good faith from people perfectly able to make them.

He waved off Whitewater as a trifling nuisance. My notes say, "He didn't seem particularly upset or interested." Nor was I. Neither of us had a clue that Whitewater soon would become the linchpin for investigations to mark and convulse his presidency. In a further irony, talk of Arkansas did prompt a clairvoyant disgression into more personal attacks. Clinton said the agitation over Whitewater was being churned along by the same two people who had promoted the election year uproar about a sexual affair with Gennifer Flowers. Cliff Jackson and Sheffield Nelson were his lifelong peers, both of whom turned from Democrats to failed Republican candidates. Clinton attended Oxford University with Jackson, and had defeated Nelson badly for governor in 1990. He called them dedicated enemies. "They don't have anything else going in their lives," he said, "but trying to bring me down." They were approaching state troopers from his security detail at the governor's mansion—"telling them, 'Bill Clinton has gone up to Washington, and he's high and mighty, but you're stuck down here and he hasn't given *you* one of those big jobs. We can get you one.' " In exchange for stories about Clinton's private life, he said, these people were offering jobs, vacations, money, "and everything else," mostly as conduits for Republican interests. He expected them to foment more scandal.

All this was a revelation to me, except the name Gennifer Flowers. The president said Jackson and Nelson had cooperated in funneling similar offers to her, and he believed he had traced the sources of funds. He said Flowers had called him at the governor's mansion before any of it became public, when she was still holding out, and he talked with her from the bedroom phone with Hillary sitting right there. Publicity from and about Flowers eventually threatened to derail his candidacy before the New Hampshire primary, forcing his joint appearance with Hillary on CBS's *60 Minutes* in January of 1992. While describing that interview, the president mentioned that one of the high lamps backlighting the stage fell on their sofa. He had pulled Hillary out of the way, and people quipped that the accident was a metaphor for the campaign— they were besieged under the falling hot beam of the press.

Clinton slipped into another discourse on the news media. He said scandal fever sprang from a convergence of the cash-paying tabloids and mainstream outlets. Once the Gennifer Flowers story surfaced, he and Hillary had switched their Flowers interview from CNN to CBS at the last minute, augmenting the audience tenfold, after which the CNN people vowed to get even with Clinton for ruining their scoop. He said CNN's president, Tom Johnson, made no secret of his determination, and the network pushed scandal stories among other barbs for several weeks. Either Jackson or Nelson—I neglected to put in my notes which one he identified—then leaked to CNN a list of five women alleged to have had affairs with him in Arkansas. One of them—a young staff member—told him that a *Washington Post* reporter was promising her confidentiality if she confessed an affair with Clinton, but was threatening otherwise to expose her. When I told him these tactics struck me as aggressive but fairly standard, the president cited a book called *Feeding Frenzy* by University of Virginia professor Larry Sabato, which argued that attack journalism was transforming American politics. I said I would not know such a book these days, being utterly absorbed in work on the 1960s. He noted that it was published in the Bush administration, meaning he was not so paranoid as to think these trends were invented solely for his torment. There has always been sensationalism, he acknowledged, and he needed to understand the changing dynamics for reporters no less than for politicians, but Clinton insisted that roller-coaster entertainment was bad for journalism and the country.

His outburst subsided, having bounced from Whitewater to women and partisan intrigues with the press. Clinton responded briefly about prospects for the Brady Bill on handguns, but said he was too tired to record anything about the June 26 missile attacks on Baghdad. So was I. Heading home after one in the morning, I reflected that the president had signaled worry in two strikingly different ways: quiet puzzlement over a blackout of his extraordinary people skills with China's Jiang Zemin, followed by a careening survey of personal vulnerability. The latter disclosures had unfolded with few intervening questions from me, and his initiative made me wonder again about my role. Should I intrude to seek clarification in this area? "He didn't flat out say he'd never had an affair," I dictated in my notes, "but he said many charges were untrue." I told myself that the president himself had preserved on the tapes telling details about genesis of these stories, with an attitude of defensive alarm. They underscored a hope I had salvaged with nervous friends of Clinton during the Flowers scare—that this ongoing threat, plus the gigantic stakes, would make him behave in the White House and confine the prurient questions to his past.

OUR SESSION TWO weeks later in early December lasted only an hour. Waiting in the Treaty Room, I picked up a new memoir by the ninety-year-old artist Leni Riefenstahl about her propaganda work for Adolf Hitler, with photographs of the grandiose Nazi rally at Nuremberg, while taking in the contrast of fresh Christmas lights around Washington's landmarks outside the window. About nine-thirty, President Clinton walked in a sorry sight. His eyes were running and puffy. His nose was red, and he walked stiffly with a list to one side. He said he had tried to call me to cancel. "I'm up to my ass in alligators," he groaned, mostly over North Korea's nuclear program, but he waved off my offer to come back another time. Exasperated and miserable, he said that although he had asked pointedly for no natural greenery, the magnificent new White House decorations triggered his severe allergies to pollen and pine on the return yesterday from California, where he had aggravated an old back injury—the origin of his interest in rocking chairs—while leaning over to take off his socks.

Before I could ask about these unusual afflictions, Chelsea and Hillary came in from an inspection tour of the formal rooms downstairs. They were full of enthusiasm for the holiday artistry, dampened with sympathy for his compounded plagues. Hillary wore an exercise outfit, looking as chipper as he seemed pathetic. After the three of them exchanged good night hugs, she asked me to let him sleep soon. "He's a very tired POTUS," she said several times, fashioning an endearment from the Secret Service acronym for President of the United States. "Don't keep him up late."

He and I stayed on to record in the Treaty Room for the first time. Clinton, who found it less uncomfortable to stand, hobbled around a good bit to make sure the festive new wreaths were artificial, touching and retouching them in compulsive distraction. I verified that the recorders were picking up his voice at a distance, but his answers were largely pro forma. Of his first Thanksgiving at Camp David, he said the turkey "was cooked very nicely." No, he did not ask Gore to take over a failed foreign policy, as alleged, but to improve public presentations by his troika of "bad talkers": shy National Security Adviser Tony Lake, boring Secretary of State Warren Christopher, and disorganized Defense Secretary Les Aspin. Spanish prime minister Felipe González had given him a hard time today over the thirty-year U.S. embargo against Fidel Castro's Cuba—calling it illogical, counterproductive, lonely, and wrong—but now was not the time to change. He was very happy to have passed and signed the Brady Bill* at last on November 30. Only domestic politics stimulated the president to reveal much beyond public reports. He traced a substantial Indian Sikh community near tiny Bernalillo, New Mexico, recalling even the Sikh voting percentages in adjacent districts, and described his recent audience of distinctive white turbans mingled with Native American costumes and Southwestern string neckties. "Democratic functions in New Mexico are quite a sight," he said brightly, mentioning specific people and exchanges, but the energy soon faded.

Clinton apologized that his spongy head felt too awful to go through the Baghdad missile attacks. He wanted to summon his doctors again in the hope of sleeping. While rewinding the tapes, I made small talk that his comments on one minor topic, a speech on violence in movies, embarrassed me as an author for the trashy tone of our current best-seller list in nonfiction. The president laughed, but he said you could always

---

* The Brady Handgun Violence Prevention Act of 1993 was named for White House Press Secretary James Brady, who became a gun control advocate after being wounded with President Ronald Reagan in an assassination attempt in 1981.

find good books. He agreed that Hollywood sometimes transcended its lowbrow reputation to explore the most difficult subjects, such as AIDS in the forthcoming *Philadelphia,* and the Holocaust in *Schindler's List.* Having attended advance screenings for both, Clinton gave capsule previews of *Philadelphia* as a good film with two Oscar-caliber performances, and *Schindler's List* as a great film that delivers a stunning message. By then, headed toward the elevator, the president thanked me profusely for coming down. "This is good," he kept saying—good to get something down, good to have the discipline. I left before he dredged up his last reserves.

Doorman John Fanning, in his working white tie and tails, stopped at the first floor to show me the White House decorations. We wandered empty halls covered by temporary rubber pathways to protect the floor from the thousands of daily visitors in those years before terrorism interrupted public tours. There was a showpiece national tree in the Blue Room with ornaments from across the United States, plus eight or nine trees in the East Room and, in the State Dining Room, a giant gingerbread pastry shaped like the White House. John shared gossip about a battle of potentates over Clinton's allergies. The medical staff and the first lady's office wanted to spray fake white snow on the decorations, he had heard, to cut down on pine vapors, but the political people vetoed it because the Bush administration had drawn criticism for bad taste in doing so.

CHAPTER SIX

A MOTHER'S DEATH AND THE SPECIAL PROSECUTOR

Monday, December 27, 1993

Friday, January 28, 1994

Saturday, January 29, 1994

Our eighth session stretched over a pivotal month. On December 27, with the South Lawn closed off for the presidential helicopter, I was diverted to street parking and the entrance through West Wing security. Trouble started there with two wrapped Christmas presents in my briefcase, intended for the president and first lady. Conferences ensued. While officers with earpieces took them away for X-ray or worse, others obliged me to wait on the unstated premise that I was suspect until the gifts proved innocent. My telephone inquiries brought mixed consolation that President Clinton was himself overdue from a duck-hunting excursion to the Eastern Shore of Maryland. His delays outlasted mine, until a soldier came by my station in full camouflage with a matching shotgun case. He stopped long enough to indicate in clipped stories that it was no small undertaking to move a president with armed guests into a duck blind by dawn, then safely home, hinting that POTUS was unhappy with other units on this mission for mishaps in traffic and transportation. I could not decide whether Clinton really liked to shoot at ducks, which was a disappointing thought, or had steeled himself in political dedication to woo hunters for his gun control measures. Bulletins kept me in a holding pattern while he juggled a backlog of appointments. Our session was shifted, squeezed, and finally aborted.

"Can you ever forgive me?" asked the president. "I'm sorry. I've wasted your day." He darted about his small study next to the Oval Office, sorting through boxes and shelves for items to stuff into a large duffel on the desk, which he called his "Santa Claus bag," for people in Arkansas. He was scrambling to depart again—this time with a holiday entourage that included his ailing mother—with small logistical armies already mobilized on a coordinated timetable for Air Force One. Clinton fussed that he had mislaid some things and couldn't find others. When he called out for help, personal aides came in to shrug before rushing on with last-minute travel bags bound for the helicopter. I told him not to fret about the lost session, but suggested that we set no more of them for the daytime. He agreed that we did much better at night in the privacy of the residence, and he wanted to keep current. "I'm anxious to talk to you about this shit with the troopers," he said eagerly.

This comment took me aback. I knew from titillating stories in the mainstream press that a small conservative magazine called *The American Spectator* had just published trooper-based allegations of wild philandering with unnamed women. The story was testing the limits of national appetite for soap opera in politics, and I had assumed Clinton would recoil from its tawdry embarrassment above all other subjects. On the contrary, he raised it himself more than once. "There is some really good stuff here," he said, "and we've got to get it down." We talked of rescheduling another session soon, especially since his allergies had abbreviated the last one. While he packed the duffel, I showed him our son's citation in the ten-year-old division of the Maryland chess tournament, and the president seemed excited that Franklin had found a sports outlet compatible with his hip disease. "This is the greatest thing," he said. "I've got to write him a note." He picked busily through little stacks of presents, asking out loud for his pens gone astray. My pride as a father overcame any reluctance to impose, but when I offered him my own pen, the president stared blankly. He said he meant a different kind, and finally located several boxes of presidential logo pins to supplement the stash of knickknack presents. Deflated, I realized his mind had raced so quickly past thoughts of a note for Franklin that he didn't notice our mixing up of pen and pin.

His secretary, Betty Currie, hurried in with an armload of identical, finely wrapped gifts and a hug. (I had known her when she worked at the Peace Corps under Carter.) The president signed one of the gifts for me—a fresh collection of favorite speeches from his first year in office— and I handed him in return my two wrapped survivors from the Secret Service security. A minute or two later, eyeing them warily under a pile of things to be left behind, I told him he could open mine now. He paused to smile. "Oh, I can?" he asked, teasing me. His face lit up when he examined the old parchment inside. "Where did you find this?" he exclaimed. It was an original 1826 edition of Daniel Webster's memorial tribute to John Adams and Thomas Jefferson after their famously coin- cidental deaths on July 4, 1826, the fiftieth anniversary of the vote by the 1776 Continental Congress to approve their drafting committee's Declaration of Independence. Clinton mentioned the subsequent elec- tion of 1800 among many fateful dramas in the tempestuous relation- ship between these two Founders. I told him Webster ranged over such themes in this classic oration at Boston's Faneuil Hall on August 2, 1826, which date in turn marked exactly fifty years since Jefferson, Adams, John Hancock, and most other delegates had reconvened to sign the finished Declaration.

Beaming, Clinton reached for my other gift, zipped up the duffel, and swept out past valets coming to fetch his gear. We stopped in the Oval Office long enough to wish each other happy holidays above the noise of the Marine One helicopter engines on the landing pad outside. I told him Hillary's present was a dictation machine like the two we were using, and encouraged him to support my plea for her to record her own oral history with it, even if she never told a soul. He nodded. "I'm sorry again for standing you up," said the president.

CLINTON BEGAN WITH solemn directness when we resumed at the residence in the early evening of Friday, January 28, in the new year of 1994. He said we had a lot to do. The month since our last session had been an important, traumatic period in his life—with the death of his mother, a long trip to Europe, the establishment of a Whitewater special prosecutor, and his State of the Union Address, among many lesser events. He wanted to take two or three hours to get the highlights straight, but our time tonight was short. His first lively responses addressed key personnel transitions, beginning with the new deputy chief of staff. Harold Ickes, son of FDR's interior secretary, was precisely the sort of crack-the-whip administrator needed to make government function well, Clinton observed, but the appointment had been held up for months because of a complicated investigation at Ickes's New York law firm. Then, with the obstacles finally removed, Ickes unaccountably had lost his brash, self-assured manner, telling both the president and Hillary that he was afraid to take the job. They were baffled. Ickes reconsidered, refused again, and sank into a kind of limbo. The president said it took quite an effort to coax him into the White House with restored confidence for the major legislative tasks ahead: health care, the crime bill, welfare reform. "He's doing great now," Clinton added, "but this illustrates for me how hard it can be to read the character of people here in Washington—even people you've known for a long time."

He commented glumly on his second failed nomination to head the Civil Rights Division at the Justice Department. Sponsors in the civil rights community, especially the Congressional Black Caucus, had remained deadlocked long after it emerged that John Payton had not voted for ten years—very likely, said Clinton, because the sponsors did not want to acknowledge their own glaring oversight. Worse, he added, they turned against their nominee for the wrong reason, only when key legislators decided that Payton might not be vigilant enough about buttressing their incumbency advantages in specially carved districts. Clinton said such objections rested on a selfish distortion of the 1965 Voting Rights Act. Its central purpose was to guarantee representation broadly for *voters*, he explained, not for officeholders. The president disputed a conventional wisdom equating fairness with "safe" seats in heavily minority districts. He said constituents from such districts could be taken for granted, and he criticized minority Democrats for colluding with Republicans in several states to create sinecures on both sides of the aisle. The voters would be better served by some impartial way to maximize rather than minimize competitive districts, Clinton observed, but he would not dispute the raw politics on Payton's flawed credentials. In fact, he said he remained so heartsick from the Lani Guinier controversy that he was leaving this problematic selection to Janet Reno through regular channels.

Conflict also dogged some bigger transitions at the Pentagon. Clinton recalled quiet discussions with Tony Lake and others about replacing Defense Secretary Les Aspin even before the Black Hawk helicopter losses in Somalia. He said Aspin had never made a good impression at the National Security Council, where his meandering presentations had an aimless quality that obscured any managerial talent or drive. Some people even doubted Aspin's attachment to his post, but the president discovered otherwise when he asked privately for a resignation on December 15. Aspin reacted with what Clinton called a "character transplant," arguing forcefully and cogently why he should be retained. He had given up a House chairmanship to help Clinton adjust the military posture after the Cold War, Aspin reminded him, tackling a challenge that might well determine the next election. The president said he conceded some of the strengths Aspin claimed for himself, then told him directly that his reactions in moments of crisis had instilled confusion and doubt instead of purpose, which Clinton believed would happen again if permitted. He said it took more than one insistent, painful conversation to achieve a clean severance.

The president's announced choice to replace Aspin lasted one bizarre month. He said retired admiral Bobby Ray Inman had drawn unanimous enthusiasm from the foreign policy establishment, including members of Congress from both parties. A Texas Republican, Inman had headed the super-secret National Security Agency under Reagan, served as deputy director of the CIA, and enjoyed a reputation for lean, skillful administration. Clinton said Inman's fervent supporters ran the gamut from contracting specialists and four-star military officers to general advisers like David Gergen and Strobe Talbott, the new deputy secretary of state. He digressed briefly to note that the recent promotion of Talbott—his old schoolmate in England, my longtime acquaintance in journalism—came solely on the initiative of Secretary Christopher, against Clinton's reservations about elevating Talbott above his proven specialty as the administration's troubleshooter for all things Russian. Clinton switched back to the Pentagon appointment before I could tell whether he was worried about charges of cronyism, or genuinely feared some lapse without Talbott focused on the vast and vital transformation of Russia. Clinton said that only Mack McLarty had expressed misgiving about the preliminary interviews with Inman, finding him oddly detached in manner–"kind of dreamy," as Clinton put it–but a strong consensus of national security experts overwhelmed his vague instincts.

The Inman nomination went forward to general acclaim, although Clinton did find it nettlesome when, at their joint announcement, the admiral pronounced himself satisfied that the president could be entrusted with the nation's safety, as though Inman occupied some superior position to make the judgment. Then, ten days ago on January 18, Inman abruptly renounced his appointment with a tirade against "modern McCarthyism," naming Senator Dole and *New York Times* columnist William Safire among conspirators plotting to ruin him. Inman's outburst stunned observers. Not a single senator was opposed to his confirmation, and the few press quibbles were lost in a sea of public praise, but dramatic shifts had occurred out of sight. The president said Inman changed from the moment Dole agreed to allow questions from Republican senators, becoming so agitated that the administration's background investigators returned to Inman several times about rumors that he was gay. The admiral denied them convincingly, said Clinton, but did acknowledge a closeted relative, whose status was unknown to his mother, and Inman came unhinged with fear that disclosures from the confirmation process would destroy his family. Many secrets, both real ones and decoys, simply vanished with him beneath a volley of stories bidding good riddance to his mysterious, prickly paranoia.

President Clinton expressed no great remorse over Inman's departure. He seemed much relieved to have appointed a successor already, and was full of compliments for William Perry. The incoming defense secretary was not only safe–reliable and experienced as the current Pentagon deputy–but also an innovator with whom the president enjoyed talking military strategy. While Clinton was glad that Inman ducked a prolonged scandal for himself and the administration, he could not help musing that political changes rushed by on fever and whim. No discipline or balance guided attention to significant issues buried in the Inman saga, such as how for decades so brittle a figure had mastered the most sensitive spy agencies. Almost inevitably, the president related this abbreviated affair to his own troubles in Whitewater. He said that although the press never ignited the allegations against Inman in public, reporters had created a subterranean political force by circulating the rumors of homosexuality. This was not nearly as pervasive or sinister as McCarthyism, he said, but hidden agendas advanced unchecked on sensationalism. To that degree, he sympathized with Inman.

There was extra bite in tonight's roving lament on Whitewater, which consumed nearly an hour. Under duress, the president had just consented to a special prosecutor—Robert Fiske—named by Attorney General Reno eight days ago on January 20. Even Clinton, with his runaway gripes, could not anticipate a seven-year investigation that would outlast his presidency, but he was plenty upset. Now Fiske must hire a new staff and start all over again on the land deal questions from 1978, plus new ones that undoubtedly would be raised, and Clinton fumed that he and Hillary would wind up spending most of their net worth defending against charges yet to be specified because there was nothing there. He gave numerous theories on causes and combinations behind the latest outcry for a special prosecutor. Scoffing at the standard rationale—that some clarifying authority was urgently needed, and harmless, *because* Whitewater was incomprehensible—he speculated that the outcry borrowed drumbeat energy from sex rumors beneath the surface. There was no logical connection between them, but that was his point. What they had in common was a feverish, hidden agenda, reminiscent of Inman's demise, abetted by what the president called a prevailing condescension toward Arkansas people as hillbillies still rooted in backwardness, promiscuous and corrupt, epitomized by Clinton.

A Whitewater chorus had intensified above the furtive pulse of revelations from the Arkansas state troopers, and here Clinton delved into the discoveries he had mentioned the last time we spoke. He said the first warnings had come in a report from his Arkansas political director that Danny Ferguson, a trooper in the former security detail at the governor's mansion, had left a message with the White House pleading to discuss an unspecified emergency. Clinton returned the call, expecting some personal or family petition, and heard instead Ferguson's anguished confession-turned-warning that he had been among four troopers meeting clandestinely with Cliff Jackson and various reporters. Ferguson told him Jackson was connected to a political network that was well organized and well financed—dangling dream jobs, book contracts, and even movie deals for the troopers, offering as much as $300,000 to women if they would say publicly they had slept with Clinton. The president said he had since confirmed some of this, and that Ferguson—battered by temptation, peer pressure, guilt, and fear—refused to be a named source for the *American Spectator* story, only to have two of the remaining troopers expose him anyway as their cold-footed confederate.

Ferguson told him, Clinton continued, that the troopers had been encouraged to volunteer speculation and uncorroborated gossip so long as they could agree on the specifics. The overriding goal was to get the sex tales into the news media, which required them to be provocative and consistent but not necessarily accurate. This point sent Clinton on another tangent about the press. "The reporters would just stampede and print anything," he seethed. One juicy story had spread from the *Spectator* into many mainstream outlets, alleging that the president-elect had slipped off with a judge's wife at his farewell party in Little Rock, so brazenly that Hillary had called the woman a whore. He said every bit of that was ridiculous. The farewell party had jammed several hundred couples into a one-room airplane hangar. Chelsea was there. The judge and his wife continued by charter flight to Washington for the inauguration. The wife, like the other women indirectly described by the *Spectator*, but carefully not named, flatly denied an affair with Clinton. She went so far as to warn CNN that the charge was a slander garnished with absurd details, but Tom Johnson, president of CNN News, gave her a laconic response, something like, "Well, I guess that means you won't let us use your name." The president qualified this attributed quote, saying he heard it only secondhand, but he believed the substance by CNN's rush to broadcast the story.

Clinton's rants against the press conveyed more than a touch of disappointment. He was accustomed to war from political enemies, but it seemed that he had looked up to big-time newspapers as truth seekers of greater refinement. The *Washington Post* and *New York Times* had been "a little better" on the sex stories, he observed. They did not brandish them on the front page with lurid headlines like the tabloids, and they noted reservations about the troopers' veracity. He complained, on the other hand, that these premier newspapers had led the charge for a Whitewater special prosecutor with compensating gusto and indignation, as though nurturing a more respectable crusade to keep pace. On Whitewater, Clinton looked forward to fairer treatment from Fiske.

The president stood, late for engagements. There were so many more subjects, he said, pacing while I rewound the tapes, and he wanted to talk especially about his mother. He said he called her every Sunday night, but the funeral went by in such a blur of crises over NATO and Russia and scandals that it did not hit him until he returned from Europe late on a Sunday, with no one to call—how much he missed her. Could I come back in a few hours, and perhaps stay over? This was feasible because of my speaking engagement there in Washington that same night, around which we had scheduled our session, and arrangements were quickly made. I drove to a nearby synagogue for *yortzheit* services honoring Rabbi Abraham Heschel on the approximate anniversary of his death. On my return, an usher said President Clinton was too tired to work and in fact had gone to bed while his guests watched the film *Grumpy Old Men*. He showed me to the Queens' Bedroom, which I had not seen since our whirlwind inspection on inauguration day.

EARLY THE NEXT morning, I made my way to the far end of the long yellow corridor to search for coffee. In the small upstairs kitchen, across from the master bedroom, I came upon two butlers standing near Clinton, who sat hunched over the breakfast table clad in boxer shorts and a hooded sweatshirt. He greeted me with a barely decipherable rasp, saying his voice was gone and he had stayed up through the night because his cold medicine failed to work and Hillary had come home from a health care trip at five o'clock. He said he hoped to record something, but he felt pretty bad. I had no doubt of that. Wordless, the butlers gave me stricken looks tinged with reproach, signaling that I had intruded

upon their custody of the president's intimate, vulnerable state. I retreated hastily from the image of his bare feet on the cold floor beneath
strikingly pale, hairless legs—old man's legs—far too spindly it seemed for
the torso above, which was larger than mine, or for his leonine, sniffling
head. I told Clinton I would await his instructions back in the Queens'
Bedroom, and much to my surprise a transformed president appeared
there an hour later, dressed to befit the high office. He beckoned me to
set up the recorders quickly in a hallway landing nearby, where we could
hide until the staff rounded him up for his Saturday morning radio address.

The president reviewed his mother's illness. Virginia Kelley had a
mastectomy upon being diagnosed with breast cancer in 1990, and new
symptoms had revealed a malignancy spreading into her bones. He said
she was very sick when she came to Washington for the inauguration a
year ago. The cancer was attacking her bone marrow's capacity to replace
red blood cells, which would have killed her swiftly if the doctors had
not given her transfusions. Each of these provided a tonic jolt from the
donated red blood cells, and Clinton said he knew on one level that the
treatment masked her underlying condition. She was frail, and her hair
fell out from the chemotherapy. Yet she was proud of her nice-looking
wig, and seemed to be having such a good time—flying all around the
country—that he decided she might last a few more years. Besides, she
was his mother, and he believed the best until an improbable encounter
at November's APEC meetings in Seattle. An Arkansas doctor he knew,
who attended on one of many state delegations seeking commercial
concessions with Asian nations, had emphatically waved off Clinton's
rosy report on her health. He had just seen Virginia Kelley's charts. She
had essentially no bone marrow function, and, barring a miracle by lot-
tery from experimental drugs, was unlikely to survive more than three
months. The doctor thought it was important for the family to know.

"This really brought me up short," said the president. He tried to
discuss these grim prospects with his mother, but she deflected him. At
Camp David for Thanksgiving, she shrugged off his updated reports that
she was getting as many as two transfusions per day. When they flew
home together after Christmas, she joined a raucous pizza dinner as
usual but then shooed him off to go bowling with his old high school

friends. They finally had a mother-son visit for three hours the next morning, alone at her home in Hot Springs. "We talked about everything except the fact that she was dying," Clinton recalled, with regret. She wanted to live her remaining time normally, and he took consolation from her goodbye trip to Las Vegas for Barbra Streisand's New Year's concerts. The president said that while it was easy for the press to sneer at the Streisand friendship as a Hollywood publicity stunt, she and his mother sustained an odd-couple bond. They talked constantly for a year. He said the same was true of the only other famous person at his mother's funeral, Buffalo Bills owner Ralph Wilson. By the second quarter of Wilson's disastrous Super Bowl XXVII—a blowout loss to the Dallas Cowboys—the owner was surprised to learn that his Arkansas guest, Clinton's mother, was not only a diehard Bills fan but also "fairly tight" already from trips to the bar, sharing a compatible outlook on life's hardships.

Notice of her death reached Clinton after midnight on January 6. He spent time at home comforting his brother, who had leaned heavily on their mother through his own severe troubles with drug use and imprisonment. "Roger hated our father a lot more than I did," said Clinton, explaining that the violent, alcoholic tantrums of the senior Clinton had fallen hard on his younger sibling. The president said he had made a strenuous plea for self-control just before the funeral. "This day is for Mother," he told Roger, "but if we argue or yell or break down, then the whole thing is going to be about us." Separately, he praised his stepfather Richard Kelley—Virginia's fourth husband—for leadership through an emotional impasse about whether her grave should lie among the Clintons in Hot Springs, or elsewhere. Kelley took Clinton aside to defer, saying she should be buried in Hope next to the president's biological father and namesake, William Jefferson Blythe, who had died in a car crash before Clinton was born. "He was the first and great love of her life," Kelley told him magnanimously. "It's proper for you to decide, and we'll worry later about where I'll be buried." That settled, the family pulled together for the funeral, and Clinton described its joyful service of tribute. A preacher said Virginia Kelley once caught him at the racetrack when he was supposed to be at a ministerial convention. Janice Sjostrand sang the Pentecostal hymn "Holy Ground," in a reprise of her performance at the inaugural prayer service at Metropolitan AME, moving Streisand to express awe that such music could come from human beings. A post-burial reception filled the Western Sizzlin steak house.

From Arkansas, Air Force One stopped over in Washington just long enough to exchange passengers while Clinton gathered up some items for his diplomatic tour of Europe. The presidential party took off again within hours, amid a crescendo of demands to formalize the Whitewater investigation. On our tape, the president complained that Republican leaders—Iowa's Jim Leach and Georgia's Newt Gingrich in the House, Bob Dole in the Senate—"kept up their flacking" on talk shows right through the funeral, pushing for a special prosecutor. "The guy couldn't even let me bury my mother," he said bitterly of Dole. He said Al Gore, probably to calm him down, postulated wryly from their service together in the Senate that Dole had "a nice streak." Gore detected generous sparks within Dole's flinty disposition, which amused Clinton. "Maybe nobody gave Dole any presents this year," Clinton quipped. "He's been really nasty since Christmas. I wish I had sent him a present myself."

The president sketched his tightrope mission abroad. He lobbied NATO officials in Belgium on a delicate timetable for adding new members from the former Soviet empire—rapidly enough to ease their fears of being isolated or reabsorbed, slowly enough not to topple Yeltsin beneath Russia's ultranationalist revival stoked by Vladimir Zhirinovsky. In Moscow, he assuaged Yeltsin while pushing him to recall troops from the three tiny Baltic nations occupied by Russia for nearly fifty years. In Kiev, he closed a deal for Ukraine to surrender stockpiles of Soviet nuclear weapons. In Minsk, he addressed leaders of newly independent Belarus. In Geneva, his personal introduction to Syria's President Asad lasted through five hours of intense talks on the Middle East.

All the while, Clinton carried with him political and personal grief from home. He said his mother's death left him keenly attuned to nostalgia. On a Sunday's walking tour of Brussels, he stopped outside a toy shop he recognized from a visit more than two decades earlier. It was closed, but commotion drew the owners downstairs from their apartment to open for him. The president said he still remembered the decor inside, and bought something to honor the owners' courtesy. He appreciated a timely gift of two saxophones from Dinant, Belgium, where the instrument had been invented. Their soothing tone was nearly as rich as the world-class Yamahas, he observed, adding that most saxophones were made lately either in Paris or a small town in Indiana, where, for obscure reasons he knew, the sax makers affiliated with the United Auto Workers union. Clinton said he made extra time to play the sax in the Czech Republic, visiting coffeehouses with Czech president Václav Havel. His official business there was to persuade the presidents of Poland, Hungary, and Slovakia to accept a carefully protracted entry into NATO, but he dwelled instead on a walk from Prague Castle over the storied Charles Bridge with U.N. ambassador Madeleine Albright. She spoke fluent Czech more than fifty years after fleeing the Nazis as a little girl, and was plainly overcome by this return to her birthplace liberated from Soviet rule—accompanied in grand style by the president of her adopted country along with Havel, the poetic dissident turned architect of new democracy. Albright exchanged tales about a similar odyssey for General Shalikashvili, a childhood refugee from Poland. On a lesser arc, Clinton said he recalled a youthful pilgrimage to this romantic city in 1970, when Prague was Communist and his mother was alive.

American politics overtook the president in Prague. Incessant clamor about Whitewater forced an international conference call with his closest advisers on January 11, which Clinton described as a heated continuation of the stalemate over how to respond to the trooper stories. Half the inner circle argued that he should ignore the fray, and refuse to get "down in the gutter" with his detractors, while the other half said he could win only by fighting every accusation. Clinton said it was impossible to do both. In this fierce debate, he added, Hillary remained the staunchest opponent of agreeing to a special prosecutor for Whitewater—steadier than his lawyers. From her legal work on the House impeachment staff in the Nixon era, she insisted that presidents must be investigated, and impeached if warranted, for misuse of their unique powers in office. The vague Whitewater allegations were miles beneath this standard, rooted in actions long before Clinton's term, and she said a special prosecutor on these facts was not only foolish but wrong. It would invite open-ended persecution while tampering with constitutional balance. On the other side, Clinton's political advisers foresaw unstoppable decline so long as opponents and critics could keep up cries that he must be hiding something. Democratic allies were joining Republican demands that he put suspicions to rest, while Whitewater dominated press conferences even in Europe. The president said he merely went through the motions on the showdown phone conference. Sleepwalking half the time, he chose to invite an independent investigation even though he agreed with Hillary. The Whitewater special prosecutor "is setting a terrible precedent," he believed, but it was the only way to calm the uproar. He had given in for relief.

The president asked whether I had seen a column by E. J. Dionne at the end of December, speculating about why Republicans hate him so much. He endorsed its thesis that Republicans focus on Clinton's character because they feel threatened by his agenda. Clinton is trying to restore confidence that politics and government matter broadly to citizens, and Republicans feel handicapped in such competition—largely because they really want to shrink the public agenda toward the basics of war and ceremony. Therefore, Dionne argued, any success by Clinton incites them to harsher attacks on stronger ground, which for them is personal. Clinton nodded. This was why he should expect some recycled scandal whenever his approval ratings get too high, but here he recognized a drawback to his Whitewater decision. The special investigation rewarded character politics. It would reinforce the divide between substance and diversion.

There was stirring at the far end of the yellow hallway. Aides hovered with his script—doubtless still in revision—anxious to get him over to the Oval Office for the live radio broadcast. (It opened with a confession that he was still hoarse from Tuesday's State of the Union Address.) The president said we should wrap up, reserving some topics for later. They included the State of the Union—with its publicized gesture of his pen raised aloft, challenging Congress not to make him veto a health care bill providing less than universal coverage—and especially his grueling talk with Syria's President Asad, but Clinton wanted to mention something not on my list. He said he had picked up a bad feeling on the trip to Russia. He called it just an ominous sixth sense. "I had it, and Hillary had it, too," he said. They worried about long-term prospects for Russia and parts of Central Europe. "Democracy may make it there," he mused,

"but you can begin to feel why patterns of history repeat themselves."
He said we must bear in mind that these nations have been invaded
many times, unlike the United States, and it was hard for Russia to get
through the shock of establishing markets and openly functioning government, away from evaluating herself by military threats and dominion
over surrounding countries. "I think this is what the twenty-first century
is going to be about," the president concluded. "How freedom will survive all these pressures where it's never really been tested."

These historical forebodings reminded me of President Clinton's
somber mood about China in an earlier session. He said his reactions
were similar but distinct. As opposed to inward dangers to Russia, and
within Russia, he was more preoccupied with outward projections of
Chinese power. When I asked if he could elaborate on anything Jiang
Zemin might have said along these lines, the president vividly recalled
their private meeting. He said Jiang was well aware that mammoth size
and rapid growth destined his economy to become the largest on earth.
Jiang's rhetoric in Seattle had invoked this future so lucidly that Clinton
conceded to him the possibility of a very different summit in fifty years,
when some leader might try to cajole a U.S. president to "reform" *our*
Constitution and laws along Chinese lines. Jiang declared that Chinese
rulers believed in discipline for their people, not from them, and he
bluntly diminished American self-government as a small and dubious
blip on the Chinese calendar, not a monument of world history. In my
notes, dictated moments later on the way home, I said I could only approximate the eloquent force of President Clinton's relayed quotation.
"Look," Jiang told him. "It's wonderful that you have all this freedom,
and all this money, but what do you do with it? You have 33,000 homi-
cides by guns. Your cities are uninhabitable. Your schools don't work.
You have rampant drug use, and you can't control your population.
Who is to say that your freedom is worth it?"

CHAPTER SEVEN

CLINTON AND THE PRESS

Wednesday, February 16, 1994

Wednesday, March 16, 1994

Sports delayed the February 16 session. I found the president in the parlor room with Jim Blair, whose wife, Diane, I knew as a professor and confidante of both Clintons. The two men were talking to the television set, deeply immersed in a men's basketball game pitting Arkansas against Alabama. They shouted like fans—"When you go up, you've got to go up *hard*!"—while second-guessing each other about the subtleties of the zone defense and clock management. President Clinton seemed much more of a passionate expert about college basketball than, say, Major League Baseball, where his comments drifted just above the politician's norm. He and Blair told stories about the Arkansas basketball players—their families, high schools, recruitment histories, and career highlights so far. Number 3 had worked four years in a grocery store saving money for college, talked his way into a tryout, and now had a green light to take the three-point shot. They said Coach Nolan Richardson had won 74 percent of his games despite losing seasons the first two years, while enduring not only venomous abuse as Arkansas's first black coach but also the slow loss of a daughter, Chelsea's age, to leukemia.

During commercials, President Clinton used the remote control to switch back and forth to the Winter Olympics in Lillehammer, Norway. He admired the athletes, especially those who overcame injuries, and criticized a trial event in which skiers bounced downhill over constant bumps, calling it torture instead of sport. When I confessed never noticing that Arkansas had transferred from the Southwest Conference to the Southeastern, Blair ascribed the move to one word, "Money." He said he had been chairman of the Arkansas board of regents when Southwest schools like Rice and SMU deemphasized football because they could not compete with local NFL teams for ticket sales. Arkansas had left a shrinking Southwest revenue pool at the right moment, he added, when the paired addition of South Carolina gave the Southeastern Conference enough teams for a two-division championship playoff and therefore a huge extra payout for each member school. He recited precise figures with a blunt emphasis I thought vaguely unbecoming to higher education. Then he explained small black armbands on the Arkansas players as a mourning gesture for Virginia Kelley, which startled the president. "Has that been announced?" asked Clinton. "I didn't know."

Blair left when the game finally ended—a lopsided victory for Arkansas—and the president asked me to look at one of his eyes. He had been complaining of discomfort, wiping away tears. I saw no obstruction, but he decided to call for medical assistance because he felt something hard scratching the eyeball. Apologizing for our slow start, he noted that February had been chaotic and rough. The health care initiative was "coming apart already," and the opposition managed to surface a "new bimbo" he said he didn't even recognize. (This was Paula Jones, whom Cliff Jackson had introduced to reporters at the annual convention of NCPAC, the National Conservative Political Action Committee. Identifying herself as the "Paula" mentioned in *The American Spectator,* as the willing invitee to a trooper-arranged hotel rendezvous with Governor Clinton, Jones claimed defamation.) Plus, Clinton said, the North Korea crisis worsened for several days, and a Serb artillery shell on February 5 killed sixty-eight civilians and wounded two hundred, mostly Muslims, in the Markale marketplace of Sarajevo—by far the worst single atrocity in the bloody two-year siege of Bosnia's capital city. This outrage was provoking the Western nations to act at last, said the president. Against them, Boris Yeltsin threatened to retaliate with "all-out war" if NATO mounted air strikes against Serb artillery positions around Sarajevo, but

Clinton attributed some of this to political bluster. He said Yeltsin had to react angrily because his nationalist opposition supported Russia's traditional Serb allies almost blindly, notwithstanding their primary responsibility for the genocidal ethnic cleansing in the Balkan wars since 1992.

A crisp, pleasant military doctor arrived in a uniform I did not recognize, featuring a white blouse with red and blue stripes brocaded down the button line. She flushed the president's eye with solution from a fierce-looking syringe in her bag. My job was holding a towel to catch the splatter. She promised to return, and reminded Clinton that the main goal was to remove secretions before they dried beneath his eyelid. I asked whether this infection was publicly known. He said probably so. On tape, he said his recent phone calls with King Fahd of Saudi Arabia definitely were related to the announcement today of a Saudi contract to order new commercial aircraft from the United States. There had been infighting for months. President Mitterrand pushed a rival bid by the European Airbus company, said Clinton, and the French paid very large incentives to Saudi intermediaries. Now that American companies had won the business, Clinton said, the French were likely to criticize a separate agreement for the U.S. government to renegotiate the Saudi debt on previous purchases of military aircraft, calling it an indirect bribe. The president called our approach smarter, and legal.

He told new stories about his trip to Europe in January, with descriptions of Moscow's white spires and his formal entrance into Georgy Hall at the Kremlin, facing Yeltsin across the vast floor, walking past ornate walls embossed in gold with the names of Russian military heroes back through Gen. Mikhail Kutuzov, who defeated Napoléon, to Peter the Great. He said the pride of Mother Russia made her current hard times more poignant. War in Bosnia complicated military and market transitions that were difficult already, as Yeltsin lurched between arduous reform and his frustration that free institutions would not spring up preinstalled by decree. Politics currently obliged Yeltsin to roar against NATO, but Clinton thought Yeltsin also wanted a larger role for Russia than merely defender of the Bosnian Serbs—something parallel to NATO but not subservient. This made negotiations tricky, if not quixotic.

The president emphasized the volatile atmosphere of his journey through a changing Europe. He had insisted on seeing the patriarch of the Russian Orthodox Church, despite criticism that church officials had collaborated with the Soviet KGB under Communism. At one restoration site, where Stalin had destroyed a cathedral to build a public toilet, Clinton said he could see and feel the Russian church coming back to life. He visited Belarus to reward its initiative in surrendering Soviet nuclear weapons on its territory, and stopped at a mass grave in a pine forest commemorating some 250,000 Belarusians killed by Stalin. There was controversy in Minsk about whether he should have paid homage first to victims of the Nazis, said Clinton, and it was a shame that press coverage of such trips omitted so many rich details. "Or maybe only somebody like me would care," he mused, calling Belarus a "heavily warred area" that lay across the historic invasion route to Moscow. Already punished by Stalin as a stronghold for the White Army during the Russian Revolution, Belarus went on to lose a quarter of its population in World War II. The scars of suffering and hardship had become more evident as Clinton worked his way eastward across Europe, but he noticed at his public ceremonies that the musical bands steadily improved in quality and cohesion, despite every disadvantage. He took solace from this small, improbable trend.

Of his January 16 private summit in Geneva, Clinton said he found Syria's President Hafez al-Asad relentless and direct as advertised. Despite his poor health, Asad had talked nonstop for nearly five hours without refreshment or a bathroom break. Terrorism was a principal subject. Asad claimed vindication in the ongoing investigation of the 1988 bombing over Lockerbie, Scotland,* whose chief suspects now were agents of Libya. While he disavowed the use of any terrorists abroad, Asad bluntly asserted a right to host Hezbollah, Islamic Jihad, and other such radical Islamic groups in Syria, insisting that he could not tell others how to fight their battles. From a standoff on this point—that the United States would never normalize relations so long as Syria harbored terrorists—the presi-

---

* On December 21, 1988, a bomb destroyed Pan Am Flight 103 shortly after takeoff from London, bound for New York, killing all 259 people on board and eleven victims at the Lockerbie crash site. For the United States, it would remain the deadliest terror attack until September 11, 2001.

dent said they made limited headway on Syria's continuing state of war with Israel. Clinton thought Asad really did want to make peace, but he said Asad's conspiratorial mind feared that Israel's recent breakthrough talks with the Palestinians would leave Syria isolated among Arab countries in the Middle East. In fact, Asad dropped hints about sabotaging the Palestinian-Israeli peace track to preserve Syria's leverage—and did so with relish, said Clinton, because Asad despised Yasir Arafat as a bumbling nomad. He fondly recalled having Arafat in a Syrian jail, and wondered why he ever let him go. The president said he had done his best to convince Asad that Syria had a stake in Palestinian success, because failure would ruin peacemakers like Yitzhak Rabin in Israel, leaving no one to bargain with for the Golan Heights.

Clinton reviewed more Syrian nuances than I could remember, then lamented that everything was scrambled a week later by the sudden death in a car crash of Asad's older son and carefully groomed successor, Basil. A shaken, grieving Asad called him at the White House, said the president, in the fretful grip of dictator politics. Under family duress for the funeral, Asad was obliged to readmit to Syria his own exiled brother Rifaat, the ruthless former spy chief who had tried to overthrow him in a 1984 coup. Asad told Clinton he loathed but feared Rifaat. He worried incessantly that Rifaat would seize power either from him or soon from his younger son, Bashar, Rifaat's nephew, an aspiring ophthalmologist in London. With his ferocious will, Asad resolved to live until he could toughen Bashar for a new destiny.* Clinton, for his part, reassessed the ruler of Syria—absolute yet insecure, and distracted. He wondered how and when Asad might risk peace with Israel for the dream of his country made whole.

My questions shifted topics. Somewhat to my surprise, the president complimented a *Washington Post* series on the previous year's disastrous military raid in Mogadishu, Somalia. He considered the reporting generally accurate and the criticism fair. Separately, Clinton described the collapse of trade talks with Japan, which he predicted may doom an-

---

* Asad survived six more years, until June 10, 2000. His son Bashar, who shifted from eye care to the army after Basil's death, and rose to the rank of colonel, did succeed him in the presidency.

other Japanese government.* "He talked about Motorola," my notes record. "He talked about cellular phones," which were then a new
invention. The president said that only wispy, toothless reforms could
get through the current Japanese Diet, where members denounced as
"quotas" any more specific targets toward free trade. He likened the impasse to racial disputes over affirmative action in domestic politics.

On another matter of governance, Clinton described his rearguard
action to head off a balanced budget amendment to the Constitution.
"It's going to be nip and tuck," he said. If the proposal won approval in
Congress, Clinton said the states would ratify the amendment overwhelmingly, and this outcome would ratchet up the level of cynicism,
subjecting the Constitution itself to ridicule when the same legislators
inevitably concocted ways to avoid compliance. After all, most of those
pushing the amendment had ducked or opposed every one of Clinton's
budget bills, which had reduced the annual deficit already by 40 percent.
A balanced budget was right in front of them, he charged, but they sidestepped the work and responsibility in favor of a rhetorical pose.

I asked whether it might be possible to shift public opinion on the
balanced budget amendment with a major presidential address—noting
that his recent State of the Union message had raised support for Hillary's health care bill by more than twenty points. Clinton shook his
head like a disappointed teacher. He planned no such speech for several
reasons. First, public opinion on the deficit was not subject to quick
change because three decades of campaign debate had cemented the
language around attitudes rather than performance. He said there was a
better chance to head off the balanced budget amendment by a coalition with his political adversaries. They valued their issue and its slogans
far above actual success, just as anti-abortion politicians always knew to
stop short of any criminalizing legislation that might actually send
mothers or nurses to jail. Second, the president said his State of the
Union bump was wearing off in the polls. Support eroded quickly because the health proposal was complex, which meant hard to remem-

---

* Morihiro Hosokawa, who had become prime minister on August 9, 1993,
soon fell from power on April 28, 1994. His successor, Tsutomu Hata, lasted
two months.

ber and easy to attack. Clinton said insurance companies had spent $100 million to skewer the bill as socialized medicine. With simple sound bites, their "Harry & Louise" ads cultivated the same fearful attitude that distorted anti-deficit politics—a ritual contempt for "big government"—and the administration could not compete effectively with its big words like "comprehensive" and "universal." In retrospect, said the president, perhaps he should have started with a small piece of health reform, generating positive sound bites about safer and better coverage for more people. He was beginning months of effort to salvage the health initiative, but he sounded pessimistic. "There's a reason why this hasn't been done in sixty years," he said.

His eyes looked worse than before. I told him one in particular had something yellowish in the lash, and I was concerned he would wake up with his lids matted together. He decided to call the medical staff again, then spoke briefly about his perilous decision to put three hundred U.S. soldiers in the former Yugoslav province of Macedonia—to prevent war with Greece over irredentist claims and flag symbols that somehow angered even his urbane friend Andreas Papandreou, the aging Greek premier. He also mentioned talks with Federal Reserve Chairman Alan Greenspan. Like all presidents, he found a hike in interest rates painful. It would retard an economy positioned for sustained growth, and Greenspan himself had detected no warning signs of inflation. He said the chairman claimed to be under heavy pressure because of inflated values in the stock market—and the recent rate hike did knock 100 points off a Dow Jones peak of 3,900—but Clinton half-suspected that the true motive was to remind everyone that the Fed was important. Still, he would not protest too much. The Fed was good to him overall, and Greenspan had supported Clinton's omnibus budget bill.

In the bathroom, examining his eyes while the tapes rewound, we talked about Haiti. I saved this topic for spare moments, apologizing for my personal interest, but this time Clinton was fully engaged. He said he would spend much of the next day on the festering crisis over Haitian refugees, and that the few people in his government who cared tended to blame its exiled president, Aristide, for failing to negotiate his way back into office. I replied that such blame, which permeated news coverage, undermined any chance that Haiti's military rulers would think we were serious about restoring Aristide. Maybe so, said the president, but the hamstrung negotiations left him only two bad choices: invade to evict the generals, or sink poor Haiti to its knees with sanctions. Aristide, a pacifist former priest, "wants me to invade his country without him asking," Clinton fussed. Even if he were willing to send troops, he added, "I can't just invade and then pull out and leave people there to have a bloodbath that I would be responsible for." Groping for a response, I said nobody wanted that. The president quizzed me about how Aristide discussed these pitfalls in private. Did he have a convincing scenario in which tighter U.S. sanctions could force the Haitian generals to resign? I agreed to find out.

I DROVE BACK down to Washington on Sunday afternoon. Two Secret Service agents guarded the entrance to Aristide's downtown apartment-in-exile, and others inside made the protective unit oddly more visible than at the White House. The presence of armed Americans added to frictions over spying and mistrust among Haitian emissaries, many of whom believed they risked their lives or families back home to visit the ousted president. Aristide himself was calm, as usual. He outlined a letter of immediate response to the questions I posed to him from Clinton, and I found myself typing a draft dictated by Aristide's young lawyer, Mildred Trouillot. She asked for suggestions on what points might bother Clinton. I struggled with a computer keyboard geared for French. Aristide made minor changes, emphasizing that the best hope to avoid violence was to speak with one determined voice about a restoration plan with clear definitions and broad international support. While the finished text was being prepared, he invited me to see something in his library. Opening a history book, he ran his finger down the long list of his predecessors since 1804–all driven from office, each downfall preserved in an unbroken string of French words for "assassinated," "overthrown," or "forced into exile." He said there were special reasons for his euphemisms to Clinton about Haiti's reliance on American muscle as "further unspecified steps if necessary." It was hard to create new democracy by force, especially with another country's army, and Aristide had promised Haitian voters a nonviolent war of independence from tyranny. Fighting the Haitian military would only continue the bloodshed, even if the people could win. "But with the United States," he said, "we have a chance to break the cycle of two centuries."

From Aristide's apartment, I called the White House switchboard and asked to speak with President Clinton. A skeptical cross-examination by the operator turned into a long wait, during which I confessed to Mildred Trouillot that this may not work, as all my previous contacts had been at the president's initiative, not mine. Finally, a voice announced the first lady, and Hillary came on the line to say Clinton was asleep, tired from working on Bosnia. When I told her of the letter, and offered to send it through Tony Lake, she told me to drop by instead and she would take it if Bill did not wake up. Her clearance whisked me along through the Southwest Gate to park under the Truman Balcony, then up through the Usher's Office to find the yellow hallway silent with the doors closed. John the Doorman walked uncertainly back and forth, saying he was trained not to disturb, but eventually he heard water running in the bathroom and knocked. The president emerged, apologizing that he could not shake hands because he had conjunctivitis. His eyes looked worse than Wednesday. He called himself hopeful now that the Bosnian Serbs had taken down nearly all their artillery sites around Sarajevo. I told him of hearing radio bulletins minutes ago that full Serb compliance was expected before the NATO deadline for air strikes. "They said that?" he asked, sounding pleased. He held up Aristide's letter. "I'll read this tonight," he said. "Are you coming back this week for another session? We have a lot to do on this Bosnia stuff." I promised to ask Nancy Hernreich about his schedule.

SHE SECURED NO diary slot for almost a month. I next saw President Clinton shortly before ten o'clock on Wednesday night, March 16, standing in the yellow hallway with a book titled *Executive Privilege* by Mark Rozell under one arm, intently sorting through a list of jazz performers with the White House social secretary, Capricia Marshall. For an upcoming dinner, he wanted to select entertainers whose music would not confuse or repel strangers to jazz—something not too highbrow. Marshall made notes on his capsule reviews. I could only shrug when he glanced at me, but I told him on our way to the parlor that I hated to see him reading a book about the doctrine used by presidents to resist investigation. He laughed. This was not like the Watergate books, he said. It was "very exciting" legal history, although some of the cases arose from trivial matters. He cited years of amusing contention over a forty-dollar mirror given to President James Monroe. Such levity and perspective soon vanished for much of our session. On this night, the president detoured into long bouts of woeful rage over the pandemic investigations of him, howling mostly against the press.

Hillary came in as we began, still in her topcoat and scarf, flushed from a stressful event. We stood, and I fidgeted through their mysteriously long embrace. When he asked about her evening, she said she had been teary through the whole wonderful program. Sidwell Friends had staged its mother-daughter banquet, she explained for my benefit, with skits and speeches built around moms and their senior girls facing the big world beyond high school. She already felt the impact of separation even though Chelsea was only a freshman, with three years left. Hillary smiled in disbelief, asking how she could be a mess so far ahead. Three years left, she repeated. Clinton chimed in with his own wry complaint that the school held three separate banquets—mother-daughter, father-son, and mother-son: one for each permutation *except* father-daughter. He said gender bias blocked his only chance, and vowed to organize something before Chelsea graduated.

On tape, the president resumed his tale of fragile progress in Bosnia. He felt relieved and lucky on two crucial tests already this year. First, by removing their artillery around Sarajevo, the Bosnian Serbs had spared NATO from carrying out its ultimatum to launch air strikes against those siege guns. Clinton said the bombing would have severely strained relations within NATO, because the ultimatum was partly a bluff stitched over strong objections from countries with troops deployed as peacekeepers in Bosnia, vulnerable to retaliation, especially England and France. Second, NATO's military engagement began afterward with a victory in the air. Clinton said that when the Bosnian Serbs violated the U.N. no-fly zone in strafing missions against Muslim targets—probably to show some peevish defiance after backing down on the artillery, and to flaunt their superior weapons—U.S. fighters under NATO command swiftly shot down four Serb warplanes on February 28. This was the first real combat in the entire forty-five-year history of the NATO alliance.

The president gave thanks for these results. They were decisive, showing the Bosnian Serbs that NATO finally meant business. They were relatively clean, and low on controversy, which helped manage Clinton's swirling dance with the cantankerous Boris Yeltsin. He said Yeltsin first had wanted to move the international military command on Bosnia from the U.N. to NATO, where Russia had no responsibility, leaving Yeltsin poised to attack excesses by Russia's NATO enemies from the Cold War. Then lately, since the world applauded NATO's action to thwart ethnic cleansing, Yeltsin reversed course to demand a share of credit and control. Clinton and his allies refused. It had been hard enough to galvanize NATO, and they could not trust Yeltsin with veto power over a Bosnia policy lodged in the U.N. Security Council, especially given his fluctuating need to pacify pro-Serbian voters at home. This exclusion made an angry Yeltsin rattle mischief from Jerusalem to Washington. The president said one of his vital tasks remained to pacify Yeltsin on Bosnia, so that Russia could develop a stake in the peace process there and elsewhere. He hoped to cobble together some face-saving way for Russian peacemakers to be deployed alongside NATO soldiers. For the moment, he said, Russia was holding up as the coalition finally reached for something better than palliative measures to staunch the slaughter in Bosnia. Yeltsin had not obstructed the treaty that would be signed in Washington two days hence between the warring Muslims and Croatians, and this would raise hopes for a peace settlement with the militant Bosnian Serbs.

I expressed surprise about the impending Muslim-Croat treaty. Though admittedly preoccupied with my own work, I found it strange to have heard nothing about it, and suggested that perhaps his foreign policy team should have done more to trumpet the breakthrough. This remark set off a tirade on the press. His people had tried, said Clinton, but nobody was interested because the media was obsessed this month with Whitewater. Headlines centered on the parade of Hillary's staff members to testify before the Whitewater grand jury convened by special prosecutor Robert Fiske, and other news gravitated to scandal and titillation. He said respectable newspapers like the *Washington Post* were reporting ghoulish theories that the Clintons may have concealed their own murder of Vince Foster as a suicide. (The *Post* profiled grizzled conspiracy buffs shifting to Whitewater from decades on the Kennedy assassination, and a story leading its business section began: "Whitewater splashed over Wall Street today, buffeting stocks, bonds and the dollar.") Even a recent shake-up of the White House chefs was presented as a potential Whitewater matter evidencing Hillary's high-handed character, complained the president, who said all he knew was that the kitchen personnel were always threatening each other with lawsuits. On top of everything else, Hillary's former law partner Webb Hubbell had been forced to resign as associate attorney general.

The president's exasperation subsided into a sketch of Hubbell, with a stated aim to be objective about the faults suddenly revealed. He said Hubbell, like Vince Foster, had been a star back home—the youngest mayor of Little Rock, youngest chief justice in Arkansas history. In retrospect, Clinton said Hubbell's first mistake was to mix family with business by representing his wife's wealthy father, Seth Ward, who owned one of the nation's two parking meter companies, in a major contingency lawsuit. When Hubbell lost the case, Ward refused to pay even the office expenses incurred by the firm, and Hubbell's partners demanded that he make good for his father-in-law. Through this part of the story, Clinton considered Hubbell an honest man caught in a nasty catfight. He said Ward was irascible, and darn near crazy, while the Rose Law Firm was hard-pressed for money, having lost not only its fees in the Ward case but also three top-earning partners to Washington in Hillary, Hubbell, and Vince Foster. It was sad to see such a squabble, said the president, but his sympathy turned to shock when told that audits by the Rose firm turned up billing fraud in Hubbell's other cases. Clinton could not fathom such a criminal lapse.* He said Hubbell remained an inspirational figure to many at the Justice Department, where he received a ten-minute standing ovation after his resignation on Monday. Hubbell's disgrace was coincidental to Whitewater, the president insisted, but Fiske was opening a collateral investigation, and news stories folded Hubbell into generic suspicion of the Clintons. White House

---

* Hubbell pleaded guilty to mail fraud and tax evasion charges on nearly half a million dollars in billings from the Rose Law Firm. In June of 1995, he was sentenced to twenty-one months in prison.

polls showed that most people were influenced by the press even though they didn't like it. People said Whitewater was confusing and overblown, but they also thought Clinton must have done something wrong or it wouldn't be such a big deal. Already, the scattershot scandals had hurt his approval rates among working women, Clinton noted, and damaged Hillary's reputation.

About the sensational spy case of Aldrich Ames, the president said he had received progress briefings on a high-tension search for the worst double agent, or mole, in CIA history. Since 1985, the KGB had paid Ames some $5 million to betray the names of every Soviet citizen spying for the United States. The KGB had killed many of these people—known as "assets" to the CIA, traitors to Russia—before the collapse of the Soviet Union in 1991. Clinton said Ames had passed CIA lie detector tests while under suspicion, which proved "the box" to be a flawed instrument for detecting truth under stress. The interrogation of Ames after his arrest on February 21 could have been a movie scene, said the president, as the CIA-FBI task force confronted their colleague in a closed room plastered with blown-up surveillance photos. This elaborate display, while dramatic, camouflaged the underlying weakness that the task force never managed to catch Ames in an actual spy drop with his Soviet handlers. If they had, they wouldn't have needed to bluff and intimidate the suspect. Still, Clinton said he had congratulated the task force, confident that Ames could be convicted on the money trail.*

The president's hidden duty was giving a delicate, last-minute notification of the arrest to Boris Yeltsin, who demanded that the entire Ames case be hushed up to minimize embarrassment for Russia. When Clinton tried to explain that this was beyond his power or inclination—and why the capture of a KGB traitor at the CIA inevitably would be front-page news—he said Yeltsin turned belligerent. Ames was only a spy, Yeltsin snorted, and spies were routine for every government. He invited Clinton to have Ames shot or locked away as he pleased, so long as the disposal remained quiet. On our tapes, the president used the Ames case

---

* Ames pleaded guilty to espionage on April 28, 1994, and received a life sentence. His case inspired several books and the Hollywood film *Aldrich Ames: Traitor Within*, starring Timothy Hutton (1998).

to illustrate the seesaw battle between Yeltsin's autocratic side and the reformist courage he had shown facing down Soviet tanks at the birth of Russian democracy. Yeltsin personified the transition from Russia's authoritarian past, and, with the historical outcome far from assured, his unstable image compounded an enormous challenge for U.S. foreign policy. If Americans perceived Yeltsin as a petty tyrant, Clinton explained, they would not understand or approve the international cooperation needed to build democratic institutions in Russia.

Worries about Yeltsin spilled into collateral events. With Clinton's private encouragement, former president Richard Nixon recently had toured many countries newly carved from the Soviet Union. Clinton said Nixon, while a strong supporter of Yeltsin, was free as a private citizen to meet with leaders and dissidents across the political spectrum, including Aleksandr Rutskoi, a former vice president who had turned against Yeltsin to join an aborted coup in the Duma. This meeting so infuriated Yeltsin that he refused to see Nixon, which in turn irritated Nixon, and now Clinton fretted that Nixon may come home to brand Yeltsin a fraud—a throwback czar at heart, masquerading as a democrat. He thought Nixon might be able to rally Republicans in Congress, tipping the political balance on Russia, because there would be more than a grain of truth in his charges. In the Middle East, for instance, he said Yeltsin's way of asserting Russian influence was to stoke the wrath of Arab governments over the recent massacre near Hebron's Tomb of Abraham, sacred to Jews and Muslims alike. Baruch Goldstein, an Israeli settler and physician, had entered its mosque alone with concealed weapons on February 25 to interrupt prayers with gunfire that killed 29 Muslim worshippers, wounding another 150. The president said he had spent much of today with Israel's prime minister, Yitzhak Rabin, striving to calm the bloody uproar on both sides, hoping somehow to salvage the Palestinian-Israeli protocols signed in September. He described a perilous vote ahead at the United Nations, where nonaligned countries, egged on by Russia, were trying to spike a consensus resolution on the massacre with an emended preamble calling Jerusalem the capital of "occupied Palestine." Clinton was maneuvering for less inflammatory language. By mass murder, he said, Goldstein may have accomplished his goal to derail the peace process.

Further on, into renewed troubles over China and North Korea, I mentioned that a number of quandaries seemed to be converging, and this careless remark touched off another lament about the press. Clinton said reporters were discarding issues of consequence and drama to pursue juicy diversions from the past, freely ascribing dark personal motives to him and Hillary. At a private briefing, when newspaper executives received detailed assurances that the Clintons had never interfered with Jim McDougal's management of the Whitewater investments, *Washington Post* editor Len Downie bluntly told Hillary that he did not believe her. The president shrugged, wondering how he could defend against that. He claimed no quarrel with scandal-mongering political opponents like Republican senators Alfonse D'Amato of New York and Phil Gramm of Texas, conceding their professional right to seek votes by any strategy, fair or foul, but he blamed the press corps for stooping to be eager patsies, and especially the *Washington Post* and *New York Times* for making the tabloid atmosphere respectable. He disclosed that the *Times* had sent the reporter for the original Whitewater story, Jeff Gerth, back down to Arkansas to investigate investments made fifteen years ago. From memory, Clinton presented a bizarre saga—that Hillary, on advice from their friend Jim Blair, who had made and lost fortunes in the treacherous commodities market for agricultural futures, had run up some hundred thousand dollars in profit before the risky streak sapped her nerve. Clinton said the *Times* was determined for two reasons to allege something crooked about the windfall. First, true or not, charges of scandal would boost the scoop into Whitewater's journalistic surf. Second, the *Times* relied on political sources who promoted interpretations of corruption at every level. The investment story had not yet appeared, fumed Clinton, and Cliff Jackson was boasting already that he had Gerth eating from his hand.*

The president repeated his profession of lifelong admiration for the *Times* and the *Post*. He called himself disillusioned. They may not have a political agenda, he allowed, but they had fallen prey to one. Or been

---

* The *New York Times* published Gerth's dispatch two days later on March 16, under a front-page headline: "Top Arkansas Lawyer Helped Hillary Clinton Turn Big Profit."

stampeded. Or turned cynical. Overwrought, he groped for words to comprehend their motives and express his dismay. "You know," he said, "I've never done anything remotely like Phil Gramm did—getting a developer to subsidize his house for him, and just weaseling out of it." The press arbitrarily dropped that, he groaned. Nobody mentions it—even when Gramm gets up on the Senate floor to proclaim Clinton so rotten and false that he should not serve out the balance of his term.

The president raised his hands, stood up, and walked away to compose himself. I muttered advice about not giving in to bitterness. I told him I could hardly speak for journalism, but to me reporters still were people of many types and talents, under pressure and not always curious. Lacking an adequate theory to explain what did seem a broadly corrosive attitude toward Clinton, I thought his preoccupation with the press could do him more harm than good. All presidents felt abused by the media, but those who stewed and withdrew only injured themselves. It was better to engage reporters with strategic charm and constant material for good stories. Feed or bleed, I quipped lamely. The president sat down again. "I'm mad about it," he said with a sigh. "I can't hide it."

Uncomfortable moments passed before he waved the subject aside. "Well, I function in here every day," he said, as though snapping from hypnosis. "We've got all these other things going on. You know, we've gotten a little rebound in the last few days from the G-7 meeting in Detroit." This summit was about jobs in the global economy, and Clinton said the assembled leaders of rich countries felt something close to panic over the steady loss of jobs to poor countries. His fellow heads of state were reluctant even to acknowledge the problem for fear of provoking their own corporate heads to jump ahead of its outward flow. They agreed, at least, that hiding was no solution, and Clinton described small signs of progress.

Before midnight, when fatigue halted our session, he also mentioned Northern Ireland in connection with a visit from the British prime minister. John Major still bristled against Clinton's recent decision to grant a U.S. visa for Gerry Adams, head of the Sinn Fein political wing of the Irish Republican Army, and the president said most of his own government had opposed the visa, too, agreeing with England that normalized travel would "reward" Adams for the IRA's terrorist crimes against British soldiers and Protestants in Northern Ireland. To his surprise, Clinton was swayed by Nancy Soderberg, a deputy on Tony Lake's staff, who argued that terror and repression would remain deadlocked unless someone took risks toward settlement. On balance, she thought Adams himself would take risks worth matching, but rarely did a president defy the foreign policy establishment on the hunch of a second-tier deputy. He took the chance partly to escape tradition's lockstep endorsement of the dead-end British policy, Clinton recorded, then hosted Major as his first foreign counterpart to spend the night at the White House. He said the two of them patched relations in spite of press chatter across the Atlantic that they would be frosty at best. It was ridiculous to suggest that each nation's most important bilateral partnership would fall hostage to one dispute, or to party differences, and Clinton said he sort of liked Major, anyway. He found the prime minister quirky and unpredictable, with an odd background. A child waif, the son of a circus performer who sold garden ornaments, Major had lived on relief in Pittsburgh before moving back to England. Now, after his rise in British politics, Clinton saw Major as the sacrificial victim of machinations by fellow Tories devoted to his predecessor, Margaret Thatcher, who were fixed on proving no mortal was worthy to succeed her. The president referred to a controversy about a necklace, saying it was orchestrated to make Major look bad.

As he left the parlor moments later, the president called out that he was hearing strange things about Haiti. Aristide apparently *did* want him to invade if necessary, but now officials doubted that Aristide himself really wanted to go back, and such a failure of purpose would negate the whole point of restoring an elected government. These comments made me hurry to deliver tonight's rewound tapes to Clinton. He was in the closet, hanging up gift neckties from the Johns Hopkins Children's Hospital. I told him I felt certain about Aristide's resolve, and summarized the story of his finger running down the list of deposed presidents. It seemed that people judged Aristide by their own convenience. The president cross-examined me about confidence and channels of communication. While the complexity between governments was far beyond my compass, I volunteered to give Tony Lake my firsthand witness on simple points of contention. The president named several. "I wish you would," he said.

CHAPTER EIGHT

MISSILES IN BAGHDAD

Wednesday, April 20, 1994

Tuesday, April 26, 1994

Assorted crises buffeted both sessions in April. President Clinton came into the parlor at 9:20 still in his business suit, chewing an unlit cigar to keep awake. He said he had been up three nights running. Serb militias were about to overrun Gorazde in Bosnia. His crime bill was squeezing through one house, education through another, and American pilots had mistakenly shot down two Black Hawk helicopters over Iraq, killing twenty-six allied soldiers. The president had tried to cancel me at the last minute, when I was already en route and impossible to reach. Now he urged me to skim for highlights until he gave out or needed to quit.

I asked about his second nomination to the Supreme Court, which would turn out to be his last. Clinton, far from embracing the historic choice ahead, strikingly regretted the resignation of Justice Harry Blackmun, who had been his only friend on the Court. He described Blackmun as an old-fashioned progressive Republican, strong-willed and congenial, and recalled the bond of conversations at seminars and social events going back some time. The justice had come in the previous year to talk about quitting, but now his mind was made up, and Clinton outlined his ensuing negotiations with the Senate majority leader, George Mitchell of Maine. The president said his approach had been straightforward but perhaps unfairly vague. He told Mitchell "flat out" that he was his first choice—that Mitchell was perfect as a respected former judge who also would meet Clinton's goal of seasoning the Court with justices of political experience—unless Mitchell's subtraction from the Senate figured to doom the national health care bill. They first weighed this condition together, sifting likely ramifications, and then Mitchell withdrew to ponder alone. A fiendishly difficult task required him to project interdependent outcomes objectively, from assumptions with and without his own Senate leadership, but Clinton said he returned in person with a comprehensive analysis. While Mitchell could not say that his loss from the Senate would be decisive for the health care bill, he did predict that the pending shift to the Court would injure the president's chances for reelection in 1996. Mitchell concluded, therefore, not to accept the seat even though he aspired to be on the Court. Mitchell's selfless decision was forceful, statesmanlike, and persuasive, said Clinton—yet all the more wrenching because it embodied everything he hoped for in a Supreme Court justice.

When I asked about his latest efforts to promote the health care bill, the president took more respite than I expected or wished. From bare mention of a forum in Deerfield Beach, Florida, he remembered that day's round of golf with PGA tour professional Raymond Floyd, which triggered an animated description of the course complete with a stroke-by-stroke replay of one hole. It was a short par-4 of 225 or 230 yards over a pond to a fairway that doglegged sharply around trees. He said most players used an iron from the tee to cross the water safely, then a second shot to the green, but he had emulated Floyd's daring long shot over both the water and trees to reach the green in one. While he replayed the club selection and trajectory, for his shot as well as Floyd's, I debated my own role as usual. Should I nudge him back to a more presidential subject, especially given the time pressure? Or would future historians find it revealing that the president's mind refracted to golf from an impasse between health care and a Supreme Court choice? Did it reflect his earlier pessimism about the bill, or simply his enthusiasm for golf? Should I ask if he regretted not appointing Senator Mitchell without condition, which would imply that Clinton ought to accept early defeat on his major initiative for the year? In the end, as he was re-creating his long putt for eagle, I interrupted merely to suggest that we return to choices for the Court. (The golf story would remain unfinished until a future session, when the president said he had three-putted for par and Floyd made birdie. Clinton was satisfied with four, given the tricky contours, and stated convincingly more than once that his three putts did not diminish the thrill of driving the green.)

Since Mitchell, Clinton had been evaluating U.S. District Court Judge José Cabranes of Connecticut. He thought the first Hispanic justice would be a step forward, but doubtful asides punctuated his glowing review of Cabranes's career and legal opinions. The president said Cabranes was an assimilated patrician who did not even consider himself Hispanic. He noted rumors of political horse trading by Cabranes, emphasizing that they were rumors. Impulsively, I observed that Clinton's tone seemed to undercut his words of praise, like a brief without enthusiasm. Was he trying to talk himself into Cabranes? I reproached myself as soon as this impertinent comment silenced the president. Having affirmed only moments ago that my main function was to stimulate a candid flow of his recollections, I now found myself distorting the record.

From an awkward pause, I stressed the value of preserving his thoughts on the Supreme Court selection, and the president homed in for half an hour. He described the vetting procedures, the regular councils with his delegated staff, and mostly his own examination of various candidates. Still seeking a political justice, he said he had explored Speaker Tom Foley and former Democratic governor Gerald Baliles of Virginia. From the Senate, he discussed Pat Leahy of Vermont and Paul Sarbanes of Maryland, both Democrats as well. He had thought about Solicitor General Drew Days, saying he admired his mind and would not recoil from two African-American justices at once, but Clinton decided that recent arguments by Days before the Court would raise complicated problems for Senate confirmation. Of sitting judges, the president sketched a black female from New York, but his personal favorite clearly was U.S. Court of Appeals Judge Richard Arnold from the Eighth Circuit. Arnold was "far and away the best lawyer and best judge in the country"—but with two drawbacks. First, he suffered a dormant but dangerous form of lymphoma, which clouded his future. Second, Arnold was from Arkansas. The *Washington Post* had endorsed Arnold as the preeminent candidate, dismissing potential charges of cronyism, but the president was not sure the advance exoneration would hold up. He said he was still wrestling with the intertwined questions.

We recalled last year's near-choice of Bruce Babbitt to fill Byron White's seat on the Court. As with George Mitchell and others, Clinton's goal of a political justice ran into the political cost of the appointment. He said Babbitt was still too valuable at the Interior Department, even though his presumed wizardry had failed to prevent revolts over grazing fees and timber policy. Clinton thought it was almost impossible for an environmentalist Democrat to appoint *any* interior secretary without losing the West. "I've decided that grazing fees are like Bosnia," he said with a sigh. "Nobody can handle it."

We switched to the ongoing death struggle around the Muslim city of Gorazde in eastern Bosnia. Today, more than a week into emergency consultations, Clinton had held a press conference to shore up support in Western countries for more NATO intervention. Ironically, said the president, the recent partial treaty had intensified the fighting in many parts, because the Muslim and Croat armies—once they stopped fighting each other—turned aggressively to recapture territories lost to the Serbs since 1991. And the Serbs, who controlled more than 70 percent of Bosnia already, tightened their strangleholds in response. Earlier this month, U.S. jets struck the siege guns around Gorazde with NATO authorization. It was a halfhearted attack, said Clinton. Air strikes spectacularly obliterated a Serb tank, but three bombs didn't even go off. It was mostly to show that NATO finally could act, and the Serbs retaliated as feared by seizing U.N. peacekeepers on the ground. Now, despite these hostages, NATO gave the Serbs an ultimatum threatening further air strikes unless the siege guns pulled back within forty-eight hours. Clinton said they were trying to save Gorazde with bluff and baling wire.

On other worries, the president reviewed fierce lobbying on both sides of his recent decision not to grant clemency for the imprisoned Jonathan Pollard.* He was philosophical about three hikes in national

---

* Pollard, a civilian analyst for the Naval Criminal Investigative Service, pleaded guilty in 1987 to one charge of espionage, for selling U.S. military secrets to Israel, and received a life sentence.

interest rates since our last meeting—an unprecedented cluster—saying the Federal Reserve had been certain to clamp down on the economy after figures showed a 7 percent growth rate for the fourth-quarter GDP. Of the ongoing rampage against Rwandan Tutsis in central Africa, Clinton commended the U.S. ambassador there for a remarkable job evacuating American citizens. This was not a very positive mission, he added, but it was all that could be done in the midst of the chaotic tribal warfare. The president thought more Rwandans had been killed since the April 6 uprising than in either of the protracted wars in Somalia and Angola. CNN seldom showed pictures of the bodies on television, he said, so fewer people cared.

His digressions on the press were shorter and more cerebral. He expected the Whitewater coverage, which had receded for weeks, to surge again before summer. He said Floyd Brown, who had produced the notorious Willie Horton attack ads for the Bush campaign in 1988, had attached a Washington staff of twenty-six to the formidable array of publicists, think tanks, and lawyers pushing the generic scandal. Summarizing a book on the trivialization of press culture,* Clinton grandly improvised contrasting news bulletins—a "classic" one of facts impacting the world, then a "spin" version of the same event: "In a desperate attempt to rescue his faltering campaign, Senator Kennedy accused Vice President Nixon . . ." He dissected the book's thesis that modern news tilted to pamper consumers rather than inform citizens, with entertainment and subjective gamesmanship. On this point, Clinton cited a line from radio host Garrison Keillor's recent speech to the American Society of Newspaper Editors, decrying that our fellow baby boomers were "the sort of people who will stand in an aisle at the grocery store and argue the merits of two different brands of olive oil."

Sheepishly, the president admitted that he was wrong to answer yesterday's televised question about whether he wore boxers or briefs. He should have ducked. He should have said he was too old to discuss underwear, but then, he didn't think of himself as old. To him, anyone even a year younger than he was young, and old people were from his parents' generation. He grimaced and grinned. Now he had set off a lit-

---

* Thomas E. Patterson, *Out of Order* (New York: Alfred A. Knopf, 1993).

tle press frenzy himself, foreclosing any chance for a sober dialogue about the MTV youth audience. He said they really were different. They seemed surrounded by uncertainty and decay. Their devil-may-care attitude had a streak of nihilism that was not part of Clinton's own youth.

He delved into the friendly fire disaster in the skies over Iraq. Not nearly all the facts were known yet, as the two U.S. F-15s had shot down the two U.S. Black Hawk helicopters less than a week ago, on April 14. Clinton said he had to call President Mitterrand personally, because a few of the twenty-six victims were French soldiers. Most (fifteen) were Americans, but others included British soldiers with some Turkish soldiers and Kurdish civilians. The president had been meeting with Turkish prime minister Tansu Ciller when incoming cables confirmed the grim tragedy. He said he had promised the foreign leaders representatives on an international commission of inquiry. Now his purpose was to make sure that the commission, along with parallel U.S. investigations, uncovered every pertinent error in order to prevent a recurrence. He said many questions were murky. Why were the planes so anxious to shoot down helicopters that made no hostile moves? Were the helicopters fitted with extra tanks to resemble the Russian Hind-24s flown by Iraq? Why didn't they answer requests for a friendly signal? Were the helicopters not painted with normal U.S. insignia? Did they make unscheduled desert stops in a mission to prevent attacks on Kurdish outposts by Saddam Hussein? He said there was much at stake beyond justice for the victims and their families, including trust for multinational military operations. Clinton believed the pilots would always have these deaths on their conscience. He was circumspect, but his questions themselves suggested that secrecy may have contributed to the deadly mistake.*

The president wearily asked me to stop the tapes. He had work to finish before bed, and he did not expect Richard Nixon to live through

---

* Relatives would press demands for accountability through many investigations, but the Pentagon blocked testimony by key witnesses. One crew member, from an AWACS communications plane guiding the F-15s, was tried and acquitted on dereliction of duty charges by a 1995 court-martial. Private donors built a memorial at Giebelstadt Air Base, Germany, for the twenty-six victims, and moved it to Fort Rucker, Alabama, in 2006.

the night. As I packed up, he told me the former president had suffered an edema similar to the one that killed Hillary's father. This kind of stroke was deceptive, he explained, because it could leave a good bit of brain capacity intact and raise hopes for recovery. However, pressure would build up slowly as blood pushed against the skull, shutting down bodily functions one by one. Clinton said the loss would sadden him, as he was getting along fairly well with our old antagonist from the Vietnam era. A month ago today, he had received from Nixon a letter about Russia that Clinton called the most brilliant communication on foreign policy to reach him as president. Nothing else came close, he said. It was about planning for a "post-Yeltsin era," with penetrating studies of political characters and fledgling countries. Nixon anticipated that subnationalist movements aimed to break up the old Soviet Union still further, and Clinton wished he could talk more with Nixon about his recommendations. He said he had shared the letter only with Al Gore. So far, to guard against distortion and leaks, he was keeping it from his own foreign policy team—even Tony Lake.

An afterthought wafted from the bathroom. Sadly, Clinton called out, Nixon loved Pat so much that he seemed to decline quickly since she died last year. When I delivered tonight's finished tapes, Clinton reflected that Nixon always had a hard time with his emotions. "He was one of those husbands," said the president, "who couldn't live with or without his wife."

PRESIDENT CLINTON SEEMED distracted in our brief session six nights later. Following up on the friendly fire losses in Iraq, we finally reviewed his June 26 decision of the previous year to order a missile attack on the Baghdad headquarters of the Iraqi intelligence service. He recounted the background—how Kuwaiti authorities had arrested nearly a dozen Iraqis and six Kuwaitis about a year ago, just before a visit to the region by Clinton's predecessor, George Bush. Two months later, classified reports found that bomb materials possessed by the detainees dovetailed with other evidence of an active plot to kill Bush on the orders of Saddam Hussein. When I mentioned the doubts raised subsequently by journalist Seymour Hersh, who argued in *The New Yorker* that the suspects were too unprofessional to be convincing assassins, and the official connections too weak, the president said he had shared that reaction at first. He found it ridiculous that Saddam Hussein would entrust the ultimate spy mission to a ragtag group of truck drivers and bar owners. Surely, he had thought, the Iraqi dictator must have a stable of more authentic killers, but his investigators informed him that Iraq's terrorism was confined almost entirely to the military repression of its own people. Unlike Syria and Iran, Saddam did not maintain a network of highly trained civilians for terrorist operations abroad, and therefore he had no better alternative unless he was willing to send traceable and highly visible officers from his own army.

Three of the twenty-three U.S. Tomahawk cruise missiles had gone astray with their half-ton warheads, killing at least eight Iraqi civilians who lived near the target. "I regret the loss of life," President Clinton said. His tone was wooden and mechanical. It sounded like an official statement for the record, with barely a trace of feeling, but he repeated the phrase several times. I could not be sure whether he was still hardening himself to the weight of presidential power. He seemed less familiar to me for a moment, with the gulf between us yawning wide. The reports had been unanimous, he emphasized. Even the CIA and FBI had risen above their habitual feuds to agree that the case in evidence amounted to an act of war against the United States, demanding a response. Clinton's minor complaint was an exasperating aloofness by the Joint Chiefs, who, though pressed hard for a recommendation, steadfastly repeated the full range of options. While he could not state that General Powell, who was still chairman of the Joint Chiefs at the time, was hedging for protection in hindsight, the president said carefully, no straightforward opinion could be extracted, and Clinton alone chose to mount a single-strike retaliation against the site of operational control. Doing less would invite further attacks, he decided, but more would be bellicose and wrong, especially since the plot had been foiled well short of success. He thought his course remained prudent. "At least it has stood the test of nine months' time," he concluded. "We don't know how it will look later."

Chelsea came in somewhat flustered, asking when her mother would be home. Clinton told her that Hillary would return from California tomorrow after a three-day trip for the health care bill. (This update, together with the playing cards and crossword puzzles strewn among his reading folders, made me speculate that a restless Clinton had summoned me for company.) In her absence, Chelsea spilled a confession that she had left her biology books at school overnight, which meant she had to get up before dawn to get there when the doors opened, as only then could she study for a make-up exam being offered because her class had scored the lowest average grade—67—in the history of Sidwell Friends biology. The president asked what her own grade had been, and she replied with a wince: 82. Quite sensibly, I thought, Clinton offered consolation that her situation was not so bad, being fifteen points above average, but Chelsea rolled her eyes. Her dismissive look said he was not the one who could appreciate the crisis. "I love you, Daddy," she said. "Good night." He and I exchanged semi-baffled nods in her wake.

On the tapes, the president presented no big developments in his search for a new Supreme Court appointment. He dispensed briskly with numerous subjects before a routine question opened a trail of sustained thought. The president first scribbled a note to himself that Strobe Talbott owed him a report on his recent trip to South Asia. He called this the one region on the globe facing a serious threat of nuclear war between two nations, India and Pakistan. Their mutual enmity was historically constant, yet chillingly erratic. In private, he disclosed, Indian officials spoke of knowing roughly how many nuclear bombs the Pakistanis possessed, from which they calculated that a doomsday nuclear volley would kill 300 to 500 million Indians while annihilating all 120 million Pakistanis. The Indians would thus claim "victory" on the strength of several hundred million countrymen they figured would be left over. But on the other side, the Pakistanis insisted that their rugged mountain terrain would shield more survivors than the exposed plains of India. "They really *talk* that way." Clinton sighed.

"We have bad relations with both of them," he continued. Locked in their arms race, India was furious that the United States had agreed to sell F-16 fighter planes to Pakistan, and Pakistan was no less enraged that the United States refused to deliver the planes years after receiving payment. Such transfers remained blocked since 1990 under the Pressler Amendment, which prohibited military sales to any country found to be developing nuclear weapons in violation of the Nuclear Non-Proliferation

Treaty. Even worse for the Pakistanis, said Clinton, U.S. law obliged his administration to collect storage payments from Pakistan on its impounded F-16s gathering rust in American custody. The president hoped to devise a rebate or remedy for these grossly unfair charges, which he called a diplomatic insult, but he saw no cure for the larger strategic impasse over South Asia. He said the United States was trying to hold the line on a treaty that fed hostility and opportunism. If we didn't try to enforce the ban on nuclear proliferation, plenty of countries would rush to sell the required technologies on our example. As long as we did try, however, we would draw upon ourselves some of the extraordinary venom between India and Pakistan. Clinton said this issue demanded persistence. His impression was that Talbott's trip turned up little of promise, but he wanted the details.

When I asked whether Clinton paid much attention to the worldwide trade in nonnuclear, conventional arms, his answer seemed resigned. He had sent representatives to a worthy conference last year in Paris without much notice. Everybody peddles weapons, he allowed. We try to restrict them to our allies, but the flooded market leaks contraband through every barrier and restraint. And even if you could shut down new trade entirely, those who misuse weapons tend to have plenty already. Before discussing Bosnia as a potential exception, the president linked Pakistan to the general question of Muslim countries threatened by fundamentalist movements. He said the purpose of Turkish prime minister Tansu Ciller's recent visit was to seek U.S. aid for her country in a way that would dampen rather than inflame the fundamentalist opposition to her government.

"I really like her," Clinton kept saying. Characteristically, he alternated between personal connections and abstract analysis, burrowing into Turkish politics through stories about Ciller. He sketched her career as a pioneer female of Western education with Muslim roots in Istanbul, citing their shared memories of Yale, where Ciller once taught economics, and also the names of her key partners in Turkey's modernist True Path Party. The president said she was adored or reviled by large rival factions at home, where her need for U.S. aid, like her gender and striking good looks, cut both ways in public opinion. It gave Clinton leverage to insist that Ciller's government improve treatment of the Kurdish minority along Turkey's border with Iraq, but it also made her more vulnerable to the fundamentalist Muslim parties. The president specified how many seats these parties had gained recently in the Turkish Parliament on their campaign pledge to suppress the dissident Kurds more thoroughly than Ciller. To protect Turkish democracy from theocrats, Clinton said he was obliged to balance U.S. interests with Ciller's political needs, including her foreign policy. Because Turkey ardently sought membership in the European Union, which ran into fierce opposition led by Greece, Clinton himself worked to mediate their chronic clashes over the Mediterranean island of Cyprus. He listed dealings with more Greek Cypriot and Turkish Cypriot leaders than I could remember for my notes. He confessed inadvertently telling Papandreou of Greece, before Ciller had properly communicated her goodwill gesture, that Turkey would disarm its patrol flights over the island.

The headaches were worthwhile, said the president, because Turkey was a strategic fulcrum. He called it the fifth or sixth most important country in the world. Along with Egypt, Indonesia, and to a lesser extent Pakistan, Turkey gave the United States a fighting chance to help reconcile Islamic societies with modern democracy, and this, he said, was the long-range hope to outgrow the backward drag of tyrannical fundamentalists. For Clinton, Bosnia mattered in part because of repercussions in the pivotal Muslim nations. I asked whether Ciller of Turkey tried to make Bosnia a contingent factor in their private negotiations. No, he replied, but Bosnia did permeate their conversations. He said it affected her personally and politically, citing verified reports that Ciller had walked openly through the cratered streets of Sarajevo while it was being shelled, together with Pakistan's prime minister, Benazir Bhutto. For these two gutsy women, said the president, Bosnia was more than a religious kinship. Bosnia tested their reform platforms against fundamentalist propaganda that Western democracy was a facade for corrupt, postcolonial domination of Muslim nations.

In Bosnia, Serb gunners had just pulled back from besieged Gorazde under the NATO ultimatum. The president flinched when I mentioned that New York senator Pat Moynihan was calling for the United States to lift the international arms embargo unilaterally so that the Bosnians could fight for themselves. "That's just a freebie for him," snapped Clinton, "and he knows it." Moynihan made headlines by belittling the tenuous, hard-won reprieve for Gorazde, and he played politics by advocating steps that sounded tough but risked and accomplished nothing. The president said Moynihan understood all the reasons why his recommended course would be wrong. First, "unilateral lift" was a euphemism for violating the embargo. Doing so would compel Russia and other countries to send offsetting weapons to the Serbs, and it would undermine international compacts all over the world. Clinton said the right way to lift the embargo was by repeal at the United Nations, where it originated. Repeal there might be possible, he added, because Russia and Serbia had come to resent the notorious blood lust and greed of their Bosnian Serb allies. (They had helped force the siege gunners back from Gorazde.) Still, Clinton expressed new misgivings about any "responsible" lift of the embargo. If repeal was accomplished, NATO and the U.N. would extract peacekeepers swiftly from the crossfire, and Serb forces would press their advantage before the Bosnians could import weapons to defend themselves. In effect, the world would abandon Bosnia to let the three ethnic armies fight it out. Clinton predicted that such a grim precedent would haunt us there and elsewhere.

He thought Moynihan's sly outburst betrayed early anxiety for the 1994 election. Several incumbent Democratic senators had vented political worries to Clinton on a recent retreat in Colonial Williamsburg. They complained of being pilloried by association with the president, whose biggest triumph—the anti-deficit package—was called nothing but a tax increase. They said the National Rifle Association was hammering them over the Brady Bill and the ongoing drive to ban assault weapons. Clinton reeled off Democratic figures by state on the NRA's laserlike powers of retribution. He said Harris Wofford of Pennsylvania was in trouble. So was Frank Lautenberg of New Jersey, and Virginia's Chuck Robb confided that he might not survive a challenge in the Democratic primary.

The president summoned up gallows humor from these political woes. On the retreat, he said, the other senators had marveled in whispers at Robb's strange decision, upon hearing that the *Washington Post* was investigating his private life, to release a preemptive confession of misdeeds back into his tenure as governor—where and why he had been around illegal drugs at wild parties, which specific sex acts he considered outright adultery as opposed to lesser sins like petting, and how he squared all this with his wife, Lynda, daughter of the late President Lyndon Johnson. Clinton said they attributed the political mistake to Robb's spartan reserve as a stiffly formal ex-Marine, unforgiving toward himself. Way out on a Williamsburg golf course, he recalled, two foursomes of senators rushed up to an outdoor relief station. They deferred to the president, who entered the men's room alone, but Senator Robb was in such distress that he yelled to find out if there were any women using the other side. Just then, trying to be helpful, Clinton called out—"There's two in here!"—and Robb blushed crimson long after he realized that the president meant urinals instead of women. Clinton said he emerged to find all the senators, including Robb, dissolved in laughter.

Carolyn Huber came in while Clinton discussed Haiti. She had managed the governor's mansion for the Clintons in Little Rock, and now showed him her preliminary edit of some 1,400 photographs from his brother, Roger's, recent wedding at the Dallas Arboretum, featuring the president as best man and a radiant bride nearly seven months pregnant. Looking through the giant album, guided by Huber, Clinton said he had been irritated of late by "my diplomats." They proposed to scuttle a package of tighter sanctions against Haiti's military regime, telling Clinton that exiled President Aristide did not deserve such help just now because his partisans were criticizing U.S. refugee policy as racially biased in favor of white Cubans over black Haitians. The president sharply countermanded the diplomats. On the other hand, he refused to be bullied by the publicized hunger strike of anti-apartheid activist Randall Robinson, who had vowed for nearly three weeks not to eat again until Clinton did justice by Aristide. Robinson's reported medical condition was sinking slowly, but Clinton cited a number of steps beyond sanctions that should give him reason not to starve himself. If Robinson wanted to commit suicide anyway, the president added rather coldly, that was his own business.

In a parallel conversation, Huber was pointing out photographs from the wedding of an adorable four-year-old with ugly head wounds. The president, much affected, said he had forgotten to write her family. Making a note to himself, he told me the girl had my name with a different spelling—he and Huber worked out something like "T-A-L-O-U-R"—and suffered from a disorder that caused her to pull out large patches of hair.

Clinton rose to search his bedroom bookshelves intently. As he did, I tried to offer some encouragement about Haiti, where desperate refugees were again fleeing on flimsy rafts, but Clinton replied that most U.S. politicians saw no hope in the restoration of Aristide. They wanted to jettison him, even though his election victory was Haiti's sole birth credential for democracy. Senator John Kerry (Democrat of Massachusetts) had urged Clinton the other night to secure Aristide's resignation in exchange for the junta's promise of new elections, and before I could respond, the president returned from his bedroom with a book about leprosy. He said the only U.S. leprosarium was in Carville, Louisiana, hometown of his political consultant James Carville, and this British author had studied lepers there for twenty-five years. Only 5 percent of the population lacked natural immunity to the disease. If exposed, 80 percent of new lepers would recover, but it was critical for the endangered few to heed their residual sense of pain. Otherwise, they would scrape off numb flesh from diminishing stumps.

Pain is your friend, said the president. Little Talour did not have leprosy, but he wanted to tell the family that her heartrending cries were a warning system against self-aggravated wounds and infection. His ongoing explanation further tongue-tied me. Could I, or should I, try to see some analogy between these horrible symptoms and Haiti—with its street executions and grisly mutilations, Robinson's self-starvation, and our impulse to avoid the whole subject? Was there a concise insight to render Haiti's political pain into something positive, even historic? If so, I could not find the words while Clinton and Huber were completing their tour of the wedding album, and we all left shortly thereafter. The president needed to work on tomorrow's eulogy for Richard Nixon. Both of the former president's daughters had called, asking him to speak even though it was not a state funeral. He wanted to address Nixon's life as a whole, arguing that any lasting fault lay in his affront to the Constitution rather than any political differences, even about Vietnam.

President Clinton walked me across the hall to his elevator, with an arm around my shoulder. He kept saying that tonight's session was pretty good, pretty valuable, and we were pretty well caught up. His comments seemed half-questions and half-statements, seeking reassurance for us both. I sensed that his mind was drifting somewhere else.

CHAPTER NINE

SUPREME COURT CHOICES

Tuesday, May 31, 1994

Early in May, three of the president's speechwriters—Don Baer, Carolyn Curiel, and Carter Wilkie—held a small seminar at the White House on rhetorical themes from the civil rights era, and this daytime visit allowed me to drop in on Nancy Hernreich. She wanted an update on the oral history project, being its sole liaison, and I welcomed the chance to speak freely. We exchanged thoughts on the recording experience so far—frequency and logistics, the balance between security and detail, the president's freewheeling mind against his desperate need for rest. Nancy apologized tersely for extra interruptions. She said the whole West Wing was a madhouse because of Clinton's longtime adviser Bruce Lindsey, who, in a fresh media storm, had appealed for public donations to fight the sexual harassment lawsuit just filed by Paula Jones against the president. Hernreich's exaggerated calm commanded sympathy, but I stammered vaguely about the suit, which charged that Clinton had exposed himself to Jones during a hotel room rendezvous. I felt squeamish like Senator Robb. When I managed to convey my reservations, Hernreich asked me to repeat them. In fact, she had me escorted within minutes to see the new White House counsel, Lloyd Cutler. We knew each other well enough to explore the gaps between history and law. He was worried about Lindsey's defense fund, too.

"By the way," said Cutler, "are you the president's diarist?" His question struck me dumb. He was nodding already, as though I need not

bother to lie. Cutler said the Whitewater special prosecutor had subpoenaed a broad range of materials on specified topics, and he had a professional duty to seek disclosure of all responsive items in the president's
knowledge or possession. This plunged me into nightmares of imminent
exposure and ruin for the project. The president and I did talk from time
to time, I replied evasively. Cutler should direct his specific question to
Clinton himself, I said, but it would be a great loss to history if legal
threats precluded any compilation of presidential notes.

Cutler steered me back to the Paula Jones lawsuit. From his soundings at the Justice Department, it appeared that the most Clinton could
ask for was a postponement. Fine, I reiterated, still in shock: citizen
Clinton was not above the law, and must answer the courts, but a sitting
president should be accountable for the exercise of constitutional powers. The Framers, in designing three coordinated branches of government, had vested the executive branch uniquely in one person, the
president, and it would violate constitutional balance for the courts to
ensnarl that officeholder in a lawsuit—or, potentially, ten lawsuits—over
private conduct. In other words, legitimate presidential investigations
must be framed toward the logical extremity of impeachment for abuse
of power, and everything else could wait. Cutler said he tended to agree.
Whatever the true facts, the Jones case was about personal *and* pre-
presidential behavior, but there were political costs in that stance. To
seek delay until he left office would make Clinton look like he was hiding from Paula Jones. It would elevate her sordid accusations into a test
of constitutional law. The president wanted to assert his innocence now,
said Cutler, and he might lose the postponement anyway. Even so, I
stressed a positive obligation to defend the office. Embarrassment was
no excuse to equivocate about the separation of powers.

My head seemed to implode outside Cutler's office. What had I
done? I reproached myself for intruding on the turf of a thousand experts. Now that my eager freelance spiel had jeopardized the one secret
in my trust, it was small comfort to think that the special prosecutor's
subpoena may have doomed the oral history project regardless. I called
Nancy Hernreich about the dreadful surprise, half-expecting an explosion already—an angry cancellation of our work, or news of a requisition
for all the Clinton tapes, perhaps even a subpoena for me. She urged

calm. Nothing had exploded yet, and nothing happened for three weeks. Just when my grandiose anxiety dissipated, Hernreich's assistant summoned me on a few hours' notice. If there was anything unusual in store for the May 31 session, she could not or would not tell me, and President Clinton let on that there was nothing amiss. He was bustling in the parlor before a trip to Europe, headed first with Hillary to see Pope John Paul II. Nonplussed, I tried to remind him indirectly of the legal crisis, by asking for once about Whitewater, but this prompted a standard reprise on cynical press coverage. The president said he was being hit with conspiracy theories about Vince Foster's death that would make your flesh crawl, and I disgorged my encounter with the White House counsel.

Clinton's face fell. "Oh, shit," he said. How did Cutler find out? Did I think Nancy told him? Exactly what did I say before he used the word "diarist"? As he cross-examined me, I wondered how no one had informed him. Was it avoidance, or simply the crush of more important things? We agreed that several staff people had seen the two of us talking, but we could not figure who leaked such a precise, loaded term to Cutler. Nor did our speculation really matter. The president absorbed all he wanted and then beckoned me to get on with tonight's recording. I hesitated. Now that our tapes were compromised—presumably headed to the special prosecutor, and from there almost anywhere—I thought he would panic, or at least restrict our talks. He waved such thoughts aside to presume nothing, see what came, and fix what he could. This gave me a small taste of what he meant by pressing forward through bombardment.

The president brightened with recollections from early May. By persevering through terrorist trauma and haggling technicalities alike, the Israelis and Palestinians miraculously had met a deadline fixed by their breakthrough accord the previous fall. The interim agreement, signed in Egypt, established Israeli security zones in the West Bank and created a structure for Palestinian civil administration leading toward full self-government. By mutual recognition, the new Palestinian Authority bestowed a formal job and title upon Chairman Yasir Arafat, who migrated back to ancient Jericho from two decades of exile in Tunisia.

Almost simultaneously, at home, the House of Representatives had cleared a historic hurdle to ban nineteen kinds of assault weaponry. Beaming, Clinton said he had not thought he could win before the May 5 roll call actually began on the House floor. An anguished Andy Jacobs, Democrat of Indiana, called to say he would switch his vote to support the bill, because he believed Clinton was being vilified hysterically like our best presidents, Lincoln and FDR. Off this fulsome, if backhanded, praise, the president detoured into some nasty press coverage before reliving the drama of his razor-thin House victory, 216–214. He said our old friend from Texas, Democratic representative Jack Brooks, never dreamed the gun lobby could lose. "I love Jack Brooks," said Clinton chuckling, "but he's very close to the NRA and he's just dumbfounded." More warily, he predicted that Brooks would connive with senators hoping to keep the assault weapons ban out of the final crime legislation. The NRA was stirring up gun lovers like hornets to scare off the huge public majority–80 percent, said Clinton, backed by nearly all the sheriffs and police chiefs–who wanted to curtail these murderous weapons.

He waxed rhapsodic about one obscure item on my agenda: his all-day reception on April 29 for the representatives of some 547 Native American tribes. Never had there been such an event, and its prior arrangements alone were an adventure for the federal government. The Interior Department was nominally in charge, but Clinton said its officials proved to be culturally lost beyond processing their regular programs and paperwork. For once, he traced performance down into the bureaucracy. He said the invitations had been spearheaded by members of the White House staff, who catalogued a whole new protocol for introductions and ceremonies–intertribal customs, rankings, seating charts, translators, rights to the "council" floor, and what languages must be spoken. Every U.S. cabinet member attended except Secretary of State Christopher, who was meeting with President Asad of Syria about the Golan Heights. Most of the guests referred to themselves by tribal names, Clinton recalled, and preferred the term "Indian" to "Native American." There were shallow, reflexive speeches for and against the "sovereign" legal status of tribes–its pitfalls as well as the broken promise–but most of the discussion was thoughtfully fresh. Speakers explored the paradox of yearning for citizenship while trying to maintain their Indian identity. The president said these issues, like the Indian day itself, were widely ignored, but he hoped they would grow on the American public. He called the event moving and provocative, like a naturalization ceremony with an edge. It was also politically smart, he added, listing surprise districts from Florida to Montana where Indians comprised a potential swing vote.

The president turned somber again about China. Five days earlier, he had abandoned his trial effort to hold Chinese trade privileges contingent upon satisfactory improvement in basic human rights. In policy jargon, his May 26 proclamation "de-linked" trade from the government's annual human rights review, making China eligible for a permanent MFN (Most Favored Nation) agreement with the United States, and this opened the path to full Chinese participation in global commerce. Politically for Clinton, the proclamation marked a stinging retreat. He had criticized President Bush in the 1992 campaign for a weak response to the infamous repression of pro-democracy vigils in Beijing.* Having vowed to honor the martyrs of Tiananmen Square, and stand tall for human rights, Clinton said he had fought like the devil to keep that high ground.

On tape, he examined a stalemate since butting heads with Jiang Zemin in Seattle. There was one scrap of progress. The Chinese government agreed to subscribe to the International Court of Justice on human rights standards, but Clinton said this amounted to little more than words—"to beat them over the head with"—toward later, unspecified reforms. Other gains were marginal at best. While his administration helped negotiate the release of numerous political prisoners, including some important ones, Clinton said the Chinese arrested more democratic activists than they released. The Chinese army did promise to reduce forced labor in military prisons, but the overall abuse there seemed

---

* The 1989 pro-democracy movement was stimulated by Soviet leader Mikhail Gorbachev's glasnost reforms, with Chinese students using nonviolent sit-in tactics adapted from the U.S. civil rights movement of the early 1960s. Demonstrations spread across China between April and early June, when the government launched a crackdown. Graphic news photographs fixed worldwide outrage on Tiananmen Square in Beijing, where infantry and tank units killed at least two hundred protesters.

worse than original estimates. The net result was doubtful, and Clinton was reluctant to claim a positive impact for fear of drawing attention. To be honest, he said, human rights had gone backward in several areas including Tibet. Clinton had been talking secretly with the Dalai Lama, who wanted badly to open a dialogue with China. When the Dalai Lama agreed to a key condition brokered by the administration—that he not publicly assert the right of Tibetan independence—the Chinese government reneged. "They upped the ante," said the president, sighing. Now China refused to meet until the Dalai Lama first announced that Tibet was and should be its loyal, subordinate province. A standoff hardened. The Chinese stepped up persecution of ethnic Tibetans and the Dalai Lama's religious orders.

Jiang Zemin's government refused to budge on human rights. Clinton said he and his security advisers had underestimated several psychological factors behind the resistance. One was the impending death of Deng Xiaoping, China's seminal leader since Mao Zedong. Deng had survived wars, assassination attempts, and at least three bloody purges as a "capitalist roader" branded disloyal to Mao. (His son was a paraplegic, tortured and thrown from a fourth-floor window by zealous Red Guards during Mao's Cultural Revolution.) Restored to power through the 1980s, Deng had launched his "socialist market economy," revving up national enterprise that he contained with ruthless political intimidation such as the Tiananmen Square massacre. President Clinton said all the Chinese leaders now were on tenterhooks for the ferocious infighting sure to follow the death of Deng Xiaoping.* Any contender for power who supported human rights concessions would be marked as a target for the hard-liners and, worse, as a stooge of the United States. China could hope for no positive credit at home or abroad, because every reform would be discounted as capitulation. The American linkage between trade and freedom threw down a publicized gauntlet. Additionally, it contradicted Deng's core premise that authoritarian rule was indispensable both for order and prosperity.

Clinton singled out the counsel of Treasury Secretary Lloyd Bent-

---

* Deng Xiaoping would survive nearly three more years, until February 19, 1997.

sen, who suggested that he weigh each alternative by the likely outcome if everything he hoped for went wrong. Under that assumption, de-linkage would lead to setbacks for human rights and every new trade agreement would invite protest that we compromised democracy. Continued linkage might sour also the whole strategic relationship with China, including the delicate multilateral efforts to restrain North Korea's nuclear weapons program. The latter would be worse, and perhaps irreversible. Of the many allies involved in negotiations with China over North Korea, none really favored Clinton's linkage. Jimmy Carter had advised him to break it, and so did Richard Nixon.

The president finished a grim tale. Having decided weeks ago to de-link, he pushed hard to obtain face-saving gestures in return. The Chinese government still balked. A secret envoy for Clinton, former ambassador Michael Armacost, offered Beijing a "goodie bag" of enticements to no avail. The Chinese said they craved the prestige of a state visit from the President of the United States—but not enough to release any political prisoners, which was a chastening comment on Clinton's relative value. More gall followed when he prepared sanctions against China to offset the de-linkage proclamation. Representative Nancy Pelosi, Democrat of California, and other human rights advocates called for stiff measures, and Tony Lake recommended a tariff package strong enough at least to uphold the credibility of U.S. sanctions elsewhere in the world. Clinton, however, succumbed to the logic of clean defeat. Any steps beyond the actual tokens of displeasure (banning the import of Chinese weaponry) risked reprisals from China. He might reap the worst of all worlds: a self-defeating trade war, with no improvement in human rights, plus criticism for trying to have it both ways and getting neither. He resolved instead to take his lumps for flip-flopping and failure, from gleeful opponents who had scorned the effort all along. Former secretary of state Alexander Haig assured business clients in China that human rights was not a proper concern of foreign policy. Clinton said he could only maneuver for another chance, hoping that continued trade and internal change would build the leverage for human rights.

By comparison, it seemed a relief for him to tell me about putting a new justice on the Supreme Court, and President Clinton marched on tape through the final stages of his choice. He had concluded that he could not in good conscience recommend Judge José Cabranes. Nor could he find another Hispanic judge yet able to meet the high standards. After that, the president concentrated at length on three finalists from earlier rounds: Babbitt, Arnold, and Breyer. He reaffirmed his close decision to keep Babbitt at Interior, in part to conserve political strength. Babbitt's controversial management of Western lands would have provoked a battle for Senate confirmation into the fall, diverting focus and support from Clinton's endangered health care bill.

He turned to his sentimental favorite, Richard Arnold of Arkansas. On merit, Clinton thought a vote of sitting U.S. judges would put Arnold highest among them for elevation to the Supreme Court. Although he had always admired Judge Arnold, they were not close personally or in politics. He would have gone forward with the appointment, and braved the inevitable charges of cronyism, were it not for the uncertain state of the judge's lymphoma. Arnold had received another round of radiation treatments in 1993. The disease was said to be in remission, but Clinton sought and received permission for a team of outside specialists to review Arnold's medical records. When the news leaked, there was a groundswell of home state excitement. Rumblings made the judge a celebrity in Arkansas, where no local citizen had ever served on the U.S. Supreme Court. Even the president's worst enemies beseeched him to make Arnold the first, and loudest among cheerleaders spoke the *Arkansas Democrat-Gazette.* Clinton pointedly called that newspaper his chief tormentor for decades, and digressed to say that its owners, with a smug agenda carried over from their ardent defense of racial segregation, also crusaded shamefully against Arkansas basketball coach Nolan Richardson. Headlines derided the coach ("Nolan Wrong As Rain"), while stories mocked his looks, diction, and coaching style, which the paper variously called "rat ball," "ghetto ball," and a "Globetrotters" carnival. "They did everything but call him a 'nigger,' " said Clinton, adding that for him—and for Hillary, too—a crowning satisfaction of Arkansas's first national basketball championship last month* was getting to watch the

---

* The University of Arkansas defeated Duke, 76–72, in the title game on April 4, 1994.

Democrat-Gazette eat all the hateful things it had written about the victorious coach.

Something else gnawed at Clinton about the newspaper. It had amused him at first that his nemesis made common cause in friendly editorials on behalf of Judge Arnold. He said the publisher, Walter Hussman, lobbied friends in the right-wing press. Hussman called editors at *The Wall Street Journal* to promote a Clinton-Arnold choice as good for the country and for their common point of view, touting his family connection. Hussman's sister had been Richard Arnold's first wife, and was the mother of his two daughters. This was all fine, said the president, but these newspeople were blindly selective about the personal consequences of their politics. He said the *Journal* editors had hounded Vince Foster to death with malice, and this was just as bad. Puzzled, I asked how. Mack McLarty knew the whole thing, said Clinton. As White House chief of staff, he was rightly aghast that the president wanted to confront Hussman. But the president called Hussman anyway, determined to upbraid him for entangling so many lives in Faulknerian plots.

Judge Arnold's current wife, Clinton said gravely, was the woman all-but-named in the trooper-based allegations about a tryst with him as president-elect at his farewell party in Little Rock. She was the one who had called CNN heatedly to deny it. This meant that Hussman had been willing to promote a scandal by implicating his own near and former relations. Clinton notified Hussman on the phone that he wanted to put Judge Arnold on the Court, and that his chances depended mostly on the medical review, but now there was poison spreading everywhere. "If I name Richard Arnold," he said he told Hussman, "the press will descend down there in a host, and they will ferret out that it's his wife—your ex-brother-in-law's wife—that you implicated in the trooper story. There's no way it won't come out."

Clinton quoted Hussman's smooth reply: "Well, Mr. President, don't worry about that. The troopers say that Kay Arnold was misidentified in the original stories." The president paused, looking agitated. He said he asked Hussman if he realized what he was saying. This was the whole point. "You people," he told him, "have these troopers where they will allege and deny things at your convenience, and therefore your vendetta against me has come back to haunt our state, and the long-run interests of the United States." The president said he gave Hussman a piece of his mind. He talked about collusion, political payrolls, and utter disregard for the truth. Moments later, my post-session dictation concluded succinctly: "Clinton got very worked up in recounting this story."

More calmly, he said the medical reports turned out to be mixed. Judge Arnold might survive only a few more years, or he might beat the lymphoma with aggressive treatments that nonetheless would hinder his work on the bench.* Clinton first called the two U.S. senators from Arkansas with his regrets. He said they were deeply disappointed, especially Dale Bumpers, for whom Arnold had worked on his congressional staff. Both urged him to substitute their Senate colleague, Paul Sarbanes of Maryland, as a surprise choice. Sarbanes was a first-rate lawyer and model politician. As a political bonus, they thought the Maryland governor, Donald Schaefer, would appoint Clinton's friend, Mayor Kurt Schmoke of Baltimore, to replace Sarbanes in the Senate. The president said he toyed briefly with the suggestion, but Hillary warned him that it was late in the process to introduce a new name. She also doubted that Governor Schaefer would appoint Schmoke. Schaefer was famously cantankerous, and might even appoint a Republican.

The president fell back one notch. He said their peers ranked Judge Stephen Breyer second only to Arnold in legal temperament and skill. He admired Breyer's graceful comportment when passed over for Justice Ginsburg's seat. Of countless petitions that filtered across his desk, Clinton was impressed by a Breyer recommendation from Hillary's friend and colleague Marian Wright Edelman, head of the Children's Defense Fund. He also retained an eloquent, handwritten letter from a fellow Rhodes Scholar, Rick Stearns, who had been instrumental in sending Clinton and me to Texas long ago. Ironically, a clinching qualification turned out to be Breyer's predicted ease in winning Senate confirmation. His nanny tax problems from the previous year seemed forgotten, or at least overshadowed by bipartisan esteem for him as a former chief counsel to the Senate Judiciary Committee. That was it, said President Clin-

---

* Judge Arnold retired to senior status in 2001. He died on September 23, 2004, at the age of sixty-eight.

ton. He named his choice on May 13, and the Senate would confirm Justice Breyer on July 29 by a vote of 87–9.

Clinton lingered on Vince Foster and the *Democrat-Gazette*. He said it was mortifying to have people accuse you of murdering your friend, and then be forced to run up personal debts defending yourself from a special counsel created out of your own government and funded by the taxpayers. More philosophically, he said there were only two conceivable kernels of substance buried in all the charges: first, that he knowingly received political money funneled through the Whitewater bank, and second, that he used improper state influence to benefit the bank. He had done neither, said Clinton, and eventually he would prove it, but he predicted that the vindication would be stale. Exoneration was a mirage, he mused, because the substance itself was largely beside the point. His critics simply rummaged for more accusations. The driving motive all along was some mix of partisan strategy and prurient indulgence, sustained by people above or indifferent to the country's real political problems. Clinton said the scandal machine had taken a lot of the joy out of being president.

Chelsea stopped by, neat as a pin, talking about an exam on Spanish verbs. She said good night and a preliminary goodbye for his long trip. When she was gone, Clinton said former president Bush had been encouraging him to spend more time at Camp David. Bush was hearing of low morale in its vast, attentive support staff, which remained isolated and idle because the Clintons almost never visited. The president said that while he appreciated such concerns, he saw few opportunities to change soon. Chelsea was fourteen years old. The last thing she wished for was a weekend at Camp David, which to her was the middle of nowhere. She stayed home, and her parents wanted to be apart from her as little as possible. So Camp David must wait.

He touched lightly on his two funerals the previous month. There were persistent grumbles that his eulogy for Richard Nixon was too soft, especially about the Vietnam War, but the president said he wanted to frame Nixon as the last liberal in a larger historical cycle, by highlighting his innovative proposals for the environment, income maintenance, and comprehensive health insurance. As for Jacqueline Kennedy Onassis, who had died of lymphoma at sixty-four, the president said he knew her mostly as an iconic figure, having met her only in glancing encounters on vacation last summer. By contrast, he said Hillary and Jackie had become friends. They had talked frequently on the telephone about coping with life in the White House, and he was grateful for that.

Hillary walked in from the bedroom and froze. She was wearing her bathrobe, a head towel, and a layer of grayish face cream with a few white spots. Neither she nor the president spoke, but I said "Excuse me" as she retreated. I apologized for staying so late on the night before their departure for the fiftieth anniversary of D-Day. President Clinton had capped off his preparations with a White House dinner for leading World War II scholars, and he relished the whole evening. He said all the experts agreed with the blunt assessment of historian Stephen Ambrose that the main purpose for the bloody invasion of Italy in 1943 was to keep Winston Churchill happy. They called this goal—odd as it may seem now—an acceptable policy back when leaders with all their foibles were more dominant figures on the world stage. I sensed a trace of wistfulness in Clinton's voice. Across Europe, he would speak for the United States at ceremonies to commemorate one of the most pivotal events of the twentieth century.

From France, he said, Sam Gibbons of Florida had called earlier today with news of his election at last to chair the House Ways and Means Committee. Having parachuted into Carentan, France, behind the D-Day invasion, the former Captain Gibbons was back there early for reunions with surviving Army buddies from the 101st Airborne Division. In their honor, he vowed now to pass the health care legislation. The president said Gibbons was an old-time fighter in the mold of Harry Truman, and very smart, but political pros doubted that he would wield the raw clout of his predecessor. (Dan Rostenkowski had just resigned to fight a corruption indictment that would ultimately send him to prison.) Clinton hoped Gibbons's gritty ego would pass the bill and prove them wrong. He pictured the old soldier jumping again into a desperate, noble cause. This image stuck with me among hundreds from a session I still feared might be our last. On my way home, I wished we had covered more topics.

CHAPTER TEN

FOREIGN TRAVELS

Thursday, June 30, 1994

Thursday, July 21, 1994

We worked in the Treaty Room on the last night of June, because Chelsea was watching a movie in the family parlor. With my recorders and notebooks spread on the coffee table before me, I sat on a sofa beneath the signature painting of treaty ceremonies to end the Spanish-American War of 1898. President Clinton arrived in jeans and running shoes, with his unlit cigar. He took a large armchair across from me and put his feet up, clearly in a good mood. Just that day, Chairman Sam Gibbons pushed the administration's massive health care bill through the Ways and Means Committee by a strict party-line vote, 20–18. This was a big hurdle, said the president, but things would get tougher from here.

Had I heard yet from David Kendall? The question startled me. Kendall had been in all the newspapers as the lawyer retained personally by the Clintons for the Whitewater investigations. I told the president that by coincidence I had bumped into him last week down at the thirtieth anniversary of Mississippi Freedom Summer, a student mobilization at the peak of the civil rights movement. Clinton understood why I would go there to gather material for my work, but he looked puzzled. "Oh, what was he doing there?" he asked, speaking of Kendall. I hesitated, unsure how much the president knew or wanted to know about his defender. While a student at tiny Wabash College, Kendall had been among the intrepid volunteers beaten and jailed that summer of 1964 in witness against Mississippi's primitive segregation.* President Clinton nodded. He had met Kendall as a fellow Rhodes Scholar, and seemed impressed to hear of such early passion in a Washington lawyer now known for schoolmaster looks and quiet tenacity. Clinton digressed sadly on trends of racism surfacing lately in his polling data. Then he said Kendall had found out somehow about our history tapes—probably from Lloyd Cutler—and would be calling me about the special prosecutor's subpoena. Did my notes indicate which tapes had "substantive" remarks about Whitewater or the death of Vince Foster? He said Kendall may insist on listening to some of them. We sagged into a dozen ominous questions. If leaks from a legal submission revealed the existence of his diary, Clinton feared that Congress would demand all the tapes. He rehearsed a backup argument that he, unlike Senator Packwood, did not relinquish his privacy rights due to voluntary disclosure. Kendall was an excellent lawyer, he kept saying. Maybe he could avoid such a fight.

We suspended these hypothetical dangers. On cue, he said Sam Gibbons could not move the health care bill to the House floor anytime soon. Members of the lower chamber, gripped by a persecution complex that Clinton called partly justified, wanted the Senate to go first. Too many times they hazarded "hard votes" on some controversial bill only to watch the "prima donna" Senate dodge final passage, leaving the representatives politically exposed for nothing. The health care bill was stuck in the Senate Finance Committee, chaired by Pat Moynihan of New York, who was finding no majority for any version of the bill. Clinton analyzed Moynihan's performance with sympathy, observing that he was saddled with bad luck. On the Democratic side, his committee was composed heavily of members from small rural states—Max Baucus of Montana, Kent Conrad of North Dakota, David Boren of Oklahoma,

---

* Andrew Goodman, Kendall's roommate during the nonviolent training sessions in Ohio, had been one of three young civil rights workers notoriously lynched on the very first night of the summer project, June 21, 1964. The Klan posse included Mississippi constables who pretended to investigate their own crime.

and to some extent John Breaux of Louisiana—who were vulnerable to well-financed opposition campaigns by insurance companies. The small-state senators also faced disproportionate resistance to employer-mandated health coverage, because they represented fewer large companies to share the burden on small business.

In Senator Boren, Clinton said Moynihan faced still more committee headaches from a temperamental maverick. Boren insisted upon a bipartisan bill, irrespective of content, and would support no measure that failed to attract some shifting number of Republican senators. His stance amounted to a health care veto for the opposition, whose goal was to block rather than shape the legislation. Newt Gingrich, the House Republican leader, openly stated that he would marshal party discipline to make the bill "unpassable." Only yesterday, Bob Dole finally introduced his alternative health care legislation in the Senate, but Clinton said this was only window dressing. What really mattered was that Dole had secured the loyalty of nearly every Republican senator. Moreover, chance gave Dole an extra advantage to stop Clinton's bill with this partisan phalanx. The president observed wryly that the senior Republicans on Moynihan's Finance Committee were "politically impaired." Dole had put Senator Packwood of Oregon on strict notice that the Senate ethics case for sexual harassment would intensify—during his uphill reelection campaign—if Packwood cooperated with Democrats inside the Finance Committee. The next ranking Republican, David Durenberger of Minnesota, was not seeking reelection owing to his legal disbarment, and censure by the Senate, for misuse of public finds. Still, Clinton described Durenberger as beholden to Dole in advance—therefore useless to Moynihan—for help with post-Senate employment and character references at his impending trial.

Raw politics left President Clinton somber about the prospects for his legislation. Although a substantial public majority still favored the component principles in the health care bill, he said pinpricks of intense and distorted opposition turned victory toward defeat. He likened the dynamics to gun control battles, in which the NRA war chests and mailing lists punched holes in broad but thin support. Clinton homed in on the challenge of public presentation. Not many advocates understood the complexities of the health care bill, he said, and few of these could shine a clear spotlight on its merits: universal coverage, cost containment, patient choice, and payment simplification. More than once in our session, the president drifted into his own practice speeches. He said he and Hillary were experimenting with new forums. He praised Senator Robb's spirited riposte in a recent debate when senatorial opponent Oliver North called him a lackey who voted mostly with Clinton. Robb replied that he had voted mostly with President Bush, too, because his duty was to help presidents where he could, not tear them down. He and Clinton were working to create jobs for Virginians, cut bureaucracy, and assure everyone of quality health care. Robb fought squarely. He did not cavil or mince words, said Clinton, predicting he would win.*

The president's enthusiasm crested with memories of his D-Day anniversary trip to Europe. He dwelled largely on private encounters, such as a spontaneous forum with several hundred aspiring priests inside the Vatican. This audience with John Paul II was neither as intimate nor wide-ranging as others to follow in later years. Clinton thought the pope's recently broken leg was a severe injury, because, over his protests, John Paul struggled mightily to stand when Clinton entered and left. Otherwise, the pope did not move, and the president guessed he had been carried to his seat. They exchanged courtesies, and discussed many issues including Bosnia, but Clinton's foray on abortion and birth control fell flat. While he supported, and would enforce, a woman's recourse to legal and safe abortion, Clinton tried to clarify that he yearned to reduce drastically the number undergone by voluntary means. He believed most women did, too, and toward that goal he hoped John Paul II could consider relaxing church doctrines against birth control, so they could seek cooperative ways to discourage unwanted pregnancy. At this notion, Clinton said the pope furrowed and frowned silently. John Paul spoke very good English, and yet Clinton could not be sure whether the pope was pondering the compromise or merely checking his grasp of language, and the eventual response veered off into an attack on a forthcoming U.N. birth control conference in Cairo, Egypt. The pope be-

---

* Senator Robb did defeat North in the 1994 general elections, when barely half the Senate's Democratic incumbents survived. Republicans gained eight Senate seats held by Democrats, and lost none.

came quite agitated about feminist affronts to church authority. He finally told Clinton he could bless only one new form of conception—the alleviation of world poverty, which would cause people to limit their families naturally. He did not specify how they would do so without birth control.

In Rome, the president met the new Italian leader, Silvio Berlusconi, who projected a naive quality, asking why politics could not be as simple as business. He owned all three Italian television networks, plus a villa in the Bahamas near Ross Perot. Clinton thought even Perot was more sophisticated than Berlusconi. The president's memories dwelled on subsequent tours of the Italian countryside with World War II soldiers. He said veterans of the Italian campaign felt overshadowed, somewhat like Russians about the eastern theater of the war. They had forced Nazi soldiers out of Rome two days before the landing in France. Clinton recalled walking through the cemetery at Nettuno with a handful of veterans. One soldier found the grave of his sergeant, who, unable to sleep, had asked to swap patrol duty. Had he not agreed, the soldier said, his sergeant might be there strolling instead. Similarly, the president described walks along French beaches at Normandy, far from the press, listening to veterans tell stories about what happened coming ashore into the murderous enemy fire. During pauses, they leaned over absently to form what became a small cross of stones. Up past an escarpment, where veterans told how they had spiked the German artillery guns, a soldier Clinton remembered by name described waking up delirious in an Army hospital, with grievous wounds, to see his brother standing over him among the doctors—then always waking unharmed to realize that his brother had died near him on the beach. The soldier hoped somehow this reunion might cure his recurring dream of fifty years.

The president skimmed over a night aboard Queen Elizabeth's royal yacht with Charles and Diana, who were separated, and his own remarks at the formal D-Day ceremonies ("When they were young, these men saved the world"). He was more animated about the subsequent trip back to Oxford for an honorary degree, which brought a rush of memory about campus life and British customs. Two students from Singapore attacked him for cultural imperialism, prompting a lively debate. One Oxford friend from long ago, amazed that the president still knew his name, congratulated him for a fine job in all respects but one. He hated the Irish policy, saying Clinton never should have let the Sinn Fein "terrorist" Gerry Adams into the United States. This touched off another of many political arguments well into the night. Clinton said the arguments rejuvenated him, and it seemed to rejuvenate him again merely to sketch the fine points of contention. The students held their own on scores of subjects, while he wore out the mass of reporters who tried to keep up. The same thing happened at marathon press conferences in France. Exhausted reporters said they expected American politics to be more superficial.

A call from Tokyo intruded. The president left me in the Treaty Room, hidden from Deputy National Security Adviser Sandy Berger and other aides waiting to attend the introductory conference with Tomiichi Murayama, who had been chosen yesterday to become Japan's fourth prime minister within the past year. Clinton returned fifteen minutes later, smiling. From the photographs in his briefing book, he said Murayama had big bushy eyebrows like the old union boss John L. Lewis. They had gotten along well in this, their first contact, though the president wondered why a socialist like Murayama headed a coalition government of so many conservative parties. Murayama kept saying how much it meant to talk with the American president about basic issues before them, which reminded Clinton that even strong countries looked to the United States as a bulwark. Contrary to our stumbling, bumbling image, we were regularly outperforming the developed economies. Over the past year, he said, the United States accounted for 40 percent of aggregate production and *all* the net growth in jobs among the G-7 nations, with the lowest rate of inflation.

When Chelsea stopped by, the president tried to set a time to play cards, or just to talk. He said he had not seen her for a while, but she excused herself to get up early. Clinton looked a bit forlorn, telling me she had a summer job at the National Institutes of Health. On tape, we turned to the major shuffling of the White House staff announced on June 27. Its centerpiece was the shift of Budget Director Leon Panetta to replace Mack McLarty as chief of staff. Clinton disclosed that he had sought advice before his D-Day trip, asking Hillary's chief of staff, Maggie Williams, to compile confidential suggestions. Panetta was her idea.

When I asked how unusual it was for the first lady's office to be involved, he replied that there was no easy blueprint for reorganizing the organizers. Williams was shrewd, discreet, and efficient. She recommended Panetta for his steady application of good humor and ramrod toughness to shrink the budget deficit. McLarty, despite his executive background, was more a business ambassador than a hard-nosed manager. Harold Ickes was mean enough, but too narrow and project-oriented for overall command. McLarty never wanted to be chief of staff, the president concluded with a sigh.

Clinton said he should have made this change eight months ago. It was his fault. He also agreed with management specialists who said the White House had too many general advisers running around. David Gergen was the odd one out this time, moved from the White House to the State Department. The president seemed pained for him. Not very convincingly, he said Gergen was showing strong interest in foreign affairs. The two of them thought much alike, and worked well in close contact, but Gergen on his own had found himself in chronic conflict with the other staff generalists. Now Bruce Lindsey would concentrate on personnel matters, working from the counsel's office. George Stephanopoulos, having already lost his role as a public spokesperson, would report to Panetta. The president expressed confidence that Panetta would tighten lines of responsibility, but he seemed uncomfortable talking about firings and friction, happy the ordeal was behind him. He was more expansive about economist Alice Rivlin's qualifications to take over for Panetta at the OMB, the Office of Management and Budget.

The president shortened his answers, signaling fatigue. He said far more people cared about welfare reform than campaign finance reform. His crime bill was stuck on racial justice amendments to the sections about capital punishment. He was plugging away to dislodge at least one of these bills in Congress, which he said would "get my fighting blood back up" to refocus the country on politics. On North Korea, he said Jimmy Carter had initiated his own recent trip with a call to Al Gore, and Clinton had approved the volunteer mission to break through North Korea's extreme isolation. He said the administration was receiving other private signals—oddly from evangelist Billy Graham—that North Korea feared shriveling away like "another East Germany." Sure enough, Carter did reach North Korean dictator Kim Il-sung, who proposed to allow inspection of North Korea's nuclear facilities in exchange for relief from the harsh economic sanctions. The only hitch was that Carter announced the terms to CNN before they became official, adding gratuitously that he never had agreed with sanctions in the first place. News stories had the White House seething, but Clinton made light of the spat. He said the deal was since ratified by an exchange of letters, and he did not believe Carter would criticize official policy "if the game were still in doubt."

In a casual aside, the president said he had played golf recently in San Diego with O. J. Simpson, the movie actor and former football star, and maybe we could talk about that next time. (We didn't.) He was reacting to a jarring cultural phenomenon while Carter was in North Korea. Media outlets—including CNN—suspended all other world news for an entire afternoon to show a white Ford Bronco trailed by an armada of L.A. police vehicles, meandering along freeways until Simpson surrendered on suspicion that he had slashed his wife and her friend to death.

Clinton interrupted my listing of state visits to record that he had shared an emotional moment in the Oval Office with President Eduardo Frei of Chile. Back in the 1960s, Frei told him, when the Chilean constitution required presidents to obtain parliamentary permission for any trip abroad, a combination of Socialists and military conservatives had blocked the first President Frei from accepting invitations to the White House. The newly elected Frei wished his father had lived long enough to accompany him now. On another small note, Clinton winced when asked about his formal testimony to the Whitewater special prosecutor. They had met here in the Treaty Room on June 13, he said, pointing to chairs. Robert Fiske brought a couple of his guys and put him under oath. He answered all their questions. So did Hillary. Presidents before him had submitted to such interrogation, he emphasized—Carter four times on some peanut inquiry. The president seemed touchy, eager to move on. I left shortly after midnight.

THREE WEEKS LATER, delays knocked our July session off routine. A line of sedans filled my usual parking area beneath the Truman Balcony, and no doorman waited inside to take me upstairs. There were Secret Service

agents instead, posted at the diplomatic entrance, who told me the ushers were with the president and first lady next door in the Map Room.
Occasional laughter spilled through the walls from the place where FDR
had tracked World War II with huge charts and battle zone models. I
waited with the agents in the lower hallway. New ones arrived when they
rotated positions—some stone-faced, some chatty. One said the White
House may be a career ticket but the counterfeiting detail was more fun.
Another joked that their eight-hour schedules were synchronized with
hospital nurses, and the graveyard shift was about to come on duty.
Legislators began to slip out of the Map Room every few minutes, followed by White House usher Dennis Freemyer. He said the meeting was
about to break up, and hurried me to his office so that he could rush
back downstairs to operate the president's elevator. George Hannie, one
of the butlers, came along as the hubbub below grew louder. "Mrs. Clinton would like me to take you to the kitchen," he said.

It was quiet in the utilitarian kitchen across the grand hallway from
their bedroom. Hillary arrived shortly, famished, apologizing that the
health care strategy session ran late as always. We sat at a small breakfast
table next to the refrigerator. She said Chelsea was due back tomorrow
from a summer trip to Europe. We caught up on children and schools,
then drifted somehow into Major League Baseball's long-simmering
labor dispute. Team owners had proposed to implement a salary cap,
which the players rejected with an imminent vote to go on strike. Hillary
was upset as a lifelong Cubs fan, and she still stung from her experience
on opening day. After the thrill of throwing out the first pitch at Wrigley
Field, she heard about nothing but taxes from players in the Cubs locker
room. Multimillionaires in their twenties accosted her: "Your husband
raised my taxes! What are we going to do about it?" Most of them were
thoughtless and spoiled, she said. They refused to consider any comparative public needs of the country making it so fantastically lucrative
for them to play with a ball.

The president arrived to eat. He said he had gotten an earful about
taxes from the players, too, but he made light of it. The country did
pretty well in the golden years before Kennedy *lowered* the maximum tax
rate to 70 percent, and now it was below 40 percent. "If the players want
to lower their taxes," he quipped, "they should give more to their

churches." His reports warned of a devastating strike likely to ruin base-ball's exciting season in progress. Not until last night did he realize that the Padres' Tony Gwynn was hitting over .390, or that the lowly Mon-treal Expos had the best record in baseball with the second lowest team payroll. Our conversation glanced from books to movie gossip as the Clintons ate warmed-over plates of fish. Hannie set a third place for me, insisting that it would be impolite to decline dessert. The pastry chef sent up an elaborate chiffon cake covered in huge blackberries—safely without dairy products, because of Clinton's allergies—which turned out to be gooey inside. We picked at it. The president asked for some vanilla yogurt, but Hannie could find only exotic flavors. They both seemed stoic about the haphazard meal, and mixed talk of personal health and national care. We were going in the wrong direction. They said insurance covered 88 percent of the people ten years ago, and health took 9 per-cent of GDP, whereas health now took 14 percent of GDP with only 83 percent covered. Clinton had met an older man today who maintained his high school weight of 140 pounds simply by banishing all snacks from the kitchen, even an apple. Hillary frowned as we mulled over the idea. "That sounds really boring," she said. "Having no food in the house."

In the parlor room, while setting up my recorders on the card table, I offered soberly to resign my volunteer role. David Kendall had called several times about which tapes to review. He judged some material "plainly disclosable," which put the president's confidential memories in jeopardy, and I felt terrible as a participant in the project. While stress-ing that I had told no unauthorized person about the diary tapes, out of both personal and professional conviction, I said my assurances were irrelevant. What mattered was his confidence. He had talked once of finding a diarist in the White House, and if he wanted to make that change, or any other, I would stand quietly aside. A silence hung be-tween us. "That's understood," was all he said.

We sat down to continue. On tape, the president made striking ob-servations about his European economic meetings early in July. He loved his public reception in the newly independent Baltic nations—especially at Riga, the capital of Latvia—where knowledgeable crowds cheered him for his persistent efforts to secure the withdrawal of the still

occupying Russian soldiers, but he discovered himself eclipsed in some
quarters by a relatively new subordinate. Everyone was asking for FBI
Director Louis Freeh. No kidding, said Clinton. Into Poland, and all
through the former Soviet satellites, people spoke of Director Freeh like
a rock star. Clinton said their yearning reflected deep social fears where
the birth of liberty brought disorder, meaning freedom to steal or be
stolen from, and people clamored for the FBI because organized crime
preyed on their wobbly institutions. Taking no public or private transac-
tion for granted—that a bus driver would not demand a bribe, that a
bank would pay checks to the designated party—they clutched at the
hope that Freeh could help.

In Warsaw, Clinton found that hardship had wilted the first bloom
of Polish liberation. Markets did not yet function. Unemployment was
rising above 15 percent where it could be measured, and President Lech
Walesa, who had plummeted from the hero of the Solidarity freedom
movement to approval ratings beneath 5 percent, battered Clinton in
private for protection for his country within NATO. For all but twenty-
six years of the previous two centuries, Poland had been conquered
whole or splintered by foreign powers, and Walesa insisted that imperial
Russia would try again if Poland did not disintegrate first. At his state
dinner, Clinton had been seated between Walesa's wife, Danuta, and the
speaker of the lower Polish parliament, or Sejm, when the latter observed bitterly that Poland was better off under Communism. Danuta
rose up in her chair to vent fury at the speaker. She called him ignorant
of the deep wounds Communism had inflicted on the Polish people.

"I thought she was going to belt him," said the president, who recalled stepping in to referee a wonkish truce. On learning that the
speaker was a potato farmer, Clinton reminded him that the Soviet system had allowed Poles to own their farms, sparing them the worst of
totalitarian collectivism. The state had bought all their crops at a guaranteed price, but Poland did not need a Communist dictatorship to restore
those benefits. Every country in the world where farmers are not dirt
poor had devised some sort of stabilized marketing system for agriculture, and the miracles of fair competition could blossom only when
rules were established for basic sectors of the economy. This required
hard work. Although Poland was suffering in transition, Clinton tried to

assure the speaker that prosperity and political freedom were necessary partners in the long run.

The president kept eyeing Bob Woodward's new book, *The Agenda,* which was lying among my papers on the card table. Clearly he had received reports. When he asked my opinion, I hedged to sound out his own judgments. Clinton agreed that he was lucky to have a reporter of Woodward's stature unearth the hidden battles over his omnibus antideficit bill of 1993, which was a dry subject for general readers. He also agreed that major sources for Woodward probably were those advisers rewarded with flattering roles in the text: Stephanopoulos, political consultant Paul Begala, and especially Fed Chairman Alan Greenspan, who came off as Clinton's patient tutor in economics. None of this seemed to bother the president much. He thought his finance adviser Robert Rubin had talked with Woodward very little ("He's too smart"), and Mack McLarty perhaps not at all, because McLarty's portrayal was the least sympathetic.

What upset him was an obsessive focus on style above substance, especially in media discussion of *The Agenda*. Debates within his administration were lampooned as contests of seesaw mismanagement suited to a romper room, full of temper tantrums and panicky showdowns pitting "true Democrats" against coldhearted bankers, or realists against doctrinaire liberals. The president objected first to exaggeration. He said fierce argument is healthy for free government—and infighting inherent— even on small matters. "It's the nature of the beast," he said. By fair comparison with the hacks of many administrations, or even the talented backstabbers around Lincoln and FDR, the president called his budget advisers models of decorous public service. Their victory in Congress had momentous stakes for every citizen. Could the package really tame our deficit? Might we dare to balance the national budget for the first time in two generations? At what cost? How would it affect tomorrow's grandchildren to be spared trillions in public debt? Clinton lamented that the Woodward reviews ignored these core questions. They buried the central issue under a mountain of finger pointing and factional scorekeeping.

I tried to resume the account of his European journey to the G-7 summit in Naples, but President Clinton veered off into side trips with

Hillary and Chelsea. They visited Caserta, the eighteenth-century palace built for King Charles VII, with some 1,200 opulent rooms approached by landscaped fountains he likened to the Lincoln Memorial Reflecting Pool—except eight miles long—and before I could absorb these colossal dimensions he described the ruins of ancient Pompeii. There was no lava. A flash of hot pellets had killed everything, followed by a flood of ash that preserved death moments with eerie precision, sometimes molding a grayish texture on skeletons to replace departed flesh. Clinton retained stores of archaeological detail. He explained how excavators had pegged one shop as a kind of fast food outlet by reconstituting its window shelf fitted for pickup bowls along a public walkway. A whorehouse was the only two-story building, and whitewash covered layers of political posters along the streets. Clinton seemed fascinated that scientists might decipher the actual campaign slogans for municipal elections under way in Pompeii's final year of 79 CE. He expressed excitement for once about presidential modes of travel, recalling a helicopter flight along the Rhine River to Helmut Kohl's house in Ludwigshafen, above "castle after castle" like aerial scenes from a storybook. Clinton said Chancellor Kohl and his wife, Hannelore, seemed to be tough, well-matched partners, still very much in love after twenty-nine years. She was full of inquisitive energy, despite a mysterious skin ailment.[*]

Kohl, unlike most European leaders, supported Poland's petition for expedited admission to NATO. Clinton said the basic reason was simple: Kohl did not like being exposed on the easternmost flank of the Western alliance, while still completing the reunification of Germany. Strategically, and politically, Kohl was sensitive about authoritarian tendencies in the non-NATO countries. Everything else about NATO was complicated, of course, and the president spent much of his summit dancing between Yeltsin's anxiety about an expanded NATO and NATO's anxiety about resurgent Russia. One small gesture in Naples was to mollify Yeltsin by reconstituting the G-7 forum of seven nations into the G-8, with Russia permanently added. Clinton noted a further

---

[*] Hannelore Kohl suffered from photodermatitis, an acute sensitivity to sunlight thought to be caused by a reaction to penicillin. She would commit suicide in Ludwigshafen on July 5, 2001, at the age of sixty-eight.

ramification of NATO—that as Poland looked to the west, Ukraine lay ever more isolated on the southeast with her sixty million people, driven perhaps to seek a protective alliance with Russia. He described his telephone initiative earlier that day to make friends with Leonid Kuchma, the newly elected president of independent Ukraine. Because of size, demographics, and strategic location, he added that much of current European diplomacy revolved around two nations: Turkey and Ukraine. Every decision that touched either one seemed to reverberate from London to Mecca.

The G-8 leaders fashioned several economic agreements to stabilize and woo Ukraine. Then again, he added, the deliberations in Naples were overshadowed by external events. North Korea's founding leader, Kim Il-sung, though constitutionally unchanged as "Eternal President of the Republic," had ended forty-six years of earthly rule with his sudden death on July 8. The president said he still thought it was right to endure Jimmy Carter's preening to secure the freelance deal in June. Now he had been assured that North Korea was not likely to violate its nuclear agreements until it buried Kim. Otherwise, the intelligence reports so far merely pawed the ground, calling the son and heir, Kim Jong-il, either a weak bon vivant or a ruthless killer who had overcompensated for his pampered youth. A simultaneous hemorrhage of Caribbean refugees was so massive that the G-8 leaders had suspended their lofty calendar to notice tiny Haiti. Something terrible was driving a whole year's human flotsam to rafts *every day,* with 140 Haitians drowned on July 4 alone and some 16,000 plucked from the sea by July 7.

From Europe, President Clinton had ordered his new special envoy on Haiti, former Pennsylvania Democratic congressman William Gray, to announce that the United States no longer would accept Haitians adrift. They were being shipped temporarily instead to the U.S. naval base at Guantánamo, Cuba. Clinton reviewed a telephone spat with the outgoing president of Panama, Guillermo Endara, who had reneged on his public promise to grant asylum for ten thousand Haitians, and there were subtle lessons from the administration's quiet effort to disperse Haitian refugees among Latin nations. The president said most of the leaders expressed fitful reservations about U.S. intervention anywhere in the hemisphere, citing popular resentment of prior invasions under the

Monroe Doctrine. However, these same leaders confided a counter-vailing worry about the permanent displacement of an elected govern-ment by Haiti's military. Nearly all the Latin American democracies had been overthrown at least once in recent decades, and the elected civil-ians were keenly attuned to any recurring atmosphere in the region for coups. They talked constantly among themselves to share readings on each country's military establishment, while soldiers from the Latin American armies watched developments in Haiti, too. Clinton said he had not realized how broadly the Haitian crisis might affect civilian-military relations.

Today, said the president, Ambassador Madeleine Albright had in-troduced in the United Nations Security Council a two-tiered resolution that would authorize force to restore the Aristide government, followed by a multinational deployment to keep peace. He thought the odds were slightly against passage. Tomorrow, he would announce the dispatch of four thousand American troops to assist relief efforts in Rwanda. The Pentagon was far from enthusiastic about a mission to either Haiti or Rwanda, especially on top of the ever-shifting contingency plans to en-force some kind of peace settlement in Bosnia. Nevertheless, the top generals and admirals were cooperating. They worked with national se-curity appointees to define clear tasks of acceptable duration and risk, and Clinton pushed to distinguish their military responsibilities from political goals. He said he looked forward to meetings with the Joint Chiefs. Their rapport had come a long way since the initial friction over gay soldiers. The president shook his head wistfully. "I'm getting along a lot better with the military than with the press."

He had received a grim report on the atrocities in Rwanda. Already, despite the chaos, some five hundred Rwandan leaders were reliably identified with evidence of substantial war crimes, or even genocide—nearly all by Hutus against the Tutsi minority. Clinton hoped for trials there, as well as Bosnia, observing that the charges and jurisdiction would be different from the case the U.N. hoped to mount against Gen-eral Aidid, the Somali warlord. He paused, looking perplexed. "I'm em-barrassed," he said. "I can't remember exactly under what auspices Aidid would have been tried."

When I asked about the disturbing Census Bureau report on the

American family, he spouted statistics from memory. Did I mean the 70 percent growth since 1983 in the number of children living with a never married single parent? There were now 6.3 million such children, up from a quarter of a million in 1960. The president perceived an isolated culture of poverty deteriorating under its own weight, depriving families of eligible males. He associated the decay, which was proportional to poverty rates across ethnic groups, with the stubborn abortion rate of 27 percent for all pregnancies. We had talked about that before, he said, and so skimmed on to bottlenecks in the health care legislation. This time he seemed less forgiving of the Senate Finance Committee. Echoing comments by Hillary at dinner, he faulted Senator Moynihan for aimless hearings conducted without a strategy or theme. Only Ted Kennedy, South Dakota's Tom Daschle, and West Virginia's Jay Rockefeller knew enough about the subject to carry a floor debate, whereas Moynihan aired his doubts about the comprehensive bill. Of late, he also resisted Clinton's entreaties to move some minimalist version out of committee. *Any* bill, said the president, hinting at fallback options such as an experimental plan for children only, with a phase-in period extended over a number of years.

Clinton doubted he would get a chance to pass health care reform in the next Congress. His mood was so grave that I offered a stab at condolence, predicting that he would gain credit for massive political groundwork. He squelched such talk as premature, or patronizing. Maybe he was just tired, but he brightened over a surprise from Jordan. He thought a breakthrough was imminent and real, even though he confessed having no sense of it during King Hussein's quiet visit less than a month ago. They had retreated for lunch as two couples—the Clintons, with the king and his wife, Queen Noor—in the family dining room across the hall, next to the little kitchen. Their agenda was a delicate race between Hussein's failing health and his desire to make peace with Israel. The president said he and Hillary pounded away on symptoms of national estrangement: closed borders, water disputes, travel barriers, war grievances, contested airspace, sealed electrical grids, and so on. Hussein gave them a feast of goodwill without commitment on any point.

Clinton wondered what had changed between then and six days ago, when Hussein arranged at last to see a prime minister of Israel in person. Something gave way, or fell into place, but the president agreed with all his experts that it was serious. They knew because the weakened king was hastening back across the Atlantic Ocean, and Yitzhak Rabin was coming all the way from Israel to meet him at the White House. Clinton himself felt a backlash from Syria's President Asad. Somehow—out of simple avoidance, or a fear of irresolution—King Hussein had failed to notify his neighboring ruler of the momentous decision to explore peace with Israel, and that unpleasant task fell to Clinton. Rage burned through the telephone line as Asad berated Hussein to Clinton for betraying a fellow Arab. Asad's worst fear was that Jordan and the Palestinians would follow Egypt's example to make peace, isolating him, and that Israel then would stiffen its terms enough to retain Syria's precious Golan Heights. The president said he had walked a fine line through the tempestuous phone call. He first warned Asad that he would spare no effort to promote the sudden Israel-Jordan summit. Rabin and King Hussein would address Congress jointly. Clinton would shore up support for Rabin among American Jews, while helping Hussein win debt relief and other legislative sweeteners for the deal. Secretary of State Christopher would broker a formal end to belligerency, to be followed soon by a full-fledged peace treaty.* The United States would sponsor and witness all these things, which would be bitter for Syria, but Asad should hear the full truth. This included Clinton's balancing assurance that no peace in the region would be complete without Syria. He promised to keep pushing on that front, independently of other agreements.

The president stepped from his closet a few minutes later, barefoot in suit trousers and a T-shirt. He had been undressing while I rewound and labeled the twin tapes. "Wait here a minute," he instructed, heading down the hall. Back he came shortly with one of the two storage boxes I had provided for his oral history cassettes. I put one of tonight's tapes inside, and counted the others quickly to make sure the set was com-

---

* Four days after this session, Hussein, Rabin, and Clinton signed the Washington Declaration to terminate the perpetual state of war between Israel and Jordan. They reconvened sixty days later at the Wadi Araba border near the Dead Sea, where the two countries concluded their peace treaty on October 26, 1994.

plete. He took tonight's other cassette in his hand. Only a few nights earlier, Clinton explained, he had taken David Kendall down to the Lincoln Bedroom so the lawyer could listen to selected tapes. Kendall worked there alone, making his own little transcripts, which he was incorporating into Clinton's response to the subpoena from Special Prosecutor Fiske. The exposure would be nerve-racking, but we agreed that Kendall's punctilious compliance was wise. Without it, the tapes would become legally tainted. He would never have been able to open them for historical research without inviting charges that he should have surrendered the Whitewater comments under subpoena. Evasion or suppression would defeat our whole purpose. Instead, we had to take our chances with disclosure.

The president had instructed Kendall where to hide the cassettes when he finished. My visit reminded the president that he forgot them temporarily, and now he secured both boxes somewhere in a closet. Clinton's reassurance hung uneasily with my awareness that I was at his disposal on a project that might blow up. On my way home, I pictured Kendall hunching over a recorder in the Lincoln Bedroom, Hillary arguing taxes with Cubs players, and Jimmy Carter huddling with a dying, deified recluse in North Korea. Was the presidency more than the blur of events happening to and around Clinton?

CHAPTER ELEVEN

HILLARY'S DREAM

Friday, August 26, 1994

White House Picnic
Saturday, September 10, 1994

More than a month passed. Nancy Hernreich said the president was locked away in crisis meetings nearly every night. To avoid falling another twelve days behind, she proposed to squeeze in a session before the Clintons' summer vacation on Martha's Vineyard. Although we had resolved to avoid daytime visits, she said the only available slot was for a getaway afternoon. I found the Marine One presidential helicopter waiting on the South Lawn, which attracted several hundred tourists to peer through the fence for a glimpse of the first family's departure. From the White House residence, where aides carried messages and satchels, the president led me through the Yellow Oval Room to record privately outdoors in the heat, high on the Truman Balcony.

With Justice Breyer confirmed, the Jordan-Israel accord so far a success, and refugee riots suppressed at the U.S. naval base in Guantánamo Bay, Clinton picked up his narrative with a shocking August 11 defeat. Fifty-eight Democrats opposed his signature crime bill on the House floor, while only eleven Republicans voted in favor. Combined with a downward stall on health care, the unexpected short tally of 210–225 had pitched Clinton into emergency salvage. He said he resisted urgent pleas to resubmit the crime bill without its ban on assault weapons.

Speaker Foley and Majority Leader Gephardt pushed this option with most of the White House staff. By concentrating on the more popular elements—100,000 new community police officers, plus more prisons, prevention and treatment programs, and tougher penalties for terrorist crimes—they sought to recapture members from those rural districts most vulnerable to the gun lobby. They hoped to pass the heart of his crime bill on a party-line vote, without having to bargain for Republicans, and take chances separately on the assault weapons ban.

That may have been the only way for the House, but Clinton fretted about the Senate. There he needed sixty votes to overcome a looming filibuster, and a narrowly Democratic bill from the House would make it almost impossible to attract the vital Republican senators. Taking out the assault weapons ban might secure only a Pyrrhic victory, and the president plunged into a complex calculus of personality and tactics. Logically, he thought the ban belonged in the comprehensive crime bill. Symbolically, he knew that removing it would raise a storm about his caving in to the gun lobby—even from those who had not wanted to challenge the NRA in the first place. Politically, he received unflinching notice that House Republican leader Newt Gingrich would enforce party discipline against any resubmitted crime bill, with or without the assault weapons ban. Even so, Gingrich had predicted, "You might be able to do business with a few Republicans." Clinton worried that Gingrich was luring him into a mirage of Republican votes, away from Democrats, but he decided feverishly to pursue both groups. He reviewed some successes and his ultimately failed negotiations with Republican John Kasich of Ohio. He described wrenching talks with liberal Democrats who had voted against the crime bill because of its new provisions for the death penalty. Some opposed all capital punishment. Others believed death sentences were racially skewed. Some did both, like Representative John Lewis of Georgia. Lewis and others ultimately could not bear to stand with the gun lobby against the bill, especially with Clinton holding firm to include the assault weapons ban. A ten-day flurry of deals and torn consciences changed twenty-five votes for a dramatic reversal last Sunday in the House, 235–195.

That left a crush in the Senate before its Labor Day recess. Clinton called the politics there pretty naked, stripped to the flimsiest pretext of concern for merit or substance. The Senate had passed his crime bill overwhelmingly last year, 93–4, with only two Republicans in opposition, but he said Dole and Phil Gramm of Texas were vying for the title of "Mr. No," with their eyes on the Republican presidential nomination in 1996. They attacked anything Clinton was for, from a presumption that any government initiative was a fraudulent curse, and the forty-two Republicans who had supported the 1993 crime bill now branded it full of "pork." Dole claimed to have signed pledges from all his caucus that they would not permit a floor vote, and he demanded first to consider ten "anti-pork" amendments. His ultimatum set off turmoil in the administration, because even one successful amendment would send the whole bill back into the maw of the House for reconciliation. This was a terrible risk. The bill could flounder between a stubborn, partisan Senate and the freshly bruised, divided House, but Senator George Mitchell, the beleaguered Democratic leader, found no other prospect to pry away the five Republican votes needed to avert a filibuster. With deep misgiving, he and Clinton agreed to schedule floor votes on the ten Republican amendments to the crime bill.

Then Dole reversed course. He blocked votes on his own amendments. The crime prevention and drug treatment programs in question were popular, and of minor cost, so that Dole's amendments to kill them would fail. Worse, each would fail so badly that Mitchell could spare extra votes. Mitchell could allow selected Democrats—those in tough reelection races—to vote for some of the "anti-pork" amendments without endangering the bill. So Dole fell back on his filibuster pledge to prevent a vote, said the president, but his switch exposed a dozen moderate Republicans who claimed still to support the overall crime bill if they could get votes on the amendments. Clinton, having pleaded desperately with these senators not to block the measure on pure politics, fumed that he could not persuade William Cohen of Maine to defy his party leadership. He said Bob Packwood was helpless, still in Dole's pocket. He conceded Mark Hatfield of Oregon as a sincere vote against the death penalty. He said his team cornered William Roth of Delaware, who was running against a Democratic prosecutor. Arlen Specter, a former prosecutor in Pennsylvania, broke with Dole, joined by John Chafee of Rhode Island and Jim Jeffords of Vermont. The legislation teetered through the Senate debate.

Clinton saluted those who withstood the withering pressure of the gun lobby. Conceding that his own popularity was "near zero" in Alabama, he reenacted a courageous speech by one of the endangered Southern Democrats. Howell Heflin told his fellow senators he loved guns. He hated to ban any. When he looked down the list of six hundred weapons that were explicitly *not* banned by the bill, Heflin said he recognized familiar names. They were trusty guns. But when he examined the nineteen assault weapons to be outlawed, they were alien. He said nobody in Alabama hunted deer with Tec-9s spraying ammo heavy enough to pulverize an armored vest, and he declared these guns nothing but artillery for "heinous crimes." Clinton merrily imitated his oratorical version of the word "heee-nusss," stretched out with a dramatic shake of the jowls. He said Heflin stood up to the NRA for the crime bill, which gained final victory only yesterday, 61–38. When the president called to thank Kansas's Nancy Kassebaum, the last of six Republicans who provided the necessary margin, she told him her phones were ringing off the hook with angry Kansans insisting the new law was a sham. People simply denied that there would be any new police or prisons. She said there was a lot of hate and distortion out there. "Well, Nancy," Clinton replied, "you know where that came from, don't you?"

The president believed the new law would reduce crime significantly across the United States within a year or two. Yet he seemed resigned to consider it a dodged bullet more than a triumph or promise fulfilled. He said the political culture discounted empirical benefits. The health care bill was a bigger bill, and it was sinking, which kept the focus on his travails. Clinton himself confided that his bipartisan approach to the crime bill would be good coping practice in case Republicans gained seats in the midterm elections ahead. He was preoccupied already with Fidel Castro, who suddenly disgorged daily flotillas with hundreds of Cuban criminals, misfits, and incompetents on rafts bound for Florida. The president noted proudly that it had taken only three days of Castro's miserable expulsions—in the midst of the final strains on the crime bill—to change the U.S. immigration policy that automatically accepted Cubans rescued at sea. By contrast, it had taken more than a year to change the opposite policy of automatic rejection for Haitians. Now the

Coast Guard diverted Cubans and Haitians alike to Guantánamo for immigration hearings.

The new policy provided at least some filter to identify legitimate political refugees, but discouragement alone did not shut down the mass exodus. Seven thousand Cubans had reached Guantánamo only two days ago, inundating its facilities. Frustrated, the president disclosed that he had devised his own communication over the silent wall of nonrecognition between the United States and Cuba. He called Carlos Salinas, the outgoing president of Mexico, with confidential questions for Castro about his hostile initiative. Salinas was "tight with Castro," he said. Back came word that Castro thought the U.S. embargo was ruining his economy. Clinton argued through Salinas that Cuba had access to trade and investment from every other country in the world. Castro's real problem was a dysfunctional economic system and a lost Soviet subsidy. Cuba would be a pauper with or without the U.S. embargo, Clinton insisted, but Salinas said Castro claimed double victory by expelling the dregs of Cuba to punish the United States. The president relayed his final stance. He said he did not "have a hard-on for Castro." He did not want a fight. He was open to exploratory talks and exchanges on the side, but he served notice on the expulsions. Clinton advised Castro to use the weekend's bad weather as an excuse to stop the flotillas, because he would refuse to let Castro dictate the immigration policy of the United States. "I don't care if I have to put fifty thousand Cubans in Guantánamo," he said.

The president was sensitive about the Cuban refugees. We discussed his vivid memories from the Mariel boatlift of 1980, when Clinton was governor. He ascribed his failed bid for reelection more to other factors, but it did not help that Cuban convicts and mental patients had rioted in Arkansas prisons. On another matter, I asked whether Clinton had been tempted to let the Republicans kill the crime bill and then run against them as obstructionists. Well, it was close, he replied, but that was their game, not his. As president, you have to persevere and produce. Besides, having won on the crime bill, he had better footing to go on the offensive against negativity and obstructionism in the off-year elections.

Nancy Hernreich sidled onto the balcony with a reminder that the president had to record tomorrow's radio address before leaving. It was past time. He beckoned me to let him look over my notepad on the way inside, regretting that we did not get to numerous topics great and small: Bosnia, the new Mike Espy scandal, Clinton's forty-eighth birthday and thirtieth high school reunion, or the Federal Reserve's fifth jump in interest rates for the year. And especially Haiti. The U.N. Security Council had approved his resolution authorizing the use of force, and now he was running out of time. He said Congress strongly opposed any intervention to restore Aristide, which would put him in the position of going against the democratic will in his own country to enforce it in someone else's. If I thought the Republicans were maneuvering to pounce on him about crime, where their positions were close, Clinton said, I should imagine what they would do on Haiti. Militarily, the restoration would be an easy day's work, but the aftermath would be full of peril. "We've got to do something," he said, "but it could mean the end of the whole administration."

He asked me to leave tonight's rewound tapes next to his travel grip, but I found the family parlor already emptied. Chelsea came in singing show tunes with a friend from school. Bubbling with anticipation of a holiday together, they selected CDs of Broadway productions for the trip to Martha's Vineyard. Hillary stopped by later, at loose ends, ready to go, and our conversation wandered idly as we waited for Clinton to return from the West Wing. We discussed Chelsea's precocious musical phases and the first lady's collection of frog statues displayed there on shelves—frogs of glass, silver, and ceramics, leaping or in repose, solemn and ridiculous, some in pairs, many with whimsical memories of how they were acquired. She knew a lot about the variety and lore of frogs.

When she asked about the book next to my briefcase, I recommended it—H. R. "Bob" Haldeman's meticulous record of service as chief of staff in the Nixon White House.* There was much in the shorthand diary to verify his image as a robotic functionary who wrote memos on the exact dimensions required for bars of soap at Camp David, but I found his clinical detachment to be surprisingly charming. To me, his

---

* H. R. Haldeman, *The Haldeman Diaries: Inside the Nixon White House*, foreword by Stephen E. Ambrose (New York: Penguin, 1994).

laconic anecdotes brought the petty obsessions of bureaucratic warfare alive with original personality sketches, and Hillary warmed to samples about the gargantuan ego of Henry Kissinger. She said she had heard that Kissinger, noticing looks of awe when his air caravan landed in Egypt, once casually offered a magnificent government helicopter to President Anwar Sadat, saying, "Here, you can have it." The story may be apocryphal, but its affectation rang true as she braced for Kissinger's inescapable presence on Martha's Vineyard. Last year, at a dinner party, he had leaned over to whisper sadly that if the administration's health care reform became law, Kissinger would never again be permitted to see his personal physician. Hillary had rolled her eyes at first, and explained why this was a paranoid concoction, but she said Kissinger merely scowled and growled behind his "game face" of impregnable secret knowledge.

The impasse stuck with her. She said it was interesting, in fact, that she had dreamed about Kissinger only a few nights before. His visage turned suddenly effervescent at a banquet, announcing gladly that his worries were over because the Clinton health care bill was dying. "Oh, no, Dr. Kissinger," she replied coolly. "Don't be sure that it's dead. We'll keep fighting, and there's always light at the end of the tunnel." She said Kissinger blanched, speechless at her deft reminder of the Vietnam War. Famously, he had sighted nonexistent beacons of victory for hawks and doves alike. Now at last, in Hillary's dream, it registered that his strategic designs had spewed carnage and venom for seven needless years. The slogan of a lighted tunnel left Vietnam no less Communist—and no more a threat to Americans—than if Nixon and Kissinger had withdrawn boldly to fulfill their alleged 1968 plan for peace.

"That's what I dreamed," Hillary repeated, lost in thought. "You know, I always get my revenge in dreams, but never in real life." She dispelled this generational burden with a lighter memory of Kissinger before his prominence in government. As a Wellesley student in the mid-1960s, she once ventured to the Harvard campus for a lecture titled "The Future of Europe," and stood afterward in line for a private word. She nodded wide-eyed to me, aware that the story revealed in her a delayed extreme of Girl Scout earnestness, late among peers to rebellion. When her turn came, she noted that Kissinger had not mentioned

East or West Germany at all, and wondered how these central countries might affect the future of Europe. She said the professor looked at her gravely. "I am sorry," he intoned, "but all my thoughts on Germany are classified."

I laughed in waves. This tale was like one of Haldeman's tidy little surprises about Kissinger, except that it captured an early glimpse of two historic figures at once. The first lady raised her hand to attest by scout's honor, smiling, but she also gritted her teeth as though still nettled. It was beyond me to sort out the layers of Vietnam and health care, life and death, reality and dream. Instead, I broached to her my worries about the presidential tapes project. To my knowledge, only she and Nancy Hernreich knew about David Kendall's submission under subpoena. Hillary corrected me. She said Nancy knew the arrangements for our tapes, of course, but not about Kendall's submission. This gave me pause. In that case, the circle was even smaller. I told her that although we were coming to accept Kendall's disclosure as inevitable, someone in the White House—not me—had leaked something to Lloyd Cutler. Suspicion was corrosive, I added, emphasizing my hope that she and the president could trust my commitment to honor them and their secrets now, for the sake of better history.

We went back and forth on the tensions between duty and friendship. She thought Bill would risk a lot to continue the recordings. I told her Kendall had instructed me to avoid Whitewater discussions on tape, lest further disclosures be legally required. Thus, an open-ended subpoena was silencing the President of the United States in his own diary. It meant, for instance, that I could not ask Clinton today about two significant events this month: the sudden dismissal of special prosecutor Robert Fiske, and the quick decision by his replacement to investigate the 1990 governor's race in Arkansas. If we discussed these topics off the tapes, we would waste precious time on presidential words that would be lost to future historians. If we skipped them, we would truncate the record on issues affecting the presidency. Boxed in, I told Hillary what a relief it was just to speak freely. She was privy to the diary's secrets and steeped in constitutional theory. Both seemed to face a pernicious threat from an investigation that had slipped its moorings.

"Of course!" she said emphatically. "That's why I was against a special prosecutor in the first place." She reviewed the internal debates of January, confirming the president's account that she had been a holdout dissenter against the request for a Whitewater special prosecutor. She said she had urged Bill to resist political pressure. Now, as then, she based her view on her formative experience at the House Judiciary Committee during the full-blown constitutional crisis in 1974, when her team of staff lawyers drafted preliminary rules for the inquiry toward Nixon's impeachment. She said much of the raw evidence still remained sealed twenty years later. The committee had narrowed its scope to specific allegations that Nixon had abused presidential powers, adopting careful standards to reduce partisan bickering, and, more important, to confine the dangers inherent to the struggle between the branches of government. Hillary said her husband knew very well that Whitewater had no such framework, but he had resisted her argument that accepting a special prosecutor would be a grave disservice to future presidents. Beyond any calculation of damage or risk to the president himself, she called his yielding a dereliction of duty. Nevertheless, he not only gave in but also compounded the error by signing the Independent Counsel Act of 1994. This law transferred responsibility for special counsels, including Fiske, from the attorney general to a panel of judges appointed by Chief Justice William Rehnquist. Hillary said she had warned that the judges would get rid of Fiske to perpetuate Whitewater.

I was blinking in confusion. Hillary's background analysis seemed shrewd and comforting, but her passionate discourse on judicial politics was foreign to me. Did she really predict that the judges would fire Fiske? She said she did. "In fact," she added, "if you and I had been doing the tape project we once talked about, you'd have me on record saying they would fire Fiske as soon as he began to shut things down. Everybody around here thought I was crazy." Sure enough, Fiske was gone soon after he released an interim finding that Vince Foster had killed himself. Hillary said he was too professional for his intended role. Fiske was a hard-nosed, experienced, Republican prosecutor, trained to investigate and dispose of allegations briskly on the evidence. His replacement, Kenneth Starr, had never prosecuted a single case, but he was an ideologue who would recycle the Foster conspiracy theories and otherwise keep Whitewater going. Hillary said that when she had tried to warn of this danger in the Independent Counsel Act, the White House counsel, Lloyd Cutler, told her he would "eat his hat" if federal judges acted from such blatantly partisan bias.* But when they did, Cutler's shock had no more practical effect than the widespread public criticism.

Hillary said the essential design of checks and balances was fatefully skewed, starting with the absence of a proper mandate. Because Whitewater never pretended to be defined by alleged abuses of presidential power, it could become anything. Because the judges with sole authority to fire Fiske enjoyed lifetime tenure, they faced no legal or political restraint. Because the president himself was targeted, the executive branch of government was broadly disqualified from the process, and the only acceptable orientation from the Clintons was a bared neck of unconditional cooperation. These combined flaws left a heavy responsibility upon the Congress to provide oversight and balance, or at least perspective, but Hillary said the legislators utterly failed. She was especially scornful of the Democrats, and quoted a number of them. Senator Moynihan, for instance, publicly said the Clintons were nice people and he was sure they had nothing to hide. "Why not have an investigation?" he often asked. She said Moynihan skated blithely on the surface, never produced results in Congress, and could not withstand such scrutiny himself for five minutes, living in an apartment secured through his chairmanship of the Pennsylvania Avenue Development Corporation. On top of everything else, she said the congressional Democrats stood by and let Clinton get pilloried for their weakness. Here was a president who had taken on the gun lobby four times in his first two years, plus the "hopeless" deficit, the Middle East, his own allies on NAFTA, the tobacco moguls, and all the health care special interests. How could Democrats be so spineless?

Hillary pursued these points methodically, with greater emphasis on

---

* President Clinton signed the Independent Counsel Reauthorization Act, its official name, on June 30, 1994. Doing so, he wrote in his autobiography ten years later, "drove another nail in my own coffin." On August 5, 1994, the panel of judges headed by David Sentelle of North Carolina dismissed Fiske in favor of Starr, who served more than five years, until October 18, 1999. Lloyd Cutler resigned on August 11, 1994. He did not eat his hat.

logic than personality. Her remark about tapes suggested that Clinton had been correct about her reticence to compile a diary in the White House. She came to a weary pause and looked out the window. "I'm sorry," she said. "The helicopter is cranking up." Downstairs, where a precautionary fleet of emergency vehicles had assembled for the presidential takeoff, I maneuvered around Fire Engine 13 to exit.

THE CLINTONS RETURNED from vacation to host the preview screening of *Baseball*, a new documentary by Ken Burns, on Saturday, September 10. They entered the packed National Theatre to cheers for the president's musical salute, "Ruffles and Flourishes," with accents of tension beneath its festive strains. By freakish coincidence, this series celebrating baseball was previewed (and then aired) during a historic players' strike that had shut down all major league games for a month, with no prospects for a settlement. The opening scenes traced baseball's origins in the sepia-toned pluck of the Civil War era, when Lincoln was shot at a theater only four blocks away. Dan Okrent, who had commissioned my *Life* magazine article about the Clinton inauguration, now sheepishly watched himself on the big screen as a talking head raconteur for baseball. With my wife, Christy, and Becky Okrent, we joined National Security Adviser Tony Lake in what would have been a reunion of friendly families except that Lake's wife had retreated to rural Massachusetts. She thought he was too much married to the job, he said with a twinge of melancholy. Lake recovered his chipper control for calls into the White House Situation Room, applying deadpan military jargon to commandeer updates on the Michigan–Notre Dame football game.

One Haiti question dotted an otherwise social afternoon. A rash of punditry and government news sources now foresaw that President Aristide, if restored to power, would demand to extend his term by at least the three years he had lost in exile. Some insisted that he would never leave voluntarily. Lake perked up when I recalled two or three instances when Aristide had told me it was more important in a fledgling democracy for a president to surrender power than to hold it. Would Aristide say so in writing? I hesitated, fearful that Lake was putting me on. He had a droll way of humoring amateurs before puncturing their illusions, but this time he stayed serious about a mission that soon took me back to the guarded apartment-in-exile, with its French computer keyboard. Aristide reiterated his determination to hand over Haiti's presidential sash on the constitutionally appointed date in 1996, even if he had been restored to office only the day before, and Lake would call the faxed commitment a minor help in calming the opposition. Many commentators scorned or ignored the promise by Aristide, however, assuming blandly that it was a concession wrenched from his dictatorial nature by the full power of the United States.

We walked to a picnic for *Baseball* on the White House South Lawn, where more than a thousand guests mingled under balmy afternoon skies. The Dodworth Saxhorn Band, featuring muttonchops and military tunics, played old-fashioned quadrilles on over-the-shoulder brass horns. President Clinton stepped away from a long receiving line to greet us, which made me uneasy in several respects. Might we offend those waiting behind, or speak too freely about the diary? He glided over trivia and politics alike—reaching a long par-5 in two shots, outmaneuvering the pope at a birth control conference in Cairo. Quickly, before turning back, the president leaned forward with a tight smile. "Christy," he whispered, "you are looking at half the white men in Washington who are for us on Haiti."

CHAPTER TWELVE

HAITI: THE BRINK OF WAR

Wednesday, September 14, 1994

Strange news on the radio distracted my journey to the next session. Experts were hinting that surface-to-air missiles should have destroyed a Cessna 150 before it hit the White House. Security procedures were under review. Meanwhile, analysts dissected today's formal cancellation of the remaining 1994 baseball season. Because of the ongoing strike, there would be no World Series for the first time in ninety years.

These would seem bad omens in retrospect, but not now. My drive down to Washington always carried a buzz of anticipation. Another sudden notice had yanked me from solitary enthrallment with the past into a charged encounter at the White House, storing memories for history's future. The dual missions made me a kind of time traveler. There was no way of telling how the tapes project would evolve or be evaluated, and I never knew what to expect. A sitting president's reactions tended to enliven almost any subject. Would Clinton see a role for himself in the baseball strike?

As I parked near the Truman Balcony, Monday's suicide flight changed from disembodied news speak to spotlighted remains. Yellow tape sealed off an ugly tear in the lawn, aligned with the mangled low limbs on a magnolia tree and burned gouges in the White House wall beneath the family parlor. Frank Corder, a thirty-eight-year-old truck driver distraught by his wife's death from cancer, had found the keys in a Cessna parked at an airfield and managed to kill himself "in a big way," flying on crack cocaine instead of a pilot's license, navigating restricted airspace to crash on one bounce at full forward throttle. He reportedly bore the Clintons no ill will, but would that be a comfort?

Such questions faded in a hurry. President Clinton, breaking our after-hours routine, waved me sharply into the Treaty Room. He was on the phone with Senate majority leader George Mitchell, pleading for time. Could Mitchell hold off for six days? The president said fifteen thousand U.S. troops were moving toward Haiti with final orders, and any halt now inevitably would leak. How binding was the resolution of disapproval? Could it be softened with the promise of a swift report on national security? From Mitchell, Clinton switched lines to thank Senator Chris Dodd for his valiant defense on the Senate floor, "getting beaten up all day" with few allies beyond Tom Harkin of Iowa and Bob Graham of Florida. He indulged in some gallows humor about Davy Crockett at the Alamo. His phone calls jumped between Mitchell and other senators for nearly an hour. Without a respite in sight, I started my recorders on the big desk where I had tested them before our first session. We probably squeezed in our standard introduction about the date and session number, but my list of topics lay untouched. There would be few stories or reflections on this night, when crisis overran the oral history project.

"Nobody is for this," the president moaned. "Nobody." His enemies were gleeful, while his allies were furious or dismayed. He said friends called him "three turns short of loopy," asking why he would focus on Haiti before the off-term elections. If he was so eager to invade, they said, he should have gotten in and out months ago. Well, maybe so, but there were good reasons for delay. The president reenacted arguments with himself, ticking off points emphatically on his long fingers. First, he didn't want to go in alone "like the ugly American." Second, it took months to build support among the wary small countries in our hemisphere. He said representatives from seventeen CARICOM (Caribbean Community) nations were gathering in Washington on Friday to approve the Haiti intervention. Third, it took even longer to win the improbable 12–0 mandate from the U.N. Security Council, with troop commitments from five countries including Canada and France. Fourth, a price of the international coalition was endless coordination. Fifth, his own government was unruly and divided on Haiti. Sixth, while he was beating the diplomatic drum for a new policy to remove Haiti's dictators, what mobilized in public opinion was overwhelming opposition instead of support. "This is a sack of shit," he concluded with disgust. The politics were all wrong. He didn't have his head screwed on right.

His only chance to shift the political balance was a televised address scheduled for tomorrow night. This was news to me. The president recalled comments after our previous sessions, during personal moments off the tapes. "What did you say about how there's no question who's a Haitian and who's not?" he asked. Why was Haiti not like Somalia? How was it different from invading to liberate Cuba? His questions hit me with sudden, flattening weight. They reversed perspective and role to throw me on the witness stand, looking ahead. I scrambled for clarity. In Haiti, there were no borders or tribes in dispute. Unlike Cuba, Haiti had achieved a fair and open expression of popular will in its first national election, certified by international monitors. Our purpose was not to create, impose, or guarantee democracy. The mission was strictly limited—to remove the obstacle of a weak but intimidating military regime. We sought only a first breath for the Haitians, giving them a chance to build their free political institutions.

President Clinton's nods gave way to disappointment, as though he had hoped to hear something new. Already, on this one issue, he said he had forfeited any chance that Colin Powell would support him for reelection in 1996. Powell was telling him that Haiti was a worthless, miserable country governable only by the military—that Aristide was insane and it would be unconscionable to put American soldiers at risk for him. Clinton said Senator Dale Bumpers, his best friend in politics, had just warned of censure and perhaps impeachment. Bumpers thought Clinton would be lucky if fifteen senators stood with him against a resolution of disapproval. Mitchell's count was the same, with a similar margin in the House, and these numbers exposed Clinton to political rebuke even harsher than last year's debacle on homosexual soldiers. Bumpers, trying to be polite, advised that elected Democrats weren't simply running away on an unpopular issue. "He said this time they're hopping mad," said the president. "They feel I'm doing this to *them*. Nobody in

North Dakota or anywhere wants to defend losing Americans in a piss-ant little country like Haiti." Democratic candidates had been running scared already, upset that Whitewater gave them a black eye instead of a boost from the White House, and now Clinton was dumping Haiti on them just before the election.

He paused. My face must have looked queasy and pale. "I'm going to do it anyway," he said gently. "It's the right thing. I still believe in it, but I let the politics get away from me." He fumbled for the correct words to capture his predicament—maximum risk for minimal gain, with less than 10 percent support in some polls. The Haiti venture was off the scales, beyond unwise. It was nonsense and gibberish, incomprehensible to lifelong peers like Bumpers. This alien reception was humiliating for Clinton, who treasured his standing among political professionals.

Reviewing the bureaucratic history, he said Tony Lake had favored invading Haiti for some time. Sandy Berger and Strobe Talbott had come to agree, in part to stop the chronic irritation over Haiti. Christopher at State went along. At the Pentagon, Secretary Perry thought the politics were terrible for Clinton, but his people were dutiful and optimistic about plans that featured quick replacement of the U.S. military by an international peacekeeping force. The president said an academic consensus had muddled along on floating contingencies until a week ago, when he returned from vacation. Suddenly, the internal dynamics shifted to pressure. Congress was threatening to pass resolution to hamstring Clinton before recessing for the fall campaigns, and if it did, the international coalition for Haiti would come unraveled. The national security team said invasion was now or never, and Clinton recoiled from the timing more than the policy. He said he knew it was a mistake to let his advisers maneuver him into a situation where he was racing to invade Haiti ahead of a congressional vote. There was no room for judgment, especially political judgment. "I've never been in anything like this before," said the president. "I keep telling you, nobody is for it."

I asked him what Hillary thought. He said the pell-mell rush to invade was crazy to her. Reacting against the pressure, the lack of options, and his sense of being trapped, she said he was badly served by his foreign policy staff. He said she observed with some suspicion that the chief sponsors of the invasion—Lake, Berger, and Talbott—were the same people who had pushed the ill-fated appointment of Bobby Ray Inman as defense secretary.

On a more positive note, Clinton said political communication with Aristide was improving. He appreciated the message that Aristide considered Haiti's second free election even more important than the first. Some doubters in the United States might be reassured by his commitment to a timely, peaceful transfer of power to an elected successor, and Aristide stated publicly that was a crucial step to institutionalize respect for the vote. Clinton himself welcomed private signals that Aristide could blend guile with principle, like a politician. While he could not openly welcome the invasion of his own country, for instance, Aristide was meeting quietly with Joint Chiefs chairman General John Shalikashvili and others about military logistics. Also, Aristide resisted pressure from reporters to comment on his plans for the Haitian generals who had overthrown him, but he asked American officials confidentially to remove them to exile before Aristide returned to Haiti. "Between you and me, Mr. President," he told Clinton, "I don't want custody of those people." To say he wanted them would raise talk of vengeance. To say otherwise would advertise the fearful, stark frailty of Haiti, where the courts were dysfunctional and no concept of an impartial criminal investigation yet existed. Clinton said he had reports that some three thousand civilian officials, including the mayor of Port-au-Prince, still lived in hiding from military goon squads in Haiti. I said the atrocities were so widespread that Aristide dampened expectations for punishment or justice. He hoped to create public forums for truth telling and amnesty, modeled on the reconciliation commissions in post-apartheid South Africa. Clinton agreed with this modest approach. He hoped to put Aristide in touch with Nelson Mandela.

I tried to stimulate optimism for tomorrow's address to the nation on Haiti. Perhaps the public was cold to intervention because Clinton had not yet stated his case. He could speak to the misgivings across the board. He could explain why oppression and destitution so near our border made Haiti an American problem. He could confront the twin fears from Vietnam—baffling, bloody defeat and moral quicksand—with the pledge of quick multinational action. He might even try to cultivate sympathy and identification with Haitians. I mentioned our intertwined history. Haiti had been America's second largest trading partner before the American Revolution. Napoléon, seeking to fortify his holdings west of the Mississippi River, sent a massive expedition first to subdue the slave revolt in France's richest colony, which then produced 40 percent of the world's sugar—only to have fifty thousand of the eighty thousand French soldiers die in the conflict with Haitian guerrilla armies. The shell-shocked Napoléon abandoned his scheme for a Western empire in 1803, selling the vast Louisiana Territory to Thomas Jefferson. For this historic gift, our thanks to Haiti was a strangling quarantine to protect slavery in the southern United States. Not until 1863, after the Emancipation Proclamation, did Lincoln recognize the world's first black republic. France did worse. She imposed a treaty of reparations that charged Haiti almost twice the price of Louisiana for lost colonial property, including the value of the former slaves themselves. To service this spiteful debt, France expropriated from the Haitian government more than half its annual revenue for the next century.

The president fidgeted. This was when he often quipped that I should stick to writing, which was different from politics. I rushed to say his speech could appeal to American optimism. Haiti was the ultimate underdog. If democracy could take root there, it would nurture hope everywhere from Saudi Arabia to China. It was understandable that people cringed from the downtrodden, and scoffed at their prospects, but the civil rights movement had stunned the world with waves of new freedom. Aristide, like Martin Luther King, was an apostle of nonviolence contending with entrenched power. Haiti aspired to another miracle from the bright side of our heritage.

Clinton said I missed the point. He had been making these arguments for months, and would make them again, but U.S. public opinion was an enormous ship. No presidential speech could turn it around overnight. If he spoke forcefully enough to convert five senators, eighty would still be against him. This meant Haiti was a foregone loser in American politics, and he was trying to limit the damage. It was a great relief when Senator Mitchell called back to say he might be able to postpone a vote on the hostile resolution. Clinton thanked him profusely. "That's all I can ask," he said. "If you can just hold off until Tuesday." There were moves in the works to be on the way out of Haiti by then.

Signing off, he confessed lessons. "We never should have stopped the refugees," the president told Mitchell.

He explained to me that national polls had favored a U.S. invasion of Haiti briefly last summer, when thousands of desperate Haitians were washing up on the shores of Florida. People from Maine to California were frightened and angry. But then Clinton had changed the immigration policy to buy time for sanctions and the international coalition. The Coast Guard started diverting refugees to Guantánamo. "We've got sixteen thousand Haitians there now," said the president, "and nobody wants to go live in those camps." So the exodus dried up, and public concern vanished in the United States. People didn't want to hear about Haiti anymore. Clinton said a congressman berated him just today for trampling on three days of good campaign news, asking, "Can't you think about anything else?" People had cared about the refugees because they were black, and now they don't care because *Haiti* is black. "We've got racism working against us instead of for us," the president fumed. Race alone had accomplished a transformation far beyond his power. "If I just wanted to invade," he added, "the smart thing to do would be to stimulate a big tide of refugees and then march right in without asking Congress at all, saying it threatened national security."

Seeking to lighten the mood, I asked about the blandest topic on my list: his trip on July 23 to Hot Springs High School for the thirtieth reunion of his 1964 graduating class. The president said he had been signing photographs and letters from that event just before I arrived. He remembered names. Fifteen of his 325 classmates had died, including four killed in Vietnam. He talked about who showed up, who teased him for needing a nap, and where a bunch of them went out for barbecue at two in the morning. He said he didn't dance because he was self-conscious, fearful that movie cameras might provide fodder for undignified "Bubba" stories. Mostly he had talked. For three or four minutes, Clinton recalled jovial stories in precise detail. He said several of the incoming reunion letters expressed surprise that he was such a regular person who shared old yarns and gossip instead of pretending to live in a world above them. They told him he had been demonized. They hardly recognized him from the news.

Seized by a notion, Clinton churned with speculation against the

grain. Maybe he was too regular–too much himself. Maybe the press demonized him because he did not play a grand role in the White House.
He applied this theory to the Bob Woodward book, which portrayed him
as messy and indecisive because he struggled with the deficit. Maybe Clinton would have done better to conceal the leadership process until he
could make a pronouncement from on high. Similarly, he never pretended
that progress was certain in Haiti. He did not minimize the dangers of
military intervention or the inherent difficulty of using force to incubate
a democracy. Maybe he should hide during the real process of government. Let someone else have the visible arguments. Then he could come
in from the blue, deliver some sweeping command, and ride off into the
sunset. "My problem is I'm not a good enough actor," declared the president. "I'm not John Wayne." In a cynical era, he said, the press would tear
down any president who did not intimidate them as a military hero.

My questions on other subjects failed to take hold. Clinton's fabled
gift of compartmentalization had deserted him for once, and he seemed
too weary or discouraged to jump between complex worlds. Recurring
gloom dragged us down until he called a halt for the night. While re-
packing my equipment, casting about for relief, I volunteered to work
on his televised address about Haiti. Since he was committed already to
the invasion, I shrugged and said that he might as well try to give a fighting Harry Truman speech–however late or impractical my suggestions
might be. The president smiled benignly. By all means, he said. I should
contact Lake and David Gergen, or send faxes through Nancy Hernreich. He indulged my needy hopes without showing much interest.
Rhetoric was marginal to him, because Americans would be killed even
in a near-perfect military operation. "When the first soldier dies," said
the president, "I'm a dead duck." He walked me out with his usual
thanks, apologizing that we had covered so little ground. Nothing I said
lifted his spirits. "I'll get through this," he told me at the door. "Don't
worry about it. I can always find something else to do to make a living."

Everything was quiet downstairs. Yellow tape still guarded the crash
scene on a serene night, and I felt numb before dictating my notes. "It's
11:08 on September 14," I began. "Now I'm driving out of the South
Lawn with a splitting headache."

At home, I pitched myself into a flurry of phone calls and faxes

about successive drafts for the president's speech. My friend John Shattuck, the assistant secretary of state for human rights, told me of Clinton's visceral reaction to a grisly photo spread of political murders
committed by Haitian goon squads, most often with machetes. He
thought the president was holding firm through political anguish, determined to act. Happily for me, everyone wanted to make the speech
shorter and simpler. One draft seemed to lose focus in generalized sentences about democracy, such as, "Our government has actively promoted and supported that trend." By late morning, I wrote Gergen,
Lake, and Berger that the speech "needs to sharpen around four watch-
words: CLEAR, NEAR, MERE, DEAR." The first three justified the
mission by reduction. The fourth addressed vital but elusive hopes for
new freedom, where easy answers never exist.

Revisions disappeared into the White House, usually without response. For me, the activity itself helped contain stress all through
Thursday, when the likelihood of an invasion registered ominously on
the public airwaves. President Clinton's image came on television that
night from the Oval Office. Trying to calm Americans for the showdown, he vowed that U.S. soldiers would not become the world's police-
men or get bogged down rebuilding the Haitian economy. He announced
that President Aristide, if restored, had pledged to step down when his
term ended. While emphasizing limited objectives and international
support, he denounced the coup leaders for suppressing free elections
with "a horrible intimidation campaign of rape, torture, and mutilation." His address was streamlined and blunt at its heart. "The message
of the United States to the Haitian dictators is clear," said the president.
"Your time is up. Leave now, or we will force you from power."

We stared at our television screen as commentators absorbed daunting prospects for Haiti. The president was risking American lives for a
wisp of freedom in a land of perpetual tyranny and voodoo, the poorest
country in our hemisphere if not the world. My first urge was to reach
through the electric aftermath to Clinton himself. His lonely foreboding
must have intensified since our talk, but thoughts of consolation fell
lame. Any attempt to sound wise would be ridiculous or self-serving.
The outcome hung in the balance, with stakes far exceeding my novice's
grasp on Haiti. Compulsion led me to hazard something flippant and

personal, hoping it might convey truer respect for his leap into the un-known. I called Nancy Hernreich that night to send him a handwritten fax on the private line: "Bravo! If they run you out of town, I promise to supply all your golf balls."

Political and military upheaval consumed the next several days. I did not hear from the president, but I talked by phone with several of the principals including President Aristide and Tony Lake. Aristide was tucked away in Washington while Americans negotiated with Haiti's military regime. Members from both parties in Congress branded him an ingrate for failure to salute the U.S. soldiers landing on his behalf. Some called for a clean sweep to remove Aristide and the dictators in favor of newly installed regents, following a well-worn historical pattern. One front-page story in the *New York Times* whiplashed him as both a tyrant and hapless visionary: "Aristide Adopts a New Role: From Robes-pierre to Gandhi."

Aristide's lawyer, Mildred Trouillot, called me at night in distress. Lake had arrived seeking patience and a statement of support for the military operation. He was in the next room, talking. She said Aristide was inclined to trust him, and in any case was utterly beholden to the United States. Still, it was hard to praise a foreign invasion of your coun-try, especially with so many rumors of deals afoot, and Aristide felt obliged first to represent the faceless Haitians who had given him their votes. All I could recommend was careful public optimism and private candor. No one could read all the colliding forces ahead, but I would vouch for Lake's integrity. He had resigned from the White House staff to protest the escalation of the Vietnam War, when I first knew him. As an observer, from outside the government, I believed he would quit again now if ordered to break his word.

"That's interesting," Trouillot replied. "Mr. Lake has said that twice in the last half-hour. He told President Aristide he would resign before letting him down."

CHAPTER THIRTEEN

YELTSIN AND THE GINGRICH REVOLUTION

Tuesday, October 18, 1994

Thursday, November 10, 1994

John the Doorman whisked me upstairs to the Solarium, where the Clintons were finishing a late dinner with several couples from Arkansas. Attention centered on a mild-looking gentleman of advanced years. The president said he had allowed his old campaign pilot to take control of Air Force One on the flight home today, touching off rowdy jokes from the group about brushes with death at the hands of a retiree cleared only for puddle jumpers. Apparently the man had a reputation for hijinks, such as filing fake flight plans to deceive Clinton's barnstorming rivals. The pilot smiled through the yarns about him. Clinton later told me he was a terminal cancer patient being celebrated with friends and his wife, who suffered from Lou Gehrig's disease.

The president introduced me as an old friend just back from Haiti, and I did my best when invited to share highlights of the mission to restore Aristide as its first elected president. Everything was new for me—my first trip to Andrews Air Force Base, first ride in a government plane, first landing in Haiti, with Secretary of State Christopher, Aristide, and a host of dignitaries at an airfield dotted with dug-in U.S. soldiers. On the runway, Aristide poignantly received welcome-home bouquets from two young boys who lived in an orphanage he had founded as a priest. Because of security threats, our motorcade became a convoy of ten U.S. Black Hawk helicopters–another first for me–flying over a lurid expanse of squatters jammed with garbage and livestock in Cité Soleil (Sun City) to restoration ceremonies for Aristide on the vast lawn of the whitewashed presidential palace. Six hours later, throngs of Haitians still cheered around the perimeter–crying, "Aristide c'est bon ... Democracy c'est bon ... America c'est bon!"–reaching through the fence to clutch any hand in jubilation. Not since the 1944 liberation of Paris, said a military historian attached to the 82nd Airborne Division, did the battle records for his unit contain anything like this month-long welcome.

The Solarium guests nodded politely that Clinton's policy had turned out all right after all. Haiti itself seemed too foreign or exotic for them. They were subdued until I mentioned that the State Department's protocol officer had lamented our congressional delegation as the first single-party group on record for a flag ceremony abroad, confiding that Republican leaders had blocked all requests by their members to attend. This political tidbit stirred the Arkansans. They cussed Republicans for bad manners, and conversation turned to haughty insurance companies until President Clinton excused the two of us shortly after ten o'clock.

Downstairs in the family parlor, he recorded sad observations about the recent downfall of his agriculture secretary, Mike Espy. Leon Panetta recommended that Espy must go, and Clinton agreed. Espy had accepted corporate favors that might have been routine for him in Congress, and may never have traded government influence for football tickets or a free hotel, but the appearance of conflict of interest was ruinous to a cabinet executive. Clinton said the clinching revelation was a $1,200 graduate scholarship awarded to Espy's girlfriend by Tyson Foods, at a time when chicken inspectors under Espy held sway over Tyson's business. Tyson chickens came from Arkansas, as the president well knew from his friend Jim Blair, and all its goodwill scholarships went to Arkansas people–except for this one to Espy's girlfriend up in Maryland. ("Maryland is Perdue country," Clinton said with a sigh.) Worse than fishy, this distant gift derailed a pioneer of special promise. Espy had been the first black Mississippian elected to Congress since

Reconstruction. After the 1990 census, he was the only member of the Congressional Black Caucus to request a *lower* percentage of minority voters in his district, the Fifth. Clinton had been impressed that Espy, when asked why, said a close ethnic balance would make him a better politician. Within two years, as the youngest secretary of agriculture in history, and the first black leader of a sleepy plantation bureaucracy, Espy had eliminated 7,500 unnecessary jobs while pushing through vital reforms in food and farm regulation. The president said he still admired him, and regretted his loss.

Clinton had hosted Russian president Boris Yeltsin for two days at the end of September. By this, their fifth meeting, he said Yeltsin had learned to frame his objectives as requirements for political survival, knowing that Clinton respected such candor among professionals. To beat back the challenge of hard-liners pining for the lost Soviet empire, Yeltsin pressed a need to assert "special influence" over surrounding countries. He called this policy his "Monroesky Doctrine," mimicking James Monroe's historic assertion of U.S. dominance in the Western Hemisphere. Paradoxically, Yeltsin argued that he must look and talk like an emperor to nurture Russia's fledging democracy. He walked a thin line between theatrical poses and reasonable demands.

President Clinton said he tried his best to accommodate Yeltsin's pretensions while advancing a peaceful agenda. He tolerated public claims of benevolent protection in the Baltic nations, for instance, but pushed Yeltsin successfully to remove the last of the occupying Russian troops from there. He endured pronouncements about Russia's right to intervene across borders in conflicts that might compromise her security, but insisted on the need for international observers to make sure any Russian military presence was benign. He contested the sale of covert Russian arms to Islamic fundamentalists in Iran, wrangling over Yeltsin's stance that he must honor contracts negotiated by his predecessor, Mikhail Gorbachev. Clinton tried to prune back Yeltsin's campaign for equal participation in Bosnia, and soothed Russian fears of NATO expansion with hints of eventual membership.

On issue after issue, from nuclear weapons safety to the development of commercial institutions, the president said he pressed Yeltsin to dismantle the old Soviet apparatus. Even in theory, this was a difficult task. Clinton said we did not yet have a name for our period in history. We still defined our "post–Cold War era" by what had ended, and Clinton was prodding scholars and diplomats to help coin a term for the challenges ahead. He said grand labels could be a useful tool in politics. Hoping for something like the age of global democracy, he said no strategic clarity had emerged. Meanwhile, he and Yeltsin navigated a perilous transition on grit and instinct. They made headway with a flurry of deals and submerged their differences in personal rapport. Yeltsin straddled a huge gap between the mighty Soviet image and the threadbare reality of democratic Russia, with unpredictable bluster that made their joint press conferences a spectacle nicknamed "The Bill and Boris Show." (The Russian president entertained White House reporters with his take on the recent summit: "Looking into the future, we tried not to float above this sinful earth.")

Yeltsin did not always cope with the pressure. President Clinton said his chronic escapes into alcohol were far more serious than the cultivated pose of a jolly Russian. They were worrisome for political stability, as only luck had prevented scandal or worse on both nights of this visit. Clinton had received notice of a major predawn security alarm when Secret Service agents discovered Yeltsin alone on Pennsylvania Avenue, dead drunk, clad in his underwear, yelling for a taxi. Yeltsin slurred his words in a loud argument with the baffled agents. He did not want to go back into Blair House, where he was staying. He wanted a taxi to go out for pizza. I asked what became of the standoff. "Well," the president said, shrugging, "he got his pizza."

Amazingly, he said, Yeltsin slipped away again on the second night. Eluding security, he made his way down the back stairs into the Blair House basement, where a building guard mistook him for a drunken intruder. Yeltsin was briefly endangered until converging Russian and American agents sorted out everyone's affiliation. Clinton thought this incident, although contained within Blair House, exposed even greater risk than the pizza quest. When I asked whether he saw fit to counsel Yeltsin personally about the alcohol, the president said no. He was not sure of his place or the consequences. My question about consultations with Mrs. Yeltsin elicited a carefully indirect response. Clinton called her forceful. As a shadow entrepreneur in the old Soviet Union, she built a contracting business that did not officially exist. Naina Yeltsin agonized about her husband, said the president, while remaining fiercely devoted to him.

On Haiti, President Clinton said he was too tired to review the detailed chronology since our September session on the night before his invasion speech. He did remember that Jimmy Carter had called several times before then, volunteering to seek a last-minute truce as a special emissary. Vice President Gore pushed vociferously to reject the offer, stating that Carter had exceeded his mandate in the nuclear negotiations with North Korea, and Secretary of State Christopher supported Gore. He said Carter should not be trusted a second time. Carter, probably anticipating such opposition, recruited Gen. Colin Powell and Senator Sam Nunn to buttress his team, which prompted Clinton to overrule his own national security advisers. He called all three of the freelance diplomats for hurried talks. He told them their prior criticism of his Haiti policy actually would strengthen the bargaining position of the United States, so long as they accepted the terms for their proposed mission. The goal was to secure the certain abdication of the illegal junta in Haiti. An international military expedition, led by the United States, was under way to do so by force if necessary, and Haiti's rulers were vowing to mount a suicidal defense of their homeland. If the Carter team could induce the junta's top three generals to order a stand-down instead, in exchange for a guarantee of safe conduct into exile, Clinton would embrace such a deal to reduce the risk of casualties.

Ahead of the troop carriers, Carter's group flew into Haiti for frenzied negotiations over the weekend of September 17–18. Their status reports echoed the Haitian generals' position that the United States was bluffing—that an invasion had no support in Congress or the press, making it foolhardy to support Aristide, whom they called the real tyrant, against a junta preserving hope for a free Haiti. President Clinton said Powell played the bad guy, telling the generals they may be right about the politics but he knew Clinton and the command structure of the United States. Powell warned the military officers about exactly how much firepower was about to obliterate Haiti's tiny army along with the command headquarters where they were sitting. By Sunday afternoon, a fax from Carter to the White House endorsed the junta's final offer, which was to step down whenever the reconstituted political authorities of Haiti ordered them to do so. Clinton said he rejected these terms as the same vague smokescreen of the past two years. He used the word "clientitis," meaning that Carter had come to sympathize with the Haitian generals, and was pushing the United States on their behalf in a reversal of his proper role. It seemed to Clinton that Carter was smitten with Yannick Cedras, the influential wife of Raoul Cedras, the top Haitian general, to the point of insisting that these pleasant people could not possibly rule by murder and mutilation as alleged in Clinton's speech. The president said Carter resisted instructions to break off talks and leave Haiti. Clinton told Carter he was in danger of being captured. Friction escalated to the point that he threatened to have Carter evacuated against his will. He said he wanted his ass out of there.

Only then did the Haitian generals submit. They agreed to order stacked arms, respect the multinational task force on arrival, and leave Haiti permanently within a month. The president said U.S. intelligence had predicted wrongly that the Haitians would demand large bribes. They held out instead for a tissue of legality by pretending to await the commands of the figurehead civilian they had installed in Aristide's place. This sham consumed more time under duress, after which Carter asked to stay on and welcome the soldiers arriving unopposed. Clinton refused. If the deal went sour, Carter would be a target. If it held, he would be a distracting proconsul. The three negotiators flew back to Washington late Sunday, and Carter, invited to stay over at the White House, called CNN's Judy Woodruff after midnight to arrange an interview the next morning before he reported to Clinton on his mission. This conduct, the president said tersely, was not right.

We skimmed over the month-long occupation since, during which the Haitian army's few rusty big guns were slowly confiscated and the coup leaders in fact did depart. I told Clinton of my introduction to Agency for International Development (AID) administrator Brian Atwood on the memorable trip down to Port-au-Prince. Atwood, while serving among international monitors for Haiti's first trial election in 1987, had been rescued from panicked crowds when the infamous Tonton Macoutes aborted that contest by hacking to death at least thirty-four would-be voters at the polls. Atwood said he had never been so scared in his life—and that over the seven years since, his admiration had grown for the nonviolent tenacity of poor Haitians seeking democracy in the face of such terror. Professionally, he saw a land of human potential trapped in misery for lack of the most basic infrastructure—water, roads, sanitation, electricity—stripped of trees and much of its topsoil. He hoped careful international assistance could spark development toward Aristide's modest goal of "poverty with dignity," building now on the minor miracle of a multinational military operation with zero casualties thus far.

Zero casualties. Clinton frowned when I asked whether this stark empirical success, if not America's traditional sympathy for the underdog, might turn his gamble on Haiti into an asset. He said I still underestimated political resistance. The press was full of retrospective stories about friction between him and his three prominent negotiators, brimming with innuendo that the entire venture had been needless or misguided. He said the current newsweeklies lapped up criticism by Carter as an embarrassment to Clinton, and this pervasive climate left him wryly philosophical. He said he looked bad but felt lucky. To have averted disaster in Haiti brought enormous relief, and it was folly to expect more positive results.

Many of his advisers griped that Jimmy Carter thought he was still president, but Clinton found this criticism too jaundiced. Carter had spoken with restraint at their joint press conference, he allowed, exhibiting a keen political ear. ("The key to our success," Carter told White House reporters, "to the extent it was successful, was the inexorability of the entry of the forces into Haiti.") To Clinton, Carter simply felt that he had earned the right to speak his mind as an international statesman, even about a mission he had accepted for the United States government complete with an Air Force jet. This sense of entitlement could make Carter a thorn, but Clinton thought his value far outweighed the political annoyance. He considered Carter a sterling ex-president. More particularly on Haiti, he said Carter's team had secured a safer landing for U.S. soldiers in a foreign country. This goal alone justified the Carter mission, and success was a bonus. Clinton said he would make the same decision again. He called it a no-brainer.

The president mulled a larger point. He said he still made a lot of mistakes, and his leadership was not what it ought to be, but he did not hesitate to promote other leaders or make them look good. This was a hard lesson, as most politicians do not like rivals and subordinates to shine. Presidents above all tend to hoard credit, but Clinton thought it was smart to give Al Gore choice assignments. And he did not mind sending Colin Powell to Haiti, despite knowing in advance that the sheer visibility would raise Powell's stature as a potential presidential candidate against Clinton in 1996. This is precisely what happened, he said, reeling off poll numbers. The president presented no easy formula for such choices. He valued political loyalty as the essential glue in politics. Still, in conflicts between people and issues, he kept telling himself that positive outcomes for the country generated the truest measure of success.

We covered some personnel transitions and the recent state dinner with South Africa's new president, Nelson Mandela, who had regaled Clinton with tales of his childhood admiration for the American boxer Joe Louis. The president closed with a mordant summary of the 103rd Congress. Both houses had adjourned in deadlock shortly after Senator George Mitchell conceded defeat for the two-year struggle to pass health care reform. Clinton described the political dynamics as vexing but simple. He said the Republicans, upon losing the crime bill in August, had resolved to let nothing else pass. As a unified minority, they blocked routine confirmations, delayed votes, and objected to parliamentary shortcuts. They mounted successful filibusters against sixteen bills and turned abruptly against their own legislation. On "Gridlock Day," October 5, they stopped everything. They postponed the popular Superfund reform for environmental reclamation, and the Senate killed a public disclosure act that had passed 94–6 on a preliminary vote. Clinton said lobbyists cheered Senator Jesse Helms of North Carolina when he left the Senate floor in triumph, having brazenly praised their secretive clout as a shield against meddlesome big government.

Unfortunately, the president concluded, his polls vindicated Republicans so far on the politics. Public majorities favored the legislation they were obstructing, but their scorched-earth tactics played to disgust with Washington as a whole. Clinton said Republicans were betting that voters would hold Democrats responsible for national bickering, anxiety, and stalled hopes. ("Most Americans want us to get out of town," declared Senator John McCain. "They think we have done enough harm.") House leader Newt Gingrich had assembled some 350 Republican congressional candidates to endorse a ten-point "Contract With America" for the fall campaign, promising to end gridlock with tax cuts, term limits, and other curbs on professional politicians. Clinton said he had three weeks left to convince voters that this contract, by milking cynicism, would only produce more of it.

First, he must go to Jordan for the breakthrough toward peace. As our session broke up, a strange note of fatalism crept into his parting words. He said he had addressed many items from his ambitious agenda for the first term. If he could revive a few bills set aside at the end of this Congress, he might not feel compelled to seek a comparable mandate for 1996. In that case, he said, it would matter less whether he got reelected or not.

MY NEXT SUMMONS, on November 10, came only two days after a historic rebuff to President Clinton's leadership. Nowhere in the 1994 elections did a Republican incumbent lose for Congress or governor, while Democrats across the country lost eight senators, eight governors, and fifty-four representatives. Republicans gained control of both legislative chambers in the biggest midterm shift since 1946, the year Clinton was born. At the White House, usher Skip Allen presented an awkward dilemma to me and a tailor from Saks Fifth Avenue. He said our evening appointments were backed up because the president had fallen asleep in the barber's chair and no one could rouse him.

The three of us trooped upstairs to the little beauty salon next to the dining room, across from the family parlor. We took turns trying to wake the president just enough to ascertain his wishes, offering simultaneously to let him sleep. He rallied across the hall to a large pile of suits in his closet, saying some of them needed overnight alterations before his departure to the Philippines. The diminutive tailor agreed, reaching up to make adjustments. Chalk flew from his deft tucks and tugs as the president stepped in and out of trousers, then jackets. Somehow his chest had shrunk, leaving his coats too loose, but he needed more room in the waist because he had not exercised in weeks. Clinton groaned that everything was backward, and the brisk fitting awakened him to gallows humor about an election to match his sagging body. What a great start for a presidency—with five million new jobs, peace initiatives around the world, headed into a third year of unprecedented deficit reduction—until the crash on Tuesday's election. He had tried to grin through the shock in a speech at his alma mater, Georgetown University. Newt Gingrich whipped his ass, he said. You didn't need to be as bright as a tree full of owls to see that. The voters had clubbed him with a two-by-four.

On tape, his energy carried him through his recent travels in the Middle East. Before the peace ceremony in Jordan on October 26, the president had stopped in Egypt to nurse along the Palestinians on their parallel track with Israel. Without much success, he tried to enlist Egyptian president Hosni Mubarak to press his guest, PLO chairman Yasir Arafat, toward greater administrative responsibility in the Palestinian territories. Clinton thought Mubarak and Arafat were temperamental opposites. Mubarak suppressed Islamic fundamentalists ruthlessly, while belittling their danger, and said the Egyptian state, resting on three thousand years of bureaucracy and culture, was largely immune to terror or theocracy. Clinton worried that Mubarak was overconfident. Arafat, by contrast, was obsessed by the threat of religious zealots in Palestine. If he came down too hard on Hamas,* which advocated religious war against Israel, Arafat said he would be out of power himself. Clinton said Arafat resisted talk of practical governance in the territories, which was vital to establish his nation, because he felt out of his element. Arafat preferred to discuss plots, deals, and especially money. In fact, laughed the president, Arafat chafed lately because international assistance flowed to the new Palestinian Authority through official channels, with auditors and accountants. He was much happier with the old spy methods, haggling over bundles of cash.

From Egypt, President Clinton flew to the Wadi Araba in the Great Rift Valley, for the treaty signing at the border between Eilat, Israel, and Aqaba, Jordan. He said the United States, mostly through Secretary of State Christopher, had been more involved in the minutiae of this peace agreement than in the Israeli-Palestinian negotiations. We were the guar-

---

* A foreign-backed group created from the 1987 intifada among Palestinians.

antor for security arrangements and complex transfers—150 square miles of land and 65 million cubic meters of water. The ceremonial platform, outdoors near one of King Hussein's summer palaces, overlooked mountains rising from the Red Sea all the way to Saudi Arabia and Egypt. For Clinton, the only drawback to the spectacular setting was the hot desert sun that beat down through the preliminary speeches. Prime Minister Rabin wore a baseball hat for protection. The president, on the advice of handlers, tried to get by with sun lotion until perspiration carried stinging rivulets into his eyes. Worse, the glare off the treaty parchment blinded him into dizzy spells, and he finally called for sunglasses. "I didn't want to look like a Mafia person up there," he said, "but I was going to ruin the ceremony."

The treaty formally ended forty-six years of war status and nonrecognition between the two countries, since the founding of Israel in 1948. Among other effects, it opened borders that had been permanently sealed with minefields and vast coils of barbed wire, the latter still visible at the Wadi Araba. With the documents finally signed, said the president, strange noises continued in the distance after the cheers and applause died down. They were haunting, ululating cries. King Hussein waved at figures in the distance, and Clinton leaned over to Rabin. "Yitzhak, who are those people?" he asked, and he imitated the reply with an affectionately heavy accent. "Those are the Bedouin," growled Rabin. "Some are ours. Some are theirs. They live on opposite sides of the border, many from the same family. For years they've been getting together only at night. Now they can come and go as they will, and they are very happy."

President Clinton addressed the Jordanian parliament and the Israeli Knesset on the historic significance of this second peace treaty, after Egypt, with Israel's Arab neighbors. ("We respect Islam," he told the Jordanian legislators to thunderous applause, adding that every morning across the United States, "millions of our own citizens answer the call to Muslim prayer.") Then he pursued negotiations on another front with President Asad of Syria. In Damascus, visiting a palace built for Asad by a Lebanese billionaire, the president said he felt Asad's extraordinary dominance. Asad controlled everything, having long since imposed his will on a country of simmering ethnic differences. Syria had one of the lowest crime rates in the world, and this manicured order helped explain why Asad was impatient with the raucous, ever-shifting democracy in Israel and the United States. He thought the elusive treaty with Israel would be a simple swap of land for peace on the Golan Heights, which should take about three minutes. He could not understand the political constraints of Israeli leaders, or why their biblical forebears under Moses had argued and feuded for forty years in the wilderness.

The Syrian-Israeli negotiations, said Clinton, were stuck somewhere between three minutes and forty years. In their private talks, when he pressed for a condemnation of terrorism, Asad replied that he opposed the killing of innocent civilians anywhere, anytime, and they rehearsed answers for the huge contingent of international reporters traveling with Clinton. At a joint press conference, Asad managed to keep his composure until the second question, from Rita Braver of CBS News. Clinton told me it amounted to, "Are you still a terrorist?"* Asad exploded with rage to deny that he and Clinton had even discussed terrorism, which he called a pretext for slander against Syria. His outburst obliged Clinton to split hairs between truth and a public rebuke, explaining hastily that Asad meant they did not discuss specific charges of terrorism by the Syrian regime. Afterward, citing enormous stakes for the Middle East, he pleaded with reporters not to emphasize this contradiction. The president wished he had coached Asad more aggressively in advance. He should have prepared him for blunt, snippy, and hostile questions, recognizing that he was accustomed to fawning indulgence. "His press conferences are like Castro's."

Despite its stormy conclusion, the president considered the Damascus summit a step forward. Asad still wanted to make peace with Israel before he died. Neither he nor his wife, Anisah, seemed to have much confidence that their son Bashar, the eye doctor and newly designated heir, would have the strength to do so. Clinton, for his part, stressed the urgency of an Israel-Syria treaty to build some sort of stable structure for

---

* The official transcript preserves Braver's actual questions to President Asad: "Did you in this discussion promise not to sponsor terrorism anymore? Did you acknowledge that you, in fact, do? And can you tell us what the Syrian view is of terrorist activities?"

the Middle East before either Iraq or Iran attacked the whole region. Both those large countries were shaky beneath the surface, menaced by poverty, sectarian divisions, and conflict between modernists and mullahs, but the president thought Iran was more likely to boil over or disintegrate.

A month before, on October 7, Iraq's president, Saddam Hussein, had sent troops suddenly toward the border with Kuwait in a virtual replay of the Gulf War, spreading shock and disbelief that he would challenge the world with the bulk of his army killed or disabled. The Iraqis backed down within days, once the United States deployed a rapid strike force of Marines, missiles, and 350 new fighter planes with the *George Washington* Carrier Strike Group. Intelligence analysts were still debating Saddam's mysterious, futile maneuver, and one school held that he had misinterpreted U.S. policy in Haiti as an exploitable aversion to military conflict. This notion amused the president. "I guess he figured that if he mounted a provocation," he remarked, "I would send Jimmy Carter over there to make a deal, and he could wheedle something out of us."

The president strangely fell asleep again—in mid-sentence, while speaking on a topic that engaged him. Alarmed, and puzzled, I offered to stop our session. It was unclear whether or not Clinton heard me, but he started awake and pushed doggedly into his postmortem on the mid term elections.

A foul omen greeted his return from the Middle East. On Saturday afternoon, October 29, a disturbed man pulled a Chinese SKS rifle from beneath his trench coat and fired twenty-seven shots wildly through the fence along Pennsylvania Avenue. Seven rounds hit the White House before citizens and agents subdued Francisco Duran, a twenty-six-year-old native of New Mexico. Duran, apparently on a loner's quest to punish Clinton for banning assault weapons, had driven from Colorado with his rifle, literature from the anti-government militia movement, and a bumper sticker that mocked the prophet Isaiah's vision of peace: "Those who beat their guns into plows will plow for those who don't."*

The president said he had been here in the parlor room when the

---

* A trial jury in 1995 convicted Duran on multiple charges, including the attempted murder of a U.S. president. He received a forty-year sentence.

shots rang out, and he heard the muffled sound of at least two bullets striking the stucco—or whatever the north wall of the White House is made of—before agents rushed in to surround him, talking on their radios. He was sorry for the Secret Service, which endured a barrage of criticism for this attack on top of the suicide plane crash. Clinton never sensed physical danger, but, ironically, he felt very much threatened politically by gun zealots like Duran. In Tuesday's elections, the National Rifle Association had picked off at least twenty incumbent members of Congress on gun issues alone. This was a chilling feat. The president said the NRA stealthily harvested votes from paranoia. "If you don't smoke them out and confront them," he ruefully observed, "they'll cut you to death."

Clinton claimed his share of blame for the historic midterm debacle. There were too many little scandals. Health care had failed. He said several times that he had pushed change too rapidly for voters to digest, and he confessed a key error most recently in the decision not to deliver a televised address on his return from abroad. There was important news other than the Israel-Jordan peace treaty and the face-down of Saddam Hussein. North Korea had just signed an agreement to surrender eight thousand nuclear fuel rods and accept international inspection of its nuclear facilities. These foreign successes elevated Clinton's approval rates above either party in Congress. Each was complex. To explain them to the nation was certainly a political opportunity, and arguably a duty, but the president decided that he must choose between statesmanship and campaigning. Trying to do both seemed tawdry. With only ten days left before the election, it might backfire if he followed a presidential address with partisan stump speeches. So Clinton omitted his speech to hit the campaign trail.

The president called this a mistake on every front. The bloom quickly wore off the foreign triumphs for lack of attention. Why should voters appreciate great stakes in North Korea or the Middle East when the president himself preferred to discuss a congressional race in Ohio? Worse, he said, the Democratic candidates steadfastly refused to unite behind a campaign message. Blaming him for their unpopularity, they all demanded to tailor their own individual campaigns, but their disparate slogans seemed puny against Gingrich's unified call for smaller government and lower taxes. Clinton said he never should have let the Democratic National Committee pass along the money he raised to individual candidates. Most of them wasted it on poorly conceived ideas, and he had sensed momentum fading toward the end. If the campaign had lasted any longer, he thought, the Republicans would have gained even more seats.

Again and again, he fell asleep while talking. His irises rolled up beneath his eyelids and he would be gone for ten or fifteen seconds. I stopped the tapes on my own initiative, saying he needed to rest, but he perked up each time with more theories on the calamity. The Democrats had no centralized message to match the Republicans. Their slogan from campaign consultant Paul Begala—that the nation must go forward instead of backward—did not wash. Gingrich was power-mad, and would make many mistakes. The voters were hurting, and they wanted their government to hurt, too. ("Well, I'm sure hurting now," he said.) Republicans were channeling widespread anxiety into resentment of minorities, cities, and government. He would have to counterpunch from the center.

The president asked me what I thought of his press appearances since the election. There was a plaintive tone of uncertainty, mixed with political gloom. He kept talking even as I left.

On the way home, I began my dictation by noting that it was scary to see him slip in and out of sudden trances as though hypnotized, or suffering from narcolepsy. "Still combative," I said. "Still trying to figure out what happened in the election, where the mistakes were. But I think fragile and vulnerable in his exhaustion."

CHAPTER FOURTEEN

TIRADES:
"I REALLY LET
THEM HAVE IT"

Wednesday, November 30, 1994

Christmas Movie
Sunday, December 25, 1994

Sunday, January 1, 1995

These grim political themes continued three weeks later. President Clinton, escorting our mutual friend Eli Segal, stopped by the Yellow Oval Room, where I had been deposited to wait. Eli, the founding director of Clinton's national service program for young people—AmeriCorps—reminded Clinton that he and I had met straight out of graduate school in a low-stakes poker game of political activists with more ambition than money. By convention, no one mentioned our respective business with the president. We talked warmly of old times and our children. I passed along a message from Chelsea that she wanted a moment with her father whenever he could slip away. The president summarized historic artifacts and architecture like a gracious tour guide, telling Eli that this was President Franklin Roosevelt's favorite room in the White House. Its bank of rounded windows looked down across the Mall to the tidal basin of the Potomac River, where FDR had built the Jefferson Memorial so that he could gaze upon it from here.

Clinton visited Chelsea and changed into blue jeans before the two of us sat down to work in the parlor. Much disgusted, he said the Democratic National Committee had blown even more than his entire $80 million war chest to lose all those seats in the midterm elections. Its leaders also ran up substantial debts, he was discovering, so that now, to repair the party for 1996, he must ask fund-raiser Eli Segal to leave his dream job at least six months early. Clinton said his own personal finances looked no better. With Republicans announcing plans for Whitewater hearings when they took over congressional committees in January, he fully expected the family legal bills to exceed $2 million soon. Incredibly, he fumed, the new special prosecutor wanted to reinvestigate the Vince Foster suicide while foraging through the history of a failed S&L owned by Jim and Susan McDougal, his former partners in the Whitewater development. Ken Starr was about to immunize Susan McDougal, who was penniless in distress, squeezing her to make accusations under threat of jail.

The president called Starr's tactics a diversion in search of a crime. He said the Republicans were doing the same thing to Mike Espy. Not content with driving him from the cabinet, they had established another special prosecutor who was hiring no fewer than thirty-three assistants to subpoena the backlist of plaintiffs from employment disputes at Tyson Foods. Blatantly, said Clinton, they were trolling for people angry enough with the company to say something bad about Espy. This was a dragnet worthy of Joe McCarthy, built on a scholarship peccadillo, playing to cynicism rather than fear. He said they would keep going until they found something.

This tirade seemed tamer than ones from prior sessions. There was less ranting, with a resigned air and moments of wonkish reflection. President Clinton said Whitewater trivialized vital issues still pending from the S&L collapse of the 1980s. The Reagan and Bush administrations, by deregulating financial businesses while leaving public guarantees intact, essentially had let bankers gamble freely with several hundred billion dollars of the taxpayers' money. He said the McDougal S&L accounted for only 8 percent of bankruptcy failure from the state of Arkansas, which in turn was less than one percent of losses charged to the public nationwide. I asked what he meant. Was he shifting the question from guilt to proportion, saying Whitewater was overblown? No, Clinton meant Whitewater was a snipe hunt—we were chasing stray hillbillies to taint a Democratic president.

On tape, he managed to highlight upbeat, personal aspects of recent travels in the Pacific. He took both of his White House valets with him, so they could see their Filipino families for the first time in years. After his flight dropped low over the island of Corregidor into Manila Bay, he stayed in a hotel suite draped with medals and ribbons bestowed on General Douglas MacArthur, donated by his widow. In Jakarta, he visited the world's largest Muslim mosque, with five prayer levels spreading beneath a huge dome forty-five meters in diameter. He told stories about the provenance and cultural lore of many new gifts of state strewn around us in the parlor, including a carved wooden mask from Indonesia. Although his summit with Chinese president Jiang Zemin reached another opaque standoff, he seemed less flustered as he surveyed for openings on trade and human rights. His memories of Suharto, Indonesia's famously authoritarian leader, betrayed a twinge of longing for the ease with which the old general flicked aside troublesome questions from the press, especially about violent repression in East Timor. Clinton anticipated post-Suharto Indonesia as a strategic crossroads, like Turkey in the West. On the way home, he had mingled affably with soldiers at Alaska's Elmendorf Air Force Base, including one who wore a T-shirt from a school Clinton had founded in Arkansas. The president noted the alluring effect of military postings on settlement patterns in Alaska, and reviewed his dinner in an Anchorage restaurant owned by the new governor, Tony Knowles, an upstart Democrat with an excellent recipe for reindeer stew.

His energy lapsed, matching the content of his stories. On the first day of vacation in Hawaii, he said he had played twenty-seven holes of golf like a walking zombie, dead tired, wearing a blister through his glove. He played eighteen holes the second day before collapsing on the third with Hillary staring from the porch of their villa as gale force winds howled constantly ashore from the Pacific. At home again, Clinton pitched back into consultations with experts about what had gone wrong in the midterm elections. Citing rafts of statistics, he said there really was an empirical base for the political phenomenon of the "angry white

male." Incomes for breadwinners without a college education had fallen
14 percent over the past decade. In the last year alone, the median wage
had dropped one percent, even though the average was rising. This, he
explained, was because the rich few pulled the average up with enormous gains. A typical CEO in 1970 had commanded the combined
salary of thirty-five employees; now it took 150 workers to match the
average boss. If you looked back over the sweep of the twentieth century,
he said—from the world wars and the Depression through the civil rights
movement—the indices of middle-class health and security were vastly
improved, but people no longer *felt* a personal stake in their government. Clinton's economic recovery plan, with its five million new jobs
created already, seemed abstract. Even white-collar managers were insecure in a changing economy.

He did not believe the Republicans were a lasting majority, because
their "Contract With America" was negative and contradictory. Many
Republicans themselves did not support the promised legislation, he
said, but they were schooled in its rhetoric. Gingrich had crisp slogans
you could say in ten seconds, and the president asked whether I had
tried my hand to suggest any competitive ideas for him. I said yes, reaching for my briefcase, flattered that he remembered asking. He responded
favorably to one of five or six quick notions—how Americans needed a
federal government that was "lean but not mean"—weighing various advantages and disadvantages out loud. Then he asked whether I thought
Pennsylvania senator Harris Wofford, a Democratic casualty of the recent elections, would make a good replacement for Eli Segal at Ameri-
Corps. Almost certainly, I replied. Wofford's career dedication made
him a good fit, but I did not know if he had Eli's management skills.
Clinton nodded. What about Dr. Joycelyn Elders, his surgeon general
from Arkansas? She had been everybody's wise mama until her comment that masturbation for teenagers was safer than intercourse and
more realistic than abstinence. Should he replace her? I squirmed—
probably so.

Should he fire CIA director James Woolsey? Still hesitating, I said
yes. Who should replace Woolsey? I drew a blank, and the president
smiled. He knew of my belief that we had corrupted the word "intelligence" in our postwar devotion to spies. "Not your field, eh?" Clinton

said gently. He turned to the cabinet feud over a plan by Labor Secretary Robert Reich to attack "corporate welfare." Treasury Secretary Lloyd Bentsen, while endorsing most of its provisions, objected to the emphasis on division and punishment. He favored language about opportunity, seeking to kick-start a national debate on the proper balance between public and private needs. Reich said politics demanded villains. The Republicans would ridicule any public need except military spending, he argued, and make mincemeat of Bentsen's fair-minded approach. I sided generally with Bentsen.

Clinton cross-examined me, debating changes. A complicating nuance for him was that Bentsen was about to leave the cabinet, whereas Reich wanted to stay.* For me, flattery gave way to worries about a shift in my role. Would future historians consider my opinions intrusive and impertinent? Or would they find it instructive that the president groped for answers from his oral historian? Were these clues to his state of mind more important than memories for the record?

When I steered him back to the calendar, with questions about the sixth hike in interest rates so far this year, the president said Alan Greenspan of the Federal Reserve adjusted rates to keep a "natural" unemployment rate of 6 percent. Clinton cited global price competition and the decline of unions to argue that unemployment could go lower without touching off inflation. He thought stale economic theory was punishing minimum wage workers, 40 percent of whom were the sole support for families, but he lobbied Greenspan carefully because of the Fed's insulated power. For different reasons, the president said he muted his response to a televised attack from Senator Jesse Helms, who called Clinton "unfit" to command the armed forces. Helms was a significant national figure—the incoming chair of the Foreign Relations Committee—and to denounce him from the White House would magnify conduct suited to a banana republic.

---

* On December 6, 1994, a week after our session, news leaked that President Clinton chose Robert Rubin, formerly of Goldman Sachs, to succeed Bentsen as secretary of the treasury. Three days later, the White House announced the resignation of Surgeon General Elders. CIA director Woolsey resigned on December 28. Harris Wofford replaced Eli Segal at AmeriCorps in July 1995.

Clinton told me he appreciated General Shalikashvili of the Joint Chiefs, along with many leading newspapers, for statements of support, but Helms defiantly escalated the rhetorical assault. He warned that President Clinton would not be safe on any military base in North Carolina.* The president shrugged off the ominous barb, even professing a touch of fondness for "ol' Jesse." Incredulous, I pressed him about false bravado. Surely, Helms violated some taboo in civil-military relations, if not basic decorum. His veiled threat, I said, delivered on the anniversary of President Kennedy's assassination, could be construed as incitement to crackpots or even military revolt. Clinton insisted that it was no worse than Whitewater—personal contempt, impervious to political balance or constitutional norms. He said insult was their program, and Helms was just more honest than his fellow Republicans.

The president fondly remembered one particular golf hole in Hawaii. On the tee, his host told him not to worry about a big gully some three hundred yards down the fairway, because no one reached it. But Clinton did, to his immense satisfaction. Like any mediocre, macho golfer, he chuckled, he preferred to hit the ball a long way, even into a ditch, rather than play with intelligent restraint. He was already happy before his shot from the gully somehow landed on the green and he sank a seventy-five-foot putt for birdie. Three successive marvels raised delirious joy. He said he was going to live off the story for months. As he recounted his approach to each shot, and the vivid topography, I found myself conflicted. Clinton's digression crowded out important topics at a moment of crisis in his presidency, and historians might censure us both for boyish escape. On the other hand, his tonics and diversions were part of the record, too. He was running on nervous fumes, clearly drained, and I myself was telling him that he needed rest. We had conflicting roles. Why shouldn't he talk about golf?

The president returned briefly to my list. On budgets, he said the ascendant Republican leaders warned that they would try to eliminate not only whole programs, like AmeriCorps, but whole departments, like Education. On Bosnia, he said a precarious truce seemed to be falling

---

* "Mr. Clinton better watch out if he comes down here," Helms told the *Raleigh News & Observer*. "He'd better have a bodyguard."

apart in the week since his return from Asia. With separatist Serb armies converging on the Muslim town of Bihac, a designated hospital zone west of Sarajevo, the peacekeeping nations remained tangled in paralysis. Logistical disputes foiled protective air strikes. The Russians demanded parity. To justify inaction, some U.N. commanders accepted claims that the Bosnians were shelling their own towns in a play for international sympathy. Clinton thought the Balkan war would be judged a crucial failure for the United Nations and a transitional test for NATO. He said the hardest part now was to endure the hypocrisy of the British and French, who used their troops on the ground as a shield to preside over the slow dismemberment of Bosnia. Most of their leaders only pretended to care about the survival of a Muslim nation. He said the preeminent strategic interest of the United States was to keep the war from spreading.

The subject visibly wore him down. "I'm sorry, I'm giving out," he said, calling a halt. While the tapes rewound, the president mused again about a government that would be "lean but not mean." He asked to keep my little suggestion sheet.

THERE WAS CONSIDERABLE debate in my family about taking the bird feeder to Washington on Christmas night. Could we get it through security in the back of our pickup? If so, what then? What were the risks of damage and embarrassment? Would either Clinton have the slightest chance or inclination to look? Our two children, Macy and Franklin, voted for adventure in the jump seats. I decided the president could use some levity. Christy made me promise to temper expectations, knowing how proud I was of my dad's woodcraft. It had taken him many months to build a White House of impressive architectural detail, with feeding perches around a seed trough under the North Portico.

We joined about twenty guests in the Family Theater to watch a new film, *Little Women*, featuring Winona Ryder and a child actress named Kirsten Dunst. By serendipity, walking afterward to a reception, President Clinton greeted the four of us as we passed the diplomatic entrance, and he agreed to duck away for the surprise parked just outside under the Truman Balcony, where he made a big, satisfying fuss over the bird feeder, patted the pickup, and posed for photos—all within a minute or two. Back inside, Hillary asked Macy about her new high school. When the Clintons confided that eleven-year-old Franklin seemed to walk normally, we said he was blessed with recovery almost three years into his hip disease, such that he was resuming noncontact sports. Yearning to teach him golf, I bemoaned my once-a-year game with its incurable slice, and this remark produced a spontaneous lesson. The president demonstrated his stance, grip, and address to the ball, instructing me to rotate my right hand a quarter-turn clockwise on the imaginary club, then to draw the head back slowly and low along the hallway floor outside the China Room. Ignoring the usual clamor around him, he coached me through several practice swings. Christy, while later confessing some discomfort herself, said Franklin stared at us in unabashed wonder.

THE RECENT ELECTION disaster registered with force a week later, on New Year's night, 1995. Half our three-hour session took place off the tapes, because the president wanted to vent about Whitewater and persecution, which was forbidden to us by his lawyers, while he labored out loud to find his bearings. Again, as of late, he reversed our practice by asking me questions about political dilemmas. I felt a citizen's duty to respond forthrightly to any president, and beyond that a growing commitment to him, but there were drawbacks. Turning off the tape made me a sounding board, counselor, or simply a companion. The shift seemed glamorous at times, but it was also curious—and worrisome—to feel a president so smart grasping for amateur opinions, including mine. At a minimum, our unrecorded consultations subtracted from the record we sought to preserve in the president's own words. They exposed our history project to the friction of presidential politics. On this night, my reactions caused or released in Clinton a towering rage that left me shaken in my driveway at 1:43 on the morning of January 2, finishing dictation. "It was not fun," I said.

We began innocently enough with transitions before the new Congress convened in January. He described at some length his choice to replace the seasoned judgment and personal trust of Lloyd Bentsen at Treasury with the renowned brainpower of Wall Street's Robert Rubin. His choice of Representative Dan Glickman to replace Espy at Agriculture was more esoteric and abstract to me, centered in geography. Glickman was a Democrat from Kansas, home of the incoming Republican chair of the Agriculture Committee, and his ties might salvage the agriculture appropriations bill. ("I'm never going to carry Kansas, anyway," said Clinton.) The president gave a mixed review of the departing White House press secretary, Dee Dee Myers. She was skillful, loyal, and discreet—not given to the immature leaks that permeated his White House staff. Even so, Clinton resolved that a hip young female projected the wrong image, and he disputed news stories that suggested he had implored her to stay on. Instead, they made a clean break once she declined transfer to another job. The president said he was happy so far with the grayer tone of his new spokesman, Mike McCurry.

McCurry reminded him of a nettlesome issue. Should he grant a last-minute interview to *Washington Post* reporter David Maraniss for his forthcoming biography of Clinton, *First in His Class*? He seemed irritated with his staff. Stephanopoulos and Mark Gearan in particular had blocked the request, but Clinton said he could not coax out of them a good reason. They thought he should save everything for his own autobiography, and they told him the only way for a journalist to get ahead was to crap on the president. Clinton thought the latter was a dead-end formula, playing to his paranoia. Did I know Maraniss? Not well, I replied, but I had talked with him myself about my memories of Clinton in the 1972 campaign—several times, in fact, because he seemed fairminded. It galled me that I had forgotten where our apartment was in Austin. I could picture the place but not the address. The president said Hillary would know. We reminisced a little about Texas, and he asked whether I would call Maraniss for him if needed. Of course. He said he was consulting McCurry, and picked up the phone just long enough to ask a White House operator to find him.

The president reviewed his surprisingly lopsided Senate victory, 76–24, merging ad hoc trade agreements into a comprehensive new World Trade Organization. Clinton said this bill was bigger for the economy than NAFTA, which had been a nastier fight. Of his quick visit to Budapest, Clinton said Yeltsin had "acted up" again on NATO at a bad time, with Europe a mess of seething divisions over Bosnia. "I had to use all my discipline not to react," he confessed, so he could shepherd Yeltsin through more important business on nuclear disarmament in

Ukraine. He said this chapter of the Yeltsin chronicles was like a visit to the dentist.

More positively, the president sketched the first-anniversary celebrations for the repair of the Hubble space telescope. He seemed to know technical terms for the maddening foul-ups—fluttering gyroscopes, lenses ground microns too thin—but he said the success already revolutionized our database for studying the cosmos, with crystal clear photographs, free of atmospheric obstruction, peering thousands of light-years into space. On recent gun stories, Clinton dimly recalled being awakened before dawn when another bullet struck the White House on December 18—this time a 9mm round, nearly spent, one of four apparently fired from somewhere on the Mall. He reacted more effusively to the lone rifleman who walked from one Boston abortion clinic to another on December 30, killing two receptionists, wounding five others, and then disappeared.* Clinton said Rush Limbaugh and other journalists, by demonizing opponents, excused and even egged on their zealots. I prepared for another tangent on the right-wing press, but he circled elsewhere. He said many sincere, nonviolent opponents of abortion—Pentecostals and Catholics, among others of conscience—would be tarred unfairly with this crazed rifleman, just as the other side portrayed every abortion as the work of murderous fiends. Clinton expounded against hate mongering, calling it both the essence and negation of politics, unresolved in tension. Later, in dictation, I regretted that my memory was not good enough to capture his burst of eloquent language on these themes.

The mood darkened over his two major speeches in response to the midterm elections. He said speechwriter Don Baer wrote several drafts for a televised address, titled "The Middle Class Bill of Rights," but Clinton didn't like any of them. He said he wound up writing most of the speech himself. There was "significant disagreement" among his policy advisers over its central proposals for tax cuts, centered on education. Some people opposed them all, he said. They called the initiative

---

* John Salvi III was later captured, convicted, and sentenced to two life terms. He committed suicide in prison on November 29, 1996.

a repudiation of his commitment to fiscal responsibility, and he had to override them.

We turned to his second speech, an overtly partisan and political address at the Democratic Leadership Council (DLC). This was a centrist group Clinton had helped to create. Its leaders were his key allies, so familiar to him that I missed a number of his shorthand references to inside disputes. The speech itself was full of folksy humor. Still, there was a bristling tension over responsibility for the election losses. The president said he understood why DLC leader Dave McCurdy was angry. Less than four years ago, many people thought the popular Oklahoma congressman should run for president instead of Clinton, and now McCurdy was finished, trounced in a race for the Senate. Clinton's unpopularity in Oklahoma hurt, he conceded, but McCurdy never asked his advice on whether to run and never stood up to fight on anything. He lost meekly to a primitive campaign by James Inhofe on what the president called "God, gays, and guns." Now McCurdy blamed Clinton so openly that the president couldn't give him a consolation job. All he could do with McCurdy was "string him up," as Vernon Jordan put it. Democrats tended to carry on their feuds in public, Clinton groaned, and he had dressed down the DLC leaders after the event. He reminded them that he already had enacted most of the DLC platform—from deficit reduction to the "motor-voter" law—but all they did was "suck lemons." He called them ingrates and sunshine patriots. He said they hid their light under a bushel, afraid of being called liberals. "I really let them have it," said the president.

Worked up, he told me to stop the tapes. A long update on new Whitewater subpoenas and the Espy dragnet at Tyson Foods gave way to hard choices ahead. Who should succeed the able but weary Warren Christopher as secretary of state? Preemptively, he told me not to think of recommending Colin Powell. Clinton knew Powell would refuse, preserving his option to run against him for president in 1996, probably as an independent. I said I did not really know the potential successors, but I endorsed Madeleine Albright for her ability to speak articulately in public. She might raise the profile of foreign policy, answering a deficiency among the national security advisers. Clinton nodded. What about the Democratic National Committee? Fumbling, I recommended

Senator Chris Dodd for the same reason. He was a well-spoken, fair-minded fighter, with the ability to confront irrational stampedes like Whitewater. When the president asked if I had any thoughts for general public themes, as we had discussed last time, I gave him a half-page memo on three words—"simplify, fix, affirm"—applied both to government and democratic principles. This prescription certainly applied to the successful repair of the Hubble telescope, he said, playing with the ideas before he set the memo aside. I volunteered a briefing on baseball from my contacts in Baltimore, warning that the season ahead was in jeopardy now, with both sides locked in the spiraling impasse that had ruined the 1994 World Series. The owners had just implemented a unilateral salary cap, whereupon the players vowed to sit out another season for their freedom to bargain. Already, spring training cities in Florida and Arizona felt hints of catastrophic loss from lost tourism. The president had few options, I said, but nobody else seemed able to jar the antagonists from mutual destruction.

The phone rang somewhere in these exchanges. Listening, his face fell into exaggerated calm. "No, Mr. McCurry *was* the State Department spokesman," he corrected. "Now he's the White House press secretary." He hung up, disgusted over the hapless search, and ridiculed legends about magically swift White House operators who could track down a flea in the desert. "It's all a pack of lies," said Clinton.

The president returned to his Middle Class Bill of Rights. Having sensed my misgivings, he pressed for my true reaction. Euphemistically, I said it did not strike me as one of his better efforts. It felt gimmicky, geared to short-run politics. When he persisted, I said the speech seemed transparently to imitate the Republicans in giving away tax cuts. Instead of reminding voters that they must secure the future, he invited them to forget his historic anti-deficit achievement and fleece their heirs some more. The president baited me—did I mean he was pandering? I said, well, it was a sugar-daddy speech. He was seducing voters to feel good by running down the government.

He erupted in rebuttal. If the voters cared so much about the future, why did they throw out the first people who really grappled with the deficit? Why did they elect a whole phalanx of sugar-daddy Republicans? The voters were sovereign, Clinton declared. They were the boss. He would give them what they wanted, even if it was stupid.

Clinton calmed into simmering reflection, as was his habit. He said November's harsh rejection at the polls opened a new angle on his political mistakes. He should have postponed the quest for health care reform until he hammered home public appreciation for the 1993 budget reform package–telling people over and over that it reduced taxes on most Americans, and increased them only for the wealthiest one percent in order to shore up the whole country's long-term fiscal strength. By neglecting that educational task through the year-long push for health care reform, Clinton said he allowed the Republicans to lump both initiatives together as nothing but "big government" tax increases. Their distortions deprived him of public credit for the budget achievement while torpedoing his health bill to boot. He dissected these lessons, then abruptly reversed course to embrace the propaganda. He would imitate Republican salesmanship to give the voters a borrowed gift. To do so, he would make middle-class tax cuts the centerpiece of his legislative program in the upcoming State of the Union Address.

Reeling, I tried to mediate between Clinton and the voters. I said he was entitled to howl against their rejection as unwise or unfair, but they were entitled to be wrong. No democratic axiom claimed that any electorate was infallible–only that the public will must be respected through corrections and adjustments. The president demanded to know why I insinuated that his Middle Class Bill of Rights violated democratic principle. I blurted out that a bill of rights is fundamental. It should not be for one social class, excluding others. And even if it were, it shouldn't be a string of tax cuts.

He told me I was wrong. "I can *pay* for my tax cuts," he said. "The Republicans can't pay for theirs. They don't care. I do." His fury spilled over at fate more than me. "I believe in the Middle Class Bill of Rights," the president declared. "And by God, I'm going to see it through."

CHAPTER FIFTEEN

BAILOUT, BOMBS, AND RECOVERY

Thursday, February 2, 1995

Monday, March 6, 1995

Monday, March 27, 1995

Wednesday, April 19, 1995

President Clinton beckoned me into the Treaty Room while he talked on the phone, juggling calls about an emergency loan to Mexico and the forthcoming biography of him by *Washington Post* reporter David Maraniss. He said tomorrow's *Post* would have a front-page story alleging that he tried to suppress the book's revelations about "bimbo" girl-friends in Arkansas. White House staff members were scouring for other land mines, and some thirty or forty paper clips protruded from Clinton's advance copy. When I asked whether all these marked potential controversy or objections, however, the president said no—these were passages he liked. He read from them in rapt nostalgia, as though freshly discovering his youth. "Gosh, I wonder where he got that quote from," mused Clinton. The account of his escape from conscription was slightly askew, but he did not blame Maraniss. Two friends who knew most about Clinton's moral and patriotic turmoil over Vietnam were not available to the author, because they had since died.

The president regretted his decision not to grant an interview, which had forced Maraniss to assess him from afar. Clinton thought the *Post*, as usual, was trying to crank up a titillating scandal on the side, but he considered the book itself more than fair. Oddly, in fact, he wondered whether he should ask Maraniss to become his administration's official historian. They did not know each other. There would be an appearance of public friction over the book, and perhaps that was good. Was there any chance he might accept such an offer? Nonplussed, I spoke highly of Maraniss again without commenting directly on the prospects. Clinton certainly remembered that I had counseled against the whole idea of recruiting a White House historian, and his inquiry conveyed to me a hint of lingering dissatisfaction. Not only had I declined this role myself, in favor of the taping project, but we had quarreled sharply last time about his Middle Class Bill of Rights. I felt tension. A president deserves both candid rapport and an objective diary, but it was hard for me to nurture them both.

We breezed above these undercurrents on tape. Clinton described at length the preparation for last Tuesday's State of the Union Address to the first Republican Congress in forty years. He called it a pivotal test since the landslide defeat. Without saying so explicitly, he had de-emphasized his Bill of Rights proposal and its tax cuts to concentrate on a statement of core values. He experimented with language all through January, most notably at Carl Sandburg College in Illinois. The president said the country's community colleges were a burgeoning sign of national pluck and adaptation, which made them a good political barometer. He tried out self-deprecating humor to salve the sting of the election. (Being president is like running a cemetery, he told the Sandburg students: "You've got a lot of people under you, and nobody is listening.") He reprised themes from the 1992 campaign about a New Covenant between voters and government, stressing accountability, economy, and hope. He said he worked feverishly on drafts by Don Baer, his chief speechwriter, to acknowledge the "Gingrich revolution" while upholding his own mandate for change. He pledged to cooperate whenever base principles were respected on both sides.

Clinton thought the address to Congress began his political recovery. I asked whether any congressional leaders had told him so privately that night, and he said no—that those conversations were almost entirely ceremonial—but he did recall significant eye contact with one of the two new Republican senators from Tennessee. Fred Thompson was a gifted politician and a pretty good stage actor, said Clinton. He seemed to be grinning up at him about thirty minutes into the State of the Union Address, mildly surprised that Clinton might prove himself a worthy adversary after all, by neither cursing fate nor rolling over in surrender. Most pundits panned the address as a laundry list of excessive length (eighty minutes) from a repudiated president, but Clinton said the voters agreed with Thompson that the address made a connection. His polls jumped above 50 percent approval for the first time in months. All through January, his approval rate climbed as Newt Gingrich's numbers slipped. Strangely, said the president, his polls also climbed whenever Gingrich recovered favor. Voters seemed to feel that Clinton was more reasonable than the flamboyant new House speaker, or, alternatively, that he was cooperating to overcome political gridlock. Vice President Gore had quipped to him that at long last the public was "grading us on the curve," relative to the Republicans now running Congress.

In triumph, Gingrich helped strip away his own campaign polish. He vowed to remake American history by rolling back changes from the 1960s as personified by Bill and Hillary Clinton, whom he branded "counterculture McGoverniks." His mother, Kathleen Gingrich, said in a CBS television interview that Newt considered Hillary a "bitch," after which the Clintons gained public sympathy by inviting mother and son to tour the White House residence. The president identified with the speaker's hardscrabble family background—born to teenage parents, adopted, a childhood bouncing around as an Army brat. Already, said Clinton, reporters had unearthed salacious details about Gingrich's first marriage to his former geometry teacher, with allegations that he had pressed her for a divorce in the hospital as she received cancer treatments, telling her she was too fat to suit his political ambitions. Other news stories had compelled Gingrich to surrender a $4.5 million book contract from media baron Rupert Murdoch—because of potential conflict with Murdoch's legislative petitions before Congress—and also to jettison the speaker's chosen historian for the House of Representatives, owing to his published skepticism about the Holocaust. A relentless public spotlight would challenge Gingrich to temper hubris and extremism, said the presi-

dent, and watching the speaker fulminate against the media had crystal-
lized lessons for him, too. He could no longer allow himself to get
emotionally distracted by the press. To do so was worse than a flaw or self-
defeating mistake. It was a dereliction of duty. Clinton said he resolved to
focus on the people's business, getting up each day ready to work.

THE FINANCIAL CRISIS in Mexico consumed most of January. The president,
though tired, cogently summarized how a fundamentally sound national economy could face sudden ruin over the management of public
debt. Chronic budget deficits had weakened the Mexican peso for years.
Mexico's leaders stalled on the necessary devaluation of currency until
after their 1994 elections, then overdid the correction in a single jolt.
The result was a speculative run against the peso, whose value plummeted, which in turn made it prohibitively expensive to service Mexico's
debts calibrated in ever more expensive dollars. National default quickly
loomed. That would mean contagious financial collapse in neighboring
countries, massive layoffs, and perhaps a fivefold surge of desperate
aliens across the U.S. border. Robert Rubin, the new treasury secretary,
masterfully explained to congressional leaders how a calamity could be
averted by $40 billion in temporary loan guarantees from the United
States. Speaker Gingrich and Senator Dole agreed to support emergency
legislation, joined by their new counterparts for the minority Democrats, Representative Dick Gephardt and Senator Tom Daschle. They all
found the package scary but rational and imperative.

From there, said Clinton, this crisis test of bipartisan governance
went swiftly down the toilet. Neither party's leaders could deliver their
rank-and-file members, whose visceral reactions prevailed. Gingrich
faced revolt from some seventy freshman Republicans, nearly all conservative ideologues, who had just arrived in Washington primed to eviscer-
ate "big government." How could they explain that their first major vote
was a huge "bailout" for Mexicans? They demanded extraneous amendments, such as a guarantee that no indirect benefit could give comfort to
Fidel Castro, and the president recorded that most of the Democrats
were nearly as bad. "The truth is, they didn't want to do anything," he
told me. "So they just kept thinking up new questions to ask."

The stall lasted until nearly midnight on January 30, only three days before this taping session. Secretary Rubin warned congressional leaders that Mexico would begin to implode within forty-eight hours, and that collateral pressures already had weakened the government of Argentina. With Congress paralyzed, the only conceivable remedy was for President Clinton to secure the necessary loan guarantees on his own authority, using the U.S. Exchange Stabilization Fund. These reserves were intended to shore up the American dollar in the event of speculative panic and decline. (As an aside, Clinton noted that an equivalent devaluation crisis for the giant U.S. economy, which was roughly twenty times the size of Mexico's, would require staggering stabilization bets approaching a trillion dollars.) Rubin advised that a guarantee by Clinton should calm the markets, secure the peso, and revive Mexico's credit without actually drawing on the U.S. collateral. Most economists and national security experts endorsed the risk. So did state governors, including Republicans Bill Weld of Massachusetts and George W. Bush of Texas. However, American voters did not yet appreciate their own vulnerability in an interdependent global economy. They opposed the Mexican guarantee by poll margins exceeding four to one.

Clinton said his midnight meeting was quick. He approved the entire package by executive order, and debate turned to its political aftermath when congressional leaders reassembled for a public announcement the next day. How should they answer complaints from their members that Clinton bypassed Congress altogether, trampling their constitutional prerogatives? Both Democrats and Republicans worried about potential revolt until Gephardt exploded. "Here's what we tell them," he roared. "We tell them, 'Have a nice day!' We tell them the president picked up this big rock off the floor and we don't have to vote on it." Clinton said Gephardt's line provoked merry agreement. Now, in the early anxiety over results from Mexico, observers hedged their appraisal. The *Washington Post*, which called the guarantee itself farsighted and essential, nevertheless pronounced its unilateral execution "another political setback for Clinton [that] still leaves a huge economic cloud over Mexico and, to a lesser extent, the world economy." Even if the rescue proved successful, the *Post* said, it reserved censure for "slipshod handling" that failed to include Congress. This petulant review was the sort of media distraction Clinton had just resolved to ignore.

He described a pained reaction to the two suicide bombings in Israel on January 22. At Beit Lid Junction, a bus crossroads between Tel Aviv and Haifa, one traveler feigned illness to draw a crowd before detonating himself, and a second bomber exploded among bystanders converging to attend the wounded. To mark their new political alliance, Hamas and Islamic Jihad claimed joint responsibility for this carnage, which killed twenty Israeli soldiers returning to duty from weekend leave. (A third bomb failed to go off a day later when Israeli prime minister Rabin visited the site of the devastation.)

President Clinton had spent most of the past week trying to salvage the skeletal peace process. He said Rabin spoke bravely against giving in to the terrorists' scheme for hatred. In shock, Rabin maintained a pretext of civil contact with Arafat. The president had written a letter to President Mubarak of Egypt, pleading with him to go to Jerusalem and sponsor rededicated negotiations. Mubarak had never been to Israel. The drama of his first visit might help preserve the agreed framework toward a Palestinian-Israeli treaty, but Mubarak steadfastly refused to go. As a pallid substitute, he invited negotiators again to Cairo. Mubarak's secret fear, Clinton believed, was that he would receive in Israel a less tumultuous welcome than his predecessor, Anwar Sadat, in 1977, diminishing himself by comparison. On another front, Clinton was imploring Asad of Syria to restore communications with Israel, which had broken down in recriminations over Beit Lid. Asad knew his time was running short to recover Syria's Golan Heights, and Clinton reminded him that each spasm of terror made Rabin more fragile. "I don't know how much longer he's going to be around," he told Asad, adding, for that matter, that Clinton was not sure how much longer he would be around himself. "But I damn sure know you're going to get a better deal from us than from whoever comes after us." He said Asad remained noncommittal, forever cagey and hard to read.

The president wearily regretted that we had started so late tonight. Skimming over political headlines, he expressed relief that former defense secretary Dick Cheney had removed himself from the Republican presidential race in 1996. He thought Cheney would have made a formidable opponent. We skipped major events on my list, such as an earthquake that killed three thousand people in Japan, and did not have time to mention the growing national obsession with the O. J. Simpson murder trial, the opening statements to the jury having just concluded before Clinton's State of the Union Address. On only one subject—baseball—did the president manifest his rattled state since the election. He asked whether the owners and players would settle the strike by a February 6 deadline, in time for spring training. I thought not. Should he impose the terms recommended by his mediator? No, there was too much greed and too little authority for a president to impose anything. He asked me to fax him another memo of suggestions through Nancy Hernreich, and I sent him a Bible verse to use in his public exhortations: "There is no umpire between us, who might lay his hand upon us both."*

OUR CONSULTATIONS ON baseball continued sporadically through two more taping sessions, the first on March 6. At the president's behest, I scouted for solutions informally with Donald Fehr, head of the baseball players union, and Peter Angelos, owner of the Baltimore Orioles. Fehr thought Clinton's mediator, William Usery, leaned heavily against the players because of a far-fetched antilabor conspiracy he traced through an owner of the Kansas City Royals to Wal-Mart in Arkansas. Angelos said most of his fellow owners were prepared to write off the entire 1995 season to break the players union. The president once called me for an update by radiophone from his motorcade in San Francisco, letting his aide Bruce Lindsey explain why it was impractical to nudge the baseball owners with subtle threats to take away their antitrust exemption. Lindsey said Anne Bingaman, the administration's chief antitrust lawyer, was not likely to back down once she challenged the amateur draft among baseball's specialized restraints of trade. In a separate call, Vice President Gore scolded me for encouraging the president to risk his prestige in a scorpion fight. He considered settlement hopes wildly optimistic even before the teams recruited castoffs and old-timers for spring training. By the end of March, internal strife within baseball menaced a season now scheduled without any major league players. Sparky Anderson of the Detroit Tigers refused to manage strikebreakers. The Toronto Blue Jays scrambled to move their home games to Florida because of adverse

---

* Job 9:33.

labor laws in Canada. Angelos announced that the Orioles would not field a replacement team, in part to spare the star shortstop, Cal Ripken Jr., a devil's choice between loyalty to striking peers and his pursuit of Lou Gehrig's historic record.

At the White House, the president asked what kind of record Gehrig held. He feigned no expertise about baseball, and I concealed my surprise to discover him a superficial fan. Clinton was impressed to hear that Gehrig had played in 2,130 consecutive games for the New York Yankees—never missing a day through more than a dozen broken bones, suffering numerous beanballs in an era before protective helmets, enduring the early ravages of the fatal disease since named for him. Gehrig's legendary "Iron Man" feat had been unassailable for decades, but Ripken stood poised to break it if some miracle could resurrect the 1995 season. The president, while not steeped in his usual omniscient detail, fully grasped its symbolic stakes for national character. An indulgent squabble among millionaires was threatening to spoil a paragon example of renewed workhorse excellence.

Prospects were bleak also in Mexico. On tape, Clinton said the whole country had turned into a soap opera in the midst of its financial crisis. Raúl Salinas, brother of the former president, was arrested for murdering the socially prominent head of a political party, who had scandalously divorced Salinas's sister. The prosecutor on the case was the victim's brother, which set tongues wagging even before Raúl Salinas absconded under suspicion of laundering millions in drug cartel money himself, to be captured in New Jersey on March 3. Since then, ex-president Carlos Salinas launched a sensational hunger strike against his successor, Ernesto Zedillo, demanding vindication of his family's honor, but Salinas called off the strike after only one missed meal. This made him the butt of ridicule on top of swirling charges that his administration had corrupted both justice and the national economy. Clinton said that while he liked Salinas personally, his conduct eroded the precarious confidence within the international currency and capital markets. Because Mexico, unlike many Asian countries, did not finance its economy out of savings, the whole country remained at the mercy of traders. The stabilization program was slipping again, said Clinton, and his guaranteed loans might not hold.

At home, he measured political trouble by the number of Republicans who were jumping into the presidential race nearly two years before the election. Senator Phil Gramm of Texas already had announced, followed by former Tennessee governor Lamar Alexander, Senator Richard Lugar of Indiana, and anti-abortion activist Alan Keyes. Pete Wilson, the new governor of California, declared his ambition after a heavily publicized inaugural speech proclaiming his state sovereign, "and not a colony of Washington." Wilson appealed to resentments in coded language pioneered by the segregationist Alabama governor George Wallace. He stressed his goal to end affirmative action programs for minorities, calling them reverse discrimination, and Senator Dole, the Republican front-runner, pushed the same theme nationally in exploratory speeches. ("Race counting," said Dole, "has gone too far.") Clinton said affirmative action was proving a potent wedge issue. By retreating, defensive about any badge of liberalism, Democrats offered opponents essentially a free line of attack. The president described the windfall with another of his Southernisms that had escaped me growing up in Georgia. For Republican candidates, he said, affirmative action was like finding "a bird's nest on the ground."

His opponents were multiplying for obvious reasons. Each one saw the GOP nomination as tantamount to election. "They all think they can beat me," he said. "They have weakened me with health care and the midterms, so they'll just finish me off in 1996." The notion permeated politics, though Clinton professed his doubts. He wryly described the private dialogue when Senator Ben Nighthorse Campbell switched parties earlier in March. Campbell kept assuring him of undiminished admiration, saying his jump to the Republicans should not be interpreted as a political defection from the president. Clinton told him the press would declare otherwise, but Campbell insisted that he would continue to back the president on at least 80 percent of votes in the Senate. His rare dissent, except on Western issues such as guns and grazing fees, tended to occur when Campbell felt the president was too conservative on trade and the budget. Precisely, Clinton replied. Republicans had seduced Campbell with flattery, he teased, and the Senate's only Native American would find himself uncomfortable among the naysayers on the other side of the aisle. When Campbell said he had been promised fraternal welcome as a Republican "of conscience," like Oregon's Mark Hatfield, Clinton pointed out to no avail that Hatfield was an isolated relic in his party. "I like Ben," the president told me, "but I can't figure him out." His best guess was that Campbell—a Colorado rancher—was succumbing to heady entitlements peculiar to the big-sky states, swelled by overrepresentation in Congress and subsidies from public land.

The president had just completed his annual checkup at Bethesda Naval Hospital. He said his blood pressure was 113/78 and his standing pulse rate was 55, which were okay. The doctors did fuss a little that his weight was up by six pounds to 216, but Clinton claimed offsetting progress on his waistline from doing crunches in a new weight room on the third floor. There were several small scabs on his face where skin lesions had been removed, which he dismissed as harmless. He said he felt fine. From up close, across the card table, I noticed that his hands were especially pale and yellowish, almost jaundiced, in contrast with his ruddy face, but overall he seemed less splotchy and battered than on previous occasions. The office was taking a toll on his youth.

Clinton said Boris Yeltsin was drinking heavily again since his troops stalled in the drive against separatist rebels in the Russian province of Chechnya. There had been brutal fighting in the Chechen capital of Grozny, and Clinton said he appealed often in private for Senator Dole not to make Yeltsin a partisan issue in the United States. He asked how Dole could expect him to oppose Russia's first elected president. To what end? He acknowledged a political impulse to cultivate hostilities left over from the Cold War, by branding Yeltsin a bloodthirsty tyrant and demanding freedom for Chechnya. But Clinton argued to Dole that the case was not so simple. Unlike Hungary and other Cold War conquests, or even the Soviet republics added since 1917, Chechnya had been part of Russia for more than two hundred years. Its war for independence was more like secession from the United States by Hawaii or Alaska, or by the Confederate states. Did we not fight to protect our own country from dismemberment? Clinton said he was pushing Yeltsin for negotiation and restraint—while trying also to convince Dole that not every secession was virtuous. He complained of unexamined tides in political culture. Partisan urges, floating on press sympathy for Chechen rebels, tempted politicians to exploit anything bad for Russia.

Separatist tensions marked his recent visit to Canada, where he and Prime Minister Jean Chrétien had worked on severe trade and budget imbalances. Canada's economic problems dragged down the performance of NAFTA, perhaps as much as Mexico's, but were much less publicized. They were complicated by a fault line between Canadians who spoke French rather than English, and Clinton said his address to Parliament walked a tightrope of identity politics. Although he went a little further than most U.S. presidents to promote Canadian unity, he tried to stop short of inflaming the French-speaking separatists centered in the province of Quebec. This task involved nuances of delivery and response in a divided chamber, he recalled with a smile. Depending on your inflection, some may perceive a rebuke of French separatists when you say, "Long live Canada," but others may be upset that you did not specify a "*united* Canada."

THE PRESIDENT EXPANDED on this idea late in March. He said he had been thinking for several months about larger trends in world politics. Just today, before a guest assembly of state attorneys general at the White House, he tried out his evolving theory that the central challenge of the next fifty years would be to handle the colliding forces of integration and disintegration. The shrinking world was coming together and apart at the same time. He sketched dozens of examples on each side. Positively, technology and trade knitted strangers together in a massive new kinship, lifting whole continents from poverty, spawning businesses and millionaires in stupendous numbers. The United States had generated six million new jobs since he became president, most of them paying high wages, with inflation and unemployment both trending downward, and yet people at every level felt increasingly insecure. Similar trends gripped China and Russia—economic miracles with lots of anxiety. The same global markets that created opportunity could flatten industries and countries, which left people feeling vulnerable and detached.

Clinton himself managed a dizzying array of simultaneous pursuits. When I arrived at ten o'clock, he was eating a late dinner alone in the kitchen upstairs—steak, he announced with gusto, sneaked in for him now that Hillary and Chelsea were off touring South Asia. He played solitaire briskly, three cards at a time, and kept one eye on a muted broadcast of the Academy Awards, flashing the remote when something looked good enough to hear—all the while hopscotching verbal topics from silly to grave. *Forrest Gump* was winning all the big Oscars, he remarked, and his explanation slipped into a semi-apology that he did not like *Pulp Fiction,* however hip the film may be. For him, its vulgarity blotted out the naughty fun along with any subtle message of redemption. When a butler cleared the small table between us, I tentatively showed him several photographs of my dad's latest patriotic bird feeder, doubtful that he would even remember his glimpse of its predecessor, but he focused intently on the Lincoln Memorial like a guest in one of his receiving lines. He noticed architectural details, such as the garlanded roll of states above its frieze. There were twelve per side, listing the forty-eight admitted before the 1922 dedication, above thirty-six Doric columns representing the states Lincoln had kept in the Union. Clinton explained why he thought this replica surpassed the White House feeder for accuracy and skill. Observing that rounded surfaces are the most difficult aspect of woodcraft, he wondered whether my dad might ever tackle the dome of a Jefferson Memorial bird feeder. If so, he would welcome it for placement on the South Lawn, looking toward the original. I told him I would be pleased to ask, so long as he understood that my dad voted Republican. The president laughed. So much the better, he said. Pop could tell his friends Clinton was for the birds.

Chelsea and Hillary had called the previous night from Pakistan, demanding first to hear an update on the NCAA basketball tournament. The president joyfully told them how Arkansas made it to the national semifinals again, against my alma mater, North Carolina. For them, and for me, he handicapped the Final Four games ahead with all the sophistication he lacked for baseball. He pronounced Hillary's trip doubly important. First, she could begin to repair poor U.S. relations with a volatile region of the globe—Pakistan, India, Sri Lanka, Nepal, and Bangladesh. Chelsea had been studying Asian religions diligently at Sidwell Friends, he said, reading the Q'uran every night. Personally, Clinton thought the trip would help revive Hillary from the major disappointment of the health care defeat. Her schedule was far more demanding than ceremonial, pushing both conflict resolution and civic empowerment for downtrodden women. She was planning a book, and he asked me whether the latter topic would be suitable. I thought she should write more broadly about civic responsibility for children. She could cover much of the same ground without so easily being caricatured as a feminist, by addressing all adults about a democratic society's obligations to youth. She could tie together her issues as a fundamental test of democratic principle, measuring how a self-governing society cares for those denied the vote because they are not yet self-governing. Americans, while professing boundless devotion to our young, shortchange them in every public arena from education and health to mountains of intergenerational debt.

As we rummaged through ideas for Hillary's book, the president related almost everything to his larger thesis about disruptions in a shrinking world. Off the tapes, he erupted when I mentioned the Arkansas banker Neil Ainley, who had cashed checks totaling some $50,000 for Clinton's 1990 gubernatorial campaign. All the money was spent legally, and itemized in the campaign's public reports, but the independent counsel, Ken Starr, indicted Ainley for failure to notify the IRS of cash transactions under a statute used to trace illicit drug money. It was the first prosecution in history on the technical violation itself, apart from any racketeering or conspiracy, and Clinton called it a runaway dragnet. "Don't get me started on Whitewater," he said. "Did you hear what they did to Chris Wade?" A former salesman for the Whitewater land parcels, Wade had gone broke years ago, then settled his debts, but Starr indicted him for misstating assets on his withdrawn petition for bankruptcy. This was beyond far-fetched, charged Clinton, and Wade pleaded guilty to minor misdemeanors only because Starr threatened to indict his wife. Neither the Ainley case, nor Wade's, bore the slightest connection to the Whitewater mandate, vague as it was.

These indictments were patently draconian, said Clinton. Horrendous. Yet the *Washington Post* and *New York Times* refused to say so. "I think these papers have corrupted themselves over Whitewater," he said. The president was shaking. "Don't get me started," he repeated, and his fury calmed. He had been thinking a lot about the press. For two years, he had interpreted hostile coverage as malicious or opportunistic. They were out to get him, or just trying to sell newspapers. Now he suspected that the news media were caught up in the same insecurity that plagued a changing world. Their markets were splintering. They obsessed daily over the O. J. Simpson trial. Like Japan, which had miniaturized global circuits and bought New York, only to sink back into paralysis, they fell prey to the rewards of high technology. He was coming to believe that the media, too, were victims of a larger collision between global integration and displacement. Instead of manipulating the news, perhaps they were acting out the anxiety—egging it on. No longer sure of their bearings, or objective standards, they projected worry outward in feverish waves.

THE PRESIDENT PURSUED his theory about tension in an era of rapid change, especially since the end of the Cold War, ranging from the press to affirmative action and even the budget. When the Republicans under President Nixon introduced widespread programs for affirmative action, he said, they had pictured the future as an upward escalator that would accommodate women and minorities on the widening edges of prosperity. Now, however, they foresaw crowding on narrower steps. He said a lot of corporate downsizing for white-collar workers was disguised as affirmative action to deflect responsibility. By contrast, the president had mandated an interagency study of affirmative action, which he analyzed from every angle—history, justification, rules, clarity, fairness, competition, controversy, and results. There were scores of affirmative action programs for different industries and employment groups. So far, he had canceled some, renewed others, and modified many. He gave several examples from across the government, saying the process was nearly complete. When I expressed surprise that he was so eager to talk about affirmative action in detail, he said that was the point. He loved sifting the record. He was proud of its many accomplishments. People responded to statistics of stark exclusion by race and gender since the era of segregation, and it was rightly an occasion to celebrate whenever an honest evaluation showed enough progress to discontinue affirmative action. He said opponents avoided both assessment and appreciation by reducing affirmative action to a silver bullet for political campaigns. They tended to skip the past, skim the facts, and look for something to justify resentment.

Similarly, said Clinton, the Republican "Contract With America" was proving to be more about attitude than governance. Most of its fanfare was grinding to a halt in the new Congress. Having vowed to punish Washington by setting term limits, Republicans divided over the wisdom and constitutionality of evicting themselves from office. All their exertions fell just short of approving a constitutional amendment that, if ratified, would require them to balance future budgets, while they dodged the ruling party's duty to present congressional guidelines for the actual budget now. The president perceived treacherous gaps between promise and performance. He summarized a scholarly article by Senator Moynihan about fiscal conduct throughout U.S. history, concluding that chronic deficits had appeared only in the 1970s and "structural deficits" in the 1980s. Two centuries indicated that harmful debt came from poor choice rather than any constitutional defect, and Clinton said he had met the deadline to produce a national budget only twenty-seven days after he took office. Then he rammed through the Omnibus Budget Act* without a single Republican vote, "I made all those Democrats walk the plank," he said, "and the Republicans took the Congress away."

Just today, he noted, Gingrich admitted privately that he had been wrong to call the omnibus bill a Clinton power grab that would ruin the national economy. Results proved the opposite on both counts, and the annual deficit would have declined even more if not for all the interest rate hikes by the Federal Reserve. (Every time Reserve chairman Alan Greenspan tightened credit, the president lamented, it closed a few Head Start programs and cost billions of dollars more to finance the accumulated debt.) Clinton wanted Congress to propose budget guidelines as required, thus sharing responsibility for hard choices. All they had done so far was float rumors of massive cuts in school lunch programs, to please their hard-liner base, while postponing commitment behind a mask of conflicts between the House and Senate. The president quoted one wag that the Republican approach to budget cutting gave a cruel twist to the survival motto "Women and children first." He vowed to hold their feet to the fire. "I told them they've got to submit their bud-

---

* Formally known as the Omnibus Reconciliation Budget Act of 1993.

get," he declared emphatically. "They've got to come to work. They've got to quit just talking. All they've gotten right is the politics."

This analysis seemed to reinvigorate Clinton on several issues, including the peace process for Northern Ireland. He shrugged off hysterical charges that he had frayed the vital U.S. alliance with England by permitting the Sinn Fein leader, Gerry Adams, to solicit donations on his second visit to the United States. Legally, he said, Adams could raise money in England itself, because he retained citizenship rights there under the same British rule that Sinn Fein opposed, but London wanted the United States to restrict Adams here as an Irish terrorist. Sinn Fein, long the political wing of the shadowy Provisional Irish Republican Army, had honored its own cease-fire for seven months now, since August. To stimulate peace talks, Adams had agreed recently to place on the agenda a complete surrender of IRA weaponry, but the British government insisted that such disarmament must precede any talks. Clinton found the British positions illogical, geared to freeze hostilities at low political risk. He said Prime Minister John Major peevishly refused for a week to take his call explaining the decision to let Adams travel unfettered. The president rolled his eyes. Major was venting frustration out of political weakness, he said, and public pressure on all sides eventually would push the talks forward. He cited spontaneous demonstrations of hope when Adams and the Irish prime minister, the taoiseach,* John Bruton, visited Washington over St. Patrick's Day.

Similarly, the president gamely defended his decision to stick with the nomination of Dr. Henry Foster for surgeon general to replace Joycelyn Elders, despite Phil Gramm's filibuster against confirmation in the Senate. Gramm portrayed Foster as a coldhearted abortionist. Erskine Bowles, Clinton's deputy chief of staff, concluded after a painstaking second look that Foster was a skilled, honorable obstetrician, admired by colleagues and beloved by parents, who never dissembled about performing some forty abortions and sterilizations while delivering thousands of babies since the 1950s. Bowles, a former banker in North Carolina, vouched for Foster as an exemplary person, which sealed Clinton's commitment. "I have enormous confidence in Erskine's judg-

---

* Pronounced "tee-shock."

ment," he said, in what struck me as a rare statement of unqualified praise for his staff. As long as Dr. Foster stayed willing, Clinton said he would push for a vote. He thought Gramm could block the Senate majority favoring confirmation only by a determined filibuster, which would injure him as a presidential candidate.* Most voters thought there was something unfairly obstructionist about a filibuster, he observed, which was why Democrats previously had chosen to fight Supreme Court nominees Robert Bork and Clarence Thomas by straightforward votes.

The president sketched his ordeal to replace CIA director James Woolsey. He kept going back to his first choice, Deputy Defense Secretary John Deutch, who did not want the prize. Deutch, a chemical engineer and former provost at MIT, loved scientific challenges, cutting-edge energy systems, and large-scale weapons design. He considered the CIA a glorified "security job," full of hype and clubby old myths. He knew that the CIA's opinions on world matters were far from Clinton's top priority. Therefore, Deutch bluntly declined an offer that most national security experts coveted beyond measure. The president wryly admired his grit. Incidentally, he remarked, the CIA had just briefed him for an upcoming trip to Haiti—in which Clinton would become only the second U.S. president ever to visit the island, sixty years after FDR landed to promise the removal of the Marines—and it almost killed the CIA officials to report that President Aristide was governing well against all their dire warnings, pushing reconciliation within the law.

In Deutch, Clinton confronted the unusual wonk who could match his fountain of arguments. So he reduced the contest to a test of personal will. "I told him, 'This is your country, and I need you over there,' " he recalled. He told him the CIA was a mess. With the Soviet Union's demise had vanished its defining purpose since the post–World War II birth of institutional spying in the United States. Clinton bore in on Deutch being his indispensable choice to make major repairs. "I'll get

---

* Gramm did succeed in blocking a Senate vote on the Foster nomination, but he withdrew from the Republican presidential race before the New Hampshire primary in 1996. No surgeon general would be confirmed for nearly three years, until Adm. David Satcher in February of 1998.

you out of there as soon as I can," he promised, "but you don't want to turn your president down, and I know you won't." Deutch finally yielded. Sheepishly, Clinton said it had taken him a while to develop an effective version of Lyndon Johnson's relentless, swarming, presidential "treatment."

His tone made me ask impulsively if he thought he would still be in the White House two years from now. The president paused. "Yes, I do," he replied. "I really do." He didn't initially think so, but his mind had shifted in the last month. He said millions of people still weren't sure. They may not like him but still agree with his positions, or vice versa. On balance, he decided he could win.

BEFORE OUR NEXT session, I saw President Clinton from afar in Haiti. Early on March 31, our delegation of mostly diplomats and politicians left Andrews Air Force Base for Port-au-Prince, whose airstrip had been cleared of foxholes and barbed wire coils since the military landings six months earlier. This time, improved security allowed us to ride buses into the city, past families cooking on charcoal fires along the streets while they tended rows of miscellaneous hubcaps for sale, and little jars of oil, with milling crowds as far as the eye could see. "Lots of pigs and chickens and goats," recorded my notes. "Several donkeys, some of them tethered. Cows right there in the city. I saw a great big sow in the street, rooting around in one of the piles of rubble." Of the Haitians we passed closely, about three of every four broke from blank stares into animated smiles and waves.

Clinton arrived separately on Air Force One from an event in Florida, and we all converged at Haiti's presidential palace. It had been handsomely spiffed up since October, but signs in several languages still warned not to drink the tap water. The forbidding military barracks across the way, where Jimmy Carter had negotiated with the Haitian generals, had been whitewashed and converted into a national ministry for women. Aristide was abolishing the army. Haiti's first class of police cadets drilled in formation on the grassy plaza, drawing applause along the iron fence. In a flag ceremony, U.S. commanders transferred peace-keeping authority to a U.N. force as honor guards from its thirty component nations marched by the outdoor reviewing stand in distinctive uniforms and gaits—notably from India and Pakistan, Bangladesh and Greece, Trinidad and Senegal, plus the United States and Canada. One of many doves released to symbolize peaceful democracy landed on a tuba player's head. Inside the palace, United Nations Secretary-General Boutros Boutros-Ghali surprised me with a toast whose spirited eloquence surpassed both those of Clinton and Aristide, quoting a new hit tune in France about Haitians recovering their song. The national security adviser, Tony Lake, approached on the rear fringe of business and political groups being exhorted by Clinton to build Haiti from the ground up. She was gone, Lake whispered forlornly. His wife had moved back to Massachusetts. We commiserated over the broken marriage before Bruce Lindsey appeared with brighter news that a federal judge, Sonia Sotomayor, had ended the baseball strike after 230 days. In a detour back at the airport, President Clinton thanked an entire unit of American troops, and behind him plunged Carrie Meek, Democratic representative from Florida, to sort through them with maternal hugs, calling, "Whose children are you?"

WEEKS LATER, ON April 19, on the drive to Washington, news of destruction in Oklahoma City eclipsed these vivid memories. Hundreds were said to be trapped inside the Alfred P. Murrah Federal Building, and experts on the radio inferred from the mangled, smoking structure that a huge bomb had been detonated. They cited many earmarks of a major terrorist attack, while some broadcasters lapsed into the shaken humanity of a transcendent event. Familiar correspondents apologized for confusion. Conflicting reports put the number of dead so far up to twenty, including somewhere between six and seventeen children of federal workers who had been crushed in a day care center. Bulletins said President Clinton called upon all Americans to pray for the victims.

I reached the White House fully expecting to be sent back home, but eventually he called down for me. To my surprise, the usher on duty dispensed with the usual escort and simply waved me toward the stairwell. Protocol was forgotten in the rattling emergency, it seemed, or, perhaps, my night visits were becoming routine. There was an empty hush upstairs. Finding the pocket doors almost closed in the yellow hallway, I saw the president with a phone, huddled next to Hillary on a sofa outside the family rooms, nodding to my signal that I would wait down the corridor. In what became a long, solitary vigil, I wandered two or three times into each stately room to the east. In the Lincoln Bedroom, I studied the muted debate between a plaque beneath the mantel, declaring that here Lincoln signed the proclamation to end slavery, and the notice on a nightstand nearby, quibbling that his proclamation freed slaves only in the Confederate states. Elsewhere, tables held displays of new state gifts, including Roman-era pottery from the mayor of Jerusalem and several treasures not yet labeled—four or five Greek icons painted on wood, and a jeweled sword with a wavy blade and matching dagger.

Of the paintings, what held me longest was a mid-nineteenth-century encampment of Flathead Indians by George Catlin, hung outside the Treaty Room. The American artist had captured realism and dignity in the Flatheads even as his countrymen were subjugating them, and a tension between raw conflict and serene ideals echoed from today's shock in Oklahoma City. Somehow, our history had refined from ghastly collisions a tempered freedom symbolized by these elegant corridors, where every president since John Adams had walked. Having witnessed and absorbed everything, they remained silently unfazed even tonight. I recorded later a mental note that the place itself gave me goose bumps more than the people, wondering why I was comparatively calm about hours alone with President Clinton.

The president came into the Treaty Room muttering about a terrible day. He barely mentioned Oklahoma City in our preliminary talks, however, perhaps for relief. In the press of other topics, the first question that engaged him on tape concerned his speeches of late about the administrative trend toward block grants for the states. He said President Nixon had originated a political stratagem advertising hostility to federal control from Washington, converting federal programs into lump disbursements for states and cities. Clinton had loved the freedom to spend block grants as a governor in Arkansas. He said they opened many useful innovations along with wasteful toys such as the computerized light shows that had replaced simple domes on city police cars. In a speech to the Florida legislature, he warned that block grants were seductively skewed. Their allocation formulas tilted heavily toward rural areas over cities and toward small, stable populations over rapidly growing states. He explained how block grants violated conservative principles of governance, with officials from one jurisdiction unaccountably spending tax dollars raised somewhere else.

Clinton said block grants were all the rage again in the new Republican Congress. He paid grudging tribute to Newt Gingrich, who had persuaded the networks to carry his report on its First Hundred Days in the first solo address from Congress ever broadcast nationwide. The speaker claimed a triumphant start for his quest to "totally remake the federal government," with aggressive political marketing that Clinton conceded was shrewder than his own. He said Gingrich had papered over differences among House Republicans to obtain 97 percent compliance on votes for his "Contract With America," arguing that it was paramount to amassing a record of completed bills regardless of their subsequent fate. Of the few that cleared the Senate, Clinton cited a modest but messy tax cut measure with loopholes to benefit, among others, Australian media mogul Rupert Murdoch, the Viacom corporation, and music impresario Quincy Jones. Although Clinton loved him, Quincy Jones did not need a tax break, and the president said he would have removed each of these loopholes surgically if he possessed a line item veto. As it was, House Democrats had urged him passionately to veto the entire bill. Their main argument was an expatriate provision in current law that allowed millionaires and even billionaires to evade taxes by renouncing their U.S. citizenship. A Democratic amendment to repeal the exclusion had passed both houses, only to be removed in conference committee at the behest of two prominent Republican lobbyists, and former members of Congress, Steve Symms and Guy Vander Jagt, benefiting their client, one of the largest contributors to the Republican National Committee. The secret removal was outrageous, Clinton agreed, but it stretched logic to veto a bill for what it did *not* include. Still, he harbored regrets for signing the law, and he contemplated political ads to expose the unsavory deals behind it.

More Republicans had jumped early into the 1996 presidential race. Clinton passed over an announcement by Pennsylvania senator Arlen Specter, and, of California representative Robert Dornan, said only that he had neglected his rabies shot before attacking rivals in both parties as draft dodgers and country club softies. The president spoke in much greater detail about the painful loss by Arkansas to UCLA in the championship game of the NCAA men's basketball tournament. "I never thought I would see Arkansas force twenty turnovers and lose," he said with a sigh. Describing his quick state visit to Haiti, he said a trip there with Hillary twenty years earlier had prepared him for the gut-wrenching poverty, but he was jolted by the airborne view of a country stripped bare. Fifty thousand workers could plant trees for a year and hardly begin to repair the eroded landscape. With foreign companies still reluctant to return, Clinton feared that starving vigilantes would tear the country apart. He was groping to find a specialist who could "bird-dog" Haiti's economy and environment the way special envoy Bill Gray had worked to restore its politics.

John Major of England had visited recently. As usual, the president's description mixed his fascination with character into the swirling politics. "I kind of like old John," said Clinton, "but a lot of people don't." The prime minister was a big, galumphing man, whose hapless image was so well established that he seemed clerkish and wimpy. In private, they had set aside frictions over Northern Ireland and Gerry Adams to concentrate on Yeltsin, scheming for ways to stop Russia from selling nuclear technology to Iran. Clinton said Britain and Germany cooperated smoothly in this vital task, pointedly excluding France, and soon he expounded at length on troubles with Pakistan. His guest in Washington last week, Prime Minister Benazir Bhutto, had interrupted their discussions to praise Chelsea and Hillary. She told him Chelsea's knowledge of Islam had made a positive impression all over South Asia, especially in Pakistan. By contrast with a superficial American press, which portrayed Hillary as a demure tourist of no policy significance in exotic Asia, Bhutto said she had touched essential political chords with whirlwind encouragements for citizenship groups and small-scale economic development.* Clinton called Pakistan an uphill struggle. He said it was

---

* The *New York Times* set a patronizing tone with its summary of the South Asia tour on April 6: "In stop after stop, she has played the traditional role of First Lady as wife and mother, emphasizing the importance of educating girls and women, with her 15-year-old daughter, Chelsea, almost constantly by her side."

a poor Muslim nation entrenched in patriarchal culture, yet governed precariously by a woman, and so were Bangladesh and Sri Lanka, plus Turkey. The broad advancement of women would foster democratic progress as well as stability in all these countries, but U.S. policy seemed hostage to warlords.

Pakistan was still paying a heavy price, said the president, for its steadfast support of our surrogate war in the 1980s against the Soviet Union in Afghanistan. First it was overrun by refugees, then by drug dealers, until a diverted poppy trade created some three million heroin addicts in Pakistan. Bhutto's government had just extradited to the United States the captured fugitive Ramzi Yousef, an alleged master-mind of the 1993 truck bomb that killed six people and injured a thousand in New York's World Trade Center.* Clinton reeled off details of significant cooperation for which the Pakistanis deserved credit. Separately, he said they "feel screwed on Kashmir," because the United States has long deferred to annexation by India against the majority wish of the Kashmiris. Also, it was fundamentally unfair that the U.S. Pressler Amendment punished Pakistan and not India for the development of nuclear weapons. Pakistan still offered a nuclear-free South Asia, complete with international inspections, but India insisted that she needed nuclear weapons to deter China. Benazir Bhutto's main purpose in Washington was to seek relief for Pakistan's F-16 aircraft confiscated under the Pressler Amendment after the full $1 billion purchase price had been paid to Lockheed Martin. Bhutto, desperate for foreign exchange, secretly preferred a refund to possession of the planes, but current U.S. law blocked either course. "If I couldn't get an exception to the Pressler Amendment through a Democratic Congress," lamented the president, "I sure can't get one through now." Legislators loved to boast about striking a blow against nuclear proliferation, he said, to the point

---

* Yousef, convicted twice by jury in 1996 and 1997, was sentenced to life without parole and imprisoned at the Supermax facility in Florence, Colorado. Yousef's uncle, Khalid Sheikh Mohammed, would be captured by Pakistani agents and transferred to U.S. custody in March of 2003. The 9/11 Commission Report branded Mohammed "the principal architect of the 9/11 attacks" in 2001.

of outright thievery. All he could do for Bhutto was scrap her rusting planes and seek to return a pittance from their value in salvage.

MORE HAPPILY, PRESIDENT Clinton looked forward to the return of Major League Baseball after the longest suspension in history. He asked whether he should throw out the first ball on April 25 at the delayed opening day for an abbreviated 1995 season. I said no. Latent hostilities on both sides threatened a renewed stoppage. There was enormous ill will from fans over two squelched seasons, and the president would probably have to cross a picket line because the owners were still locking out the umpires to break their union. With so many negative associations, I recommended that he wait for a better mood. Clinton disagreed. A president should not base ceremonial decisions on frailty or mistakes. Beyond politics, his job was to stand for continuity in hope. He wanted to welcome baseball back, whatever happened next.

Chelsea came in fretting about homework. In an exercise to hone succinct composition, she was writing an essay of no more than one page on the best and worst qualities in the legendary character Dr. Frankenstein, with illustrative passages from the Mary Shelley novel. Chelsea said her draft spilled stubbornly onto a second page, which was unacceptable, and she expressed doubt about her choice of quotations. The president paused to give counsel, and I left the recorders on as he read most of her essay out loud. He liked its cited images of Frankenstein's passion for learning, enthralled in his lab, cheeks sallow with intense discovery, but he thought Chelsea was slightly ambiguous about whether his best quality was curiosity or ambition. On the negative side, where she wisely pinpointed an overbearing pride as the chief fault, he said she might find shorter, more precise quotes. We both complimented her language about the progressive blindness of Frankenstein's zeal. Instead of creating life, Chelsea concluded, the mad doctor faced a "monster who had become his bane." She went off to make revisions, and Clinton promised to consult her again before saying good night.

Offhandedly, the president wondered whether these tape sessions were doing any good. His sudden question unnerved me, in part because I was not sure what he meant. Was his emphasis on *these* sessions, indicating that they should be better, or on *any* good, suggesting that our whole venture might be a waste of time? If the latter, I suspected from his tone that he may be doubting the usefulness to him now, in his current duties, as though he had hoped to derive some peculiar guidance from our long-term perspective. This notion was disturbing. Should I try to safeguard the history project by behaving more like a once-a-month, amateur adviser? Surely not. Our sessions took energy and respite from his perpetual job, which bothered me already. My role was to invite comfortable, candid memories. Reflexively, I told him I thought the tapes would preserve texture in the presidential record, and future readers would find many revelations in his exact words. He moved along, probably from an idle comment.

The president looked gamely past media lack of interest in his latest televised press conference, which attracted a small audience on the lone network to broadcast it. Today's breakfast meeting with financial donors had been upbeat, he said, followed by a state meeting with Prime Minister Tansu Ciller of Turkey. She was on the verge of agreeing to withdraw Turkish troops from Iraq, where they had pursued Kurdish rebel armies of the PKK, the Kurdistan Workers' Party, which wanted to establish an independent Kurdish nation from parts of Turkey, Iraq, Syria, and Iran, when Leon Panetta abruptly stood up next to Clinton and left the Cabinet Room. Someone had mentioned a bomb on the way in, the president recalled, but he sensed something awful the instant Panetta left a tense negotiation without ceremony or excuse. Schedules sagged. The first photographs of the Murrah Building made his stomach cringe. It looked like a jagged wreck from World War II's battle of Stalingrad, swarming with rescue workers. Over and over, Clinton said the United States was one of the few anchors for stability in the world. Angry forces resented our role in peace negotiations from Bosnia to the Middle East and even Algeria. From reports in the first few hours, he feared the case was heading overseas. He said we do have some leads, then checked himself. If a terrorist group was involved, the president said carefully, he fervently hoped that it was not one affiliated with a foreign government. The hand of a government would make this bomb an act of war, rather than a heinous crime, triggering obligations to retaliate. He said the distinction had profound implications, because a war could open tears in the fragile world economy and order.

So far, at the scene of devastation, Clinton had spoken by telephone only with Oklahoma governor Frank Keating. He knew the governor as a right-wing Republican from their overlapping studies at Georgetown twenty-five years ago. They had little in common, and minimal contact since. Keating was tough as nails, but this trauma dissolved their differences. Many calls waited from members of Congress, added the president, and he would begin to return them when I left.

CHAPTER SIXTEEN

OKLAHOMA CITY

Monday, May 22, 1995

Tuesday, June 13, 1995

Monday, July 24, 1995

Oklahoma City did not lead overseas as President Clinton had feared, but domestic terror did spawn confusion and denial. Casualties shot up overnight to 853 people injured, many severely, plus 168 confirmed deaths and the unmatched leg from an anonymous 169th victim. News outlets around the world circulated the photograph of a burly firefighter cradling toddler Baylee Almon—one of nineteen child corpses pulled from the wreckage of the Murrah Building. Public outrage marched in lockstep behind what former Oklahoma representative Dave McCurdy called "very clear evidence" of a fiendish Muslim plot—with scattered American mosques ransacked by mobs, and an Iraqi-American woman, one of 2,700 Arab immigrants in Oklahoma City, suffering a miscarriage when rocks crashed through her home windows—until the first arrested suspect turned out to be Timothy McVeigh, a twenty-six-year-old Army veteran with corn-fed looks from Iowa. Even then, *New York Times* editor Abe Rosenthal wrote that Americans would suffer until the West committed fully to war upon Middle Eastern terrorists, declaring that "the era of forgiveness is over."

After a security review of the potential death radius from truck bombs, our next session fell on the day when permanent new rules routed vehicular traffic away from the White House. Critics debated a loss of republican access against the requirements of modern security, but twin rows of Stalinesque concrete slabs decisively blocked off Pennsylvania Avenue. Detours and additional screenings eventually let me upstairs into the family parlor, where Clinton arrived in jeans and a T-shirt advertising some musical group lost to memory in my notes. He described the complex reaction to Oklahoma City among various branches of government, then launched into a tirade about the stunted public response to McVeigh.

When the chief suspect turned out to be a blond American instead of a bearded foreigner, and also a right-winger steeped in bitterness against the federal government, the president said many pundits and politicians lost interest. They changed the subject. His tone seemed strangely benign for so grave a complaint. I couldn't tell whether he was guarded or genuinely bemused, but the situation reminded him of his overnight guest watching television right then in the Solarium, who was such a die-hard Democrat that he refused to stay in the Lincoln Bedroom. This goodhearted geezer finally conceded that Lincoln was the best the Republicans had to offer, Clinton chortled, but still wasn't good enough for him to sleep there. So they had to find him another room. Stubborn human nature helped keep Arkansas the only state that never had elected a Republican to the U.S. Senate, the president declared, although, in a complicated aside, he said Ken Starr might facilitate a Republican breakthrough by conjuring some way to indict the best Democratic candidates in his Whitewater investigation.*

Clinton allowed that he had expected partisanship to continue through the tragedy. On the Saturday after the bombing, he and Hillary met in the White House with children of federal employees like those killed in Oklahoma City, hearing their fearful reactions to the pictures on television, assuring them there were more good people than bad in the world, after which they both proceeded to the Treaty Room for separate Whitewater examinations under oath—with questions still, remarkably, emphasizing conspiracy allegations in the death of Vince Foster.

---

* Starr did indict Governor Jim Guy Tucker later in 1995, and in 1996 Lieutenant Governor Tim Hutchinson became the first Arkansas Republican elected to the Senate.

When these tense interviews ended, the president invited Starr and his prosecutors to tour the Lincoln Bedroom. Despite mild grumbling from Hillary, said Clinton, he strained to observe courtesies in the midst of warfare, but even he expressed shock at the disinterest in the political motives of Timothy McVeigh. Early profiles revealed the bomb suspect to be a survivalist from the militia movement, who demonized Washington as the tyrannical promoter of secularism, Jews, and racial minorities. Among McVeigh's papers at his capture were climactic pages from *The Turner Diaries,* a white supremacist novel about a militia-led holy war against the FBI and Pentagon, culminating in triumphant slaughter of everyone but "Aryan patriots" across the country. The Oklahoma City bomb was detonated on the second anniversary of the FBI raid near Waco, in which eighty members of the Branch Davidian cult had perished inside a besieged fortress. Because the Murrah Federal Building housed some of the federal agents involved, the mass destruction of their colleagues and children seemed to be a triggering call for the book's apocalyptic rebellion.

Of course, the bomb triggered horror and revulsion instead. Americans were aghast over the terrorist carnage at home, and baffled by McVeigh, but commentators reacted shrilly against reasonable inquiry, and scorned even the president's appeals for civil discourse. They said it was wrong to single out or admonish hate groups, because scrutiny would inhibit freedom to denounce the government. Rush Limbaugh indignantly told listeners that "liberals intend to use this tragedy," and conservative columnist Charles Krauthammer accused the president of ghoulish profiteering: "Clinton has found his weapon: the dead of Oklahoma." By twisting questions about origin and motive into exploitation, the public chorus stifled inquiry into a manifestly political crime.

The president said this was only the start. Within a week of discovering that Oklahoma City was the handiwork of anti-government zealots, his opponents decided the real issue was Waco, and they crusaded to extend investigations of the disastrous 1993 raid. A leader of the National Rifle Association branded the federal agents "jack-booted government thugs . . . wearing Nazi bucket helmets and black storm-trooper uniforms," who preyed upon innocent civilians. This attack was so extreme that the elder George Bush resigned in protest from the NRA, for

which Clinton was grateful, but the cries about Waco swelled into accusations that the president himself sanctioned murder. With "unmiti-
gated gall," he said, Republican leaders scheduled new congressional
hearings on Waco—not Oklahoma City. Politically, Clinton admitted, he
had to credit a move that so brazenly reversed sympathy and suspicion.
It diverted attention from McVeigh—and also from a thousand Oklahoma victims as public servants with neighbors and families. By substi-
tuting the usual diatribes against government officials as inherently
parasitic and oppressive, the switch implicitly condoned McVeigh's fury.
Amazed, President Clinton resolved never to sneer casually at "federal
bureaucrats."

He said eight or nine previous hearings about Waco found fault on
all sides. The crisis had begun with four Treasury agents shot dead when
they tried to serve a search warrant for illegal military weapons at the
Branch Davidian compound. The U.S. task force then waited seven
weeks for cult members to come out peacefully—and should have waited
longer. Clinton said the FBI reports of child abuse turned out to be a
flimsy cover for impatience to end the standoff, but the tear gas raid itself did not cause disaster. The cult leader inside was indeed maniacal,
and evidence showed that his obedient followers set fires to immolate
their own compound from within. Further hearings would add neither
balance nor accuracy, but Clinton said that was the whole point. His
opponents abhorred balance and craved rhetoric. They cussed big government rather than discuss its actual size, or address its performance, or
debate the changing mix of public and private needs. He said the fixa-
tion on Waco above Oklahoma City showed how hard their politics
worked to stir up fearful resentment, painting civilian government as an
irksome threat without any of its constitutional purpose or glory.

AN ODDLY SIMILAR fight loomed in foreign policy. Clinton said China ve-
hemently opposed an impending trip to New York in June by Taiwan's
president, Lee Teng-hui. Lee's reception would imply American sympathy for Taiwanese independence, argued Chinese officials, which would
violate their prized commitment from the United States—since the
Nixon era—to a strict "one China" policy. China considered Taiwan a
rogue internal province, and American governments had danced along

a tripwire between humoring its claims and protecting Taiwan from sub-jugation by force. Clinton said the Chinese brushed aside all assurances that Lee would receive no diplomatic notice. He would not come to Washington, and no U.S. official of any rank—let alone President Clinton—would come anywhere near him. In fact, Lee was being consid-ered only for a three-day tourist visa to receive an honorary degree from Cornell, where he had attended graduate school. Still, this private status did not satisfy Chinese officials. Earlier, during Lee's international flight to another country, they insisted he not even leave his airplane during a stopover in Hawaii, and they still thought his very presence on U.S. soil might somehow breach the "one China" accord. They wanted him banned. They were outraged that Clinton would even consider the visit against their wishes, and the president said his foreign policy wonks fa-vored concession. They figured one man's pleasure trip was not worth reprisals from an enormous, strategic nation.

Against his advisers, Clinton said he sympathized with a rare bipar-tisan groundswell behind Lee in the Congress. He kept pondering the uproar over his decision to let Gerry Adams into the country. "Poor Lee hasn't done any of the terrible things the IRA has done," he recorded on our tapes. "All he wants to do is come here and get his honorary degree, but they're saying he can't do it." He said the Chinese were hypersensi-tive about Lee in particular. For nearly forty years, the rival governments of both mainland China and anti-Communist Taiwan had ruled by au-thoritarian decree, but now Lee pushed through reforms toward Taiwan's first popular presidential election in 1996. He embodied the American position that free enterprise and democratic freedom reinforced each other's strengths, which made him anathema to Beijing. Clinton said he had experienced icy disdain while standing next to Chinese president Jiang Zemin in Moscow during fiftieth-anniversary celebrations of vic-tory in World War II. Jiang did not acknowledge Lee's name at all, and he treated Clinton's remarks on many subjects like a passing trifle. He was tough and arrogant, sighed the president, who wryly recalled a se-rene appraisal of the French Revolution from China's Maoist premier Zhou Enlai: "It's too early to tell."

Lee's visit may be a small personal matter, and to grant his visa may be posturing. Unlike the visa for Gerry Adams, it would advance no strategic vision like the peace process in Northern Ireland. Still, the symbolic impasse touched core democratic values of free travel and speech. For better or worse, it was one human rights choice that would command notice in Beijing. So Clinton had instructed Tony Lake to inform the Chinese ambassador that the United States would grant Lee's visa. China was furious, and the president said he did not know where retaliations might lead.

More positively, he told sentimental stories about the commemorations for World War II. Among the posthumous honorees on VE Day at Arlington Cemetery was an American soldier named Ellington, the son of a slave, who had rescued a survivor at Dachau by pulling him into a tank. Clinton mentioned intricate connections to descendants on both sides of the story, including one who worked in the administration. He described an endless parade of Soviet veterans past the Tomb of the Unknown Soldier in Moscow's Red Square—men's units and women's units, all grizzled in their seventies or older. It was striking that the men especially marched in close formation, huddled and clumped together, holding hands. "Many of us were crying there," said the president. He said the American press conveyed very little of the war's lingering emotional force among Europeans. Perhaps because of the long, poisonous atmosphere of the intervening Cold War, we have a diminished feeling for the Soviet Union's wartime loss of 27 million casualties relative to our 280,000, and a distant war across the oceans leaves no visual reminders of battles and atrocities in our midst.

At the Babi Yar Memorial, on May 12, Clinton saw remnants of the ravine where German soldiers had pushed naked bodies of civilian prisoners—more than thirty thousand exterminated in the first three days—to create a mass grave of Jews and Gypsies. He said it lies quiet now in a beautiful forest near Kiev, Ukraine, which, he noted, has a higher proportion of trees to landmass than any national capital in the world except Washington. Students at Kiev University had gathered in a pouring rain to cheer the American president so exuberantly that unnerved police officers manhandled and beat them over Clinton's objections. Ukrainian experts told him that Americans did not understand the rigors of local security, and the president said he had to break off his speech and wade into the square, pleading for calm on both sides.

The whole trip was edgy, with moments of grace suspended above danger. In their seventh round of business meetings, Clinton essentially finessed differences with Yeltsin over NATO and Iran. Yeltsin grudgingly suspended the Russian contract with Iran for a nuclear centrifuge—but not for a light-water reactor. Anything more would backfire in Russian politics, perhaps dooming Yeltsin as a stooge of the United States. Meanwhile, back home, Senator Dole attacked Clinton as a stooge of Yeltsin. The president said Dole was upset because he had aspired to represent the United States at the Moscow ceremonies himself. "He is always bitter about something these days," said Clinton. Dole pushed for new Waco hearings, and was "sticking his finger in the eye of the Middle East peace process" with a bill mandating transfer of the U.S. embassy in Israel to Jerusalem. The latter was a merely fund-raising showpiece, but Dole nearly had passed his tort reform legislation built on contributions from the insurance industry. Democrats killed it with a label: "the Drunk Driver's Protection Act."

What Clinton called a nasty spell with Dole stimulated him for political competition. "This is how I see it on May 22, 1995," he said, as his mind ranged over the reelection campaign more than a year ahead. He had blunted all three prongs of the coordinated attack in the modern Republican victory strategy: fiscal conservatism, crime, and strong national defense. On balancing the budget, in fact, he had outperformed them by historic margins made plain in the scrambled budgets then being drafted by a Republican Congress. None of them repealed his landmark reconciliation package of 1993, even though not a single Republican had voted for it, because any plan to end the deficit would become a laughingstock if they did.

On social issues, he said Democrats were learning to stand up for themselves. They still fought Senator Gramm's ongoing filibuster against Dr. Henry Foster's nomination to become surgeon general. This was one filibuster that helped Democrats politically, turning voters slowly against the Republicans as vituperative and extreme on abortion. Clinton said Gramm was only hurting himself, and he hoped—futilely, in the end—to win confirmation for Foster. The president thought gays in the military remained his biggest vulnerability among social conservatives, but he cited a tip that the damage from 1993 may be fading. Governor Lawton

Chiles, a Democrat, had just consulted one of his bellwether farmers in Florida, who consistently swore not to vote for Clinton because of "queers in the Army," but now might change his mind if Clinton kept confronting "the Japanese bastards" on trade. The president said Chiles was famously savvy about finding the pulse of average voters. Much amused, he described trade representative Mickey Kantor's bare-knuckled negotiations to pry open the one-sided Japanese markets with European allies cheering from the rear, quietly, lest they offend Japan.

His take on Democratic issues was positive. "If you just look at the objective record," he said, "I've already done enough to justify getting reelected." Ticking off a list of accomplishments toward a sound, broad-based economy—the earned income tax credit, family leave reform, streamlined government, educational and environmental investment—he claimed an honest, healthy start on fulfilling his pledge to retool America for a new century. He anticipated two chief obstacles to that message in 1996: the media did not care about his agenda as much as the voters, and Republicans were more unified than Democrats in their talk. Witness the concerted shift of public attention from Oklahoma City to Waco.

Other questions on tape covered topics from Cuba to a spike in gun violence among children. His answers were sometimes elaborate, but his thoughts never strayed too far from the reelection contest. Its first phase would be a joust with Congress over appropriations and the budget. Each side faced temptation to demagogue the other as spendthrift liberals or heartless reactionaries and then hide in the fog of political gridlock. Republican leaders still disagreed among themselves about their initial proposals—or pretended to—daring Clinton to go first. The president said he must keep a constant, veto-proof majority behind him, making sure not to lose too many Republicans for cutting too little or too many Democrats for cutting too much. If the Republicans insisted on punishing education and the environment to finance tax breaks for their contributors, Clinton vowed to veto and win. "Short of that," he added, "I'm ready to negotiate."

He suddenly looked tired. "We've talked too long tonight," he said.

WE RECORDED NEXT in the upstairs kitchen. A theme of the June session was euphoria tempered by forebodings on every front. The president was eating a late supper alone, ravenous, he said, because he had fasted to keep himself lean and hungry for his five-minute address to the nation at nine o'clock. He said the leap was done. Against ferocious resistance from his own staff, he had just announced the release of a detailed plan to balance the federal budget in ten years or less by conservative projections, without new taxes, barring cuts in education, health, and the environment. Most political advisers thought he was forfeiting a golden chance to avenge the 1994 election disaster. If he had kept stalling until Congress adopted its own unified budget as required, then Democrats could have flayed Republicans for the inevitable hard choices, spotlighting their proposed cuts in Medicare or school lunches. By going first yet again, Clinton made Democrats the target for renewed demagoguery.

Maybe so, said the president. But you could only dodge so long when claiming leadership and demanding responsibility in others. Evasions on the budget made it hard for him to hold press conferences. They fed cynicism and paralysis. Henceforth, an honest fiscal blueprint would be a requirement—he called it "the ticket of admission"—for any serious presidential candidate. Even if polls showed that voters didn't like the individual measures, you needed a credible record. Liberals must show they could pay for their programs and conservatives must answer their own call to fiscal discipline. Proud of the plan, Clinton praised his budget director, Alice Rivlin, for her tireless work without a single leak.

While he shrugged off Dole's rebuttal speech as a partisan distortion, the private scorn of Democrats clearly rankled the president. Only Louisiana's Senator John Breaux had called to support his initiative. All but two Democratic governors were opposed. They said he was trading payback for the hot seat. Governor Chiles told Clinton he should have waited, because losing statesmanship is worthless, and congressional Democrats seethed at Clinton for putting them gratuitously in danger. For the first time, said the president, he expected challengers in next year's primaries: Jesse Jackson and Representative Dick Gephardt. He said he didn't care. Offering his budget plan was the right thing to do. A tone of defiant isolation reminded me of his misery before invading Haiti.

Questions about Bosnia elicited stories from a roller-coaster month.

On June 2, Serb gunners had shot down an American F-16 fighter pa-
trolling the no-fly zone over Bosnia, and Clinton said he was obliged to
defend his policy through days of excruciating tension over the unknown fate of its pilot, Capt. Scott O'Grady. This would be the first U.S.
casualty so far in some 69,000 sorties flown by the U.N.-NATO joint
command to keep Serb aircraft from bombing Muslim and Croatian
villages. They had helped reduce war deaths on the ground from roughly
130,000 in 1992 to 3,000 in 1994, but, with no end to the brutal conflict
in sight, the shaky peacemakers' coalition teetered with rumors that the
Serbs intended to make a spectacle of O'Grady's body, or worse, turn
him over alive to Serbian war widows for public torture. Miraculously,
on June 8, a faint radio signal from O'Grady's locator allowed a flying
rescue squadron to extract him safely from the woods. President Clinton
and Tony Lake celebrated with cigars on the Truman Balcony.

Only the day before, Clinton had hosted a hero's welcome at the
White House. When a whole bunch of O'Gradys and friends wouldn't
fit in the family dining room, he said, butlers set up tables for a private
lunch in the Yellow Oval Room, across the hall. There the captain recalled seeing Serb soldiers stand on his parachute within three minutes
of hitting the ground, which meant they knew he was alive and nearby
from the outset of a frantic six-day manhunt. O'Grady ate berries and a
few ants. The president noted merrily that reporters, hearing of this detail, got carried away with images of primitive derring-do, but O'Grady's
tale was more prosaic.* By training, he put on gloves and hugged a tree
for many hours at a time, motionless and silent, with searchers all
around. He became so dehydrated that he could not swallow some of
the few things he found to eat. He perceived his gun as a danger and his
ordeal as more spiritual than military.

---

* In *Behind Enemy Lines*, a 2001 Hollywood film starring Owen Wilson and
Gene Hackman, the character based loosely on O'Grady kills pursuers Rambo-
style across Bosnia while villainous politicians and international bureaucrats
hamstring the effort to rescue him. In fact, O'Grady stayed in the woods, never
interacted with anyone on the ground, and was liberated within hours after the
24th Marine Expeditionary Unit picked up his radio signal. He sued the film
producers for defamation.

O'Grady was reflective, said Clinton, and disarmingly honest. Walking together from the lunch to the West Wing, he furtively consulted Clinton about the photographers waiting ahead. He did not want to look unkempt in the White House. Still weak, he fretted about his heavy stubble and the thick eyebrows merging on his forehead. The president, laughing, said he advised O'Grady to relax and enjoy his moment as the most popular American: "They'd all think you look great even with a ten-day beard." Alone with Clinton in the Oval Office, asking permission to speak frankly, O'Grady said that while he supported the war aim to preserve Bosnia, he worried that any U.S. combat troops ever sent there would get bogged down in the terrible terrain.

The president worried about Bosnia, too. On tape, he updated the terrible impasse in far greater complexity than I could remember for dictation later that night. He spoke of ironies and maddening deception. Overall, he said the latest crisis sprang from a positive turn in the military balance. The Bosnian Croats and Muslims seemed to have reached rock bottom after surrendering more than 70 percent of Bosnian territory to the attacking Bosnian Serbs. Now they were slowly gaining strength in spite of the international arms embargo. Concentrated into strongholds, they had agreed to stop fighting each other and were even contemplating a counteroffensive. The Serbs, by contrast, had spread themselves thin by conquest. In May, frustrated by the inability to finish off their enemies, they violated the hard-won international truce with renewed artillery bombardment of Sarajevo and other Muslim enclaves. When NATO and U.N. forces mobilized air strikes to stop them, Serb militias seized more than three hundred European peacekeepers and chained them to targets on the ground—artillery sites and ammunition dumps—daring NATO to bomb its own allies. In the midst of this tangled mess, Captain O'Grady had been shot down.

Now the Europeans threatened to pull out their peacekeepers entirely, and were bargaining for logistical assistance from the United States. The president said such a withdrawal might bring hidden benefits, because the peacekeepers—with their strict orders not to resist attack—were often more hindrance than help. They were also a focus of political intrigue, with credible reports that U.N. commanders secretly promised the Bosnian Serbs immunity from future air strikes if they left the peacekeepers unharmed. On the other hand, Clinton said the Serbs would mount an all-out attack as soon as the peacekeepers left, especially if the arms embargo was lifted or broken, and non-Serbs may not survive at all in Bosnia. The president said Jimmy Carter and others were pressuring him to open direct talks with the Bosnian Serbs, who had won most of their territorial demands already, and make the best deal he could for the Muslims. Carter reflected a strong current of realism, or fatalism, about the Muslim cause there. ("I don't give two cents about Bosnia," wrote *New York Times* columnist Thomas Friedman. "Not two cents. The people there have brought on their own troubles.") Clinton said Carter may be right. It was a huge gamble to hold out for the Bosnian Muslims to grow stronger, but he could not yet bring himself to seek peace from the Bosnian Serbs. He called them "pretty thuggish" aggressors, by far the predominant instigators of ethnic cleansing. Jewish legislators, alert to ugly parallels with the Holocaust in World War II, had become the ardent, ironic champions of Muslim Bosnia in Congress. Given the intractable hostilities radiating from the Middle East, the president thought they were relieved to be for Muslims somewhere in the world.

On the Middle East, he said he had called President Asad a week ago to push for the revival of peace talks stalled since December. He urged him to take advantage of a brief political window ahead. Prime Minister Rabin of Israel was running strong for reelection in December, he told Asad, and, despite whatever rumors and polls might reach Syria, Clinton figured to win reelection himself. This gave Asad two stable partners for the arduous labor of a peace treaty. However, they must act decisively to finish before the summer of 1996. By then, Clinton would be preoccupied with his presidential campaign, and Rabin may face serious new impediments to any treaty with Syria. Rabin's opponent from the Likud Party, Benjamin Netanyahu, was building a movement to require that any peace instrument involving the Golan Heights must be approved either by seventy votes in the Knesset—which Rabin did not have—or by a special referendum in Israel. To me, Clinton described Netanyahu's bill as the procedural equivalent of the balanced budget amendment, ingeniously designed to frustrate its stated goal. To Asad, he argued that time was short. Rabin had taken the risk of announcing that he would consider token withdrawals of Israel forces from the Golan Heights as a catalyst. After his call, Clinton sent Secretary of State Christopher to Damascus for talks in person, and Asad had just agreed to resume negotiations with Israel.

Hillary came into the little kitchen while the president was discussing domestic politics. He predicted that Dole would have the Republican nomination locked up by March because his rivals had devised no way to take him on except lame boasts to be better Republicans. Meanwhile, Dole skillfully assembled a preemptive war chest. While scolding Hollywood gently for loose morals, said Clinton, Dole was amassing contributions from the cable networks, film studios, and broadcasters. Hillary seemed well versed in fund-raising. She said any unscrupulous dullard could milk the vulnerable communications industry, citing the bonanza reaped by a new Senate committee chair, Larry Pressler of South Dakota, as he marked up a telecommunications bill with lucrative subsidies for Time Warner and other companies—ten-year licenses, more generous fees, and fewer restrictions on local monopolies.

Two calls came through for the president. A pollster told him his national numbers were up again, almost to match the Republicans now on fighting the deficit. Senator Chris Dodd complimented tonight's budget speech. Clinton said his was only the second positive call. We're going to take a lot of grief, Hillary said with a sigh, because Democrats were afraid to stand up. He said not a soul had called from the House. In fact, added the president, Gephardt was so mad that he had refused to take Clinton's call explaining the reasons for the speech. "Gephardt is an asshole," Hillary commented. The president, pointing to my recorders, advised gently that the tapes were on. She winced but shrugged with a smile. "Well, he is," she insisted. In an awkward silence, I backed up both machines to erase the first lady's epithet. Moving on, we discussed the actress Anna Deavere Smith for some reason, plus experiments with "benchmark" governance in Oregon. Hillary wanted to know whether Kurt Schmoke, with whom the Clintons had overlapped at Yale, was likely to be reelected mayor of Baltimore.

The president dissected the last two moves by the Federal Reserve to raise interest rates. He considered them both overkill against a nonexistent threat of inflation. With economic growth already at a paltry 1.5

percent, down from 5.1 percent at the end of 1994, the rate hikes had
choked off factory orders before two straight months of declining national employment. More than a hundred thousand jobs had disappeared in May, reversing the upward trend of 6.7 million new jobs
toward Clinton's huge first-term goal of eight million. Clinton said he
had called Fed chairman Alan Greenspan only today. While previewing
tonight's budget speech, he suggested why lower interest rates were essential to attack the deficit. They reduced it outright, of course, with
smaller financing costs on the national debt. More delicately, lower rates
gave Clinton political room for extra budget cuts, because they generated economic growth to compensate constituents for lost government
spending. On both fronts, Fed policy could reinforce budget calculations. Together, budget cuts and lower interest rates had whittled down
the annual shortfall by a third—slowly at first—and further coordination
could reverse the momentum of perpetual deficits. The president said he
thought Greenspan agreed.

He reviewed a strange event with Speaker Gingrich. Its genesis was a
throwaway question from a press interview, asking Clinton what advice
he might give for Gingrich's exploratory visit to New Hampshire. The
president had waxed nostalgic, replying that he should first seek folk
wisdom at Mary Hill's grocery store in Concord, and the speaker, seeing
the subsequent story, called to propose a joint appearance. Clinton said
this novel idea pitched his White House staff into revolt. Most suspected
an ambush, figuring Gingrich would concoct a scheme to elevate his
presidential ambitions at Clinton's expense, but the president overruled
them. He went from his commencement address at Dartmouth to a senior citizens picnic in the woods near Claremont, sitting with Gingrich
to answer questions on everything from Medicare to the line item veto.
There were sharp disagreements in an atmosphere of folksy banter. The
audience loved it, said Clinton, but reporters wrote disappointed articles
with wobbly spin on the "love fest." Partisans attacked their own side for
being too friendly. The president, noticing anxieties in common between pundits and political advisers, resolved to discount them relative
to his feel for the voters themselves. He said this notion fortified him to
release tonight's budget blueprint in spite of strenuous objection from
the political pros.

Well through his first term, Clinton had just vetoed his first bill from Congress. It was a bipartisan test to make token cuts of some $16 billion—about one percent—from current appropriations. In response to my questions, the president said they had identified mutually acceptable savings when Congress proposed to add new spending heavily concentrated in the districts and states of Republican leaders themselves. This was politics, he said, but they wanted to pay for their pet projects by eliminating Clinton's AmeriCorps youth service along with his college tuition program, and it was also politics for him to refuse. Clinton said he negotiated them down to about $700 million in patronage projects—mostly courthouses and new highways—but then the leaders could not agree among themselves on whose pork would be eliminated. So he vetoed the bill. Then the leaders, still trying to revive it, had come back two days ago asking him to take less in education so they could accommodate each other. To pacify their base, they also wanted some anti-environmental language they passed off as trivial. The president refused, telling the speaker that too many House Republicans believed all Gingrich's rhetoric on confronting the evil Democrats. There would be plenty to fight about with Gingrich.

TWO SURPRISES INTERVENED shortly before the July session. First, Clinton's college friend Tommy Caplan invited my wife, Christy, and me to dinner at Washington's Jockey Club on a Monday night. What Bill and Hillary really needed, he decided, was a quiet social evening outside the White House, free of protocol. This would be no small feat, as President Clinton was glued to a motorcade and his Secret Service detail, not to mention the nuclear codes, but Caplan brushed aside my skepticism. Just come, he said, and we found a little back room partitioned off from the main restaurant, with a dozen place settings around an oval table. The waiters buzzed before the Clintons arrived. I was seated next to Nancy Hernreich, and our secret partnership on the oral history project made it a special pleasure to get acquainted. Other guests nearby included novelist Susan Shreve and the head of the National Institutes of Health, Dr. Harold Varmus, who discussed the scientific basis for regulating tobacco products.

The president walked around behind me during the meal. "Did you see that?" he whispered, leaning over. I said no. Emmett Tyrrell, publisher of *The American Spectator*, had slipped through the partition to ask whether Clinton had read his new article, "The Arkansas Drug Shuttle," in which ex-trooper L. D. Brown conveniently vouched for the most lurid anti-Clinton fantasies in circulation, about how the former governor had nurtured a drugs-and-murder CIA ring from the airport in Mena, Arkansas. The president replied that he didn't need to read it, because Brown was a liar who had injured people including his own family all his life, but, he said, Tyrrell persistently boasted that his story already was being picked up by mainstream newspapers. If so, Clinton told him, this revealed fault in the media rather than merit in Tyrrell's article. Almost gasping, he said Tyrrell had brought two young teenage girls with him like shields, which made it hard to fend him off. The intrusion punctured Caplan's design for a respite of normalcy, but he and the president recovered to exchange humorous toasts on the lasting bond from their adventures as paired oddballs at Georgetown University.

That Friday, July 21, beginning a bizarre fling with Clinton's government, official alarm poured into my writing roost from Deputy Secretary of State Strobe Talbott, followed quickly by AID Administrator Brian Atwood, Ambassador James Dobbins, Sandy Berger, and AID's Haiti officer, Mark Schneider—each one calling me for the first time at home, upset about a story in the *New York Times*. It said Robert Pastor, a foreign policy specialist now affiliated with the Carter Center in Atlanta, had criticized Haiti's parliamentary elections in June as chaotic and flawed, which gave Republicans in Congress nonpartisan grist to claim that Clinton's Haiti policy had failed. Would I go see President Aristide to address the problems Pastor identified? Stunned, I begged off. Such a mission was the ambassador's job, and besides, I didn't even have a passport. Ambassador Bill Swing introduced himself by telephone from Haiti to say he welcomed help, and coded faxes soon rescued me from several airport interrogation rooms to board an international flight without travel documents of any kind. Well into Saturday night, at President Aristide's home outside Port-au-Prince, Aristide and his lawyer, Mildred Trouillot, briefed me on the irregularities bursting from the poor country's premier election with eleven thousand candidates from twenty-seven parties vying for some two thousand offices.

All Sunday morning, political and security officers reviewed the principal disputes from our embassy's point of view. They said the major parties wanted "do-overs" in some districts, threatening to boycott runoff elections, and Aristide needed to make deals with his political opponents to legitimize the election results. Abouja, a "street priest" recommended by film director Jonathan Demme, located several of these party leaders for me by signals reminiscent of a Graham Greene spy novel. Evans Paul, the mayor of Port-au-Prince, seemed to be in hiding with deputies after receiving only 18 percent of the vote for reelection. Paul was a democratic activist familiar to many foreigners, having been jailed by dictators and later managed Aristide's presidential campaign before repositioning his own party to succeed Aristide. His crushing loss to a wandering folksinger disturbed Bob Pastor as evidence of foul play, but Paul himself shied away from seeking new or fairer balloting. For three sweaty hours, arguing that the folksinger had cast a spell over voters, he envisioned political adjustments instead through some sort of ad hoc executive council.

Ambassador Swing confirmed over Sunday dinner that the folksinger novice probably did win in a landslide, even without an endorsement from Aristide, because the city's poor masses had turned against Evans Paul as an ingrate. He said Haiti faced an acute "George Washington problem": how to instill democratic norms when the founding hero is revered like a monarch. Swing told stories of its echo in South Africa, where he had begun his diplomatic career during the 1964 apartheid trial of Nelson Mandela, returning decades later as U.S. ambassador when Mandela emerged from prison to launch his miracle of biracial democracy. Having counseled both leaders, Swing thought Mandela had been blessed, paradoxically, with a larger popular opposition than Aristide. In Haiti, elections exposed a crucial flaw in the role of its customary leaders: they had virtually no public support. Swing endorsed one compromise proposal that had appealed to Evans Paul, and coached me all the way to the airport, still without a passport. Aristide could not simply fire the imperious, incompetent head of the national elections board, which was legally independent. To do so would undermine any nascent respect for elections by reinforcing Haiti's stubborn custom of "vote sharing." Instead, Aristide needed to persuade several other members of the elections board to resign voluntarily along with the head. This would observe legalities and cushion the politics, while giving the disgruntled party leaders a scapegoat for electoral failure.

After a flurry of consultations, Sandy Berger and Jim Dobbins instructed me to tell Aristide that the international community would announce support for the desired changes in the elections board. Nancy Hernreich then provided an escort to a third-floor bedroom in the White House residence, where I would spend Monday night before returning home to Baltimore. A knock from President Clinton found me hours later, somewhat dazed, waiting with my recorders. Downstairs, he changed into jeans and a Special Olympics T-shirt. "Do you really think we need to get rid of the head of the elections commission down there?" he asked. Yes, I replied, but it was complicated. He nodded, and we were pretty much finished with Haiti for this session. He said the shit was hitting the fan in Bosnia.

The president was exercised that night about a sudden offensive against three remaining Muslim enclaves in eastern Bosnia, near its border with greater Serbia. Bosnian Serb armies had overrun the designated U.N. "safe area" of Srebrenica two weeks ago, seizing Dutch peacekeepers as hostages against retaliation, and uncorroborated horror stories on the fate of Muslim villagers seeped through a news blackout. Now the Bosnian Serbs were driving into Zepa while tightening their encirclement around Gorazde. To stop them, the new French president, Jacques Chirac, publicly offered to take the blue U.N. helmets off a thousand French troops and let them fight, provided that the United States could airlift them into Gorazde. Clinton, for his part, labored to simplify the cumbersome "two-key" command structure that required both NATO and U.N. approval for air strikes. He wanted NATO to control the bombing on military logic. Its leaders were more aggressive, knowing that the Bosnian Serbs would stay reluctant to harm U.N. hostages so long as NATO credibly threatened to pulverize their command and supply centers to the rear.

Almost on cue, a Bosnia phone call came through from Secretary of State Christopher. I left the tapes running to record the president's side.

No, he kept saying, he did *not* agree to restore the U.N. sign-off for air strikes. Who said he did? Why would he want to get Boutros-Ghali back in there? Clinton repeatedly assured Christopher that he had not wavered on scrapping the two-key agreement. He said this sabotage must be Chirac. It was Chirac's way of acting tough but then wiggling out behind some ruse. During pauses, when Christopher apparently tracked his sources, the president chewed an unlit cigar while glancing at his *New York Times* crossword puzzle, which he finished and laid aside. Then he dealt solitaire busily on the table as he traded thoughts with Christopher on how to stamp out the rumors of backsliding. He spun out reasons why they were wrong on fact, substance, and now the politics, because a stronger U.N. role in Bosnia would abet a congressional challenge to his policy. The president hung up, holding his cards, which snapped me out of a reverie that this was extreme multitasking even for him. "That's what it's like," he said, of Bosnia. "Terrible and never ending."

Should he go at last to the United Nations, declaring that its peacekeepers only hampered this war crisis, seeking repeal of the multinational arms embargo in order to let the Bosnians defend themselves? That would be more honest, Clinton replied, but not necessarily more effective even if it could pass. In the event of repeal, weapons would flow first to Bosnian Serbs from the armories of their allies next door in Serbia. Because of politics, and timing, Clinton longed for something like FDR's Lend-Lease program of military supplies for England before World War II—some way to help the Bosnians without overtly breaking the embargo—but it was harder now to get away with violations of neutrality. "I think about Roosevelt all the time," he said wistfully.

He reviewed clashes with China. The government had recalled its ambassador from Washington when Clinton let President Lee of Taiwan visit the United States. Clinton said Beijing reacted hysterically, out of all proportion. Following public threats of reprisal, China first arrested the democratic activist Harry Wu, who had been imprisoned for nineteen years under Mao. Against diplomatic protocol, jail guards abused the U.S. consuls who tried to visit Wu, a naturalized American citizen. The Chinese ambassador, on his return to Washington, excused treason charges against Wu as insignificant while venting official fury to Clinton over "the renegade" from Taiwan. Lee's statements of democratic principle at Cornell* were especially insolent to Beijing's ear, and the president said he argued with the ambassador to a blunt, worrisome standoff. Whenever Americans offer any criticism on human rights, Clinton told him, Chinese officials say we must respect their internal prerogatives and try to understand how their culture venerates social control above individual liberties. Well, now the Chinese should try to understand how much Americans value free speech and the right to travel. Clinton said the ambassador did not think well of his explanation.

In sharp contrast, the president had received very little protest over his decision to exchange full diplomatic recognition with Vietnam—twenty years after its Communist government consolidated an epic victory over foes including the United States. U.S. war veterans from both parties praised the move eloquently at the White House ceremony, with Senator John McCain flanked by Senators John Kerry and Chuck Robb, and Clinton said most Americans seemed to approve, quietly, sensing the time was right, without dwelling on reminders of a war that still scarred our generation. He asked why there was such controversy instead over Robert McNamara's confessional memoir—"We were wrong, terribly wrong"—about his seminal role in the Vietnam War. I thought it was because McNamara admitted willful public deception, which was bad enough, on whether the American war effort in Vietnam was winnable, which remains a sensitive political topic. Beyond that, McNamara was silent on the deeper questions of purpose—when and how it can be justified to pursue systemic political goals for another country by war, winnable or not. The president said he had not read enough of the book to understand the vitriol against McNamara for going as far as he did. Most architects of major wars don't question themselves in public at all, he

---

* "My years at Cornell from 1965 to 1968 made an indelible impression on me," President Lee declared in his university lecture on June 9, 1995. "This was a time of social turbulence in the United States, with the civil rights movement and the Vietnam War protest. Yet, despite that turbulence, the American democratic system prevailed. It was also the time I first recognized that full democracy could engender ultimately peaceful change, and that lack of democracy must be confronted with democratic methods, and lack of freedom must be confronted by the idea of freedom."

observed, and deep passions, though sometimes submerged, still dis-placed healing reflection on this war. He saw them poignantly in the dogged search for the remaining 2,200 American MIAs in Southeast Asia. By comparison, the victorious Vietnamese ignored their own 300,000 MIAs, as we overlooked our 79,000 MIAs from World War II, where they dug and sifted across their land for U.S. dog tags or scraps of bone. Whatever its other faults, the Vietnamese government patiently obliged us despite the vanishing odds of any plausible recovery. "There's never been anything like this in the history of warfare," said Clinton.

RAW POLITICS DOMINATED several subjects. House hearings on Waco had just begun with a pronouncement by Chairman William Zeliff of New Hampshire that "all these deaths were the direct result of federal govern-ment action." Elsewhere, Clinton conceded defeat for his nomination of Dr. Henry Foster to become surgeon general, observing that an un-breakable Senate filibuster was all about the Republican presidential nomination. Dole simply could not allow an up-or-down vote, which might risk his own support from the anti-abortion Republican base. The president's only consolation was a farewell weekend in Arkansas with the gracious Dr. Foster, who was "not a half-bad golfer." On abortion itself, he bemoaned his failure to move beyond the rigid ideological standoff. He had gained no public traction by commending the United Pentecostal Church for its cooperative campaign to adopt unwanted ba-bies without discrimination or stigma. He said he had reviewed debates back through the original abortion statutes here and abroad, tracing dis-tinctive laws all over Europe that outlaw abortions after the tenth or twelfth week of pregnancy, whereas American states permit them until the third trimester, or twenty-fifth week. After describing the gnarled obstacles to his goal of making terminated pregnancy "safe, legal, and rare," Clinton said he would "remove the thorn of abortion" if he could, but he had not yet figured out a way.

The president berated himself for naiveté in the closing of military installations made obsolete by the end of the Cold War. By choosing an independent defense analyst to supervise the preparation of the "hit list," he reaped the worst of both worlds—no influence, yet sanctimo-nious press charges that his public suggestions corrupted a neutral zone carefully insulated from selfish politics. What really happened was ugly. When they lost the Congress, leading Democrats and their staff ran over to the Base Closure Commission to protect their interests. He said they screwed Connecticut because it had no defense Democrats or Republicans. They screwed California by assigning it fully half the bases to be closed. Clinton said he didn't need those bases to win California, but nobody else pointed out the gross disparity in economic impact, with the California unemployment rate already above the national average by 40 percent. He also protested the commission's devastating impact on Texas, which he had no chance to win, because the proposed cutbacks there targeted impoverished areas around San Antonio, where nearly half of all Hispanic soldiers lived. Clinton groaned, "I snookered myself politically. I should have appointed someone who would be loyal to me."

The reelection campaign was quietly under way, and details of fundraising events rolled easily from his tongue. He said he had given a lot of thought to shape and structure but was not yet committed. The only way to set a political course was to hire people, he said, and that was too expensive this early. The consultants were all around, chipping in. He mentioned Paul Begala, Stanley Greenberg, James Carville, and Frank Greer, among others, saying he loved Greer for suggesting the "common ground" theme. No, Dick Morris was not his "favorite" political adviser, as mischievously rumored by colleagues who had more or less blackballed him. Morris was irascible and abrasive, but fearless. He was the only consultant who had warned bluntly that the Senate was foregone to turn Republican, saying Clinton's one slim chance to keep the House was to ignore its floundering Democratic candidates and bask in a presidential glow from the peace treaty between Israel and Jordan. Clinton disregarded this advice, probably unwisely he thought, but Morris's rivals fed reporters what they wanted to hear about his Svengali influence. In fact, said the president, Morris knew his place, and all you had to do was tell him no when his recommendations got out of line.

He scoffed at reports that Morris was writing his speeches. This was a time for testing potential issues before the election year, and Clinton said he was writing most of them himself. His July 12 address on religious freedom, at James Madison High School in Virginia, pictured a two-sided coin of uniquely American balance, which safeguarded the free exercise of religion while prohibiting its establishment. The Constitution did not mandate a religion-free country, as some wanted to believe, nor prefer any theology or belief as such. Clinton bemoaned a widespread lack of sophistication on the difference between state-sponsored religion and individual religious initiative within a state-sponsored context such as a school. He said too many principals would snatch Bibles or yarmulkes from students for fear of implied endorsement, just as teachers often distorted history by omitting its powerful religious currents. We discussed Martin Luther King as a marvel at the opposite extreme. He had invoked democracy and religion daily on the most radioactive controversies—reaping hatred, applause, and refraction of every kind, but miraculously no criticism for mixing church and state. I thought it was because King's ingenious oratory never subordinated one to the other. Clinton said the public was becoming more comfortable with religious pluralism than the press, which remained at once skittish, sensational, and patronizing about matters of faith.

Of his major speech on race and affirmative action, the president said he had rewritten the final draft after cross-examining Deval Patrick and Chris Edley among other legal experts on all 130 affirmative action programs. He hadn't even known so many existed, but he resolved to decide each one on its merits. Most of them deserved continuation with a few changes, and he offered straightforward support for the program as a whole. ("Let me be clear," he declared at the National Archives. "Affirmative action has been good for America.") On the tapes, Clinton said he knew this comprehensive approach may not lift his poll numbers on affirmative action much above 30 percent. So be it, he said. He wanted to serve notice that if the Republicans attacked him next year, he would be eager to respond head-on, in detail, having laid out the history and the numbers by economic sector for females, Asians, and Hispanics, as well as African-Americans. White males still held 95 percent of the top management positions in corporate America. Black unemployment was twice white unemployment, and females earned roughly a third less than men for comparable jobs. Clinton's limited aim was confining the opposition to its hit-and-run flares from two blatantly contradictory poles, that discrimination was either solved or unsolvable.

He commended one press commentary on the pitfalls of reverse discrimination. At close angle, wrote *Washington Post* columnist Jonathan Yardley, each dose of affirmative action displaces some qualified person. Therefore, logic bedevils affirmative action in its own fair cause, and only gut experience or a larger perspective can argue otherwise.

The president bristled at news stories insinuating that he pursued the crime issue for shallow political motives, to look more like a Republican. No Republican president ever broke with the National Rifle Association, he said, at least not while in office. Having done so to pass the Brady Bill, and then the assault weapons ban, Clinton resolved early to stay on the offensive against the NRA's renowned political muscle as he headed into the 1996 election. He proposed to outlaw "cop-killer" bullets with a bill that almost certainly would fail in this Congress, but he wanted people to know exactly why he was for it. On tape, he recalled introducing the idea at a June 30 memorial rally for a Chicago police officer killed by armor-piercing ammunition through his Kevlar bulletproof vest, fired from a Tec-9 assault weapon. His speech there drew attention with what he called a calculated line to reassure hunters frightened by NRA propaganda. ("I'm almost fifty years old," he declared, "and I've never seen a deer, a duck, or a wild turkey wearing a Kevlar vest in my life. You do not need these bullets.") The jest was effective in the press, but he volunteered that all his remarks were a dramatic letdown from the introduction by a black police captain with an Irish name, who told of surviving military service twenty years apart in Vietnam and Iraq's Desert Storm, only to answer a call a block away in the 15th Precinct, where, "within ten seconds I had eleven bullets in my body and my partner over there had four." The president quoted his tale of survival, his tribute to slain friends, and his confession that he never dreamed of making a political speech until shamed by the wrongheaded hysteria to preserve these assault weapons. This introduction had melted the audience, Clinton allowed, before he said a word.

CHAPTER SEVENTEEN

GIRDING FOR SHOWDOWN

Monday, August 14, 1995

Usher Skip Allen, who was knitting a rug, escorted me upstairs to the Treaty Room, but President Clinton shifted our August 14 session to the West Wing because he had work to finish there. Walking over from the residence, he assuaged my fretful comments about trying to work in the fishbowl ahead. It was getaway night before his family vacation started tomorrow in Wyoming, and everyone was gone—even Nancy Hernreich. In the deserted Oval Office, Clinton dragged over a high-backed chair, saying his upper back hurt too much for him to use the soft chairs or sofas around the fireplace. He sat rigidly upright, chewing his unlit cigar. As I arranged recording materials on the coffee table, he noticed my new drugstore spectacles and asked to try them. I said close vision for me had succumbed to age and many years staring at typewriters or computer screens. He squinted and blinked, finding that he could read through one lens but not the other. His own superior eyesight had fallen apart unevenly, he said with a sigh, so that now he needed prescription glasses to correct each eye for reading.

Tonight's stinging preoccupation was Bosnia. In July, even while the international tribunal at The Hague was indicting the Bosnian Serb leader Radovan Karadzic for war crimes committed years earlier, Karadzic's militias overran the desperately besieged U.N. protectorate of Zepa. The president said investigators were assembling credible reports that the militias massacred and raped thousands of Muslim civilians there and in Srebrenica.* Enough disaster was known already to throw the international peacekeepers into a humiliating crisis, and a fog of complexity shielded posturing of every kind. Clinton said he was obliged to get "downright testy" with French president Jacques Chirac, who kept touting his public offer of elite French soldiers to save Gorazde, the last of eastern Bosnia's three Muslim enclaves. Privately, Chirac admitted that his own generals considered his plan militarily unsound. A thousand soldiers were not nearly enough, and they could reach Gorazde only by hitching a ride through the mountains aboard U.S. helicopters that would be easy targets for Serb gunners. Chirac would never go through with it, even if he could, but he loved to look macho. His nickname was "Le Bulldozer." He had just shocked the world by scheduling tests of nuclear weapons on French possessions in the Pacific Islands. His prime minister announced that the Bosnian war already would be won "if the Americans had lifted their little finger." The effete American press laps up criticism from France, Clinton quipped, and the right-wingers love to say that even the French make Clinton look wimpy.

Speaker Gingrich breezily declared that he could think of twenty ways to fix Bosnia without risking a single American soldier. He and Senator Dole, ignoring Clinton's pleas, pushed a bill through Congress to break the arms embargo on Bosnia unilaterally. The president, explaining again why he was opposed, vetoed it. Among his lesser considerations was the eagerness of the French to reciprocate by breaking the U.N. arms embargo on Iraq, in place since the Gulf War, so they could make money off Saddam Hussein. Yeltsin could provide no help from Russia, where his own parliament was passing chest-thumping resolutions to guarantee victory for the Serbs. Only Senator Dick Lugar of Indiana, the Republican chair of Foreign Relations, had proposed a consistent, logical course to resolve the religious war in Bosnia. Clinton said

---

* Eventually, the Red Cross and other agencies verified more than seven thousand victims from trench graves near Srebrenica alone, making it the largest mass murder in Europe since World War II. In 2007, the World Court designated these executions a crime of genocide.

Lugar wanted to replace the U.N. peacekeepers with U.S. combat troops, which was real enough to leave him isolated and ignored.

Overall, the president used a strange metaphor to characterize the international imbroglio. I labored afterward to recall the name for my dictation. It had the feel of Russian roulette applied to dancing—something like a Hungarian standoff. Many bad ideas held each other hostage. Meanwhile, a hundred thousand Croatian soldiers had launched an offensive in the Krajina region to recover lost territory for Bosnia, and the Bosnian government itself cobbled together enough arms to outfit more soldiers than the Bosnian Serbs. The British and French lobbied intensely for the United States to stop these counteroffensives, arguing that they may incite greater Serbia to invade from the other side, but Clinton said he refused. Beneath the sensational crimes around Srebrenica, the surprising military success of the Croats and Bosnian government pushed Bosnia slowly toward its original shape. He had sent Tony Lake to Europe with stern demands for more aggressive NATO air strikes to stave off mortal threats to Gorazde, Sarajevo, and other Muslim areas encircled by Bosnian Serbs. At home, the president faced daily threats that Congress would lift the arms embargo unilaterally by overriding his veto. That measure still sounded virile and easy, but he believed the Republicans would stop themselves just short of a victory that would make them responsible for the consequences, most of which were likely to be bad. Clinton concluded that Bosnia remained delicate, lethal, and tense. To accomplish anything was like threading a needle.

He answered questions about domestic battles over tobacco, which now overlapped his Bosnia negotiations with Dole and Gingrich. They had begun in July with ferocious political debates inside the White House. By coincidence, the Justice Department was completing perjury investigations of tobacco executives just as Food and Drug Administration Commissioner David Kessler proposed federal regulations to curtail cigarette marketing aimed at children. Clinton said the numbers are grim. Youth smoking remains a hidden epidemic. Although the fifty states have criminal laws against selling cigarettes to minors, three thousand new teenagers take up smoking every day, incurring addictions that eventually kill one-third of each day's recruits. Of all two million Americans who die annually, 400,000 die of tobacco-related causes, and since virtually no smokers begin the habit as adults, only fresh youth can replenish the wide river of brown lungs and shortened lives. Indispensably for tobacco companies, this wholly illegal market perpetuates the largest preventable health disaster in history.

The president said Al Gore excused himself from the internal arguments because his sister, Nancy, had died of lung cancer. Before leaving, Gore outlined the economic hardships learned from childhood on his family's tobacco farm in Tennessee. Tobacco is still a lucrative, stable cash crop for small farmers, although the growers receive less than a nickel on each pack of cigarettes sold. This harsh combination frustrates every inventive design to wean family farms to alternative crops by subsidy or transitional allowance. The president outlined several failed schemes. He said tobacco farmers, cruelly, were concentrated in several states being contested after a century of "solid South" hegemony for Democrats: Kentucky, Tennessee, Virginia, and North Carolina. Numerous tobacco state Democrats begged the White House to leave tobacco alone, and Clinton said most of his staff agreed. They called the proposed regulations political suicide, however worthy the goal. Big tobacco was like the gun lobby. It mobilizes mountains of money behind high-intensity "bullet voters" who care much more about their single issue than your tepid reformers with multiple priorities.

I asked how much our generation's partisan shift influenced his choice. He and I had grown up in the South when local Democrats were so universal that the word "Republican" was a synonym for "Yankee"— with GOP officials unknown, GOP candidates rare, and ordinary Republicans considered eccentric. Since the civil rights era, however, Southern Republicans had sprung up from nothing to become the presumptive party of white voters, until, coldly speaking, a Democratic president had little left to lose. True, said Clinton, the cost was reduced, but he could not simply write off the entire tobacco South, with inevitable ripples into Florida and Missouri. Nor could he drive away good people from those states who wanted to stay Democrats, such as Senator Wendell Ford of Kentucky and Governor Jim Hunt of North Carolina.

He had tried to soften the political risk by putting the tobacco reforms into law, which would require Republican support, and this move touched off clawing behind the scenes. Only Commissioner Kessler was generously pragmatic, said Clinton, offering to surrender his prospective FDA jurisdiction in exchange for a statute that would take effect immediately on stronger political ground. The tobacco companies feuded among themselves. Philip Morris, the richest one, favored the anti-tobacco legislation as a strategic retreat to avoid the precedent of FDA jurisdiction. Its abiding fear was that FDA control would expand inexorably from children to adults, one day sweeping tobacco products entirely from the shelves like disease-tainted fruit or a defective drug. Smaller tobacco companies preferred to fight on all fronts, against the FDA in court and the legislation in Congress. The president said its lobbyists made alliances with new Republicans rising in the tobacco states. These were the shock troops from the Gingrich revolution, who wanted Clinton alone to promulgate new FDA rules so their allies could win more seats by branding Democrats the anti-tobacco party. As they argued with more established Republicans, many of whom favored the bill to protect children, the president said one thing was certain: Gingrich and Dole would not let their party divide on so potent an issue. They would either invoke discipline to pass a bipartisan law, neutralizing tobacco politics, or they would discard the bill without allowing any recorded votes.

The shock troops narrowly shelved the legislation, whereupon Clinton, overriding a final spasm of protest from his White House staff, publicly authorized Kessler to initiate FDA regulations on tobacco marketing to minors. Tobacco companies immediately sued to block them. Republicans denounced "big government," and the political landscape heaved to adjust. Within the past forty-eight hours, factions from all sides had pressed Clinton to revive the legislation. He was distressed enough to seek help from one of his bitterest critics, Ralph Reed of the Christian Coalition, but religious conservatives ducked this cause. Committed, the president said the regulations if sustained promised at least modest curbs on youth smoking. They would effectively banish cigarette vending machines, billboards, and child-targeted ads such as the cartoon icon Joe Camel, a cool siren of tobacco recognized by more six-year-olds than Mickey Mouse.* Politically, Clinton hoped to earn credit

---

* After two years of rearguard litigation to save Joe Camel, R.J. Reynolds Tobacco Company erased the advertising image from public view on July 12, 1997.

with the voters by tackling the tough issues at home and abroad. Uncannily, he remarked, many domestic ones highlighted children—"the least of these"—from public health to the debt burden. Gunshots kill an American youth every two hours, and two children start smoking every minute.

CONGRESS WAS OPEN for business in anticipation of the election year, and the president analyzed a number of pending bills that he called anti-competitive in the guise of competition. On telecommunications reform, for instance, a veritable flood of political money had allowed the regional "Baby Bells" to gain decisive advantages over the long-distance companies. "They just completely rolled them," he said, positioning the Bells to acquire more local monopolies. He recalled meeting a number of long-distance executives at a recent fund-raiser, all lifelong Republicans, sulking that they lost in spite of hiring as their chief lobbyists Marlin Fitzwater, President Reagan's former spokesman, and the celebrated GOP leader Howard Baker. These executives confessed surprise when Clinton recited numerous details of the bill he found unfair to them, endorsing their point of view, and they hinted astonishment when he vowed to seek redress from the opposing political camp, gratis. They had expected no recourse or solace by their rules. Bluntly, said the president, the difference between the two political parties is that the Democrats sell access and the Republicans sell control. "Businesspeople know a bargain when they see one," Clinton observed. "They'd rather have control, and they're willing to pay a premium for it."

The president anticipated a clash with Congress over the purpose of government itself. Only six weeks before the end of the fiscal year, the thirteen annual appropriations bills needed to keep federal agencies running still languished somewhere between the Republican House and Senate. Given the ominous tensions, I asked what it was like to play golf with a central negotiator on the other side in Louisiana's Bob Livingston, chairman of the House Appropriations Committee. My question, perhaps poorly chosen, led to a spirited reminiscence on the golf at TPC Sawgrass in Florida, starting with its layout and beauty. He said Livingston did not play much. He had been trying to teach the chairman a few ways to improve his swing, but then Clinton's own game failed him all day. Nothing went straight, and the new course, however famous on television, was unfamiliar to him as a player. His only consolation was that he clearly impressed Livingston with long drives on a few holes.

As to the impasse over appropriations, Clinton said the pivotal figure was Speaker Gingrich, who had marshaled steadfast pressure behind a test bill on education, refusing all pleas from the few Republican moderates to soften cuts in student loans and other popular programs. Gingrich hammered and cajoled for unity to vindicate the 1994 landslide, until he reached the magic number of 218 for passage. When you're in the majority, said Clinton, you can usually win the close votes by holding firm, and this outcome set a course toward a broad, historic meltdown. The president said Gingrich and Dole now were lining up the appropriations bills for a political version of chicken, after the fabled teenage duels in which hot rod drivers speed headlong at each other to see who swerves first. He predicted they would send him a Medicare appropriations bill just before the annual funds expired, forcing Clinton to sign its draconian cuts or let Medicare lapse entirely. In a rush, they would send punitive, last-minute appropriations also for regulatory agencies and civilian departments, forcing Clinton to capitulate or shutter them with a veto. He thought they would spare only their own congressional budget, plus the military aspects of government.

Even these bedrock functions might not be safe, the president warned. He said few Republicans in Congress had ever voted to raise the legal ceiling for public debt, as required periodically to finance new deficits on top of the old ones being recycled. This unwelcome duty had belonged to the majority Democrats for most of the past sixty years, allowing Republicans to stand innocently aside. Now a determined wing bridled at governing responsibly. Out of old habit and new ideological zeal, they kept fiercely aloof as the debt ceiling converged with the end of the fiscal year, vowing to ignore Uncle Sam's credit card even if it pitched the United States into default on all its obligations. Unless Gingrich could be induced to tone down his right-wing freshman caucus, Clinton feared, they would shut down federal offices literally from the Treasury to Fort Greely, Alaska.

He said he really needed his vacation before these battles. The August heat was taking its toll, and he found himself thinking a lot about

the election year ahead. I asked whether he focused on the grand strategies or the daily polls and individual states. "All of those," he replied. "I
think about all of those." He said he had weathered the latest congressional hearings on Whitewater and Waco pretty well so far. He thought
Dole would be most formidable if he ran with Colin Powell, but that
Powell would have a hard time over his support for abortion and affirmative action. In fact, the president remarked, many of the Republican
governors themselves were upset with the national party for stirring
up wedge issues they had managed pretty well back home. Only Kirk
Fordice of Mississippi, George W. Bush of Texas, and Pete Wilson of
California supported Dole's initiative to repeal all the laws on affirmative action. Last time, said Clinton, he won all five Mississippi River
states stacked from Minnesota down to Louisiana, but as of now he figured to lose Louisiana and Missouri. Adverse politics in the grazing
states would make it impossible for him to win Montana or Colorado a
second time. Prospects were good on the West Coast and in New England except New Hampshire, where he saw a chance only if a Ross Perot
third-party run drained votes from the Republican advantage. The president thought he had a shot in Florida, a message for Pennsylvania and
New Jersey, and a chance to salvage Kentucky and Tennessee again from
the Deep South. He gained momentum as he sketched nearly all the
states, recalling vote totals and swing districts, ending with a prediction
that the whole election might turn on Ohio.* Although Bosnia had hurt
him lately with dissatisfaction in the polls, Clinton said a strong campaign could make him the first Democrat since FDR to win consecutive
terms. Joining Roosevelt and Woodrow Wilson, he added pensively, he
could become only the fourth since 1832, going all the way back to Andrew Jackson.

The president excused himself to his desk after a few more topics,
taking with him a souvenir from my research files. On its front page of
December 17, 1964, the *New York Times* pictured Senator Ted Kennedy
walking unaided for the first time since a plane crash left him with a
broken back. Next to the thirty-year-old photograph was a news story

---

* These hunches for 1996 turned out to be cautious. President Clinton won all
the states mentioned except Colorado and Montana.

that cigarette companies were adopting a code to eliminate sales pitches aimed at young people, including suggestions that smoking enhanced fitness, success, and eye-popping romance. Wryly amused, the president noted Kennedy's boyish looks back when tobacco first promised reforms.

Moments later, stepping over to hand him the finished tapes, I asked gingerly if he was open to advice about his public messages of late. Absorbed elsewhere, he said yes with a nod that meant make it quick. I said his trial speeches about "common ground" were getting trivialized as an expedient search for some happy medium where everyone can get along. On his main goals, from Bosnia to cop-killer bullets, he should emphasize that common ground demanded an arduous stretch of antagonists just to stay in the same unfamiliar room, creating a threshold for constructive politics. The president said he agreed. His glance hinted that it was easier to express than to make heard. He looked down at his papers as I left, thanking me as usual for my troubles on his project

Hillary's aide Capricia Marshall blocked my exit through the residence. She pulled me surreptitiously aside, lest any of the ushers overhear her mission to get my spontaneous historical advice. The official Bush portraits finally had arrived, presenting complex choices over placement that Hillary wanted to resolve before she left for the family vacation in Wyoming. Nonplussed, I followed down the cross hall outside the Blue Room and Green Room, past the portraits of Jimmy Carter, Lyndon Johnson, and Gerald Ford. Capricia said these three had to stay, despite their inferior quality, because they were the only modern ones small enough to fit the wall space. In the grand East Room, the new Bushes sat lonely on separate easels. Barbara Bush was complaining that the artist made her look fat, said Capricia, pausing as though to invite objective judgment. Perhaps so, I hesitantly replied, but she also seemed graver if not wiser than this smirking version of her husband. I learned that President Bush was now scheduled for Harry Truman's spot in the Entrance Hall, and Kennedy would replace FDR on the other side coming in from the North Portico. Capricia said Kennedy needed a prominent display because so many tourists asked about JFK's famously brooding pose not long before his assassination.

Our footsteps echoed in night stillness back to the stairwell leading up from the Entrance Hall. Truman was bumping Ronald Reagan from its alcove, Capricia informed me. Eisenhower was retiring Herbert Hoover from one of two archways above the landing, but there was some question about Woodrow Wilson in the other one. I confessed mixed feelings. Historically, Wilson's idealism was severely compromised—at home by his segregation of Washington and the federal government, abroad by his role in imposing artificial colonial boundaries that still plague the world. To my amateur eye, however, a haunting depth of character lifted this portrait high for artistry in the presidential series. Wilson might stay, Capricia guessed, but a problem remained with Nixon, who presently faced Kennedy in the Cross Hall going west toward the State Dining Room. Reagan would move to Kennedy's vacated place, and Hillary planned to balance Reagan with FDR, but she wanted to know if she could get away with hiding Nixon someplace upstairs, out of sight. We dithered over factors from etiquette to partisan pique. To propose a compromise, I took Capricia downstairs to the ground-floor hallway past the White House theater, where a second FDR hung next to Andrew Johnson. Nixon could supplant either one of these, I suggested. Capricia seemed doubtful. We agreed that every president winds up a flat, movable portrait of debatable fidelity.

CHAPTER EIGHTEEN

POPE JOHN PAUL II: "TELL ME HOW YOU SEE THE WORLD"

Wednesday, October 4, 1995

Tuesday, October 31, 1995

Seven weeks later, after an aborted session in September, the pulsing roar of a helicopter sounded about nine o'clock, long past schedule, followed by clatter as the arriving presidential entourage dispersed near the White House Map Room, where I was secluded to organize my questions. The hubbub evaporated before we met for a solo meal in the small kitchen upstairs. President Clinton took out a Coca-Cola and two bottles of water to go with his warmed-over plate. Still energized, he had just come from his third meeting with Pope John Paul II, in Newark, New Jersey. He said they finally had achieved some rapport on many issues, including abortion. He essentially made peace, he said, and started but stopped two or three papal stories. I asked him to wait until I could get the recorders running on the breakfast table, and he was not sure he wanted the sounds of his cutting and chewing on the tapes for posterity. We temporized while he hurried through a roasted half-chicken with a sizable helping of fresh English peas. Doorman John Fanning brought some bread. At the president's invitation, I briefed him about my latest troubleshooter expedition to Haiti for Deputy Secretary of State Strobe Talbott.

This was a delicate delay. I didn't want to distract Clinton from the pope, nor distort his oral history with my peculiar interest. He already knew his Haiti policy was gnarled in politics, improbably through the FBI, because Congress, by something called the Dole Amendment, restricted U.S. assistance until Haiti could meet certain standards of governance. To demonstrate good faith, President Aristide had invited the FBI to help investigate his country's political murders, but the FBI demanded to conduct the criminal interviews alone, treating the Haitian government itself as a suspect.

The evidence in these cases was sensitive and complicated, yet vague. Talbott had ground me through the security mill for a high-level clearance needed to review classified material with the NSC's Richard Clarke and other U.S. security experts, but I told Clinton that the whole dispute seemed to fall on two miserable FBI agents huddled in a trailer at Camp Democracy, outside Port-au-Prince. They told me no one from the embassy ever visited. Dispatched from Miami, they had orders to work only on the murder of a prominent conservative who had supported the 1991 coup against Aristide, and to demand exclusive FBI control—"by the book"—even though they spoke no French or Creole. President Clinton interjected that he understood why Aristide could not single out one murder above others, especially when his own justice minister was among thousands of victims in unsolved cases. If the circumstances were reversed, Americans would never dream of granting foreign jurisdiction in any criminal matter, with or without such political overtones. I said I had commended discretion by analogy with Watergate, when the FBI had developed cases first against the actual burglars in order to build factual pressure methodically on superiors all the way up to President Nixon. That approach was prudent, the agents replied, but their brass made it a test of FBI prerogative for them to grill all possible conspirators from the start. The ensuing standoff suited anyone who preferred to ignore Haiti. It blocked U.S. aid under the Dole Amendment, including help routed through multinational agencies, and so did the continuing fights over Haiti's parliament. Since Aristide had implemented the U.S.-brokered changes in the election commission, splinter parties discovered new reasons to boycott the polls.

I tried to relay impressions the president was not likely to get through official channels, such as the solemnly brave atmosphere at Haiti's Truth and Reconciliation Commission, modeled on tribunals in South Africa. In what felt like a church basement, matronly volunteers gathered affidavits from maimed victims and terrified witnesses to political violence—five thousand of them so far—on a shoestring budget without a nickel from the United States. Merely to speak openly of such crimes was a healing leap in Haiti, where schoolteachers had not been paid for eighteen months. Aristide himself confessed that national justice remained primitive and corrupt. Loyalty still ran to people rather than institutions, and new recruits labored to grasp police methods more objective than arresting whoever the boss said was guilty. With everyone and yet no one to blame, some of the same Clinton officials who had feared tyranny in Aristide now agitated, ironically, for him to extend his term as an emergency anchor of stability. These trial balloons alarmed Ambassador Swing, I reported, and Aristide was determined to step down precisely on time in January. The local ambassador from Pope John Paul II, the papal nuncio, stalled his presentation of credentials until that successor could take office, making the Vatican the only government on earth to recognize Haiti's rogue junta but never its elected Catholic priest. I omitted mentioning this puzzling snub, given Clinton's fresh enthusiasm about the pope, but I did pass along a note of surreal surprise. Only yesterday, as I left Camp Democracy, a young Marine with an earpiece predicted mayhem back home because a jury had just acquitted O. J. Simpson of murder.

On tape, with the dishes cleared, President Clinton said the pontiff was greatly changed from the enfeebled old man of last year's private audience. His hearing seemed faulty at times, but he displayed mental vigor from his first words when they were alone: "Tell me how you see the world." Clinton said this was a sharp departure in several respects. Nearly all his summit partners brought some petition for the United States government, and for that reason they did at least two-thirds of the talking. Clinton said he usually considered it rude to diminish their limited time for anything other than clarification, but here was Pope John Paul II prompting him instead for a detailed survey by region, beginning with Europe.

The president responded eagerly with sketches of Yeltsin and Russia, NATO, Kohl of Germany, and the early negotiations in Northern Ireland. He said the pope quizzed him about IRA and Sinn Fein personalities involved, seconding his view that street hunger for peace outpaced the leadership thus far. On Bosnia, Clinton summarized a pivotal month. Two shocks in August—the death of three U.S. envoys trying to reach besieged Sarajevo, and a Bosnian Serb mortar that killed thirty-seven civilians in a Sarajevo marketplace—finally galvanized the United Nations to hide or bunker its European peacekeepers so that NATO could launch air strikes against the heavy guns of the Bosnian Serb aggressors. American pilots led the largest military operation in NATO history, and the president said John Paul did not flinch at his justification for the ongoing concussions through September, including NATO's Tomahawk cruise missile attacks on strongholds near Banja Luka. Meanwhile, rapid ground offensives by Croatian and Bosnian soldiers recaptured 1,300 square miles that had been lost to Serbs since 1992—some 20 percent of all Bosnian territory. As the war map restored Bosnia's former intermingling of three religious groups, Clinton said the pope's influence may be needed to tip its Roman Catholic participants—the Croats—from the heat of battle into a peace agreement.* He said John Paul promised to do all he could. The world could not let the twentieth century end as it had begun, he told Clinton, with another checkerboard conflagration out of Sarajevo.

Clinton said his global briefing for the pope continued through the dramatic events lately in the Middle East, with implications for Iraq.

---

* Because the three main populations share a common language and genetic heritage, ethnic differences in Bosnia spring from religion. Nearly all its Croats, like neighboring Croatia to the west, are Roman Catholics. Its Serbs, like Serbia to the east, belong to the Eastern Orthodox Church. Its Muslims have no nation of co-religionists nearby, but they outnumber both Croats and Serbs scattered across Bosnia.

John Paul interrupted on Africa, he recalled, with worries that the former colonial powers would abandon the continent entirely to the ravages of poverty, tribal war, and disease. Most memorably, Clinton said the pope praised Hillary's September 5 speech in Beijing at the U.N.'s 4th World Conference on Women. She hit all the right notes, said John Paul, with her bold declaration that families would flourish as women gained freedom from ignorance, oppression, and all forms of violence.

Here the president digressed into the prior controversy about whether Hillary should visit China at all. Dole and Gingrich had called publicly for her to stay home, saying the first lady's presence would reward China's wretched performance on human rights. White House advisers mounted what Clinton called a pincer argument. Hillary would validate China, and yet any forthright criticism on human rights would infuriate the Chinese government to the detriment of vital progress on trade. The president had deferred a decision on her travel until their vacation in Wyoming, where Hillary said the focus should be bigger than China. She was only too happy to meet his request for a balanced speech that would neither shrink from China's forced abortions nor dwell unduly on its shortcomings. She discussed harsh reality everywhere, from genital mutilation in Africa to domestic violence in the United States. Females comprise 70 percent of the illiterate, unhealthy, and poor. While she prepared such an address, said Clinton, the Chinese government shrewdly finessed diplomatic pressures by pronouncing Harry Wu guilty of espionage but then expelling him back home to the United States. This made it easier for the president to weather attacks on Hillary's trip from both the political left and right. He said the approval numbers for her speech were high, especially among women, as Hillary's ratings were skewed by a gender gap larger than his own.

The pope, having absorbed a full tour of world politics, responded with blunt encouragement for Clinton in his domestic battles with Congress. He decried Republican efforts to repeal or curtail safety net programs across the board—school lunches, Head Start classes, Medicare, Medicaid, food stamps, and the tax credits for the working poor. His bishops and cardinals could not tell Americans how to vote, the pope conceded, but they would issue statements urging the rich countries to set examples of strength and compassion. Their governments should care for the vulnerable, uphold the weak, and rise above violence. This would make them beacons for faith and democracy alike, said the pope, which was why he thought so well of Hillary's speech in Beijing.

Clinton clearly relished the breadth and intensity of this endorsement. He quoted biblical phrases to indicate that the pope was sincere in spirit, but he seemed equally transported by the political communion. He said John Paul II exemplified the central art missing in modern politics. While not denying deep disagreements, he looked beyond them for ways to make a difference in the world. The pope headed a church that systematically excluded women from authority, but he embraced Hillary's call for their global human rights. He still opposed Clinton on abortion rights and homosexuality, but he cultivated common cause as peacemakers. The president said he tried to reciprocate by understanding that the church aimed consistently to value each soul. "That's why the life of the poor is more important than the luxuries of the rich," he said, "and why the life of the unborn child is more important than the convenience of the parents." Clinton went so far as to forecast a renaissance for Catholicism. In every era of upheaval, he said, people turn crassly materialistic but eventually yearn for something deeper.

Only too soon, they were extracted from the one-on-one consultation so that John Paul II could preside at vespers there in Newark's Cathedral Basilica of the Sacred Heart. On the feast day of St. Francis, overlapping the Jewish Day of Atonement, Yom Kippur, the pope delivered a religious homily, but the heat combined with the swirling incense gave Clinton an allergic seizure. Coughing and choking, he clutched Hillary beside him in the pew. He said it was hard to breathe. Now, hours later, he still looked puffy and flushed. He recalled the departing pope's interaction with the electrified crowds, including nuns from the reclusive Carmelite order, who, by special dispensation, were permitted to leave a cloister for the first time in decades to gaze rapturously on their pontiff. Outside in the rain, John Paul climbed into the bubbled Popemobile, and a glance back at Clinton seemed to stimulate waves of affection for them both. Appraising the spectacle with a politician's eye, Clinton said, "I sure as hell would hate to be running against him for mayor anywhere."

•   •   •

THE PRESIDENT ENGAGED questions about the September 28 interim agreement between Israel and the Palestinian Authority. He had decided to
hold the formal ceremony in the East Room, hoping to trim back comparisons with the dramatic outdoor handshake two years ago between
Chairman Arafat and Prime Minister Rabin. After all, this was only a
step toward a peace treaty, but Clinton called it a crucial one. Negotiators had parceled every inch of the Israeli-occupied West Bank and Gaza
into zones designating three different levels of divided government. The
Palestinians would assume full powers including police enforcement in
some areas, mostly the larger cities. The Israelis generally would retain
control of the unpopulated regions, and they would reserve overriding
security jurisdiction in many small towns and villages, where the Palestinians otherwise would take over civil functions from roads and utilities
to schools. Clinton said these agreements were codified in no fewer than
twenty-six maps of intricate detail, down to individual bridges, each one
to be signed by Rabin and Arafat. The maps themselves were a significant undertaking, he added, because they reflected thousands of exchanges over the precise habits and places of the separated populations.
If nothing else, the process created a mutual sense of administrative
competence. Clinton thought this was especially important to Rabin,
who had fretted early that the Palestinians might not be able to perform
the duties necessary for stable coexistence, because they had never run
anything close to the scale of a nation.

Two years of bickering also created personal relationships in both
delegations, all the way up to Arafat and Rabin. They were no longer the
dehumanized strangers of permanent war, for whom proximity itself was
a combustible ordeal. In fact, said the president, they were the most
comfortable pairing among the four Middle Eastern leaders who huddled with him in the Oval Office before the ceremony. He was sure this
quartet had never gathered before. King Hussein of Jordan was kindly
but reserved by nature, especially around Arafat, and President Mubarak
of Egypt stuck gruffly to business. In an aside, Clinton said Mubarak
kept vowing to "deal with" unnamed plotters who had tried to assassinate him recently in Ethiopia, leaving no doubt that his retribution
would be bloody. Hinting at intelligence reports, Clinton said Mubarak
was incredibly tough. So were the others, but Rabin and Arafat turned

the Oval Office into something of a bull session. Arafat joked that he wanted to live one day near Rabin, the president recalled, because he knew it would be a safe neighborhood. Rabin replied that he felt less like Arafat's neighbor than his cousin, because in Israel that meant quarrelsome but close. Well, said Arafat, maybe they were cousins from somewhere far back, through Moses or Abraham. Clinton said this notion touched off banter about common lineage traced through respective scriptures, and whose family lines were legitimate or illegitimate.

The president harped on the glaring absence of Syria. No Syrians of rank joined the foreign dignitaries to witness the Israeli-Palestinian signing. Just today, he remarked, he had spent another hour on the phone with President Asad, cajoling him to clamp down on terrorist attacks in the West Bank. Suicide attacks by Hezbollah and other groups made them unwitting allies of Israeli hard-liners desperate to stop the peace process. Without an enemy, said Clinton, "they'd be all dressed up with nowhere to go." Asad mumbled agreement that he must confront them with a better vision—inevitably, but not now. In the Oval Office, the president recalled, Mubarak had volunteered to go see Asad and push him along, but Rabin confessed helplessness on the Syrian track. He was barely surviving progress with the Palestinians, despite worldwide praise, and figured to beat back a parliamentary challenge on the current agreement by no more than three votes. Clinton said he elicited more gallows humor by confiding that U.S. experts thought Rabin's margin had shrunk from three votes to one.*

Unexpectedly, a commotion had burst into the Oval Office from the Cabinet Room, with Israeli foreign minister Shimon Peres apologizing grimly that the negotiators were making rather than solving problems for the heads of state. Clinton excused himself with only Rabin and Arafat into his little private dining room off the Oval Office, where they began to argue about fine print on one of the map annexes. The dispute had something to do with whether Palestinian police must seek permission from the Israelis, or merely notify them, when moving between certain zones in an emergency. Its familiar crux was a volatile tension

---

* On October 5, the day after this oral history session, Rabin's government narrowly won a vote of confidence in the 120-member Israeli Knesset, 61–59.

over status—whether Rabin would resort to conqueror's language, or Arafat would rage against humiliation in his own land, and the president made a snap judgment to leave. "I'll let the two of you work this out," he told them. A few agonizing moments later, they emerged all smiles with a compromise word. After a pleasantly trivial debate about Israeli dress standards, Rabin borrowed a necktie from Clinton, and the delegations were ready to face news cameras in the East Room.

Of his related meetings the next day, the president stressed a private consultation with King Hussein of Jordan. He said they sifted intrigue over the king's grant of emergency exile to two high-profile defectors from Iraq, each one married to a daughter of dictator Saddam Hussein. Despite their similar names, the rulers of Jordan and Iraq were far from relatives or friends. Jordan's Hussein represented ancient Muslim royalty out of Mecca, from a Hashemite line traceable back to the Prophet Muhammad. Saddam Hussein, by contrast, was a secular politician who had risen to power in the wake of a savage 1958 coup against the last king of Iraq, who, until slaughtered with much of his family, was both a first cousin and childhood friend to Hussein of Jordan. As schoolmates after World War II, at London's elite Harrow School, the two young princes had dreamed of uniting their family's adjacent countries. Now, fifty years later, President Clinton said he felt obliged to mention intelligence reports that King Hussein's hidden goal was to overthrow Saddam. The acceptance of these particular Iraqi defectors—if not their active recruitment—had the world's spy agencies crackling over more than family ties. One of Saddam's rebellious in-laws was an army general who had headed the war industries of Iraq since 1987, including all production of chemical and biological weapons. With this intelligence coup, King Hussein might hope to avenge his cousin and even restore Hashemite rule over Baghdad.

Hussein denied such ambitions, the president recalled, but he confessed very complicated feelings about Iraq. He said Arab countries in the region wanted Iraq to stay weak. In private, they applauded the U.N.'s military and economic sanctions since the Gulf War, because they contained a proven threat, and Arab leaders did not really care what happened to Saddam so long as Iraq was feeble. On the other hand, they realized that a weakened Iraq would always be unstable, vulnerable to disintegration and external plots. If Saddam were to die or be removed, Hussein said Syria would move in from the west and ethnic Kurds would renew their chronic drive to secede. Iraq's Shia majority would align with religious cohorts next door in Iran, while the minority Sunni Muslims would gravitate toward Jordan and Saudi Arabia. King Hussein reminded Clinton that Iraq was not a natural country. After World War I, when the victorious Allied Powers carved up the globe with new borders, Great Britain had installed a spare foreign prince—Hussein's great-uncle—as the founding monarch over Mesopotamian provinces bundled together for their oilfields. Hussein regretted that the arbitrary designs of rulers still could inflict so much misery on ordinary citizens, especially in Iraq.

QUESTIONS ABOUT CUBA opened a bumpy transition to domestic affairs. The president explained why he had slightly relaxed the thirty-year-old economic embargo against Fidel Castro's regime by allowing Western Union to open offices in Havana. This would facilitate communication for divided families, he said, along with financial transfers to create goodwill on the island, but these very benefits infuriated Cuban-American leaders in the United States. Representative Bob Menendez of New Jersey, a Democrat, had just called to protest, Clinton disclosed, but this was nothing new. They got along very well on every other issue, but Menendez "kicks the shit out of me every two or three days to be harder on Castro, like clockwork, no matter what I do." To Menendez, Clinton always defended his Cuba policies as tougher than either Reagan's or Bush's, but he confided on tape that the embargo was a foolish, pandering failure. It had allowed Castro to demonize the United States for decades, propping up his government with an all-purpose excuse for one-party rule. The president said anybody "with half a brain" could see the embargo was counterproductive. It defied wiser policies of engagement that we had pursued with some Communist countries even at the height of the Cold War. It helped no one, did nothing to open Cuba or prepare the nation for life after Castro, and left Clinton straddling the worst of both worlds. His dead-end policy was hostage to bullet-voting Cuban exiles in two swing states—Florida and New Jersey—and yet he never won them over, anyway, because Republicans always found ways to out-posture him in hostility. Flailing about, he recalled asking today whether John Paul II really intended to make a dramatic visit to the stranded island, but the pope said Castro did not want him.

Sour politics carried over to a surprise retirement announced by New Jersey Democratic senator Bill Bradley. The president said he was angry with Bradley for quitting—disgusted, in fact, by Bradley's speeches proclaiming himself detached from both political parties and yet somehow uniquely in tune with the American people. This was pabulum, said Clinton. Although he and Bradley agreed on nearly every stance that actually divided the parties, he said, Bradley lacked the fight to make them concrete for voters. Clinton thought Bradley regretted his decisions not to run for president in 1988 or 1992, and now, facing an uphill battle simply for reelection in New Jersey, was positioning himself in the wings as a national candidate of maverick integrity, marching to a different drummer. Bradley was talking privately to Colin Powell about a progressive independent ticket in 1996. The president said he knew so from his periodic talks with Powell himself about the presidential race. With characteristic zest and detachment, Clinton summarized his clinical explorations with Powell about Powell's chances to beat Clinton. Bradley could not help Powell, he advised, even with the cosmetic politics. If the mass of voters truly wanted an independent candidate, they would much prefer Powell's striking authority to Bradley's vaguely pure mind.

The president said much more than I expected about the sudden resignation of Oregon senator Bob Packwood. Senator Mitch McConnell of Kentucky, chair of the Ethics Committee, was all lined up to take a dive on Packwood's diaries, he said, avoiding an investigation or a report of any kind, when fresh writings by Packwood surfaced his unwanted attention to a sixteen-year-old girl. Then, abruptly reversing course, McConnell orchestrated a motion to expel Packwood in a clean sacrifice. Both extremes spared colleagues from any fair investigation of a fellow Republican, charged Clinton, who said he had no respect for McConnell. Surprisingly, the president added that he himself had been reading Packwood's diaries. He thought they verified a private assessment from Packwood's wise senior senator and former teacher, Mark Hatfield, who told Clinton that Packwood always had combined a precocious, forceful intelligence with an arrested personality.

You could feel that assessment in the diaries, said Clinton. There was an infantile quality in many passages, as though Packwood was puffing himself up to sound like a smooth libertine. With graphic but awkward descriptions, Packwood meticulously recorded efforts to subdue mistresses and young staff aides. He had immersed himself in politics so young, and had pursued his career with such single-minded intensity, that his personal instincts never comparably developed or matured. This was the gist of Hatfield's diagnosis, and Clinton said he identified with Packwood in this respect. He, too, had found an obsessive refuge and gift in politics, straight from his own troubled childhood in Arkansas. He could see a timid nature buried in Packwood's diary. Many of the entries plainly conveyed a domineering abuse, he said, but you sensed that Packwood would have complied if the women had commanded him to stop. His aggressiveness seemed largely a bluff, observed Clinton, adding that the senator could not begin to carry off the rogue bravado of his colleague John Breaux. He said Breaux frequently ridiculed Packwood with jokes, calling him a flop with women, and the president bemoaned something pathetic here. Unsettled, I tried to clarify where he meant Packwood or Breaux, but my questions broke the spell of reflection. Even so, Clinton's meditation on the diary struck me as his most personal comments for the record so far.

He had mentioned O. J. Simpson over dinner, fretting that the trial might exacerbate racial conflict over American standards of justice. On tape, smiling, the president said he had invoked O. J. lately to keep Senator Sam Nunn of Georgia from early retirement. Unlike Bill Bradley, Nunn could waltz to reelection with a home state approval rating of 78 percent, but he was advertising reluctance. Only Democrats recoiled from the burdens of power, groused Clinton, which made him appreciate tenacious right-wingers like Jesse Helms for enduring decades stoically on the back benches. The president said Nunn acknowledged the error of his impulsive promise to raise no money unless he decided firmly to run, which boxed off options with needless constraint. His career resolve had weakened with regret, Nunn confided, since a halfhearted lobbying effort to become Clinton's secretary of state. He and Clinton dangled afterward in semantics, somewhere between an offer to run for another term and the promise of a cabinet post. The president listed reasons why it would be imprudent to make an explicit deal so far in advance of the election. To compensate, he praised Nunn's stature in the Senate, urging continuity so that doors could open at the right time. When that failed, he said he became desperate. "Tell Sam not to announce he's leaving," he begged Nunn's chief backer in Georgia. "Not only do I need him, but the Simpson verdict is coming down any day. It would be a travesty to end one of the great legislative careers, only to have no one care because the whole country is obsessed with O. J."

Today the chief backer was interpreting the Simpson verdict plaintively to Nunn as a "sign from God" for him to run again. Clinton quipped that he did not endorse such a fantastic claim, but he did not try to stop it, either. Nunn's loss would cost far more than a single Democratic seat, because he was one of the Senate's few statesmen. The president cited a contentious meeting with congressional leaders on Bosnia last week, at which Nunn made more sense in five minutes than all the others combined. While colleagues still angled to split or exploit differences among themselves, Nunn looked for combinations to stabilize conditions on the ground. Clinton thought the senator performed best inside the government, under maximum pressure, and Bosnia was making him shine. Until lately, the president said, the Balkan wars had been a kind of low-grade fever for the White House, marked by occasional press caricatures to tweak Clinton for impotence in a tangled mess. Now a concentrated summer of haunting massacres and NATO bombardment pushed Bosnia to the brink of clarity or disaster. Siege guns no longer killed pedestrians in Sarajevo, but Serb militias still blocked the main roads and all electric power into a capital darkened three full years. With military advantage teetering across the map, U.S. envoy Richard Holbrooke was in Belgrade to meet indicted war criminals for the first time, including Serb president Slobodan Milosevic. Clinton said he dearly hoped to announce a cease-fire by morning.

Collisions began simultaneously at home. Past the dawn of a new fiscal year on October 1, Gingrich and Dole held back all thirteen annual funding bills needed to run federal operations. Clinton said the stakes rose over their professed mandate to crush big government, or at least big civilian government. Two days later, with his signature, the Pentagon finally gained lawful appropriations to pay its soldiers and employees, but all other departments including the White House limped day to day on stopgap resolutions. Shutdowns and layoffs loomed. Negotiations over big cuts in Medicare and Medicaid appropriations were so sensitive that the president ordered no one but Gore and Leon Panetta to discuss them even within the administration. He had just received and vetoed a separate bill to fund the legislative branch. Clinton did not object to the numbers so much, but he called it unconscionable for congressional leaders to secure their own pocketbooks while injuring millions of citizens. The president said he was ready to fight. If Dole and Gingrich wanted to play chicken, they had to stay in the car.

CONFLICTS OVER BOSNIA and the budget intensified steadily through Halloween night. The president came into the Treaty Room wearing jeans and a bright shirt advertising a cantina called La Sierra. He slumped wearily in a chair beneath the signature painting, turned slightly toward my recorders on the coffee table. His posture accented a noticeable paunch. I told him Christy had charged me to advise more rest. She was alarmed by how tired he looked at today's sendoff ceremony for Secretary Christopher and Ambassador Holbrooke, who were convening the major belligerents from Bosnia for comprehensive peace talks beginning the next day near Dayton, Ohio. The House had just magnified the political hazards of American sponsorship of the peace process with a resolution opposing the deployment of U.S. troops to help NATO guarantee any future settlement. Speaker Gingrich called the restriction a measure of comprehensive mistrust toward Clinton, and the president simultaneously denounced Gingrich and Dole for blackmail, citing their steps to pitch the Treasury into a historic default unless he deferred to them on the stalled appropriations bills. Politics were nasty across the board, said Clinton, but what Christy noticed was probably his miserable reaction to pollen. He braced for attacks until winter started. I asked if he meant ended, recalling that Christmas decorations had waterlogged his head. No, those were different allergies, and a short respite usually spared him between first frost and the holidays. "I'm allergic to everything," he said with a sigh.

I asked about cryptic reports of a "donnybrook" argument with New York's Senator Moynihan. News stories were speculative and vague about its nature, but lingering resentment provoked Clinton to fill in details intermittently for the rest of the night. It had started aboard a helicopter flight to New York for ceremonies at the United Nations. The president said he never raised his voice, but he upbraided the senator for a catalytic role in another press spasm. This one sprang from Clinton's fund-raising speech in Texas about his difficult and unpopular decisions so far, from NAFTA to the Brady Bill—how no one wanted to invade Haiti and everyone hated to raise taxes. In fact, Clinton had told the donors, he would have raised taxes less in the big budget package of 1993 if even a few Republicans in Congress had given him leverage for more spending cuts instead. This extemporaneous remark was literally true, the president said on tape, but it was a mistake. No president should raise hypothetical wishes about controversial decisions in the past.

He said critics and columnists stampeded with the error. They inflated his marginal wish into a statement of central regret. They said he was repudiating his own prescription for the economy and sound government. Those who never embraced the anti-deficit package rushed to declare that Clinton had abandoned its high ground, proving himself a vacillator to the core. "He doesn't understand," Moynihan told reporters, "that he's conceding the principles." The president said he confronted him about blithe disregard for substance and context. Moynihan knew exactly what he was doing, Clinton charged. He was feeding the beast of hostile presumption about Clinton's motives. The president told him such personal attacks poisoned the whole climate for politics. Nebraska senator Bob Kerrey, who joined in Moynihan's scornful diagnosis of the Texas speech, had cast the deciding vote against raising the minimum wage, but Clinton said he never ascribed to him a foul or selfish purpose. Nor did he impugn Moynihan for announcing just yesterday that Republican proposals for Medicaid would not be so damaging to the poor. Clinton thought he was flat wrong, but he reserved personal invective for Moynihan's own ears.

Of course it hurt, said the president, that this furor erupted on the approaching crest of his duel with Congress over these same key issues. Both sides claimed to move toward a balanced budget without new taxes on the middle class, but the Republicans were trying to ram through a

$245 billion tax cut when they were $580 billion apart on spending. Whenever they approached serious negotiations, he said, Gingrich faced revolt from a substantial wing of his party that did not want to reach agreement with Clinton on anything. They believed he would fold on the budget, and they did not really care if the government shut down for lack of appropriations or public credit. Their primary goal was to punish all but the military hierarchies, and many of them saw no legitimate role for the civilian agencies, anyway, to the point that they really believed the country would be rejuvenated without them. He said pride and ideology blinded them to common purpose, including their own dependence on public services from markets and meat inspectors to sewerage.

Exasperated, Clinton said he tried to warn Gingrich from the standpoint of Republican self-interest. To justify massive cuts, the GOP was projecting runaway inflation in health costs with virtually no economic growth. How could Gingrich hope to campaign on that message? If he and Dole persisted, the president vowed to veto their appropriations bills with or without a new debt ceiling. He would bet on the public reaction when the FBI agents and air traffic controllers went home, let alone when the Social Security checks stopped coming. The Constitution wisely called for balance as well as checks, and he was ready. "I think I'm beating them to death on the politics," he said.

In spite of this confidence, the president dwelled on two factors that might cost him reelection in 1996. One was latent resentment of his 1993 stand on gays in the military. The other was his adverse public image. He said it was becoming a fixture in political culture, sustained on Whitewater allegations and cultivated daily by the establishment media. People made him a feckless character of elastic beliefs, like a cartoon satire from the 1960s, whereas General Colin Powell floated on a stronger image from the same era—hip and familiar, but strong. Powell would make a formidable candidate running as a more genial version of Gingrich and Dole. A third, independent ticket might run to the right, but Clinton thought Ross Perot would drop out in deference to Powell, being instinctively pro-military. Clearly, the private poll numbers looked grim. While his mind processed odds for Powell actually to run, and calibrated conservative resistance to deny him the Republican nomination, Clinton's pessimism anticipated the stark choice in a head-to-head contest. "If the American people really want someone to preside over a kinder, gentler dismantlement of the federal government," he said, "they should get another president." Let Powell do it. Clinton said he would not compete for that ground. Too many people make politics a game of bystanders, forgetting its actual and potential stakes for millions of lives. Becoming emotional, he said repeatedly that it was wrong.

The president never said he felt isolated or abandoned. On the contrary, he praised congressional Democrats for standing ready to sustain his vetoes. The emotional tripwire for him seemed to be his image. He relished the unprecedented clashes ahead over shutting the entire government, despite its heavy burdens, but the prospect of being compared with Powell by media made Clinton let loose a stream of complaints, railing against images that were stubborn and unfair, even backward. How could the initiator of lasting controversy be portrayed as a changeling? How could he take so many unpopular stands and yet stand for nothing? If anything, he stood for too much.

Off this point, I tried to steer him back to political calculus by asking about the Employment Non-Discrimination Act. The president had just endorsed Senator Ted Kennedy's bill to prohibit the dismissal of employees solely for their sexual orientation, by public and private institutions above a certain size, excluding the military. It stood zero chance of passage in this Congress, as Republican leaders openly refused to grant even a hearing. Did Clinton consider withholding his endorsement until Kennedy could mobilize more support? Should he ever say, "Show me this bill has a chance and I'll fight for it, but I'm not going to absorb significant damage for a purely symbolic position"? In response, Clinton instantly recognized the historical precedent for this dilemma. It was FDR saying "Make me do it" during World War II, challenging civil rights leaders to arouse a citizen's movement for integrating employment in the defense industries. Clinton agreed with FDR that there were times when embracing a farsighted goal could be wrong, even in principle, because the reaction would undermine a leader's strength for many other causes. He said the Kennedy bill was certainly impolitic for him. If he had declined to back it, the equality groups would have accused him of having no guts, but he hoped that was not the reason he consented.

Improbably, the president detoured into tales of his late father-in-law. Hugh Rodham had been such a right-winger that he didn't even like Catholic "papists," said Clinton, let alone Jews, black people, or homosexuals, but he had changed over time—as shown most dramatically by his interaction with his caretakers during his terminal illness. He bonded with everyone from orderlies to a nurse with a Purple Heart. Even old Hugh learned to evaluate people by conduct and spirit rather than labels. This was the right standard, Clinton insisted. He would stick up for the Kennedy bill, and people could attack him all they wanted. He told more Rodham stories. If they were meant to illustrate the president's sense of exposure on principles, he did not say so. I could not tell whether family memories sharpened his sense of persecution by the press, or vice versa, but he was nearly maudlin. My bid to rekindle his roving intellect had backfired.

He soon ranged over assorted topics. Mexico's President Ernesto Zedillo had just visited with an early repayment of $700 million on Mexico's stabilization loans. Clinton analyzed the investigation of an Amtrak train sabotaged in Arizona, and he thought Christy's employer, Mayor Schmoke of Baltimore, had been right to attend the Million Man March for black males that month on the Mall in Washington. It had been a remarkable event, defying frightful visions of invective and riot. The president wondered why so many Christian ministers had surrendered vital issues of self-responsibility and atonement to the sectarian Muslim leader Louis Farrakhan. We glided past Sam Nunn's final decision to leave the Senate—"I'm sorry," he said tersely, "I like him"—but a question about Hillary's birthday inspired a full rhapsody on the toasts and decorations. She had arrived in a knockout Dolly Parton wig, he said, which made him joke that his real dream since boyhood was not being president but exactly this—having a rodeo girl. He described his selection of presents. Some faded before midnight dictation, but I remembered a print of Lincoln's "Meditation on the Divine Will," plus a whistle shaped like a woman holding up the world. He said it reminded him of Hillary.

WE CLOSED ON his trip to New York the previous week. President Clinton recalled fun in the midst of serious business, epitomized by a gigantic photo shoot to commemorate the fiftieth anniversary of the United Nations. With no fewer than 189 heads of state assembled in one room, the renowned photographer Paul Skipworth frantically waved his arms to shoo away a jumbled army of assistants and security officers, yelling at the befuddled world leaders "like they were Cousin Joe and Aunt Marty." Clinton, standing next to China's president, Jiang Zemin, discovered that Jiang's English was good enough for him to appreciate a running commentary as U.N. culture met the humorous traditions of an American family portrait. Skipworth mugged to get cheesy smiles from the heads of state. Every time he repositioned a subject for a better view, as too skinny or short, Clinton said, shudders ran through protocol chiefs over diplomatic slights. French president Jacques Chirac already seemed a bit uneasy, Clinton whispered to Jiang, over the broad condemnation of his nuclear tests in the Pacific. Through this informal opening, the president said he almost—but not quite—persuaded China to accede with Russia and newly chastened France in a strict moratorium on nuclear explosions.

By helicopter, Clinton flew to a secluded interval with Boris Yeltsin at Franklin Roosevelt's Hyde Park estate. Indulging his taste for historical memorabilia, he showed Yeltsin a letter from the library in which Roosevelt had notified Joseph Stalin of the time fixed at last for D-Day to open a western front against Hitler—pointing out how FDR had made handwritten changes in the typed draft. At the briefing for this meeting, said the president, his advance team had offered to display the actual chairs in which Roosevelt plotted war strategy with Winston Churchill, and Clinton stipulated that the chairs must be sturdy. If Yeltsin saw them, he would demand to sit there and revel. And so, on a spectacular fall day, the two chairs were placed in a picturesque spot overlooking the Hudson River. Walking toward them, Clinton said it was almost like Julie Andrews's mountaintop scene to open *The Sound of Music,* except that Yeltsin suddenly had a stricken look on his face. The president offered his arm, fearing the onset of a heart attack or stroke, but he did not beckon help from the aides following at a distance.

Their talks on the bluff covered ongoing projects to keep Russia afloat in the wake of the Soviet collapse, and the president said he felt deeply for Yeltsin on many fronts. He knew how much it preyed on

Yeltsin to receive so little credit for starting a democracy despite what Clinton called "hideous problems" with Russia's economy, infrastructure, and basic political order. One of these was nationalism seething at home over the lost Slavic empire, which simultaneously spurred and blocked Yeltsin's desire to reclaim a place among the great nations. He wanted badly to take part if an international consortium were to guarantee a settlement in the Balkans. Over substantial opposition, he told Clinton, Russian troops would join peacekeepers deployed to Bosnia, but under no circumstances could they serve under NATO command. To Russians, NATO was a former enemy that now excluded them, and such humiliation would be fatal for Yeltsin's career. Clinton understood, but he replied with opposing barriers of equal strength. NATO was his only hope. The worst day of his presidency, he told Yeltsin, was watching U.S. soldiers killed in the U.N.'s Somalia mission get dragged through the streets of Mogadishu. Now, even under NATO, he must battle Congress to send any U.S. troops into Bosnia, and no other command was remotely feasible. At loggerheads, he and Yeltsin nearly exhausted their imaginations before they concocted a fig leaf of formal NATO command with some ban on actual orders to its Slavic brigades. Russians would be confined to mine clearance, or logistics, or whatever the subordinate generals could work out. Keeping this flimsy hope to themselves, the two leaders confronted reporters waiting at Hyde Park, and Yeltsin, with typical bluster, rebutted predictions of a disastrous summit. "*You're* a disaster," he told them, clearly inebriated.

Back in New York City, Clinton tried to encourage two of the warring presidents bound for peace talks in Dayton. Franjo Tudjman of Croatia and Alija Izetbegovic of Bosnia had much in common. Each had served two prison terms for nationalist agitation against Marshal Tito's Communist regime in greater Yugoslavia. Their kinsmen had been slaughtered separately and together by Bosnian Serbs in the wars of ethnic cleansing, which made them allies. Even so, Clinton said, they could scarcely abide each other in his presence, which increased his forebodings about their prospects cooped up in Ohio with their Serb enemies for open-ended negotiations. The lights were back on in Sarajevo, but Bosnia hovered at the edge of chronic war. On tape, the president said he had asked for and received a big diplomatic favor from Tudjman and

Izetbegovic. They agreed to fly to Dayton by way of Moscow, so they could meet and pay tribute to Yeltsin. Their errand would have been a salve for Yeltsin's sidelined status in both the Dayton talks and NATO, said Clinton, except that Yeltsin had fallen sick again on his return home. Tonight, the leaders were flying straight to Dayton instead, to commence talks there while Gingrich and Dole bargained at the White House over the shutdown of the federal government.

The president closed with a private memory of Jiang Zemin, from the same day he met the Balkan presidents in New York. Once again, he made no progress whatsoever on human rights. Jiang deflected him. Clinton said he renewed his anthem of friendship, distinguishing between disputed issues and hostility. He listed many things to fix about the relationship, from pirated CDs and movies to persecution in Tibet, but he insisted that the United States wanted to be China's friend. We wanted China in the World Trade Organization. If we were hostile, he joked, we would not allow this huge trade deficit, and there was only one area in which Clinton considered China a threat to the national security of the United States. He said this comment startled the Chinese president, who asked briskly what that could be. Jiang's glaze softened. Clinton said he felt human contact for the first time on affairs of state, perhaps building on their informal banter during the photo session. "You are growing China into a wealthy economy," he told Jiang. "It's not your fault, but if you don't find a better way to do it than the rich countries before you, then you will ruin the planet."

CHAPTER NINETEEN

THE MURDER
OF RABIN

Monday, November 20, 1995

Rebecca Cameron, Nancy Hernreich's assistant, apologized again for the short notice. She said the week-long shutdown of government had jumbled an already precarious schedule. Yesterday's stopgap deal with Congress brought 800,000 federal workers back to work for one day of chaotic recovery, until midnight, but prickly negotiations threatened to send them all back home on involuntary furlough, including Cameron herself. By law, voided authority would reempty many offices to leave a cavernously quiet, crippled White House. There would be no one to clear me through its gates or up into the residence. Our confidential project might become a minor casualty of the gridlock, said Cameron, and President Clinton hoped to squeeze in a session before tonight's deadline.

He entered the Treaty Room briskly, still wearing his suit, clearly in the grip of business, and made notes at his desk while I waited with my recorders on the sofa beneath Chartran's painting. Things were going badly in Dayton, he remarked. After three intense weeks, he may have to break off the talks in failure tomorrow. Bosnia almost certainly would relapse into war. He thought that outcome would mark an end to NATO as an alliance of credible purpose in the world, certainly under U.S. leadership. After all, he said, he kept telling members of Congress that he had tried to keep Americans out of the Balkan wars, and had tried to get Europeans to engineer a settlement, but it was only when he sent

Tony Lake to get the NATO bombs going against the Serb bullies—and when he put Richard Holbrooke in to crack heads toward negotiations—that anything positive happened. Now, he said sharply, the few members of Congress who had championed the Bosnians recoiled from an agreement to save the country. Many saw nothing but the worst under pressure. They opposed letting U.S. soldiers become "sitting ducks" in an ethnic crossfire, on any mission to safeguard Bosnian victims, whom they discounted privately as misfit Muslims, untrustworthy and "probably in cahoots with Iran." Ironically, fumed the president, the Bosnians turned out to be the final stumbling block at Dayton. President Alija Izetbegovic was too bitter to accept his own rescue. That was the sad secret.

He came over to his chair on my right, and I stifled questions about Bosnia for the moment. On tape, we began with the November 4 assassination of Yitzhak Rabin. Fragmentary bulletins had reached him in the Oval Office after his Saturday radio address two weekends ago. Three gunshots at an outdoor rally in Tel Aviv. The prime minister hospitalized, fighting for his life. Shock and suspense so unnerved Clinton that he moved his agitated pacing outdoors to the putting green, where soon the look on the face of the approaching Tony Lake told him Rabin was dead. The president broke down before Lake could utter a word. He said he wept openly for Rabin. He called Yitzhak an old soldier who embraced enormous risks for peace. He recalled poignant moments—Rabin saying, "It will all work out," before the last signing ceremony, borrowing a necktie, joking with Arafat, pushing forward. By contrast, Clinton said, President Izetbegovic still sat frozen behind every imaginary bunker on the disputed map of Bosnia, expecting the Serbs to open fire.

Some details of official grief had become public. The president and Hillary, rushing to sign a condolence book at the Israeli embassy in Washington, consulted friends about a Hebrew word to convey their feelings, and settled on *haver*, which means "friend" or "comrade" with connotations of togetherness beyond any term in English. Clinton's short statement—ending "*shalom, haver*, goodbye, friend"—struck such a chord that "*shalom, haver*" sprouted on Israeli walls, billboards, and even bumper stickers, one of which had arrived already with a heartfelt inscription by Rabin's widow, Leah. He treasured the memento, and wanted to show me. It was down the hall in the family parlor. Shaking off that notion, he remembered his call to demand firmly that Mubarak of Egypt attend the funeral—knowing well that Mubarak had never set foot in Israel, and that his predecessor, Anwar Sadat, had been assassinated by fellow Egyptians enraged over his peace journey to Jerusalem.

Peacemakers on all sides, said Clinton, faced violence from their own extremists. The killer of Rabin was not an Arab terrorist but a fervently Orthodox Israeli Jew, claiming a religious mandate to prevent compromise with God's enemies, and King Hussein of Jordan, as a teenager in 1951, had survived a street ambush in which Palestinian nationalists gunned down his grandfather lest he recognize young Israel's claim to a share of Palestinian territory. At Rabin's funeral, Hussein confided to Clinton that this was a wrenching ordeal for him on many levels. He had not seen Jerusalem since the Six Day War of 1967. Nearby, said Clinton, Hussein's wife, Queen Noor, cried softly through the entire ceremony. He thought the emotional assembly of five thousand foreign dignitaries, including Mubarak, visibly reassured shaken people in tiny, isolated Israel.

A phone call from Dayton intruded. It was Secretary of State Christopher, and Clinton's side of the conversation made clear that the impasse over Bosnia had hardened. "I thought he had agreed to 51/49 a year ago," he said to Christopher, plainly annoyed. "That's right, isn't it?" They were discussing proposed boundaries for the ethnic militias, separating the central government's Muslim/Croat federation from the rebellious Bosnian Serbs. These lines would determine the vital starting point of military control, from which Bosnia hoped to rebuild the common currency and infrastructure of a single nation. Previously, when President Izetbegovic and his Croatian allies held only 30 percent of their territory, they had accepted 51 percent as a wispy, acceptable goal, but their counteroffensives since then had lifted them to 55–56 percent, above target. In Dayton, thousands of miles from bloodshed on the ground, three weeks of land swaps and head butting had failed to close the gap. "I can't believe he won't make peace over this small amount," the president told Christopher. Izetbegovic needed a lesson from Yitzhak Rabin about the courage to take risks. "The leaders who deserve to be called by the name," said Clinton, "know when these moments come." He instructed Christopher to make sure Izetbegovic understood that the deal on the table was fleeting, retractable by all parties. "If he rejects these terms now," he said, "he may never get them back."

Several times, while Christopher consulted his diplomats, Clinton filled me in on the proceedings so far. He said his own role was limited. While keeping abreast of the talks in Dayton, he had intervened sparingly to address logjams with the other heads of state. Just today, for instance, in a phone call, he had secured grudging assent from Croatia's Franjo Tudjman to abandon nearly eight hundred square miles of thinly populated mountains that his Croatian soldiers had overrun in Bosnia. The president called Tudjman a tough old buzzard. Whatever happened in Dayton, he remarked, Tudjman might prove to be the bad guy of eventual negotiations over his stray conquests in neighboring Slovenia. For the moment, however, Tudjman's surrender of "worthless" land put the three warring parties agonizingly close. They were less than one percent away from a settlement, and the final transfers need not involve key population centers or symbolic sites. Still, Izetbegovic balked at surrendering even an inch toward the goal. Clinton described him as shell-shocked, righteous, and morally entrenched. He had spent nine years in Yugoslav prisons under Communism. Now near death, he could scarcely imagine a restoration he would never see. His government seethed with internal divisions on the brink of peace. To Izetbegovic, Milosevic and the Bosnian Serbs had usurped half his nation by butchery, and he could not bring himself to participate in that result. Clinton said he shared his basic outlook, but blame was not enough. Paralyzed grievance offered neither realism nor hope, and the trick was to make Izetbegovic see that.

Would Clinton try persuasion himself, as with Tudjman? No, he replied, reviewing that option closely. He was satisfied that Christopher and Holbrooke had battered Izetbegovic with every objective argument. Not only would the prospective deal save besieged Gorazde from likely extermination, but Milosevic had offered a stunning concession to pull troops out of Serb enclaves within greater Sarajevo. Clinton believed the resistance of Izetbegovic was psychological. He said any direct presidential diplomacy would leak, and, if successful, be interpreted as a bullying attempt by Clinton to impose a settlement. This would stiffen congressional opposition that was fierce already. Some Democrats joined Republicans accusing him of grandiose ambitions to expose twenty thousand U.S. soldiers in foolhardy "nation building." His own White House staff emphasized polls running heavily against troop deployments to Bosnia. On balance, the president concluded, his direct intervention could gain a Pyrrhic victory at most. He resolved to hold back.

Public pressure would backfire, too. Clinton said he could not afford to expose Izetbegovic as the last problem in Dayton, because this surprising news would revive popular suspicion that the Bosnians must be complicit in their own demise. A strong undercurrent of prejudice would reinforce the temptation to stand aside while the only Muslim state in Europe regrettably succumbed to "ancient Balkan hatreds." The president called this image of the past erroneous but powerfully convenient, strong enough to unravel the peacekeeping coalition. No one would be able to mold the European nations into another one, certainly not the Russians. Therefore, he reasoned, the anguished holdout by Izetbegovic must be concealed to the bitter end, so long as there was any chance for settlement.

History gave Clinton a sliver of leverage. He said Izetbegovic must be warned that his protective treatment would expire once the Dayton talks failed. "If he doesn't take this peace," the president told Christopher, "I want him to know that sooner or later I may have to tell the world who's responsible." Picturing such a grim aftermath made Clinton steadily more upset on the phone. No one really cared about Bosnia in this lull, he said, but the whole world would erupt if war resumed. The same people who resist involvement would bristle with blame. "When the killing starts, it's bad for my administration," he said. He told Christopher they had risked too much and done too much for peace—leading horses right up to the drinking trough—getting more for Bosnia than anyone thought possible. "I'll be damned if I'm going to sit by and get torn to shreds over this," he vowed. He reeled off a checklist for the overnight ultimatum. Could Izetbegovic be made sure we weren't bluffing? Would his teeth rattle over the consequences of failure? Did all the allies see him as the obstacle? Were they agreed that something deep in his nature blocked assent?

The president listened to Christopher, nodding. He paused only slightly. "Well, Chris, go ahead and do it," he said. "Walk away. I trust you. I'll back you up. Eventually, you've got to shut it down if they won't take the peace." His tone mixed relief and resignation.

I YEARNED TO dwell on these decisions about Bosnia, captured raw, but too many topics beckoned from the list. Our compressed focus must delve erratically, mimicking his job.

We returned to the Rabin funeral. Clinton scoffed at a press conniption over whether he had slighted Dole and Gingrich by forcing them to use a rear door of Air Force One. He said protocol people handled such things. As he remembered it, only those on the helicopter went straight into his compartment, and everybody else in the huge delegation, including former presidents Carter and Bush, boarded through other doors. But he was less dismissive of complaints that he had snubbed Gingrich and Dole on the long flight home from Israel. He said he had been tired. He recalled a long phone conversation with Yasir Arafat just after liftoff. He did play cards, though, and he called it a mistake not to have said a word to Gingrich or Dole. On the other hand, he wanted to send them a message on the budget impasse. Clinton said he was sick of stories pitting the resolute conservatives against a vacillating president. In truth, Gingrich and Dole had failed to do their most basic work. They were stalled on the annual appropriations six weeks into a new fiscal year, and he was far from desperate to make a deal. Indeed, he sounded still glad that his silence made them howl. Any regret seemed conflicted and unresolved, like the government shutdown itself.

The president confirmed a press report of heated negotiations. He said Gingrich and Al Gore nearly came to blows. While trading barbs over extremism, Gore once tartly observed that at least no Democrat ever accused the speaker of drowning babies in South Carolina, and Gingrich exploded over the reminder of his gaffe in the Susan Smith case. (She had killed her own toddler sons and then blamed a fictitious African-American carjacker. Days before the 1994 elections, Gingrich attributed her infamous crime to permissiveness from the 1960s, soliciting Republican votes as the ideal remedy.) On tape, Clinton said he had pleaded for calm, and he described the climactic confrontation since as deceptively quiet. A week ago tonight, he almost whispered to Gingrich and Dole his reasons to veto their last, loaded resolutions keeping the government afloat. "You're not the only people with convictions," he told them. His spiel extended full credit for sincerity to the other side. They all wanted to balance the budget, but they could finish the job without riders to the budget that would throw 380,000 kids out of Head Start. Or slash college loans and Medicaid. If he must close the government to uphold countervailing values, so be it. He promised Gingrich and Dole that they would feel his priorities before this was over.

Gingrich especially seemed shaken by the final notice. They were going over the cliff after all, and the speaker quickly confided his surprise. All his calculations had assumed Clinton would bend or fold. Clinton said he thought Gingrich and his caucus were fooled by their own propaganda about the moral force of their proclaimed crusade. In the past week of shock and shutdown, as the president's approval ratings skyrocketed while those of Congress plummeted, they clung to hopes that the adverse reaction was temporary panic. The president thought the mainstream press fed their delusion by attributing his success to nimble posturing and salesmanship—seeing anything but a strong stand on principle. His theory produced a darting tangent on the mainstream media. He said the flagship *New York Times*, having sponsored an original tide of cynicism with Whitewater allegations, was showing signs of mitigating fairness in its reports, for instance, about how much of the budget fight was buried in economic forecasts. Since the 1980s, Republican administrations projected absurdly high growth and low inflation in order to conceal their massive accumulation of public debt, while the Republican Congress now was predicting years of low growth and high inflation to justify their maximum cuts in nonmilitary programs. Clinton perceived less balance at the *Washington Post* on the real impact of these debates. He guessed few editors there knew anyone in a Head Start family. "As a governor for years in a very poor state," he said, "I know a hell of a lot more about Medicare and welfare than they do."

He relished the outcome so far. Public hostility to the shutdown refuted decades of orchestrated myth about harmful government. Citizens badgered legislators to reopen their passport office, Arlington Cemetery, or Yellowstone. Who would mail the next veterans' checks? What about courthouses and weather satellites? Republicans had scrambled to reprieve federal workers today while vowing to reimpose a shutdown for their cause. If national elections were held now, said the president, Gingrich would not be speaker. Republicans would lose the House and maybe even the Senate. His polls had shot up nearly to 70 percent with the likeliest voters, fifty-five and older, even though he had not yet gotten to veto appropriations slashing Medicare and Medicaid. He said these shutdown vetoes were magnificent teaching tools. He looked forward to vetoing the current environmental appropriations bill, to amplify his message that conservatives were failing their first duty to conserve. If the next continuing resolution included more poisoned riders as the price of reopening the government, he would veto that, too, gaining a platform to explain. "There are horrible things in there," he said. "People have no idea." I floated the notion of a hypothetical line item veto, suggesting that perhaps he could illustrate the provisions he would have struck if he had such power. He paused, smiling. He thought I opposed the line item veto on constitutional grounds, whereas he favored it. True, I replied, but I was caught up in the possibilities from this crisis.

His political optimism carried over to Colin Powell's recent announcement that he would not run in 1996. The president had not called Powell since, fearing that a leak would advertise his relief. He had figured wrongly that Powell would oppose him, Clinton disclosed, whereas both Hillary and Al Gore argued otherwise. They thought Powell would realize sooner or later that he was not really a political animal, nor comfortable among Republicans, who would tear the gloss off his reputation if he became a candidate. They saw in Powell a highly structured man, devoted to appearances and proprieties, who might worry about becoming the first top general to run against his former commander since George McClellan tried to oust Abraham Lincoln in 1864, sealing McClellan's place among history's most vainglorious losers. The mistaken prediction about Powell seemed to gnaw at Clinton. He wanted to reread David McCullough's biography of Truman about the decision by General Eisenhower to stay at Columbia University in 1948. Maybe Eisenhower declined to politicize the modern military with a race against Truman, which might have made future presidents hesitate over appointments to the Joint Chiefs. Clinton nursed doubts that Powell was so scrupulous. Indeed, he faulted Powell's blockbuster autobiography for revealing presidential confidences from his service on the Joint Chiefs, saying these details should have waited at least until Clinton left office. His mental churn pulled up a fresh clue. Every upward step for Powell had been paved by patronage and appointment, observed Clinton, including his post in the Reagan White House. Powell was a career staff officer at heart, perhaps unsuited to the solo leap that a presidential bid rightly requires.

Powell's exit gave Dole a bump in polls for the Republican nomination, but it lasted only three or four days. His numbers against Clinton jumped, then sagged, and Dole barely won the recent Republican straw primary in Florida against a weak field headed by Senator Phil Gramm. The president said Dole was suffering with voters from his performance as Newt Gingrich's passive sidekick in the budget crisis. Dole had become a fixture on television, standing by while the speaker spouted his aggressively professorial retreat from the government shutdown. He could not look very presidential as second banana, especially since voters were tiring of Gingrich in droves. Clinton expected this image to haunt Dole through the election, and he thought solidarity with Gingrich was a political mistake. Dole should have broken with the firebrands to stake out a middle ground for the "grown-ups." That would show independence and leadership, managing differences to get things done. Ironically, said the president, bold cooperation with Clinton now might have helped Dole beat him in the race next year.

WE SKIPPED AND skimmed through remaining topics from the month. A car bomb had killed five U.S. soldiers at a training base near Riyadh, Saudi Arabia. Of the announcement that Attorney General Janet Reno had been diagnosed with Parkinson's, Clinton noted that Senator Alan Simpson, who had a knack for personal diversion across partisan lines, was comforting her with yarns about his father's three active decades with the disease. Separately, there was a failed international effort to keep Nigerian dictator Sani Abacha from hanging nine political and environmental activists for the Ogoni people, including the writer Ken Saro-Wiwa. With some chagrin, the president described his spontaneous phone call to discuss *Values Matter Most,* a new book by the neoconservative political strategist Ben Wattenberg, which had led to a running press flap over Wattenberg's claim that Clinton confessed himself a values relativist of zigzag belief. Strangely, said the president, he liked Wattenberg in spite of this predictable distortion and uproar. I speculated that they shared a rare enthrallment with campaign statistics. Clinton said no—he found Wattenberg engaging but not snide like most pundits. Besides, he thought he learned something. Wattenberg denied any values content in Clinton's major initiatives, from NAFTA and Bosnia to the assault weapons ban, calling them political maneuvers. Whereas Clinton approached values from the standpoint of civic standards for a republic, designed to protect and manage controversy, he thought Wattenberg confined them to community standards for private conduct, as in a small-town congregation, designed to condemn deviation as taboo.

His response on one domestic issue veered off to Japan and back into a family argument over Chelsea. *The Wall Street Journal* had mounted a campaign to force the resignation of Energy Secretary Hazel O'Leary over what Clinton called "a tempest in a teapot." He said he delegated the internal review to Al Gore, authorizing him to speak in his name, and the vice president determined to support O'Leary, which reminded Clinton that he sent Gore as his substitute to last week's economic summit in Japan. Gore came back with a very unpleasant report. The heads of state were openly hostile to him, affronted that Clinton himself stayed home during his emergency government shutdown. They said everybody has political troubles. Australian prime minister Paul Keating hotly told Gore he had come to Osaka despite a dock strike and paralyzed economy back home. Where was Clinton? The regional host, Prime Minister Tomiichi Murayama of Japan, faced chronic economic stagnation, corruption scandals, and outrage toward the United States for CIA operatives caught spying on trade talks, plus seething resentment over the rape of a twelve-year-old Japanese girl by three U.S. soldiers. The rape case was ugly, sighed Clinton. The soldiers had stalked the victim, beaten her, and stifled screams with tape they brought along to cover her mouth. Their commanding admiral had been cashiered within hours of his breezy comment that it would have been cheaper for them to hire an Okinawa prostitute.

Murayama was furious over the likely fall of his government, and Gore admonished Clinton that superpowers too easily overlook the impact of their gestures. His absence had insulted all of Japan, where culture ascribes great importance to symbolic forms of respect. A festering wound could damage sensitive U.S.-Japanese relations for years, Gore warned. Clinton must visit Japan quickly to make amends. Just today, the president told me, he and Gore had tramped back and forth over a crowded calendar. December was out because of nightly Christmas parties, and so on, until Clinton circled dates next April. Horrified, Gore said that would be months too late, especially since the White House was announcing a peace trip to Europe for next week. Why not substitute Japan for Northern Ireland? Alternatively, Gore zeroed in on three lightly committed January days, but the president pronounced them vital to Chelsea's schoolwork. Gore blinked. So what? He stared through Clinton's halting explanation why this would be a bad time—because Hillary must join him in Japan, and junior-year midterms are the most pressure-packed events in all of high school. Mutual exasperation spiked. "Al," Clinton told him, "I am *not* going to Japan and leave Chelsea by herself to take these exams." Gore erupted. He thought Clinton had lost his bearings. They had a big fight, said the president, and were still wrangling about dates for Japan.

Clearly distraught, he sifted implications like a medieval scholastic. It was a choice between public duty on a vast scale and the most personal devotion, with potential hurt feelings on all sides. There were rare times when no tutor or telephone could substitute for a father's presence. Somewhere during this appraisal, Doorman John Fanning appeared in his working white tie and tails. He explained shyly that he had been ordered to interrupt because the president must sign the continuing resolution before midnight. From a large envelope, he brought over the formal documents on an oversized cardboard framing mat. A White House memo certified the underlying legislation to be free of tricks. The United States Congress cleanly authorized the federal government to stay open at current levels until December 15, pending further negotiation on the overdue appropriations. Clinton did not look beneath the signing page, and I noticed penmanship while he affixed his approval. At the top, for the House of Representatives, the speaker had left a cartoonish contrast worthy of Dr. Seuss, from his long and angular "Newt" down to a tiny, scrunched "Gingrich." Below him, for the Senate, "James

Strom Thurmond" trailed off in the wobbly preschool print of a ninety-two-year-old patriarch, the former lion of white supremacy. Momentarily, with Clinton's brisk, vertical, left-handed strokes, the instrumental power to move our whole government seemed bizarrely human.

As always, while rewinding tonight's tapes for the president, I tried to defer reflection. My immediate goal was to hold empirical details in mind for dictation on the way home, but one stubborn impression lingered. President Clinton seemed off balance toward the end. It struck me already that he launched into his call to Ben Wattenberg, admitting that he had babbled vulnerably on the record, straight from describing a prior resolve with his staff to make himself drastically more reticent—more carefully "on message," as he put it—in his public comments. This juncture was too close to be accidental, and it was not like Clinton to pass over so blatant a contradiction. His discourse about Wattenberg led straight into the argument about Chelsea's exams. The latter was remarkable and funny to me, yet also touching about Chelsea and certainly disturbing to Gore. Both stories were passionately analytical on conflicts between public and private values. Even with hindsight on that theme, I doubt that it would have helped my interpretive stabs if Clinton had telescoped some hint of fateful news more than two years ahead. The shutdown for the past six days had stripped the White House of most paid employees to leave a small coterie of volunteer interns, which had just facilitated his first two groping assignations with young Monica Lewinsky.

I thought his odd state might simply vanish like other moods in the whirlwind. He was waiting in the upstairs kitchen for me to drop off the finished tapes—sitting up late for developments in Dayton, watching television, mulling over budget options to avert another shutdown. While saying good night, I complimented him for a line in his Rabin eulogy, which warned that those who hate enemies "risk sowing the seeds of hatred among themselves." The president merely nodded without comment, which made me hesitate. I figured this line must have come from a speechwriter, not him. Venturing again, I suggested that these convergent crises may be a blessing in disguise. Perhaps they could help him restore our nation's pathbreaking political experiment. He could balance its core discipline for self-government with the common purpose inherent in democratic values. True, this grueling task might not be as exciting for him as an election, but its heritage of freedom was our lifelong inspiration from the civil rights era. Clinton looked up and smiled. He could tell I was trying to cheer him up, and the reaction surprised me. "No," he said. "This is more exciting than a campaign."

CHAPTER TWENTY

TRIUMPH AND FURY: "YOU LIVE TO HAVE ONLY A FEW DAYS LIKE THAT"

Thursday, December 28, 1995

Tuesday, January 30, 1996

We resumed in confusion three nights after Christmas, eleven days into the second shutdown, with an early session scheduled to finish before the president's supper with Senator Chris Dodd. Aides advised me to allow an extra half-hour to clear security by a temporary route into the White House grounds next to the Treasury Building, through a gate tended by a skeletal staff of stand-ins who would not know me. I arrived earlier still, assuming that tonight's special cargo would test even a seasoned bureaucracy. It took a while to explain the unfamiliar van with Georgia plates, registered to someone else, and a large shrouded sculpture in back. The bomb dogs behaved badly, it was said, because the shutdown had deprived them of regular handlers, but they finally tired of sniffing my father's newly completed Jefferson Memorial bird feeder. Then I sat marooned under the Truman Balcony until usher Skip Allen himself produced a dolly and helped me roll this structure down into the dark, labyrinthine basement for storage among rugs and furniture in Room B-14. He said the custodians were still furloughed, along with Park Service groundskeepers and nearly half the federal workforce. Regardless of the president's wishes, he warned, at least a dozen offices, from architects and preservationists to gift lawyers, would have a say before the bird feeder moved again.

This stark reality discouraged me, but Allen brightened as soon as he stepped from the elevator upstairs into the yellow central hall. He said "the house" never looked better. Just recently, he had overheard a moviegoer claim inside knowledge that *The American President,* starring Annette Bening and Michael Douglas, had been shot right here to get the lush White House interiors precisely right. He shuddered and said that this was not true, of course. It would have destroyed the place. The film erroneously depicted swinging doors across this hall toward the master bedroom, said Allen, pointing to the actual recessed pocket doors. Several paintings were absent or substantially different on the screen, he added, but the look was generally authentic. Director Rob Reiner had been granted a tour for his crew to take notes but not photographs, and the resulting sets were so expensively good that Allen thought Oliver Stone had used them again in *Nixon.* For better or worse, Hollywood had at least a physical model for genuine White House drama.

President Clinton swept by to pick me up, preoccupied with his own timetable. "Leave your stuff here," he said. "I want to take you upstairs." I waded behind him through incoming and outgoing presents stacked along the third-floor corridors, past a room full of golf clubs. He was making notes about late surprises, plotting thank-yous and reciprocal gestures, concentrating heavily on the people involved rather than the gifts themselves. Distressed to hear that I knew nothing of any Windbreaker with the presidential seal, Clinton told me to call him if no package came in the next few days. He kept trying to unload bounty in the meantime, and virtually insisted that I take a framed photograph of William Faulkner riding a horse. Mainly, he wanted to show a fellow music lover this year's present from his staff—a small room wired, equipped, and soundproofed so he could blow his heart out on the saxophone without bothering anyone.

On the way back downstairs, I barely mentioned the bird feeder in limbo, saying we had begun transfer despite the shutdown because my dad needed his van back in Atlanta. Whitewater was the topic of pressing opportunity. Curiously, I told him, there were more Whitewater news stories now than in any month since March of 1994, notwithstanding a cold trail without major developments. We had done pretty well following David Kendall's advice not to discuss legal matters, lest the tapes themselves fall subject to subpoena, but what about our fallback idea to record separately about Whitewater, isolating any exposure to discovery? Clinton heartily approved. We should do that. He had many things stored up. We discussed whether we could make two sets of tapes in a single session, to avoid falling behind.

He detoured hurriedly into the Yellow Oval Room. His allergies were mercifully calm this season, and at last they had a family tree big enough for their twenty-five-year collection of ornaments. He highlighted for me only three small crystalline wreaths holding intricate peace figures, which came from the widows of the U.S. envoys killed in Bosnia last August. Biting his lip, he turned proudly to a first copy of the forthcoming *It Takes a Village,* standing on the nearby fireplace mantel with a cover of Victorian blue bordered by striking illustrations. He said Hillary had worked hard to make her book more substantive than a first lady's traditional fare. Next to it was Hillary's commissioned present for him this year of a life-sized dove with an olive branch—sculpted not in the usual repose, he explained, but roughly, turned sideways, flapping her wings in labored effort to symbolize the ongoing peace initiatives in Bosnia, Northern Ireland, Haiti, and the Middle East. Next door in the Treaty Room, he described an ornate glass vase that made him a lifetime member at one of the world's ten best golf courses, where he was yet to play because he had rushed from Northern Ireland to visit Bosnia-bound troops in Germany. I asked, while setting up the recorders, about two new items on the wall to my left. He said one was a photograph of President Kennedy addressing the Irish Parliament. The other was a handwritten memento from an author excerpting his own poem, "A

Chorus," with a personal inscription: "To President Bill Clinton with highest regard, it was a fortunate wind that blew you here, Seamus Heaney, Dublin, 1 December 1995."

WE BEGAN ON tape with Bosnia. Had the president changed his mind about calling Izetbegovic? He said no. He remained convinced that doing so would have made any peace even harder to hold. What happened was simple but dramatic: Warren Christopher dragged the Bosnian president through the dire alternatives until Izetbegovic caved at dawn, saying he was against the unjust terms but his people needed peace, and everyone scurried to confirm and leave Dayton before he changed his mind. Since then, Clinton called it a fire drill under siege to implement the agreement through NATO. At home, he had barely survived the heated resistance that overlapped the second shutdown of the federal government. Speaker Gingrich knew the Bosnia agreement was right, said the president, but his House had turned harshly isolationist. It was all the administration could do, with a fervent national address by Clinton on November 27, to defeat a resolution that would have cut off every dollar of support for U.S. troops there, 218–210. The president said he fared better in the Senate, where Dole pushed through a backhanded resolution of support for the troops laced with doubt about the mission. Dole called it "laying a marker" to blame Clinton if something went wrong. He and the president had come to fraternize across the battle lines, like opposing lawyers on a lunch break. "We acknowledge that he wants to be president—wants to be the commander, wants to be treated that way," Clinton stated. "Dole knows the only way he's going to get elected is if the economy tanks, or Bosnia falls apart, or if there's some other unforeseen disaster. Otherwise, it's going to be hard to beat me. And he's pretty frank about that."

Two incidents abroad provoked ruminations on stability. South Korea's Kim Young-sam, the first civilian president in a generation, had just arrested his two immediate predecessors—both military dictators—on charges of capital treason and corruption. One of them, Gen. Roh Taewoo, reportedly amassed a corporate slush fund in excess of $600 million, and Clinton mentioned systematic payoffs on a large scale. He thought punishment and reform were urgently needed, and yet we must bear in mind that a partnership between warlords and giant cartels had developed the economic miracle of South Korea from its primitive, war-torn starvation of 1953. Graft lubricated a crude but effective form of military capitalism. Clinton remembered leading a trade mission from Arkansas shortly before the Seoul Olympic Games in 1988. He said General Roh, who was then president, had kept his own Olympic team waiting an extra half-hour while he cross-examined Clinton on the presidential race between George H. W. Bush and Michael Dukakis. A war veteran, Roh had fought in Vietnam at the behest of the United States. Although he had since commanded the violent suppression of pro-democracy demonstrations in 1980, Roh was considered a modernist, and Clinton, looking ahead, thought President Kim faced a very delicate decision about whether to let his predecessors slip away into exile. The tough alternative—sticking for jail, or even execution—would risk backlash from humiliated leaders of a cartel system that many Koreans still associated with national prosperity. Clinton fretted that Kim already had squandered a good bit of his electoral mandate, possessing neither the shrewd resolution of the generals nor the immense moral prestige of his pro-democracy colleague and rival, the nearly martyred Kim Dae-jung, whom the president bluntly called a hero. From this complex intersection of Korean forces and personalities, Clinton narrowly expected the current President Kim to push forward through the next stage of reform.

In Turkey, a surge by the Islamic Welfare Party had just wiped out the parliamentary majority supporting Prime Minister Tansu Ciller. She may yet be asked to form another government, said Clinton, because many Turkish parties did not want to work with a rigid Islamist agenda, but he perceived a broadly troublesome trend in this election, alongside the resurgence of Communist parties across Russia and the defeat of President Lech Walesa in Poland. Remarkably, he said, Walesa lost despite the unprecedented, open support of the organized church in Europe's most Catholic country. It was a supreme consolation that all these electoral mandates were being honored, but Clinton noticed a common mood of anxiety above the political differences. He said global transitions were displacing great masses of people in the midst of new prosperity. We often forget that in our industrial era of new railroads and bustling great fortunes, there are people starving in tenements, too. He said the marginalized populations remain disproportionately old and poor, plus children, and we never hear that in the midst of China's economic upsurge, fifty thousand people sometimes sleep in the railroad stations of Shanghai. It would be well to remember that people can take only so much strain, especially where the social fabric is weak. In this context, Clinton interpreted the recent elections not so much as mandates for Communism or Islamic fundamentalism as a reaction to the pace of global change.

We turned to the formal signing of the Bosnia peace treaty in Paris on December 14. The president said he had flown all night to see his distinguished friend and appointee, Ambassador Pamela Harriman, in the midst of a paralyzing French transportation strike. Apart from the formal ceremonies, he focused on his lengthy introduction to Slobodan Milosevic. The Serb president spoke better English than Izetbegovic and Tudjman, said Clinton. Milosevic brusquely treated the whole war and peace as craziness now put necessarily aside to escape the crippling sanctions against his country. "You could really see how he was the lead dog in the fight over there," the president observed. He found Milosevic very crafty and full of life, with a steely look.

Clinton recalled telling Milosevic of his overnight visit that week from the widow Leah Rabin. She was especially close to Hillary. Recovering from shock, she joined long, therapeutic conversations in the private dining room at the White House, but one of her two children still seemed barely able to speak. By way of condolence, said the president, Milosevic wished lightning speed to the Israelis in tracking Rabin's real killer inside the Mossad, their secret service. Taken aback, Clinton asked how he knew of such a plot. Was not the murder more likely an uncontrollable event, or at worst a security lapse? "Absolutely not," Milosevic replied. "No head of state in that political situation gets killed without being betrayed in his own household." He promptly cited the Kennedy assassination, asserting that elements of the CIA had killed JFK amid swirling passions over Cuba, Vietnam, and the underworld. "You Americans have done a good job of covering it up all these years," Milosevic concluded, "but everybody knows that's what happened." He spoke with a calm assurance that Clinton found sad and chilling. For Milosevic, he said, conspiracy and violence filled the entire political landscape.

More positively, the president saluted the swift deployment of NATO's IFOR (Implementation Force) coalition to enforce the peace agreement in Bosnia. A third of its sixty thousand troops already had moved through transport to operational stations. U.S. soldiers had been on the ground three weeks. He praised the Pentagon for amazingly detailed blueprints and realistic training in the mountains of Germany, designed to simulate Bosnia's harsh winter terrain. He explained intricate incentives for the treaty partners to make verified withdrawals of armament from the war zones. There had been no signs of resistance so far, nor any glitches in the joint protocols among the NATO commanders. Only two casualties had been sustained, both from a jeep that struck a land mine. One British soldier may lose a leg, Clinton reported, but otherwise the mission proceeded smoothly.

Continued success would magnify a ripple of optimism, which the president called "America is back." He said he felt its outpouring in Germany. Even the sophisticated countries of Europe were not yet capable of maintaining regional security agreements without U.S. leadership, he said, and our assurance means more to them than we realize. In a striking theme, Clinton said the desire for peaceful cooperation had tapped public emotions so deep that politicians had not yet figured out how to give them structure and form. This was a lesson he kept repeating from his trip to the British Isles, whose highlights he recalled for at least twenty minutes.

EXPECTATIONS BEGAN LOW. The president said he had called in his speechwriters before leaving the White House. He loved them all, he said, but their draft for his November 29 address to the British Parliament was terrible—a wooden list of things to do. Where was the magic of their prose for the Middle East? Did they think bland food defined our rich history with England? Their work vastly improved, said Clinton, but he stayed up all night to rewrite his speech during the flight across the Atlantic. The moment was important to him personally from his studies at Oxford, being steeped in the great speeches of Gladstone, Disraeli, and Churchill. He said he was nervous. Beyond that, he wanted to break through a wall of cynicism. The British press, which he called the only media more juvenile than our own, had stirred feverish suspicion that

Clinton supported the Irish peace process only to punish the Tories for conniving against him in the 1992 election. To complement such non-sense, he thought the warm-up speakers at Westminster introduced him with cursory remarks on a proper Anglo partnership. The president said he worked hard to wake them up. His jokes clicked. So did an emotional summary of the twentieth century's wars against dictators, Fascism, and Communism. Then he summoned them to confront an array of global threats to freedom and prosperity, bigger than any clash of armies.* Its breakthrough was his pledge never again to retreat into isolationism. Our forebears won the war, he told them, and now we must win the peace. These lines electrified MPs from both houses and all parties. Some of them pronounced his reception the best for a foreign leader in British history. To follow its momentum, his memories on tape passed lightly over social events with Queen Elizabeth.

Astonishing crowds gathered in Belfast. Catholics mingled openly with Protestants, the president said, as he and Hillary shook hands on streets that had been deserted for fear of snipers fifteen months earlier, like the wartime markets of Sarajevo. A truce was holding. Goodwill swelled with un-shuttered shops and a vigorous revival of jobs, plus the British government's agreement to join two-track talks that separated arms disputes from political questions, mediated by former senator George Mitchell. The first U.S. president ever to visit Northern Ireland came with a purpose. Children pressed forward with petitions for peace, and the reversal accelerated to warp speed. Instead of priming a creaky pump in London, he was swept along on a torrent of euphoria.

At one public meeting, he told me, the hard-line separatist Ian Paisley lectured him for twenty minutes on fickle crowds and fleeting dreams, saying the Protestants always returned to their leaders for safety. Paisley silenced a restive audience, but then the mayor of Belfast went on sourly about how the benighted Catholics did not really understand Christmas

---

* "We see it," Clinton told Parliament, "in the growth of ethnic hatred, extreme nationalism, and religious fanaticism, which most recently took the life of one of the greatest champions of peace in the entire world, the prime minister of Israel. We see it in the terrorism that just in recent months has murdered inno-cent people from Islamabad to Paris, from Riyadh to Oklahoma City."

in this month of Immanuel. His own people hooted him down. "Save it for Sunday!" they shouted, and, "We want Bill!" Clinton said he walked a tightrope in reply, figuring the mayor had hated him even before this stunning rebuke. He tried to channel the hostile sermon toward Immanuel's central message of loving your enemies. Protestants may know Clinton only for giving a visa to their enemy Gerry Adams, he admitted to them bluntly, but he sought no peace that they would not embrace, too. They could answer sound politics as well as their better angels, because Protestants were down to 51 percent in Northern Ireland, and would become a minority. On these hybrid notes, he managed to restore cheers for everyone.

Moments of awe and acclaim surged with him into the walled city of Derry, or Londonderry. The president recalled a sudden silence of anticipation in the packed square, noticing people jammed also in streets all the way up a steep hill. Perhaps half the city's divided population had turned out. Clinton spoke of their native son, William Penn, a warrior who had converted to Quaker pacifism and laid out the city of Philadelphia. He praised its contemporary hero John Hume, Northern Ireland's most eloquent voice for nonviolence, along with his Protestant counterpart for negotiations, David Trimble. On tape, the president preserved memories in far greater detail than I could duplicate in my notes, including the name of an Irish tenor who sang a cappella at the last stop in Dublin. "I've never heard anybody sing better," he said. "There wasn't a dry eye in the house when he was done." He finished in a rush about speeches on College Green and in the Irish Parliament, with the taoiseach (prime minister), John Bruton, of their determination to persevere with treacherous but historic negotiations. He went to Cassidy's Pub, after his mother's maiden name, and he felt that Van Morrison was peeved when Clinton declined to play the sax with his band. Thousands bobbed along with Hillary and him through Dublin's giant Phoenix Park. There was a quiet retreat with the newest Nobel laureate, Seamus Heaney, before flights to Germany, Madrid, and home. The president called the Irish visit shimmering. "You live to have only a few days like that," he said.

Breaking off well after eight o'clock, we left the tapes on rewind to seek the president's date for supper. Butler James Selmon, who was patiently tending an empty table set for two, agreed to put out a call for

Senator Dodd. On our way back down the hall, I said Bob Woodward had called me several times about his book on next year's presidential campaign. He had interviewed Senator Dole many times, and was pressing to speak with Clinton. The president nodded on the move. Did I think he should agree? He said they had really screwed him on *The Agenda*, when his staff members gave Woodward government documents without permission. I told him the book itself had been a pretty straightforward account of the big budget fight, but Clinton said the sales spin was terrible. Ignoring the actual outcome, not to mention the historic potential, it touted a theme of disorderly vacillation that became the default premise for news about Clinton. I said that was a bigger problem than Woodward, who was rummaging again among a talkative White House staff. We returned to the Treaty Room, debating his options as the president disappeared through a hidden door in the wall. He called out from a bathroom that I had never noticed, asking if I vouched for Woodward. I thought he was trustworthy. Well then, did I believe his account in *Veil* that CIA Director William Casey had confessed the Iran-contra scandal to Woodward alone in the hospital, with his dying breath? I squirmed. That may be far-fetched, I replied, but he seemed free of general animus against Clinton. The president teased me above the sound of a steady stream. So I thought Woodward stretched the truth, he asked merrily, with unbiased little fibs?

TEN DAYS BEFORE our next session, Christy and I ran into Tony Lake while making a connection at Miami International Airport on our way to Aristide's wedding. The national security adviser was slipping away from world duties on his own time, because the Haiti mission had grown on him. All of us dipped into savings for the commercial flight into Port-au-Prince, and we were summoned hours later to find President Aristide pacing serenely in welcome, insisting that he needed visitors before the ceremony. Priests milled around their former colleague. Aristide smiled at the street gossip about the sudden marriage to his lawyer, Mildred Trouillot. Folk poems and graffiti bemoaned the love of one woman for ruining a chaste marriage between the president-priest and Haiti herself.

"Would you like to see Minush?" he asked. Waving aside our protests about bridal seclusion, he led us eagerly upstairs to behold her attended by parents, a sister, and several other relatives, photographing each other. The formidable Ms. Trouillot coyly dodged questions about the origins of her endearment by the nickname Minush, except to insist that romance had surprised them both. Ambassador Bill Swing blocked our awkward attempts to retreat. We were not imposing, he assured us. Aristide would tell us when to leave. When he did, guests joined assorted dignitaries seated on folding chairs outside Aristide's home for a wedding service in several languages, and Swing's wife, Yuen, herded six of us, including two uniformed generals, back to the embassy residence for a very late supper. The question at table was why Americans cared so little about Haiti's first steps from bloody tyranny. Joseph Kinzer of the Fifth U.S. Army, commanding the U.N. forces in Haiti, said the victory had been too cheap. Finding no drama in the battle for a defenseless country, he drifted into conversation with Christy about her escapades as a skydiver. On Haiti, Gen. Jack Sheehan said American politicians failed to engage public interest in what he called "the Mother Teresa aspects" of foreign affairs. Lake's deputy, Nancy Soderberg, bridled, countering that Americans wanted policy framed in the language of "interests." She said soft goals wouldn't work in the long run, but Sheehan insisted that Mother Teresa deserved equal weight. Otherwise, our commitment to democratic governance was merely window dressing for military power. Christy looked at Sheehan with fresh admiration.

General Kinzer mentioned one staff sergeant renowned for delivering a Haitian baby. I recalled hearing Gen. Hugh Shelton tell Aristide that the welcome of Haitians had converted his grumbling soldiers to their mission. Sheehan cautioned us not to get carried away. To him, the defining moment had occurred here when ten armed paramilitaries challenged newly landed U.S. troops on the streets of Cap Haitien, to their swift and ultimate regret. At the formal transfer of remains, when asked why there were eleven body bags, Sheehan said he informed the assembled Haitian generals that the extra one contained unmatched fragments and limbs. He felt "all the starch go out of Cedras," the dictator, and there had been no casualties or trouble to speak of since then.

THE PRESIDENT'S EDGINESS surprised me on January 30 because I had expected his triumphant approval ratings to generate an ebullient mood.

He was distracted. The Arkansas-LSU basketball game was about to start, and he wished Nancy Hernreich had scheduled us earlier tonight. He said he had other things to do, but his tone softened for personal inquiries while he finished dinner in the private kitchen. Not for the first time, he consoled me through bumps in the marathon quest to make films of my work on the civil rights movement—offering theories about why race was a barrier for Hollywood, along with suggestions for a director to replace Jonathan Demme. Clinton said he admired Phil Robinson's 1989 baseball classic, *Field of Dreams,* enough to visit the director's set of *Sneakers* during production, and he commended the texture of Carl Franklin's film noir of 1992, *Devil in a Blue Dress.* Beyond talent and timing, he traced the biggest movie obstacles to finance, which generally meant studios, and kindly volunteered to consult Steven Spielberg at his new venture called DreamWorks. He mentioned contacts elsewhere, including a good friend of Al Gore's high on the business side of Disney.

On tape, in the Treaty Room, we reviewed the second government shutdown, which had lasted into the new year. There were stories from his fifty hours of intense budget negotiations with Gingrich and Dole, but he emphasized a consistent pattern. The president said Dole misread presidential politics by choosing the shutdown over a constructive deal. He still thought Dole would eke out a victory for the Republican nomination, but only because his rivals were so weak. Senator Gramm was fizzling, he said, and magazine heir Steve Forbes could not last on his chirpy message that rich people were good for the country. Former governor Lamar Alexander had blown any chance to overtake Dole, Clinton believed, by packaging himself as a phony backwoodsman from Tennessee.

As for Gingrich, Clinton said the speaker had aimed consciously all last year to close the government, knowing that Republicans did not have the votes to override presidential vetoes on the budget. Now he was paying a political price. The public blamed Republicans for dereliction and extremism, while their ideologues blamed them for retreat. Clinton thought the outcome also spoiled Gingrich's "Contract With America." He found it hard to gauge the resulting political tension between Gingrich and Dole, noting that the two of them persisted in their parallel course toward financial default. They had refused to act as the national debt rose above the legal ceiling authorized by Congress. In fact, Republican leaders denounced Treasury Secretary Robert Rubin for staving off disaster with ingenious gimmicks, and Representative Gerald Solomon of New York, chair of the House Rules Committee, actually vowed to impeach Rubin unless he let the Treasury fall toward bankruptcy. This posture amazed Clinton. He said Rubin was performing a heroic public service, as sane bankers and economists well knew, and he was also protecting Republicans from themselves. Default would boomerang against them. Any breach in the full faith and credit of the United States—even a slight downgrade in the rating of Treasury securities—would reverberate with pain. Government services may evaporate, and the spike in interest rates surely would add crippling burdens to the federal deficit, business loans, and millions of home mortgages.

These dire effects were obvious in advance, said the president, but Congress enjoyed a strange sense of impunity. This, too, was a pattern. Since the savings and loan debacle of the 1980s, and the government shutdowns lately, Republicans did not seem to worry about calamity ahead when they carried out their rhetorical scorn for government. Even now, the public threats against Rubin drew respectful news coverage for hard-nosed politics as they played chicken to precipitate default in the national treasury. Clinton was not sure he could thwart them, but he claimed one certainty: he would have been eviscerated for advocating anything remotely so irresponsible.

A nettled foreboding crept into his analysis of some positive trends. At long last, he said, President Asad had moved to join the Middle East peace process. His Syrian generals had been huddled with Israeli generals for more than a month now at the Wye Plantation on Maryland's Eastern Shore, getting to know each other as they narrowed the security issues for a peaceful transfer of the Golan Heights. Asad was in a good mood, said the president, and Israeli prime minister Shimon Peres enjoyed a twenty-point lead in the afterglow for his martyred predecessor, Yitzhak Rabin. Here lay the seeds of a dilemma. Clinton said Peres must hold national elections by October. Alternatively, under the Israeli system, he could call early elections for spring to secure his own mandate. Peres knew, however, that his aura from Rabin would dissipate rapidly when he became a candidate for power. The Likud opposition, led by Benjamin Netanyahu, would attack unpopular concessions to Syria before a treaty itself could be achieved. Moreover, Peres would have to freeze the Wye talks during the ferocious Israeli campaign season, which would infuriate Asad. The president himself could see no way out for Peres. Every choice, including a current paralysis within the Israeli cabinet, doomed prospects for Syrian peace along with the political advantage from Rabin's sacrifice.

On other topics, Clinton described his recent journey to the Balkans—its meetings with Croatian president Franjo Tudjman in Zagreb, troops in Tuzla and Aviano, mayors in Hungary. He contrasted the nervous apprehensions there with the pulsing optimism on the streets of Northern Ireland. Every small move in Bosnia was calibrated not to provoke renewed fighting. Land mines were the greatest danger to the NATO troops, he said, followed by accidents and snipers.

At home, the president lamented an extraordinary, bipartisan exit by incumbent members of Congress. Thirty-five representatives already had announced retirement, and William Cohen of Maine had just become the thirteenth senator to quit, leaving a safe Republican seat. Democrats were understandably forlorn over lost powers since 1994, but Republicans joined the evacuation, too, abandoning coveted new committee chairs and privileges. Clinton said the place had become too mean-spirited. Subliminally, he thought, some Republicans clung to marginal differences in negotiation because a budget agreement would exhaust their positive agenda. Without it, they reverted to generic sneers at Washington and the folly of politics, which Clinton called "kind of stomping on the government." This was insidious. In the long run, said the president, politicians harmed everyone by belittling their own profession.

Grim habits had earned Senator Dole a dismal public reaction for his televised response to the president's State of the Union Address. Dole tried to make Clinton the straw man for suffocating, omnipotent government—branding him "the rear guard of the welfare state." By contrast, Clinton aimed to shift the framework of a political generation. "The era of big government is over," he told Congress and the nation. "But we cannot go back to the time when our citizens were left to fend for themselves." The president dissected this formulation on tape, calling it a two-step prescription. First, he consigned the mantra of "big government" to the past by proclaiming consensus against the dangers of compounded debt. The budget fights had been tumultuous, but he embraced steady and measurable progress toward a dramatic goal, saying we must eliminate structural deficits before their cumulative burden saddled future generations with an unsustainable national economy. At the same time, he rejected anti-government individualism as an unpatriotic fantasy in the shrinking world. One emphatic vow in his State of the Union Address—"Never, ever shut the federal government down again"—had triggered a standing ovation from the assembled legislators in both parties.

THE PRESIDENT HAD sought in one speech to define the 1996 election. This was what he would disclose about his approach to the campaign, he remarked, if he decided to give Bob Woodward a book interview for the record. (He never did.*) For Clinton, the election's most essential choice boiled down to a single question: what is the role of government between the two outmoded extremes? The bulk of his address set forth seven urgent public challenges for the twenty-first century.† They were all daunting, he said, and far too complex for easy answers. Each one called for a mix of debate and experimentation, private responsibility, bold initiative, and political discipline. Still, he exhorted citizens to tackle these challenges with American optimism. He said the administration had cut the federal deficit in half so far, while turning a recession into eight million new jobs with the lowest inflation and unemployment since 1969. This record helped raise the traditional proclamation of our strong national union into a springboard for oratorical heights. Members of the House and Senate, though dominated by Republican opposition, interrupted him with applause almost eighty times. Their enthusiasm spanned the entire seven-part address, at roughly ten ovations per challenge.

---

* The book, *The Choice*, was published in 1996 by Simon & Schuster.

† (1) Protect children and families. (2) Reform education. (3) Revamp economic opportunity and security. (4) Reduce crime. (5) Rescue the environment. (6) Maintain global leadership for democratic values. (7) Reinvent streamlined government.

Clinton reviewed his extraordinary success. He ascribed some of it to surprise, because the speech did not leak in advance. Some was presentation, because for once a timely draft gave him several days to practice. Brevity helped. He said none of the rehearsals had exceeded thirty-seven minutes, including generous pauses, but the extra cascades of approval pushed the actual delivery toward an hour. I asked about his chosen sequence for the seven challenges. Was that important? Did he try to seduce the audience by starting with familiar issues like crime before newer ones like peacemaking and the environment? The president minimized this factor. There were plenty of strong disagreements throughout, he said, and what mattered more was his effort to break the gridlock embedded in political labels. After decades of rising federal deficits, he said, Republicans were losing their excuse to hammer government as the enemy. They were exposed in a blind rut. Ultimately, our government was our common refuge and the instrument of freedom. Solutions demanded help from everyone.

His address had resonated for a week. Clinton said the entrenched political culture conceded as much, calling him "a communicator" as it scrambled to recover familiar themes and slogans. Press critics accused him of abandoning liberalism with his farewell to big government, while Bob Dole insisted that Clinton remained its captive. The president looked past all that to savor a connection directly with voters. Weekly polls showed support well above 60 percent for most of his agenda—rising to 70 percent on some initiatives. He said heavy majorities favored his approach to the array of challenges, which emphasized questions and alternatives rather than dogma. Clinton relished a host of possibilities from the public response. They were practical as well as ambitious. They could move the whole country. They revived his enthrallment with politics as life's greatest arena.

Then abruptly, his mood collapsed in conversation with his attorney in the Paula Jones lawsuit, Bob Bennett. "When he came out of that phone call," I dictated later, "it was like he was a changed person." Reminders of scandal turned his high ground from the speech into quicksand. He was seething and sinking. Two or three more calls—one to Chief of Staff Leon Panetta, another from Bennett—made him vent on several fronts. Apparently, Press Secretary Mike McCurry had apologized for a procedural misstatement about the investigation now known as Travelgate, about the firing of the White House Travel Office employees, guaranteeing a flare of accusatory publicity for tomorrow. Clinton flared himself, into the sort of wounded monologue that had marked some of our earliest sessions. He called it a sham inquisition stretched over nearly three years. It was already longer than Watergate, but you would never know from the coverage, he said, that the employees of the Travel Office served at his pleasure and could be dismissed legally without cause. The reporters thought the Travel Office worked for *them*, he charged, not for the president or the taxpayers.

Somewhere in this protest, I tossed a bromide that substance eventually would prevail. Last month, I pointed out, he made headway by observing in public that the Gingrich Congress had held thirty-four hearings on the recycled trivia of Whitewater last year, against only two on the impending Social Security crisis. The president looked at me with disappointment, and my calming effort backfired. He said Whitewater was never about substance. It was a perpetual diversion. Only last month, he pointed out, the final report of the government's Resolution Trust Corporation concluded that the underlying facts of Whitewater supported no charges, as the Clintons had maintained all along. Why was there not a speck of coverage about this central fact? Because, he fumed, reporters never had to admit error. They could simply move on to another pretext in tandem with Special Prosecutor Ken Starr. That's what happened when his aide Carolyn Huber, while cleaning out boxes upstairs on the third floor, found a missing copy of Hillary's billing records from her old law firm in Little Rock. Nobody cared that the records, like the RTC report, supported Hillary on the facts. Nobody asked whether it made sense that she would hide exculpatory evidence for two years and then surrender it voluntarily. Instead, the press went wild with suspicions of cover-up, and Starr ramped up his flagging political theater by calling Hillary before the grand jury. He could have questioned her again at the White House, said Clinton. But no. Starr made a first lady—for the first time in history—wade through an ocean of reporters last Friday to face the grand jury under subpoena, in secret, creating the illusion of something deeply sinister and conspiratorial. The president moaned. Look what they were doing to Hillary.

"We've got to get this over with," he said, waving at my list of questions, but he did not want to stop. He beckoned me to hurry. Reeling, I asked about several of the tamer events. Clinton mentioned nice music at the funeral for Barbara Jordan, whom we had met together during the campaign in Texas years ago. He had little to say about the death of *New York Times* editor James Reston. Clearly, he had lost heart for recording presidential stories, but he kept boiling over about Starr and the press. "Are you getting this down?" he asked. "Are you keeping these chronologies?" Brushing aside our plan to save Whitewater for a separate tape, he circled back through the scandals in detail. A torrent of outrage dissolved his practiced veneer. He said the whole thing was stacked against him. It was not enough to do his job after all, nor was it an accident that these persecutions had reared up just in time to spoil his hard-won political gains. Both to me and to his lawyer on the phone, he railed against the stance of patient cooperation. He called it naïve, vowing to fight. More than once he exploded, "I'm tired of this limp-dick shit." McCurry was good, he conceded in a rush, and he liked him, but Mike tended to give in too much. Clinton pleaded for an aggressive army. "I want somebody to stand up to these people," he cried. "This is ridiculous."

Was there anything else? Did I have more questions? The president wanted to stop, but then he raised a final topic himself. Two weeks ago, he had attended the holiday commemoration at Martin Luther King's old church in Atlanta, Ebenezer Baptist. He softened and smiled. The service went on too long, of course, but he said it was a wonderful event of historical poignancy, featuring the music of his gifted friend Wintley Phipps. His lyrical description seemed like a moment of recovery or grace, culminating when someone had mentioned Hillary from King's pulpit. The whole audience stood instantly with a wallop of noise—not polite applause, but a heartfelt roar. He could tell the difference, and it meant a lot. Emotion welled up. That was all.

HAVING DICTATED MY notes, I could not put this session out of my mind. Previous nights had affected me—notably the ordeal before invading Haiti, and our dispute over the Middle Class Bill of Rights—but their discomfort had passed in the blur of decisions and events, leaving only hints of a president's burden. This one lingered. The peaks and valleys were so close together. Clinton seemed conflicted, slipping backward. My consolation was that perspective would allow future historians to mine rich material from these tapes, but what about now? Was he asking for help? Not from me, I scoffed to myself. Not now, anyway, and perhaps my impulse to volunteer was simply a loss of objectivity. After many sessions together, it was jarring and painful to see him so overwrought. Sifting the clues, I worried that he was about to terminate our history project. I even speculated that he knew Hillary faced indictment from some discovered secret.

Strobe Talbott unwittingly focused my resolve a few days later. At his invitation, I would spend the night at his home before our predawn flight from Andrews Air Force Base to Haiti, and this gave me a chance to compose personal thoughts for delivery to President Clinton by hand. "Dear Bill," I began. "Please allow me to step beyond my role as your historical sounding board. As your friend, I have been troubled about finding you in such private anguish the other night just when you have created a positive watershed for your presidency."

In Washington, Nancy Hernreich cleared me into the West Wing through the daytime security. She took my letter, introduced me to Janis Kearney, and asked me to wait. Kearney bravely filled a new position in White House meetings as the first official diarist, which was one of the recommendations from our ad hoc history group in 1993. While she sketched her progress against ongoing bureaucratic resistance, my divided thoughts followed Hernreich with the letter, which aimed neither to intrude with guesswork nor mince words with a president's time. The first paragraph continued: "You may have forgotten already, given your resilience, but I think you must guard relentlessly against effects of a recurring dark mood that may endanger your chance for both historic and personal triumph."

Nancy returned. The president had started reading the letter on the spot, but he did not finish before participants for his current meeting filed into the Oval Office. She said he slipped the letter into his pocket. I thanked her profusely, guessing that a two-page letter was probably too long. On the way out, I regretted placing my central advice several hundred words into the text. "Your biggest weakness," I wrote, "is a tendency to lump 'the press' together with your political opponents." I recommended a strategy to distinguish them. Basically, he could attack opponents but not the press. He must feed or charm reporters. Perseverance with his constructive agenda was essential on both fronts, I concluded. History would not celebrate Lincoln's wisdom, or generosity of spirit, if he had lost his war.

Strobe and I left the next morning, February 7, with a delegation headed by U.N. Ambassador Madeleine Albright. We saw the presiding officer solemnly don a bowler hat to begin Haiti's first peaceful transfer of elected power. Aristide shifted the presidential sash from his shoulder to René Préval. They embraced and then led everyone to a ceremonial Te Deum at the National Cathedral, where barefoot young men and women slowly proceeded down the center aisle to present samples of everything produced in Haiti—fruits, vegetables, baseballs, on finally to paintings and novel musical instruments made of iron. Later, by chance, Strobe and I were ushered in for our greeting just as Préval took his congratulatory phone call from President Clinton.

Back home, the mail brought me a handwritten note from the White House: "Thanks for your words of encouragement during the past week." Much to my surprise, it was from Hillary.

1

On inauguration morning, 1993, President-elect Clinton rehearses his address in the Blair House library (*above*). Listeners from left are myself (*under the bust of Jefferson*), George Stephanopoulos, Rodney Slater (*head only, in foreground*), Michael Sheehan (*standing*), Tommy Caplan, and Vice President–elect Al Gore, with aide Degee Wilhelm in the far doorway. That evening, now president, Clinton records impressions of his first hours in office (*below*), seated in the third-floor Solarium at the White House residence.

2

3

Dressed to leave for the inaugural balls. In the yellow central hall of her new home, the first lady waits with me for the president (*above*). On October 20, 1993 (*below*), I have concealed both recorders after a photographer and several aides unexpectedly joined our interview in the Oval Office. We learned to tape elsewhere in seclusion, at night. The first storage box for Clinton's microcassettes lies on the desk next to his glass. He soon needed bigger ones.

4

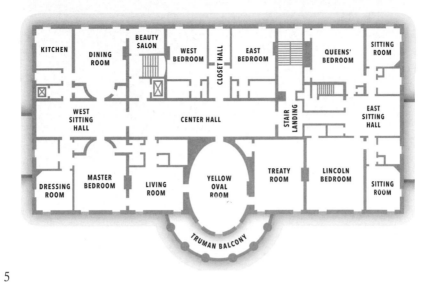

A diagram of the main residential floor at the White House (*above*), where we taped nearly all the presidential interviews. Our favorite spot is prepared for a session (*below*) in the president's private office called the Treaty Room. My chronologies, recorders, and notes are on the coffee table. The president usually sat in the wing chair.

7

The Treaty Room during the Clinton presidency (*above*). Benjamin Wilson's portrait of Benjamin Franklin (1759) hangs on the south wall, behind Ulysses Grant's desk. The table we used during interviews is visible in the lower right corner. Nancy Hernreich (*center*) handled arrangements for the presidential taping sessions. Social Secretary Capricia Marshall (*below, left*) poses with usher's-office staff during Christmas holidays in 1998: (*l-r*) Dennis Freemyer, Gary Walters, President Clinton, Daniel Shanks, James "Skip" Allen, Worthington White. (Not shown: Nancy Mitchell)

8

9

10

Bird Feeders. On Christmas night, 1994, President Clinton steps outside to pose under the Truman Balcony (*above*) with my father's novel gift to our Baltimore family (*l-r, son Franklin, daughter Macy, my wife Christy*): a bird feeder shaped like the White House. In 1996, Frank Branch (1922–2003) gives his latest creation, a Jefferson Memorial bird feeder, to President Clinton on the South Lawn (*below*). Socks the cat is tethered in the background.

11

12

End of "the Gore Administration." President Clinton hugs Hillary and Chelsea (*above*) at his second inauguration, on January 20, 1997. Because he took the oath slightly after noon, there were jokes that Vice President Gore (*center*) held office for three or four minutes. Platform dignitaries are Senator John Warner of Virginia (*left*) and Speaker Newt Gingrich (*at right with Marianne Gingrich and House Majority Leader Dick Armey*). In February of 1998, the Clintons roast me at a publication party for one of my books on the Martin Luther King era (*below*).

13

Son for a day. President Clinton shows Franklin where to hit the ball (*above*) at the Army Navy Country Club on November 11, 1998. We watch one of Franklin's shots (*below*).

To Taylor
Thanks for a great round of golf, *Bill*

16

With her chief of staff, Melanne Verveer, Hillary studies last-minute changes drafted by Christy (*left*) for a speech to the United Nations on March 4, 1999 (*above*). Later that year (*below*), the president and I huddle at one of our few public events together at the White House.

17

CHAPTER TWENTY-ONE

FAMILY FEUDS: FROM GREENSPAN TO SADDAM HUSSEIN

Wednesday, February 28, 1996

The ushers sent me straight up to the third-floor Solarium, where I found President Clinton watching the Grammy Awards telecast with Hillary and Jim Blair. He wore blue jeans, and they were in suits— Blair with a guest pass around his neck. The Tyson Foods executive seemed more lighthearted than I remembered from his earlier power talk around the president. He saluted Hillary for a best-selling debut, *It Takes a Village,* in the literary world, teasing about her new place in the arts alongside this bumper crop of female musicians nominated for awards, including Mariah Carey, Alanis Morissette, Shania Twain, and a close-harmony group called TLC. Hillary allowed that it felt much better to be an author than a targeted witness before the grand jury. She happily signed two books I had brought along for charity auctions in Baltimore, but then she disclosed an undertow.

Sally Quinn of the *Washington Post* was spreading rumors that Hillary had not written her own book. Worse, she was saying Hillary had denied proper credit to its collaborator, a friend of Quinn's named Bar-

bara Feinman. The book company, Simon & Schuster, had recommended
Feinman on the strength of her prior work with its other Washington
authors including Bob Woodward and Quinn's husband, Ben Bradlee,
the *Post* editor renowned for witty bravado during the Watergate scandal.
However, said Hillary, Feinman had withdrawn mysteriously from the
project since an early promise to spend the weekend editing at Ben and
Sally's. Her retelling wryly identified that location as local shorthand for
Washington's social headquarters. Fortunately, she said, the White House
had retained draft chapters in Hillary's own hand, and her computer-
illiteracy became a blessing for once. To verify authorship, she was going
through those manuscripts now with ABC News correspondent Barbara
Walters. Some of the original content was embarrassing, she winced, like
an overgrown garden, and many friends and advisers had helped her cull
the weeds. Still, she was countering Quinn's charge.

What did I think of this mess, which implicated me loosely on several fronts as a former ghostwriter and Washington journalist now writing
books also for Simon & Schuster? Stammering, I ducked the publishing
dispute. Multiparty book contracts were notoriously complicated, and I
knew nothing of Feinman or the editorial process for *It Takes a Village*. On
the feud with Quinn, I expressed a passing wish that Hillary could include Ben Bradlee in direct mediation. He seemed to me amiably detached from Washington's obsession with status. I confided that years
ago, when he was already famous, Bradlee had howled at me over a harsh
review of his memoir about President Kennedy. Then he laughed, said
maybe I was right, and launched a spirited debate about being too spellbound or disillusioned by JFK. I thought the Clintons could find rapport
with Bradlee because he loved journalism the way they loved a good
political fight. Quinn would be harder. Even to me, on occasion, she had
said she could spare the Clintons from grave mistakes. She took her exclusion from the White House as proof that neither Clinton understood
the codes of Washington—which charity boards mattered, whom to entertain, the dynamics within various political couples.

The reply was decisive. "You know," declared Hillary, "she has been
hostile since the moment we got here. Why would we invite somebody
like that into our home? How could she expect us to?" From my heels,
I suggested that Hillary approach the Washington press corps like swing

voters in a tough campaign, but she rejected the analogy. She said Quinn
and her friends simply invented gossip for their dinner circuit. They had
launched one juicy affair between Hillary and a female veterinarian attending Socks, the Clinton family cat, with tales about how somebody
discovered them in flagrante on a bedroom floor in the White House.
There was no end to it. Jim Blair, perhaps to rescue me, said stuff almost
that bad got printed. He cited a *New Yorker* essay full of barbed quotes
about Hillary from Quinn and Elizabeth Dole, the senator's wife, plus a
popular new novel about the 1992 election, *Primary Colors*. All she knew
of that book, said Hillary, was that she cussed like a sailor and was portrayed in a graphic one-night stand with George Stephanopoulos, of all
people. Her aggrieved mood dissolved into mirth. Blair summarized the
book, saying its purportedly anonymous author (Joe Klein) did not
know Hillary very well but did capture the wildness inside Clinton's
presidential race with thinly disguised portraits built around a staff character just released from an asylum. And so now, laughed Hillary, they
have her carrying on both with George and a lesbian vet.

He had not read *Primary Colors,* the president chimed in, but the
bitterness of their critics signaled that he and Hillary must be doing
something right. With his remote control device, he turned up the television volume to hear Whitney Houston perform a gospel medley, and
he detected a Bob Dylan quality in Joan Osborne's offbeat pop song
about religion, "One of Us." When the show finally ended, I tried to
hurry things along by excusing myself ahead to the Treaty Room. Waiting there, the question was whether to pursue alone with him my hand-
delivered letter's warning about dark moods and the media. I decided to
leave it alone. The Grammys had preempted more than an hour of taping already. Starting late and tired, we faced a heavy backlog.

THE PRESIDENT SEIZED on questions about this month's threats to peace.
He was upset first about Northern Ireland. Three bombs in London had
killed two people, injuring more than a hundred, with the first explosion
only an hour after the Irish Republican Army publicly terminated the
year-old cease-fire. Just before that, Gerry Adams of the IRA's political
wing called the White House with a "heads-up" for impending violence.
It was a tense, mournful conversation. Adams still opposed the move

internally, Clinton believed, but proved powerless to stop IRA military commanders who were determined to blame England for the stalled talks. They were at loggerheads with British prime minister John Major over requirements for "unconditional" negotiations—whether the cease-fire itself was enough, or must be attested by some surrender of the IRA's clandestine arms. Clinton bemoaned the artificial impasse. He said the renewed terror dropped sympathy for Adams well below 25 percent among Catholics in Northern Ireland, marginalizing his Sinn Fein Party with less than 10 percent of the total vote. The bombs created only a brief spike of sympathy in England before Major's government was likely to fall. As for the IRA, its commanders virtually confessed their bankrupt strategy by sending word through Adams that they had delayed violence until a decent interval after Clinton's visit in November. (Before that trip, the president recalled, U.S. intelligence warned that the most extreme IRA factions wanted to break the truce while he was there.) Now he salvaged one hopeful surprise: huge, spontaneous peace rallies in ten cities across Northern Ireland. Catholics marched with Protestants. They created pressure to revive negotiations, prodding the stale imagination of their leaders. In that part of the world, said the president, public wisdom ran well ahead of the politicians.

Bombs also struck Israel only four days ago—one in Jerusalem, another in Ashkelon—killing twenty-six civilians. Hamas claimed responsibility for suicide strikes in its avowed mission to destroy Israel, and the president analyzed trauma reverberating across national borders. He said Hamas sought to undermine not only the Israeli government but also Yasir Arafat among fellow Palestinians. Its leaders calculated that suicide bombs would force Israel to quarantine the Gaza Strip, closing off Palestinians from their jobs and as much as 40 percent of their economy, intensifying the desperate poverty, which would turn Palestinians against Arafat because of his cooperation with Israel. He said the bombs weakened Arafat in everyone's eyes. Separately, Hamas aimed to bring a conservative Likud government to power in Israel, because Likud also opposed the peace process. Since Shimon Peres of the Labor Party had called for early elections, the bombs accelerated the erosion of his popular majority. Peres was vulnerable. If he could squeak out a victory in May, Clinton predicted, Peres would conclude a treaty with Asad of

Syria, but a loss would hurt negotiations on every front. Ironically, said the president, the Likud candidate, Benjamin Netanyahu, had favored Clinton in the U.S. elections of 1992, mostly because former president Bush made no secret of his preference for Yitzhak Rabin. Now, however, Netanyahu opposed the peace alliance on both sides of the Atlantic. While he legitimately attacked Peres in the Israeli campaign—emphasizing the danger of potential concessions to Syria—his Likud agents in the United States joined Republicans eager to stir up suspicion against Clinton's Middle East diplomacy. So far, said the president, they had not made much headway with Jewish voters, but he called it scandalous electioneering by and with a foreign political party.

He traced a neighboring intrigue from Jordan to Baghdad. "I can't believe those guys were dumb enough to think Saddam Hussein meant his promise to forgive them," Clinton scoffed, speaking of the two Kamel brothers who had defected to Jordan last August from high positions in the Iraqi army. General Hussein Kamel fully intended to overthrow Saddam, which at first made him attractive to his Jordanian host, King Hussein, but the leading Iraqi exiles recoiled from association with Kamel. They mistrusted him as one of Saddam's most brutal subordinates, and the isolated, haughty Kamel became such a nuisance that the king encouraged him to leave. Clinton kept track of the separate Husseins down into their volatile family relations. Last week, blandishments from the dictator Saddam lured home his prodigal kinfolk—each Kamel brother was married to one of Saddam's sisters—to a royal welcome followed swiftly by extermination in a military ambush. Reportedly, Saddam's more ruthless son, Uday Hussein, was hunting down the surviving relatives of his slain in-laws. The president worried that such raw political violence dampened hopes for political progress in the whole region. On the other hand, he thought Saddam's bloody flash of nature would help the international community maintain and defend sanctions to contain his regime.

Then there was Castro. Last Friday, Cuba's air force had shot down two little Cessnas flown by anti-Castro exiles from the United States. Clinton said most Americans remained calm through the ensuing upheaval. Regardless of international law, many seemed to feel that countries had a right to defend their airspace from trespass, and the Cessna pilots, from a group called Brothers to the Rescue, had buzzed Cuban territory illegally for years to earn bragging rights back in Miami. These flights irritated U.S. authorities, whose efforts to revoke the pilots' licenses were ensnarled on appeal, and they infuriated Castro. The president said you could hear anger in the intercepted radio orders from his ground commanders to Cuba's jet fighters, which followed none of the procedures for confronting unarmed civilian aircraft. "They blew them to smithereens," he said. Air-to-air rockets obliterated the Cessnas and pilots so completely that only small bits of wreckage could be recovered from Caribbean waters. More than the transgression itself, what roused disgust for Cuba was its wanton display of mismatched force. The president said he warned Castro privately that the next such action would meet a military response directly from the United States.

I asked about risks. If his message leaked, might it actually encourage anti-Castro exiles to mount new harassment missions in the hope of drawing U.S. might into a showdown with Castro? After all, this had been a quixotic dream since the Bay of Pigs. Clinton minimized such danger. The communications were secure, and he doubted that Miami's weekend warriors would trade their lives for a slim chance to provoke war. Still, his threat to Castro seemed to make him uncomfortable with posturing on all sides. He reflected sourly on the paradox of violence. The people who were so bloodthirsty toward Castro, demanding unrelieved hostility as the only effective cure, now cried out that this cruel attack disgraced him as an impotent bully. At the same time they helped tighten the noose of the embargo against Cuba, which further isolated us as a bully in the eyes of the world. Especially since Reagan, said the president, Republicans had harvested the Cuban exile vote by snarling at Castro, but it was only noise. No one bothered to think forward about consequence.

Already, at giant memorial rallies, Clinton's opponents blamed the Cessna martyrdom on the weakness of Democrats while trumpeting a five-day rush of bipartisan legislation to strengthen the forty-five-year-old embargo against trade with Cuba. "Adios, Fidel," chairman of the Senate Foreign Relations Committee Jesse Helms had cried today on final passage of his bill. Cosponsored in the House by Indiana's Dan Burton, the law froze assets and blocked U.S. travel for the executives of foreign companies doing business with Cuba. In retreat, Clinton said he had been negotiating to allow exceptions for some personal contact, such as phone calls to relatives still in Cuba, but he would sign the Helms-Burton Act. Castro had brought the hardship on his own people, said the president, but his regime thrived on U.S. persecution and would probably outlive Helms. Clinton felt backed into a policy of proven failure, which he had lamented privately for closing off political engagement toward a peaceful transition in Cuba.

FOR RELIEF, SKIPPING over two gruesome car bombs in Algeria, I asked about recent ceremonial visits from championship sports teams. The Dallas Cowboys managed not to tear up the White House. They behaved like gentlemen, he quipped, to befit the team's many Arkansas ties. An assistant coach came from Arkansas State, and head coach Barry Switzer had grown up under harsh deprivation in the last Arkansas county with an active Ku Klux Klan. Clinton said Switzer's father had been a bootlegger who ran into a tree and killed himself in a car chase leaving the home of his black mistress. Left behind, young Barry was rough-cut and quiet, but he was a lot smarter about football than sports pundits commonly insinuated. His players, no less than the president himself, were flabbergasted by a toast from the team's Republican owner, Jerry Jones. Clinton said Jones had bought the Cowboys with money made drilling oil in Arkansas on licenses from Clinton's arch-nemesis Sheffield Nelson, who presumably kept him steeped in the most lurid Whitewater allegations. Despite all that, Jones pronounced Clinton good for the Cowboys, and said they must get him reelected to keep winning Super Bowls.

The Atlanta Braves visited two weeks later, and Clinton was fascinated by banter that only one member of the team, relief pitcher Mark Wohlers, had voted for him in 1992. He offered the pitchers a subtle analysis. On a tour for the upcoming Atlanta Olympics, the president told them, he had noticed very little foul territory in the stadium being built for the summer games to serve as the Braves' future home. In fact, engineers had confirmed that there would be only forty-five feet from the baselines to the stands—well below the major league average of seventy feet. The new configuration meant fewer foul pops would be caught for outs, diminishing the advantage of a superior pitching staff. Would it be harder for the Braves to win more World Series? Clinton said his observations drew appreciative comments from all four of the Braves' starting pitchers—Steve Avery, Tom Glavine, Greg Maddux, and John Smoltz—while the Braves' hitters jumped in to argue the other side. Clinton did not expect to win many votes in the rich dugouts and locker rooms of modern sports, but he did seem pleased to impress insiders about baseball.

He turned serious on economics. Three key appointments had just converged for him at the Federal Reserve Board of Governors, including the chair and vice chair. Clinton had wanted badly to replace chairman Alan Greenspan with Felix Rohatyn, the shrewd investment banker from Lazard Frères, but he ran into vexing constraints everywhere. Rohatyn himself advised Clinton to reappoint Greenspan instead, arguing that the Republican Senate would confirm no one else. Wall Street could not elect a U.S. president, Rohatyn told him, but it could surely un-elect one. If threatened, financial powers would sacrifice short-term profits to drive interest rates high, hurting blue-collar workers with layoffs and shaky pension funds. In the end, Rohatyn refused appointment to both posts, and Clinton suspected that Greenspan had engineered this result by warning of political friction and terrible drudgery at the Fed. He thought the wily incumbent protected his brittle ego from comparative scrutiny alongside Rohatyn, who was just as accomplished and a far more persuasive, attractive public speaker.

Resigned to keep Greenspan at the top, Clinton described his fall-back choice of Budget Director Alice Rivlin for the vice chair position. If she could win confirmation, on her proven expertise as a pro-growth fighter against deficits, she would provide an able counterweight to the tight-money bankers. He further tempered disappointment by noting that Greenspan was not the most extreme of the monetarist ideologues at the Fed, anyway. The chairman could be appeased if handled carefully, and they were managing steady growth with lower deficits. Still, the president confessed lost enthusiasm for the third Fed appointment, which he left entirely to his economics adviser, Laura Tyson. He called her an unsung public servant—skilled and fair-minded in approach, while passionate about the common good—to underscore a contrasting appraisal of Rohatyn. "I was committed to him, and I really think he ducked this fight," Clinton said with lingering dismay. "He backed out too soon. He didn't have the stomach for it."

On politics, the president assessed the primaries and caucuses on the Republican side. "Play" seemed to be his word for the night in handicapping each race, as in, "[Lamar] Alexander didn't have the money to play in the Dakotas." Steve Forbes was the only one playing with a sense of enjoyment. Gramm had dropped out, hopeless. Pat Buchanan was mad. Dole was upset. Alexander was overwrought. Forbes, running blithely on his narrow message to cut everyone's taxes, pulled off a win in Arizona, and Buchanan shocked the party establishment with an upset in New Hampshire. Clinton thought the contests so far exposed weaknesses in all his potential opponents. He said Dole was trying to play with only one lackluster idea, which boiled down to "I've been around a long time and deserve to be president." Clinton still figured him to win the nomination. He said Republicans tended to favor orderly succession, and Dole had accumulated many friends among the superdelegate party officials, who always weighed heavily at their convention. Republicans also relied on an early start for saturation by repetitive message, which required plenty of money.

By contrast, the president recalled, he had not visited New Hampshire until October of 1991, about a year before the general election. He reminisced about campaigning in New Hampshire, as usual, but his point was that it took him months beforehand to hone a presentation for the voters—why he was running, what he would do. Now, while updating that presentation for a second term, Clinton used an incumbent's free ride through primary season to raise and husband as much campaign money as possible. He said he hoped to cut into an adverse funding ratio that could reach four to one against him if Ross Perot ran again on a third-party ticket.

Campaign finances spilled over into President Clinton's review of the Telecommunications Reform Act of 1996, which he had just signed into law. He attributed most of its balance and promise to Al Gore, saying the vice president had warned of legislative danger shortly after the disastrous 1994 election. The major broadcasting networks, Gore predicted, would team up with the regional Bell companies to push a freighted agenda through the new Republican Congress. In the guise of free markets, they would strip away the government's power to promote competition in their rapidly changing industry. Gore called the plan a Trojan horse. Before most people realized the scope of the impending change in communications, he said, the established companies would gobble up outlets for upstart alternatives such as cable and cellular services. By extending control over the potential competition from new technology, they hoped to prevent or slow down the dilution of their markets. Huge sums were at stake, said Clinton, which made for a titanic lobbying struggle in Congress. New companies were springing up to buy licenses into this uncharted territory Gore called "the information superhighway." They were paying far more than anticipated already, which Clinton called a bonanza for the taxpayers. The only drawback he perceived was that the high prices made it difficult to include small stakeholders.

The president said he was mystified by a dramatic public offer this week from the Australian-American media mogul Rupert Murdoch: free airtime for all the presidential candidates on his Fox network. Murdoch's declared purpose, to "curb the cancer" of money in the political system, angered his fellow broadcasters and touched off an uproar among Republicans, who traditionally opposed limits on campaign spending. Suddenly, they murmured against Murdoch as an apostate, foreign opportunist, or worse. Clinton welcomed the offer while pondering its motive. He said Murdoch had played very heavily to Gingrich's side on the telecommunications bill, which meant big contributions to Republicans. They had failed to produce all Murdoch wanted, and perhaps he intended to even his bets.

Clinton saw promise in Murdoch's idea if it could be coupled with requirements for the candidates themselves to speak directly to voters on camera, without produced images or sounds. Was it possible for such a combination to stigmatize, or crowd out, the advertising techniques that drove so much cost and distortion in political races? Could it be constitutional? Clinton grappled on tape for some fair revision of the Supreme Court's decision in *Buckley v. Valeo*, which prohibited restrictions on political free speech. Our session gave out somewhere in these thickets of the First Amendment.

CHAPTER TWENTY-TWO

PRIMARY SEASON

Monday, May 27, 1996

A month passed before the next contact, when Robyn Dickey of the White House Social Office arranged an event to coincide with my parents' weekend visit in Baltimore. Our whole family drove to Washington on Saturday morning, March 30. We cleared security into the West Wing for a briefing about broadcast decorum—what to expect, cues for silence, warnings not to trip over cables on the floor—then crowded into the Oval Office to watch live delivery of the nationwide radio address. President Clinton argued for legislation to raise the minimum wage from $4.25 to $5.15 per hour. Afterward, by another cue, our group was last among nearly a hundred guests to greet and pose with him on the big blue rug, so that we could duck outside together through the Rose Garden for a brief presentation. The Jefferson Memorial bird feeder, on a rounded white table, waited in gleaming isolation against the dark green South Lawn. Clinton circled it several times with admiring looks, and my dad, while not visibly nervous, mumbled unusually brief replies to questions about architectural details. My mother slid easily from maternal encouragement into Southern chitchat with the president. Macy, then fifteen, leaned over to peer inside at the miniature statue of Jefferson. Franklin was distracted by Socks the cat, who was tethered under a nearby tree with a long rope around his neck. Aides orchestrated photographs. Christy and I beamed at everyone before Clinton was hustled off to the next appointment.

Two more months passed. Our sessions grew sparse through the election year. Campaign frenzy, aides told me, added to fierce competition over a sitting president's schedule, but it occurred to me that his interest may be waning. Could I blame him? There was a macabre side to our project. We were compiling a million words to be hidden away for distant years, mostly when both of us would be dead. How durable was his intent to leave this record behind? Did he seek a fresh angle? Must I improve our reflection? Was our companionship useful? I kept these preoccupations to myself. Trips to the White House usually upended them, anyway. I never knew what to expect.

A summons came late on Memorial Day. It yanked my working mind three decades forward from the Martin Luther King era, and I rushed to organize questions from a pile of contemporary notes. So much had occurred. At the White House that night, escorted quickly up to the Treaty Room, I hoped to finish last-minute preparations during the usual wait, but President Clinton was already there, talking intently on the phone about poll data in Israel. District by district, he kept asking if that was all, writing down the numbers. Apparently, Shimon Peres had done well in the only debate scheduled with his challenger, Benjamin Netanyahu. The prime minister held his own by every key indicator. He had gained one point overall in the post-debate polls, building his nationwide lead to 3 percent.

The president looked resigned when he hung up. Three points were not enough, he said. Israeli elections always closed in the last few days toward the war party, Likud. As of today, Peres would lose the election, which Clinton considered a disaster. It would retard the peace process on all fronts, especially with Syria, as Netanyahu was pledging to make no agreement that would cede back any part of the Golan Heights. He said President Asad of Syria could be too brilliant for his own good. Asad was always holding out for the extra ounce. He should have made peace last year.

Clinton was pacing. I asked him to save this material until I could get set up for him to speak directly into my recorders, and he switched subjects. Bob Woodward's book on the forthcoming campaign was supposed to be coming out soon, but a new letter had come seeking a last-minute interview. He said he would fish it out for me, but his eyes wandered while he touched papers on his desk. I had seen this fidgety mood before. Both his thoughts and his fingertips seemed to jump

around. He walked from one shelf to another fussing with his books—
feeling them, examining them, rearranging them, even taking scissors to
cut out one autographed page for some reason, which made me cringe.
On the move, he said his chief of staff, Leon Panetta, had picked up
from Woodward that the book would include strange passages about
Hillary and Eleanor Roosevelt. The bare truth was that Hillary had asked
herself a few times how her predecessor might have handled some crisis,
just as Clinton said he had been asked once at a governors conference
what Thomas Jefferson might do, but Woodward planned to present this
exercise as some sort of witchcraft, as though Hillary held séances to
commune with the dead. These were telltale signals about the book.
Panetta was trying to talk Woodward out of its most egregious errors, he
said, but corrections would never catch up with a sensational focus and
tone.

On tape, sitting down, the president reviewed bumpy events leading
up to the Israeli elections. In March, to answer the spate of suicide
bombings, President Mubarak of Egypt had hosted what was billed as a
summit of the peacemakers at Sharm al-Sheikh on the Red Sea. He welcomed Clinton among the leaders of twenty-nine countries. In a historic
precedent, Israel and fourteen Arab nations not only met there for talks—
with the notable exception of Syria—but also joined the group's public
declaration of measures to combat terrorism. There was progress behind
closed doors as well, said Clinton. Yasir Arafat helped restore momentum on the Palestinian front with convincing efforts to crack down on
Hamas violence in Gaza. Arafat also vowed to beat a May 1 deadline
from the Oslo Accords—by pushing through a formal amendment of the
PLO charter to accept coexistence with Israel—and he kept that promise
in spite of upheavals shortly ahead. From the summit, Clinton continued his trip to reassure Israelis shaken by the suicide bombs. He described an emotional visit to Yitzhak Rabin's grave. Privately, he pledged
a consistent U.S. policy if the opposition won the upcoming election—
vowing never to impose peace terms on Israel—and Netanyahu committed in return to honor the agreements already in process.

No sooner did he leave Israel than Lebanon-based Hezbollah began
to fire Katyusha rockets into the cities and towns of northern Israel. Israel suffered some two hundred deaths from random attacks over several

weeks, which was roughly equivalent to twenty thousand casualties in the United States. Clinton said Israel had to retaliate. In fact, Peres probably waited weeks too long in anguished deliberations. But then, in April, Peres launched sustained artillery and air strikes without consultation or notice for the United States. His Operation Grapes of Wrath was designed explicitly to drive civilians from southern Lebanon north toward Beirut in numbers massive enough to force pleas from the Lebanese government to President Asad of Syria, who in turn would intercede with Hezbollah to stop the Katyusha rockets. President Clinton called it a Rube Goldberg scheme—far too complicated to work, blind to larger resentments, guaranteed to backfire. By turning nearly a half-million Lebanese into refugees amid credible reports of large-scale civilian fatalities from Israeli howitzers, the bombardment antagonized the Arab states, which had just labored at Sharm al-Sheikh to diminish hostility. Military failure kept Peres from winning over Israeli hawks, and Israeli-Arab voters deserted him in droves. They thought the cold-blooded disproportion showed Peres to be no better than Likud. Arab citizens made up 14 percent of Israel's population, said Clinton, and 7 percent of its likely voters. Their weakened support could be the margin of defeat for Peres.

A SOMBER MOOD continued through his account of two funerals. The president checked himself briefly, upset that he could not remember exactly how he learned of Commerce Secretary Ron Brown's death in a plane crash near Dubrovnik, Croatia. This was why we must carve out time for extra sessions to catch up, he said, as though making a note to both of us. He did not like losing memory for the feel and flow of these things, but he recovered a host of stories about Brown—from his rise to head the Democratic Party down to Clinton's own journeys with Hillary to visit families of thirty-four others killed on the trade mission with Brown. Before a ceremony to receive the bodies at Dover Air Force Base, Brown's young son swaggered to be brave for his toddler sister, who did not understand, until the caskets started rolling down off the plane and the boy crumbled, wailing, "I want my daddy back." That was a tough moment, said Clinton. Abruptly, he shifted to rare praise for the *Washington Post*. He said editors there played the postmortem stories straight. They did

not hide from their prior criticism of Brown, and in fact reprised unsuc-
cessful efforts to nail him for corruption, but they added new reports
about how Brown had permanently changed Commerce from a stodgy
little dead-end department into an energizing ambassador for business
development overseas. They quoted witnesses in and out of politics
about how much Brown's service meant. The president expressed grati-
tude for the balance, wondering again why such attention to actual government had disappeared from most public discourse.

Later, Clinton explored the May 16 suicide of Adm. Jeremy "Mike"
Boorda, chief of naval operations. Biographical tidbits spilled forth in a
restless search that seemed almost tactile, like his hands wandering over
the bookshelves for something invisible. He knew, for instance, that
Boorda had married at seventeen and talked his way into underage Navy
enlistment in San Diego—she a Southern Baptist, Boorda Jewish. When
his best friend's wife bridled at a Navy assignment to landlocked Oklahoma, young Boorda swapped to take the posting himself. Somehow, it
was established that one of Boorda's Southern relations had sung with
Clinton one year in an Arkansas youth choir. The president sketched an
extraordinary rise from seaman to top rank, driven in part by the need
to keep Navy health care for a firstborn with severe disabilities. As chief
of naval operations, in the aftermath of the Cold War, Boorda came to
lead a service torn by conflicts from grand weapons strategy down to
cheating scandals at Annapolis and intramilitary strife over the Navy's
annual Tailhook convention for young officers. He supported a radioactive investigation into competing claims that Tailhook's bacchanal
rituals instilled command cohesion or shielded hazing to extremes of
assault and rape.

In a hidden swarm of disputes over honor, Boorda suddenly shot
himself, and the president compared his own helpless, recurring postmortem to Vince Foster's suicide nearly three years ago. He sensed in
both cases a fleeting, spur-of-the-moment despair. At home alone,
Boorda had learned of impending media charges that he bent Navy rules
to wear two small "V" ribbons for valor. Clinton thought a word of conversation, even a chance phone call, may have allowed the fatal impulse
to pass. He saw Boorda, like Foster, as a workaholic who did not realize
the extent of his physical and emotional depletion. Deeper than that, he

said, some mysterious weight in them plunged through normal defenses along with any understanding that these attacks were just politics.

We escaped to memories of his trip with Hillary through Asia in April. There was something perfunctory about his update of policies in South Korea, Japan, and Russia. He sketched familiar complexities of trade and political reform, scarcely pausing even to describe a visit to the wondrous Hermitage Museum in St. Petersburg. The president kept mentioning a standard omission from his Asian itinerary—China. "You know, I haven't been there," he said. The Chinese government—furious over the reelection of President Lee Teng-hui in Taiwan—had swapped saber-rattling statements with Taiwan during Clinton's trip. Clearly nagged, he said he would not go there before the election, but everything may change. Maybe he should be more candid about this emerging great power. Just because we are profoundly upset, he said, by the violent suppression of democracy at Tiananmen Square, that doesn't mean we can gain much influence over China's internal behavior on human rights. On the other hand, the United States is only 22 percent of the world's economy, but we are buying more than 40 percent of all China's exports. We should get something for that.

He digressed at length into this unmet challenge, from the details of two thousand AK-47s smuggled recently into San Francisco all the way back to the general outlook from Chinese history. They still feel humiliated to have been occupied by foreign powers since the nineteenth century, most recently Japan, and they are fearful—terribly fearful—of breaking up again into warlord territories. That's why their leaders, said Clinton, are determined to maintain political control—all the more so because they sense an inevitable loss of economic control. Mountains of new money are breaking loose from the old state-run bureaucracy. In that context, the president reviewed his impasse with China's leader, Jiang Zemin. Everywhere else in the world, he would stand or fall on his best efforts to blend personal interaction with strategic interest. Not China. "If I've made one mistake in foreign policy," he declared earnestly, "it's a failure to develop a relationship with China, and specifically with Jiang Zemin."

I asked about stories that President Yeltsin of Russia had just begun his reelection campaign with infinitesimal support in the polls, measured as low as one percent. Could that be true? No, said Clinton. Boris was never that bad. His negatives did start above 70 percent, with Russians furious about the brutal transition from the old Soviet system, but hard campaigning had reduced that number. The opponents, led by the hard-line Communist Gennady Zyuganov, still figured to win, and the president disclosed reports, in fact, that Yeltsin threatened to hold power by canceling the elections in advance. Clinton said he had called Moscow immediately to remonstrate over the Russian constitution. He reminded Yeltsin that all four statues in his Kremlin office honored seminal reformers in Russian history. There was no Communist like Lenin, nor any socialist. The four were Peter the Great and Catherine the Great, plus Alexander II, who freed the serfs, and Nicholas II, who pushed for a republican Duma before getting overthrown by the Bolsheviks. They were all czars. "Boris," Clinton told him, "you can still have those guys as your heroes, but you can't throw out the elections." Reformers don't go backward, he argued, and Yeltsin recanted toward the end. "Yes," said the Russian president. "I put in the constitution, and I must live or die by it."

CLINTON PAUSED TO take a phone call from state senator Charlotte Pritt of West Virginia, congratulating her for victory in the gubernatorial primary. It was all over now, he said repeatedly, and he would urge her fellow Democratic leaders to "get in the same boat and row." Hanging up, he remarked (correctly) that she may lose because of ill will from her "terrible mistake" four years ago, when she opposed West Virginia's popular Democratic incumbent. Skimming through collateral events, the president said Al Gore had endured gibes since a security presentation on the infamous domestic terrorist called the Unabomber, who turned out to be a fellow Harvard graduate.* Wags teased Gore that Harvard had too many students, including demented ones, and would train them for

---

* Theodore Kaczynski, a former math professor, had sent sixteen mail bombs for more than a decade to targets mostly at airlines and universities, killing three people and injuring twenty-three. FBI agents arrested him at his remote cabin in Montana on April 3, 1996. Kaczynski was sentenced to life without parole. His cabin became an exhibit at the Newseum in Washington, D.C.

anything. Clinton did linger fondly over a round of golf with actor James Garner, who scored 78 despite advanced age and bad knees from years of performing his own film stunts. The president fared many strokes worse. For our record, he recalled individual shots plus random details about Garner's older brother, a 3-handicap and club pro at seventy.

We covered one belated achievement from Newt Gingrich's "Contract With America." Asked why the line item veto suddenly passed without explanation, after being stalled more than a year, he said the answer was simple. He had made a private deal with Gingrich and Dole not to use the new veto powers at all in 1996. Until this promise, he said, Republicans had stifled their own legislative majority for fear that Clinton would veto their pork barrel projects selectively in the election year. From the president's perspective, it was worth the wait to secure a new deficit-fighting tool for the future. Republicans eagerly hid their motive for the deal. They may denounce spending, and ridicule governance itself, Clinton said, shrugging, but an awful lot of them love federal projects before elections. In fact, he and Leon Panetta had been joking that they should use the line item veto only in districts whose representatives hate the government, to help cure hypocrisy. When I asked whether the line item veto would make much difference, he said it was hard to say. If the law survived challenge in the courts, he thought the first applications would be crucial to set an evenhanded precedent. At best, he expected marginal restraint on the budget as a whole, and he noted subtle evasions already in the works. Republicans had rigged the law to make line item vetoes more difficult on tax preferences than on regular expenditures, which would steer more new programs into the tax code.

The arrangement with Dole led us into presidential politics. President Clinton reminded me that he had expected Dole to prevail for the nomination even in February, just after he lost the New Hampshire primary. The GOP rivals just didn't "have any tall," he said, in a new Clintonism I took to mean they lacked stature or command. He said Forbes and Alexander didn't have any tall in South Carolina, for instance, certainly not with the Christian Coalition. Dole's hold on the nomination was secured so early that he had spent weeks experimenting with issues for a general election campaign against Clinton. His delivery was still poor, the president observed clinically, and his two trial speeches on shame had flopped. First, Dole's address on the shame of Clinton's liberal judges drew minuscule attention, partly because he was too mannerly at heart to demagogue on abortion. It was probably unnecessary for the president to answer, but he insisted that every attack be parried at once. Surrogates cited surveys finding Clinton's appointments to be more moderate—representing the electorate—and far more qualified than judges from Reagan and Bush. "We killed him on that," the president concluded. He thought Dole gained some traction with the second speech, on welfare as the shame of liberalism, by attacking Clinton for his veto of a Republican welfare bill. Democrats were airing rebuttal ads to point out that experimental waivers to thirty-eight states had helped reduce the welfare population by 1.5 million people, reciting Clinton's objections to the GOP's punitive approach.

He said Dole was staking out "free enterprise" positions on three salient issues—tobacco, guns, and gambling—by arguing that government should not interfere with business or consumer choice. Clearly, Dole believed it was good politics to collect these ample war chests, and history supported his judgment. No presidential candidate of either party had campaigned actively against these industries, but Clinton resolved to be first. Committed already, he had appeared at rallies to defend the Brady Bill and the assault weapons ban from repeal. On tobacco, he described his recent speech at "Kick Butts Day" in New Jersey, plus a White House conference with state officials on ways to combat teenage smoking. Here Clinton stressed the merits. He vowed to oppose the illegal sale of cigarettes to minors as a growing, predatory epidemic, which was sadly ignored or blamed on the minors themselves. As for gambling, the president said he would push through—despite scalding objections—a first comprehensive study on the modern era's proliferation of casinos and state-sponsored lotteries.* Gaming interests were mobilized to block or hamstring the inquiry. They accused Clinton of treating legitimate corporations like gangsters. Their lobby, while led by Republicans, in-

---

* Two months later, on August 3, President Clinton signed the National Gambling Impact Study Commission Act of 1996. The commission published its final report in 1999.

cluded plenty of Democrats because the neon lure of jackpots was brighter than partisanship. The president himself sheepishly volunteered that he had accepted a lunch in Las Vegas with casino magnate Steve Wynn, who had raised "a ton of money for Dole."

Dole also had hired three attack ad consultants, including one expert in anti-gay messages. Clinton said the working premise, based on two decades of poll trends, was that roughly 45 percent of the voting population remained viscerally offended by the gay lifestyle, with far less remorse and misgiving than other haters, which offered a base toward winning elections. Still, all these experimental issues so far did not add up to a big enough vision for a presidential campaign. To complement the hard, specialized tactics, Clinton expected Dole to emphasize character themes on the stump. He might spice up his ticket by running with a moderate Republican woman—such as former governor Christie Todd Whitman of New Jersey—but the president thought it would be smarter for Dole to pick Senator John McCain. A ticket of paired war heroes would drive home the contrast with Clinton's nonservice in Vietnam. The president had pioneered this novel strategy of matched strengths, rather than bookend balance, with his wonkish peer Al Gore from Tennessee, right next door to Arkansas.

Most people thought Dole was correct to resign from the Senate in order to concentrate on the presidential race. He had explained the rationale to Clinton in a courtesy call just before the announcement on May 15. First, Dole did not have time to be a presidential candidate while also serving as majority leader, which required him to manage a hundred egos and fool with Gingrich every day. Second, he realized that he did not want to be in the Senate if he had to step down as leader, which more or less made the decision for him. This seemed candid and reasonable, the president told me, although he wondered whether anyone would appreciate that he, Clinton, also was running a campaign, plus the entire executive branch, while fending off about six lines of torment on Whitewater. He and Dole merely wished each other well. Theirs was a remarkably civil competition, he said, especially since Dole's recent letter apologizing for his televised attacks back on the day Clinton's mother died. On tape, Clinton paraphrased Dole's gracious wish that both their mothers could have lived to see them contend for the presidency. He also quoted from the thanks he gave Dole in person, confessing that this particular injury had eaten at him for more than two years. "Bob, I'm going to let that go now," he said. "I won't mention it or carry it around anymore."

DURING THIS PREVIEW of the campaign, Chelsea popped in the doorway to say she was sorry she may have disturbed us. She had been singing to herself in the hall, and did not realize we were here. Before he could reply, she vanished, and while I was rewinding the tapes shortly afterward, the president rummaged around the big Ulysses Grant desk. A decade ago, when she was about six, he said Chelsea had skipped into a ceremony at the governor's office with a briefcase, which he was obliged to open in front of everyone. He showed me a photograph of little Chelsea doubled over in laughter as Clinton squeamishly displayed a boa constrictor inside. His daughter was cheerful and courteous, he said, but she was mischievous, too.

He had fooled me in turn. I said I thought he was searching again for his letter from Bob Woodward. No, and he was pretty sure he would decline the interview. Woodward's book was shaped already around the Republicans, as he had completed about a dozen talks with Dole before approaching Clinton. The president thought any interview now would give a false impression of parity, and his feelers drew no contrary advice from me. It seemed too late for him to gain much, and I shifted to parting concerns. *Esquire* had approached me to write the pro-Clinton essay for its election issue, I began, and the president quickly interrupted. He knew more about the magazine's internal plans than I did. Richard Ben Cramer had agreed to argue for Dole, he informed me. Cramer was good, and he liked Dole in a folksy way that would be effective. The president hoped I would defend him, but I demurred. How could it be done without jeopardizing his oral history? Nearly everything I knew about his presidency came from these interviews taped for posterity, whose existence was a precarious secret in the White House fishbowl. With David Kendall's help, we had been lucky so far. On my end, when curious friends asked about a canceled dinner, or sudden trip to Washington, I got by on a truthful capsule summary about renewing old acquaintances through confidential talks on historical preservation.

However, if I put firsthand stories from our sessions into print, people rightly would question my access to such detail.

Feeling trapped, I divulged risk on another front. Senator Alfonse D'Amato's Banking Committee had subpoenaed me for its Whitewater investigation. In fact, FBI agents had visited me already at home. This news seemed to shock President Clinton for once, although I tried to make light by telling him that I had framed my summons from D'Amato as a trophy of the absurd. The myriad questions were about Hillary's law firm records—had I seen them, or something like them, in specified rooms, on certain days, or discussed anything similar, with people not limited to the following? Utterly foreign to me, they were all answerable no a thousand times. According to Paul Sarbanes, my Democratic senator from Maryland, Republicans on the committee had voted to interrogate me along with everyone else who had spent a night at the White House when the records may have been there, including some two dozen of Chelsea's sleepovers. Sarbanes was negotiating to quash subpoenas for these girls, and spurned my impish notion that he might do better to acquiesce. Perhaps such a spectacle—the televised inquisition of teenagers—could break the fever of Whitewater at last into farce.

Clinton sighed. Democrats were too nice at times, but Sarbanes was right to oppose a gratuitous ordeal for the kids. By then, as I was leaving, he had absorbed my concerns and withdrawn to his thoughts, brooding again on the move, with a golf club from a stack in the corner. It was a driver, the last club Ron Brown had acquired. "Ron was worse than I am," the president mused, "both as an addict of golf and a terrible player." Even by mail order, Brown was always stockpiling new clubs. They were like magazines now—everybody sold them. Clinton took several swings on the Treaty Room's Heriz rug. "I can hit it pretty far," he said, "but this club's a little short for me."

CHAPTER TWENTY-THREE

TERRORISM, WELFARE REFORM, AND THE CHICAGO CONVENTION

Monday, July 1, 1996

Friday, August 2, 1996

Democratic National Convention,
Chicago
August 26–29, 1996

Clinton surprised me early in June with a phone call at home. There were troubles with the *Esquire* election issue. They had found no suitable writer to defend him, and he ran through snags with the latest possibilities: Texas columnist Molly Ivins, Harvard professor Thomas Patterson, and the eminent crime author John Grisham. Would I reconsider? I was on the fence, worried about how to navigate between temporary secrecy and journalism. We explored ideas to generate a responsible article without inviting discovery and ruin for the oral history project. Eventually, we settled on a plan to turn our next session into a standard interview, arranged through the White House press office. This would sacrifice candor, because the president would be speaking for the record with staff observers and a stenographer. In return, we would obtain a usable supply of stories and quotations on themes for *Esquire*. I called the pretext honorable. We were laundering historical notes for a preview.

Nancy Hernreich made arrangements for this decidedly new experience on Monday evening, July 1. There were special procedures along with aides and onlookers, even after-hours. Susan from the press office set up her equipment as directed outside on the Truman Balcony, next to a table with my notes and recorders. The president arrived with Deputy Chief of Staff Erskine Bowles, in jeans and a green pullover. He said they were exhausted, having cut short the G-7 summit meetings in France to fly back yesterday for a heart-wrenching memorial service at Florida's Eglin Air Force Base. A massive truck bomb last week had destroyed the Khobar Towers housing complex near the Saudi oilfields at Dhahran, killing nineteen U.S. soldiers and injuring 372. Responsibility was claimed by the local branch of Hezbollah, with ties to Syria and Iran. Rumors also implicated a group called al Qaeda, which embraced terrorism to punish both the U.S. and Saudi governments for the military presence of foreigners on Islamic home soil.

The Khobar Towers investigation, while destined to be a news item for years, failed to displace more entertaining FBI stories at home. Gary Aldrich, a former FBI agent assigned to conduct background checks at the White House, had just published a book claiming, among other things, that the Clintons decorated their Christmas tree with sex toys, and that the president smuggled himself out of the White House to meet mistresses at a Washington hotel.* Aldrich was being discredited already as a hostile fantasist, repudiated by his own sources, but the allegations drove media interest along with Bob Woodward's book and a new FBI scandal dubbed Filegate.

The president sharply distinguished the latter. FBI background files on former Bush employees had been discovered in the Clinton personnel office. Unlike the prurient books, or Whitewater, which he called "a

* Gary Aldrich, *Unlimited Access: An FBI Agent Inside the Clinton White House* (Washington, D.C.: Regnery, 1996).

political deal from start to finish," this inquiry was legitimate because those files did not belong at the White House. He had just made this point again at a press conference in Lyons, France, where even the foreign reporters clamored about suspicious shenanigans with FBI secrets. His administration should and would be held accountable, he said, and he could only hope the facts confirmed his current understanding. When the outgoing Bush people took all their personnel files with them, Clinton's new employees had asked the FBI for replacements to facilitate clearances into the White House, and the FBI erroneously included some three hundred Bush visitors, including government officials, in the large batch sent to restock the personnel office. These should have been isolated and returned immediately, said Clinton, but that offense in itself was relatively benign. So far, there was no evidence that any of the files had been requested, singled out, or used at all. If such misdeeds did emerge, they should be punished. If not, people should get over speculating about blackmail schemes.

Clinton walked a fine line on other attacks, seeking neither to feed them nor hide. He called them distortions—as well as distractions from the country's pressing business. Both news fixations from the Woodward book, for instance, were marginal at best to its stated goal of preparing readers for the 1996 election. Clinton said it was ludicrous to suggest that he had submitted to a political makeover by consultant Dick Morris, and trivially indulgent to characterize the administration by Hillary's alleged "channeling" with the ghost of Eleanor Roosevelt. He said Hillary had been targeted painfully and unfairly from the start—branded willy-nilly too masculine or too feminine, mocked with condescension but also hauled before the grand jury.

I asked whether the personal trials had strained his marriage. To my knowledge, I added, this Aldrich book contained the first public charges of infidelity, however flimsy and vague, since they moved to Washington. Well, there had been some tough days for both of them, the president replied, "but I think we are closer today than we were the day we showed up." They relied on commitment like any other marriage, and tried hard to purge themselves of bitterness over daily criticism. "Something like this either breaks you down or builds you up," he said, "and I think it has built us up." I could not speak for the romance, I told him, but I had been struck by their flow of warm conversation, like partners, and by small gestures like holding hands in the elevator. He shrugged. That had not changed much between them. He said he was amazed by the common assumption that everything about a politician was calculated.

I asked him to translate some Clintonisms. I asked what he read in the Bible. He reviewed preferences since youth, and mentioned so many passages about overcoming enemies that I remarked on them as a theme in his peacemaking diplomacy. "Some people think it's a big mistake," he said dryly, because many of his advisers considered the cultivation of enemies a staple of successful politics. I asked him to describe some of the hardest decisions of his first term, such as Haiti and the big budget deal that nakedly summoned Democrats to walk the plank. You had to honor their sacrifice, he said, try to keep them involved, and move on. I asked how he would frame the campaign ahead. During his answer, we could see timekeepers stirring inside. Several hurried from the air-conditioning when I took out my camera. No photographs, they said, except through the White House. *Esquire* must choose from the institutional portraits. On the way out, I slipped my camera to the president with a spontaneous covert wish. Did he dare let Hillary or his mischievous daughter take a candid shot of him instead?

HIS VOICE SURPRISED me again on Sunday, July 7. He had just finished testifying by videotape for one of the Whitewater criminal trials, in which Ken Starr's deputy prosecutors were trying to tar him with far-fetched charges against Arkansas bankers. The president was tired, and really needed to spend time with Chelsea. So we must cancel our session tonight. He vowed to catch up soon. Of course, I replied. His staff always handled such logistics, but for some reason he delivered this notice himself.

We resumed on the first Friday in August, the 2nd. An usher kept me downstairs because the motorcade was late returning from a ballet, and subsequent reports had Clinton detained in the Oval Office. Finally, a butler escorted me up. In the yellow hallway, with a dubious nod, he said his instructions were to shoo me right into the bedroom, where I found the president leaning on the bed to steady himself as he changed into jeans. He wanted a head start on our preliminaries. Aside from packing in campaign money with nonstop fund-raisers through a heavy legislative week, he had stayed up the awful night of Saturday's bombing at the Atlanta Olympics. He said he was a zombie ever since, and I should keep talking to help him stay awake.

He led me into the big closet to find his sneakers. Then he called out from the bathroom, asking if the *Esquire* article was really finished already. Oh, yes, and I told him half-jokingly that the editors were less excited about my text than the accompanying photograph by Chelsea. Already, well before publication, they called the picture an advance scoop of worldwide interest. Newspapers were lining up for previews, and White House officials scrambled against them to guard Chelsea's photographic copyright. I had heard they were blocking every request for access or a comment, determined to limit the breach in her protective cocoon.

He emerged smiling. They were right to shield her, but he thought a photograph in the magazine couldn't hurt. Was it the one of him with a golf club? Yes. I did not know of any others, as my camera had been returned without the film, but the picture from the magazine proofs showed him holding an iron on the Treaty Room rug, posed in front of the coffee table where we worked. What the editors treasured was his blissful expression as he looked into a lens held by his daughter. Alternatively, I teased, he may simply have been relishing that particular golf club.

Clinton told stories about Chelsea on our way down the hall. He and Hillary had just returned from her ballet recital. "She's not an ideal body for a ballerina," he reflected. "Far from it." Chelsea was bigger than most of the other girls, who were flat-chested and tiny. She had big bones. Her feet had bled after practice ever since she was a little girl. Nevertheless, she pursued ballet above other arts or sports for which she was more naturally suited. "I've always admired that," he said. "I've wondered whether I could ever stick with something for its own sake." He was inclined to obsess about competitive standing and talent, he said, whereas Chelsea, though smartly aware of her limits, loved everything about ballet including the hard work.

He sagged into the usual Treaty Room chair, grumbling about old age. His fiftieth birthday was coming up this month. A friend in Arkansas had told him that all he did since turning fifty-five was stay near a bathroom and try to remember the name of the last son of a bitch he had met. The president said he wasn't nearly so bad yet, but some days were hard. This seemed like one of them to me. His eyes already fluttered upward in mid-sentence, as they had done once strikingly before. Fatigue made him twitch at times, chewing his unlit cigar to keep awake. I thought more than once about calling off the session to let him rest, but rationalized that he was too restless to sleep anyway. Sure enough, presidential talk cranked up his mind and slowly revived his body.

First came the welfare reform bill, which the president had just resolved to sign. I asked whether the internal debate in the White House had been vigorous, as opposed to predetermined, and what correctives he would leave behind for the accounts printed so far. Well, some people may have anticipated all along that he would sign, but he called the arguments fierce. No one seemed inhibited, and nearly everyone wanted him to veto this welfare bill like the two before it. The opposition included Vice President Gore, he said, contrary to information in the *New York Times,* along with health secretary Donna Shalala, housing secretary Henry Cisneros, and, much to his surprise, the economics adviser Laura Tyson. She had mounted a sophisticated defense of welfare on Keynesian grounds. Tyson concluded that welfare, more than other entitlement programs, reacted early to signs of general economic stress with finely calibrated payments that stimulated recovery. Quite apart from compassion or political factors, she urged Clinton to veto the bill in order to preserve this vital tool against recession. Without the welfare structure, she said it would be harder to reverse any severe downward spiral in the national economy.

Tyson's unexpected opinion encouraged Stephanopoulos among many opponents of the bill. The president said Leon Panetta, as the son of immigrants, was especially incensed about the disqualification of legal immigrants from all forms of government assistance including welfare and Medicaid. Pleading for a veto, Panetta argued that such a cutoff would betray the welcoming heritage of freedom. On the other side, Republicans in Congress objected that some immigrants welshed on their pledge not to become charges upon our government. To address substance in this complaint, Clinton offered to conjoin the income of each immigrant's required sponsor within the United States—usually family members or prospective employers—when measuring eligibility for public assistance, but Republicans rejected this offer. They held firm for an absolute ban on aid to legal immigrants as a class, even in cases of catastrophic injury or illness. Clinton said he agreed with Panetta. This ban was ad hominem politics, milked from anti-foreign sentiment, and therefore unconscionable.

The Republicans also inserted a provision to eliminate nutrition supplements for low-income working families. This was mostly food stamps for single mothers with children—in large numbers—and it had nothing to do with welfare reform. All those to be affected had jobs already, but simply did not earn enough to afford a healthy diet. They were precisely the people who needed support in their efforts to climb out of poverty, and Clinton discerned only two motives for this extraneous penalty. Both were ugly. First, he thought Republicans wanted the program savings to help finance their tax cut proposals. Second, he detected an element of sheer malice against constituents who were not their voters. In fact, only a low percentage of them voted at all, and many of the indirect victims would be children. The president said this last factor still haunted him. He did not want any lasting effect of his presidency to hurt children. No matter how long or hard he had studied the welfare system, there could be no certainty about net consequences once a reform law touched off fundamental change.

Of his close advisers, only Bruce Reed urged him fervently to sign rather than veto the bill. Some campaign advisers did favor the new law for strictly political reasons—to shore up moderate support by fulfilling Clinton's 1992 promise to "end welfare as we know it"—but not even these strategists were united. Regardless, the president said he had tuned out the political arguments fairly early in the process, not from altruism or disinterest, but because he decided he could beat Dole either way. This was his first step toward judgment. He felt enough credibility on welfare to neutralize the issue, by explaining to most voters either a third veto or the reasons why he approved this bill above the previous two.

On the merits, he sketched legislative details too technical for me to retain, and I was glad to leave them on his tapes. Clinton vowed never to hide or excuse the two major defects still embedded—a cutoff of all benefits to legal immigrants and food assistance to working families. These provisions were so egregiously mean-spirited, in fact, that he believed he could overturn them separately after winning the election. He parsed final options that translated to me as sign-and-repair against veto-and-start-over. Some features may never again be obtained, he feared, such as an extra $4 billion for child care, plus incentives for state experiments in retraining and job transition. The current bill balanced work requirements with practical measures to foster opportunity from hardship.

Clinton stressed Hillary's prior support for his decision to sign. He said the welfare bill, which frayed their relations with many Democrats, was particularly hard for Hillary because of her long partnership with civil rights advocates such as our mutual friend Marian Wright Edelman of the Children's Defense Fund. Edelman, too, was an expert on struggling families. Her problem was not with the structure of welfare, said Clinton, but with funding levels she considered woefully inadequate. The issue split her from both Clintons, who, at the crux, concluded first that welfare had nurtured and perpetuated a debilitating cycle of dependence. Moreover, they believed they could engineer wholesale improvement by moving people from welfare to work. Clinton pronounced this gamble rightly controversial. For him, welfare reform risked only political reputation and stature, but it would destabilize daily patterns of life support for the most vulnerable families, many at the edge of survival. It was daunting. It had generated charges of rupture and betrayal. The president said his friend Congressman Charlie Rangel of Harlem had called him a cracker and many other bad names right on the House floor.

Welfare demanded raw judgment by champions for the poor. Clinton accepted clashes with them on the issue, but he decried popular assumptions making the current system a barometer of decency. Pundits on all sides said Clinton's reform would abandon liberal principles. They reduced liberalism to racial sympathy, associating welfare with black people as a detached, dependent set, which projected on minorities a permanent need and desire for welfare. Ironically, this conceit was superficial and patronizing to the point of racism. The president's welfare audiences, both in seminars and great halls, pulsed with the opposite yearning for dignified work. Nobody hated welfare more than the people on it, he said, and our stunted public debate revealed more about disjointed history than the nature of welfare. In our youth, during the 1960s, a black-led popular movement had catalyzed liberal politics of lasting impact, such that almost no one wanted to restore segregation, or ban women again from West Point, or return the prestige professions to white males. Yet the authors and heirs of all this refined freedom did not know how to claim the achievement. Trapped in old conflicts, they let liberalism sink to the bottom of modern politics. Candidates everywhere fled and flung its label like a plague. Some citizens desperately attached its husk to welfare mothers. This baggage tilted the current fight, where Clinton hoped to restore balance. He said he would take his chances.

THESE WERE TOUGH ideas about tangled themes. Shifting to terrorism was almost a relief.

The president recalled vivid reports on the crash two weeks ago when TWA Flight 800 plunged into the waters off Long Island shortly after takeoff, killing all 230 people on board. A huge consortium of investigators converged first to recover bodies and then to salvage the plane. This was a mammoth but urgent task. Clinton said it had taken more than a week to prove bomb sabotage eight years ago in Scotland, when the wreckage of a Pan Am flight lay accessibly on the ground near Lockerbie. By contrast, this TWA plane was strewn across miles of the ocean floor, rinsed and scattered by the tides. In dark waters, with less than two feet of visibility, divers still groped for blasted fragments as well as large chunks of fuselage—several million pieces, eventually—seeking clues. Unless some telltale chemical residue survived the brine, said Clinton, they must try to reassemble the plane to determine the cause. It may have been an accident, but proof of terrorism would make this a crime even deadlier than the Oklahoma City bombing. On one ominous front, he said the FBI was rechecking its interviews with some fifteen ground witnesses who saw a bright streak in the sky near the plane. If corroborated, and independent, these reports could indicate a missile rather than an onboard bomb. Technical factors ruled out a Stinger missile fired from land, said the president, but a SAM, a surface-to-air missile, from the sea was possible.*

Early apprehensions carried his thoughts abroad. Intelligence focused suspicion in the TWA crash, as in the Khobar Towers bombing, upon elements within the government of Iran. If true, he said gravely, this result could force a military response to further destabilize the whole Middle East—which was precisely the goal of Islamic fundamentalists in Iran and elsewhere. On motive, his security briefings on the TWA crash assessed reported plans to undermine Clinton's chances for reelection because he was pushing the Middle East peace process. "They want war," he said, and of course they also opposed the agreements at Sharm al-Sheikh to make terrorists the world's common enemy. They might target his administration on both counts, and it was chilling, said Clinton, to think they could aim at him through the deaths of all the innocent people on that plane.

Separately, on the Khobar Towers bombing, he said Iranian fundamentalists would like nothing better than to topple the Saudi monarchy, hoping to create another radical Islamic regime. This attack served a dual purpose by striking both U.S. soldiers and the control of Saudi oilfields. When I asked about Saudi politics, the president spoke of worries going back twenty years. One of his classmates at Georgetown University had been a member of the royal family, Prince Turki al-Faisal, who was now chief of intelligence for the kingdom. Clinton liked him then and now. Turki was a generous sophisticate dodging an inescapable contradiction. For decades, when thousands of nonroyal young Saudis returned from Western universities, asking why their homeland could not be more modern and democratic, Turki's family temporized. "They kicked the can down the road," Clinton said repeatedly, by covering up the symptoms. First they shut off the flow of young Saudis to schools abroad,

---

* Sixteen months later, having pieced together most of the aircraft in a hangar, U.S. experts concluded that the TWA 747 exploded by accident, not by terrorist act, from a known malfunction in one of the belly fuel tanks. James Kallstrom, head of the FBI task force, said the ground witnesses had mistaken flaming fragments dispersed *after* the explosion for a missile headed toward the plane.

throwing up orthodox universities for them at home instead. Then the royals diverted a huge stream of new OPEC oil money to put an entire stratum of educated nonroyals essentially on welfare, with fancy desks and salaries but little to do. A sham economy gave people money without purpose, and discontent seethed beneath the brittle monarchy. Clinton said kicking the can down the road sometimes just creates bigger problems later. Unfortunately, a delayed reckoning may await not just the Saudi system but also the U.S. economy, which remained addicted to Saudi oil. We had a different can, but we were kicking ours, too.

Terrorism struck home again with the pipe bomb right in the middle of Atlanta's festive Olympic Games last week, killing two people, wounding 111. Leon Panetta woke him before two o'clock with the news. The president said he had stayed up all that Friday and well into most nights since. Theories chased fears, with no clues yet on the perpetrator or motive. Despite the crisis, as Olympic athletes and spectators bravely continued the games, Clinton's anti-terrorism bill remained stalled in Congress. It had been crafted earlier in the summer from the twenty-five recommendations adopted at Sharm al-Sheikh. He called its wiretap provisions fairly moderate—basically extending to terrorism the procedures for organized crime cases. Al Gore was working on airport security, but the impasse centered on a proposal for "taggants," or traceable identifiers, to be embedded in all manufactured explosives. There were objections about safety, and scientific reliability, but Clinton called them thin cover for the National Rifle Association's absolutist claim that any such regulation would set a precedent endangering the traffic in arms. He said I could safely bet that he would try to expose these obstructions during the campaign.

The president confessed losing his temper at a press conference yesterday. To begin, he had announced robust economic growth of 4.2 percent in the second quarter, with inflation still low, real wages rising (for the first time in a decade), and the federal deficit now running less than half what he had inherited in 1993. He tried to explain why progress was beginning to compound in a cycle of higher growth from lower deficits and interest rates, which in turn eased the burden of public debt. Reporters ignored this good news, he complained, along with the bomb cases and climactic action on several major bills—welfare, terrorism, the minimum wage, water quality, and children's health insurance—to ask six times whether Clinton would reimburse the fired employees of the White House Travel Office for legal expenses. The president balked. Reporters insisted that he had promised. No, he told them. He supported fair reimbursement for *all* the public employees not charged in the Whitewater investigations. What about his innocent staff people still scraping and borrowing to defend themselves from Ken Starr? Why reimburse only the travel employees? This was blatant favoritism. Clinton said his resentment boiled over, and it was all he could do not to ignite more controversy with a reminder that $50,000 of public funds was found diverted into the accounts of the Travel Office chief, among many other irregularities. On tape, but not at the press conference, he cited a conclusion from the *Columbia Journalism Review* that in a sane news world, the president would be congratulated rather than vilified for cashiering such a miscreant.

REVVED UP, PRESIDENT Clinton continued with summaries of two recent trials in the Whitewater investigation. Should I remind him of our intention to save this legally sensitive material for a separate tape? Part of me bridled at censorship. As he talked, I merely scribbled a note on my pad, "* 1st WW comments," in case his lawyer David Kendall ever asked me which tapes he needed to review. I tried to remain on guard, perhaps to interrupt if he made specific comments that might be incriminating, which of course begged for a definition of Whitewater itself. The president was convincing first in his effort to position these trials miles from the real, utterly neglected, policy issues left over from the savings and loan debacle of the 1980s. Back then, federal deregulation had tempted thrift owners to reap windfalls from wild speculations with their depositors' money. Arkansas accounted for a minuscule fraction of the gargantuan losses that ensued across the nation by mismanagement, fraud, or outright theft, and a small part of the Arkansas tab bankrupted thrift institutions associated with the Whitewater land development. The current prosecutions, finally, were not about correction or restitution for any of these failures, which fell against the taxpayers. On the contrary, said Clinton, they were Ken Starr's attempt to squeeze vulnerable bankers into making some kind of allegation against Clinton, on promise of leniency.

The trials themselves, as described by the president, were such a dense thicket that I found myself secretly appreciating Kendall's gag order. It had deprived future specialists of mountainous detail, some of which I heard off the tapes, but many other historical subjects filled that vacated space. The exchange was a selfish boon to me, I realized, for the same reason that I skipped most Whitewater stories in the newspapers. Naturally, the president was elated by yesterday's acquittal of bankers Herbie Branscum and Rob Hill on most charges that they had not filed the proper paperwork for legal withdrawals from their own bank. The prosecution must have hoped to stampede the jury. If so, the verdict was embarrassing, and Clinton predicted (accurately) that Starr never would seek retrial on any of the remaining deadlocked counts.

As for the earlier trial, which did secure extra convictions against Clinton's former Whitewater partners Jim and Susan McDougal, the president said Starr managed to rope in his successor as governor, Jim Guy Tucker, on charges of falsifying loan applications at the McDougal bank. He said this prosecution was nearly as technical and arbitrary as the Branscum case. The business loans in question were legal, and long since repaid, but some money had been used for work not stated on the application. If every party to such fungible transactions were marked for felony indictment, said Clinton, we would need a supplementary prison system. He called the trial a mess. The chief accuser was convicted of big-time theft. Half the witnesses were mentally infirm. Tucker, though articulate and respected, mistakenly refused to testify in his defense. The president said he felt bad for Tucker, and then he lost me in arcane issues for appeal that made Arkansas sound like a dysfunctional family. One juror supposedly had served even though she was angry with Tucker for not pardoning her boyfriend.

He regained stride with a buoyant description of Boris Yeltsin's re-election campaign in Russia. Once Yeltsin struggled into a runoff, he made a deal with the third-place finisher, Gen. Alexander Lebed. This was the right move, said Clinton, and so was Yeltsin's quick, decisive purge of three hard-liners within his government. They were putschists and authoritarians. The president believed Yeltsin was making slow headway against corruption in substance, but these dismissals gained him political momentum as well. Yeltsin painted himself the steadfast reformer against a backward-looking Communist functionary in Gennady Zyuganov. To win a miraculous, uphill victory, he campaigned vigorously to the end across all eleven time zones within the enormous Russian Federation—using an airplane, Clinton noted, that was slower and less comfortable than Air Force One. The president pronounced Yeltsin a marvel of stamina and determination. Clinton was more than fifteen years younger than his Russian counterpart—just as driven, in far better health—and yet he conceded that he was dead on his feet already in the U.S. campaign. His reports indicated that Yeltsin's symptoms were more likely from constricted arteries than a disease, such as cancer, and he hoped surgery to remove blockages could restore his energy. For now, he recalled toasts to Boris. They had talked a lot through and since the election. To Clinton, Yeltsin's win was good for the United States.

Not so the narrow victory by Benjamin "Bibi" Netanyahu to become the new prime minister of Israel. The president did not dwell on his disappointment. They had known each other before the campaign, he said, and all their conversations since had explored ways for Netanyahu to keep some aspect of the peace process moving forward. Otherwise, hopes for stability would begin to unravel for the Israelis as well as for the Palestinians. Clinton accepted basic new political realities, such as a dead end with Syria. Netanyahu had campaigned against the Golan swap for peace, and therefore Asad fell to the back of the line. Clinton's private argument was that Netanyahu needed to find some way to reposition Yasir Arafat into a partner, because the alternative was to have none but implacable enemies on the Palestinian side. Arafat was slowly building a record of competent cooperation that could benefit Israel, and his replacement would be embattled at best, or an outright foe of the process.

Bibi understood, said the president, but he was toying with ideas to start first a separate track of negotiations for Israeli withdrawal from Lebanon. Politically, this notion was attractive because it would address problems exacerbated by Shimon Peres and the Labor Party. Its drawback was that delays on the Palestinian front would feed on themselves.

Benchmarks would be missed from the Oslo timetables, and the steady expansion of Israeli settlements would make compliance even less palatable to the Likud Party. Clinton clung to a glimmer of optimism from his reading of the new prime minister. He was convinced that Bibi wanted badly to maneuver against "crazies" within his own coalition. Netanyahu complained constantly that Gen. Ariel Sharon forced his way into the cabinet, for instance, and had made nothing but trouble since, dreaming of an Israeli settlement on every corner in the West Bank.

Clinton scrounged up a final consolation. President Mubarak of Egypt was reasserting leadership. Always ambitious, Mubarak yearned to forge a united front for all the Arab nations like his famous predecessor, Gen. Gamal Abdel Nasser—only this time for peace instead of war. Frankly, said Clinton, Mubarak had sulked a bit on the sidelines so long as Rabin and Peres ruled Israel, reaching one agreement after another with their Arab adversaries. Now, however, the Netanyahu crisis seemed to reenergize the indispensable man. Mubarak already had convened an Arab summit to press the Israelis for negotiations.

As usual, our session broke off with topics unchecked on my notepad. We skipped entirely the G-7 conference in Lyons, France, along with a terrible rash of Klan-style arsons that had destroyed some thirty black churches across the South. Afterward, off the tapes, Clinton said he was satisfied with the diligent work by the FBI to solve these cases, and he shrugged off partisan attacks that his visits to the ruins were poll-driven gimmicks for the election. He looked suddenly drained again, yet walked me all the way downstairs to my truck saying he wanted to tell me something about the *Esquire* article. This made me nervous.

On the way, I raised a suggestion from our talk about the TWA crash investigation. An astonishing team was gathered more or less spontaneously to address vital questions of terrorism and safety. There were Navy dive teams, FBI agents, Coast Guard cutters, and scientists from the National Transportation Safety Board, plus assorted reinforcements from local fire departments, police, medical examiners, and even volunteer sanitation haulers. Some risked life and equilibrium to retrieve human remains for the comfort of relatives. Others tackled the seemingly impossible mission to reconstruct the plane. All were on the public payroll. As bureaucrats, they were habitually derided in scornful rhetoric about government and taxes. Should Clinton honor them for their mission? Could presidential ceremony lift up the value of public service again?

He commented favorably. My other notions fared worse, and I feared he wanted to quiz me about the slant or content of my *Esquire* article. Although it was openly an endorsement, we had agreed to avoid any hint of collaboration. Now he worried about my interviews following publication. If reporters bore down hard on me about the nature of our contacts, it might compromise our historical work. I nodded, puzzled. We had discussed this hazard at length. And there was something else. Visibility on his behalf would heighten my risk of becoming a target in the press. That was simply a fact of personalized politics. If I said anything to excite controversy in the campaign, one side or both would make snide remarks about my motivation and character, or appearance, or anything they could think of. "I don't want to see that happen to you," he said. With this caveat, he trusted my judgment on doing interviews or not. I thanked him, chastened for my prior suspicion. He looked tired, I said. He should get some rest.

The president headed toward the Oval Office. I doubled back upstairs to call home from the Usher's Office. We were finished a little early tonight. When I drove past the Truman Balcony minutes later, a clump of watchful Secret Service agents caught my eye. There were five of them on the lawn to the west—more than usual, I figured, because of the recent bombings. About a hundred feet away, alone and clearly running on fumes, Clinton chipped golf balls methodically toward his little green.

A WHITE HOUSE operator called three weeks later, and the president followed to say he had just finished reading my article in *Esquire.** He thanked me. He thought it would do some good. Shrewdly, he identified two basic choices in the presentation. A "conversion" theme emphasized my initial reservations about his presidency, adding weight to judgments later. He did not mind the setup, and the stories were okay, although a reader might wonder how old friends came to discuss the Mexican bailout. The artifice to conceal our project made me sound at

---

* "Clinton Without Apologies," *Esquire*, September 1996.

times like one of the reporters divining his innermost thoughts. Clinton also perceived why the article was aimed at journalists. I was writing about skewed perceptions, he said, trying to make people think.

Looking back beneath the surface, a dozen years later, this written portrait would appear more than ever a mirrored discovery about our respective life choices. When we parted from Texas in 1972, I had considered my friend Clinton both naïve and cynical in his obsession with elective politics. Disillusioned myself, after our formative decade had crashed into Vietnam, assassination plots, and constitutional scandals, I sought integrity through the written word. It was a hard shock, therefore, to find Clinton at work a nobler figure than I or my fellow scribes. A politician? Less cynical than oracles of public conscience? More reflective than specialists in free thought? It was hard to fathom, coming against the presumption of my own career. Yet most images of Clinton collapsed into formula and hype, however pervasive. They were myths. They put me, I wrote for *Esquire*, "on a different planet from the president I have seen."

On his phone call, the president said Dole seemed to be switching back and forth about whether his top priority was tax cuts or a balanced budget. Our sessions would become even harder to schedule once the campaign began in earnest, he predicted, urging me to consult Nancy Hernreich. He wanted to squeeze some in. I replied that we were already talking. In fact, Nancy had offered Christy and me a guest room at the convention if we could spring for the airfare. He was surprised to hear it. I hoped none of the disclosures in my article would come back to bite him. It had been hard to balance candor and risk through the minefield of political topics, I confessed, while writing properly in isolation. He said not to worry. Maybe he would send for me in Chicago. I had not attended a national convention since the upheaval there in 1968, weeks after finishing college, when our Julian Bond challenge delegation* was

---

* Julian Bond, then a young civil rights activist and state legislator, led a challenge to the delegation appointed by Georgia's segregationist governor, Lester Maddox. The 1968 Democratic National Convention seated both delegations in a compromise, each with half-votes. Bond was elected board chair of the NAACP thirty years later, in 1998.

seated from Georgia. Clinton remembered that. For Hillary, of course, Chicago was home, and they were about to ride a train all the way there from West Virginia. He loved whistlestops, he said eagerly, signing off.

I went first to New York for a TV interview about the *Esquire* article with Charlie Rose, which aired nationwide on PBS. Rose was thorough and inquisitive, as usual. On fairly good rapport, from years of acquaintance, we bantered through my Clinton stories with amusement on both sides. He called most of them fresh, and I acknowledged that they could be interpreted many ways. We skirted two areas of friction. First, he repeated a litany that President Clinton had brought much of his trouble on himself by withholding information about Whitewater—inviting charges of cover-up, and so forth—and by failing to see that forthright disclosure could have resolved all this long ago. I mounted a glancing defense that nobody could, or would, define the basic question, which rendered such resolution always a mirage. Next, Rose invoked Bob Woodward to correct my comments on pollster Dick Morris. What about Clinton's dependence on campaign advisers? Did not his famous resilience spring from amoral flexibility in their hands? This, too, was a mantra—that the president was an empty vessel, a chameleon colored by Morris—supported by drumbeat assertions in the Woodward book. ("Dick Morris continued trying to reshape Clinton's image. . . . Morris was in charge of the big picture, the thematic speeches and bully pulpit and the presidential schedule.") Here I jousted more aggressively. The president seldom mentioned Morris at all. I thought Morris's influence was vastly overblown, and the notion of a rudderless Clinton simply ignored his personal conduct through unpopular storms over the deficit, Haiti, assault weapons, Northern Ireland, and Mexico, among others. To me this Svengali consensus smacked of a bargain between hungry reporters and Morris, who fed them in ardent self-promotion. I credited him with ample brains to scatter tidbits they could not resist.

Fateful misgivings about the interview trailed me into Chicago two days later, on the 28th. Would my harshness about Morris provoke a senseless spat in the next interview? Was I trading one cynicism for another? Dense crowds and formidable security accented the high stakes. There were dump trucks parked along Columbus Drive, forcing traffic through zigzag checkpoints. I walked the last several blocks to the Sheraton Towers, where screening lines and detectors in the lobby filtered access to a bank of express elevators for the twenty-ninth floor, opening upon a quieter gauntlet of ID checks and searches required for the coded badge of admittance to five presidential floors above. It took more than an hour to reach my appointed sanctum. A fancy name placard greeted me on the door of room 3326, across the hall from a placard inscribed "Morris."

This gave me pause. We had never met. It seemed fitting somehow to turn up the neighbor of a man I had just belittled in public. I thought I owed him at least a straightforward offer to talk it out if he wished. In rehearsing the likely confrontation, it was easy to defend my stance that Morris should not be advertising whatever influence he had with Clinton. This was inherently disloyal, and plainly injurious to the president. On the other hand, I shrank from jockeying with him over Clinton's favor. What a sordid, gossipy prospect—even without the added constraint of protecting the history project. So I headed instead for Wednesday night's convention events at the United Center. They included the formal renomination of the Clinton-Gore ticket by roll call vote, plus Al Gore's unusually personal address about his family journey from a storied tobacco farm through the poignant loss of his sister to lung cancer. Several speechwriters passed through the staff boxes in a possessed frenzy, looking for someone else. They needed scripture on a theme of repair—building a bridge for the future. I found a Bible in the United Center, which was not easy, and a courier to submit a suggested verse, Nehemiah 2:18. Carolyn Curiel, another speechwriter, advised me to spare the effort. Moping, she said the "white boys" had hijacked Clinton's acceptance speech. Morris was hurling edicts and curses at rivals who discarded his drafts. There would be no chance for outsiders like Curiel, a Hispanic female, unless President Clinton himself intervened in the turf wars.

Thursday morning, I knocked resolutely on Morris's door. There was no answer. Partly relieved, I stopped by the twenty-ninth-floor security area to make sure Christy's name had been added to the manifest for her arrival today. Much to my dismay, it was missing. I pictured her expelled to the streets until a gatekeeper confided to me some curious good news. My wife, Christy Macy, did appear elsewhere on the manifest. She would be staying across the hall with Mr. Morris! I nearly collapsed between laughter and frustration. There must be some silly mistake. The two last names did begin with the same letter, but my wife would not find it funny to be housed with a stranger. I said somebody needed to consult Nancy Hernreich, who had made the arrangements, only to be advised against pressing the issue myself. The agents nearby, with guns and ear-pieces, had a lengthy protocol for those who demanded changes in room assignments on the presidential floors.

Retreating in wonder, I hurried off to the Hyatt Regency for a National Public Radio interview about the *Esquire* article. Correspondent Linda Wertheimer seemed distracted from the start. Aides and technicians exchanged frozen whispers in the background. Finally, someone brandished the morning *New York Post* with a front-page picture of Dick Morris and a gigantic headline: "Bill's Bad Boy." Our interview dissolved in a hemorrhage of breaking news. Morris had been exposed—even photographed—on regular visits to a prostitute at the Jefferson Hotel in Washington. No detail was too salacious. To impress the prostitute, Morris proved he could get President Clinton on the phone from their bed, letting her overhear. He had a fetish for sucking toes. Both these images collided in tabloid delight with this week's solemn cover story on Morris in *Time* magazine: "The Man Who Has Clinton's Ear." I rushed back to the Sheraton Towers, where people looked stricken in the hallways upstairs. Erskine Bowles looked like he had just bitten a raw persimmon. He had been up before dawn in crisis meetings, and now his lips were pursed so tightly that I barely said hello. Helpless, I went to check the placards outside my room, nursing mad thoughts of a lifetime keepsake if the super-efficient gnomes had installed a "Morris/Macy" version, but there was no placard at all. Every vestige of Morris was gone.

THAT AFTERNOON, CHRISTY cleared security into our room. We moved around that night in the staff boxes at the convention, sitting at times with Leon Panetta, Sandy Berger's wife, Susan, and the president's secretary, Betty Currie. Everyone shook their heads about Morris before marveling how normal the convention seemed. Someone—I think it was John Podesta—described what it took to prepare $250,000 of tricolor balloons to drop simultaneously from the United Center's rafters. Lacking a current draft of tonight's acceptance speech, we wondered how the president would cope. He came onstage with recollections of "unmet challenges and a rising tide of cynicism" four years ago, bracketed with stories from his train ride to Chicago, including one whistlestop when two preschoolers read proudly to him from *The Little Engine That Could.*

Clinton claimed a record on this track: ten million new jobs, the smallest federal workforce since JFK, 1.8 million people moved from welfare to work, a budget deficit "down 60 percent on the way to zero," life expectancy doubled for AIDS patients, a miraculous supercomputer in the works. More than twenty times, he exhorted the television audience to build a bridge of engagement toward the twenty-first century just four years ahead. I fretted out loud that this overworked metaphor was making the address too long, but others said you must hammer home a campaign theme by repetition. Besides, Clinton chugged masterfully between huge ovations, turning near the end to uphold leadership abroad. "We cannot save all the world's children," he said, "but we can save many of them." He linked five ongoing peace missions to the heritage of freedom at home. "In our own country, we have seen America pay a terrible price for any form of discrimination," the president declared. "And we have seen us grow stronger as we have steadily let more and more of our hatreds and fears go, as we have given more and more of our people a chance to live their dreams." Less than two minutes later, tons of confetti fell with the balloons into sustained bedlam on the convention floor.

Seeking coffee before an early flight home the next morning, Christy and I located a strangely hushed hospitality room on our floor. President Clinton stood with a plate and fork, flanked by a Secret Service detail but no aides or celebrities. A few shy guests approached him in turns. He hugged Christy, who asked him as a speechwriter about the construction of last night's address. After a few stories, he remarked to me again that we needed to catch up. I told him I thought Dr. King would have approved the ecumenical lift in his closing themes. He thought it came out all right. Our quiet interlude did not last long before anxious handlers converged, as though tracking down a runaway, and swallowed him off to the campaign for two months. We were left in a surreal, blended world of shrill punditry superimposed on daily snapshots of history in the making—crowd estimates, swing voters estimated in millions, poll numbers with Clinton consistently ahead of Dole and his lackluster campaign.

The vortex of the campaign itself was remote. I thought often of Clinton's private appreciation for Boris Yeltsin in Russia, humping gamely across all those time zones. Punditry was far more immediate, and drenched with emotion, although my own role dried up instantly in the wake of the Morris scandal. What survived was a small packet of letters from readers and listeners about my *Esquire* article. A Clinton supporter printed in a child's hand on lined paper: "Travelgate! Travelgate! Who gives a darn! We could not care less about any of this nonsense rubbish." Greater agitation and numbers fell on the other side. Marvin of Tennessee found me "a complete blooming idiot in your excuses for the criminal actions of our current Socialist draft dodger, Bill Clinton." An anonymous respondent was more direct: "Branch. You stupid asshole. MLK and Clinton. You are a sick shitbag. If Slick Willie dropped his drawers to you, would YOU take the bait? I bet you would." Several vulgar ones aimed racial threats without specifying a cause—probably from general disposition.

Senator Dole, running behind in late October, summoned voters to "rise up" against the press. He urged a boycott of television news, and denounced liberal bias particularly in elite publications like the *New York Times*. They printed bad news about him, Dole charged, to set a tone favoring Clinton. His final pleas earned a puzzled column by the *Washington Post*'s sensible media critic, Howard Kurtz, who listed a string of anti-Clinton stories in the *Times*. After all, the news publications deemed most favorable to Clinton had been driving the Whitewater scandals for years, and something downright perverse took flight from their opinion pages. A bemused, backward tribute in *The New Yorker* began the rehabilitation of Dick Morris toward sober authority as a perpetual media source for character faults in both Clintons. At the *Times*, columnist William Safire exposed what he called "the penetration of the White House by Asian interests." Also at the *Times*, the former boss Abe Rosenthal assailed Clinton for giving militant Islam "its first European beachhead" in Bosnia—and also for betraying the poor—while Maureen Dowd subjected Clinton to whirligig scorn. She called him "President

Pothole," a fixer of tiny things, and the "Limbo President" who slowly lowered the bar on every national standard. "We pretty much know that the Clintons did something wrong in Whitewater," she announced without a hint of irony.

An intimate rage crested broadly in the interpretive classes, driving pundits into fits also at Kurtz's newspaper, the *Washington Post*. "Clinton: Not a Flicker of Moral Life," proclaimed a guest editorial by Andrew Sullivan of the liberal flagship *The New Republic*. Sullivan said Clinton had perfected a "moral nihilism" so wicked that it crippled the entire political process, including journalism. "The media reports cynically on process," he wrote, "because that is what they learned from this president, a man whose convictions are plucked from focus groups." On November 4, the *Post* columnist and book critic Jonathan Yardley took my sad prize for confident venom. I wondered how Clinton might react if shown this attack on his flight home to vote in Arkansas—having once praised a Yardley column on the subtleties of affirmative action. I could only sigh. Yardley and I were friends—neighbors in Baltimore, both steeped in the civil rights era, fellow UNC alumni and Orioles fans—but we could not talk about Clinton. Like Sullivan, he conceded first a legacy of solid achievement in the first term, and emphasized his distaste for the Republican candidate. Why, then, would he vote for Dole tomorrow? "Because he isn't Bill Clinton, stupid," wrote Yardley. The president was "a buffoon." Most people did not have the foggiest idea how to evaluate true character, he added, scoffing at "amatory peccadilloes." Yardley detected instead a monstrous fault "at the very core of his being," and he thundered against Clinton in peroration: "He is a man who does not believe in anything, to whom 'principle' is a word as foreign as any in Sanskrit or Esperanto, who has never met a promise he did not like, whose sole gyroscope is expediency."

CHAPTER TWENTY-FOUR

REELECTION 1996

Friday, November 15, 1996

Thursday, December 19, 1996

His victory led to a chaotic transition of euphoria mixed with ennui. Nancy scheduled us for ten o'clock on the second Thursday after the election, and, toward midnight, a prolonged lapse in distant phone conversations drew me from my waiting seat in the yellow hallway. The president looked up from notes at his Treaty Room desk, alone, still wearing a suit. He apologized profusely. The outside world gave him no respite, and he was upset about his appointments. This combination had kept him up past two o'clock every night. He was too tired to start taping now, but could I stay over and talk early tomorrow? Otherwise, a back-log of detail may soon be forgotten.

Yes, I replied, and his thanks slipped into these preoccupations for at least twenty minutes. Vote tallies bubbled up by state and district—up here from 1992, down there, and why. He had lost Virginia by only three points, for instance, despite pro-Republican mobilizations by its celebrity evangelists Pat Robertson and Jerry Falwell. This was a harbinger, he purred, that Democrats could reclaim Virginia after a post-1960s hiatus of thirty years. Clinton was far less encouraged about the cabinet, especially his core team for national security. William Perry would stay on at Defense no more than another six months. At CIA, the president would send Tony Lake to replace John Deutch, who wanted out, and move Sandy Berger into Lake's job at the White House, but Lake may have confirmation problems. Against a dearth of top candidates for these jobs, Clinton sifted at least four worthy aspirants to replace Warren Christopher as secretary of state: George Mitchell, Sam Nunn, Madeleine Albright, and Richard Holbrooke.

Perhaps he could apply one problem to another, I suggested, by appointing Nunn to head the Pentagon. The president said no, for many reasons, but the counsel that stuck with me was a letter from Massachusetts representative Barney Frank, one of the few openly gay members of Congress. Frank pleaded against Nunn. He had absorbed a torrent of abuse for supporting Clinton, Frank wrote, ever since the don't-ask-don't-tell compromise over gay and lesbian soldiers. What bothered him were not so much conventional opinions as Nunn's ostentatious distaste for the idea of gay soldiers. Nunn was the only senator younger than seventy to vote for one harsh piece of throwaway legislation, and his appointment would pitch the gay community into lasting revolt, Frank warned, complete with rumors that Nunn felt compelled to display extra virility.

It was State or nothing for Nunn, said the president, and there were inevitable objections that Madeleine Albright could not be "tough enough" as our first female foreign minister, or at least that foreigners would not take her seriously. Here he cited distinctive advice from Senator Barbara Mikulski of Maryland, who believed Albright would break barriers in communication as well as gender. Her manner and words resonated with Mikulski's constituents on the docks of Baltimore. She could make ordinary people feel a stake in world affairs. This potential was attractive to Clinton, who often chafed that his foreign policy leaders were too unpracticed and inarticulate for outreach in plain language, beyond the confines of professional jargon.

He complained about Janet Reno—made it clear, in fact, that he felt alienated from his own attorney general. If he removed her, however, the pending decision on yet another special prosecutor would fall to Reno's deputy, Jamie Gorelick, who, Clinton feared, may share Reno's wholesale devotion to outside control for any case in which the president himself may become a target. If so, she would establish an open-ended investigation of the Clinton-Gore campaign based on vague but insistent press reports about improper or suspicious contributions from immigrants and foreigners, especially Asians. If he removed both Reno *and*

Gorelick, to start fresh, it would touch off a firestorm of protest like Nixon's Saturday Night Massacre of Justice Department officials during the Watergate scandal. That was not an option.

Clinton heeded my plea to save this material for his tapes, and I raised my own transition as we said good night. Now that he was about to become a two-term president, the oral history project took on added significance, and I felt compelled to say we had managed only four or five sessions this year. He should consider any step to make these first-hand recordings easier and more convenient, including a replacement for me. The president smiled, while nodding that the offer was appropriate. No, he wanted to keep going, perhaps in smaller, more frequent dollops. We should each speak with Nancy.

HE TOOK ME early on Friday to the third-floor Solarium. Clinton gripped his belly, remarking that he had gained six pounds during the campaign and taken three of them back off. So he had not done too badly. His posture and carriage seemed relatively fit to me, though he yawned frequently from lack of sleep. My unspoken health concern was his complexion, which was more splotchy than usual around a large nose. The bright morning sunshine made his face disappear at times into an ornate red tapestry behind him. On tape, he reprised troubles on the cabinet transition, and he doubled back to record his impression of events collateral to the campaign. A week of rioting in Jerusalem, for instance, had killed some seventy people and wounded more than three hundred, both Palestinians and Israelis, after a sudden Israeli excavation on September 25 through a sealed gate into the ancient Hasmonean Tunnel beneath the Temple Mount.

This entire crisis was calculated in advance, said the president. The Israeli government, giving the United States no notice, pretended the operation was routine even though it was accomplished by sudden stealth with troops guarding the excavators. Prime Minister Netanyahu, having decamped nonchalantly for Europe, feigned shock over the lethal uproar, but Clinton said he was paying debts to right-wing parties in his cabinet with an aggressive show of Israeli sovereignty across the fault lines between Jews and Muslims. By digging unilaterally under the common foundation for the Temple Mount and the Muslim Dome of the

Rock, Netanyahu's government asserted new leverage on the final status of Jerusalem. Like the Jewish settlements, which were called "facts on the ground" as they spread through the occupied West Bank, this excavation was an empirical statement *under* the ground, designed to provoke and override protest.

Clinton said it was all he could do in the midst of his own campaign to gather a truce summit at the White House. Mubarak of Egypt refused to come, citing deficiencies in the hasty preparations, but Clinton thought he simply refused to be part of a likely failure. In spite of Mubarak's absence, the summit achieved some calm, with renewed public commitment to the timetable for peace negotiations. The president said he had left Netanyahu and Arafat alone together in the library for three hours, forcing them to get acquainted as they could never at home. He recalled impassioned private speeches by King Hussein of Jordan to both the chief antagonists. Hussein told Arafat he had been fighting all his life. Hussein was old enough to be Netanyahu's father, and he knew younger generations would revile their addiction to fruitless war. There would be no victory for you, he told them, even with the support of the bloodiest factions on both sides. Later, in dictation, I regretted my inability to recapture the force of Clinton's language here.

He reacted to news of conquest in Afghanistan, when Kabul fell suddenly to the fundamentalist Taliban militia on September 26. His State Department expressed hope for an end to seventeen years of war and anarchy, but they were telling Clinton within a month that the cure proved worse than the disease. The new regime summarily executed opponents and draped bloated corpses from lampposts, while confining all women under an extreme version of Islamic Sharia law. It was highly ironic, said the president, to see fundamentalist groups across Asia turn hostile after cooperating with us against the Soviet Union through the Cold War. Dogmatism hardened them for war, and some militias—even in sophisticated Turkey—provided better schools and garbage service than complacent secular governments. The political elements for democratic stability, Clinton observed, remained elusive in many parts of the world.

At home, Dole and his running mate, Jack Kemp, never gained traction from any of five or six experimental attack themes against the president, whose job approval held firmly above 60 percent. Clinton drew what he called big "October crowds" in September, and he figured the press got bored with a race that was never in doubt, barring a miracle. To spice things up, journalists tried a bit of healthy competition over the unsolved mystery of the TWA airline disaster, with the *New York Times* sensing a terrorist plot, against skeptical rejoinders in the *Washington Post*. This foray died out, but the leading papers did capture an audience with their tandem suspicious about Clinton's Asian donors. He sighed again over an artificial scandal buttressed by politics. While its adverse effects included depressed voter turnout in some districts, Clinton drew satisfaction from a decisive margin in the Electoral College, 379 votes to 159 for Dole.* His net increase of nine electoral votes above 1992 all came from Florida, where victory more than offset the loss of Georgia.

Only three other states switched their electoral vote for president this time—all from the Mountain Time Zone. Not since Truman in 1948 had a Democrat won Arizona. Clinton merely winced at defeat in Montana, but he groaned over a two-point loss in Colorado despite its popular Democratic governor, Roy Romer. He analyzed this result in minute detail, until a diverting question evoked memories off the campaign trail. Vice President Gore's introduction had inspired spontaneous remarks at the September 18 dedication ceremonies for a 1.7-million-acre Grand Staircase–Escalante National Monument. Clinton said he described his first visit to the Southwest. On a 1971 trek to see his brand-new girlfriend, Hillary, who was in California that summer, he had lain alone for two hours at the rocky rim to watch a setting sun transform the Grand Canyon every few seconds in spectacular shades of red and yellow. He once read, and could easily believe, that Teddy Roosevelt had cried when he made the Grand Canyon a national monument. Clinton said his only comparable experience of natural beauty came later in Granada, Spain, again watching late afternoon sunlight as it played from the golden Alhambra Palace down a valley filled with lemon and lime groves.

---

* By comparison, Ronald Reagan amassed a record 525 electoral votes for his 1984 reelection. The first President Bush won with 426 electoral votes in 1988. His son captured 271 in 2000—one above the minimum—and 286 four years later. In 2008, Barack Obama won the presidency with 365 electoral votes.

The election was never far away. Higher margins more than offset lower turnout in specific parts of greater Philadelphia, holding Pennsylvania barely above the NRA's gun vote through its rural center. He rationalized negative TV ads restricted to selected markets on the Social Security issue, saying they do work. He second-guessed his own choices late in the campaign. With victory assured, he did not hold rallies in safe big states like California and New York, where a small boost of enthusiasm might have given him a national majority above the combined popular vote for Dole and Ross Perot.* Nor did he finish with trips to neck-and-neck states like Georgia, where a late Dole surge surpassed Clinton by one percent. Instead, the president had tried to bolster key congressional candidates in Kentucky, Iowa, and South Dakota, with mixed results. He failed to ensure defeat for New Hampshire's "mean, mean" Republican senator Bob Smith, but this regret opened fond thoughts from the New Hampshire primary of 1992. "I love that little state," he said, clearly in the grip of nostalgic remorse. Already, at the age of fifty, he could never run again. He retold sentimental stories about young Michael Morrison, the New Hampshire volunteer who canvassed in a wheelchair, and Paul Begala's "Comeback Kid" slogan to revive Clinton's 1992 campaign from the brink of extinction.

What memories would stand out this time? Well, this election proved again how remarkable it had been for Clinton to run so well in that 1992 New Hampshire primary next door to Massachusetts, the home state of his opponent Paul Tsongas. Dole did not have a chance near Arkansas, said the president, ticking off lopsided results in surrounding areas such as Memphis, where Clinton carried 83 percent of the vote. When I pressed for something more personal, recollections surfaced slowly from a blur of names, statistics, and noisy campaign stops. He cited two from historic black churches. At Newark's New Hope Baptist Church, Dionne Warwick sat in the congregation and Whitney Houston's mother directed the choir. Clinton said the music was so good that it lifted every trace of fatigue from his bones—and he told them so.

---

* Perot, running again on a third-party ticket, dropped to 10 percent of the popular vote from 19 percent in 1992. President Clinton's 47 million votes left him just short of half the national total, at 49.24 percent.

At a church rally in Tampa, two days before the election, the president said a scripture reading moved him to speak extemporaneously. He told them this story had inspired him to seek out the Healing Pool of Bethesda. It is still in Jerusalem, full of lore. According to the book of John,* a cripple once told Jesus he had been there for decades, unable to join the mad rushes to bathe whenever a mysterious healing power stirred the waters. Clinton told Tampa the parable reminded him of the election. Everyone must do their part, but no one should be abandoned to fend entirely for themselves. While the cripple lacked a sound body, he still had his mind and his faith. He tried again when Jesus told him to rise and walk. If modern citizens worked hard, Clinton told them, there shouldn't be an underclass. There shouldn't be welfare rolls, or a huge prison population. We must all tend the healing waters. Everybody should rise and walk.

The president soared off briefly in recital on tape. Yet another poor, minority audience had cheered his message on work and opportunity, he said, but the mainstream media ignored such stories in favor of Whitewater, the presidential horse race, and suspicious Asian donors. When he delved into grievances about the press, I asked about military strikes against Iraqi forces in September. Clinton's summary emphasized an array of poor choices. He said Saddam Hussein brutally exploited rivalries to suppress the Kurdish opposition. In a switchback deal with the intermittently pro-American Kurdistan Democratic Party (KDP), Saddam sent thirty thousand Iraqi troops against the intermittently pro-Iranian Patriotic Union of Kurdistan (PUK), seizing the city of Erbil and executing political opponents with their families, as identified by KDP agents. These persecutions were genocidal in nature, prohibited by U.N. guarantees ending the Gulf War, but Saddam shielded himself from direct reprisal by dispersing his troops among the Kurdish populations, carefully within Iraq's border. With support only from England, Clinton attacked Saddam's capability for larger military offensives. To expand the no-fly restrictions, he sent cruise missiles against air-defense installations. B-52 bombers, flying round-trip from Guam, reinforced the missile strikes near Baghdad for two days.

---

* John 5:1–9.

When President Chirac of France had called to protest, the exchange was blunt on both sides. Chirac accused Clinton of staging gratuitous military action for political reasons—to look tough before the presidential election. Clinton told Chirac his charge was nasty and ridiculous. It would have been far easier to do nothing, like Chirac and most allies. While conceding that no available response could answer this crime precisely, Clinton defended missile strikes as the best practical alternative. Doing nothing, he said, would only encourage Saddam Hussein to disregard the Security Council's pledge of collective protection for Iraqi civilians.

Clinton fussed to me about Chirac's penchant for grandstand postures, such as refusing Israeli security guards on a visit to Jerusalem. The French president was usually better in private talks, he mused, and had been helpful toward the end on the Bosnia settlement. This thought apparently reminded him to place two phone calls through a White House operator. With the Dayton peace agreement holding steady, he was seeking congressional approval to extend the U.S. peace mission in Bosnia beyond its allotted year. The scourge of violence was spent, or deterred, and land mines were being cleared, but political progress remained slow against fresh wounds and resentments. Clinton said its sturdiest partner, President Tudjman of Croatia, was in such fragile health that we had smuggled him into the United States for emergency treatment of his advanced cancer. Sometimes, he remarked, there was a delicate trade-off between medical necessity and national honor. Boris Yeltsin, after confidential consultations with Dr. Michael DeBakey and others, had demanded that Russian surgeons perform his heart operation (on the day of Clinton's reelection). Quietly, however, Yeltsin accepted a team of U.S. Navy doctors for his postoperative care. Russia's medical infrastructure had deteriorated beneath the skill of its personnel, Clinton confided, to the point that lives were lost unnecessarily after surgery. He said he owed Yeltsin a call in the next few days. Viktor Chernomyrdin, his premier, thought the medical prognosis was strong enough for Yeltsin to get through Russia's presidential transition without a coup.

The president's call came through from Senate majority leader Trent Lott of Mississippi. Almost simultaneously, Leon Panetta and Erskine Bowles marched up the inclined passage to the Solarium in identically plain dark suits and spit-shined black shoes, like twin morticians, except that Panetta was smiling. I wondered whether Clinton's buzz for a White House operator had tipped off our whereabouts. The outgoing and incoming chiefs of staff, respectively, came to fetch the president for his morning schedule, and both discreetly ignored my materials while I rewound the tapes. Bowles and I quietly talked UNC basketball, being fellow alumni. Panetta reminisced about his two years in the Nixon Justice Department, back when I wrote my first articles about its civil rights enforcement. Then a Republican, Panetta had been whipsawed between Nixon's Southern strategy and breakthrough momentum in desegregation cases. All the Justice Department lawyers, Panetta marveled, had been instructed to Scotch-tape their car hoods to detect bombs planted by the Klan.

Clinton finished his call. "I really learned something," he announced. Lott had assured him that the Bosnia extension would pass. His Republican majority would flay the administration about "mission creep" and other dangers, but only for show, and if Clinton played his cards right he could win approval for at least another eighteen months. Lott said the U.S. mission in Bosnia had performed well with negligible casualties, and the United States enjoyed too big an investment to jeopardize the Dayton accord. Even better, said Clinton, Lott confided in detail how he relied on two colleagues for policy judgments as opposed to politics: Senators Slade Gorton of Washington and Bill Cohen of Maine. The affinity was a major surprise, given Cohen's reputation as a loner isolated from Lott's conservative bloc. Bulbs lit for everyone but me, until someone explained that they were considering Cohen for secretary of defense. "Well, I don't guess we'll have any confirmation problems there," said the president, beaming.

TOWARD 10 P.M. on December 19, I was escorted mysteriously to what I presumed was a closet beside the master bedroom at the far southwest corner of the residence, across the yellow hall from the family kitchen. The door opened to Hillary alone among ribbons, cards, wrapping, and last-minute gifts for Christmas. Excusing the cluttered chamber, she said Bess Truman had slept here. So had Eleanor Roosevelt and other first ladies whose husbands preferred separate bedrooms, but Hillary, like

Jackie Kennedy, used the space for a hideaway office. She asked about the gift in my hand for Bill, promising not to tell—a first edition of collected speeches by ex-president Theodore Roosevelt in 1910, called *The New Nationalism*—and she opened forthwith her own present of two sculpted frogs jumping over one another. I told her Christy had found it somewhere in her travels. This produced smiles and several stories, including one about a remote Bolivian village, where, with the Spanish translator stumped by the Indian language, Hillary and a tribal artist communicated in gestures about frogs depicted as universal symbols of hope. Wherever the atmosphere is not literally boiling, Hillary quipped, frogs bring forth life and personality. Chelsea popped in to say she had appropriated money for takeout food from mom's purse, the White House kitchen being closed. Was that okay? Of course. Hillary inquired of me about Christy's report on a state experiment in streamlined government called the Oregon Option, and she reiterated her long-lost constitutional dissent on Whitewater. Now, entering the fourth year since Bill had let himself get stampeded into a special prosecutor, they must try to keep going until craziness from that error played out. She sighed in stoic determination.

By telephone, Hillary traced the president's delay to the West Wing. Moving there at her suggestion, to make myself a physical reminder of our appointment, I encountered a night bustle of revolving huddles. Nobody sat down. Betty Currie relayed phone calls, and Nancy Hernreich managed traffic in a bright red outfit that accented the holiday decorations. Erskine Bowles and the outgoing HUD secretary, Henry Cisneros, wore suits with festive Christmas neckties, which made me self-conscious in my jeans for normally secluded work at the residence. Erskine's deputy, Sylvia Mathews, stood beside a desk making several calls, evidently recruiting prospects for the transition. Making a phone call in the Oval Office, Vice President Gore attracted all eyes with a lively pantomime of a sport fisherman at sea. Cradling the receiver to an ear, he strained backward as though fighting a mighty blue marlin—then lurched forward to reel in his catch with frantic hands and soothing words. "I just about got him," Gore joked. President Clinton sidled over during a lull and proposed to try some interim recording across the coffee table. "Mr. President," I replied, "I'll be happy to talk here, but won't all these people want to know what you're doing?" He pondered briefly, and conferred with Nancy before directing me into his adjacent study.

The president picked at a half-eaten supper while I set up the recorders. On tape, he ranged over the second term's cabinet shifts. Final selections would be announced tomorrow. He said New York's Andrew Cuomo was far from his first choice to replace Cisneros at HUD. Mickey Kantor, bored at Commerce, wanted to be attorney general, but Clinton suggested that Kantor might be too partisan on his behalf—and therefore too political to be a credible corrective for Janet Reno. He commented favorably again on my offhand suggestion that he might neutralize the politics by appointing a Republican like Bill Weld, the current governor of Massachusetts, who was a fiscal conservative, supporter of women's rights, and generally a stickler for good government. The president said he liked Weld, but felt stuck with Reno, despite his resentments that had accumulated over her handling of requests for special prosecutors. He said he had not been able to trust her for four years. If he tried to have an honest conversation with her, she would leak it. He said she had no sense of a healthy, combative politics, and therefore she had surrendered vital authority to external ideologues as well as her subordinates at the FBI.

His burning example was the Henry Cisneros case, which had dragged on for years. The president called Cisneros a brilliant public servant, qualified to be president. At his confirmation hearings in 1993, Cisneros verified widespread reports that he had supported a mistress in the past. With his subsequent approval by the Senate, this public confession would have ended the matter except that the FBI pursued discrepancies in the overall amount Cisneros admitted having paid her. His estimates, recalled from painful and prolonged contention with the former mistress, turned out less than the sum pieced together by FBI agents. Clinton said the difference was immaterial even to the Republican committee chairman, Alfonse D'Amato, who, though chief among Clinton's partisan tormentors, had written formally to Attorney General Reno that the error by Cisneros was of no consequence. It would not have affected the confirmation vote of any senator, D'Amato specified, which meant it failed a legal test for deceit. The ethics division at Justice agreed. Even so, the president fairly howled, FBI Director Louis Freeh told Reno that Cisneros should have done more homework before his background check by FBI agents. Above statutory requirements, or integrity in the Senate confirmation process, Freeh considered any discrepancy an affront to the FBI, and he demanded not only the expulsion of Cisneros from government but also a special prosecutor to sustain a criminal dragnet through his life.

This was only a beginning. The president said Freeh and Reno had done the same thing to Agriculture Secretary Mike Espy. Far from measured justice, the establishment of separate prosecutors with teams of FBI investigators made for impervious, open-ended persecutions driven by arrogance and ideology. Espy remained so pinioned by suspicion and legal bills that he could not earn a living. There was no end in sight.* Worse, Clinton charged, insulation hid shocking abuse. When the special prosecutor had brought witnesses to Washington for testimony in the Cisneros case, he said FBI agents ransacked their offices and apartments in Texas, without a warrant. Impunity rendered these misdeeds brazen but safe, reminiscent of the J. Edgar Hoover era.

I was reeling. Could such extremes be true? The president hurried on to describe his private audience with Janet Reno a week ago, on December 12. He deliberately made her wait until last, after Reno declined to seek a special prosecutor for the Asian donors. This was a pretty simple decision, Clinton observed, because the allegations had mentioned no public officials listed in the triggering provisions of the law. His opening remarks rebuked Reno for public statements about her desire to stay on the job. "I told her I didn't like that one damn bit," the president said tersely. "I didn't hire her to work for the *New York Times* and *Washington Post*. I hired her to work for me." Soon after, reining in his agitation, he said he had given Reno credit for good traits and achievements: rebuilding relations with local and state agencies, expanding enforcement on spousal abuse, plus skilled coordination with the U.S. attorneys and her educational speeches about why America could not simply jail its way out of crime problems.

On Whitewater, Clinton told Reno that of course he did not blame

---

* The office of special prosecutor Donald Smaltz spent four years and $20 million to prosecute thirty counts of receiving improper gifts, including sports tickets and lodging. A 1998 jury acquitted Espy on all charges.

her for the original special prosecutor. This was his mistake, made during a lapse in the statute, but he did blame her for abdicating responsibility to supervise the investigations ever since, letting mandates multiply almost at will. She had accepted criteria that were ludicrous and crassly partisan. Reno had failed to defend the presidency itself—not Clinton personally, but the institution—and by extension the entire executive branch including her own Justice Department. In our system of checks and balances, passivity could be far worse than aggressive politics. He told me she had no clue what he meant. His advisers considered her more naïve than upright, and the fuzziness of that distinction seemed to save her. Since the Civil War, Clinton told Reno, only two of her predecessors had served longer than four years. He invited her to stay on as attorney general, but he expected to replace her within a year. She should prepare herself for that.

This anticlimactic result hung briefly between us. Well, didn't he need to make a change now? He would take a huge political hit to nominate even a Republican like Bill Weld for attorney general, but fresh independence might correct the horrendous wrongs he had just portrayed. Weld was a family acquaintance,* and I did not mean to push him, but replacing the attorney general would only get harder. Meanwhile, could Clinton uphold the executive authority vested in him by the Constitution? Yes, he replied. He had asserted control. He put Reno on notice. I hesitated. If she concluded, on the contrary, that he wanted to fire her but could not, his lecture might actually compound the problem—advertising his paralysis, diminishing any chance to correct the runaway impunity in the Cisneros case or anywhere else. The FBI already felt free to refract its own failures back against the president— with political leaks, for instance, that the White House had "victimized" the bureau in the Filegate scandal, and "hamstrung" its antidrug performance.

Clinton said the FBI worked for him, too, though problems were daunting. He mentioned Richard Jewell as one tip of a big iceberg. FBI leaks had fueled press hysteria that nearly lynched this innocent security

---

* He was then married to Susan Roosevelt, a friend of my wife, Christy, since childhood.

guard for terrorism at the Atlanta Olympics, until Reno and Freeh fobbed off an apology by underlings.* Only now, five months later, did the FBI revive a dead-end investigation by publicizing surveillance photographs of the knapsack bomb. Clinton said the bureau hated honest appeals for help. It preferred leaks to guard prideful secrets among experts. Against an admittedly strong combination of political hubris and prurient media, the president insisted on progress toward reform. He could fire Director Freeh, if necessary, like Judge Sessions before him. This seemed dubious, but we moved on to other cabinet posts.

CLINTON SAID NEW Mexico congressman Bill Richardson originally wanted Commerce, spurning the U.N. as a dreamy outpost, but changed his mind. He reviewed conversations with all the candidates for State, where his choice boiled down to Richard Holbrooke or Madeleine Albright. Clinton said he hesitated mostly because of Strobe Talbott's ardent support for Holbrooke. Citing more than his stellar performance at Dayton, Talbott believed he would inject needed focus and energy into the conduct of foreign affairs. The president said he had not seen Strobe so passionate since his anguished attempts to understand the suicide of their mutual friend at Oxford, Frank Aller. Bringing Holbrooke back for closer examination, Clinton had asked whether he would wind up taking grief for his secretary's abrasive reputation. "Oh, Mr. President," scoffed Holbrooke, "that only happened in Bosnia because I was told to be more aggressive with the press." No, Clinton persisted. People said more generally that he could be arrogant and irritating. Holbrooke looked sheepish in his reply: "Well, I kind of understand." They reached a candid bargain from there, and Clinton secured Talbott's pledge to remain his administrative anchor for Holbrooke at State. Finally, however, the president discerned slightly more promise in the notion of Deputy Talbott paired with a Secretary Albright. He said everyone took his decision with grace.

---

* Reno did apologize for these leaks at a press conference in July 1997. NBC News paid Jewell $500,000 because of statements by Tom Brokaw. The *New York Post* settled a $15 million claim for an undisclosed sum. Jewell's defamation suit against the *Atlanta Journal-Constitution* was pending at his death in 2007.

The vice president's head appeared at the door. "Excuse me," he said. "I've made four calls and here's where we are." They were trying to persuade Transportation Secretary Federico Peña to head the Energy Department, replacing Hazel O'Leary. Erskine Bowles followed Gore and stood over me. "Here's our pitch," he told the president, ticking off factors including the disposition of subordinate slots. Plenty of cabinet officers had switched jobs, mastering new issues. "I think you can close it, Mr. President," said Gore, and the three of them vanished toward the Oval Office. Alone, I examined the little study. A huge purplish sword from Yeltsin hung on one wall, etched with elaborate swirls. There was a strange antique card game from Mexico, called Balance the Budget, plus a framed report by Mary Lasker on 1968 government programs for children, inscribed with a thank-you from President Johnson.

Looking outside toward the putting green and private garden, I must have stepped close to the door because a steward rushed in with reassurance. Someone had tripped an alarm under the rug, but he vouched for me with the Secret Service. We had ample time to chat between muffled hurrahs from the Oval Office, which must have signaled success in the recruitment of Peña. The steward said his father had come from the Philippines to try out for the senior golf tour. He corrected a wall clock that still showed Daylight Saving Time, setting it back an hour to just after midnight.

President Clinton returned to plow through new topics on tape. Yes, the United States did scuttle a second term for U.N. Secretary-General Boutros Boutros-Ghali, and we were lucky to secure Ghana's Kofi Annan in his place. Clinton appreciated Annan for his skillful pressures to advance peace in Bosnia, but he said the complex U.N. politics often turned on esoteric questions such as who was a "real" African and who spoke better French. Elsewhere, Clinton's diplomats were "working like dogs" to defuse a crisis in Serbia, where mass marches had swelled daily since President Slobodan Milosevic annulled municipal elections on November 17. The dictator injured himself at home and abroad, mused Clinton, by refusing to let elected critics assume even minor posts. Although they posed no logical or overt threat, Milosevic feared obsessively that the slightest opposition would make him look weak, inviting jackals to swarm. He would repress all dissent if he could get away with it. The president said he had been discussing Milosevic's autocratic psyche with Holbrooke. They had walked a tight line in pushing him to make a face-saving deal, because, ironically, the chief instigator of the ethnic wars in Bosnia had become a key link for compliance with the Dayton peace accords.

On a twelve-day trip to Asia, the Clintons had snorkled the Great Barrier Reef off Australia and held a koala at Port Douglas Wildlife Park. Their stop in Thailand spanned King Bhumibol's grand palace down to Hillary's visit with child prostitutes suffering from AIDS. In describing the lengthy Asia-Pacific Economic Cooperation (APEC) meetings at Manila, Clinton called President Kim Young-sam of South Korea "very excitable" in private talks about harassments from North Korea, nuclear negotiations, and political tensions over the fate of his indicted predecessors. Prime Minister Ryutaro Hashimoto of Japan sounded beleaguered, as usual, and there seemed to be a lot of bargaining over new international air routes for Federal Express. Clinton's renewed sessions with Jiang Zemin of China produced a schedule for an exchange of future visits, beginning with Vice President Gore. I reminded the president of his resolve to push for a deeper grasp of Jiang's character in relation to Chinese policy. Well, he replied, the Chinese leader had pleaded insecurity because Deng Xiaoping was still holding power in the shadows. Jiang promised to be more forthright after the Communist Party Congress next fall. Did he mean it? That was hard to say. He could be inventing excuses, Clinton acknowledged, with no intention to change. Were there any new clues about Jiang's nature? Progress was slow. With a vow to keep at it, the president deflected further questions about China.

He was far more expansive on Greg Norman, the golf champion nicknamed the Shark. In Australia, Norman had offered him the choice between a scoring round for fun and a teaching round for conversation. Clinton chose the latter, and they plunged deeply into subjects from preparation and club selection to the psychology of recovery—whether from losing both houses of Congress or the 1996 Masters. They birdied the same hole. Norman flattered Clinton's weak spot, complimenting him for limberness to hit the ball so far at his age. This led to a comparison of stretching techniques, said the president, to the point of lying on the thirteenth green to demonstrate their respective calisthenics in front of astonished caddies and Secret Service agents.

Gore reentered in triumph. I left the tapes running to capture the final details on the second-term cabinet, complete with his burst from song into a short but animated victory dance. The president asked how much criticism to expect over the late cobbling of Peña over to Energy, keeping two Hispanics. There would be some of that, Gore predicted, but it wouldn't last long because Peña was very well respected. Clinton asked bluntly whether this cabinet matched the first. Gore pondered trades out loud. Albright for Christopher at State. Rubin staying on at Treasury after Bentsen. Senator Cohen to the Pentagon for Perry, who succeeded Aspin. Effectively—with the Peña switch—Richardson for Cisneros and Rodney Slater at Transportation for O'Leary at Energy. Bill Daley at Commerce for Kantor, after Ron Brown. Gore winced. "It will have to go some, but it's close," he said. "It could be." The president seemed to agree. High-caliber but not a home run. Maybe a little less creative upside. Gore left to work on tomorrow's announcements, and Hernreich came in to say she was going home.

Clinton finished the night on Israel. He admitted a diplomatic mistake three days ago at his joint White House press conference with Prime Minister John Bruton of Ireland and Jacques Santer, president of the European Commission. In a jumble of questions bounced between them, his simple reply of yes came out confirming that the Israeli settlements themselves—rather than the *issue* of West Bank settlements—were "an obstacle to peace." Clinton blamed the ensuing tempest partly on his ears. He said the military doctors had pushed him for some time to get microscopic hearing aids. The controversial statement represented his true opinion, of course, but it probably would haunt him at some later crossroads. Therefore, he regretted the slip. In the short run, however, the public uproar might do some good. People believed—rightly—that he felt almost a religious sense of identity with Israel, and the visible outrage of American Jews might boost his leverage with Palestinians. He needed to shake up negotiations stalled dangerously over Hebron. Four hundred Israeli settlers lived there precariously among 140,000 Palestinians, in an ancient city revered by Jews and Muslims alike as the tomb site for their common patriarch, Abraham. Sacred and explosive, like a miniature Jerusalem, Hebron was the last sticking point for the timetable set in motion at the White House three years ago.

Clinton's description of the impasse peeled back layers of pretense and paradox. Every move seemed to be a feint in the opposite direction, like jujitsu. Public expectations for Hebron tilted against Israel—because of its tiny, contested presence there along with lingering infamy from the lone Israeli settler's massacre of its worshipping Muslims in 1994. Arafat had milked this advantage for the Palestinians down into details cursed or appreciated by close partisans, but then he froze. To close the current interim agreement would be cast as a victory for him, which subtly would reverse burdens in the next round. Netanyahu and the Israelis would gain credit for concessions, while civil control of Hebron inevitably would bring many headaches to the Palestinian Authority. Arafat also figured that Netanyahu's right-wing parties would bring heavy pressure again to compensate for Hebron, perhaps with an aggressive stunt like September's commando excavation under the Temple Mount, which in turn would incite attacks on the peace process by Palestinian groups like Hamas, weakening Arafat. Therefore, Clinton concluded, Arafat burrowed in where he was—on the verge of a Hebron agreement—while Netanyahu emphasized his generous terms on the table.

Dennis Ross, the able Middle East envoy, had just been dispatched with two secret letters from Clinton. The president said one warned Arafat to close the deal on Hebron or risk losing assistance from the United States. The other sharply advised Netanyahu to focus on the substantive peace process rather than quarrels within the Israeli cabinet. By taking the high road, Bibi could scarcely do worse for himself. He trailed Peres already by seven points in polls restricted to Israeli Jews, which Clinton called an unprecedented slip for a Likud prime minister. With virtually all the Israeli Arabs certain to vote for Peres, Netanyahu would lose a national election today by fifteen points. His erratic, gruff start had produced omens of such resounding political failure that many of Clinton's advisers considered him a lightweight, out of his depth. The president summarized an internal debate about Netanyahu's potential. He traced impressions from Netanyahu's early written work through their personal encounters, noting his charged legacy as a surviving brother of Lt. Col. Yonatan "Yoni" Netanyahu, the leader and only fatality among the 1976 commandos who famously rescued hijacked Israelis and French Jews from the Entebbe Airport in Uganda.* Clinton felt in Bibi the strong pull of idealized, decisive force against career experience patiently defending the policies of other Israeli governments. He said Netanyahu's shining ambition—to win reelection and become the ten-year prime minister who lifted young Israel into secure respect—was in severe jeopardy.

Once again, my predawn dictation soon would regret the groggy loss of precise language from a striking run of oratory on tape. Clinton said, he, for one, was not giving up on Netanyahu. He thought Bibi was still feeling his way along, with his head and heart often divided. In spite of their differences, Clinton identified with Netanyahu from early stumbles in the White House. He recalled his personal shock in the first transition, when the grim budget numbers convinced him to put deficit reduction ahead of the promised tax cut for the middle class. His political gut took months to accept his own rational decision. And it had been wrenching to adjust his historical logic on the destiny of gay and lesbian soldiers to a firestorm of emotional protest.

Out of these thoughts, the president expressed more than once a general lesson that leaders need to be at peace—not totally at peace, but roughly united in mind and spirit. He said torment skews judgment. If you are upset, you will lack the self-command to hear opposing views, without which you cannot even stand wisely on your own. A job like this requires a settled base inside, he kept saying, because decisions every day can offend and hurt people in very large numbers. He continued sporadically on this theme even after we packed up.

---

* The July 3–4, 1976, Entebbe raid attracted lasting study and inspired at least five feature films. All seven hijackers were killed, including two from Germany's Revolutionary Cells, along with forty-five soldiers deployed to defend them by Uganda's pro-Palestinian president, Idi Amin. The Israelis safely extricated 102 of the 105 hostages.

CHAPTER TWENTY-FIVE

BITTERSWEET RENEWAL

Wednesday, January 8, 1997

Second Inauguration
Monday, January 20, 1997

My plan went awry. Rather than belaboring him about Reno or Jiang Zemin, I had decided to recommend bold departures in the second term. Clinton was seeking ideas for his encore inaugural address, when most presidents offer modest agendas on a theme of staying the course. I thought he should hazard major initiatives instead, on the order of Kennedy's vow to land on the moon or Nixon's opening to China. Even if they stall, dramatic ventures broaden perspective. They could enhance appreciation for Clinton's ongoing peace efforts and economic achievements. Big fights of consequence to voters might even relieve tabloid fevers beneath Clinton's problem with Reno. On this reasoning, I rehearsed four ideas for the informal moments before and after our January 8 session—only to botch the presentation.

Inauspiciously, we worked in the family parlor so the president could keep an eye on the basketball game between Auburn and his Arkansas Razorbacks. Chelsea came in looking for her mother. We speculated briefly about her impending choice of college, failing to elicit much, and I remarked in her wake that both our daughters were youngest among their classmates. Just today I had taken Macy, who was a grade behind Chelsea, to get her first driver's license at sixteen. Clinton paused, saying the quick visit reminded him to buzz the White House operators. They must put through no calls to the bedroom, he instructed, because the first lady was already asleep.

On tape, the president reviewed his turnover. "It's always the ones you really wish would leave who stay," he said wanly. "And the ones you most want to stay wind up leaving." Above all, he would miss Cisneros. He said people had no idea how much he contributed to the government. At the White House, he regretted particularly the resignations of religion adviser Bill Galston, economist Laura Tyson, and chief of staff Panetta—all of whom were leaving to recover time with their families. These jobs take such a cruel toll on home life that Clinton said he could not allow himself any patriotic jawboning for them to stay. Al Gore, who shared in personnel decisions, gave him comfort about all the replacements, including chief of staff Erskine Bowles. I asked whether it bothered Clinton that Bowles so readily stressed his own doubts in soliloquies about whether he was cut out for politics. A little bit, he replied. The president called Bowles a rare example of reverse family pressure, saying his wife encouraged him to temper wealth through public service. By choosing Bowles over Panetta's other deputy, Harold Ickes, he acknowledged a sacrifice in passion. Ickes was an elemental force. Clinton traced personal ties and his deep political indebtedness to Ickes. He needed management over zeal right now, however, and no deputy should report to a former peer of the opposite temperament. There was no job for Ickes, he said with a sigh, yearning to heal the rupture over time.

I sagged inwardly. This preference for orderly deliberation did not bode well for my grand suggestions, but Clinton swerved into outrage over the final transitions yet undone. There was dereliction at the Democratic National Committee. So far, only one woman had fallen on her sword with a forthright statement that its compliance department had been shut down in mid-campaign, apparently as a cost-cutting measure. DNC chair Dan Fowler, having approved the change, was out. Clinton himself was summoning a string of officials after Fowler, but nobody had coughed up a straight answer about what happened and why. He thought fund-raiser Terry McAuliffe vaguely knew. Compliance officers performed the vital task of screening major donations for improprieties and embarrassments, such as a pending criminal case. "I don't have a hundred percent of the facts yet," Clinton kept saying. Later, taking a telephone update from campaign aide Doug Sosnik, the president actually reversed roles by relaying to Sosnik fresh inconsistencies in the accounts given him by several employees.

This issue gnawed at him all night. He said the discontinued screening was wrong, stupid, and a potentially legitimate scandal, like the improper FBI files found at the White House. He felt rightly accountable for any taint of real corruption. For negligible savings in staff salaries, the DNC had triggered a bigger press uproar than Filegate over questionable contributions totaling far less than one percent of receipts. Enterprising reporters compared gifts returned by the screeners with those later accepted, said the president, but their stories dripped with bigotry. First, they wrote exclusively about Asians, such as John Huang, a former Commerce Department employee who raised money for the DNC. Second, they hyped suspicion that political contact with Asians concealed some sinister commercial deal or spy plot. No one blinked when Clinton's Polish donors met with him about NATO expansion into Poland. His black donors talked routinely about affirmative action, Jews about Israel, and Greeks about practically nothing but Cyprus. Only Asians excited the press, he seethed, because racism and their vast numbers could make them seem scary. Stories intimated that his friend Yah Lin "Charlie" Trie sneaked into the White House with bundles of cash to foment war with China over Taiwan. Clinton remembered being one of the first customers at Trie's tiny Chinese restaurant twenty years ago. Once his businesses subsequently prospered, Trie tried to help his fellow dreamer with more enthusiasm than prudence, by corralling contributions to the Clinton Defense Fund from fellow entrepreneurs—some of whom had immigration problems, or used corporate accounts. Trie had come all the way from Little Rock in a tuxedo to go through a Christmas receiving line, just so he could tell Clinton he never meant to hurt or embarrass him. Overwrought, Trie turned away and went straight home.

To enliven a dull presidential campaign, it was a short leap from the media stampede against Asians into rampant speculation that Clinton must be selling the Lincoln Bedroom. This story "had legs" without a brain, he snorted. Every president entertains supporters more than enemies, and plenty of overnight guests never contributed a dime. No one made a credible allegation that his administration ever sold changes in government policy.

Something about Clinton provoked an antagonism spread broadly across the press, yet still unpersuasive to most voters, and he churned again through possible causes. In Washington, portrayed as an anxious club, the president found himself a repellent intruder and irksome symbol of the watershed 1960s. He sensed it keenly from the flagships *Washington Post* and *New York Times,* personified by the *Times*'s editorial page chief, Howell Raines. Somebody asked Raines about his transparent animosity toward Clinton in light of their common Southern backgrounds—both being prodigies shaped by the civil rights era, said to have grown up fond of hunting in the woods. Quoting the fabled reply—"Well, I didn't hunt like *he* did"—the president thought Raines was driven to advertise sensibilities refined well above some hillbilly Bubba from Arkansas. Writ large, this attitude sustained a herd journalism of cheap thrills in condescension.

"I am bitter about it," Clinton declared flatly, but his mind poked from a lingering torpor. He said skewed coverage certainly cost him the satisfaction of hitting 50 percent in the popular vote. It may have cost him the House, which affected legislation for many citizens. Beyond that, it helped drive down national turnout to the lowest percentage since 1924, fostering cynicism. To top things off, images of a playpen White House corrupted by Asians managed simultaneously to stoke public outrage and kill any reasonable hope for campaign reform. Clinton explained this contradictory feat from the viewpoint of Senator Mitch McConnell, the key Republican obstructionist on campaign reform. The current system favored Republicans. Their party committees outraised Democrats by $150 million in 1996, with RNC chair Haley Barbour making pitches in at least three foreign countries and the vice chair of Dole's finance committee sent to prison over a money laundering scheme out of Hong Kong. Nonetheless, Republicans not only kept their huge advantage, and skipped all the heartache of seeking change, but they also neatly dodged any blame. Why? "Because the press is shitting all over the president instead of us," said Clinton, finishing McConnell's delighted pitch. Election reform would test minds and mettle in the best of circumstances, but the press climate now blinkered all reality. Why would any sane Republican contemplate limits on money in politics? In their shoes, said the president, he would have to be against reform himself.

HIS MOOD BRIGHTENED. Once again, oddly, the president climbed from tirades at the press into more pleasant, fraternal stories about political opponents. After a White House parley, he had asked Senator Alan Simpson in confidence whether Republican strategists really believed the Clintons did something terrible in Whitewater, like theft or perjury. He mimicked the hearty response. "Oh, hell no," cried Simpson. "But our goal is to make people *think* you did, so we can pay you Democrats back for Iran-contra."* Clinton chuckled with appreciation. Politicians understood payback. Iran-contra did address alleged abuses of presidential power, unlike Whitewater, he quibbled to me, but politics waved aside such distinctions along with actual truth in the charges. He admitted running Medicare ads during the campaign to avenge Republican attacks on his 1994 health care plan, and now Republicans were vowing to stick it to him on the budget because he had distorted their Medicare proposals. Similarly, said Clinton, Democrats were about to get even with Speaker Gingrich for spearheading the 1989 ethics investigation that toppled Democratic speaker Jim Wright.† When Gingrich endured the House reprimand being negotiated, and paid its $300,000 fine for

---

* The Iran-contra affair, which came to light in 1986, linked two clandestine endeavors by high officials of the Reagan administration. They sold weapons to factions of Iran's proscribed, hostile government, hoping to secure the release of U.S. hostages held by Hezbollah. Separately, they diverted proceeds from the sales illegally to anti-Communist contra rebels fighting in Nicaragua. In late 1992, President George H. W. Bush pardoned eleven people convicted for crimes related to these transactions, including Reagan's former defense secretary Caspar Weinberger, and former national security adviser Robert "Bud" McFarlane.

† Wright was accused of arranging bulk purchases of his autobiography, *Reflections of a Public Man,* to circumvent limits on the outside income allowed for members of Congress. He resigned from the House in June of 1989, having represented Fort Worth, Texas, since 1955.

profiteering, he would keep the speaker's gavel in a severely weakened state, Clinton predicted, especially since he was never warmly admired within his own caucus.

"Our politics are like Bosnia," the president observed. Leaders were so trapped in cycles of payback for prior injuries and wrongs, with the press egging on every fight, that it was hard to see any larger context. He seemed blithely philosophical about this picture. Then again, he suggested that a Bosnia could be the epitome of politics—if, finally, you could *attain* that rare, higher plane—which reminded him of Bob Dole. After cutting each other up for years, the president and his vanquished foe were colluding to safeguard the Bosnian peace process. Dole was going there to encourage the troops. Clinton said he had come to the White House on December 20, the day after our previous session in the West Wing, for what turned out to be a sentimental roast. They swapped yarns and personal memories. Dole chortled that every time he had gotten something going for his campaign—sticking a knife in Clinton here, rousing the crowds there—Clinton would do something presidential and make him look bad again. Finally, Clinton had introduced an earnest question by praising his elder's vastly greater experience in Washington. "That's what I tried to tell people," Dole interrupted merrily, "but it didn't work." Seriously, Clinton persisted, are most politicians more or less corrupt than when Dole started in the 1950s? "Not even close," Dole replied. "They're a lot cleaner now than they were back then." What about the press? Less responsible. If their shared experience had not made them friends already, Clinton and Dole communed like songbirds over their misunderstood profession.

Apart from occasional rants about tabloid politics, his tone remained steady through trials and bad news. "I hate to say this, even on the tape," the president answered on another topic, "but I think for the first time that the whole Israeli-Palestinian track may go south." This was not a sudden hunch or independent judgment, he hastened to say. He picked up most of his outlook from Dennis Ross and other Middle East negotiators, whom he considered the best people in the world on this issue. They had battered their wits against the convoluted Hebron impasse for months. On New Year's Day, after an Israeli private inexplicably opened fire in a Hebron market, wounding more than a dozen Palestinians,

Clinton said his calls included long condolences with Yasir Arafat. The president used all his suasion urging Arafat to finish Hebron first and tackle all his other problems later, but he could elicit no response much beyond, "I understand what you are saying. Thank you for your interest." Maybe the translator made it sound more wooden than it was. Maybe time would help. Although the remaining deal points were not inherently difficult, Arafat and Netanyahu had moved into an insoluble standoff. It was a freak of political logic, and failure of the Oslo process would reverberate through the region. "I don't know where the bottom is," he said.

I gulped. We moved on to the tax system and a diplomatic crisis out of Lima, Peru, where fourteen Tupac Amaru (MRTP) guerrillas had seized four hundred hostages at a party in the Japanese ambassador's residence. On taxes, the president described a private audience with Republican Bill Archer of Houston, newly chair of the House Ways and Means Committee, who was obsessed by a dream to abolish income taxes and the IRS. Noting my flinch, Clinton said he was also a likable gentleman who loved his country. Curious, the president had drawn Archer out on his substitute plan to finance the federal government on a broad-based consumption tax. It had some good features, promising to capture revenue from the underground cash economy, and the two men confronted calculations that any consumption tax large enough would paralyze the economy with inflation. Archer resisted Clinton's notion of a much smaller consumption tax, which could eliminate income taxes for families earning up to $60,000, because his ideological goal was precisely the opposite—to liberate rich people from the IRS. Still, they detected in common some sensitive problems, such as the depressing effect of payroll taxes on jobs and small business. The president played with economic numbers of every sort. Just today, he noted, Fed chairman Alan Greenspan had come in with a well-crafted technical analysis of another idea favored by Archer—to buttress Social Security by investing its current annual surplus of $60 billion on Wall Street. Many strange consequences would offset the joy among stockbrokers. Public funds would inflate stock prices, but corporate yields would go down. Even Greenspan perceived limits on business as a rock-ribbed panacea above politics.

On Peru, international tensions had ratcheted upward for nearly a month. Clinton said Japanese officials first had demanded restraint against cries for a showdown, fearing not only for their many citizens and dignitaries held hostage but also, indirectly, for Japan's reputation, because the standoff advertised a novel South American presence that included Peru's elected president, Alberto Fujimori, who was of Japanese descent. Secretly, however, the Tokyo government had since reversed course, sensing even greater danger from Fujimori himself. A notorious hothead, Fujimori had overthrown his own regime to consolidate power in 1992, inventing the term "self-coup" ("*autogolpe*"). Now, Clinton disclosed, Hashimoto's ministers were pressing the United States to supply elite action teams for a rescue attempt before Fujimori blasted into the hostage site with Peruvian troops. Spy agencies were buzzing, but the president outlined his methodical resistance. Where was the national interest to risk lives, given no U.S. hostages? Could Fujimori be trusted for coordination in his country? "Those terrorists are as close to the hostages as I am to you," said the president. How many things could go wrong in the best-laid "mission-impossible"? The whole thing reminded him of bureaucratic inertia into the Waco disaster, which seemed ever more like his Bay of Pigs. FBI promises back then, he decided, had covered fatigue and an itch to get it over. What kind of reason was that? Lima looked worse. He was nowhere near granting approval.

Anticipating more tension, I asked about the protest resignations from high positions in the health department by Mary Jo Bane and Peter Edelman, who issued a stinging dissent against the welfare reform law. The president said he had spoken with neither of them. In fact, Edelman's wife, Marian—Clinton's longtime friend through Hillary—had started breaking off contact during deliberations on the bill last year. Did I not see his statement? The president had commended Edelman and Bane. Theirs were honestly held beliefs that the reform bill would do more harm than good, and Clinton had misgivings himself. He admitted fresh doubt that he could soon repair the law's two harsh defects—on legal immigrants, and food stamps for working mothers—because these hot-button disputes were entangled in his budget wars with Republicans. Still, short of ending poverty, the president emphasized his resolve to disentangle race and gender from the debate. He hoped to break chronic dependencies in the inner cities, but welfare was a very difficult issue.

How could he blame these people for resigning? He said they did exactly what public servants should do in such a conflict.

DISTRACTIONS RATTLED ME through the final topics. On television, after his Arkansas team won a thriller by one point, my Tar Heels blew a 22-point lead in the second half to lose by 10 points to Maryland. We could scarcely believe it, and the president could not remember so devastating a fold at UNC over the long career of Coach Dean Smith. Then, as I rewound the tapes, he mentioned his dissatisfaction with the current drafts for his second inaugural address. There was a lot of work ahead. Would I help again, if I had time for more than our talks about thematic slogans? Not yet, though. He was not quite ready with his own ideas, and he was way past worn-out for tonight.

At this invitation, in retrospect, I made my mistake. I should have volunteered simply to wait, or previewed perhaps one of my initiatives, but I chatted instead about which writers were working on the speech. Remembering his preference for the orderly integrity in Bowles, over the passion from Ickes, I debated whether a pitch for big themes was fruitless or more urgent. Also, his thorny comments just now in our session gave me pause, to say the least, on two of my four proposals: the quest for a radically simplified tax structure, and a new approach to campaign reform, beyond overblown dreams for the McCain-Feingold bill. In the end, I stalled with a tangential preface on reasons why Clinton needed to challenge or shake the country back to its senses. We had not always agreed about the likely motives behind his press criticism, I opined, nor how they fit with the political forces called Whitewater, but *Newsweek*'s cover story on Paula Jones shocked even me. I had bought a copy to verify details that seemed incredible. Sure enough, the magazine used lavish studio portraits rather than staff photographs for Jones, complete with published credits for makeup, accessories, a public relations firm, clothes, and so forth, like a movie star layout.

The president shrugged, glancing at the magazine. He knew, of course, that the Supreme Court was about to hear arguments about whether the Paula Jones defamation suit against him should go forward now, after he leaves office, or not at all. That was the news peg, but what did the story say? Well, I had only skimmed in vain for anything about the constitutional precedent. It seemed entirely personal. I stumbled to close a topic I regretted raising already.

His mind was elsewhere. "Do they say I did it?" he asked—harassed her, or had sex with her. Not that I saw, but they implied so. The story sympathized with Jones to the point of being confessional about cultural bias. How so? Well, one striking passage repented for branding her a "Dogpatch Madonna" who liked pinching boys' behinds at the Red Lobster. The writers also claimed to have downplayed her case because it was plainly sponsored by a consortium of influential right-wingers, but now they realized that the lowliest political plaintiff still deserved her day in court. Their tone of dramatic conversion felt more like a Nashville song than a national news magazine. *Newsweek* vowed to see if a two-term president would do right by Paula Jones. "What do they suggest?" asked the president. Basically, that he would have done better to apologize from the start. "Apologize for what?" he pressed. "I didn't do it. I *can't* apologize."

By then we were standing outside the president's private elevator next to the back stairwell, where he often walked me to say good night. We went back and forth on formulas of generalized remorse that might salvage a compromise, without much success. He did not believe her feelings or public shame controlled the case, anyway. We lapsed, exhausted, but I could not break off conversation now. "One more thing, Mr. President," I said. For the inaugural address, or the upcoming State of the Union, would he consider a proposal to expand his peace efforts beyond crisis missions and wars? Perhaps he could summon the world to prepare for the return of democracy in Cuba, or its birth in Myanmar (Burma), or even Saudi Arabia. No president ever had done so. Clinton need not make demands, nor claim all the answers. Indeed, a format of questions would be more democratic in spirit—surely controversial, yet perhaps more productive. What could the nations do to help? Would the pope give a blessing? How could citizens, thinkers, and international organizations encourage democracy?

He was nodding. He asked about a mutual friend, John Shattuck at his State Department,* wondering what post he might seek for the sec-

---

* Assistant secretary of state for democracy, human rights, and labor, 1993–98; U.S. ambassador to the Czech Republic, 1998–2000.

ond term, adding that we were pretty well caught up on the tapes, were we not, and thanks again so much for doing this. His farewell kindnesses made it harder to suggest finally a leap into the unknown toward alternative power—cars powered by electricity, or natural gas, getting upward of a hundred miles per gallon, rescuing the balance of payments, healing the environment. I said there was ample precedent. By exhortation and subsidy, Washington had catalyzed transformation from the earliest canals and railroads down to jet aircraft and space travel, which helped miniaturize the computer.

"Yes, we've done that in the past," the president commented. He referred to obscure theoretical research with hydrogen, and secret experiments by General Motors, but his nods turned wearily sideways. "I can't talk anymore," he said sharply. "I'm too tired." I left fretting that I had overdone it—pushed too hard—kicking myself for a foolish detour into the Paula Jones case.

THE COMPOSITION OF Clinton's second inaugural address became another rodeo ride. My early efforts never established the need for a new watchword, replacing the "bridge to the twenty-first century" from his successful campaign. Many suggestions floundered for good reason, until the speechwriters relayed objections to "New Freedom" as a stale repeat of Woodrow Wilson's campaign slogan in 1912. This struck me as overly sensitive. I asked them to reread Wilson's pretentious first inaugural ("The scales of heedlessness have fallen from our eyes"), which never mentioned freedom of any kind. By fax, I sent a gingerly appeal through Nancy Hernreich, asking President Clinton to consider the phrase a possible step forward from his 1993 theme of renewal and change. "America is always about freedom (not World Order)," I wrote, "but its challenges now are scrambled across the board, from the Cold War's end to the ongoing restructuring of politics and the economy. Therefore, we need a New Freedom."

Nothing happened. When speechwriter Don Baer forwarded early drafts of a complete address, I found no bold new initiatives, and the watchword was still a "bridge." This was only mildly disappointing. I figured myself lucky to have had input at all. For all our excitement, the inaugural freelancers of 1993 had claimed modest contributions at best, and the history project was enough volunteer politics for me. Happily, the skeleton of this speech was about history. I found its scope impressive and creative, if a tad academic. Baer said the idea came straight from the president, who wanted to set the stage for a third new century in the American experiment. While crises have shaped American politics in many eras, most obviously the Depression and our grievous wars, Clinton would say that each changeover has allowed fateful choices amid relative calm. Around 1800, the Founders shaped original institutions to accommodate a transcontinental republic. A century later, Theodore Roosevelt's Progressive movement retooled national government to balance industrial power. Now again, according to the president, Americans faced transformation in a lull of prosperity, with no whip of bombs or breadlines—this time while hurtling into a global age of technology. Fundamental choices for the millennium could be peaceful, if wise, but they were inescapable.

I faxed down a few minor suggestions on language. On Saturday the 18th, two days before the inauguration, Christy and I went down to the Smithsonian Museum for a reunion concert by Bernice Johnson Reagon and the Freedom Singers. They shook the hall with inspired music from the civil rights movement, punctuated by short, humorous tributes to historical figures in the audience, many of whom figured in my daily work—Bob Moses, James Forman, Victoria Gray Adams, Guy Carawan, Julian Bond, and others. Several of us ventured to the White House for a massive pre-inaugural reception, where, jammed elbow to elbow in conversation and cocktails, I marveled at the contrasting intimacy of my sessions upstairs. The president appeared from a swirling eye of guests, making his way hand over hand in a stream of greetings and recognition, for spare sentences of contact with us. He thanked Christy for the frog sculpture. The speech was somewhat in flux. They had tightened it. He was still thinking about my edits, and I should get the final version faxed tomorrow. Questions trailed in his wake. How much flux? Which edits? Not knowing what had gotten through, or survived, there was no way to interpret what he meant. Even up close, the modern presidency can feel like a blind man's trip to the circus.

Baer called Sunday morning to say everything had changed. Could I come down right away? Apparently, two newspaper columns had thrown the president into a tizzy—one by Garry Wills, the other by Walter Shapiro—both warning of Clinton's tendency to get by on sparkling rhetoric about policy and process to the exclusion of overarching goals. Clinton decided they were right. He was stuck on his bridge, with too many plans to describe its features and not enough vision of the other side. Now he wanted more oratory to point, lift our eyes, and summon up purpose with direction. I assumed Baer resuscitated me as an anti-bridge man, now that these columnists had made my case. Baer sighed that the morning alarm was wrenching proof of how seriously Clinton took press criticism on the merits, as opposed to ad hominem trifles.

My truck left the Truman Balcony at 1:27 the next morning, heading back to Baltimore after we worked once around the clock. Hillary had rescued me the previous noon. She said the residence was deserted because the president was napping from another long night. I should report to the West Wing basement, where Baer threw me right into the next round of assignments between rehearsals. Michael Waldman, Tommy Caplan, and Michael Sheehan, the speech coach, were back from 1993. Stephanopoulos was gone. Paul Begala and speechwriter David Shipley were new, along with Henry Cisneros, who put me close to awe as we worked on several teams together. He was razor-smart, cheerful, and serene. Without letting on about what the president had told me about his persecution, I did ask why he kept at this extra duty for several days running. He said it was what he enjoyed. Awkwardly, I asked what he would do afterward, meaning to survive the special prosecutor's onslaught. Well, he smiled, there would be sleep first, because tomorrow he would be out of a job.

The 1997 inauguration fell on the Martin Luther King holiday. Cisneros and I worked together on two paragraphs about race, among other sections in the address. Improvements there made me briefly a hero, as the presumed expert on Dr. King, until President Clinton halted a rehearsal in the White House theater. He stumbled over a phrase that racial hatreds in American history "nearly destroyed us." No, he said. This wording put them in the past. They were still with us, in diminished form, and they were part of larger forces that fuel ethnic wars and terrorism. He reworked the section again in fits and starts. "The divide of race has been America's constant curse," his final version began. Related fears and obsessions "cripple both those who hate and of course those who are hated . . ." The revisions invoked King's patriotic determination "to replace them [racial hatreds] with the generous spirit of a people who feel at home with one another."

One consultation took place in the Oval Office. It was a limited summons instead of a general fire drill, policed to the president's wish by White House aide Rahm Emanuel. He admitted Baer, Cisneros, and me. President Clinton was pacing. This was not visual enough, he said. He wanted to paint a picture, even in the history section. Sometimes, with our very survival at stake, Americans have been forced to adapt. But other times, coincidentally or providentially at the turn of centuries, we have made freer and more positive choices. Jefferson did not *have* to buy Louisiana, he emphasized, but if he didn't we'd be singing "Dixie" or speaking French. Teddy Roosevelt didn't *have* to embrace progressive new nationalism, but if he didn't we'd be fiefdoms more like Brazil. Now again, we have a chance to shape the future, and if we don't there will be consequences. We agreed that this charge should frame the whole address. Its first paragraph was the weakest. Clinton should tell the nation what he saw across the bridge. He should name it.

The task carried over several caucuses, with many suggestions revived and discarded. "New Freedom" was still out because of Wilson. Baer said they had been working on variations of "Promised Land." The president mentioned "New Balance" but quickly spiked it himself. "Age of Possibility" made a run until he told us Hillary hated both the sound and substance. Eventually he approved "New Promise," and my sole surviving draft sentence incorporated it to close the first paragraph: "Guided by the ancient vision of a promised land, let us set our sights upon a land of new promise."

President Clinton tweaked the whole address with visual images for his thematic "land of new promise." Its structure followed a division into thirds from the historical introduction on our choices at the turn of three centuries. "This is the heart of our task," began the programmatic section. "With a new vision of government, a new sense of responsibility, and a new spirit of community, we will sustain America's journey." We tried to create a picture of responsibility even to erase the federal deficit. Mark Penn, the pollster, protested loudly that phrases about peace and children laughing in safe schools sounded too Pollyannaish. Some were trimmed or polished, but most stayed through a "final" rehearsal at eleven o'clock—then two more after that.

"Fourteen minutes," shouted Sheehan with a stopwatch. "That's all?" asked Clinton, immensely pleased. He wanted three clean copies sent upstairs, with one for Chelsea. Baer kept yelling, "We're going to clear the room."

Rebecca Cameron, Nancy Hernreich's assistant, left word of tickets for Christy and me on the inaugural platform. After the briefest sleep, we headed by morning train back to Washington, and our seats made us glad we bought a disposable panoramic camera in Union Station. We were four rows behind big armchairs for the Clintons and Gores. I took photographs of the grand vista. The aisle seat next to me was empty, marked for Dr. King's son Dexter, and Jesse Jackson slipped into it just before the ceremony. Irrepressibly, he stepped into the stairwell after the benediction, ignoring the stern security instructions, to form a solo receiving line for President Clinton and the dignitaries who followed— Billy Graham, Rev. Gardner Taylor, soloist Jessye Norman, Strom Thurmond, Newt Gingrich, Chief Justice William Rehnquist, the other justices, the Joint Chiefs, and the cabinet.

Some six hours later, from a pay phone in a restaurant, I called home to check for messages from our children, but there was only a crisp instruction from a White House operator to call the president. Its tone was so startling and peremptory that I played it back to record her voice. President Clinton soon came on the line to thank me for all my work, but he nearly moaned. "The early reviews have hurt us pretty bad," he said. Already? What did they say? "Well, Doris Kearns Goodwin and Stephen Ambrose and Haynes Johnson dumped all over it," he said. They called it devoid of conviction, written after consulting the polls. Ordinary. Vague. A stump speech. Their kindest comment was that he faced no crisis and therefore had nothing to say.

I dangled, fumbling for my own reaction. This made me sorry and sad, I told him. Whatever its eventual reputation, the address did not deserve instant disdain. To lighten the moment, I said this was my first call on a cell phone, for privacy, borrowed from the restaurant owner. She was a native of Bratislava, and did not speak flawless English, but for what it's worth she said all her workers had watched the speech and were crying, very moved. The president knew her name, of course. He said the poll reactions from regular people were good, but commentators were uniformly hostile. Not just these historians. Well, their reactions sounded like prepackaged contempt, I said, but then checked myself. Even if true, this notion offered cold comfort and paranoia. More pleasantly, I thanked him for whoever had supplied such wonderful platform seats. They were a thrilling relief from my stowaway squat in 1993. I hoped to see him again soon. It was a privilege to work on the address. History would treat it and him with greater respect.

CHAPTER TWENTY-SIX

WHITEWATER TAPES: ON THE HIGH WIRE

Thursday, February 6, 1997

Thursday, March 6, 1997

Al Gore passed in the back stairwell, bounding down from the White House residence just after the usher waved me up to the Treaty Room. His greeting was so cheerful that I mentioned my historic photograph of him as President of the United States. Gore stopped. From the inauguration? Yes, I replied—on the platform while Jessye Norman sang. Gore, needing no further explanation, drew himself up to stately posture. Of course, he said. Far fewer crimes had been committed during the Gore administration than any other. Deadpan, he rattled off a star list of records and achievements. Such pleasant tranquillity had reigned that his term seemed to transpire in the blink of an eye.

The vice president's banter deceived me. Upstairs, a comment about his dry humor produced only solemn frowns. What Gore administration? Late? Clinton said the ceremony had started precisely on time. Yes, but Billy Graham's long prayer delayed the presidential oath past expiration at noon, as fixed by the Constitution, and Gore was arguably president for those next five minutes. A few dismissive questions made clear why the president had been excluded prudently from jests about a technical interregnum, and I backpedaled with compliments for the State of the Union speech only two days before. This reprise of his second inaugural allowed Clinton to shrug off the universal scorn from pundits. Perhaps the difference was extra rehearsal for the second try, he said, or visible impact in the House chamber, where his delivery commanded standing ovations from the Republican opposition. Most important, the cumulative message lifted his polls off the charts. More than 70 percent of voters approved his job performance, stated goals, and the national direction on nearly every front—by the highest figures ever reached by a second-term president in peacetime. He and Gore had been analyzing the numbers, said Clinton, which accounted for the bounce in their step.

Ebullience trumped adversity for two sessions. He said Dennis Ross had browbeaten Arafat and Netanyahu into a decent agreement on Hebron, somewhat to his surprise, after a final snag traced to Egypt. "We woke up Mubarak at two in the morning, during Ramadan," said Clinton. "He was fairly good-natured about it. I asked him not to delay it any further, and he agreed." Egypt's role in Israeli-Palestinian negotiations was psychologically gnarled, because Mubarak, who sulked when relegated to the sidelines, could be tempted by the spotlight to rally Arab grievances instead of a peacemaker's resolve. In Serbia, the dictator Milosevic had withdrawn his annulment of unfavorable municipal election results after seventy-eight consecutive days of street demonstrations. Now he was shaky amid celebrations of his retreat. It wouldn't help to tell Milosevic that losing elections and getting lambasted in the press was not the end of the world, Clinton said, laughing. Separately, he explained tensions from the Khobar Towers bombing in Saudi Arabia. The Saudi monarchs could not countenance either a domestic or international terrorist plot, especially if it originated in powerful Iran. He said the royals—being counterfeit relics to democratic reformers and Muslim fundamentalists alike—felt compelled simply to execute suspects without asking questions, but their autocratic ways blocked basic answers in the deaths of the seventeen U.S. soldiers. This terrible dilemma drove Clinton to express sympathy for once with FBI Director Louis Freeh, who had denounced Saudi obstruction. Understandably frustrated to solve the case, said the president, Freeh did not know or care that his unauthorized remarks could tip the precarious Middle East.

At home, Senate Republicans had dug in their heels against the president's proposal to restore welfare benefits for legal immigrants. They needed the savings to finance tax cuts instead, Majority Leader Trent Lott candidly advised, and Clinton was philosophical about the standoff. He said it revealed a severe shortage of substantive issues for the other party. Meanwhile, his administration conducted an internal debate about whether economic trends were too good to last. Growth in the fourth quarter held at a robust 4.7 percent. Welfare rolls dropped by 18 percent. The economy had generated eleven million new jobs since Clinton took office, with the stock market already more than double his incoming Dow Jones average of 3,200. Some advisers thought they were pushing the business cycle beyond natural limits, he said, and Greenspan's experts reflexively sought higher interest rates whenever unemployment dipped below 5.5 percent. However, no signs of systemic inflation appeared. By healthy cooperation, said Clinton, his people half-convinced the Fed that budget discipline and the constraints of international trade could expand the safe horizons of a full-employment economy.

The president carried resilient stories even through sadness, such as the recent death of Ambassador to France Pamela Harriman. He celebrated her life for nearly half an hour. In 1981, when Clinton was wounded and confused as the nation's youngest ex-governor, newly ousted in his first bid for reelection, she had invited him to meet her third husband, Averell Harriman, in their Georgetown home. Still dazzled by its art collection, the president recalled several van Goghs and a little clay model based on a dancer painted by Degas. He had volunteered to ride with Mrs. Harriman to a public television station, offering tips on the way when she professed jitters about how to conduct herself in a political interview. Pretend the camera is one person, Clinton advised, and try to win that new acquaintance to your point of view. Several days later, a thunderclap judgment reached him by telephone in Arkansas: "Your future is assured!" It was his college friend Tommy Caplan, relaying a news squib that Harriman had named Clinton to her new group formulating strategy for Democrats to recover from the Reagan landslide. Caplan pronounced it certain that the grande dame had impeccable taste for young men on the rise.

Clinton reeled off lovers from her storybook past. They included several princes and barons, the owner of Fiat, and a stage producer for *The Sound of Music*, plus Edward R. Murrow. She married Winston Churchill's son, Randolph, at the age of nineteen. More than fifty years later, with President Jacques Chirac of France, she treated the Clintons to the best meal of their lives in Paris. He said he appointed her ambassador to France in part because she so reveled in her decade there as a young postwar publisher. Her son, Winston, had notified Clinton of her sudden death by stroke before a ritual swim at the Paris Ritz, and the president reviewed everything from pending tributes—making her the first foreign diplomat awarded France's Legion of Honor—down to simmering quarrels over the burial site. Some British relatives resented Averell Harriman's posthumous control of his widow, while surviving Harrimans had sued her lawyer Clark Clifford for squandering chunks of their inheritance.

Chelsea sidled in during the Harriman tales with a take-home biology exam. "Dad, can you time me?" she asked. To escape the phone in her room, she would be in the family parlor down the hall. Clinton excused himself soon after she left, whereupon his phone rang next to me. I debated whether to answer, foreseeing trouble either way. Sure enough, there was suspicion when I said no, I was not the president. Who are you, asked the White House operator, and where is he? I dissembled squeamishly, but rising panic in her voice made me blurt out that he was right there in the Treaty Room's hideaway bathroom. I rushed back and forth to the door. Yes, he did want to take the call, from Senator Chris Dodd. They discussed news coverage of the National Prayer Breakfast, which led on tape to a synopsis of Clinton's remarks there about the prophet Isaiah, and healing the breach, and how politicians must guard against reciprocating cynicism back toward the press. He admired the event's organizer, Linda Lader, calling her a whirlwind of theological sophistication mixed with Evangelical roots he traced through several generations. Her stepmother was the late Christian author Catherine Marshall.

We rolled through assorted topics including diversity itself. His available choices for a new Democratic Party chair led into the demographic marvels of modern Virginia, complete with details of a Fairfax County school district in which students learned English from more than a hundred spoken languages. The president told of three similar districts in other states. On the big picture, and history, Clinton said his first term had refuted Reagan's supply side economics, and progress slowly was rebutting the notion of federal governance as the enemy—parasitic, incompetent, and oppressive. This resentful stance—pioneered by George Wallace, cultivated by modern Republicans since Barry Goldwater, perfected by Reagan—had won elections by mobilizing voters against their government, sneering at Washington. Clinton found its myth so established that he tacked to change direction, renouncing "big government." Now he sought the balance of our heritage, which meant repairing the image of public service along with the capacity of government to function The country was addressing once intractable problems like debt and dependence. With tempered spirit from the Constitution's Preamble, we could hope to forge vital transformations for the next fifty years, and yet he claimed only a fragile chance to set any course. "For all I know, Russia will fall apart in six months," the president mused. "Or China will invade Taiwan. And then I'll be like Lincoln—'My policy is to have no policy.' I'd be controlled by external events."

Clinton left to tell Chelsea her allotted forty-five minutes were up. When he returned, I asked the parting favor of his signature on a report by Bertram Lee, a seven-year-old in Baltimore. According to my neighbor, young Lee had nagged his mother until she bought inauguration tickets, only to fall sick with chicken pox. Mother and son were enthusiastic supporters crushed by disappointment, as Clinton could tell from the first-grader's illustrated tablet. He sat down at Grant's desk to write Bertram a letter, waving off my flummoxed reminder that an autograph would do. Conceivably, offering a White House tour could change a life. "You never know," he said. "That's what I keep telling people around here." Some blind gesture might wind up more important than their huge schemes. This was a good session, he said at the door. He wished we could have them more often. Hillary had reminded him to record something, but he forgot what it was. And please assure Mr. Allen, the usher, that the president was turning out the lights upstairs.

•   •   •

ONE MONTH LATER, the president agreed to record a separate tape on the Whitewater scandals. This was a risky venture, contrary to legal instruction from David Kendall, but we did preserve impressions, from arcane history to courthouse gossip. Clinton's tone was unusually bright. He lapsed into bitterness only about the draconian humiliations forced on Susan McDougal, the former Whitewater banker's wife, who had been jailed on contempt, strip-searched, manacled, paraded in leg irons, locked down, and threatened with endless prison—all for silently refusing to invent some allegation against Clinton. The president remembered her as a vulnerable personality, now divorced and alone. "I'll never know where she finds the strength," he said, choking up. Otherwise, he maintained a kind of gallows humor. Hillary and Bernie Nussbaum, Clinton's first White House counsel, had been right. Against their learned, passionate advice, he had been a fool to establish the Whitewater special prosecutor. He called that pliant decision the biggest mistake of his presidency. Its immediate booby prize was $4 million in personal legal bills thus far, but lasting consequences would weaken the office for every successor. Wondering how this admission would look in history, he contemplated for the first time on record his future choices about how and when to open these tapes for research.

He took minor solace that Ken Starr would look bad. We ruminated about whether the internal records of the special prosecutor's office might ever become available under sunshine laws. Any authoritative history would reveal a bizarre mix of Starr's qualities: thin-skinned, cruel, and ridiculous. Starr had just resigned prior to any findings, Clinton thought, "because he didn't want to be there when the ship went down." Having failed to indict either Clinton, or even a cabinet officer, he tried to exit on the success of his secondary mission to drag out the inquest through the 1996 election—longer than the whole Watergate saga from break-in to Nixon's resignation. This was quite a negative feat, the president wryly observed, but it was not enough. Newspapers and Republicans raised howls of protest, branding Starr a quitter. William Safire doubted his ideological manhood, and Starr retracted the resignation within days.

Now Starr was stuck. When he leaked plans to dispose of his easiest issue, the Vince Foster case, right-wingers denounced him for abandoning their pet conspiracies of Clintonian murder, while liberals ridiculed him for taking three years to verify an obvious suicide. The Foster findings were postponed again, and Clinton predicted—crazily, I thought—that Starr could prolong Whitewater through the entire second term by hunkering down to await gifts like Webb Hubbell.* He said Starr, with the indulgence of Janet Reno, had transposed a billing dispute among Hubbell's Rose Law partners into a Whitewater federal crime. This gave him prosecutorial leverage to squeeze Hubbell like Susan McDougal, and the president thought he did so with special relish. Hubbell, as deputy attorney general, had reinstated ethical restrictions on the private representation of former targets by lawyers leaving the Justice Department. These rules cost Starr some lucrative corporate clients, provoking the animus of righteous wealth, and Clinton's Southern hyperbole could make Whitewater sound like an Ozarks blood feud. "Starr is mad," he said, "that Webb's four children haven't starved to death."

Also on the separate tape, President Clinton described a potential "new" Whitewater. Publicity about Asian contributors, which had died down after the campaign, escalated drastically again from Bob Woodward's front-page allegation that the Chinese government may have funneled clandestine money into Clinton's reelection.† If true, this was serious, but the president sensed pure hype. The charges were speculative and vague, resting on top secret tips from anonymous FBI sources. Even so, the mere specter of foreign subversion renewed feverish suspicion toward all Clinton's fund-raising. Reporters hounded the White House into releasing the names of nine hundred overnight guests, and they pilloried Gore for his stiff lotus bows at a Chinese temple in California. The stories seldom addressed the necessity of fund-raising to

---

* Starr would release the Vincent Foster report seven months later, on October 10, 1997. He resigned as independent counsel on October 24, 1999. His successor, Robert Ray, resigned on March 12, 2002. Ray's successor, Julie Thomas, kept the Whitewater office open through its eleventh year, 2004.

† Bob Woodward and Brian Duffy, "Chinese Role in Contributions Probed; Planning of Foreign Donations to DNC Indicated," *Washington Post*, February 13, 1997, p. 1.

communicate with voters. The president said scandalmongers merely heated the fever. He likened them to cocaine addicts on the street. Not all reporters, of course, but enough to create waves. He said they were "surfing along now," like Starr. Clinton shrugged. Inevitably, the froth must subside, but it may take a long time. He admitted once scoffing at Whitewater.

FINANCE ISSUES SPILLED into wide-ranging history on a second set of tapes. Senator Lott, said the president, "keeps kicking me in the head to call for a special counsel on our money." Republicans had extra incentive to support drumbeat demands in the press, because only a mandated prosecutor—either Starr or a new one—could confine such scrutiny to Clinton. By contrast, even the most partisan congressional hearings sooner or later must address the practices of both parties, which the president would gladly embrace. After all, he supported systemic reform, and considered the McCain-Feingold proposals too weak. No wonder Lott yearned to institutionalize the prevailing outrage. Pundits were obsessing about whether Democrats solicited funds improperly during work hours on federal telephones, for God's sake, while Republicans trafficked safely in tobacco PAC money on the House floor.

Lott hammered Clinton as well to take the lead in renewing the five-year budget agreement. This pressure was painful, said the president, but not so easily rejected. Beneath all his differences with Gingrich and Lott festered a strategic impasse with fellow Democrats. Most of them wanted Clinton to stall, seizing a golden opportunity to repeat the miracle drubbing over the government shutdown of 1995. Under the rules, they said, Congress was required to adopt a deficit-free budget proposal by April. Inevitably, numbers would force the Republican majority to pay for their massive tax cut proposals by gutting education and the environment, or to splinter their caucus by dropping the tax cuts. Either course spelled disaster for them. Why should Clinton take their bullet? Why should he heed their plea to go first? Because, he argued, it was fool's gold to think you could pull off such a political maneuver twice—especially along the brink of government shutdowns. Despite all their bluster, he said the Republicans needed a cooperative budget. Without one, they could be exposed perhaps as too dogmatic to govern, but the president was charged to govern now. His proper course was to bargain hard with these opponents—mindful of their hidden predicament—to secure the public's business.

"If I could make a budget deal tomorrow," said Clinton, "I would do it." He insisted that success was possible in spite of a nasty press climate, obstreperous Republicans, and balky Democrats. With leadership, plus a reasonable record of achievement, political advantage could take care of itself. He answered my skeptical questions with almost a serene quality. I sensed confidence not so much in the outcome as his approach—as though, having sifted the complexities, he would fight for his best judgment and accept what came.

The president gave benignly cerebral responses on difficult topics of late, such as the aftermath of Deng Xiaoping's death in China, partial birth abortion, and Prime Minister Netanyahu's minuscule chance to "skip over" an interim stalemate into final-status negotiations with Arafat. Then he lingered on Chelsea's seventeenth birthday. Because Hillary had been late to dinner at Washington's Bombay Club, Clinton found himself the delighted sole host to a dozen high school girls in raucous discussions of love and the world. The family celebration moved to New York for two Broadway shows the next day, ending well after midnight with a privileged excursion into the bowels of the "21" Club. He said a long stick, when inserted through exactly the right holes, tripped a lever to open the two-ton door embedded in a massive brick wall built during Prohibition. Inside, Chelsea toured the alcove fortress where Mayor Jimmy Walker once entertained guests with Lucky Luciano's bootleg whiskey.

The president glided into stories wholly off my list. Chelsea's Sidwell Friends School had welcomed seniors to make two-minute spontaneous remarks at a gathering of fathers. On a theme of candid revelation, one girl told the assembly why she and her dad communicated by letter in the same house. Chelsea almost knocked Clinton over, he said, with raw eloquence cutting through the inhibitions of youth and the public eye. She confessed setting her heart all year on tryouts for a part in *The Nutcracker,* which she did not get. Life's first major disappointment, as she called it, left her depressed and sleepless, consumed by failure. She could think of nothing but wasted sacrifice. Both parents talked with her late many nights, but she was inconsolable until she woke up fitfully to a letter only an hour old, headed "3am" on her father's White House stationery. It said he could not sleep, either, being upset because she was upset. He loved her, was proud of her, and believed one day she would find new value in her years of ballet. Somehow these words dispelled a cloud of absorption, she told Sidwell. She still read the note every day. As for his work, she admired what he did in the face of so much invective, but it had not always been so. In preschool, she had cringed as the other children stood proudly to declare their parents' jobs—doctor, fireman, teacher. Not even she had a clue about governor, and so Chelsea in turn said her mom was a lawyer and her dad cooked the French fries at McDonald's. She became an instant hit, with by far the coolest dad, but of course the grown-ups made her promise not to tell lies. Apologizing later to the class, she thought her father just talked on the phone and made speeches, which got the kids briefly excited again because they thought she said he made peaches.

She had us laughing and crying almost at once, the president recalled. He thought everyone could learn something from Chelsea's generation. They mixed competitively fresh sophistication with boundless curiosity. At the Bombay Club, her friends had cross-examined him about the recent cloning of a sheep named Dolly in England, fascinated by the implications of reproduction from adult cells rather than an undifferentiated embryo. On frontiers from biology to religion, their questions pushed Clinton beyond his encyclopedic recall of briefings from the White House science office. He disclosed to them a confidential hunch from Evangelical pastor Robert Schuller, who thought the horror over cloning in religious circles was overblown. Even if genetic human copies could be stamped out in a lab, Schuller argued, they would possess distinct souls like identical twins. Clinton agreed with the teenagers' instinct that megafantasies of engineered nations would die of boredom compared with the likely wonders of microgenetics for combating disease or repairing defective organs.

The president delivered on tape a wandering rhapsody about unfettered dreams. In barely a decade, the Internet was leaping from an obscure physics experiment to world revolution. His recent speeches already proclaimed a practical goal for every American twelve-year-old to have classroom access to the World Wide Web in four years. The comparative framework of those same speeches, Clinton emphasized, was *fifty years*. He was exhorting citizens to think in compressed half-centuries. This perspective allowed glimpses of the grim price being paid by a shrinking world for its stubborn dogmas and hatreds. He said the Middle East conflict, for instance, held hostage an immense skein of vital, interconnected questions. It prevented or distorted most thought about whether democracy and Islam could be reconciled among the Muslim countries. Would Turkey settle toward Iran or Europe? What would happen to vast oil discoveries around the Caspian Sea, now paralyzed by disputes between Russia and several of Israel's enemies? The president sketched possibilities all the way to cooperation against global warming. I could only regret that my dictation summary wasn't able to capture his bursting trails of rich language.

CHAPTER TWENTY-SEVEN

"I THINK THEY'RE PRETTY GOOD RUMORS"

Wednesday, March 26, 1997

Thursday, April 3, 1997

Wednesday, April 23, 1997

Monday, May 26, 1997

Trauma shadowed all four sessions in the spring.
   I found President Clinton laid out on a special cot installed in his formal dining room next to the tiny kitchen. He said there had been one more big step than he thought from Greg Norman's patio, and so his toes went down and backward to wedge his heel at an angle against the riser. He heard a loud pop and screamed, knowing instantly that it was bad, and it would have been worse if Norman had not caught him on the way down. From stillness in shock, he heard crisp commands to drive forty minutes past two hospitals to a special facility outside Hobe Sound, Florida, where the doctor distracted him through an MRI with yarns about nearly marrying a girl from Arkansas, whose family Clinton knew, and they moved him within thirteen hours into a surgical theater-bowl at Bethesda Naval Hospital. Under epidural anesthesia, used commonly for childbirth, he listened to musical selections by Lyle Lovett

and Jimmy Buffett as he watched in a tall shiny lamp the blurred reflection of his knee being opened across the curtain. Hillary and Chelsea delayed a trip to Africa, but Clinton was cheered since by word of Chelsea's first public talk at a Tanzanian village.

A legal interpretation of the Twenty-fifth Amendment, which factored also in the choice of an epidural, held that the president could take no narcotic painkillers without transferring his powers temporarily to the vice president. To avoid this, and keep his mental faculties always subject to swift retrieval, Clinton confined himself to medicines with unfortunately strong diuretic side effects. Each bathroom trip was an ordeal, requiring medical assistance, because the slightest flex or stress in his leg sent excruciating spasms everywhere. He claimed a milestone on Tuesday—yesterday—when his sleep interruptions dropped by half to only three tedious excursions to urinate after bedtime. He was just learning how to put on his pants over a stiff knee with its thick brace, but he could not yet reach his socks. Disabled people used specialized tweezers, among many ingenious devices, and the president was citing such discoveries to comfort Greg Norman over the misfortune of his careless guest. Clinton's sudden deprivation spiked his appreciation for the hourly courage demanded from millions to accomplish simple tasks, and the merciless White House therapists had already taught him volumes about musculature. Most men were slope-shouldered because their work was too much in front of them, he told Norman. They should maintain their carriage with exercises stretching behind.

On tape, he described the March summit in Helsinki between two pathetic creatures—himself, the week after his popped knee, and a gaunt, pasty Boris Yeltsin, fifty pounds lighter after his own heart surgery. The president said they snarled at each other more than once—saying, "That's bullshit, and you know it"—but kept coming back against lowball expectations on both sides until they reached four major agreements whose significance had not yet registered. They found a winning strategy at last for ratification of the START II treaty by the Russian Duma. To do so, they outlined a surprise START III treaty, which was intended to achieve an 80 percent reduction in combined nuclear warheads. Finally, they negotiated U.S. stabilization assistance for Russia's new market structures, along with sweeteners for Russia to acquiesce in NATO expansion near her borders. Clinton marveled that Yeltsin did all this into the teeth of ferocious opposition from Russian authoritarians back home. He said old Boris may be dying, but oxygen was getting to his brain. Moreover, with emotion, the president said he felt Yeltsin's core instinct to jump alone on that tank and stare down the military coup of 1991 in Moscow.

He was comparatively acerbic about the withdrawal of his appointee to head the CIA. The president said he would have fought for Tony Lake's Senate confirmation "until the cows came home," but Lake was too beaten down by parliamentary holds that stalled his nomination in committee without a vote. Clinton called the opposition hypocrisy smeared over trench politics. Senator Richard Shelby of Alabama, a former Democrat who chaired Lake's committee, was determined to take one scalp from Clinton's second-term leadership. Lake was it. The president saw in Shelby a dogged, spiteful man supported on his panel by two "know-nothings" in Jon Kyl of Arizona and Jim Inhofe of Oklahoma. None could hold a candle to Lake, who had given thirty years of sixty- and eighty-hour weeks in national security work, losing his wife. All Clinton could do now was thank him for sterling service and wish him a farewell recovery from the wars. He would appoint the CIA's in-house candidate George Tenet to certain confirmation. "I think he can run that agency," said the president, but he was not sure Tenet could reform or control the CIA as he believed Lake would.

We discussed few topics before Bruce Lindsey came primed for a ritual of convalescence. He had rounded up only one staff lawyer working this late, and the medical aides pronounced themselves forbidden to play cards on duty. Therefore, I was drafted for one game of four-handed hearts that extended into second chances and playoffs for three hours, until nearly one o'clock. Clinton kept up a running count of unplayed cards—sometimes deceptively for sport or bluff—and pounced on habitual moves such as the low spade lead at trick two with a mocking refrain: "Pavlov! Pavlov!" Conversation tended toward swagger and gossip beneath a tissue of presidential etiquette. Respectfully, no one spoke Clinton's first name in the presence of others, but it was acceptable to growl, "Mr. President, don't you fuck me with this pass." Nancy Mitchell, the evening shift usher, stopped by to wince primly and say good night.

• • •

EIGHT NIGHTS LATER, hoping to make up for the truncated session, I found him still headquartered on the dining room cot in slippers. He hobbled on crutches to work at the breakfast table of the little kitchen next door, eating a bowl of chicken-and-bean soup. There, much of our taped conversation explored the tightening gloom in the Middle East since March 13, when a berserk Jordanian soldier had murdered seven Israeli schoolgirls hiking on a field trip near the border. Emergency cables reached Clinton in North Carolina for a speech to the state legislature, where he urged support for national testing standards in schools. After issuing an appeal for calm, he flew on late to Florida and wrecked his knee within hours. Since then, Prime Minister Netanyahu sent bulldozers to begin the construction of Israeli settlements on the Har Homa hilltop, between the Palestinian town of Bethlehem and Arab neighborhoods in East Jerusalem. Three days later, a Palestinian suicide bomber killed three Israeli women in Tel Aviv.

The president analyzed a tight vise of reprisal. Ninety percent of Israelis believed that Arafat ordered the bombing, but some 78 percent continued to support the peace process anyway. Isolating the other 22 percent, which rejected negotiation, he said *all* of them were Netanyahu voters. Consequently, the Israeli prime minister's electoral base was divided almost in half between outright opponents of a treaty and those who barely or tentatively favored one. Whenever Netanyahu inched forward, or tried to hold steady under recoil from terror, political survival imposed backward steps to reassure his governing coalition. Meanwhile, Arafat faced constant pressure to rescue his base cheaply with violence, and the overall alignment dictated regression from stalemate in spite of majorities for peace on both sides. The celebrated Oslo Accords of 1993, which prescribed a step-by-step climb from logistical relief to peace, was no longer a functional model.

He thrashed about for a new path. Just the day before yesterday, at the White House, he had heard firsthand of King Hussein's surprise journey to knock at the homes of all seven murdered schoolgirls in Israel, kneeling to beg each bereaved, astonished family to forgive not him or his deranged soldier but the wound to abiding peace. Hussein was a great man, said Clinton, whose extraordinary gesture touched hearts in

Israel but scarcely checked the diplomatic slide. Reduced to hypothetical exploration, and supposing some way to "leap-frog" into final-status talks, Hussein confided to Clinton his belief that they could settle Jerusalem. Surprised, the president said they examined the most sensitive real estate on earth. He called the detailed vision especially significant from Hussein, a linear descendant from the Prophet Muhammad who had controlled the ancient city himself until the Six Day War of 1967. Above the mutually exclusive claims of Muslims and Jews, Hussein thought a complex dual sovereignty could apportion fair boundaries and secure access to all sacred sites.

Even this wisp of hope disappeared on the Syrian front, where Clinton's review was more military and technical. Without the Golan Heights, what guarantees prevented a perfect-storm blitz to cut Israel in half from the north?

Chelsea came in to discuss college choices. She had not yet heard from Princeton or Brown. As our diary subjects succumbed to fatigue, Hillary stopped by wishing she could go to bed, but she had to get her hair done first because her roots were showing. "I love your roots," the president told her with a weary smile. He said his knee was improving, with two hours of therapy today, but he took several painkillers while we talked. I asked for two aspirin myself.

HE HAD A bowl of fruit at the same kitchen spot when we resumed toward the end of April, with his bum leg propped up on a chair in a kind of body stocking. Steve, a military aide, pumped fresh ice every twenty minutes into the nozzle of an elaborate wrapping bag. The president said his exercises now culminated in a vigorous routine to bend the knee. They had just pushed the angle to a new high of 98 degrees—more than enough to let him sit at a desk—but the pressure always made his knee stiffen and swell, requiring the ice. Exhausted, he started brusquely on tape. The Peruvians finally had stormed the Tupac Amaru two days ago, rescuing most of the hostages, killing terrorists who tried to surrender. It would strengthen President Fujimori, he said. End of story. He preempted one question by reading from my notepad about a court decision overturning the line item veto. "We're going to appeal," he said, waving me on.

His mind roved more normally over the floods in North Dakota, where the Red River crested three and a half miles wide to force the evacuation of Grand Forks. Clinton recalled even greater destruction in Arkansas, where he said biblical weather once pushed the same river more than *eight* miles beyond its banks, but North Dakota was pretty bad. The Federal Emergency Management Agency (FEMA) rescuers had to pluck a mayor's ninety-three-year-old father from the roof of a floating house. Speaking comparatively, he broke down how California mud slides cause more concentrated money damage while floods strike a higher percentage of the population. To view the devastation near Grand Forks, he first had to practice sliding backward into a helicopter. He said the journey, like his helicopter trip to the fiftieth-anniversary celebration of Jackie Robinson's major league debut, taxed his knee severely. Hillary had informed him that air travel always causes the body to swell.

The president reviewed plans to establish a blue-ribbon panel for race relations, modeled on Truman's Civil Rights Commission and the Kerner Commission of 1968. He asked me to suggest members, aiming to broaden the scope beyond black-white issues to the full interaction of immigrants and sects. For the next fifty years, many thinkers expected the nation's worst problems to come from entitlement programs, or the environment, but Clinton believed they would stay centered in race. We needed, and other countries would welcome, a blueprint for interracial democracy refined from the unique experience of the United States. The president conceded that critics would belittle the mission as both unneeded and impossible, Pollyannaish or redundant. He said evasion was a proven symptom of racial discomfort, as he and I knew from our youth, and dismissed fears that his commissioners might split into factions. Even if they did, the effort was worthwhile.

We switched to military appointments for the new term. Over a few insinuations of cronyism, President Clinton had just elevated Gen. Wesley Clark to head the NATO command. He said the prosaic truth was that he and Clark had grown up fifty miles apart, paired as freakishly rare Rhodes Scholars in that area, yet never met in Arkansas. They hardly knew each other, and Clark got the NATO post for an exemplary record capped by success in Bosnia. A deeper cause for backbiting was that some peers considered Clark too much an intellectual. The military fraternity could tilt against heroic-action types, too, and Clinton perceived a fine line between the taint of an egghead and a bully. "They want a fighting general," he said, "but they want a diplomat." He had hoped to make Jack Sheehan the first Marine ever to chair the Joint Chiefs, but Sheehan lorded over colleagues with a six-foot-five frame, nimble mind, and virile confidence. Outside a foxhole, where he was perfect, Clinton said Sheehan drew too much resentment from the dominant Army brass to survive long atop the military bureaucracy, especially on his tiny constituent base of some 185,000 in the Marine Corps.

With Army generals reluctant to push for their third straight JCS chief—after Colin Powell and John Shalikashvili—the president strongly considered Adm. Joe Prueher, who was young and sophisticated perhaps to the borderline of an egghead problem. Clinton found the Navy still shaken from Adm. Mike Boorda's suicide and roiled by promotions that had jumped the seniority list. So he looked inside the Air Force. Ron Fogelman was gutsy and honest, but fellow generals nitpicked his "people skills." The favorite among dozens overall seemed to be Air Force general Joe Ralston, with Sheehan to be a strong deputy. Then the president said everything was clouded again by sensitive new personal and interservice concerns. His survey of volatile chemistry among "my four-stars" was so esoteric for me that I hesitated to cite General Sheehan's bold praise for the "Mother Teresa aspects" of foreign policy, from our chance encounter in Haiti.

Hillary joined us for a while, curious to observe the diary process. She also wanted to look in on the president because he had suffered a devastating allergy attack this morning after the helicopter ride. He needed more rest. We touched briefly on a book they were reading about how parents could survive a child's first year in college. A *New York Times* reporter was writing about Hillary's charitable gifts of $600,000 from last year's book royalties, she said with a sigh, arguing that she could have paid less taxes and helped charity more by forming a foundation. If she had, the president chimed in, the *Times* would say she cheated the government and drove up the deficit. As we chatted, I wondered again whether I let our talks slacken into too much comfort. Where were the lines between necessary rapport, critical prodding, and wasted time? Would the future welcome these informalities, wish for more specialized

rigor on NAFTA and NATO, or not really care? We were improvising in
secret without precedent or feedback.

I asked on tape about delayed Senate ratification of the international
treaty on chemical warfare, and President Clinton reviewed his protracted negotiations in the Treaty Room with Foreign Relations chair
Jesse Helms. He had satisfied Helms on twenty-seven of thirty objections, plus half of the twenty-eighth. Not all of them were spurious or
retrograde. Some had merit for streamlining the State Department.
Helms would vote against ratification no matter what, but Clinton predicted, accurately, an overwhelming win with every Democrat and more
than half the Republicans.* The treaty's objectives had enjoyed support
from every president since 1968, plus the top military leaders and even
the chemical industry. What was remarkable to the president was the
very existence of an opposition bloc. He said some churlish senators
spurned any cooperation with the larger world.

That world could be scary. Clinton noted recent defections by
starved North Korean soldiers who weighed less than a hundred pounds,
raising fears of desperate military action or societal collapse. South Korean officials cited both specters to justify continuing their arbitrary
powers, and Clinton said they were legitimately daunted by Helmut
Kohl's reunification of Germany. The fragile prosperity of South Korea
could not aspire like West Germany to absorb and rebuild a disintegrated nation of kinfolk next door. Elsewhere, the president distinguished new sanctions against the military regime in Myanmar (Burma)
from restraint toward China. To prepare for Clinton's summit in Beijing
next year, the vice president had delivered a speech there on human
rights and economic policy, but major American newspapers covered his
visit with political reporters rather than foreign correspondents. Clinton
said he felt sorry for Gore. With a rare chance to speak for the United
States, addressing relations with the world's most populous nation, Gore
attracted updates instead about his Asian fund-raising last year.

---

* A Senate vote of 74–26 ratified the Chemical Weapons Convention the next
day, on April 24, 1997. The U.N. General Assembly had approved the negotiated treaty for submission to member nations late in 1992.

Clinton said the FBI was stoking public interest with leaked claims that its prior alerts had enabled members of Congress to dodge subversion by Chinese money. These stories almost certainly were bogus, he fumed, but they cleverly created heroes to suggest that the administration, by contrast, had not been so vigilant. By fanning suspicion, they also deflected real news about results doctored by the FBI's forensic laboratory, which opened hundreds of convictions to reversal on grounds of tainted evidence. The president renewed his charge that a politicized FBI was dysfunctional in many respects, but he could take no corrective action while Director Freeh worked for special prosecutors aimed at Clinton. Their mission effectively neutralized the president's constitutional role. When I asked about his duty to hold the bureau accountable anyway, or at least to try, he said such an effort would backfire. It was enough for now that Attorney General Reno was refusing the persistant cries for yet another special counsel to target the campaign funds.

Hillary left before the president's mordant press review. He thought the *Washington Post* showed signs of having read the statute on special prosecutors, acknowledging at least the idea of standards, whereas the *New York Times* had dropped all pretense of objectivity. Its editors called Asia-driven contributions the biggest ethical crisis since Watergate, and Clinton said the media demanded a special prosecutor no matter what, legal or not. That benchmark would validate their crusade with a perpetual font of stories, and the president speculated darkly about the relationship between his nemesis, editor Howell Raines, and a stable of indignant *Times* columnists. He said Maureen Dowd was so jaundiced that she dumped on Tiger Woods after he won the Masters by 12 strokes. Clinton digressed into reasons why the twenty-one-year-old kid would change golf—with fitness and athleticism beyond Greg Norman's exercises, plus mental focus to elevate a gentleman's game—remembering also a phone call to tell Woods that his best shot was the hug afterward for his father. Dowd had seized on Woods's regretful decline of a White House invitation to excoriate him for impertinently "dissing" the President of the United States, and she managed to double back against Clinton in the next sentence for craving the aura of celebrity athletes. She thought the two green-eyed hucksters deserved each other with their green Masters jacket and green campaign cash. I did not remember the column, but the president seemed slightly baffled.* "She must live in mortal fear," he guessed, "that there's somebody in the world living a healthy and productive life."

BUMPY OMENS STALLED an afternoon session on Memorial Day, in the bustle before President Clinton's getaway to The Hague for fiftieth-anniversary celebrations of the postwar Marshall Plan.† Unfamiliar guards at the Southeast Gate made fun of my professed appointment. "What's your business with the president?" asked one, who smirked about checking for a clearance to park this pickup near the Truman Balcony. "What does he want to see you *about*?" asked another, clearly taking me for a lunatic. Subsequent phone calls and fluster made me late, and it took a long time for the president to change from his suit into shorts. As he did, I told him he was hobbling less, looking fitter. Unwrapped, inside the brace, a five-inch vertical scar ran just outside the center of his pale right kneecap. He said extra movements today distorted the leg more than usual, swelling its knob much bigger than atrophied muscles above and below. Still, with this injury, he said he was doing better than he had any right to hope for. The Spartan therapists had forced him to lose ten pounds even while confined to sedentary exercise.

We taped in the family parlor, sparing him a walk to the Treaty Room. During his recent visit to Mexico, which had repaid its emergency loans more than three years ahead of schedule, he said drug dealers kidnapped a prosecutor and shot him 110 times in front of his wife and children, to show how brutal the cartel could be. Despite the added chill of corruption, with drug bribes estimated to reach $500 million per year, he said the administration of President Ernesto Zedillo progressed

---

* Maureen Dowd, "Tiger's Double Bogey," *New York Times,* April 19, 1997, p. 19.

† In June of 1947, President Truman's secretary of state, George C. Marshall, proposed massive U.S. assistance to rebuild Western Europe from wartime destruction. The four-year program, designed partly to contain Cold War expansion by the Soviet Union, gained a lasting reputation for economic and strategic success. Some historians also regard the Marshall Plan as a catalyst for cooperative institutions such as the Common Market and the European Union.

slowly by fortitude. Moving on, he highlighted Costa Rica's civic spirit and his enthrallment with the biological wonders of its treetop canopy. Of Barbados, where no U.S. president had landed since a teenage George Washington in 1751, Clinton tempered compliments with regret that he had not fought harder to include Caribbean nations in the NAFTA trade pact.

Back home, he relished a series of events to discourage cigarette use by children, including "Kick Butts" day in Brooklyn and a ceremony in the Roosevelt Room on the first day of the Food and Drug Administration tobacco regulations. Clinton said cigarette addiction, started in childhood, kills more Americans each year than all car accidents, murders, AIDS, suicides, and fires combined. We discussed subtle pitfalls in the prevailing exhortation strategy—urging kids not to smoke—given the very premise of laws holding minors too young for such fateful decisions. It would be more logical, but radioactive, to target adult merchants at the point of their vast illegal sales. Still, it was strikingly novel for a president to oppose the tobacco industry in public. He said historic lawsuits were complicating the politics of late, because state governments—along with their lawyers and associated anti-tobacco groups—anticipated a stake in the ability of the tobacco companies to pay huge settlements. This gave some plaintiffs second thoughts about new tobacco taxes. On the other hand, both the conservative senators from Mormon Utah were tempted to raise "sin" taxes. The president said Senator Lott, whose brother-in-law was negotiating for tobacco settlements, was "horrified" that eight of his senators may forsake the Republican anti-tax pledge, at least on cigarettes.

Clinton traced disarray in the opposition, which controlled the House and Senate. Newt Gingrich, facing responsibility to propose a balanced five-year budget, had announced that big tax cuts must be deferred. The president said this sparked internal revolt from the speaker's hefty right wing, which considered tax cuts far more important than a balanced budget. To placate the fake conservatives, who made tax liberation a feel-good mantra of contempt for Washington, Gingrich reversed course by calling for outright repeal of two taxes resented by the wealthiest Americans, on capital gains and estates. This in turn sank any Republican five-year plan deeper into fantasy, just when the speaker was scrambling for $300,000 to pay an ethics fine imposed by his own House. Behind the scenes, Gingrich's wife threatened to leave him if he borrowed that much from a bank. If he used political funds, however, and thereby guaranteed an inquiry into which contributors were financing his misdeeds, the Republican caucus vowed to oust him for a new speaker. Clinton said former president Bush had refused him a personal loan—as did Gerald Ford—because he thought Gingrich's hard-line politics may have sabotaged his reelection in 1992. Finally, Bob Dole agreed to lend Gingrich the money in a goodwill gesture, gluing together their Republican Party while Dole also helped Clinton with Bosnia and the treaty on chemical warfare. "I only hear all this by rumor," said the president, "but I think they're pretty good rumors."

Republican distress over the budget gave Clinton leverage in negotiations with Speaker Gingrich and Majority Leader Lott. They announced on May 2 the outline of a bipartisan five-year agreement to achieve and maintain fiscal balance for the first time in decades—really since the Great Depression. This once impossible goal enjoyed almost universal support, but the landmark deal touched off a titanic struggle in Congress. Attacks from every quarter, the president believed, would delay votes on approval well into summer. From the right, Senator Phil Gramm denounced minuscule tax cuts and the protected initiatives for education, the environment, and children's health insurance, plus Clinton's "hot-button" restoration of welfare benefits for qualifying legal immigrants. From the left, Democratic senators Paul Wellstone of Minnesota and Ted Kennedy decried the inclusion of Republican tax cuts as an unjust gift to the rich.

From the middle, Senator David Pryor of Arkansas, a Democrat, still pledged to vote against all tax cuts until the deficit had been eliminated. In 1981, Pryor had been one of only three congressional votes to support Ronald Reagan's painful spending reductions while opposing the larger, more popular tax cuts, and now the president found it awkward trying to talk to Pryor, his friend and mentor, out of such a principled stance. In the House, Democratic leader Dick Gephardt mobilized against the whole package to position his presidential run against Gore in 2000. Most vexing to Clinton, South Carolina Democratic senator Fritz Hollings flayed him to the bone in strategy sessions at the White

House. We Democrats, Hollings nearly shouted, did *all* the heavy lifting back in 1993 without a single Republican vote in either chamber of Congress. *Fidelity* to that measure had eliminated 77 percent of the deficit already, by his calculation, with the remainder soon to be wiped out whether they adopted a five-year agreement or *not.* So why on earth would Clinton share *any* credit with Republicans? Did he *remember* summoning Democrats to walk the plank for this? How could any president *spit* on their sacrifice and uphold the party cohesion to survive? Was he running a political *charity?*

The president emphasized each lash himself, without flinching. These were political arguments, not personal attacks, and he respected Hollings for making them. In fact, Clinton seemed strangely aglow, as though he lived for such fiery tests. Here were two pros at loggerheads over the fundamentals of politics, and I was reminded of Clinton's torment before the invasion of Haiti in 1994. Back then, dear colleagues like Senator Dale Bumpers thought Clinton was losing his bearings entirely—and with them the trust for basic communication among political leaders. Now, as then, the president labored to picture for them a sound advantage. This agreement, he argued, would disarm Republicans more than would denying them some credit. The whole political landscape would shift toward Democratic issues.

He detoured abruptly from his rosy view. There would remain one issue of significant leverage for Republicans, said the president, and it was right there twice on my notepad of current topics: partial birth abortion. Here Clinton spewed technical details like both a medical specialist and a medieval theologian, but he claimed no political magic. He said Republicans would beat him to death for vetoing bills to outlaw this gruesome procedure. His own White House staff could barely stay in the room during graphic descriptions by surgeons, and tearful recollections from women—including devoutly Catholic, anti-abortion mothers—about their late fetuses with hydrocephalic enlargements of the skull. The condition doomed the baby, and deformities became so pronounced that even cesarean delivery posed grievous harm to the mother. In this awful circumstance, occurring less than a thousand times a year nationwide, the medical protocol was to preserve the woman's life by crushing her fetus's skull inside the uterus for safe extraction—hence partial birth abortion. If this option were criminalized, all the anguished parties would face a worse choice between illegal conspiracy and lethal neglect or suicide.

Despite ardent support from Clinton, senators from opposite wings had combined to reject Senator Tom Daschle's compromise abortion bill on May 15, in a 64–36 vote. Traditional opponents of abortion said its medical exceptions for the woman's health were a ruse for continued late abortions. Traditional supporters said its ban on all third-trimester abortions—far more than the small number of partial birth procedures— would weaken privacy rights under *Roe v. Wade,* which contained no such restriction. Clinton defended Daschle with broad strokes. Procedurally, the bill would establish abortion policy in legislation, where it belonged, rather than in judicial interpretation alone. Substantively, it would buttress the right of early choice while reducing late abortions by force of law—aligning the United States firmly with countries that require the difficult private decisions to be made, as a rule, within the first six months of pregnancy. Politically, it would break decades of theatrical stalemate between the vituperative extremes.

The president criticized both sides. Some of his pro-choice allies, stuck in aggressive tactics from the upstart years of the women's movement, still defined the issue narrowly by asserting a pregnant woman's absolute right to control her body. Clinton said this approach now played into the hands of anti-abortion leaders, who called the status quo selfish by design. They said pro-choice arguments boiled down to exclusionary power, echoing the claims of slaveholders that their human property was nobody else's business. Waving vivid photographs, they said abortion defenders did not care about these tiny fetuses torn piecemeal from the womb, and if anyone doubted the weakness of the pro-choice response, Clinton lamented, they need only look to the congressional balance of power. Five days after rejecting Daschle's comprehensive bill, the U.S. Senate passed by the same overwhelming margin Pennsylvania Republican Rick Santorum's criminal ban on partial birth procedures, with no medical exceptions to save mothers.

The president rolled his eyes forlornly. Political ineptitude and insensitivity by Democrats had elevated Santorum, of all people, into the reigning statesman on abortion. He made cryptic comments about Santorum's sincerity. If Democrats were cynics, said Clinton, they would stand reasonably aside to let his criminal ban become law. Then they could wait for sensational trials of doctors and maimed mothers to expose its empty, wishful vengeance, neither saving a baby's life nor preventing any unwanted pregnancy. Instead, he promised another veto if the House concurred with Santorum's bill. Steeling himself for a torrent of emotion, the president said decent people everywhere pleaded with him to stop these outrages against helpless babies. Given a chance to marshal all his arguments, Clinton might win a slim majority to understand his overriding duty and preserve the medical protocol. Otherwise, he lost ground, and he waved aside the suggestion of a presidential speech solely on partial birth abortion. No other subject in public life had such disproportionate impact. A terrible dilemma, affecting only a few hundred people directly, trumped global questions and destabilized an entire population to the point of foreclosing rational discussion. He called it a last, potent refuge of distraction from the common good.

I was glad to close with breezier topics. Clinton endorsed a conventional view that Labour candidate Tony Blair won the recent British elections on general weariness with eighteen straight years of Tory government. He still professed a soft spot for the departing John Major, despite their political differences, and remarked oddly that Major seemed to slump forward because the back of his head was square rather than round. Elsewhere, Clinton said his security experts had split about whether the ruling ayatollahs in Iran would allow the reformer Mohammad Khatami to run for president. Now that Khatami had persevered to win 70 percent of the popular vote, they divided again on his slim chances to liberalize the fundamentalist regime. Similarly, describing maneuvers to remove the Congo (formerly Zaire) dictator Joseph Mobutu at last, after thirty-two years of degenerative plunder, Clinton said no one could tell whether the new president would discard democratic pledges like Mobutu had done.*

---

* Gen. Laurent Kabila took power in Kinshasa on May 20, 1997. His authoritarian rule ended with assassination in a 2001 coup of Congolese officers led by his cousin. Kabila's son, Joseph, assumed the presidency and was extended in office by election in 2006.

By coincidence, Chelsea came in for food as he was recalling her retirement from ballet. She said they let her keep the leotard. When she left, he was philosophical about her choice to attend distant Stanford over five Eastern colleges. It was good in premed, and the Western campus was congenial to her as an outdoor health nut. He consoled himself that she did not want to be far from home so much as to escape catfighting among the Ivy League schools. Some of them, especially Harvard, had misread her badly by offering her a favored spotlight as the president's daughter.

Our son, Franklin, burst in from school the next day, asking if I had seen Bono at the White House. A clueless shrug about the rock group U2 lowered me to embarrassment in his eyes. I recovered slightly with a memory that Hillary's aide Capricia Marshall indeed had ducked into the kitchen with a publicity photograph, saying one member of a band wanted the president's autograph before they left. I paid no attention to which one, which ended things sourly at home, but other details came to mind. It was Capricia's sixth wedding anniversary, and there was banter about separation as a key to married bliss. The president facetiously claimed credit for giving Capricia a job with even less family time than her husband, a medical resident. His appreciation drifted into a discussion of scandal after she left, which made me emend yesterday's notes with a reminder to myself that many anecdotes get lost in my dictation. I worried that my already selective recall must be poorer still after our late night sessions. In this case, President Clinton had sketched a sad estrangement between Capricia's mother and father. They were compelled separately into the same room, he said, only to support their subpoenaed daughter in testimony about some hanging trifle, and the shared ordeal helped spawn a miraculous reconciliation. "This is the only good thing that ever came out of Whitewater," said the president. "Ken Starr got Capricia's parents back together."

CHAPTER TWENTY-EIGHT

THE JONES CASE

Tuesday, June 10, 1997

Wednesday, July 23, 1997

Before our next session, the U.S. Supreme Court cleared Paula Jones's lawsuit to go forward for trial. All nine justices overturned the District Court ruling that such cases should be delayed until a president left office, and the ensuing chorus of anticipation, which hailed a pathbreaking rebuke to "Imperial Presidency," left Clinton's most partisan critic at the *New York Times* in lonely, ironic dissent. William Safire's conflicted column, "Above the Law," ruefully forswore his temptation to undermine the separation of powers by advocating a "judicial management" of Clinton. "In protecting the Presidency," Safire recommended, "we give this President a short reprieve."

The Court neatly inverted his three principal reasons. Because these sexual harassment allegations involved "purely private acts," and in fact predated Clinton's presidential term, the case could not impinge directly on any president's conduct of official duties. Also, because the few private suits against earlier presidents had been quashed or settled, there was no explicit precedent to forbid them. Finally, while recognizing that the Constitution made the executive branch uniquely personal, with presidential power vested in one person, the decision held that judicial proceedings would not unduly "burden the time and attention of the Chief Executive." Surely, wrote Justice John Paul Stevens for the Court,[*] personal liti-

---

[*] *Clinton v. Jones*, 520 U.S. 681, decided May 27, 1997.

gation would not be "as onerous" for a president to manage as the constant flux of legal issues affecting the whole nation, and a trial judge could adjust deadlines around the defendant's special responsibility.

Salacious glee stampeded through this gate. Armies of legal analysts previewed the discovery period ahead, debating how broadly the plaintiff's lawyers might be allowed to depose Clinton under oath about his sex life. Leaked stories said Jones would buttress her case with eyewitness testimony about "distinguishing characteristics" of his penis. Pundits ridiculed the idea that presidents might be too busy or dignified for such a hot seat or two. Did they not have time to play golf? *New York Times* essayist Frank Rich satirized both Clinton and the frenzy of a "desperately bored" nation. He said this presidency of empty promises, which now was "shifting from the disingenuous to the nonsensical," actually needed some distinguishing characteristics. "If Mr. Clinton isn't going to do anything else worthwhile," Rich concluded, "it behooves him to go to trial and at least fulfill his solemn obligation to entertain the country." *

These mortifying spasms were suspended ten days later within a hushed buzz of the Yellow Oval Room, as everyone called the formal chamber between the family parlor and Treaty Room of the White House residence. I stood on the fringe with Deputy Chief of Staff Sylvia Mathews, having helped her compile the guest list of some fifty ethnic leaders. One by one, many of them volunteered ideas for the president's forthcoming Advisory Board on Race, to be chaired by historian John Hope Franklin. The first voice recognized was Felix Vargas of Baldwin Park, California, who had been elected the nation's youngest city mayor at twenty-three. He urged specific solutions for chronic, extralegal violence against minorities by urban police departments.

Other greetings ran from windy to wry. Rev. Joe Lowery, Martin Luther King's marching colleague, joked about snacks stowed in his briefcase on prior warning that black folks still would get no dinner. Rhonda Whiting, of the Confederated Salish and Kootenai Tribes in Montana, welcomed the chance to talk with assorted peers rather than about them. James Zogby of the Arab American Institute lamented the absence of a positive Arab personality on network television since Danny

---

* Frank Rich, "Let the Trial Begin!" *New York Times,* June 1, 1997, p. 17.

Thomas and his eccentric guest Uncle Tonoose. Charles Kamasaki spoke of fused identities in Asian-Latino families. Bob Johnson, founder of Black Entertainment Television, pleaded to recognize the centrality of the African-American struggle with a fitting shrine in Washington, like the Vietnam War Memorial or the planned National Museum of the American Indian. President Clinton welcomed conflict and questions, recalling civil rights as the driving lesson of his public life. He traced the stubborn roots of the human compulsion to define greatness by subjugation of different peoples, as in Bosnia, Rwanda, or the old Soviet Union, and challenged the board to refine different standards. Diversity must be upgraded, for instance, from "being nice" to an essential strength for the interdependent world. Author and professor Cornel West saluted the complex agenda with a curt bow to the side, saying, "And you, too, Mr. Vice President, but here I mean primarily the vision of the president." Gore smiled abashedly. "I'm used to that," he said with a sigh, and Clinton spoke up fondly of Gore: "Well, he's getting *less* used to it, or soon will be."

Handshakes, photographs, and huddles swallowed up President Clinton after the event, making me realize how unusual it was for me to see his working routine. I awaited my call from the Usher's Office, and it was nine o'clock before the two of us started work in the upstairs kitchen. For variety, he proposed to mix together our dessert plates of dissimilar fruits scrounged up by the butler Jim Selmon. When the first lady came in from a trip to Baltimore, I said my wife, Christy, had written Mayor Schmoke's remarks about her for the ceremonies today. Hillary asked troubled questions about the writer Anthony Lukas, who had strangled himself while completing a ten-year book project, *Big Trouble*, parallel to mine for the same editor. I said this stunning news had brought home my ignorance about an otherwise vibrant friend. Apparently, Tony had not even left a note behind. This was common, replied Hillary, especially for people with clinical depression like Vince Foster. Haunted, she explored the comparative details of the two suicides. Vince had started a note but then tore it into tiny pieces. According to doctors, explained the president, a final despair grips sufferers so tightly that they have nothing left to say.

On tape, Clinton said he had gotten through the preliminary NATO agreement signed in Paris. He thought President Chirac, who tended to be haughty, was badly underestimating his weakness going into the French elections. Boris Yeltsin, while enduring the absorption of many of Moscow's former satellites into NATO, had groaned about a life expectancy down to fifty-nine years in his broken Russia. Describing a bright spot in London, the president said his private introduction to Prime Minister Tony Blair and his wife, Cherie, had engrossed them for five full hours of conversation about subjects great and small. I asked whether the topics had stretched all the way to Blair's surprise apology four days later for England's role in the Irish potato famine of 1845. Not quite, Clinton admitted, but he thought Blair's statement would be politically shrewd.

He said "the sex thing" back home had gotten out of hand in press coverage about the military. A Pentagon hotline for anonymous complaints, newly created to fight the widespread abuse of rank for coercive sexual favors, was generating also a flood of gossipy leaks. They had surfaced Gen. Joe Ralston, Clinton's nominee to chair the Joint Chiefs, for an affair with a civilian woman during his marital separation years ago. Details spilled into public from Air Force sources, compelling Mrs. Ralston to grant interviews about her conditions of forgiveness, and news accounts debated whether Defense Secretary William Cohen, by affirming Ralston's fitness to head the military, set a double standard for adultery cases when compared with a female officer recently stripped of her command. So Ralston had withdrawn the previous day, which obliged Clinton to resume his delicate search. General Shalikashvili did not want to extend for another two-year term, having picked out his retirement home in Montana, and Clinton said other top commanders were reluctant to come forward.

I turned off the recorders, mindful of instructions against collecting grist for lawsuits. This Ralston story made me ask about Paula Jones. Apart from the demerits of the Court's perspective, it pained me to read of reporters questioning Hillary about a potential court-ordered examination of his anatomy while she was in Amsterdam to visit the hiding place of the martyred Holocaust diarist Anne Frank. Clinton's reaction was brief. He thought his opponents may or may not have timed these leaks while he and Hillary were abroad representing the country. Regardless, he could not worry about that, because governing was hard enough. He and his lawyers decided recently that it might be possible to prevail on summary judgment, because the facts were so clearly in his favor, but the proceedings would be very ugly. Therefore, Clinton's fallback priorities were procedural appeals, delays, and motions that could be handled primarily by counsel. I asked whether a perception of delay was in itself damaging. Would it not be better to push for a speedy trial, especially if he was confident of winning? No, he replied. He had learned from previous outbursts when he felt slandered or poorly treated. No matter how satisfying such defenses might be, they conveyed a deeper message of energies diverted wrongly from the people's business. His official tasks must always come first. Get up every morning, the president kept saying, and come to work.

There was plenty of conflict in the job. We resumed on what he called today's "prayer meeting" with Democrats on the Senate Finance Committee, which was far from quiet or reverent. These senators came to seek wholesale changes in the pending budget plan, and Clinton remarked caustically that at least half of them thought they should be president. They brought a study showing that his agreement to pacify Republicans with tax cuts for education expenses was foolish at every turn. Their experts predicted that colleges would siphon off 10 percent of the benefits by increasing tuition. Another 40 percent would become a windfall to middle-class families with children already in school, and only 48 percent would go to families that otherwise could not afford higher education. The president said he retorted that their own study proved them wrong. Forty-eight percent was a damn good return on a tax break. Did not tax breaks for capital gains subsidize things other than new investment, and how much of the tax credit for poor families wound up spent on adults rather than children? Besides, Clinton told them, their Republican counterparts would offset any change with eager motions to reconsider *their* excluded proposals, like school vouchers and abolishing the IRS. Did Democrats forget who controlled both houses? As each senator pressed some vital exception—in ardent lectures by Pat Moynihan, Bob Kerrey, and even the mild-mannered Jay Rockefeller—

Clinton repeated that opening those doors would hurtle them backward. Their improvements would make things worse. "Things got fairly warm," he recalled.

AT OUR JULY session in the Treaty Room, the president revealed friction of late with foreign allies. By incorporating Russia at its recent Denver summit, the G-7 group of leading nations became permanently the G-8, and Clinton speculated that this cosmetic change may have seduced the press. For once, he said, the meetings were grimmer and more negative than the news coverage. Other heads of state ganged up on the United States. Surprise detractors included Tony Blair and Clinton's friend Helmut Kohl of Germany, who had been almost like a blood brother. They resented Clinton for failing to pay U.S. dues owed to the United Nations—and more for engineering a new U.N. secretary-general while delinquent. They thought the United States was crowing too much about its strong economic performance, and they battered Clinton for failure to address our country's disproportionate consumption of carbon-based energy. Kohl looked artificially good on the reduction of national air pollution, Clinton said, because Germany was getting credit for cleaning up the smokestack industries of Eastern Europe. Blair looked pretty good because of England's natural gas from the North Sea. Both leaders criticized preparations for the Kyoto negotiations to reduce greenhouse gases 30 percent by 2010. They said Clinton would resist interim standards toward the goal because we were certain to fail them. They upbraided him, said the president, even though they had no idea how they would meet their standards, either. Clinton had to bristle at his friends. While not a domineering president by temperament, he thought taking a stand could require being unpleasant. There were times when niceness did no good, and perhaps caused harm.

Disputes carried over to NATO meetings in Madrid. The president said European leaders blamed him for their own inconsistent goals, such as swift withdrawal from Bosnia and vigorous prosecution of its war criminals. They grumbled about his controlled expansion of NATO. They still smarted over his imposition of NATO Secretary General Javier Solana, even though they had come to embrace Solana as an indispensable near-genius.

A curious ambivalence marked the transition from the Cold War, said Clinton. Europeans still expected the United States to lead, and were quick to feel abandoned, but they were keenly sensitive to Yankee arrogance in an age of new partnership. He tried to strike a balance. Tony Blair had confided to him how awful it felt to watch the British flag come down after 156 years over Hong Kong. Press freedoms were curtailed there already, and although Blair had criticized authoritarian management of Hong Kong by the Foreign Office, he shared fears for the trading colony now reverted to Chinese possession. From crowds across Europe, Clinton drew loud approval that was muffled in the press back home. He described a tumultuous reception both in Poland, which was admitted to NATO, and in Romania, where they cheered even his announcement that they would have to wait for membership. Personally, he enjoyed lodging in a fifteenth-century Spanish castle, courtesy of King Juan Carlos I and Queen Sofia. At the Alhambra Palace in Granada, he recalled for Hillary and Chelsea his youthful trip there in 1969.

The president seemed positive or neutral on some domestic topics. He was pleased to install a new military head for the Joint Chiefs in Army general Hugh Shelton, who had commanded the 1994 expedition to Haiti. Shelton, who was one of General Ralston's best friends, would work with Defense Secretary Cohen to dampen witch hunts through the private lives of flag officers. Clinton also celebrated the $368 billion compensation deal struck with the major tobacco companies on June 20. No one should get carried away over final success, he cautioned. These payments, being tax-deductible, would come largely from the public treasury or from increases in the price of cigarettes, and huge challenges remained to wean farmers and smokers alike from embedded habits. He called it a milestone nevertheless to win any victory over marketing forces powerful enough to disguise deadly addiction as sex appeal and sophistication. Finally, he let loose a medley of Clintonisms about his buddy Hilary Jones down on the Buffalo River in Newton County, Arkansas, one of the poorest rural areas anywhere. A standing presidential order—drag me there, drunk or sober—had just ensured his presence to tell stories at the funeral, which was like going back in time. He said people stood around to whittle a lot, thinking.

Clinton pounced when I asked about his second personal rebuff from the Supreme Court within a month. "Yes!" he cried. "And you haven't heard a *thing* about it since, have you?" He called the case an obvious political smokescreen, like the long quest for Hillary's billing records from the Rose Law Firm. All year, insisting that the first lady was part of the administration, Ken Starr had pursued debriefing notes taken by White House lawyers from Hillary, including one set made during a break in her testimony before the Whitewater grand jury. Clinton obediently surrendered the notes intact when the Supreme Court sided with Starr, but on tape he called the case a wretched and brainless precedent. Henceforth, said the president, cabinet members and midlevel officials could not consult departmental lawyers with a normal assurance of privacy. To gain attorney-client protection for discussions of a pending decision at, say, the Commerce Department, he or she may need to hire a private lawyer.

For all this hype and harm, Starr obtained no speck of evidence to help his cause. As Clinton knew—and said a clearheaded moment could have told anyone—the notes revealed Hillary's assessment that the grand jury was being led on a wild-goose chase. The president said Starr concealed this inevitable letdown with a fresh public alarm. Two days after his Supreme Court victory, banner headlines in the *Washington Post* announced that Starr had subpoenaed Arkansas state troopers from the *American Spectator* press flurry of 1993.* Based on tips from the troopers, the story said, investigators were questioning "12 to 15 women" about whether Clinton ever had mentioned the Whitewater land deals during allegedly improper relationships as governor, dating back to 1979. Shamefully, no constitutional check or balance held Starr accountable for the blatant excursion. However, marveled the president, its legal pretext was so flimsy and prurient that some reporters balked, doubting whether justice really demanded this latest set of answers for Starr. Many news outlets emphasized instead the parallel Senate inquiry into charges of illegal contributions. On July 8, chairman Fred Thompson of Tennes-

---

* Bob Woodward and Susan Schmidt, "Starr Probes Clinton Personal Life/ Whitewater Prosecutors Question Arkansas Troopers About Women," *Washington Post*, June 25, 1997, p. 1.

see opened televised hearings with a promise to expose China's full-fledged subversion plot against the U.S. elections of 1996.

Thompson's daily theater had produced nothing but excuses and postponements. His committee and Starr were "sort of limping along," Clinton observed, like the president's legislative opposition. From questions on this topic, he stressed the story of an emergency flood relief bill loaded with extraneous riders. One provision outlawed the use of statistical techniques to count the American people. Studies by the Census Bureau had found scientific sampling to be more accurate and far cheaper than the traditional house-to-house surveys, but Speaker Gingrich especially was petrified that truer methods would find more undercounted Democrats in cities than Republicans in the suburbs. The president vetoed the flood bill less than twenty minutes after it arrived at the White House, denouncing the political games with disaster relief, and public reaction thrashed the Republican majority so raw that Congress passed a clean bill within four days. After a terrible week, Senator Lott lashed out at the president as "a spoiled brat" on Sunday television, which moved Clinton to seek a private truce. On tape, he reprised their strangely jolly conversation. Lott's senators had pestered him to cram those riders in there—didn't they—and berated him later for doing it. Then television reporters worked him over for his flip-flopping surrender to the president, which really made him mad, right? "You're goddamn right they did," Lott replied, laughing. "I didn't want to go." Well, teased Clinton, let's chalk it off. Lott probably had a headache, too. He should have slept late, gone to church, and skipped the TV interviews.

The president said his relations were less collegial on the House side, where leadership struggles squeezed nearly all the levity out of politics. Speaker Gingrich had just purged one of his own deputies, Bill Paxon of New York, for plotting a coup. Majority Leader Dick Armey of Texas publicly denied his role in the seething rebellion, and Clinton thought Gingrich may have survived thus far only because Republicans were split over a suitable successor. When I asked about the repercussions for the White House, he said the disarray cut both ways. Because the loudest squawks came from Gingrich's young right-wing ideologues, Clinton thought it would be easier to frame a congressional campaign next year against their positions deemed selfish and unfair. On the other hand, Gingrich's weakness frustrated short-term goals in Congress, because the speaker controlled less and less of the middle, where deals must be struck.

He complained of troubles also with House Democrats, whose leader, Dick Gephardt, was mounting a revolt against the budget agreement. In their cordial but terse consultations, Clinton said he freely conceded Gephardt's right to prepare a challenge to Gore for the presidential nomination, and he accepted the professional calculation behind Gephardt's dissents on NAFTA, the welfare bill, and China policy. These moves staked out the labor and liberal wings of the party, but Clinton warned Gephardt that opposition to the budget deal was a serious political blunder, perhaps fatal. It would mark him as a naysayer and spendthrift. Not only were the deal's components more popular with Democratic voters than Gephardt realized, but the overall accomplishment was a vital threshold into the future. Fiscal order would create political advantage on issues from jobs to the environment.

We closed on the marathon negotiations over the budget deal in light of dueling Republican tax cuts passed by each house of Congress. Clinton described a tense carnival of bluffs, odd alliances, and wishful thinking. The outcome was very much in doubt. Everything could fall apart, but he took solace from interpersonal drama at the bargaining sessions. The president deployed Erskine Bowles and Treasury Secretary Bob Rubin to do most of his talking—with Bowles the good-guy charmer, drawling to fellow Southerners in the Republican leadership, and Rubin the bad-guy banker, swooping in with harsh economic facts. Each of "my two guys," said Clinton, had earned personal wealth many times greater than anyone on the other side—probably more than all of them put together. Their calm authority on the workings of capitalism plainly rankled counterparts such as Gingrich, Lott, Armey, Senator Don Nickles of Oklahoma, Ways and Means chair Bill Archer, and Representative Tom DeLay of Texas. Clinton said these Republicans loathed the Earned Income Tax Credit (EITC) for the working poor as a benefit wasted on mostly Democratic voters. They resented technical explanations why the EITC suffered less "leakage" of purpose than other tax breaks, and they despised even more to hear Bowles and Rubin discount incentives for

Wall Street. "It drives them crazy." Clinton smiled. "They hate getting schooled on the real world by rich Democrats."

THE NEXT WEEK, on Friday, August 1, a phone message instructed me to contact the White House operator. Betty Currie, Clinton's personal secretary, came on the line with notice that the president wanted to speak with me between appointments later that day. I agreed to call from the road, as we were leaving to retrieve Franklin from summer camp at Haverford College. Christy and I drove north toward Pennsylvania, nonplussed and wondering. Nothing like this had occurred before. My fears pictured an imminent headline or subpoena about the history project, with inevitable suspicion that I was the leak. Or perhaps it was merely some clarification on our last session, but if so, why so urgent? When we connected, he asked first where I was calling from. Looking around, slightly paranoid, I said it was the pay phone outside a country diner just off the interstate. The president told me he was under tremendous pressure. He asked for some advice. How did I think history would regard it if he settled the Paula Jones case?

The question landed with surprising weight. I mumbled something in a stall. We had discussed many episodes of war and peace, often presented closely in very human choices, but all that became suddenly detached. This request was plaintive and intimate, yet correctly historical from a President of the United States, which made it surreal to absorb in a setting of distant cornfields and highway billboards. He briefed me, perhaps sensing my dislocation. Bruce Lindsey and White House Counsel Chuck Ruff (who had replaced Lloyd Cutler) wanted to settle. So did the Clintons' insurance company. Calculating that a trial alone would cost at least a million dollars, win or lose, they all believed it possible and prudent now to settle by paying less to Paula Jones. I responded first that a deal did not seem wrong in principle. It could be defended, and there were principled arguments *for* a settlement to short-circuit the distraction from his duties. Beyond that, the actual terms would affect the degree of long-run injury to his reputation and the presidency itself.

Clinton said the offers currently on the table involved no apology or statement from him and a payment to Jones in the vicinity of $750,000. These minimal terms reflected predictions that the judge was likely to dismiss two and perhaps three of Jones's four complaints before trial. The fourth, alleging the infliction of emotional distress, would probably stand to be contested on the evidence. He thought he would prevail there, too. If so, Jones would wind up with nothing but a mountain of legal expenses, which was why her lawyers were so eager to settle.

The president previewed a trial. "We can meet more than my legal burden," he said. In fact, they were close to proving that none of the things occurred that she said caused her emotional distress—no persecution of any kind. Very circumspectly, he said he never spoke to or about her back then, "except possibly in connection with the one incident alleged in the hotel." I wasn't sure whether he was guarding against telephone intercepts or the risk of making me a witness on the facts, but I was grateful either way. He said a trial would require him to be in Little Rock about two weeks for a circus that would obliterate his agenda. This prospect pained him most. There were only three-plus years left in his term, and he did not want to waste a day.

In the end, I thought the main historical consideration was to avoid any settlement so generous that it would encourage more private lawsuits against future presidents. Paula Jones was an aberration so far, but a rash of nonofficial cases would weaken the presidency. If so, the future would hold Clinton responsible. We chewed this over, and he asked me to send further thoughts by private fax through Nancy Hernreich, which I did later. Christy was curious back in the car. What was that all about?

CHAPTER TWENTY-NINE

CHINESE LAND MINES

Wednesday, August 13, 1997

Thursday, October 2, 1997

The tension vanished by mid-August—or was stowed away. Late on a Wednesday evening, President Clinton greeted me in the Treaty Room with bubbling good cheer. First, like a trophy, he handed me a deluxe Sunday *New York Times* crossword puzzle on the upcoming twentieth anniversary of Elvis Presley's death. Nine minutes, he glowed. He finished in nine minutes, and it would have been sooner had he not been chuckling in amazement over how much trivia about Elvis was stored in his head. Next, on the bookshelf, he demonstrated a Bang & Olufsen sound system newly gifted from the queen of Denmark. A CD spun in the vertical glass chamber, projecting k.d. lang's voice from sleek speakers with tactile clarity. He called her a great artist as he reached for a digitally remastered antique recording of "Danny Boy" by Paul Robeson. "I can hardly listen to this stuff," said the president above Robeson's resonant bass. "It makes me tear up." On our tape, he replayed his first use this week of a splendid new gadget just for presidents—the line item veto. Having excised three loopholes benefiting New York, he elaborated a strategy to use this surgical power with measured restraint, especially while it was under scrutiny from the

courts.* Clinton drew far greater satisfaction from passage of his omnibus budget and tax bills in Congress. They were law at last. He congratulated a list of collaborators. He said people did not yet realize
how big a milestone this was. My notes called him "ecstatic."

The budget struggle had ended during his Nevada trip for a speech
to the National Governors Association, while he was out on the golf
course with the host governor, Bob Miller. It was embarrassing—by far
his worst round in memory. Michael Jordan, of pro basketball's reigning
Chicago Bulls, kindly advised from knowledge of injuries that Clinton's
knee may be healed but his body still missed its confidence in the brace.
So, while the staff was fetching his contraption, the president received
yet another White House page to call Bowles and Rahm Emanuel as the
final tweaks sent both conference reports cascading to passage.† He
scored par on three of the next four holes. Clinton credited Jordan and
the brace with his turnaround, but he told me the legislative drama may
have done it alone. He has been flying since.

Just today, the latest polls showed his approval ratings well up in the
60s, with disapproval in the low 30s. Astonishingly, said Clinton, more
Americans believed he was crooked or criminal than complained about
any aspect of his job performance. They were not sure what he did, according to the detailed analysis, but it must have been bad. He said this
result, from constant pounding on Whitewater and campaign finance,
made it hard to remember the mighty Cold War presidents who sometimes ran roughshod over people with conscription and emergency powers. Now, he mused, everybody was cooperating to hamstring the
executive branch—the Supreme Court, Congress, federal prosecutors,

---

* New lawsuits soon suspended this fledgling power again, and the Supreme
Court overturned the Line Item Veto Act of 1996 by a 6–3 vote, in *Clinton v.
City of New York*, on June 25, 1998.

† On July 30, the Taxpayer Relief Act of 1997 passed the House, 389–43, and
the Senate, 85–15. Its main provisions cut the top tax rate on capital gains from
28 to 20 percent, and introduced a $400 per child tax credit for nonwealthy
families. The Balanced Budget Act of 1997, which passed by similar margins,
secured a stable balance by 2002 and contained Medicare reforms. Clinton
signed both bills on August 5, 1997.

and the press—"to the point where the smallest functionary has to hire lawyers and fight like hell just to tread water."

His mood surmounted troubles. By implicit analogy with the knee brace, he could prevail through help and perseverance. He said Erskine Bowles proclaimed the budget deal a chance for him to exit on a peak accomplishment, renewing his wish to be home in North Carolina. Bowles wanted to resign after the upcoming battle for fast track negotiating authority on trade agreements, and this time Clinton accepted his rationale. With that authority, the president could seek not only to sustain international economic growth but also to repair the environmental defects in NAFTA. Unions and environmentalists had legitimate gripes about NAFTA, Clinton conceded. Many American companies were taking jobs abroad for the freedom to pollute, as well as for cheaper labor. However, the president called it a folly of self-punishment to react by choking off trade. This was his urgent counsel to allies. Workers would lose either way by making it their number one priority to fight fast track negotiations like NAFTA, which accounted for nearly four million high-paying new jobs. And Gephardt would slit his own political throat if he ran as labor's protectionist champion.

Here he looked forward, saying it was practical to be visionary because there was no good alternative, and a flight of stories and statistics needed few questions from me. He said Al Gore joined his Nevada trip for an environmental tour of Lake Tahoe—a natural wonder, 1,600 feet deep and once crystal clear—where visibility at the surface had dropped from one hundred to seventy feet in depth, and was clouding at one foot per year. At forty feet, the whole lake would turn from blue to green with devastating ecological effects, and the plainly imminent ruin had galvanized regional politics into a nonstop forum. Local citizens across the political spectrum, said Clinton, investigated the top three causes of pollution for their economic jewel: runoff from developments, greenhouse gases from automobile traffic, and Jet-Skis. They knew that one of every five gallons of gasoline from a Jet-Ski winds up in the water. They knew how greenhouse gases dissolve. More generally, they accepted what Clinton had just publicly proclaimed—that global warming was a fact of consequence, not a theory. There remained a huge educational task for people to think and sacrifice in common to heal it, and the president thought his word would have extra punch because he was perceived to be so fixated on jobs—therefore less "green" than Gore. Stringent conservation could address about 25 percent of the problem, but the rest would be tough. Did I know that 70 percent of auto emissions come from starting and stopping my car? He lost me in a preview of technology for the hybrid gas-electric engine, soon to appear in Japan, complete with rough specs and a creative stab at the shifting mechanism. A few stories later, to illustrate energy savings possible from lighter, stronger materials for cars, he brought over Greg Norman's latest titanium driver.

Abroad, two suicide bombers had killed fifteen Israelis in Jerusalem on July 30. The president, describing intricate maneuvers behind his public denunciation, would send Dennis Ross and then Secretary Albright back into the prolonged stalemate, and he disclosed his first substantial backlash of Jewish political opposition over U.S. pressure on Netanyahu to resume negotiations with Arafat. The only wisp of leverage was a prediction that Netanyahu, by undermining Arafat, could wind up facing a Palestinian leadership heavily composed of overt terrorists. The bleak reality, Clinton said with a sigh, was that anyone who replaced Netanyahu would be better for the peace process—and anyone who replaced Arafat would be worse. Moving on to Bosnia, the president described a blunt message to Milosevic through Holbrooke that crack NATO troops were coming to arrest Serbian leader Radovan Karadzic for war crimes. The "soft" message was that Milosevic had a tacit option to remove Karadzic first. Otherwise, there would be no restraining ground rules, as there had been in Somalia, and any resistance would meet overwhelming lethal force.* In Bosnia, as opposed to the Middle East, the hard path trended upward, but Clinton delivered both assessments with stoic resolve. This, too, was part of the job.

New tidbits kept boosting his spirit. He said the budget law would be good for an economy growing robustly at 5.6 percent per year, with

---

* Karadzic avoided both public surrender and armed conflict by hiding under assumed names for eleven years. A Serb militia arrested him in Belgrade on July 18, 2008. Extradited to The Hague for trial by the International Criminal Tribunal for the Former Yugoslavia, Karadzic faced charges including responsibility for genocide against eight thousand Muslims of Srebrenica in July of 1995.

no signs of inflation. Wholesale prices had declined for seven straight months, and the national unemployment rate was down to a twenty-five-year low of 4.8 percent. If these trends held, as they should, compounded benefits would bring the federal budget into balance ahead of the 2002 schedule. Indeed, we might go into surplus while Clinton was still in the White House, which was beyond his promise or hope from either presidential campaign. He said this prize was much more significant than gold-star numbers in some government ledger, and we discussed broader measures of competence and discipline. Balancing the budget met a test of political self-government central to the American experiment itself, which should restore public confidence for tackling big problems ahead. The president thought such a seismic shift would favor Democrats. He said most of them still wanted high office to *do* things, whereas Republicans wanted mainly to occupy the high office. Decades of an ersatz, anti-government agenda left Republicans so stale and vulnerable that he predicted Democrats would recover seats in the 1998 elections. They may even take back the Congress. He stressed that any gain at all would stand out in the long record of two-party competition, since the demise of the old Federalists, because the president's party had lost every off-year congressional contest except 1934.* The sixth-year referendum on two-term presidents had been especially rough, punishing them all with marked vengeance, but Clinton aimed to buck this iron law of political history.

He kept going breezily after I ran out of questions—describing the intricacies of a UPS strike, then telling how he summoned a Treasury technocrat one day to explain why an arcane tax benefit for struggling rural cooperatives would get gobbled up by companies like Sunkist. He gave me a book to read for my reaction, and asked what qualities he should look for in his next chief of staff. In return, I commended to him a copy of Spike Lee's forthcoming documentary film on the Birmingham church bombing of 1963, *4 Little Girls*. The president was inclined to help with the promotion, and shrugged when I told him Howell

---

* Theodore Roosevelt's Republicans did add seven seats in 1902, but Democrats gained twenty-five. The anomaly of a forward loss for TR resulted from an overall increase in the number of House seats after the 1900 census.

Raines of the *Times* did a good job in on-camera commentary. He said he frequently admired Raines's work, recalling an article on disadvantaged schoolchildren, and could only speculate on the bad blood between them.

As he often did in nonpressure farewells, the president asked for updates on family and the final stages of my book. I told him almost numbly that its draft was complete, and a second volume of the King-era trilogy would be published early next year. "How is it?" he asked. "Are you happy with it?" His directness caught me short. I said the material felt way too close after fifteen years of constant obsession. He waited until my hesitation crumbled. I said this book contained more discoveries for me than *Parting the Waters*. To him, I found myself divulging a naked claim of original work on subjects from the career of Malcolm X to the arc of Dr. King's life struggle, intermingling civil rights with Vietnam. My narrative sought to rescue a transcendent, conflicted LBJ from caricature. "Do you think it will be a success?" asked Clinton. Well, that was different. There would be attention, but I was not sure how these connected strands would register. Most people separated them. This was a less sentimental part of the King story, and appreciation may be slow. The black-led movement had intensified all the fundamental questions that still dominate and paralyze national politics—about crisscrossing associations between freedom and governance, democracy and violence. Its aftermath touched Clinton in many forms, hidden and overt.

The president kept nodding. I had told him what I scarcely confessed to myself: that the book felt good but probably would not be as popular as *Parting the Waters*. While my publisher doubtless would help fashion a marketing appeal, Clinton made me cut straight to the bone. I wondered why. Was it friendship or impersonal command? Presidents can attract unguarded sincerity as well as concentrated deception. Or perhaps we reversed roles momentarily. Did he move me to answer candidly for the past, as we intended his oral history to serve the future? Out loud, I escaped with a wish to find rest and perspective once the edited book went to press. Christy and I would sneak away for a few days to our old honeymoon spot on Block Island, off the New England coast.

President Clinton brightened. His family was stopping at Block Island Sunday on the way to Martha's Vineyard. He needed rest, too, but he outlined a whirlwind vacation of dinners, working interludes, and golf on the two little courses. There was a par-5 hole he once birdied even with a penalty stroke. Hillary hated golf, said Clinton, but she usually played one round a year, and it would be interesting to see if she did this time. He asked casually for the crossword puzzle, which I had forgotten. His aide Ann Lewis did not believe he knew all that stuff about Elvis, and he wanted to show her the proof.

HILLARY LASTED ONLY nine holes, said the president at our October session, but at least she played. The three of us sparred about whether this effort revealed a surpassing love for him more than her distaste for the game. She said golf was impossible. Butler Jim Selmon served me a side plate around their little kitchen table in October, a tumultuous month after their longest vacation in twenty years. Above all else, Chelsea had enrolled in the freshman class at Stanford. Capricia Marshall already was helping them assemble a second "CARE package" of amusements, for their benefit more than Chelsea's, and they pronounced themselves less devastated by the separation than expected, probably because they had "walked through" its ritual shock in such detail that the actual passage became familiar.

The president said he stayed up the whole Wednesday night before their departure for California. He and Hillary had steeled themselves to minimize the telltale moments when parents become bothersome, such as lingering to arrange the dorm room, and they swapped impressions of orientation. One father had waved off the common worries at their parents' meeting to ask, "When are we going to talk about *sleep*?" Kids who never sleep get tired and depleted, he continued, with Clinton quoting the father in a bad Indian accent. And *then* come the sex, the drugs, the bad grades. Everybody had laughed, but sleep became a dominant theme. It turned out that Chelsea's counselor was a graduate specialist in sleep deprivation. This was probably good, said Hillary, because she had inherited her father's insomnia. All they heard about from Chelsea so far was burning the candle at both ends—not much about courses. Clinton praised her nonobtrusive Secret Service detail on campus. He called the drop-off fairly normal.

I said we were only one cycle behind them, entering the college application madhouse, and hoped to deliver Macy to some college next year. Yes, but we would still have Franklin at home after that, said Hillary. It was emotional. Refusing to mope, she said maybe she would throw me a book party. She had loved her own book parties in spite of the fuss. The president told her I had promised rich new material on the Vietnam War, drawn from painstaking transcription of LBJ's phone calls. It was sad, he remarked, that he could not preserve his own White House phone calls for posterity, but such recordings now would get discovered, seized, and ripped open prematurely. When Hillary asked for samples from the book, I paraphrased a few of President Johnson's conversations with Richard Russell and Robert McNamara. The raw anguish contrasted starkly with what these same men said in public, when they had behaved like robots pursuing the Vietnam War. They were more like us than we ever thought, feeling dragged against themselves.

Hillary was so glad she had opposed that war. We reminisced about how hard it had been to figure out what was real and right at the time, but fickle memory dulled our access. None of us could remember even where our apartment had been located in Austin during the McGovern campaign of 1972. The president had an image of a complex near the Colorado River. I recalled being on a hill past the interstate. Both of us still knew the address of our headquarters on Sixth Street, but nobody could place the home retreat. Hillary absolved us, saying we had traveled so much that the three of us were seldom there together, but our vagueness and the Vietnam tapes made her reflect on the trickiness of memoirs. If she ever wrote them, how could she reconstruct her own past accurately? Their lawyer David Kendall knew more about a surviving paper trail of her life than she did. And he remembered it better. She said Kendall was truly gifted.

This reminded me that Kendall had called me for the first time in years, warning that "our friend may be sending us another Valentine." As best I could decipher the cryptic message, he meant Starr was preparing a subpoena for Clinton records so detailed that Kendall may be obliged to review our oral history tapes again—all of them. How many did we have? He remembered listening to three or four. I said there were now about *fifty*, and this was crushing news. LBJ had taped his phone calls, I groaned, but this president could not safely keep a diary. Kendall told me not to despair yet. He was still maneuvering. From subsequent calls, he seemed to be arguing that Starr should not risk duplicating discovery if a separate prosecutor were to be appointed on campaign finance. He advised me to say a prayer for Janet Reno, but I was praying for Kendall instead.

President Clinton soothed me by expressing confidence that Kendall would find a way to shield the tapes. He said there were many upheavals going on behind Fred Thompson's Senate hearings on campaign finance, which were a bust. Mostly to Hillary, he said Al Gore was trying to hire a second criminal lawyer. She already knew he was paying the first one $30,000 per month. Clinton said Jim Neal of Tennessee, the former Watergate prosecutor, was so upset by the meandering dragnet that he volunteered to defend Gore for free. Neal's handwritten letter to the White House, explaining his offer, had not yet reached Gore but was already in the newspapers! Hillary did not know this, and exchanges quickened between the Clintons. Would charity be called a bribe if Neal's other clients had business before the government? Could Gore qualify for an "old family friend" exemption under a conflict-of-interest statute? Did legal answers help much with the politics? Who leaked the letter—a friend of Neal, a postal employee, somebody in the White House? The president and first lady batted political information back and forth in shorthand that struck me again as a remarkable communion. I chimed in only my concurrence that a White House leak was likely.

Clinton stood to leave the kitchen. He wanted to work in the family parlor to keep an eye on a playoff game between the New York Yankees and Cleveland Indians. As we were breaking up, he said this craziness brought back one of the books he had read on Martha's Vineyard: a biography of Chief Justice John Marshall by Jean Edward Smith. Marshall and other founders lived in an age of duels and wild frontier slander, said Clinton, but they had strong ideas about how to structure workable government for a republic. The president thought Marshall would be shocked by our prevailing shallowness today. You could not blame it all on the press, which was sensationalist in Marshall's time, too. Even Supreme Court justices like Sandra Day O'Connor had been giving in to corrosive attacks on government, including the Supreme Court itself.

Hillary called it a broad cynicism, which suggested that consistency mattered less if cooperative politics were treated habitually like a nuisance or illusion.

I reminded the president that we had dabbled with various interpretations in our sessions. He once charged that cushy reporters were in cahoots with his adversaries. Later, he speculated that splintering market forces pushed media coverage toward tabloid standards. We added notions from the historical overlap of information technology with the Cold War, which had anchored forty years of news in the threat of nuclear annihilation. Now, however, our political communicators had to find daily drama somewhere else. Clinton merely nodded. He referred playfully at times to an "emotional hole" theory of junk news culture.

NEWS OF LATE had been riveted by the death of England's Princess Diana in a Paris car crash. On tape, President Clinton said bulletins first reached them on vacation. Hillary knew her better, and represented them at the funeral. Now he regretted his refusal to see Diana on her visit to the White House in June because of their differences on land mines. Diana had crusaded to ban them all by an international treaty called the 1997 Ottawa Convention, and Clinton, just a few days before her crash, had announced from Martha's Vineyard one last attempt for the United States to become a signatory. His account of the subsequent failure amounted to a defensive treatise in the face of worldwide sympathy for all things Diana.

On his desk, since the first day, the president said he kept a three-dollar Chinese anti-personnel mine. It was a terrible little plastic monster, three inches around, with a screw-top opening for a tiny metal detonator. Throw it on the ground anywhere and it blows off legs, killing nearly ten thousand people last year mostly in the world's poorest countries, many of them children. Clinton wanted to outlaw them, and he said the United States paid for more than half of all de-mining operations around the globe. However, he could not join the Ottawa Convention without a specific exclusion for Korea. The U.S. mines there were the only feasible military barrier between a million North Korean soldiers and forty thousand Americans guarding the short path to Seoul. Our mines were planted conspicuously across a barren width of eighteen miles. They had self-disarming features, and would never maim wandering children years later. More technically, Clinton described military reasons for a second exclusion to permit anti-tank mines in major offensives like the Gulf War. This got very complicated, but Ottawa's refusal to grant these exclusions left Clinton lumped uncomfortably with the rogue nations that scattered the lucrative, lethal cheap mines everywhere.

Emotions were stirred on an amazing range of issues. Only six months ago, the teachers unions were denouncing his national testing standards as a threat to underperforming members, and minority leaders decried a potential stigma for their students. Now these groups have reversed course, he said, but Republican governors suddenly were agitating against the specter of a federal takeover. In charter schools, Clinton gave thanks for one educational reform that had not yet been politicized. Only one charter school existed when he took office. Now there were five hundred in the twenty-nine states that authorized them, with money in the budget deal for another three thousand. He hoped even more would rise to set an independent standard within the public schools, forcing improvement.

We noted that Susan Wright, the presiding judge in the Paula Jones case, had dismissed two of the four complaints, as predicted. The president believed she would dismiss at least one more before trial. Jones's original lawyers had bailed out when she refused to settle, but he checked my wish for a merciful deal to end the case. Nonprofit ideologues out of Dallas promptly assumed counsel for Jones, supported by political donations to keep her suit alive. The whole sprawling enterprise was being managed plainly as a right-wing cause, which Clinton insisted had been the underlying reality all along. He thought his best hope now was to win by summary judgment.* His own insurance company was testing loopholes to avoid liability. If they abandoned him, chances for settlement would drop to zero, because the president vowed not to pay a dime from his own pocket.

Of the early developments related to his new Advisory Board on

---

* Judge Wright did grant summary judgment in Clinton's favor on April 1, 1998, but by then the Jones case would be overshadowed by news of Monica Lewinsky.

Race, Clinton himself was squeamish about a police brutality case in New York. Since August, controversy had skyrocketed from the alarm of a lone nurse at Coney Island Hospital, who refused to believe police claims that a patient's condition was the result of jailhouse sex. Investigators determined instead that four police officers had arrested a Haitian immigrant named Abner Louima from the fringe of a bar fight and beaten him severely on the way to Brooklyn's 70th Precinct station. Inside, still handcuffed, Louima was sodomized savagely with a broomstick in both his rectum and mouth, leaving broken teeth and nearly fatal ripped tissues that would require surgeries over several months to repair. The shocking revelations triggered protest marches, censure from Amnesty International, and trials for years to come.* When I asked, the president corrected press reports that he had scolded his race commission for timidity in response to this incident. He hoped they could use the outrage to help overcome doubts that deep-seated prejudice was still alive.

President Clinton spoke more expansively about the fortieth anniversary of integration at Little Rock's Central High School. He called this home state event a landmark in two respects. First, it focused national and international attention on broad societal changes. Only President Eisenhower's dispatch of regular U.S. troops—the first deployment against state resistance since Reconstruction—had tipped the great struggle in 1957. Clinton recalled inviting the nine pioneer black students into his governor's mansion thirty years later to feel welcome in the citadel where violent rejection had been plotted against them. He sketched their lives, saying his friend Ernest Green had survived Central High to become a successful banker. According to Green, all the Little Rock Nine had suffered some emotional damage, but white students had concentrated their daily torments and harassment on the six black girls. Elizabeth Eckford, who had been mobbed infamously in public, lost

---

* In 1999, one NYPD officer received a thirty-year sentence for the assault. A second officer received five years; two others had convictions overturned on appeal; and a fifth was acquitted. In 2001, New York paid Abner Louima the largest civil damage award for police brutality in the city's history, $8.75 million.

much of her outgoing spirit. Only this year, said the president, did Eckford begin a cross-racial acquaintance with Hazel Bryan Massery, whose face of screaming fury behind her had been captured in one of the iconic photographs of the twentieth century. To Clinton, who blended political argument with personal stories, their painful accord marked a second phase of progress, when nameless antagonists become human to each other and everyone else. By analogy, more Americans would come to identify one day not only with Haiti's democratic aspirations but also with its people like Abner Louima, who had finished training to be an electrical engineer.

ONLY ONCE DID the president ask me to turn off the recorders. "I know a lot more about the campaign finance investigation," he said. Republicans in Congress, returning from their Labor Day recess, had ramped up their year-long campaign for a dedicated special prosecutor on 1996 fund-raising by Democrats. Their timing was maddeningly ingenious, Clinton fumed, because they were filibustering simultaneously—for the fifth straight year—against legislation he supported to curb the large "soft money" contributions raised by both parties. All forty-five Democratic senators had pledged *in writing* to vote for the McCain-Feingold reform bill, but reporters echoed a contrarian GOP chorus that Clinton and Gore were the big-money obstructionists.

Once again, Clinton accused the FBI of political distortion. He said Director Freeh's bureau played to the Republican congressional majority by lobbying for a special prosecutor on Democratic finances, while peddling sensational news stories about Chinese espionage. Such conduct was outrageous. For his own failure to corral the FBI, the president said the only defense in posterity would be that he was neutralized by the FBI's constant investigation of him. As things were, he confided, Attorney General Reno was about to extend a thirty-day inquiry on the statutory test for a special prosecutor, even though career lawyers at Justice opposed this preliminary step. They found the FBI's evidence spurious or downright concocted, but Reno yielded. Ironically, Clinton took hope from his instinct that Republicans may have browbeaten her too much. Mississippi senator Thad Cochran was demanding her resignation for what he called unconscionable delay. Reno was prickly, antipolitical, and aloof. Perhaps these qualities, which made her so incompatible with Clinton, would fortify her to stand with him now on the law.

A less sensitive impasse had doomed his nomination of Massachusetts governor William Weld to become U.S. ambassador to Mexico. Although Weld was a conservative Republican, his patrician manner or progressive views on gender irritated Senator Jesse Helms so much that he vowed to block confirmation. Eventually, said Clinton, frustration drove Weld to make stupid moves. He publicly challenged fellow Republicans to override Helms's one-man hold on the Foreign Relations Committee. Had he won John Kerry's Senate seat in 1996, Weld announced, he might not have voted to retain an arbitrary antiquarian like Helms in his chairmanship. Then Weld abruptly resigned his governorship, which Clinton called diving into an empty pool. Suicidal or not, he should have told the White House of his intention to resign. "Maybe we could have gotten something for it," said the president with a sigh. He thought Weld was impetuous, or perhaps simply bored as governor. Such behavior only provoked Senator Helms to clamp down like a snapping turtle, and the president, though sorry to lose the nomination, retained a grudging respect. If Democrats had half the tenacity of Helms, he said there would be at least four more of them in the Senate. Finally, Lott had advised capitulation, telling Clinton the Mexico post was not worth "putting a dent in the whole committee system" to wrest control from a chairman. From personal interest, having recommended Weld to replace Janet Reno, I asked whether the president had mentioned his tactical errors in their postmortem. No, he replied. Why crap on somebody once the damage is done?

From Mexico, we bounced into recent contacts with novelist Gabriel García Márquez—two of them, one at the White House and then in New York before a speech to the United Nations. The president recalled going from the latter to an opening night performance of *Carmen* at the Metropolitan Opera, starring Placido Domingo and the young mezzosoprano Denyce Graves, whose voice entranced both Bill and Hillary. He diverted into love for Bizet's music, the career arc of diva Graves from humble beginnings in Washington, and appreciation for superimposed English signs that now allowed "even a hick like me" to follow the story. Of García Márquez, he said a relationship had developed since their introduction in Martha's Vineyard three years ago, when the Nobel laureate had been so impressed by fourteen-year-old Chelsea's comments on his books that he sent her a personally inscribed set. Now, said Clinton, he could say frankly that "your buddy" Fidel Castro really screwed up by shooting down those protest planes last year, and García Márquez replied, "Don't you think he knows it?" They compared versions of miscommunication and bureaucratic error. Even his anti-Castro exile groups had been turning slowly against the embargo, observed the president, but now the spasmodic reaction to violence lamentably delayed political accommodations for years.

Separately, the novelist shared an unpublished account of political kidnappings in his native Colombia. Clinton said he secluded himself next door—pointing to the bedroom—and read the whole manuscript in one sitting. It was straightforward, without the fantastical images of García's fiction, but no less captivating in the portrait of a country torn between political institutions and ruthless drug cartels. García brought alive the parallel worlds—one built mostly on law and invisible ties, the other on raw fear and money. He made you feel the cold courage required for officials to make progress in the face of their own desperate people, who begged exceptions and deals to ransom kidnapped daughters or husbands. Clinton said García's brokenhearted realism shamed fashionable opinion in Washington that Colombians were just wishy-washy.

We closed on a survey of the globe, similar to a briefing once requested by the pope. With many specifics, President Clinton said he felt positive about Africa and Ireland, negative about the Middle East, and uncertain about Asia. He lingered over a bizarre news story about Israel's release of a Hamas prisoner in the wake of an incident—first reported as a traffic dispute involving two Canadian tourists in Amman, Jordan—that may have been a bungled assassination. Well, there was a lot more to it. He said two Mossad agents disguised as Canadians had been arrested, but at least eight others fled into the Israeli embassy after injecting an exotic poison into the ear of a Palestinian named Khaled Mashal. King Hussein, furious about the insult to Jordanian sovereignty, privately demanded that Israel identify the poison and supply an antidote, but Prime Minister Netanyahu at first refused, calling the information a state secret.

Sadly, said the president, Netanyahu had ordered this rogue attack without coordination inside his own government, which was receiving significant covert help from King Hussein to arrest Hamas terrorists within Jordan. From Arkansas, on his trip to honor the Little Rock Nine, Clinton had been enlisted to call Hussein. The king was threatening in a rage to close and expel the Israeli embassy. They managed instead to obtain the antidote from Israel and save Mashal, who, as a negotiator from the political side of Hamas, should not have been a military target even in all-out war. The attempt on his life made sense only as a political gambit to shore up Netanyahu's right-wing base, but the clumsy failure obliged Netanyahu and his mortified cabinet to free Sheikh Ahmed Yasin by way of apology. In public, Israel was downplaying the release as a goodwill gesture to a dying man, but Yasin, not quite sixty, had founded Hamas in 1987 and remained a charismatic force behind suicide bombers.* With theatrical accents from *Macbeth* and James Bond, Clinton acidly summarized this messy disaster, which strengthened the undertow of terrorism. He was amazed the cover story about Canadian tourists lasted a week.

---

* Six years later, on March 22, 2004, missiles from Israeli helicopters killed Sheikh Yasin in Gaza City.

CHAPTER THIRTY

BUDDY AND
SOCKS

Tuesday, December 16, 1997

Wednesday, January 14, 1998

O ur tour of the globe continued through winter sessions. There had
been a crisis in November when Iraq expelled U.N. weapons inspectors again. Clinton's dispatch of the carrier group *George Washington*
augmented preparations for air strikes, forcing Saddam Hussein to relent
at the deadline beneath a cloud of blandishments and schoolyard threats.
The president said compliance was by no means permanent, and he may
have to authorize military action in Iraq within the next year.

More pleasantly, he described a trip to encourage Bosnia two years
into the Dayton Accords. Clinton said he was grateful for Bob Dole's
endorsement at every stop. In plainspoken speeches, full of football
metaphors about not abandoning the field in the fourth quarter, Dole
praised a mission of hard-slogging progress with negligible casualties.
His blunt bipartisanship neutralized carping Republicans, including a
few in the presidential delegation. Bosnia was no longer a powder keg in
the heart of Europe. The 8,500 U.S. troops exhibited high morale, and
Bosnia's war-torn factions salvaged healing moments. In Sarajevo, where
the national orchestra had kept playing right through the years of siege,
Hillary and Dole joined an emotional tribute to seven killed musicians.
An empty chair honored the principal violinist, who had been shot
walking to rehearsal. Martyred artists from all three ethnic groups an-

swered snipers and artillery shells with music, President Clinton told the crowd, and their courage would help sustain Bosnia's new institutions of democracy.

We covered Jiang Zemin's state visit in October. Clinton said the Chinese media trumpeted the news that a Beijing leader was received intimately at the White House residence, where the two of them talked in the Yellow Oval Room for nearly three hours. I lost track of the economic issues he reviewed on tape, but the president approached human rights with narrow calculation. Let's set morals aside, he told Jiang with a smile. If Clinton called it wrong for China to jail political dissidents, he knew Jiang always called it immoral for the United States to have so many criminals of every kind. China believed social decay was the inevitable consequence of free debate. For now, strictly as a matter of governing China, Clinton asked Jiang how jailing dissidents gained enough security to offset criticism from around the world. Would it really affect stability for a handful of critics to be making speeches? In response, said the president, Jiang detailed enormous changes such a policy would require in his bureaucracy. A shift in prerogative implied apology for the past, which was very difficult in Chinese culture. Officials at many levels would be upset, especially because they saw only a minor cost in the controversy over human rights. Jiang insisted that complex internal reform must come slowly.

The president responded to this fresh candor by setting forth his own political imperatives. Out of respect, Clinton told Jiang, here was a preview of every criticism he would make at their joint press conference of October 29. He would warn that China's human rights policies were on the wrong side of history, and he invited Jiang to express reciprocal misgivings. "We *admit* we've got a problem with criminals," said Clinton, "and if you've got ideas why order is better than freedom, Americans would like to hear them." Finally, the president encouraged Jiang to seek spontaneous opinions from ordinary people during his visit—at Harvard, on Wall Street, out in California. Perhaps direct experience, he told me, would rebut suspicions murmured among Chinese officials that public opinion was merely a contrivance by the U.S. government to put them on the defensive. Clinton claimed small steps toward mutual confidence. For the first time, Jiang Zemin publicly admitted "mistakes" in handling the Tiananmen Square demonstrators of 1989, and he soon released China's foremost political dissident, Wei Jingsheng. The president remained cautious. Forty years from now, China probably would have the world's largest economy sitting atop Asia on the flank of Europe. If she retained the current, anti-democratic form of government, such a country posed risks of upheaval even without any imperial designs. Clinton sought a relationship beyond chronic fears of misperception and blowup, strong enough to look for openings toward healthy ties. This goal, while modest, was his first real connection with China I could remember from our sessions.

The president recalled highlights of his South American trip. In Caracas, the debonair President Rafael Caldera Rodríguez had summarized his twin odyssey through nearly sixty years of Venezuelan politics and six children with his wife, Alicia. At their state dinner, Caldera offered gracious, teasing congratulations on the Clintons' recent twenty-second anniversary, predicting wryly from experience that the hardest phase of marriage soon would subside into blissful partnership. In Brazil, Clinton saw the teeming *favelas* near Rio de Janeiro, kicked a soccer ball with world-famous Pelé, and, in the capital of Brasilia, received colorful pomp shaded by hints of resentment toward the United States—for stealing every limelight in our hemisphere, dwarfing giant Brazil, overshadowing its vibrant diversity, inhibiting its markets. "It made the politics very difficult," said the president, "but boy, did I love the tourism." From talks with Argentina's President Carlos Menem, Clinton ventured far south into storied Patagonia, fascinated by a vast forest of bark-less myrtle trees—bright orange, seeping tannin, extremely cold to the touch—with unique climate causes and sensitive implications for the atmospheric chemistry of carbon dioxide. His introduction to South America's environmental wonders came in handy, said Clinton, during the recent international summit in Japan. He sent Al Gore to fortify the U.S. representatives, while from Washington the president lobbied South American presidents among others toward the historic Kyoto Protocol announced on December 10. Two thousand quarrelsome delegates agreed to halt the pell-mell growth of carbon emissions. Rich and poor nations pledged to *reduce* greenhouse gases 5.2 percent below 1990 levels by 2012.

By a quirk of timing, interruptions piled oddly into the topics at hand. Clinton addressed an overlap of the Kyoto talks with dislocations across Asia. Three of Japan's largest securities firms collapsed in November. The Hong Kong stock market plummeted sporadically, triggering on Wall Street such a precipitous one-day drop of 550 points that the exchange closed early. Somehow, we detoured into Hillary's gift to him of a chocolate Labrador puppy—where she found it and how she sprang the news, with running repartee about who needed cheering up in Chelsea's absence. A few mornings ago, recalled the president, Hillary woke up in a moment of clarity about the latest proposal for a name. "Buddy is right," she said. "It's a good name." He asked leave only to check with Buddy Carter, one of the White House butlers on canine duty, and, just as he told of favorable reaction to a shared handle, sounds of eager yelping preceded both Buddys into the Treaty Room. Buddy Carter reported that the creature turning circles on his leash had eaten and peed but "did no business" on their walk. Then the phone rang with an incoming call from Prime Minister Ryutaro Hashimoto of Japan.

The butler retreated from the official conversation, and I wound up holding Buddy's leash while the president congratulated "Ryu" on courageous moves to kick-start the frozen Japanese credit system, thereby stabilizing economies in the region. During frequent pauses for on-line translation, Clinton covered the receiver and explained for our tapes that Japan's stagnation was chronic and intractable. Interest rates were practically zero, he said, rendering monetary stimulation useless. He also tossed little treats from his desk to the rug for Buddy, who towed me with surprising ease. The pup would be tuckered out soon, the president assured me, and Buddy indeed was asleep when we resumed at the coffee table. Clinton said the Japanese economy strangely resisted fiscal as well as monetary repair. The whole culture was averse to spending, and financial leaders squirreled away money that needed to be spent.

Asian recovery was vital to the United States, because our economy alone could not sustain the load we were carrying for the world's growth. He said we were at a peak, with unemployment down to 4.7 percent and our budget deficit accelerating downward past $20 billion toward zero. Next month, the president disclosed, he would propose a fully balanced budget for fiscal year 1999—three years ahead of the target adopted with fanfare only last summer. His budget would include proposals to reform Medicaid for the poor, double the Peace Corps, expand health coverage for children, and finance a moratorium on logging in national forests. The 1999 budget also would shore up Social Security by sparing its separate surplus of $100 billion, which had been filched annually to mask the deficit. He said the American people were wiser than presumed about the discipline needed to safeguard Social Security. His agenda was ambitious. He was sick of ridiculous stories calling him a tired lame duck.

Clinton anticipated two lines of response to budgetary balance. First, there would be pressure to build highways. This was pure politics, as both Democrats and Republicans loved new roads. Highway dollars connected networks of jobs and contributors, and you could spread projects through so many districts that a highway bill almost passed itself. "I know," he said, "because I used to do it." These bills concealed cost commitments in the outlying years, which made them deceptively irresponsible, and highway politics would be an early barometer of fiscal restraint.

Second, a sound Treasury at last would expose the Republican lack of interest in constructive political competition. So the president expected more attention to scandals. The frenzy was worse, if possible, since Fred Thompson terminated his Senate hearings into alleged Clinton corruption for lack of "a clear story line" like Watergate. In a leaked memo, FBI Director Freeh pushed Attorney General Reno to appoint a special prosecutor regardless. Transparently, the bureau claimed to discover misplaced files containing highly classified tips about Chinese efforts to buy Democrats in 1996.* When Reno announced on December 2 that the vague evidence still did not warrant a special prosecutor, howls of protest were almost universal. Such headlines may be irresistible fun to reporters, said Clinton, but it was a prime strategic choice for his opponents to step up diversions while denigrating the benefits of politics. Their congressional committees grilled Reno. Speaker Gingrich called her a fool not to establish an independent source of answers for all these

---

* Bob Woodward, "FBI Had Overlooked Key Files in Probe of Chinese Influence," *Washington Post*, November 14, 1997, p. 1.

money questions. Republicans denounced Kyoto as "big-government" folly like health reform. One special prosecutor had just indicted Henry Cisneros on eighteen flimsy charges,* and another testified shamelessly that the Justice Department impeded his eternal investigation of Mike Espy.

Clinton asked me to make a note for next time. He wanted to record observations about all the special prosecutors, not just Ken Starr, perhaps on a separate tape. He said they were working in concert with blatantly partisan sources, such as the lawyers for Paula Jones. I said fine, doing my best not to wake Buddy while the tapes rewound. The president brightened instantly when offered page proofs for *Pillar of Fire,* the second volume of my King-era history. He would treasure it, he said, spreading balm for a writer. He hoped we were doing good work.

OUTSIDE EVENTS DEFLECTED our contact in January. Arriving after supper, on short notice, I glanced at the security monitor in the Usher's Office and was startled by the panoply of lawyers cleared ahead of me into the residence: Ken Starr, David Kendall, and Bob Bennett, plus various assistants. To questions about what was going on, familiar staff members repeated the visitors list in a tone of exaggerated calm. This could mean anything, which spurred my anxious preparations for a bracketed tape on special prosecutors. Surely, the president did not intend for me to meet them, risking exposure for his diaries. I wondered whether Starr's office received these time logs of White House guests, and what questions if any might be posed about me. Later, Clinton waved all these subjects aside in the family parlor. The lawyers had been in the Treaty Room with Hillary, not him, for Starr to linger again over one of his comatose inquests. Clinton thought it was the FBI Filegate tempest from 1996.

---

* Special prosecutor David Barrett indicted Cisneros on eighteen felony counts of conspiracy, perjury, and obstruction of justice. Two years later, Barrett would accept instead a guilty plea to one misdemeanor for erroneous statements, with no jail time. The deal averted trial on terms deemed nearly complete exoneration for Cisneros. Nevertheless, Barrett continued his investigation into a record twelfth year. His final report in 2006 left a conspiratorial cloud of 120 pages redacted by court order.

On tape, the president apologized for our delay. He had been absorbed in a political meeting about the congressional elections next November. Poll by poll, race by race, analysis kindled early hopes for him to become the first sixth-year president whose party gained seats. Realistically, he discounted the Senate, with its six vulnerable Democrats against only three for Republicans, but historic victory was possible in the House. Looking both backward and forward, his numbers crunchers concluded that the single best predictor of close House elections was Clinton's approval rating. "If I stay up over sixty percent, we have a chance to do well," he said. "If I don't, we don't." He called this targeted indicator none too pleasant. It raised the stakes if he chose to get things done by spending political capital. Because other politicians had similar polls, Democratic candidates would be hypersensitive about Clinton's priorities. And clearly, he said, these numbers helped explain the Republican strategy to keep stirring the Paula Jones case along with Whitewater and various incarnations of an Asia money scandal. Clinton would not be on any ballot in 1998, but seemingly incidental distractions, by driving down his numbers, could pay dividends for Republican candidates in Oregon or Indiana.

He sensed the national fulcrum teetering, and he believed they did, too. "These Republicans think they've got the whole government now," he said. "Except for the president." They controlled both houses of Congress, a slim majority on the Supreme Court, and, from recent decades, a cumulative advantage in federal judges and the civil service. Plus, they enjoyed powerful conservative think tanks, such as the Heritage Foundation and the Federalist Society, promoting a unified theme that Democrats were spendthrift softies who could not be trusted with the economy or national security. That dominant theme also was teetering, which meant that Republicans were on the brink of consolidating power or suffering a cyclical collapse.

The uncertain tilt accounted for a hardening edge in the political wars, which Clinton saw most starkly in politics over the judiciary. The Republican Senate had confirmed not a single appellate judge all last year—and only nine district judges—stranding more than a hundred Clinton appointees to vacant bench seats across the United States. They ignored neutral cries for help with clogged dockets. Even Chief Justice

Rehnquist asked fellow Republicans to relent, and Attorney General Reno blistered the Senate's intransigence in her toughest speeches. The president smiled with appreciation. On judges, like special prosecutors, the Republicans had gotten Reno's back up. She was showing her teeth.

Still, what preoccupied Clinton was neither domestic politics nor special prosecutors. While accustomed to surprise, I was slow to perceive his knotted concentrations overseas. One question drew a full description of political massacres in Algeria, with reverberations in the Muslim world and much brainstorming about potential remedies. "I have nothing positive to report to you there," said the president, but his response on Northern Ireland detailed interactions with participants including British prime minister Tony Blair. Clinton compared its lurching progress to the Middle East when Rabin was alive. The U.S. mediator George Mitchell shepherded political talks. A special emissary worked on economics. Blair had gone to Belfast, and Sinn Fein's Gerry Adams had visited Blair in London—for the first such talks since David Lloyd George famously received the Irish rebellion leader Michael Collins in 1921. The president described encouraging signals from the past few days. Not even the sectarian murder of Gerry Adams's nephew, he said, could derail steadfast efforts by warring Catholics and Protestants to create a unified government for Northern Ireland.*

His replies delved next into Asia's financial crisis, which was rattling world markets more than the Mexican devaluation of 1995. Now, as then, proposals for U.S. assistance aroused bipartisan opposition. Republicans tended to grumble against helping foreigners, whereas Democrats fussed about rewarding the very bankers and speculators who caused default. Clinton said he could only wish these political challenges were the extent of his task. Now, for the first time, he lacked confidence in a rational strategy from which to start. His shrewdest economic advisers—Robert Rubin and Larry Summers—doubted the structural support for market solutions in South Korea and Indonesia, where

---

* Protestant and Catholic splinter groups traded retaliatory assassinations designed to stop the peace process. On January 11, 1998, one of them claimed credit for gunning down Terry Enwright, who was married to a niece of Gerry Adams, outside a pub.

huge thirty-year development projects were financed with ninety-day loans, assuming the notes could be rolled over forever. Then, when the Indonesian rupiah lost half its value in two months, companies failed in waves because they could not borrow twice their debt for tomorrow's payroll. Clinton disclosed a terrible argument with President Suharto,* Indonesia's aging dictator, who rejected his plea to create basic commercial codes and bank regulations. Suharto accused the president of imposing "Western values" to gain hegemony over Indonesian companies. Clinton shrugged. So far, we were lucky to reap a temporary windfall. Panicky investors had shifted many billions of dollars from Asia to safety in the United States. He fretted, of course, that they might pull them out again right before the fall elections.

There was a burst of reflection about Iran, whose new president, Mohammad Khatami, had just granted an extensive interview to CNN correspondent Christiane Amanpour. Clinton had "all kinds of people" within the U.S. government studying Khatami's words, sifting for buried hints that the Islamist regime may be open to relations of some sort, even secretly. After almost twenty years of frozen hostility, and nonrecognition, the president said any thaw would shift politics throughout that volatile part of the world. It could isolate Saddam Hussein in Iraq, put pressure on Syria, and help the Middle East peace process, lifting economic as well as strategic opportunities for both Iran and the United States. Our intelligence, said the president, found broad support for better relations among the Iranian people, but Khatami was maneuvering delicately between their hopes and the threat of a crackdown by fundamentalist mullahs, who still controlled the machinery of Iran's religious state.

In his interview, Khatami dodged questions about Israel with a discourse on anti-Semitism. It was a "Western concept," he told Amanpour, foreign to Muslims and developed entirely by Christians from medieval Europe down to murderous culmination in the Holocaust. There was much truth to this, said Clinton, but he could not allow

---

* Suharto had seized power in a 1965 coup followed by massive ethnic and political purges still shrouded in mystery. Protests over the 1998 hardships drove him from office on May 21. He died January 27, 2008.

Khatami any excuse—whether sophisticated or specious—for his blanket condemnation of "Zionist" people and his public goal to destroy Israel. The president explored treacherous subtleties between the errors of governments and the rights of people. Carefully, under favorable circumstances, he said he could envision progress through an exchange of national apology. We should not have overthrown Iran's government in 1953.* How angry would we be if Iran did that to us—throwing out not only our leaders but the Constitution itself? Nevertheless, Iran's mullahs should not have vented that anger against American hostages in 1979, either, consolidating their revolution behind hateful slogans toward the "Great Satan" United States.

In his discourse on the Middle East, he was nettled from the beginning. Late last year, Prime Minister Netanyahu went on American television to complain that Clinton had "humiliated" the State of Israel by declining to meet when both their airplanes were delayed conveniently on runways at the Los Angeles airport. The president told me he certainly did not object to spontaneous events. Nor did he resent so much another leader trying to manipulate his schedule. He said the reason for his refusal was just what he told Netanyahu bluntly afterward on the phone: Clinton balked at another state meeting whose sole purpose was to stall. Netanyahu, having committed to take concrete steps forward, planned to filibuster yet again with reasons why Israel must wait instead—this time for five months. His stance was designed to shore up a faltering, anti-peace political base, and when Clinton denied him the implicit blessing of the United States, Netanyahu substituted a cry of national insult. The president said this petulant outburst would gain Bibi at most a temporary bump in polls. Netanyahu was headed down.

Clinton's temper rose in anticipation of separate audiences next week with Netanyahu and Arafat. Reviewing assessments by Secretary Albright and ambassador Dennis Ross, he said that Israel—four years into the Oslo peace process—had withdrawn military forces from 27 per-

---

* The CIA and British spies ousted the elected prime minister, Mohammed Mossadegh, restoring hereditary rule by the Shah of Iran. This feat, while both celebrated and reviled among covert operations of the Cold War, was not publicly acknowledged by the United States until congressional hearings in 1976.

cent of the West Bank. Now Netanyahu blocked further withdrawals unless Arafat's interim Palestinian Authority accepted a ceiling of 13 percent more territory. For political survival, and security from terrorists, Bibi would retain full control in more than half the West Bank—60 percent—including a network of roads connecting the Israeli settlements. Clinton said no two-state deal could advance on terms so stingy. Worse, Netanyahu also claimed paralysis on gestures to alleviate suffering and mistrust. He would not let Palestinians reopen the airport in Gaza, for instance, nor authorize a highway between isolated Gaza and the West Bank. He would not even permit the construction of industrial parks in Gaza, for fear that Palestinians would divert the economic base to terrorism. These policies, groaned Clinton, undermined peace politics on both sides. When Hamas planted a bomb, the Israeli army shut down all exits from densely populated Gaza, locking a million desperately poor Palestinians away from their only available jobs. The iron logic of occupation demanded a servile psychology, but it also drove popular support from Arafat toward Hamas.

The president thrashed about for an alternative. He was openly frustrated, near despair. My notes an hour later recorded that I could not remember seeing him this upset. He said he understood why President Bush and Secretary of State Baker once announced cuts in Israel's security allotment. That extremity, however, produced spasms of fear and retrenchment in Israel. It made sense only in a package to *impose* a Middle East settlement from the outside, and Clinton's whole premise was that the parties themselves must choose and build the terms of peace. Leaving Israel's military assistance intact, the president contemplated his ultimate sanction: public withdrawal from the talks. He said it was not in the interest of the United States to dignify phony negotiations. He refused to sponsor a sham.

I asked whether he would say so to Netanyahu at the White House next week. "That's what we're arguing about," he replied. Short of this, I asked, could he suspend further U.S. contact until Netanyahu delivered smaller steps like the business permits for Gaza? Well, that option was not currently on the table. It would be new—and make sense—only as a public statement, which he said would be a pretty big deal. However camouflaged, such conditions would be a rebuke to Israel for dragging its feet on measures not essential to security. Clinton said his neutrality would be hard to recover.

He analyzed alternative messages for Netanyahu, shaving grim risks and unlikely rewards. Then he smiled. The president said he was having far better success as a peacemaker with Buddy and Socks. There had been several nasty spats, mostly to Buddy's disadvantage. He gave ample credit to his secretary Betty Currie for arranging truces in which the pets eyed each other warily across the Oval Office.

CHAPTER THIRTY-ONE

LEWINSKY

Goucher College Convocation,
Wednesday, January 21, 1998

Monday, April 6, 1998

Monday, May 11, 1998

Wednesday, June 10, 1998

Tuesday, July 7, 1998

Our January session had closed on personal transitions, with no sign that some were about to get sideswiped by others. President Clinton said how happy he and Hillary were to have Christy join the first lady's small speechwriting staff. That was her third day on the job. I said the post was a daunting thrill for both of us, and we were adjusting to the reversal in our long-established household routine. Now it was Christy who rose before dawn, so she could catch an early commuter train down to Washington, leaving off-to-school chores for me. On January 21, the day I became one of its part-time professors, Goucher College in Baltimore would award Hillary an honorary degree. I inscribed for the Clintons two finished copies of my new book, with a personal note to each of them, and welcomed a novel interlude in the classroom before resecluding myself again to start the final volume of civil rights history.

The president, while chatting about family matters, raised the possibility of collaboration on his memoirs after he left office. We had not discussed this idea in several years. The prospect still made me uncomfortable, I said, because of the several roles I was trying to keep straight already—hidden diarist, friend, sounding board, occasional messenger. Plus, his official memoirs would be a significant undertaking. Selfishly, I feared getting pulled away from a marathon life's work on the searing 1960s—when both transformation and historical distortion took hold for our era—perhaps even losing the strength to finish. And secrecy inhibited my options. Just to obtain a contingency clause in my new book contract, securing terms for a temporary leave, I would need the president's permission to confide something about our tapes project. This Clinton freely gave. Now that our work had remained confidential so long, he found the risk of discreet disclosure worthwhile to preserve options for his book. I apologized nevertheless for troublesome misgivings. He faced more than enough burdens. My job was to make it safe and easy for him to compile a candid record for the future.

Our separate whirlwinds converged strangely within a few days. The president hosted Medal of Freedom ceremonies, signed a NATO pact on the Balkans, and gave yet another speech on the catastrophic costs of youth smoking, as revealed by new internal documents about cleverly insidious tobacco advertisements. Then Clinton disappeared from public sight to answer six hours of questions under oath from the lawyers for Paula Jones, amid a blind frenzy of speculation in the press. Meanwhile, I secured a campus parking sticker and launched publication events for my first new book in nine years. That Monday, a Baltimore friend sought me out after a King holiday event at a high school. His wife worked for the United States Holocaust Memorial Museum in Washington, and he arranged for her to arrive at our home shortly after I did. She brought several copies of *Pillar of Fire* for me to sign, but mostly she unburdened distress. Yasir Arafat had announced a wish to tour the Holocaust Museum during his upcoming trip to see President Clinton, only to be branded unwelcome. The museum's director had just made world news by calling Arafat "Hitler incarnate." She said museum ideologues had trampled every principle for a public institution of learning about hatred and history. Some of her colleagues careened toward revolt. Their board chair, Miles Lerman,* was sympathetic but battered. Though he was a stranger to me, would I try to calm him? She had his number in Palm Beach.

All my dodges failed. Lerman sounded desperate but not confused. His board had bulldozed him with warnings that donors would slit the museum's throat if Arafat darkened the door. Then they vanished, leaving him to defend a position he opposed. Lerman said he would welcome Arafat personally, if needed, and guide him by the hand. He had notified people in the State Department, but they could not make amends fast enough with Netanyahu arriving in the United States—and Arafat on the way. Lerman had to get exactly the right message to President Clinton. Well then, why didn't he try a direct call, especially since he knew Clinton himself? I thought the president might make time to set right this inflammatory mistake. Lerman groaned. "I led my foundation into a swamp," he said—hurting both cause and country. "I chastise myself." He could not bring himself to impose unless the president knew in advance of his remorse.

Lerman's misery was so sincere that I agreed to try, and the president answered within the hour to hear a thirty-second bulletin. Fantastic, he replied. This ugly episode might turn out for the best. Apology would show a dramatic change of heart, and we needed movement somewhere, somehow, for the Middle East. He would run interference himself if necessary. I gave him Lerman's phone numbers. That night, I drove to Washington for a book signing at Politics & Prose on Connecticut Avenue. Afterward, by chance, Secretary of State Albright walked into the restaurant next door from a screening of the film *Amistad*. The two of us huddled briefly in the doorway, between the noise within and a pounding rain outside. She knew already of Lerman's intended reversal. I relayed precautionary worries from Clinton that Arafat might now rebuff a contrite invitation from the museum, leaving damage everywhere. She

---

* During World War II, Lerman escaped from a Nazi slave labor camp into a Jewish resistance group near Lvov, Poland. His wife survived Auschwitz. In the United States, he raised nearly $200 million as the founding board chair for the Holocaust Museum, which opened in 1993. Lerman died on January 22, 2008.

said Arafat could be just mean enough to do so, but her people would be working to prevent it.

Prime Minister Netanyahu entered the White House on Tuesday. Evangelist Jerry Falwell was rallying crowds to support him against Clinton, praising the Israeli government's resistance to phased withdrawal from the West Bank. Meanwhile, news flashes reported that a stormy board meeting at the Holocaust Museum did rescind the ban on Arafat, who would meet Albright a day ahead of his audience with President Clinton.

Well before daybreak on Wednesday, January 21, Christy left for a crazy excursion of government service—down to Washington by train just in time to join the first lady on a train back to Baltimore for the winter convocation at Goucher College. I received her call before heading to the same event. Stricken, she told me to bring in our early *Washington Post* and turn on the television. Nonstop news revealed the president's alleged affair with a twenty-four-year-old former White House intern named Monica Lewinsky. Already, Starr's jurisdiction was expanded to potential perjury about her by Clinton in his Saturday deposition for the Jones case. Hints of intrigue spilled everywhere. Starr had secret tapes of Lewinsky talking about sex. Christy said everybody in the West Wing or Old Executive Office Building was whispering, and no one knew whether Hillary would go to Baltimore or cancel. She could only wait for her over in the residence as instructed, pending a final consultation on the Goucher address. It was the first full speech she had drafted.

In the staging room beneath Goucher's gymnasium, protocol people relieved tension by repeating instructions for the march order of dignitaries, trustees, and faculty. White House advance workers tracked the progress of the train up from Washington, and reporters advised Judy Mohraz, the college president, on the extraordinary number of their colleagues staked out at Baltimore Penn Station to seek Hillary's first reaction to the scandal. The rest of us were a sea of numbness in colorful academic robes, mostly chipper but vague. We had no idea whether she would whimper, hide, or sizzle. When the motorcade finally approached, Mohraz led a small advance party outside through the rear delivery door. Her plan was for me, as the rookie professor who would be moderating questions after the ceremony, to present the first lady in turn to Mohraz and others including Senator Barbara Mikulski and Christy's old boss, Mayor Kurt Schmoke. It is possible that anxiety pushed me forward, or that the others fell back, but I found myself far ahead when Hillary out-paced her aides from the front limousine. Are you all right? She smiled but barely slowed down. "I'm fine," she said. "Let's go get 'em."

Hillary dazzled Goucher, but Monica gripped the news. There was instant talk of impeachment amid feverish speculation that Clinton would resign by the end of January. David Kendall told us to shut down our sessions while Starr's army was invading the White House inner sanctum with subpoenas for entry logs, phone records, and witnesses to prove the alleged affair. Starr bowled over legal objections to demand—and win—testimony from Clinton's lawyers, aides, and even Secret Service agents about what they had seen or heard of Lewinsky.

For weeks, stories sifted what Betty Currie, Nancy Hernreich, and Vernon Jordan among many others may have told the grand jury under duress. I winced for them at a distance, clueless. Vernon had hired me for perilous civil rights work in 1969, and I retained strong confidence in his professional integrity—that he would not suborn perjury, or lie himself. Simultaneously, I nursed apprehension over his reported role as President Clinton's go-between with Lewinsky before the scandal erupted. In our glancing associations, I had picked up from Vernon an attitude toward extramarital sex best described as lighthearted or recreational.

For me, the tension between public and private morality was familiar quicksand from years studying Martin Luther King. Most people who dogmatically separate the two spheres turn out to make exceptions. There is no hermetic seal. Intimate character and public performance doubtless can affect one another, but the causality seems as complex as human nature. In King's case, I found signs of devouring guilt that drove him to seek penance in deeds of historic sacrifice. I had no strong theories about what drove Clinton. The stories of his philandering were troublesome, and so was the arrogance of judgment from afar. A few times, with other longtime friends like Strobe Talbott, I hazarded guesses about his sex life. My only firsthand evidence was that Clinton and Hillary had been ardently amorous long ago in Texas, to the point that I remembered forlorn third-wheel moments. All I heard since were the common rumors of JFK-like affairs down in Arkansas. Without proof, I thought there was probably some truth to them. Affairs would not be unusual for a success-ful politician with big appetites. Strobe pretty much agreed, though he remained steadfastly baffled. Clinton was not among the youthful Lo-tharios even Strobe had recognized during their time together at Oxford. If subsequent rumors were true, the Clintons must carry many scars be-tween them, but we found the marriage anything but loveless. Their pri-vate partnership still seemed warm and eager, never cold, with a spark from somewhere if not libido. This struck Strobe and me as an abiding mystery, though we laughed at my amateur babble and his straitlaced discomfort with sexual conjecture. We hoped, in light of the near-fatal 1992 campaign scare over Gennifer Flowers, that Clinton's equally big brain and ambition would suppress roving habits in the White House. Until now, every scandal had been resurrected from his past.

LEWINSKY CHANGED EVERYTHING, besotting the airwaves with subplots. A month later, I faxed a short note intended to convey that the history project was more important than embarrassment for anyone: "I'm ready whenever you need me." Another six weeks went by before Nancy Hern-reich's call for the night in April, the 6th, when my book promotions finally ended with a lecture at the National Archives. Afterward, I was nervous passing through clearance to the White House grounds. It felt like longer than the three months since my last visit. I had flickering fantasies of walls marred with bullet holes and lipstick graffiti, but friendly routines led instead to the same quiet dignity of the yellow cen-ter hall. In the Treaty Room, President Clinton congratulated me for North Carolina's run to the Final Four of the NCAA men's basketball tournament. He thought UNC might have gone all the way to beat Kentucky, the eventual champion, until Utah out-rebounded the Tar Heels by twelve in the first half, and he issued in jest an executive order for Vince Carter and Antawn Jamison not to turn pro next year. Catch-ing up, I told him I was just back from a march on the thirtieth anniver-sary of Dr. King's death in Memphis, alongside King's surviving colleague Fred Shuttlesworth, who preached salty recollections the whole way. Jesse Jackson was there, just back from a trip to Africa with the president.

Clinton made sure I had not yet turned on the recorders. If asked, he wanted to tell Kendall there was nothing on the tapes about Lewinsky. He told me his relationship with Jackson was checkered. "He's been mad at me," said the president, "and I've been mad at him." But now Jesse had done something he would not forget. When the Lewinsky news broke, he called Chelsea at Stanford. Jesse was the only nonfamily adult with her cell phone number. How he got it was another story. Jesse said he knew this was terrible for her. Nothing like it had ever happened in American politics. He did not know everything involved, but he wanted to remind Chelsea how much her parents loved her. Their family needed to stick together now above all, and if she needed to counsel, rage, or pray, he was always available. He never breathed a word to the press—this was not the self-promotional Jesse—and they had several calls since. It was not easy to be pastoral for a college student as fiercely precocious as Chelsea, but she clearly appreciated him. Therefore, Clinton always would appreciate Jesse.

On tape, I asked the president in veiled language how he managed to deliver his State of the Union Address only days into scalding personal accusations. Some people doubted that he would even show up. Clinton looked puzzled. He said, matter-of-factly, that he never understood all the hype. This speech was not so hard to deliver. Perhaps the uproar made him tighten its structure a bit, which was good, but he wanted to show that he was tending the people's business at a critical moment in history. The State of the Union was robust. Every indicator was at a thirty-year best—from the lowest unemployment, crime, inflation, and welfare to unrivaled technology and world leadership. The first big applause greeted his announcement that the federal deficit, once bearing an incomprehensibly large eleven zeroes, was now, literally, zero. The second applause—much bigger—answered his pledge to use surpluses ahead first to save Social Security. Within the White House, Clinton digressed to me, there had been debate about giving a quarter of the anticipated surplus back in tax cuts, but he did not want to count chickens before they hatched. Besides, a surplus budget would give the country room to retool for the twenty-first century in education, the environment, and visionary endeavors like the human genome project.

Congress cheered all these things. The scandal played to his favor, said Clinton, because it delivered an enormous television audience with commentators perched to evaluate his defense. He did not utter a word on personal matters—never considered it—which dramatized a split between public policy and the obsessive chorus. His polls not only withstood the maelstrom, they skyrocketed. The *Chicago Tribune* showed his ratings up to 72 percent. A CNN–*Wall Street Journal* survey in February recorded job approval for Clinton at a stupefying 79 percent. These heights did not last, of course, but he said they pointed to a decisive verdict on political priorities.

The chasm between his agenda and the news was awkward for our project. My log of potential questions, being culled mostly from media reports, contained few presidential events other than the sex scandals. Starr dominated the front pages. He went so far as to haul Lewinsky's mother before the grand jury, seeking to force detailed testimony about sex in the White House, and on slow days for Starr there had been reported skirmishes over Clinton's upcoming trial in the Paula Jones case. I did ask about another Iraq crisis ending February 20, and the president seemed sensitive about the fact that U.N. secretary-general Kofi Annan—not Clinton—had negotiated Saddam Hussein's latest retreat to readmit the U.N. weapons inspectors, forestalling more air strikes by Britain and the United States. He thought Annan had done a good job in spite of mischief from the French and Russians, who ingratiated themselves with Saddam by agitating for the repeal of the U.N. sanctions. Clinton said the sanctions remained vital for the weapons inspectors to dismantle Saddam's arsenal. So far, they had located and destroyed more weapons than Saddam lost in the whole Gulf War, rendering him so weak that there was almost no support in the world for renewed military attacks, but they must finish the inspections. In his opinion, chemical and biological weapons were a greater long-range threat than Saddam's nuclear program.

The president veered into a Clausewitz-style synopsis of seesawing advantage between offensive and defensive military weapons. Then he volunteered thoughts about Iran off my abbreviated list of topics. If Iraq ever became strong enough to worry Iran again, either by deposing Saddam or somehow shedding the U.N. sanctions, Iran's fundamentalist regime might have incentive to seek better relations with the United

States. Until then, Clinton thought the slightest overtures to Iran were "dicey." Islamic courts had just arrested a moderate Iranian mayor in what U.S. intelligence considered a warning against President Khatami's suspected openness toward the West. The two countries were carefully orchestrating a goodwill exchange of amateur wrestlers, but Clinton's national security advisers vigorously opposed any presidential welcome. They believed his handshake would push too fast, elevate the politics, and compel the ayatollahs to clamp down with purges. The president was inclined to disagree. He said his team may be wound too tightly on this, but it was hard to go against unanimous opinion. The most he could do was to let Health Secretary Donna Shalala meet the Iranian wrestling team. She spoke Farsi from Peace Corps service in a small Iranian village.

I prompted him through the twelve-day tour of Africa late in March. Perhaps from fatigue, my notes captured only passing images of his toasts with Nelson Mandela, his admiration for the towering President Abdou Diouf of Senegal, and his painful meetings in Uganda with mutilated survivors of the Rwandan genocide. He confessed panic in Accra, Ghana, where for a moment he thought two women were trampled during his speech to half a million people. Hillary had a significant influence on the itinerary, said Clinton. All through Africa, they visited far more health centers, refugee camps, rural cooperatives, and small-level entrepreneurial banks than normal for a presidential tour. He was grateful, sensing immense potential. On the other hand, the president said he withdrew into Bruce Lindsey's room to take an international call at the last stop in Africa. It was his lawyer Bob Bennett, and he preferred to spare Hillary. "By God, she's thrown out the whole damn thing!" shouted Bennett. Judge Susan Wright in Arkansas had granted summary judgment for Clinton. Paula Jones, she ruled on April 1, had no case for sexual harassment even under her version of the facts.

Pending appeal, the legal platform no longer existed for freewheeling examination of a president's sex life, but this dismissal came months too late to save Clinton the risks of sworn testimony by and about Lewinsky. It removed only a commonsense pretext for Starr's newest crusade. Off the tapes, I asked whether the incremental victory explained the resumption of our sessions. Not exactly, said the president. He was acting on a mix of optimism, our continued safe passage, and irritation that we had been letting fear stop our work. I couldn't tell whether Kendall approved.

Despite a season of troubles, the president's face lit up whenever we discussed Northern Ireland. He reviewed his hopeful St. Patrick's Day meeting at the White House with the new prime minister of Ireland, Bertie Ahern, and the steady progress of talks with other negotiators—Tony Blair, Protestants and Catholics in Northern Ireland, and U.S. mediator George Mitchell. All the warring parties were nudging each other along, said Clinton, except the Protestant supremacist in Belfast, Rev. Ian Paisley. The president told me they were on the brink of a comprehensive agreement to establish a free government, weaned from England as the latent colonial power. Who would have thought it possible.

The late hour made Clinton call a halt, and we walked down a deserted center hall to close up the residence. I turned out the lights in the Lincoln Bedroom. We stared together at the Queens' Bedroom. Its bed was gone, which made the space seem cavernous, and there was a gaping hole in the floor for repairs. I found the mess unsettling. He said we should get together again soon.

ON OUR MAY tapes, his excitement grew in description of the Good Friday breakthrough in Northern Ireland, with phone calls long past midnight on Thursday about the inspirational consent of Protestant leader David Trimble, and a jangling wake-up call from Mitchell two hours later to consult Gerry Adams one last time. Tony Blair was beseeching him to campaign personally in the decisive dual plebiscite—one in Northern Ireland, another in Ireland itself—to approve this new coalition government structure of Catholics and Protestants for Northern Ireland. Clinton was sorely tempted. His popularity there ran close to 90 percent. Still, he decided not to go, weighing the marginal impact against obligations at home and a slight risk of Irish backlash against an intruder. Instead, during the G-8 summit at Birmingham, England, he and Tony Blair promoted ratification in a joint interview with television host David Frost. By June, the president was euphoric. He said Gerry Adams made only one mistake, by arranging furloughs so that IRA prisoners could exhort fellow Catholics to renounce violence. This was the correct message, but Protestant opponents attacked the peace agreement for amnesty provisions to put such "killers on the street." Politically, beamed Clinton, the overwhelming success of both plebiscites on May 22 was promising above all for the determined approval of Protestant voters. He analyzed majorities of 51–54 percent by district. For the old antagonists in Northern Ireland, he said, this milestone was the equivalent of our adoption of the 1787 Constitution. Now they must breathe life into its new government against die-hard resistance from both extremes.

Asia yanked him from euphoria. The president reacted gravely to the detonation of nuclear tests by India—three on the day of our May session. One fusion device exploded with roughly the force of the bomb that destroyed Hiroshima. The other two were fission. Measured by the hideous potential developed in the nuclear age, Clinton called them relatively small bombs, but he said these shocks near Pakistan's border upset not only the Pakistani government but its allies in China. Their bellicose messages angered Russia in turn, as politics in that vast region of the world were dominated by volatile interlocking hatreds—my enemy's friend is my enemy. By June, Clinton was fending off charges that the CIA had failed to learn of the Indian tests in advance. There was a naïve presumption that we could have stopped them had we known, but these passions were stronger than pushbutton spy tricks. The Indians realized, he said, that we did not have twenty-four-hour photo coverage of their Pokhran test range. Indeed, they knew we had only three spy satellites in rotation, and they timed the orbits shrewdly to conceal the test preparations. The president doubted that we could have stopped the tests anyway, as the Indians proved by detonating two *more* nuclear tests in spite of universal condemnation—and swift sanctions—from the nonproliferation nations over the first three blasts. Then Pakistan defied the world by setting off six nuclear bombs before the end of May, openly and pointedly one more than India. Outside leaders could only fling themselves into calming diplomacy.

At home, the president analyzed twisted political maneuvers heading toward the fall elections. He focused on Newt Gingrich. The speaker had given spring speeches across the presidential testing state of Iowa, discussing his thoughtful book about future challenges from cyberspace to the world economy. Gingrich also met with Clinton's chief of staff,

Erskine Bowles, whom the president had persuaded to stay on awhile, about a compromise legislative agenda before Congress adjourned. Bowles was optimistic, but the speaker's pollsters brought him disastrous results the same day. Clinton said he knew, because Gingrich later confirmed it himself, that all the numbers recorded a sharply negative reaction to him from core GOP voters across the nation, not just in Iowa. They rejected overwhelmingly the speaker's softer, pragmatic image. The White House had similar poll numbers, and so did House Republicans who were jockeying to replace Gingrich if he ran for president. Overnight, the speaker reverted to red-meat politics. He turned publicly against all Clinton's legislation, including a bipartisan tobacco bill sponsored by Senator John McCain. He accused Clinton of "blackmailing" Israel to help the Palestinians. He called Clinton the nation's "Defendant-in-Chief" for cover-up, corruption, and crime. He said Clinton was wrong to claim that tobacco advertising induced young people to smoke.

This was cold politics, which the president said he let pass except for the dangerous claim about tobacco ads. Clearly, Gingrich was switching back to the GOP's victorious election strategy of 1994, and Clinton conceded that parts of it were likely to work. Republicans had killed the McCain-Feingold campaign reform bill in March. With the possible exception of the anti-tobacco bill, none of the administration's major initiatives was likely to pass the Republican Congress. If stalemate discouraged Democratic voters again, driving down turnout, and if Republicans could mobilize their base by demonizing Clinton, then Gingrich might pick up more GOP seats in Congress. Maybe so, said the president, but he thought the strategy might backfire. This was not 1994. Most of the vaunted "Contract With America" had collapsed. His own record was more popular and established. There was no deficit. In their singular quest to choke off all but the military aspects of government, Republicans were reduced to invective and cries for perpetual tax cuts. Clinton hoped a proper campaign, by framing and comparing programs for the voters, could expose the Republican strategy as anemic and spent, if not cynical. Their few moderates in Congress were resigned, and the dominant conservatives were splintered. In that sense, said Clinton, we were in a post-Gingrich era already.

On rushed his continuing worries about Indonesia, and scenes from a state visit to Chile, until our taped stories lingered over a visit with Chelsea at Stanford. Sidelights included lodging on a farm owned by Steve Jobs of Apple Computers and fund-raising with Willie Mays. He said he inadvertently "outed" his daughter's personal life at the campus chapel, when the minister publicly welcomed the President of the United States "along with Chelsea and Matt." Reporters quickly staked out the homes of Matt's relatives and even his sister's pool. Matt was a world-class swimmer. The president seemed puzzled why so many of her Stanford friends were athletes, but he thought it was interesting that she met this Matthew in a class on the Gospel of St. John. As a fellow dad, I found him fairly relaxed about a college boyfriend. The stories of interaction with Chelsea seemed unaffected by the mortifying Lewinsky allegations, which he still denied.

His batteries recharged at the end of our session over a treasury of gifts from Africa, laid out in the center hall. He described the provenance of each one. There were paintings and sculptures from several countries, along with pottery of striking color and intricacy from South Africa. A woman's sinewy legs hung over the side of a glass table, with a bemused look on her wood face. He said he had never seen anything like the pottery, especially.

WHEN I RETURNED in June, the African pieces had company from other continents. There were gorgeously painted lacquer boxes. I thought they were Greek, but he said Russian—from Yeltsin, on Clinton's latest trip about the usual problems plus nuclear tests in South Asia and simmering war crimes in Kosovo.

Two giant books lay on a table outside the Treaty Room. One said simply *1630* on the cover, for the year in which the Prussian king Frederick the Great had ordered these replicas of Martin Luther's groundbreaking translation of the Bible into German. The illustrated plates were ornate and fresh, albeit more than 350 years old. Next to this Bible was a black-and-white marvel of architectural drawings for every detail of the ancient Wartburg Castle, where the excommunicated Luther had fled after nailing his Protestant theses to the door. At Wartburg, in disguise, Luther had worked on the translation commemorated by Frederick the Great a century later, and Clinton described his visit to the mountaintop castle with German chancellor Helmut Kohl, who gave him these books. On the way, he said, they toured the most efficient General Motors plant in the world. Ten thousand workers once produced seventy thousand cars a year, but now, in the retooled former East Germany, two thousand workers produced more than 170,000. Kohl had been criticized for celebrating Frederick the Great—moving his tomb to the palace outside Potsdam—which some said raised a specter of German militarism. This was ironic, quipped the president, because Frederick had been flamboyantly gay. The real reason behind Kohl's cumulative political troubles, which Clinton tried vainly to patch with a fulsome public tribute, was his role in creating the European Union with a common currency. "Yes," he said sadly, "I think the euro is going to cost him his job."

On an easel, near the books, stood a canvas of spectacular Asian calligraphy by South Korea's new president, Kim Dae-jung. It accompanied a tea set of etched silver, with an English card inside the box: "To His Excellency, Bill Clinton." The president said these gifts had been presented at last night's emotional state dinner. A South Korean opera singer had waited twenty-seven years to call Kim her president, she announced, since the government had stolen the 1971 election from him, then successively exiled him, kidnapped him from Japan, jailed him for a decade, and tried to kill him four times. Finally, Kim took office in South Korea's first peaceful transfer of power, which Clinton compared with our own tense, formative transfer from John Adams to Thomas Jefferson in 1801. He praised Kim as a personal hero alongside three luminous, long-suffering pioneers of freedom around the modern world—Lech Walesa in Poland, Václav Havel in the Czech Republic, and Nelson Mandela in South Africa. Kim's goal was to stop the fifty-year war dance with North Korea. He did not seek to reunify his country like Kohl of Germany, Clinton explained, because it lacked the economic base for success. Still, with the consolidation of South Korean democracy, a truce in this global tinderbox would be an achievement for several lifetimes.

Other than the Balkans and Northern Ireland, the president spoke extensively on tape about a new variation in the persistent effort to tarnish him with sinister Asian connections. The *New York Times* had launched a new series, based on FBI sources and the moribund Fred Thompson hearings in the Senate, alleging that Chinese campaign contributions had bought access to top secret U.S. military technology.* Clinton gave credit for ingenuity. These stories gained plausibility from a surge in commercial waivers going all the way back to the Reagan administration, balancing strategic risks and economic gains. The United States, having restricted itself to "Cadillac" rockets for the space program, needed cheaper Chinese vehicles in order to reduce a backlog of satellites awaiting launch. Pending a massive investigation, Clinton himself could not be certain that no one involved in these complex decisions had crossed paths with an Asian fund-raiser, but the hype was clearly overblown. He said not even the *Washington Post*, which was propping up Ken Starr's far-flung investigations, bought into the premise that Clinton or his top aides had turned spy for Chinese money. He noted suspiciously that Jeff Gerth, the lead reporter for the *Times* series, had launched Whitewater on innuendo without substance. Republicans were using the prestige of the *Times* to pound hard against Clinton's integrity, and his analysts said this spy theme accounted for a five-point drop in his approval ratings just before his upcoming trip to China. He and Hillary would be taking Christy in their massive entourage. The president promised to look after her.

ON JULY 7, back from China, he summoned me for a session over a late dinner in the upstairs kitchen. Hillary stopped by in blue jeans to reminisce about the trip. I skimmed through some of Christy's stories about the famous terra-cotta warriors, the constant sweeps for surveillance in her hotel rooms, and some of the frantic escapes to shop. Yes, there were some dedicated shoppers, quipped the president. Hillary noted stalwarts

---

* *New York Times* stories included the following: Jeff Gerth and Raymond Bonner, "Companies Are Investigated for Aid to China on Rockets," April 4, 1998, p. 1; Jeff Gerth, David Johnston, and Don Van Natta Jr., "Democratic Fund-Raiser Said to Name China Tie," May 15, 1998, p. 1; Jeff Gerth and David E. Sanger, "How Chinese Won Rights to Launch Satellites for U.S.," May 17, 1998, p. 1.

among the men, such as John Podesta and Bruce Lindsey. Smiley, a butler from Haiti, dropped off Buddy the Labrador. He seemed so ravenous
that the president fed him, and Clinton could only shrug when Smiley
returned to report that Buddy had just had supper downstairs. Before I
could move—standing in the crowded space—Buddy darted up to snatch
a chicken wing out of my hand, which caused a crisis because he was not
supposed to eat bones. We wrestled him down and pried out at least
some of the morsel.

On tape, we discussed mostly China. I asked whether the president's
seventh meeting with Jiang Zemin advanced the personal rapport Clinton found essential in politics. "Absolutely," Clinton replied. "I think he
trusts me now." He said Jiang was more secure now in a power troika
that included the mayor of Shanghai. Significantly, Jiang had permitted
their joint press conference to be televised live in China. Although he
knew in advance that Clinton would criticize the regime on human
rights, he judged the risk worthwhile. The president described his impressions of China's enormous scale—both in physical grandeur, like the
stunning Li River Valley, and in social dislocation. The government had
displaced two and a half million workers from state-owned industries
within the past year in Shanghai alone, but 80 percent of them already
were reabsorbed into private sector jobs.

Jiang had invited both Clintons into his family quarters in Beijing.
The president summarized bilateral talks ranging over economic and
security issues. He thought they were "singing from the same hymnal
now" on nuclear proliferation. He said they talked a good bit about religion. "Atheism" was the only relic of Communist jargon in Jiang's vocabulary. When Clinton pressed him about what benefit Jiang could
possibly derive from shunning the Dalai Lama, to offset the immense
worldwide benefit he would get just for disagreeing in person, Jiang defined the Dalai Lama as a mere theocrat. He insisted that China was
liberating Tibetan culture from feudal superstitions. Among other observations, the president recorded his surprise to hear many Chinese leaders express smoldering resentment toward Japan from World War II. In
my notes, I thought he said Jiang bitterly recalled Japanese troops killing
his father. He named several others who mentioned outrages perpetrated
on their families. From this unhealed strain, Clinton said he detected

hints of satisfaction that the Japanese economy was falling on hard times.

President Clinton said he was still out on his feet from the China trip, having returned only three days ago. We postponed yet again his stated wish to record a separate tape on all the special prosecutors, which he still called a low-grade constitutional crisis. He lamented the Republican filibuster that on June 17 had killed the legislation to curb youth smoking. Otherwise, he discussed only a few topics, including the festering violence in Kosovo. Unlike Bosnia, where the peacemakers' task was to preserve independence against dismemberment by ethnic slaughter, he said Kosovo was a legitimate province of Yugoslavia. A rebellious movement of ethnic Albanians fought for Kosovo to secede, and the dominant Serbs in Belgrade fought to subdue, kill, or expel the Albanians. The president said he had appointed Richard Holbrooke his U.N. ambassador—moving Bill Richardson to the Energy Department—largely to apply his experience from Bosnia. Since then, noticing a raft of news stories complaining of Holbrooke as a meddler and egomaniac, the president said he had dressed down Secretary of State Albright and National Security Adviser Sandy Berger. Holbrooke was a first-rate mind who delivers in the toughest predicaments, he told them. Make it work.

THE LEWINSKY INVESTIGATION derailed efforts to arrange another session before the Clintons' annual vacation in August. Until June, Lewinsky's attorney, William Ginsburg, had stood firm in a klieg-light standoff with Ken Starr, demanding full immunity for new testimony about sex with Clinton. Starr refused. Since both Clinton and Lewinsky had denied having an affair in their depositions for the Jones case, it would undermine her credibility if she alone could switch her sworn testimony without penalty. Ginsburg dared Starr in public to prosecute Lewinsky for perjury about her own private life, mocking the righteous quest to unmask "a sexual relationship between two consenting adults." I secretly admired his gumption, and Lewinsky's, which would have confined the whole scandal to gossip columns and political debate, but such prudence ran into an overwhelming itch for the drama of full disclosure. Ginsburg wound up discredited and then displaced by two seasoned lawyers who swiftly made a deal with Starr for "transactional immunity."

It allowed Lewinsky to change her sworn testimony with a fig leaf of liability and an informal guarantee of penalty-free confession. In late July, Starr took her before the grand jury as a cooperative witness, and the Lewinsky scandal, dammed up since January, spilled forth in August.

President Clinton changed course. By videotape from the White House, he testified to Starr's grand jury for four hours on August 17, then spoke briefly on national television to admit the affair. "I misled people, including even my wife," he confessed. "I deeply regret that." The Clintons left for Martha's Vineyard the next day in a vortex of national astonishment. News reports were virtually identical in tone and content with what Christy told me at home—that Hillary and her staff were speechless with rage that he betrayed her, and had lied all this time. She made him tell Chelsea. Soon after Clinton returned from a zombie's vacation, Starr submitted to Congress on September 9 an official report alleging eleven impeachable offenses by the president—all related to concealment of the affair with Lewinsky. Clinton later complained that Starr's report used the word "sex" five hundred times and never mentioned his assigned Whitewater task at all. At the time, however, the president said nothing. Whatever happened with its impeachment recommendations, Starr's report sealed his humiliation with voluminous details of sexual banter—their furtive groping near the Oval Office, her semen-stained blue dress, his unlit cigar playfully in her vagina.

I could barely stand to read the salacious headlines. Not for years would I be able to compare the dated progression of this torrid, tormented, short-lived affair—with its bizarre interlude of nearly a year before consummation in February 1997—against Clinton's state of mind as reflected in our private interviews. At the time, I dreaded the next session if there was one, and the Lewinsky scandal caused another gap of nearly three months until the last night of September. Christy was writing speeches for the first lady on a trip to Montevideo, Uruguay. I took my notes and recorders to Washington again, not knowing what to expect or say.

CHAPTER THIRTY-TWO

IMPEACHED

Wednesday, September 30, 1998

Wednesday, November 11, 1998

Tuesday, December 29, 1998

With my briefcase, I followed an usher up the inclined passage into a kind of guy's retreat in the Solarium. There was muted television and talk of the Chicago Cubs. Buddy Carter, while tending Buddy, served from the galley kitchen a late dinner of steaks, two giant ones to Hillary's brother Hugh Rodham, who was on an all-protein diet. Barefoot in shorts, Rodham circled a plastic structure of suspended letters. He moved nimbly for a big man, bobbing up and down to ponder his next move. The president, equally engrossed, tried to explain this three-dimensional version of Scrabble—called UpWords—and my helpless shrugs, though genuine, also served to dodge the snare of this open-ended diversion. Insistently, Clinton beckoned me to finish his abandoned steak while he took a phone call about impeachment proceedings in the House.

He had a hard time convincing the venerable Michigan representative John Dingell that the Lewinsky charges, even if true, did not "rise to the level" of an impeachable offense. Some arguments were evasive. Whatever he had done, the president told Dingell, it "pales in comparison" with the damage from five years of standards trampled by Republicans and the press. He pleaded for normal space to work privately on his marriage and publicly on the country's problems, but most of his appeal was raw politics. He said Newt Gingrich had convinced the GOP to run a single-minded risk heading into fall elections. So long as Republicans were more united to extend the Lewinsky scandal than were Democrats to end it, Democrats would lose a 25-point edge from voters who favored everyday priorities over this uproar. "I don't care if Democrats want to get mad at me after the election," Clinton kept saying, "but my interests and theirs are the same right now." To lead where the public wanted to go, Democrats needed the skill and nerve to distinguish embarrassment from politics. An intimidated party weakened itself. Dingell mentioned, as clarified for me later, subterranean warnings that House members should keep their indignation against Clinton alive—lest they be exposed as dupes when Starr announced imminent criminal findings in Whitewater. The president scoffed. If Starr had gleaned even a peashooter's case from those thickets, he told Dingell, it would have been fired long ago. After signing off, Clinton called John Podesta about dispatching to Capitol Hill more scholarly articles on impeachment.

Leaving apologies and promises to Hugh Rodham, President Clinton suspended his UpWords game to lead me down the incline. He walked stiffly. His back hurt, he explained, and he was wearing a brace under his shirt. We stopped at a card table in the third-floor hallway, within earshot of the Solarium, to work there for the first time. While setting up, I ventured a comment on his argument to Dingell. I thought Clinton made a mistake to debate some general scale of fault in his conduct toward Lewinsky. By design, the impeachment of a president was reserved for potential tyranny—the abuse of constitutional power, or gross neglect of duty—because its extraordinary safeguard of removal from office would supersede our only nationwide election. This Lewinsky scandal, while offensive, and however packaged as malfeasance, was about private behavior. The charges weren't even in the right ballpark for impeachment, I advised the president, and he should have his defenders say so.

Clinton smiled. It amused him that I felt more strongly than he did about the historical framework for his defense. He said Hillary did, too. Were they able to discuss the case? *Now* they could, he said with a sigh, implying a terrible ordeal at first. He said they had just gotten off the telephone, in fact, noting that our wives were together down in Uruguay. And last night, before departure, Hillary gave him a short speech about the degradation of constitutional process since her work on impeachment in 1974. *To this day,* she told him, Special Prosecutor Leon Jaworski's raw evidence against Nixon has never been released. It had been presented for confidential cross-examination in the House committee, where procedural debates had been high-minded and many votes unanimous. The only close divisions occurred on whether the evidence sustained duly framed articles of impeachment for specific abuses of power over the Justice Department, CIA, armed forces, and the IRS. By contrast, Starr and the House now were feeding grand jury testimony about sex to newspapers and television networks. The president repeated that his biggest mistake in retrospect was disregarding Hillary's advice to resist the original Whitewater independent counsel nearly five years ago. "I thought they were serious about getting to the bottom of these things," he said. "I trusted the press. I trusted the Congress. I trusted the courts. And I was wrong on all counts."

Gingerly, I asked if he wanted to discuss Lewinsky on tape. He said yes. The disgorged grand jury evidence was especially one-sided because his side had not been permitted to question any of the allegations. He mentioned a claim by Lewinsky that she had eaten lunch with Hillary. Not true. And that she once ran naked around the Oval Office. Not true. Also, he pointed out that Starr had been threatening to jail Lewinsky all year over her sworn denial of the affair. If Clinton had come forward with anything at all about their relationship, he said Starr could have turned him into a witness *against* Lewinsky, betraying her discreet silence. Such subtleties, while original, struck me as tendentious. The president never claimed chivalry as the real motive for his steadfast denials, nor did he dispute the essential truth of Lewinsky's account.

We moved to other topics on my list, beginning with simultaneous suicide bombs last month at the U.S. embassies in Kenya and Tanzania. The blasts had destroyed both chanceries, killing 220 people and wounding more than four thousand—mostly local workers. President Clinton stated flatly that Osama bin Laden, the architect of this coordinated terrorist attack, was eerily like the fictional villains in James Bond movies. He was a transnational presence suspended above allegiance to any government, with enormous private wealth and a network of operatives in many countries, including ours. All this was new to me. The president said he had received intelligence warnings for some time that bin Laden intended to strike three embassies, not two, and that reports about Albania were specific enough to evacuate the premises. He described prior negotiations about bin Laden with the governments of Sudan and Saudi Arabia.

In greater detail, the president recorded his rationale for the retaliatory strikes on August 20. A massive flight of seventy-five cruise missiles obliterated four training camps in remote Afghanistan, near Khost and Jalalabad, but apparently they missed bin Laden himself. Clinton acknowledged skeptical postmortems about a second target—the Al-Shifa pharmaceutical plant in Khartoum, Sudan. Bin Laden did not actually own the building, as believed, but the president said he would stand on the ample intelligence, including soil samples, connecting an element in nerve gas found there and in Afghanistan at similarly high concentrations. In fact, he would have destroyed a second building nearby had it not been for the many unwitting employees who worked there on a night shift. Clinton said his only regret was appearing a bit too angry when he announced the strikes on television, three days after his public admission about Lewinsky. "I was under a lot of strain," he said. His statement did, he thought, carefully distinguish the terrorist objective from Islam itself. Clinton called it a chief political goal to combat the popular belief that Arabs in particular, and Muslims in general, were fanatics under righteous compulsion to kill nonbelievers.

We shifted to the global repercussions from a meltdown in the Russian financial system at the end of August. On a single day, when the Dow Jones average dropped 357 points in New York, markets fell 5 to 10 percent from Germany and Canada to Brazil and Japan. Clinton said the first $20 billion of an emergency IMF package for Russian banks literally vanished overnight. When he hurried to Moscow for consultations, Clinton found President Yeltsin sober but feeble, sadly aged from the vigorous man he had known six years earlier. "I'm not sure enough oxygen is getting up to his brain," said the president. Yeltsin seemed so removed from urgent political tasks that both Clintons counseled him directly. "Boris," asked Hillary, "how much time do you spend with the members of the Duma?" As little as possible, Yeltsin snorted—he hated dealing with any of them. She chided him for behaving like a turtle, Clinton recalled, and extolled the necessary art of political schmoozing.

The president recounted his own talks with Yeltsin's younger colleagues, who were jockeying for succession. They would never reap the benefits of a market economy until their public institutions established reliable and transparent rules for commerce. No country could take these ties for granted. He told them Sweden could choose to tax at 50 percent of national income only because Sweden could collect that 50 percent and use the revenue efficiently to maintain its physical and social infrastructure. Russia, by contrast, taxed at 50 percent, collected 10 percent, and spent nearly 20 percent, which was a formula for disaster. In the United States, crime syndicates needed more than a generation to move from loan-sharking and primitive rackets into legitimate business, but Clinton said Russian mobs had bowled over banks and regulators alike within three years. Dysfunctional markets in turn made for political weakness, he warned, citing the burst miracle in Tokyo, where Prime Minister Hashimoto's regime was now the fifth Japanese government to fall during Clinton's tenure.

He reviewed his public speeches about the world financial crisis. Mountains of currency moved instantaneously between countries for investment and speculation, without the approval or knowledge of governments. To make these transactions visible, and keep them productive, Clinton told New York's Council on Foreign Relations that there may be a need to create an international registry. He had to be careful, he wryly told me, "not to get the black helicopter crowd stirred up"—meaning paranoid, xenophobic groups convinced that black helicopters soon would land everywhere with U.N. armies bent on forcing Americans to speak some foreign language—but his message earned rousing appreciation. Last week at the United Nations, his usual tepid reception had swelled into thunderous, standing applause. To be sure, there was extra solidarity with the United States in the wake of the terrorist carnage at our African embassies, and the president said some delegates responded to a touching personal tribute from Nelson Mandela, who pleaded for

Americans to stop obsessing over petty scandals.* Still, what Clinton felt most, and confirmed in private talks, was approval for his tenacious daily effort to make international institutions function in a perilous world.

Of his many consultations during the U.N.'s opening ceremonies, I remembered best a story about Amr Moussa. He said the Egyptian foreign minister, while a cheerleader for Clinton's global role, was lobbying persistently against renewed Israeli-Palestinian talks. Egypt's private worry was that Netanyahu of Israel, having dragged his feet for a year, would gain credit and forgiveness and reelection from any revived negotiations now. Therefore, to avoid five more years of Netanyahu, Egypt urged Arafat to resist progress. "Look here, Moussa," Clinton countered privately, "Arafat needs peace more than Netanyahu does." Arafat had 95 percent of Palestinians on only 27 percent of the land. They had no room. They had no lifelines to the outside world. Give them a start. Make peace and *then* worry about Netanyahu. The president shook his head at me, doubtful that his message succeeded. "I kind of like ol' Moussa," he said sighing, "but he enjoys a contrarian view that whatever vexes the United States must be good."

We skimmed over my list toward the end. Earlier this week, Arafat and Netanyahu had accepted an agenda for renewed face-to-face negotiations at a hideaway location in the United States, and Clinton presided today over celebrations marking an official end to the first fiscal year in surplus ($69 billion) since the budget of 1969 ($3.2 billion surplus). He summarized on tape several farewell calls to defeated German chancellor Helmut Kohl, lamenting how much he would miss Kohl's help on NATO's festering crisis in Kosovo. We skipped altogether a side trip from Moscow to the market town of Omagh in Northern Ireland, where a Saturday afternoon car bomb had inflicted the worst day's casualties—twenty-nine killed, five hundred wounded, mostly women and children—in a generation of sectarian war. Save it for next time,

---

* On September 21, while he spoke at the United Nations, Clinton's grand jury confessions were released for video replay on news screens including the Times Square JumboTron in New York. The Lewinsky scandal shared headlines with baseball's Cal Ripken Jr., who ended his consecutive game streak at 2,632.

said the president, of his visit to stabilize April's Good Friday peace accord.

He had winced periodically through this session, standing to stretch his back without evident relief. When I asked if the condition was serious, he said no, it only hurt. Several times he crossed his legs—ankle on knee—and leaned forward to push the unanchored knee down toward the floor, hard, forcing open a hip, grimacing and yet continuing his story. He seemed separated, as though in a painful trance, and recrossed his legs to reverse the process without interruption. Not knowing what to say, I shut down the recorders with yarns about delivering Macy last month to begin her first year of college at the University of Michigan. We compared memories of his family passage at Stanford the previous year. Abruptly, Clinton nursed one fleeting regret about having a lone daughter. Chelsea had no interest in golf, and he longed at times to take a child under his wing out on the golf course. Coach Clinton, I laughed. He said no, it was more fatherly than that. This made sense, because I played thumper's golf only for companionship with Franklin, who, at fifteen, could learn nothing good from me. If the president ever wanted to try a teaching round, I offered him an eager surrogate son. Clinton said he might surprise us, heading back up to three-dimensional Scrabble.

THE NEXT CALL came before noon on Veterans Day, a week after the midterm elections. Could I come early for a session, and bring Franklin with his golf clubs? This touched off a fire drill to the school office, pulling him from tenth-grade classes on a vague pretext, then a hurried drive to Washington as Franklin extracted promises that I say nothing to his friends. Even a hint would be ruinous, putting on airs. From our White House dinner long ago, he remembered the Clintons as a friendly but know-it-all trio given to remote details about important things. For him, the advance buzz here was about golf—on a school day, no less, at a new course, with lessons from a low-handicap teacher—but then we cleared the White House gates to behold the motorcade. Stretched around the driveway, limousines nestled among military jeeps and emergency vehicles including fire trucks and ambulances. Soldiers mingled with suited agents on the South Lawn, some displaying big guns. When clustered aides steered the two of us into a sedan marked "Guest One,"

I assured Franklin that this unnerving pomp was very different from my quiet arrivals at night. Our driver, a garrulous Army sergeant from the motor pool, said today's standing alert was several levels above normal. The officer next to him frowned and refused to speak. We waited. "I have to stand by a lot," observed the sergeant. Engines revved smartly to life just before President Clinton emerged from the diplomatic entrance, and motorcycle escorts, passing in continuous relays to stop traffic ahead, herded our long caravan briskly across the Potomac River.

Club pro Mel Cook hushed a spontaneous gallery on the first tee at the Army Navy Country Club. I was proudly relieved when Franklin's drive soared true to land among the three grown-ups. Ralph Alswang, one of the White House photographers, kindly offered to document a tutorial partnership between Franklin and the president, who were consulting in earnest. Between photos, Ralph shared staff gossip on the alert. All 230 U.N. weapons inspectors were being evacuated from Iraq today in anticipation of air strikes to answer Saddam Hussein's latest treaty violations, and mobile U.S. combat units were landing to defend Kuwait. These war rumbles explained eight or so extra golf carts roving near us, he said, plus a dozen solitary figures in the surrounding woods. I had missed these motionless, camouflaged sentinels with their over-sized field glasses. They were not looking for stray golf balls. It was hard to imagine a more tedious job.

From the lip of a greenside bunker, Franklin chipped in for a rare birdie on the ninth hole. There was hollering and high-fiving with the president even before Clinton sank a long putt for birdie, too. Jubilant, they challenged the opposing team of Hugh Rodham and fund-raiser Terry McAuliffe to press, or double, the bet to three dollars per hole on the back nine, and jovial trash talk still billowed when I trotted in from observing distance to salute the twin birdies. McAuliffe suspected a ringer. Rodham warned Clinton to beg no mercy for a kid. The president, claiming the hot hand of momentum, moved close to Franklin again and pointed down the fairway to elaborate on the hazards and contours of a good drive on this tenth hole. Then he lapsed into a kind of reverie on how nice it was to be out here, away from Saddam Hussein. "Franklin," he said softly, "I hate that son of a bitch." No one spoke. Saddam had his people terrorized, Clinton went on. Left alone, he would only get worse, eroding prospects for concerted popular strength far beyond his region. Snapping back, Clinton advised Franklin how to play the shot, and the foursome chased golf balls until darkness made them impossible to find.

HOURS LATER, IN the Treaty Room, our session began with a bullet-point introduction of thirteen selected topics from Hurricane Mitch to the antitrust trial of Microsoft. Elections of stunning vindication for Clinton had coincided with only the third serious move to impeach a president in two hundred years. "Yes," he replied, "we live in very strange times." He plunged so gladly into politics that I asked him to record something first about Iraq. Did he get updates just now over dinner? The president nodded with a sigh. This was hardly the first time Saddam Hussein had obstructed the search for doomsday weapons, but it made less sense. Clinton's whole government was sifting for a rational motive behind the sudden defiance of U.N. inspections since October 31, which seemed blatantly self-destructive on two fronts. First, Saddam was forfeiting his best chance yet to gain relief from crippling economic sanctions imposed after the Gulf War. Iraq's compliance had been good for most of this year, and Clinton disclosed that U.N. evaluators had been near a recommendation to pull back from full inspections to limited monitoring—at least for nuclear weapons. Although verification was less complete for chemical and biological programs—which would require continued inspections for now, with dismantlement as necessary—a nuclear-free Iraq soon would have become eligible for partial relaxation of the U.N. embargo.

Second, said the president, Saddam had to know this retaliation would be sure and severe. Unlike February, when the United States had been obliged to confront him virtually alone, most governments were now united in backing retaliation. Both the French and Russians had soured on Saddam, and Secretary of Defense William Cohen reported from a sounding tour that most Arab leaders considered him a pest, too. Their major qualm about air strikes, in fact, was that Saddam was likely to survive in power to cultivate a backlash of sympathy for the Iraqi people. In a pinch, some U.S. advisers thought Saddam must be betting that Clinton would dither and retreat, weakened by Lewinsky. The president dismissed the idea, while crediting those who said so with gumption. Others thought Saddam must have given up hope for the sanctions to be lifted—ever—no matter what he did. Even so, he was shrewd, and these theories offered no reason for him to invite a military pounding. Clinton did not mention any counterintuitive motives, and it never occurred to me to ask how the end of sanctions might really look to such a dictator. Facing official certification that his regime was defanged of terrifying secret weapons, Saddam Hussein blustered desperately. He sacrificed others now, and eventually he would risk everything to preserve his bully's illusion. That woeful lesson lay in a future war.

Clinton said his own course was committed. Since golf today, he had approved orders to dispatch more bombers and reposition ships. Allied signals were clear. He expected military strikes to win bipartisan assent, including former presidents Ford, Reagan, and Bush. "Dole will support me," he said. "Carter will probably criticize me. Carter always criticizes, but he doesn't have much positive to say." The president anticipated a break point within two or three days, in a crisis so far advanced that every outcome would be rightly controversial. Whether the U.S. attacks went heavy or light, Iraqis would be killed, and many of them did not have much choice where they worked in Saddam's economy. On the other hand, he thought more people would die for less purpose if the international community failed to back up its resolve from the Gulf War. There were no easy choices. The president hoped Saddam would back down and restore the U.N. inspectors. Here, as in Kosovo, Clinton preferred a nonmilitary resolution. He digressed to sketch hard negotiations with President Milosevic by Richard Holbrooke and Gen. Wesley Clark. Ethnic atrocities had subsided to a small fraction of the summer levels. Kosovar refugees were going home.

From my first question about the midterm elections, Clinton let loose a fountain of ecstatic detail. Over and over, he said impeachment turned into a trap for Republicans. They had nothing else to run on, having filibustered campaign finance reform again and voted down everything else from new schools to restrictions on tobacco sales to children. Two weeks before election day, when their polls revealed surprising resistance, he said Republicans boldly dramatized their sole message by running national ads *for* impeachment. They committed fully their

$110 million advantage in party funds for this cycle, which he said majority whip Tom DeLay had raised by brazen extortion of Washington's lobbyists—ordering them to fire Democratic employees, telling them exactly how much it would cost to be heard on legislation. If Democrats did stuff like that, Clinton remarked, we'd all go to jail.

Still, the GOP gamble backfired. Instead of shaming Democrats into submission, by smearing them with Clinton, their ads created adverse shifts of 7 to 15 points almost overnight. Republican ads helped defeat their own incumbents most associated with pursuing the Clinton scandals, such as New York senator Al D'Amato (defeated by Charles Schumer) and North Carolina senator Lauch Faircloth (defeated by John Edwards). If Democrats had not been so timid, and had embraced for voters this choice between impeachment and the issues, Clinton said they would have reaped even more gains. He cited a throwaway congressional race in conservative San Diego, where Republicans had held their 1996 convention, in which the safe GOP incumbent lost all but a hair of his 20-point lead by running late ads for impeachment, and the president called it a preventable tragedy that Democrats let Representative Jim Bunning narrowly win the open Senate seat in Kentucky. He said Bunning, a former baseball player, was so mean-spirited that he repulsed even his fellow know-nothings. "I tried to work with him a couple of times," said Clinton, "and he just sent shivers up my spine." Mysteriously, the president apologized to me: "I know you're a baseball fan and everything, and you don't like to hear it, but this guy is beyond the pale." *

He plumbed many hidden results. By laser-targeting his infidelity in a national campaign, Republicans helped cleanse away from Hillary the years of encrusted disapproval and doubt over Whitewater. Her negative ratings plummeted. To his joy, Clinton said the results in 1998 continued to redress the debacle of health care failure and the Gingrich revolu-

---

* Clinton mistakenly thought I knew or favored something about Bunning's political career, probably from mention of a coincidence. On June 21, 1964, the day of the infamous Chaney-Goodman-Schwerner civil rights murders in Mississippi, Bunning pitched a perfect game for Philadelphia against the New York Mets.

tion of 1994. He celebrated especially a Democratic win to reclaim
the Pennsylvania House seat once sacrificed by Marjorie Margolies-
Mezvinsky through her vote for the omnibus budget bill. Gingrich had
demonized that measure successfully as a tax hike, disparaging Clinton's
formula for economic recovery and deficit reduction, but reality peeked
through. The president predicted a reversal of interpretation, making
those 1994 elections the fluke supplanted by a bellwether 1998. A few
political pros already sensed something big. Speaker Newt Gingrich had
announced his sudden resignation from politics last Friday, after confiding graciously to Clinton his shock as both opponent and historian that
Democrats actually *gained* five seats in the House.

Such a victory had been considered impossible for any sixth-year
president. Woodrow Wilson, on the brink of Armistice Day in 1918, lost
nineteen seats; Reagan lost five in 1986. Freshly disgraced, fighting impeachment, Clinton had been figured to approach the forty-eight-seat
decline after Nixon's resignation in 1974, or even the ninety-six-seat ca-
tastrophe for scandal-plagued Ulysses Grant in 1874. To set a positive
mark instead was seismic. Voters, said the president, do not make decisions with eight-year election cycles in mind. They look for a coherent
political message to weigh, and Clinton, having studied long-range
trends all his life, stuck by the appraisal he reached before running for
president in 1992. He said the GOP's anti-government engine, which
had been dominant since the 1960s, was running on fumes. In spite of
recent elections, that exhaustion had not registered much in popular
culture because of corollary attachments to scandal, money, and a prevailing negativity about politics. Last week's elections baffled most pundits. Some praised voters too sophisticated to punish congressional
Democrats over Clinton. Others ridiculed voters too ignorant or sentimental to hold the president accountable for his sins.

We moved on to other topics, but Clinton kept remembering election stories—a pivotal race in Oregon, an upset near Princeton, the delight of South Carolina's Representative James Clyburn, who claimed
impishly that he would have paid for the GOP's pro-impeachment
ads himself. Otherwise, he discussed staff transitions—John Podesta
for Erskine Bowles as chief of staff, how much he would miss Rahm
Emanuel—and outlined the capture of several bin Laden terrorist cells

without notice in the press. With Hillary, he had attended NASA's reprise rocket launch for senator and former astronaut John Glenn, who sent the Clintons an e-mail from space. At greater length, he recorded impressions of the nine-day negotiations headed by Arafat and Netanyahu at the Wye Plantation on Maryland's Eastern Shore in October. There were all-night marathons, spy controversies, an emotional intervention by the dying King Hussein of Jordan, and finally an agreement to implement the delayed interim steps in time for "final status" talks scheduled next May.

Just today, said Clinton, the Israeli cabinet had approved the Wye Memorandum by an unusual split vote with five abstentions. He thought Netanyahu may find it impossible to act on his commitments, which would render Wye perhaps a final instance of Bibi's penchant for "kicking the can down the road." Clinton seemed resigned to a waste of Herculean effort. Speaking mostly of personal interactions with the negotiators, he dwelled positively on Arafat's intelligence chief, Mohammed Dahlan, and the Israeli defense minister, Yitzhak Mordechai. Ariel Sharon, Netanyahu's foreign minister, was charismatic and articulate, but the president said Sharon openly hated Palestinians: "He calls them a gang of thugs, and says you have to treat them like thugs." Sharon refused to shake Arafat's hand at Wye. With some coaxing, reenacted in brief, Clinton finally got the two of them to sit down and talk.

When we closed, he asked me to prepare suggested themes for his January State of the Union Address. His team was working hard on it now. If he could match the quality of last year's success, he hoped to forestall carping about any diminished energy on his part, or a stale agenda. He was determined to avoid lassitude toward the end of his second term. After goodbyes, I retrieved Franklin from the Map Room downstairs, where he had long since finished his homework.

EVERYTHING AND NOTHING was normal in December. The president, wearing jeans and a gray sweatshirt, detoured into the Yellow Oval Room to show me the family Christmas tree—describing, and often touching, many favored ornaments with pleasantly high-strung tales of their provenance. We exchanged late gifts. I presented a personalized *All on Fire*, Henry Mayer's biography of abolitionist William Lloyd Garrison, and he reciprocated with equal commendation for *My Last Chance to Be a Boy: Theodore Roosevelt's South American Expedition of 1913–1914*, by Joseph Ornig. While setting up in the Treaty Room, I indulged for him my holiday ordeal of returning from Atlanta to find our dog deathly ill at the kennel. Franklin and I had just buried him in the backyard. The president finished two business calls about his forthcoming trial. Senator John Breaux said two of Clinton's bitterest Senate antagonists, Phil Gramm and Jim Inhofe, were scheming to present graphic live testimony about "supporting" sex rumors. John Podesta, the new White House chief of staff, reported that Republicans were hopping mad over reciprocal threats by pornographer Larry Flynt to expose more of their shenanigans with paramours of both genders. Surprise, the president sighed afterward. Welcome to impeachment.

On tape, he reviewed a bizarre convergence of history with farce. We had suspended last month on the verge of warfare in Iraq. Before dawn that Saturday, November 14, he said he was rousted from bed with bulletins about a letter from Saddam Hussein, reportedly backing down. No one had yet seen the document. The U.S. bomber squadrons were in the air, speeding toward their assigned targets, and Clinton had twenty minutes to recall them. Secretaries Albright and Cohen, along with Gen. Hugh Shelton of the Joint Chiefs, all pressed to go ahead with the air strikes. An enormous logistical machine was in motion, well past fair deadlines, and Saddam's letter may be another hoax. Clinton worried, however, that the letter may be real and that civilian casualties could fall on the high end of their estimated margin for error, which meant two thousand innocent Iraqis dead. How would we explain that? He aborted the attacks, saying he would rather take political hits for restraint. It took three tries to extract straightforward promises from Saddam, but the U.N. weapons inspectors did return to Baghdad under a thirty-day mandate to verify full cooperation. Until their report, said Clinton, all the carriers and allied commanders had orders to maintain advance strike positions at full readiness.

Meanwhile, as the president had feared, Prime Minister Netanyahu buried the Wye Agreement when he returned to Israel. Far from trumpeting prospects for peace, he feigned something unfamiliar but onerous in its terms, and soon suspended implementation on a claim of Palestinian bad faith. Even so, members of his own Likud Party denounced him as a "dish rag" for Arafat. To make amends with them, Netanyahu asked Clinton to extract and witness another public affirmation by the Palestinian National Council of Israel's right to exist. The president said he was skeptical of the idea—and surprised. This council was an elected assembly, one of many new Palestinian institutions created by the Oslo Accords. For a sitting U.S. president to visit its formal deliberations could be viewed as a tacit recognition of Palestinian statehood, but Netanyahu fairly begged Clinton to make the political gesture.

He and Hillary left for the Middle East on December 12, the day after chairman Henry Hyde's Judiciary Committee sent articles of impeachment to the House floor by a party-line vote. The Clintons cut a ribbon to open the new Gaza International Airport. They visited Israeli as well as Palestinian orphans whose parents had been killed in the civil strife. Clinton gave a televised speech to the five hundred Palestinian delegates who voted for coexistence, praising their courage to rise above war and the demonstrators outside calling them traitorous collaborators with Israel. Arafat and he lit a Christmas tree at the reputed birthplace of Jesus in Palestinian Bethlehem, which the president found a bleak, run-down city. With Netanyahu, the Clintons visited King Herod's ancient mountain fortress at Masada, overlooking the Dead Sea. On our tape, the president said he half-believed the prime minister's pained declaration that he still remained helpless to fulfill his commitments made at Wye. In Clinton's judgment, part of Netanyahu made excuses because he recoiled from the peace process at heart, but the Likud coalition was also a paralyzing restraint. Bibi saw only two ways out: a unity government with the Labor Party, or new national elections. I asked whether a unity government was possible. Not now, Clinton replied, because Labor thinks it can win. Likely candidates Shimon Peres and Ehud Barak would rather beat Netanyahu than join him.

Plots tangled rapidly from December 15, when the chief U.N. weapons inspector documented almost a complete stonewall in Iraq. Saddam Hussein reneged on his November promises. By blocking access and foiling inspections, he defied once again a 15–0 vote by the U.N. Security Council to condemn his noncompliance with the Gulf War resolutions. President Clinton, still in Israel, reactivated the suspended air strikes with only one concession that diminished surprise. For diplomatic reasons, he said, no confirming orders were flashed until Air Force One left Israeli airspace. Six hundred fifty bomb sorties and four hundred cruise missiles pounded Iraq over the next four days, while political explosions greeted Clinton at home. Senate majority leader Lott sensationally opposed the military operation, voicing suspicion that Clinton had timed it to trump the House impeachment debate. Dueling accusations of wartime disloyalty swirled into the partisan mayhem over Monica Lewinsky. On Saturday, December 19, when air strikes ceased in Iraq, the Republican House majority moved to vote on impeachment, but Speaker Gingrich's newly designated replacement first confessed his own adultery with several unnamed women. Bob Livingston of Louisiana preemptively resigned, sparing himself the revelation of embarrassing details gathered by *Hustler* publisher Larry Flynt. Pandemonium reigned. "There have been so many bombshells," cried GOP representative Michael Castle of Delaware. "You can barely turn your back."

It should not have surprised me, but President Clinton's first take on all this chaos was a failure in political craft. He blamed himself for the impeachment. The vote in the House was lost, he thought, by the time we had talked in November. His mistake was assuming that the midterm elections washed impeachment away in a tide of public disapproval. Immediately, said the president, he should have sent White House people scrambling to lock in public positions from all the Republicans who recognized impeachment as a political loser. Instead, his complacency allowed the entire GOP leadership to cement an issue of party loyalty. Dick Armey and Tom DeLay, along with Gingrich, pitched impeachment as a "free vote." They said Republicans, having suffered their impeachment penalty at the polls already, should make full use of the character issue while they controlled the House.

This argument, added the president, should have tipped him off to a second missed signal—that the revolt against Gingrich came not from moderate House Republicans but from the most vociferous supporters of his disastrous impeachment ads. DeLay and Armey said any backlash in the 2000 elections would fall against Republican moderates, purifying a united core of ideological conservatives. They invoked party discipline steadily until they lost only five to twelve moderates in the key tallies, offset by five anti-Clinton Democrats. By the afternoon of December 19, two articles of impeachment passed the House by narrow party-line votes, 228–206 and 221–212.

I said it seemed surreal ten days later. Clinton's approval ratings still hovered above 60 percent, and yet he was only the second U.S. president ever impeached by the House of Representatives. His presidency was scalded, and literally more historic, bound by the Constitution for a trial by the full Senate. Could he make sense of this? How did he feel? Well, it might surprise me. He said he was not nearly as angry now as a few years ago, when he had railed so often to me about collusion between right-wing politicians and the press. Back then, he believed most things got a fair shake, and he still looked up to the *New York Times* as a model of statesmanship. If he had stayed that way, which he called overwrought and obsessed about what *other* people were doing to him, he would have gone batty. "I'd be over in Saint Elizabeths by now," he stressed. "In the nuthouse." Instead, he had to distinguish between what others did and what he had brought on himself and his family. Getting thrown out of office for the latter would be minor, he said, compared with the terrible personal price he was paying already.

This impeachment, he insisted, was about raw politics. He did not fully understand it, but we lived in a nasty political era. His best course was to concentrate on his job. He had no higher aspirations for the present, but he thought detachment was the best antidote for cynicism in the long run. If he resigned, Democrats would just go after some Republican the same way, lowering everybody. While a healthy majority of voters would rather see him fight the Republicans than resign, he said an extra 20 percent preferred for him to ignore all the malevolence and keep working. "I am utterly convinced that history will vindicate me," he concluded, "and will record that my opponents have damaged the country."

What about him and Hillary? I asked how they were coming through this. He avoided personal comments by repeating how strongly she felt about the constitutional defects of anti-Clinton investigations from Whitewater until now. He did later volunteer an odd connection to Hillary from a stopover in Guam that had escaped my notes on his itineraries. At a ceremony commemorating its grim losses in World War II, a man in the receiving line said his great-grandmother's brother was Hillary's grandfather. He drew for Clinton a complicated, intersecting genealogy, and Hillary was amazed when the president brought home the news: "I bumped into your cousin." It must be true, she said, attesting to her side of the genealogy. She had not known of any Guamanian relatives.

Clinton stood up several times to stretch—bending his knees, pulling one foot and then the other up behind him. He was less distressed than previous nights, however, sailing through captivated memories of town meetings in Japan. On China, he worried about government speeches cracking down against agitations for democracy, but he had missed some of the latest political sentences. Ten years? For giving a radio interview about farm protests? "I don't really know what's going on there with Jiang," said the president. He needed to get back into that. The U.S. economy looked good—unemployment below 4.4 percent, 1998 inflation one percent, fourth-quarter growth about 6 percent, Dow above 9,300—perhaps *too* good after five straight years. Though confident for 1999, Clinton did not want a recession to hit during Al Gore's campaign in 2000. There were a number of threatening elements. "One is steel," he said, launching a discourse on dumping rules that finally tired him. In parting, he took my spare copy of suggestions sent for his State of the Union. Mostly, they urged him to lift up new rhetorical stars equivalent to Middle East peace or a balanced budget, seeking to bolster public confidence toward visionary goals. I feared the impeachment may have mooted such things. He said no.

CHAPTER THIRTY-THREE

THE TRIAL

Tuesday, January 26, 1999

Tuesday, February 23, 1999

Chief Justice Rehnquist presided over the Senate trial of William Jefferson Clinton, according to the rules for presidential impeachment set forth in the Constitution's Article I, Section 3, Paragraph 7. Analysts dredged up precedent and protocol from dusty textbooks or scraps of correspondence between Founding Fathers. In January, halfway through the five-week spectacle, I arrived somber and unprepared for a breezy surprise. First the elderly new Doorman, Harold Hancock, balked at instructions to take me upstairs. Pressed to explain, he stalled until something popped out about the Clintons kissing. Nancy Mitchell, the White House usher tonight, studied flickering mirth at the corners of a dutiful mouth. "Well," she said, "you're going to have to take Mr. Branch up. The president sent for him." Hancock shook his head. He had just been there. "I want you to call first," he said. They went back and forth about what he had seen, which sounded like smooching in a doorway, and Mitchell formulated a plan for him to announce himself from the stairwell and then close the three Southern hallway doors— bedroom, living parlor, bathroom—for privacy. She dispatched me as backup, which relieved him, but Hancock remained both tentative and tickled on our climb.

It was mixed relief to confront the first couple nowhere on the second floor, and Hancock vanished when we finally located them with guests up in the Solarium. Any overt romance was suspended, but the

Clintons communed intensely about the latest politics of impeachment. Not only did they complete each other's shorthand sentences, but they exchanged the telephone in seamless conversations with several senators—Tom Daschle and John Breaux, I later remembered, and perhaps Chris Dodd. The president avoided other contacts to curtail leaks and inevitable charges of tampering with the Senate "jury." He said tomorrow's scheduled votes would provide the first significant tests of strength so far in the trial—on Senator Robert Byrd's motion for dismissal, and on rules governing the number of witnesses. Hillary expected to hold every Democrat except Russ Feingold for dismissal even this early, which was good. They both said many senators privately loathed the impeachment prosecutors, or "managers." Here came these thirteen House upstarts, all from safe Republican districts, with a sleazy, slapdash sex case to force votes by senators whose constituents never wanted the trial at all. Outside the South, even the Republican senators often came from states where the margins were heavy and hard to leave Clinton alone—68 percent, 72 percent. The trial was near a tipping point. Senators still could claim passive duty, subtly blaming the House initiative, but daily attention slowly exposed them to political risk, too.

The president excused the two of us to work down in the Treaty Room. On the way, in playful consolation, I speculated that his case may lead paradoxically to better understanding of the only other presidential impeachment trial in history. Andrew Johnson, acquitted by one vote in 1868, was commonly portrayed as the victim of groundless persecution by abolitionists and Reconstruction zealots in Congress. By comparison with these Lewinsky charges, however, the Johnson impeachment sprang properly from clashes over basic constitutional government. After all, Andrew Johnson tried to kill the Fourteenth Amendment, which became our legal bedrock for equal citizenship and due process. "He did?" asked Clinton. Yes, Johnson campaigned to block ratification in 1866. The president said he didn't know that, looking doubtful. We needled each other. He said I was trying to convict Andrew Johnson. I said Clinton was resisting my compliment that his impeachment was even worse than Johnson's.

On tape, he apologized in several respects for his State of the Union Address a week ago. There were not as many lofty initiatives as we had hoped, and the rhetoric did not hang together as well as some previous years. On the other hand, the speech was programmatically sound. Big things were becoming doable. He reaped a double dividend from the announcement, carefully constructed with his budget experts, that the United States could guarantee the soundness of Social Security for half a century by shoring up its reserves over the next few years with 60 percent of the projected annual budget surpluses. This commitment was so well received that the Republicans fell in line. Not even Tom DeLay objected. Finally, said Clinton, the speech went over because the state of the union was very strong indeed if you ignored the impeachment trial, which is precisely what he did. His approval ratings shot up close to 80 percent, although they had dropped back a few points since. I asked how he apportioned this huge bump between approval for the speech and disapproval for impeachment. He said a lot of both. With the Gores, he and Hillary had gone straight to huge rallies in Buffalo, New York, and Norristown, Pennsylvania. People shouted for him to ignore the trial and keep going. "I'm the only one doing any of the country's business," he said.

Clinton noted a remarkable phenomenon in American politics. "Senior members of the Republican Party are terrified of their own base," he said. Even when that base represents only 20 percent of the electorate, they consistently grumble but cave in to the angry factions. They had made a tar baby of Whitewater and now impeachment. In this light, he deconstructed the new GOP party slogan recommended in Newt Gingrich's farewell speech: "Do No Harm." This was hostility to government dressed up as medical ethics, and Republicans should stick with the demand for a 10 percent tax cut. He said tax cuts were their only idea—albeit so automatic that it amounted to the same negative reflex—but a skillful appeal might win for them. Democrats would be pressed to make a convincing case that surpluses should be secured first, with tax cuts reserved as a stimulus to fight recession. You have to be very careful, he said, how you tell people maxed out on debt that tax cuts in good times can be a bad idea.

Under charged circumstances, when an adverse Senate vote any day could materialize packers to evict the Clintons, we recorded very little about the trial. Instead, the president delivered a prognosis for all the entitlement programs to complement the fifty-five-year plan for Social Security. "Quite frankly," I dictated later, "I would love to have a transcript of the tape on that because I didn't really understand it." He covered everything from the structure of the payroll tax to administrative problems with retirement investments in Chile and other nations, leaving me "dazzled" but too distracted or confused to preserve a coherent summary. There was economic theory on using private markets to enhance public savings, citing debates with Alan Greenspan, along with political theory on the stability of compacts between generations.

When asked about his meeting today with Pope John Paul II in St. Louis, the president began with personal stories. He had arranged to introduce for an emotional blessing a Catholic priest and longtime friend from Arkansas, bald from cancer treatments. Privately, he noted, the Vatican staff was animated by some dispute in the hierarchy over Jesuit colleges, which seemed to be a prime reason for the trip. To hear the pope's feeble voice, Clinton had to sit closer than he was to me, and lean forward. "Remember, he's seventy-nine," said the president. "He's got Parkinson's. He's been shot. And he had bad knees to start with. But his mind is very sharp." They spoke a lot about Cuba. The pope criticized the U.S. embargo as spiritual violence, which Clinton said was fine. Fidel Castro wanted better relations, they agreed, swapping indirect signals about how to induce him to act toward that goal. They discussed unheralded suffering in Congo, along with growing disparity between nations not only in wealth but longevity. With health systems cracking, and life expectancy sinking into the forties, how could anyone expect desperate countries to sacrifice for ecology? Why would they care? Clinton invited the pope to scold him among Western leaders toward Christian justice for the poor. John Paul explained his opposition to the air strikes in Iraq. "You have been a twin all this time," he told Clinton at the end. "Now you must learn to live as an orphan." As the sole superpower, no longer restrained by the Soviet Union, he meant the United States needed lonely, prayerful wisdom to set an example for the world.

Telephone calls interrupted the president's account of palace intrigue in Jordan. King Hussein, breaking off intensive treatments for lymphoma at the Mayo Clinic, had just flown home to depose his brother and designated heir since 1965, Crown Prince Hassan, in favor of Hussein's own son Abdullah. The mysterious coup shocked the Arab world, exciting students of monarchy. Hussein had wanted instead to elevate his young son Hamzah, by his current wife, Queen Noor, but he feared that Hassan would overthrow the inexperienced eighteen-year-old. The king did try to make a deal with Hassan to install Hamzah as *his* crown prince, for the next generation, but Hassan's wife, Sarvath, vetoed the proposal. Naturally, she favored succession by her own son, Prince Rashid, said Clinton, and Sarvath never liked Noor anyway. So Hussein chose thirty-seven-year-old Abdullah in part for his support within the military as a career soldier. Unlike young Hamzah, a minor who would require confirmation from the Jordanian Parliament, Abdullah could be enthroned by royal fiat.

On the phone, President Clinton turned steadily more electric in conversation with DNC chair Steve Grossman. Absorbing stories, jotting down numbers, he tossed back delighted reactions that culminated in a merry wish to keep the impeachment trial going another month. Clearly, something was afoot, and he covered the receiver to pass along piecemeal blips. Grossman, in disbelief of the weekly reports, had spent the whole day at a switchboard talking with telemarketing callers, whose astonishing fervor made him believe the numbers. More small donors had come forward in the last nineteen days than any previous *year* of Clinton's service. "By God," the president told Grossman, "we ought to leak that." Afterward, Clinton giggled as he replayed for me some of the pithy, profane donor comments. "I will be very surprised, and crushed," he concluded in wonder, "if we do not win the House of Representatives in 2000."

Gravity returned over Jordan. He called it a blow to see King Hussein so weak and emaciated at sixty-three. Hillary and he had grown closer to the Husseins than to any peer couple on the world stage, not excluding the Blairs and the Kohls. They shared social and political trust almost equally four ways, treasuring the American-born Queen Noor. The king would not last, Clinton feared, until the Israeli-Palestinian talks scheduled for May, and no one else could control and push Arafat to push the Israelis forward in turn. There would be instability, he said, and every kind of loss to grieve.

Nancy Mitchell walked down with me on the way out. This was not unprecedented, but I sensed her wish to calm any lingering amusement over the blushes of Doorman Hancock, as even the sweetest gossip from this place could become political artillery. I made reassuring comments about hoarding the president's record entirely for the future. As we neared the exit, I asked about an isolated chair still sitting in the middle of the Diplomatic Reception Room. She nodded. That's where President Clinton ran into Stephen Hawking tonight on returning from his visit with the pope. Mitchell had been waiting there for a van to pick up the departing physicist, who suffers from Lou Gehrig's disease, and Clinton, spontaneously, had dragged a seat right up next to the specialized wheelchair. Hawking's face lit up with a pretty smile for forty-five minutes, she said, while they talked about everything under the sun.

THEN IT WAS over. I called President Clinton to congratulate him on his acquittal by the Senate. Ten days later, a call just before supper rushed me down to Washington, and the ushers sent me upstairs with a sandwich from the kitchen. They said the president was delayed, but he quickly entered the Treaty Room with an armload of books. "I'm rearranging a lot," he said. Did I know this cross-racial history of mid-century Atlanta politics, *Where Peachtree Meets Sweet Auburn*, by Gary Pomerantz? Yes, but I had not yet read David Remnick's book on Muhammad Ali. He continued in this vein—touching, remembering, reshelving—with commentary about thinking forward and backward now at the same time. He wanted to shape vigorous themes for his last months in office while beginning to prepare his legacy. People soon would explore plans for his presidential library, and he invited me to join an informal group of advisers.

This spurred me to ask a return favor. I said I hated to do so, especially because it involved self-interest. Clinton perked up. "Shoot," he instructed with a grin. "What is it?" Well, last year the National Archives promoted to other jobs both experts who handled the release of presidential telephone recordings. These people—Stephanie Fawcett from the JFK Library, and Mary Knill at LBJ—were vital lifelines to source material for historical writers. Neither had been replaced. Most known tapes remained unavailable. The release always was painfully slow, stretching over many years, but now progress rested on spare-time effort by staff workers assigned to other projects. Could he get the budget slots filled, if not reinforced? Clinton, grappling out loud with personnel politics many layers above individual librarians, took my memo and said he would have his deputy Maria Echaveste look into it the next day. Then he teased me about presidential history. Maybe it was overrated. Still, he understood. He would hate to put his own memoirs on hold waiting for librarians to process the tapes he and I were making now.

The wealthy music executive David Geffen, said Clinton, already had offered to negotiate his contract for those memoirs without charge. Was that a good idea? I said he had at least a year before making such decisions, which would include finding safe ways to transcribe his voluminous tapes. The president professed more doubt than hurry. "Hillary's memoirs will probably be worth more than mine," he mused. He seemed downcast—probably from the impeachment, and his memoirs were always a touchy subject. Studying him for clues, I said it was possible that the market valued his book below Hillary's for now. Clinton was battered, and most opinion leaders were heavily invested in looking down on him. Nevertheless, there would be more demand for his side of history than people realized. He asked directly how much he could get. Stammering, I guessed somewhere between $5 and $10 million. He discounted my concern that Hillary's possible run for the Senate seat in New York might inhibit his candor about her in the book. "If she runs, and wins," he realized, brightening, "she'll be sworn in as a senator while still living in the White House, before my term ends. How's that for a little history?"

On tape, he described the rush to bury King Hussein within twenty-four hours of death as prescribed by Islamic law. Former presidents Ford, Carter, and Bush flew with Clinton to Jordan, and the four got along well—mostly, he thought, because Carter, who can be supercilious and hypersensitive, was in a good mood the whole twelve-hour flight, sharing stories and sharp observations. He and the others refused Clinton's persistent offers to rotate sleep breaks on two beds in the presidential cabin of Air Force One. They broke away instead for short naps in sleeping bags, then immediately joined a procession behind Hussein's caisson, walking a long way up and down hills through narrow city streets. Ford gave out, said the president, even though he was in good shape at eighty-five. So did Mubarak of Egypt. Yeltsin did not even try, though sober, and had to be helped out of his chair. Clinton bumped into Asad of Syria, among many others. Back in the royal compound, he said Hillary and Queen Noor emerged with the bereaved family women, having been separated from the funeral by tradition, and took seats quietly on a long staircase. That sight was his most touching memory. There was political business, too, but Clinton emphasized a private aside with the deposed Hassan, who was gracious about submitting to his late brother's judgment and his young nephew's rule. He said duty was clear. Clinton thanked him for service to his country and beyond.

We reviewed several developments about race. The president did not realize that the first of four defendants was convicted today in Jasper, Texas, but he knew about the gruesome murder of James Byrd Jr., who had been stripped and dragged for three miles behind a pickup truck last year. The president asked about the racial composition of the jury. Mostly white, I thought, and they returned a unanimous verdict the first day. Good, he said. To my discomfort, he perceived a side benefit for the death penalty in the fair and impartial conviction of white supremacists for capital crimes against black victims. Such progress would reduce the empirical bias in executions—a victimization by race, controlling for all other factors—which could answer a principal line of argument against capital punishment.

From another case earlier this month, during his impeachment trial, Clinton recognized the name Amadou Diallo, an immigrant from Guinea who lived in the Bronx: "You mean the one the police shot forty-one times outside his apartment?" He asked for basic facts about why the four officers were after him. They said, from my notes, that he matched the description of a serial rapist and they thought he pulled a gun, which turned out to be his wallet. Clinton sighed, knowing there were marches and demonstrations about whether the federal government should take over the investigation of the case. That decision would probably never reach him. He thought it more than likely that Mayor Rudy Giuliani would take a political position squarely behind his police, but he trusted the local prosecutor, Robert Morgenthau. "I can't believe he would take a dive on a case like this," said the president.*

Clinton came alive when I mentioned his pardon for the first black graduate of West Point, class of 1877. "Henry Flipper!" he told me, proceeding to describe many of the sixteen Flipper descendants who came to the White House last week. Colin Powell and a brace of generals told stories of the exemplary Buffalo Soldier under terrible conditions after the Civil War. Doubling as a military engineer, they said, he was still renowned by the Army for his Flipper's Ditch reconfiguration that had saved Fort Sill from malaria. Even after he was unjustly drummed out of the Army in 1882, said the president, Flipper forged an amazing career as a scientific author and designer of petroleum equipment. The case for pardon was a no-brainer, but it had taken more than two years to dynamite it through bureaucratic resistance at Justice, State, and the Pentagon. Posthumous or not, these gestures have resonance for major institutions. Clinton winced when I chimed in that Powell was said to have had Flipper's picture in his room at West Point. "Colin didn't go to West Point," he corrected. I must mean his office at the Pentagon, but it was true that admiration ran deep. Like Powell, said the president, black members of the White House staff were circumspect about overt racial awareness, let alone advocacy, considering it unprofessional, but maids and butlers had formed a cheery line when Clinton came upstairs from that pardon ceremony.

Of his Valentine trip to Mexico, with Hillary, the president described visiting the Yucatan and a Mayan museum exhibiting some ancient computation system based on the number five. He thought Mexico's president, Ernesto Zedillo, was the most astute economic manager in all of Latin America. The problem for Zedillo was that drug cartels have so much money in proportion to his government—so much money, Clinton kept saying. Drug profits generated or floated corruption on a spectacular scale. Carlos Salinas, the former president, had fled to Ireland.

---

* Local prosecutors brought indictments for second-degree murder and reckless endangerment. A jury in Albany, after a change of venue, acquitted the four officers of all charges on February 25, 2000. In March of 2004, New York City settled a civil suit by paying Diallo's survivors $3 million.

Salinas's brother, Rául, had just been convicted last month of ordering the murder of their sister's husband by hired killers.* Zedillo was roundly criticized for allowing a prosecution that exposed so much ugly intrigue among the nation's powerful families, with witnesses and prosecutors alike disappearing by murder or with enormous fortunes. President Zedillo told Clinton he had no choice but to let the Salinas prosecution go forward. Otherwise, everybody would believe the case involved still worse things in Mexican culture, such as gay blackmail.

Iraq felt almost tame after Mexico. There were daily skirmishes over the U.N.'s no-fly zone, whose purpose was to deny Saddam Hussein the protection of air defense systems for any Iraqi weapons of mass destruction. Almost unnoticed, said Clinton, the no-fly missions in January and February had destroyed more of Saddam's military infrastructure than the concentrated bombardment of December. Was it inevitable, I asked, that a British or American pilot would be shot down? He hoped not, but Saddam was offering large cash bounties to any Iraqi gunner who could bag a U.N. trophy. So far, said the president, the gunners fired wildly. They were not locking their antiaircraft radar on the no-fly planes above. If they did, they knew the sensors in those planes would react instantly with directed missile fire at the radar source, leaving the gunner far more likely to get killed than to earn a bounty. Overall, therefore, Saddam was losing control of soldiers while his advanced weapons were being degraded. This rendered him less of an external threat—frustrated, probably, deprived of his showy military stunts—but still formidable within Iraq. Clinton defended Gen. Anthony Zinni, who warned Congress never to underestimate the difficulty of replacing Saddam. Critics accused Zinni of bucking the administration's ambition to do so. Nonsense, said the president. That was authorized testimony. While we believed there could never be peace in that part of the world with Saddam in power, our first duty was to keep him weak.

THE PRESIDENT BOUNCED off several invitations to discuss impeachment. We discussed logging policy instead, then a round of talks outside Paris about Kosovo. No, he did not follow the Senate trial more closely at the

---

* The conviction was later overturned on appeal.

end. Nor did he feel any tingle of historic relief. He said I may consider him disengaged, or irresponsible, but he knew where it was headed, and the proceedings only confirmed his belief that the case was not real from the start. So he tuned out most of the details. His tactical preferences did not matter much, anyhow, because Senate Republicans controlled procedural matters with a simple majority vote. Clinton wanted to have the final deliberations open to the public. They closed them. And so on. Still, the outcome for him wound up perhaps the best of possible worlds.

He did say that one Republican senator, Ted Stevens of Alaska, announced in the closed session that he would oppose both articles of impeachment if his vote really counted. On their own, if not in a vise grip between party discipline and adverse public opinion, Clinton figured that thirty-five to forty of the fifty-five Republican senators would have voted to convict him. He told me he was too tired to go through all this, but he mentioned a surprising source. Richard Shelby of Alabama, who despised Clinton as much as any Republican senator, had confided more or less on a professional basis, as a former prosecutor, that the objectively weak case stood no chance. He said Senator Lott convened Republicans five days before the verdict to plead for a good showing. Henry Hyde and the other managers were desperate. If their own Senate partisans rebuked them, it would make the House Republicans look even worse for bringing impeachment.

Therefore, Lott demanded party unity on one of the final votes. There were two articles of impeachment. The first charged that Clinton committed perjury in the Lewinsky case, the second that he obstructed justice. Senator Lott conceded the perjury article, saying he would let ten or more Republicans vote for Clinton if they needed to. But their caucus must stand on the second article, exerting maximum discipline to round up cosmetic votes from senators like Strom Thurmond and Ben Campbell, against their preferences. Even so, Lott lost five Republicans on obstruction. Senator Jim Jeffords of Vermont voted for acquittal on honest belief. Senator Olympia Snowe of Maine may have voted her convictions, too, but not her colleague Susan Collins. Clinton agreed with Shelby that for her, like John Chafee of Rhode Island, the vote was pure survival. Chafee loathed Clinton as much as Shelby, and dearly wanted to convict him, but the president's approval ratings were above 70 percent in both Maine and Rhode Island. Shelby split his own two votes, for and against conviction. Getting zero of the forty-five Democratic senators on either tally, Republicans reached their peak vote of 50–50 on the obstruction article, seventeen short of conviction. With Lott's ten sanctioned defections, they lost the perjury article, 45–55.

Acquitted, Clinton went straight to New Hampshire. I prodded him to tell me about the trip. Slowly at first, he said he tried but failed not to make it nostalgic. People stood up to give testimonials about his comeback in the 1992 primary. He would never forget Tricia Duff, a single mother who had never voted and came skeptical to a Clinton rally but left motivated to get off welfare. She went to nursing school, became a nurse, and by the time she told people she was now on the New Hampshire Board of Nursing, there was sheer bedlam. The president said he had never experienced anything like it in politics. He was choked up then, and again now, plus several more times on through New Hampshire memories from Merrimack, Manchester, and Dover.

He tried to end our long session, pleading exhaustion, but he kept surging with new thoughts about the political aftermath of impeachment. At a retreat with House Democrats in Virginia, Clinton said he acknowledged temptation to tread water and then run against the do-nothing Republican Congress. However, he advised, it's best to begin in politics with the assumption that you can make a case to voters on the merits. Democrats should build military strength for new peacekeeping missions *and* fight for jobs, better schools, and the environment. That was the price of leadership. Set these goals first, he exhorted them, and then worry about the politics. Democrats and Republicans could always find something to fight about before an election.

Just today, Clinton said, he had the bipartisan congressional leadership at the White House to compare legislative agendas for the year. His presentation narrowed differences on at least a dozen issues. He called it the big picture, including long-term reform of Social Security and Medicare, which he repeated on tape, and a fresh calculation that the United States could also retire the cumulative national debt within nineteen years, which would lower interest rates all along the way and free up trillions of dollars for investment in the private economy. I tried to imagine

Dennis Hastert, the new speaker of the House, absorbing this tour de force. What did he say? Well, they just listened, asking to hear Clinton's views, the president replied. Frankly, the Republicans were in disarray about a message. They knew they would get clobbered again with pro-business ideas on the environment. Lott was backing off the tax cut already, trying out proposals for missile defense. And the Republican governors were no better. The president said he had just spent the weekend with them during the National Governors Association conference in Washington.

Did not the governors tend to be more practical and substantive than members of Congress? Clinton gave me his disappointed look, for political naïfs. Sometimes, he said, but not these thirty-one Republican governors. They were all politics now. They yearned only to nominate George W. Bush for president, forget substance, and run a national Republican campaign on character issues. The president launched into impressions of Bush, finding him polished and gracious like his mother in public, but cold in private. Democratic governors said they had no across-the-aisle camaraderie with him, as they did with congenial peers like his brother Jeb, governor of Florida. They had no doubt that the Texas governor Bush would try to cut their guts out if president. On Saturday, at a White House dinner, Clinton found George W. miserable and hostile the whole time. "Of course, he's never forgiven me for beating his father," said the president, "but that's about as deep as his political conviction gets. All this 'compassionate conservative' business is phony." For God's sake, Clinton added, a president has to be much bigger than that. You work with people trying to throw you out of office. That's your job.

Could Bush's early rival for the GOP nomination, Senator John McCain, show more balance in the long run? Well, he replied, McCain could be tough, but not necessarily well organized or financed. To win, he needed to be all three at once. Clinton thought it more likely that Bush would secure early anointment to head a Republican ticket with someone like Dole's wife, Elizabeth. That would pose interesting choices and trade-offs. The president would support Hillary if she chose to run in New York—they wanted to live there, anyway—and she was probably the only Democrat who could beat Mayor Giuliani for Pat Moynihan's

Senate seat. Still, the New York campaign would waste her unique strength across the country. By the numbers, and Clinton's gut, a Gore-Hillary ticket would give Democrats their best chance to defeat Bush for the White House. "Hands down," he said, "but I don't think Al would ever do it."

CHAPTER THIRTY-FOUR

KOSOVO, COLUMBINE, AND KASHMIR

Wednesday, April 14, 1999

Wednesday, June 9, 1999

Tuesday, June 29, 1999

Wednesday, August 4, 1999

Spring arrived with war, bloodcurdling new scandal, and numbing disaster at home. In April, I found the president clinging to a respite with Hugh Rodham—previewing the NBA playoffs, debating whether Duke could have beaten Connecticut for the NCAA men's basketball championship. Hugh argued that Cleveland would be insane not to take Kentucky quarterback Tim Couch with its first pick in the NFL draft, but he withdrew once his brother-in-law started fretting to both of us about late night military updates still ahead. Hastily, on the Solarium's glass-top table, our session recorded Clinton's tense rationale for his second war to stop genocide by President Slobodan Milosevic, this time in Kosovo. For three weeks—with no end in sight—NATO jets and Toma-hawk cruise missiles had been bombarding the dictator's strategic forces right into his capital city of Belgrade. They destroyed the Interior Ministry last week. Today marked 1,700 sorties. The German Luftwaffe, under NATO command, was flying its first combat missions since World War II, alongside three brand-new partners—Poland, Hungary, and the Czech Republic—in the nineteen-nation NATO alliance. Moral, political, and logistical strains lengthened the daunting odds. Never had NATO itself conducted hostile operations. Never in military history had airpower alone undertaken such a substantial goal with success.

The president navigated a thick fog of controversy. People called the air campaign halfhearted, cruel, foolhardy, or shamefully too late—sometimes all at once. House Republicans tried to block funds for four thousand U.S. peacekeepers if needed. With a straight face, Henry Kissinger warned in congressional testimony that Kosovo could become a quagmire like Vietnam. Tom DeLay denounced the administration's foreign policy "with no focus . . . formulated by the Unabomber," and many observers conflated the two Balkan wars. In Bosnia, Clinton stressed, Milosevic had tried to dismember an independent nation in league with its dominant Serbs. Kosovo, by contrast, remained the southernmost and poorest province of Yugoslavia ("Land of the Southern Slavs"). Milosevic revoked its provincial autonomy, which had protected ethnic Albanians, who were heavily Muslim—closing their newspapers and broadcast stations, expelling them from state jobs. The ragtag Kosovo Liberation Army (KLA) sprang up to demand independence, and when Milosevic sent national troops against these separatist KLA "terrorists," chronic attacks from both sides plagued civilians through 1998. William Walker, ambassador in Belgrade, verified "an unspeakable atrocity" in January 1999—a mass grave of Kosovar Albanians, including women and children, with eyes gouged out and gunshots to the head. Clinton had feared both sides would reject truce terms forged by the Western powers. The KLA guerrillas finally agreed to defer independence, settling for restored autonomy guaranteed by NATO, but Milosevic refused to allow NATO peacekeepers on his territory. Instead of withdrawing his troops, he sent forty thousand reinforcements and three hundred tanks against Kosovo's 1.5 million non-Serb civilians.

Since March 24, NATO had bombed furiously to weaken and stop Milosevic before his soldiers finished the ethnic cleansing of Kosovo. This mismatched duel was lethal, complicated, and fraught with consequences. Some 300,000 Albanian Kosovars—nearly all Muslim—fled their homes in the first week. A thousand desperate refugees trudged every hour into neighboring Bulgaria, Albania, and Macedonia, spilling south into Greece. I would remember the outline of Clinton's argument that Kosovo heightened all three danger points to the post–Cold War quest for a stable, democratic Europe. One was the potential collapse of democracy in Russia. Two was the stubborn conflict between Greece and Turkey. Three was the proven danger of secession and ethnic hatred in the Balkans. Only on the second was Clinton at all sanguine, citing history's first cooperation between NATO members Greece and Turkey in relief efforts for Kosovo. In Russia, said the president, hard-line nationalists supported the Serb Milosevic, their fellow Slav, against all the Kosovar minorities. Demonizing Yeltsin as a stooge of NATO, they mobilized Slavic fear and resentment behind authoritarian visions of a restored Russian empire.

Clinton explored the undercurrents of war psychology. He said leaders, by raising alarms against an enemy, can build popular appeal even for their own despotism. He cited Fidel Castro, who justified forty years of arbitrary rule on his defiance of the colossal United States. Almost whimsically, Clinton said Yeltsin's tormentors in the Russian Duma reminded him of the House Republican Caucus—always snarling at strangers to rally some negative mandate. He called Ronald Reagan a hard-liner with a soft touch—such a good actor that he could inspire patriotism to invade a tiny country like Grenada, containing the inherent dangers of military force.* Later, describing his whirlwind tour of Central America, Clinton said its governments had survived for decades on wars of repression. Yes, he replied vigorously, he had apologized there for the U.S. history of political interventions. We were complicit in expropriation or

---

* Reagan invaded the Caribbean island in October of 1983, citing dangers to American students. Nineteen U.S. soldiers were killed. The action, though condemned as illegal by the U.N. General Assembly, and opposed by Reagan's fellow conservatives such as Margaret Thatcher of England, remained broadly popular in the United States. It was the first battalion-level U.S. combat since Vietnam.

worse against the native Indian populations. At long last, said the president, Central American countries were climbing out of blood feuds into a bright future. He digressed to scold Congress for shortsighted politics over trade policy and the regional aid package.

Kosovo was a world crisis, not an idle theory, and Milosevic taxed Clinton's confidence. Normally, the president took pride in the art of communing with other leaders—finding room to maneuver between personal and professional constraints—but he saw no argument or deal to offer Milosevic. Though bloodthirsty and autocratic, Milosevic was lucid. Rationally, the dictator may be correct that he could not survive a halt in the crusade to exterminate Kosovo's non-Serbs. He had put his people through years of punishment for their aggression in Bosnia, and now NATO bombers were flattening their landscape. Serb fever was Milosevic's strength, war crimes and all. The minute he backed down, his own militants would devour him. Therefore, Milosevic was desperate, impervious to diplomacy, and neither NATO nor Clinton's Pentagon would risk a ground invasion of his territory. The dictator was hard to hurt, Clinton said with a sigh, and the headstrong Albanian Kosovars made themselves hard to help. Still, the president declared one shared principle of NATO's united commitment: "You cannot lose." NATO must never submit to genocide in the heart of Europe. The stakes were so grave that its leaders were determined to bomb Yugoslavia until Milosevic, or his successor, let all Kosovo's refugees go home unmolested.

We escaped war tension only briefly in discussions about China. Jiang Zemin had just sent his new premier and economic specialist, Zhu Rongji, on a nine-day mission to the United States. The president said his own administration remained divided about whether to support China's full membership in the World Trade Organization. Aside from human rights, there were many difficult issues of commercial practice, and fresh charges of espionage poisoned the atmosphere for talks. Soon after Clinton's impeachment trial, the *New York Times* mounted a war scare built on last year's allegations about campaign contributions: "Breach at Los Alamos/China Stole Nuclear Secrets for Bombs." The Energy Department fired Wen Ho Lee, a nuclear scientist born in Taiwan, and quotes from senior officials predicted a case of nuclear treason "as bad as the Rosenbergs." * Clinton tried to tamp down public alarm until the investigation was complete. Spying was a constant hazard, he announced carefully, and the alleged nuclear theft was said to predate his administration. The *Times* answered with banner headline suggestions that he had let covert influences paralyze our defense: "President Denies Ignoring Evidence of Nuclear Spying." On tape, Clinton hoped the stories may prove grossly exaggerated. He discounted the *Times* series because its lead reporter, Jeff Gerth, had written the original Whitewater stories, packed with jaundice and hype. Maybe so, I commented, but Gerth had just won the Pulitzer Prize for his reporting on China.

The president stopped me, incredulous. He had not noticed the Pulitzer announcements two days ago, and seemed chastened when I filled him in. The Pulitzer board awarded two 1999 prizes to the *New York Times*. Gerth, leading a team of national reporters, won for "articles disclosing the sale of American technology to China with Government approval, despite national security risks." Columnist Maureen Dowd won for "commentary on the ambitions and values reflected in President Clinton's relationship with Monica S. Lewinsky." He recalled underestimating Whitewater, too, until it became an inexorable tide. Perhaps he was courting trouble again with bland assurance, said Clinton, but how do you dispel suspicions from a shadow world of spies? During Premier Zhu's visit, when reporters asked bluntly for proof of innocence, Zhu tried to make light of the uproar. He said China held $156 billion in U.S. debt. If its leaders really wanted to buy the Clinton administration, Zhu quipped, they would have shelled out "at least $10 billion U.S. for that purpose" rather than the paltry $300,000 alleged. In private, said the president, Zhu maintained a rare sense of humor about the negotiations between their polar-opposite cultures. He confided arguments within his government, mirroring Clinton's, about whether to trust foreigners on trade or anything else. Hard-liners insisted that hostile Americans really wanted to keep China "down on the farm."

---

* In the most sensational criminal case of the Cold War, Julius and Ethel Rosenberg were tried and convicted for delivering nuclear secrets to the Soviet Union. They were executed on June 19, 1953.

Any Chinese reporter who revealed these deliberations would disappear, whereas Americans could joust with leaders about everything from sex to treason. Nonplussed on tape, Clinton said the *Times* whipsawed him about Asia. Incendiary critics, following Gerth, played on anti-Chinese sentiment to accuse Clinton of laxity and corruption to the brink of treason, renewing cries for a special prosecutor. Opposing stories blithely faulted his shortage of leadership and trust to normalize commercial relations.

Undaunted, the president hacked through some of the remaining barriers to WTO membership for China, which my dictation found "very complicated." New York stocks closed above 10,000 for the first time, he noted, but worldwide recession threatened trade-based growth. "Indonesia is still a basket case," he said. Thailand was recovering, South America stable, and Clinton pushed the new G-8 design for international guidelines to prevent financial collapse. On Iraq, he said Saddam Hussein, deprived of air defenses, had been killing Shiite opponents to look tough, including clerics and students. Clinton thought these jolts of short-term intimidation fed simmering unrest.

Hillary strolled briskly into the Solarium, home late from Chicago. She and the president traded notes on things to discuss before he left in the morning for San Francisco. Then she asked me point-blank whether she should run for the Senate in New York. Fumbling, I said well, it was Robert Kennedy's old seat, primed to represent a center of national energy. As an outsider, her first political race would be the toughest, but New Yorkers tended to return hard workers like her. The Senate would be an ideal public service at a high personal cost, both financially and in personal freedom. I dodged a hard recommendation.

AT OUR SESSION early in June, he seemed troubled by her test reports from the campaign trail. Having assumed she would run, he was no longer sure. Just today, he said, she had been ambushed by thirty angry demonstrators at a trial event in Binghamton, but at other moments she had been engulfed by supporters, who could turn, as she put it, worshipful and overwrought. The tension knocked her off balance. Though seasoned by two decades in politics, she could not tell whether the intensity came from New York politics or her exposure as the candidate. Either way, she was shaken. The president kept saying he would support whatever she decided. He had pledged, he told me, not to live through her once he left the White House.

On tape, the president discussed Kosovo past midnight. Seven more weeks of pulverizing NATO bombs had cracked open a window to possible victory. Clinton quivered with restrained excitement, like a racehorse in the gate. If successful, he said, Kosovo would be the first American war without a cheerleader in the press. Nobody thought it was a good idea, including many pundits who despised Milosevic. Despite NATO bombardment, his Serb troops had displaced nearly 900,000 Albanian Kosovars in April. Make no mistake, said the president, this air campaign endured severe strains among the nineteen participating NATO nations—and also within his administration. Defense Secretary Cohen and Joint Chiefs Chairman Shelton, for instance, resented their colleague Wesley Clark, who commanded the NATO forces. Clark wanted to win so badly that he was not above leaking his doubts about their commitment, said the president. Clark browbeat them to send a reserve fleet of Army helicopters at enormous expense, which sparked divisive alarms of an imminent NATO ground invasion. These slow-flying, vulnerable AH-64 Apaches, though wisely withheld from combat, produced NATO's only two casualties in a training crash. Clinton said he spoke with Clark seldom, and formally, to minimize tension. Aside from inevitable suspicion of favoritism between Arkansas friends, there was friction over a dual chain of command into the Oval Office—one through the Pentagon, another through NATO.

Clinton said his public role was to be resolute in the face of carping that NATO's strategy defied uniform military doctrine on the limits of airpower. He defended at a press briefing the pinpoint destruction of a twenty-three-story building in downtown Belgrade as legitimate, telling reporters it housed Milosevic's media networks for propaganda along with his party headquarters. Asked how many more hours he could continue what the press termed senseless slaughter, he told them for as long as it takes. He thought he did get through, at least for a moment, when the startled reporters leaned back from his assertion that Balkan flight conditions would improve in May over April, in June over May, July over June, and so on through the summer. Total NATO air strikes swelled from 1,700 to 38,000. Meanwhile, said the president, his diplomatic job was to pacify skittish leaders from major nations outside Europe. The Chinese were frantic lest Kosovo set a precedent for greater human rights pressure on their control of Tibet, and the Russians feared second-guessing of their own nasty war to suppress the rebellious Muslim province of Chechnya. "Kosovo is not Chechnya," Clinton said he kept telling Yeltsin. "Did you order young girls raped and villages systematically destroyed? Did you order Chechen mosques and libraries burned to wipe out cultural records?" Of course not, Yeltsin replied, and Clinton cajoled the beleaguered Russian to stay neutral.

His lowest moment was notice from Sandy Berger on May 7 that NATO bombs had hit the Chinese embassy. It made him ask me, rhetorically, whether anyone could be sure God favored this cause. Outraged demonstrations spread across China, where few believed the attack was accidental. Worse, said Clinton, this air strike was the only one prepared by the CIA. He called Jiang Zemin with profuse apologies and a lame-sounding explanation that CIA experts had specified the target based on outdated city maps of Belgrade. Zemin was frosty, and no one could blame him, said the president. The attack was an unprovoked act of war under international law, which treated embassies as national territory. Accordingly, Clinton ordered a full investigation and offered compensation for the loss of life. He said we would demand no less, and shuddered to imagine how China's hard-liners would interpret this supposed wanton U.S. aggression in debates within their government. Things were bad enough in reverse. Senator Shelby was demanding the resignation of Attorney General Reno for failure to wiretap Chinese spies, who, according to the latest *New York Times* investigations, had compromised "virtually every weapon in the United States arsenal." Columnist William Safire assailed Clinton for "desperately trying to keep a lid on Chinagate." The president, patiently assessing on tape the merits of these accusations, said he had received no intelligence consistent with these claims of disaster. The Chinese were modernizing their economy, not their weapons. So far, he said, most media outlets resisted the *Times*'s crusade, which seemed shrill and manufactured.

Switching topics, I asked about April's trauma in Colorado, where two heavily armed boys terrorized Columbine High School in Littleton for two hours, killing one teacher and twelve fellow students, wounding twenty-four others, before committing suicide. Clinton had visited most of the survivors and bereaved families. Some of the victims were physically maimed, already resilient or still undone. He told of being undone himself by the pluck of one gravely wounded kid who had played dead until he could heave himself from a library window, famously on national television. Juvenile violence on this scale had a national impact beyond empathy or questions of mental health, and the president said poll numbers matched his intuition. Columbine turned public opinion more decisively against the National Rifle Association. Even some of the gun manufacturers distanced themselves from the NRA. The president said most people did not realize the NRA's crucial role in the composition of this Congress over the last three elections, beginning with its targeted defeat of Democrats who supported the breakthrough gun control laws of 1994.

Columbine flushed guns to the surface of national politics. The alienated, underage killers in Colorado had obtained their sawed-off shotguns in part through gun shows, which had been exempted from the background checks required by the Brady Bill, and the rapid fire magazines for their Tec-9 semiautomatic handgun had been excluded from the list of weapons prohibited by the Assault Weapons Ban. Clinton's proposal to close these two loopholes, though mild, passed the Senate only on Vice President Gore's tie-breaking vote, and the NRA was mounting a concentrated burst of money and mail to block the bill in the House. Clinton called the pressure anything but subtle. NRA leaders never tired of reminding Republicans who had boosted them into the majority, and Republicans from swing districts were hostage to the NRA no less than to the tobacco companies. Just yesterday, said the president, Speaker Dennis Hastert scheduled a House vote instead on the NRA's toothless alternative. Its lobbyists boasted of drafting the bill in the Judiciary Committee, whose chair, Henry Hyde, openly welcomed their assistance. Clinton hoped voters would punish this minority roadblock. He practiced out loud a speech arguing simply that guns should be regulated like highway travel. Did mandates for driver's licenses and automobile tags lead to confiscated cars or empty roads? Hardly. So why not enact commonsense regulations to track dangerous weaponry and unsafe gun users?

I quibbled that the NRA's appeal seemed more political than practical, built on a cultivated belief. Nowhere in American history did untraceable guns from citizens' closets actually thwart tyrannical government. For real crises of famine or danger, people turned to government and politics—not against them. Until then, the NRA could peddle the flattering fear that household arms guarded freedom and virtue as well as safety. The president waved these speculations aside, calling them too abstract for practical politics. He was groping for help in a treacherous climate. Could the benign image of a driver's license compete with the NRA's scary picture of defenseless dupes, deprived of guns, being shuttled into concentration camps?

Off the tapes, I fared better with a different question about myth. Did he receive the book I sent down through Nancy Hernreich, *The Bridge Betrayed*, by Michael Sells? The president beamed with recognition. Not only did he receive and love the book—he was already distributing copies with a strong recommendation. Sells, a Serb professor of religion at Haverford College, argued persuasively that his people's horrendous war crimes had been born of relatively modern, nationalist fanaticism, grafted to a much longer history of coexistence. His book debunked cynical myths of ancient and implacable Balkan hatreds. This was different from a propaganda problem like the NRA, said Clinton. Sells added perspective for hard times. As a bracing reminder of common heritage, and possibility, the president said he had sent the book to General Shelton, Secretary Albright, Secretary Cohen, and Sandy Berger, among others.

He thought the indictment of President Milosevic for war crimes, on May 27, reinforced Serbia's isolation from world standards. With NATO bombers pounding its defenses and economy into June, diplomats recruited two emissaries, President Martti Ahtisaari of Finland and Victor Chernomyrdin of Russia, to deliver nonnegotiable terms: Serb troops out of Kosovo, NATO peacekeepers in, refugees home. If Milosevic followed through on his promise of capitulation, said Clinton, the world would be a better place.

Hillary called him from New York. They talked about the end of Chelsea's sophomore year at Stanford. She was fighting for a better grade in one course, over some footnoting dispute. The president practiced for Hillary several variations on his notion to compare gun control with car registration, but mostly they discussed the frustrations of her trial campaign. His counsel grew so exercised that I stood to leave, but Clinton retreated for privacy into the bathroom off the family parlor. He was subdued on his return. "You know, I've had a lot more contact with gay people in my life than Hillary." He sighed. Her temperament had a conservative, religious core, formed before homosexual issues were even mentionable. New York politics was a tough crucible, and she was unsure what heat she could take. On the other hand, personal experience could speed adaptation. Clinton had signed the Defense of Marriage Act in 1996, but now he supported equal treatment for gay couples pretty much down the line. He had named Chicago heir James Hormel the first openly gay ambassador in U.S. history, with a recess appointment that prompted Senator James Inhofe to block Senate confirmation of *all* executive appointments, including Treasury Secretary Lawrence Summers, until Hormel was fired. Inhofe, marveled Clinton, had passed Senator Bunning on the misanthrope index.

The president un-muted his parlor television for breaking news from Paris, Brussels, and Belgrade. Serbia had accepted schedules to withdraw from Kosovo, announced a correspondent, and President Clinton was expected to announce formal agreement tomorrow from the Oval Office, ending seventy-eight consecutive days of NATO air strikes. "From the Oval Office," I repeated numbly. Clinton frowned. Should he speak somewhere else? No, no, I said. It was just odd to learn this from a reporter standing nearby on the White House driveway.

Many things could go wrong, observed the president, but the Kosovo intervention promised a new era of cooperative security. Already, the eminent British military historian John Keegan had published a stark mea culpa for his ridicule of NATO prospects. Keegan wrote that Kosovo was a turning point in military history, and began to define conditions for successful application of airpower. Beyond command of the skies, and clear political goals, he emphasized leaps in the accuracy of laser-guided ordnance, which minimized the danger of civilian casualties.

Roughly a hundred bombs had missed their targets—a fraction of one percent—with precision measured in meters. These errors killed fewer than a thousand civilians. All were regrettable, winced Clinton, but he knew of no competent authority who counted fewer than fifty thousand civilians killed during the Desert Storm invasion of Iraq. Politically, NATO's careful warfare would make it harder for Milosevic to deflect resentment. He had brought upon Serbs the systematic demolition of national assets, from bridges to power plants, as well as national pride, for a surrender available on day one. Milosevic's slim chance for survival,* in Clinton's view, was to embody the consoling image of a tragic lost cause, like Robert E. Lee.

I asked a favor as we finished. Christy had stayed late tonight at her speechwriter's office in the Executive Office Building (EOB) next door, waiting for a ride with me, but now she would scarcely get home before her regular train back in the morning. Could we sleep over instead? Of course, he said, he had an empty house. I summoned Christy by phone with a joke that the president graciously offered to turn down the sheets, and he soon joined us in the Queens' Bedroom to do precisely that. For some reason, there were no pillows on the beds there or in the Lincoln Bedroom across the hall. Clinton rummaged through closets and drawers to find one, without success. All the staff had gone home. We apologized for the imposition, offering to make our way to a bedroom upstairs, but he marched us instead down the yellow hallway. There were three pillows on their bed, plus a reclining back support on his side. Leaving a pillow for Hillary, he took two extras and insisted on carrying them back for us. He also picked up a small statue from one hall table, and led us on a detour into the Treaty Room, clutching our pillows, quizzing Christy about the content of and reception for Hillary's speeches in New York. Christy stared at me after he said good night. "What was *that*?" she whispered. Well, he's a restless night owl by himself, I replied, but the pillow search

---

* The Yugoslav military ousted Milosevic during disputed elections in 2000. In 2001, after surrendering to security forces in Belgrade, he was transferred to The Hague on multiple indictments for war crimes in Bosnia and Kosovo. Before prolonged trials ended there, Milosevic died incarcerated on March 11, 2006.

was sweet for a president. Yes, but she meant something else. What was he doing in the Treaty Room—touching things so intently, moving books and replacing them, while talking nonstop? Oh, that. I shrugged. He does it a lot.

WHEN THE TAPES rolled late in June, on the 29th, the president interrupted my standard introduction. Was this our sixty-fifth oral history? "I can't believe we've done all these," he said. "It's really something, isn't it?" He contemplated a voluminous record in progress. These recordings, while a pale imitation of phone calls, did preserve mood and detail. They would become yeast for his memoirs and eventually a centerpiece in his presidential library. With beguiling eagerness, Clinton talked about preparations for his life beyond office. Melancholy would surface sporadically in our remaining sessions, but through this night, at least, he derived an extra zest and detachment from somewhere. Perhaps it was the fresh curiosity of an altered state—still president but now feeling the ex-presidency ahead. Ninety minutes later, I noted a dazed impression that he had propelled us through about four hours of "very intense brain work," stretching constantly. His mental leaps and switchbacks exceeded my ability to recall it all later when dictating my summing up of the evening.

Vice President Gore had just launched his official candidacy for the 2000 election. The president had called twice to congratulate Gore for his kickoff events—once from Geneva, hours later from Paris. Clinton thought the only glitches were technical. Gore's logistics people had planted the network cameras too low for the home-state rally in Carthage, Tennessee, so that viewers were distracted by waving supporters in the foreground. But Gore got all the big things right. His twofold message was perfect: distinguish himself from Clinton's personal flaws, and tell voters exactly what he would do for them in the White House. The president said it was fine for Gore to call Clinton's affair with Monica Lewinsky "inexcusable." First, it was true. Second, it showed a necessary strength to criticize the boss. Third, Gore would be badgered to death until he did. "Al," Clinton had told him, "if you thought it would help in the campaign, I would let you flog me at noon right on the doorstep of the *Washington Post*." They exchanged merriment in suggesting various dramatic effects—prostrate or kneeling, shirt on or shirt off. "Maybe we'd better poll that," suggested Gore, deadpan.

Gore should ignore stories that Clinton was offended, or critical of his campaign. Pot stirring and projection were endemic on the Lewinsky material, and everybody including Gore had been disappointed by his own early performance. He trailed not only the Republican contenders but also in some polls former senator Bill Bradley for the Democratic nomination. But all this was early. Gore had streamlined the campaign staff and moved his headquarters to Tennessee. He was better organized. On tape, the president said he had confided his chief strategic worry only to Gore himself and to Gore's pollster, Mark Penn. The vice president must project his platform—where he stood, precisely how and where he would lead the country—because the Republicans would try to knock him off substance. They preferred to run on style, trends, and attitude, like a high school election.

The president often railed against Republicans because they lacked an agenda. He called them self-absorbed. He said their basic message was, "Let us rule, and we promise to be nice." Now, however, he was appraising them objectively for the campaign season. Republicans specialize in politics, he said. Not being all balled up over issues and priorities, they had developed tactical flexibility around their determination to win. Adroitly, he said, they were rehabilitating him after impeachment in order to diminish Gore. "All of a sudden, I'm the master of genius and charm," Clinton said, laughing. "They're saying I'm an immoral son of a bitch, but I can jump higher and give a better speech than anybody. They say I'm Michael Jordan and Gore is pitiful. The other Democrats are blah. They're just the rest of the Bulls without Jordan."

He said Republicans were agile enough to attack his character and praise his skills at the same time—both to Gore's disadvantage. In the long run, of course, they could not run against Gore on Lewinsky per se. They would experiment for whatever of Clinton's character defects rubbed off on Gore, and Clinton said the major press outlets would fall right in line. For now, he did not want to debate how or why, but he asserted an empirical trend. He cited a prediction from the close of our last session. If indeed he could announce the successful end of hostilities in Kosovo, he had said, Republicans would plant doubts about Gore's involvement. Sure enough, we heard quickly and often that the vice president knew little about Kosovo, and contributed less, being preoccupied with his campaign. These insinuations were easy to sell in the wake of a complicated war.

Three weeks after NATO stopped the bombs, said Clinton, nearly 80 percent of Americans believed we were still fighting. Critics played up dangers, uncertainty, and friction. Clinton could not guarantee when four thousand U.S. security forces would be home, nor easily explain why some NATO countries were delinquent with their allotted peacekeepers. Russia, having reluctantly agreed to station troops alongside former NATO enemies, to police her unruly Serb allies, rushed pell-mell past the assigned zones. In a miniature reenactment of Stalin's race for Berlin to close World War II, Russian soldiers occupied Kosovo's provincial capital of Pristina. The surprise infuriated Wesley Clark, and blocked relief flights into the Pristina airport. Poor Secretary Cohen, said Clinton, haggled for withdrawal with the Russians, who pointed fingers at each other. Russia's government was amorphous. Rivals swarmed like hedge clippers to cut down the competent prime minister, Sergei Stepashin, and Yeltsin was a dying shadow. Meanwhile, frightened Albanian Kosovars assumed the Russians were in cahoots with their Serb oppressors. President Clinton said politics obscured the big picture. Five hundred thousand refugees already were returning home. The NATO gamble did stop a genocide. Appreciation from afar would come only over time—or perhaps the definitive removal of Milosevic.

I asked about Gen. Ehud Barak, Israel's incoming prime minister, who had displaced Bibi Netanyahu. "The Israeli election was simple," said the president. "Barak campaigned as Yitzhak Rabin reincarnate, promising peace and security." Now, as a soldier even more decorated than Rabin, Barak rushed to conclude treaties with both Syria and the Palestinians before the next mandated elections. This was music to Clinton, who yearned to be part of these milestones, but he gave a cautionary primer on musical chairs in Middle East politics. Barak wanted to move first on Syria, since it was simpler, but President Asad's huge ego made him want to go last since he was already behind Egypt and Jordan. The Palestinians were still smarting from Netanyahu. Barak, falling short of a tamper-proof majority, had trouble forming a government. Both his Labor Party and Likud had lost seats to religious parties in the 120-member Israeli Knesset, and Clinton analyzed the flaws in various coalitions almost by district. So far, they had talked only by phone. "I'll know more," said the president, "after he comes to visit me shortly."

Clinton surprised me about Kashmir, the Himalayan kingdom nestled between India, Pakistan, and China. He said skirmishes there were much more serious than reported. "If they called tonight, and said I could end this thing by flying over there, I would have no choice but to jump on the plane," he said. "There is no greater responsibility for me than to reduce conflicts that threaten nuclear war, and this one certainly does." Only four months ago, the leaders of India and Pakistan had embarked on a startling peace pilgrimage, worthy of Gandhi, riding trains and buses to meet for peace talks near their border in Punjab. They pledged jointly to end the festering dispute over Kashmir, which had triggered two of their three wars since partition in 1947. This new crisis snatched fear from hope, showing how swiftly politics can change. Since May, said the president, Pakistan had sneaked military units across Kashmir's de facto Line of Control into mountain redoubts—as high as eighteen thousand feet—to shell Indian outposts in the populated valley below.

Euphoria vanished, and the governments seethed with intrigue. Civilians and generals disputed each other on both sides. Elements within Pakistan had engineered the covert war to attract international mediation, hoping to realize the popular demands of Kashmir's heavy Muslim majority for independence or annexation by Pakistan. Failing mediation, Pakistan's zealots prepared nuclear attacks to stave off annihilation by India's conventional forces. India's zealots prepared nuclear attacks to preempt Pakistan, or retaliate, or defy any mandate for India to weaken its legal rule over Kashmir. Clinton said the current intelligence reports detailed by far the gravest alarm of his presidency. He could not say more, even on these restricted tapes, but Kashmir was far from over as a threat.

We shifted to the departure of Treasury Secretary Robert Rubin. The president's tribute was glowing, as expected. He said Rubin was lonely. With his wife, Judith, staying behind in New York, Rubin chose to be a boarder all these years at Washington's Jefferson Hotel. He had left the opulent world of investment banking to defend a vast, endangered middle class, and Clinton had teased him that public service would sink Rubin into their lowly ranks. Rubin liked to argue, and he spoke with authority among his peers. Throughout impeachment—in and out of Clinton's hearing—he told fellow cabinet members not to get sucked into the artificial drama. It was extraneous to their mission and the presidency. "I don't want any of you to *think* about resigning," he said bluntly.

Clinton appreciated the loyal support—especially because Rubin had a sense for what mattered. His blind spot was elective politics. When the president had urged him to run for and easily win the New York Senate seat, Rubin recoiled. Judith would leave him, he protested, and Congress was a big step down from executive responsibility. To Rubin, politics was a distasteful scrum. He could not fathom why Hillary wanted to run now, Clinton said, which meant he overlooked a vital part of her makeup. She loves the public tumble like me, said the president. It closes the ring.

The president's answers to my questions on a number of topics varied in length. The new report on national gambling left him cold, through no fault of the commissioners. He was anti-gambling in principle, but the fever had seeped into the country through state lotteries and Indian casinos. He gave a minor discourse on the relative prosperity of Botswana, then a major one on the balky start for independence in Northern Ireland. Disputes over connotations of ordinary words threatened to bring down its new government. "They'll say the fighting is over, but they can't say the war is over," he observed glumly. His survey of domestic issues addressed a central conundrum. "The public supports our positions," said the president, "but how do we turn that into votes?" Two hundred citizens groups and a healthy majority of voters favored the Patient's Bill of Rights, but health insurers alone blocked legislation in Congress. He confronted similar impasses on gun control, birth control, environmental protection, campaign reform, some education bills, and restrictions on youth tobacco. His plan was to keep hammering.

He walked me to his private elevator, engrossed again in the approaching usefulness of these tapes. I should make a note to talk about concepts for his presidential library. He was thinking about commuting time between potential New York homes and the library site in Little Rock. Just yesterday, Hillary and Chelsea had inspected houses for sale in Westchester County, which was nice but very expensive. An ex-president would have to give a lot of pricey speeches to live there and pay off his Whitewater debts. It was time to discuss his memoirs, too. How should they be organized? Could there be two volumes—perhaps a quick topical one followed by a more comprehensive book? Would it be safe or wise for him to start next year, still in the White House?

I was full of advice for his book project until another idea popped up. Someday, after his memoir was published, he mused, I should think about writing a book on my own about these tapes. He thought the process would be interesting, as no sitting president to his knowledge had tried anything like our recorded sessions. Maybe so, I replied. The timing might work well several years down the road. Clinton warmed to the notion. In fact, he spoke so enthusiastically about his book as opposed to my book that I felt twinges of separation. Was he giving notice? Did he have another writer in mind to help him? If so, could I blame him after all my hesitancy on collaboration? Flustered, I chipped in a parting suggestion for him to attend the Women's World Cup soccer tournament, especially if the U.S. team made the final in Los Angeles.

OUR AUGUST 4 session stirred more emotion than intellect. I found President Clinton in the Solarium, finishing a take-out delicatessen dinner with two Rodham in-laws, Hugh and his mother, Dorothy. They were reviewing the first month of Hillary's official campaign in New York, especially her traumatic disaster last week. "I know exactly how it happened," said the president. Writer Lucinda Franks was married to the venerable Manhattan district attorney Robert Morgenthau. With their good friends, Nick and Lydia Katzenbach, the Morgenthaus had labored to explain why a good president like Clinton could stoop to a terrible thing like the Monica Lewinsky affair. Lydia Katzenbach was a psychoanalyst. Her husband, the former attorney general, had testified for Clinton during the impeachment proceedings. The two couples worked out an elaborate thesis, which Franks proposed as an interview topic. Hillary unwisely cooperated, hoping to dispose of the controversy about her marital choices. The published interview did just the opposite, of course, and Clinton analyzed the bellowing on the airwaves.* Pundits called Hillary an enabler. They said she rationalized her husband's infidelity as the inevitable product of his abused childhood.

The Rodhams joined in to dissect Hillary's mistakes along with distorted interpretations. It seemed casually raw, like a family crisis rehearsed wearily on stage. Hillary never excused anything he did, the president insisted, and neither did he. Confession and complaint merged into politics. A new poll found that 87 percent of New Yorkers were sick of hearing about the interview and Clinton's infidelity alike. Maybe the flurry would die down. Conventional wisdom made New York mayor Rudy Giuliani the easiest Republican contender for Hillary to run against—because of his abrasive personality and his association with police brutality scandals. The president dissented. He considered Giuliani a spirited combatant who was relatively moderate on most issues. The other GOP candidates were conventional conservatives, and he thought Hillary could beat them on the merits.

Downstairs in the family room, Clinton recorded his first impressions of Israeli prime minister Barak, who had brought Rabin's widow, Leah, to a state dinner. Private talks went well. Barak was in a hurry, which was good and bad news. He wanted to renegotiate parts of the Wye Agreement in final-status talks with Arafat next year. This would pitch Arafat into a filibuster for months, Clinton warned. Barak was fresh and decisive, but Arafat saw him as the heir to Netanyahu more than Rabin. The president relayed preapproved messages between them to cushion the setback he sensed ahead.

He was besieged on China. President Lee of Taiwan had just precipitated a spasm of war maneuvers across the Taiwan Strait with hints that he may proclaim sovereign independence from China. Lee seemed willfully obtuse about pressures on his Chinese counterpart, Jiang Zemin, who was fighting to survive the August summit of his ruling Communist Party. Clinton said he had a back channel to Jiang through Senator Dianne Feinstein, who had been mayor of San Francisco when

---

* "The Intimate Hillary" launched the premiere, September 1999 issue of *Talk* magazine, a splashy joint venture between the Hearst Corporation and Miramax Films. It ceased publication in January of 2002.

Jiang was mayor of Shanghai. She confirmed his sense of struggle against converging plots. Accused of weakness, he had ordered the arrest of 1,200 leaders from the Falun Gong meditation-and-exercise sect. (He said obscure cultural movements, though baffling to Westerners, had convulsed all of China in the "Heavenly Peace" revolt of the 1850s and the Boxer Rebellion of 1898.) Meanwhile, Jiang's militant opposition agitated to treat the United States as a permanent enemy. Surely, they said, Clinton orchestrated the provocations from Taiwan along with the bomb attack on their embassy in Belgrade. They pointed to testimony by CIA director George Tenet that his agency had prescribed the target coordinates for that one air strike among thousands. They also cited a classified report from House Republicans, led by Christopher Cox, fulminating against Clinton's complicity in Chinese subversion. Several neglected studies called the Cox report a baseless projection of political hysteria. "I suppose you noticed," a sighing Clinton said, "that [nuclear scientist] Wen Ho Lee vigorously denied giving the Chinese any information, on *60 Minutes*."

He interrupted my question about Kashmir. No, he did *not* invite Pakistan's prime minister, Nawaz Sharif, to visit, as reported, but a *Washington Post* story on the tense negotiations was a public hint of a harrowing truth. Sharif had invited himself to Washington for emergency consultations, and Clinton had explicitly instructed him not to come. "Your army is in the wrong here," he told Sharif. Clinton could not mediate the Kashmir crisis without the consent of both warring nations, and India adamantly refused. The Indians saw nothing to mediate. They were winning militarily, and Kashmir belonged to India, period. Whatever Pakistan claimed from the preferences of Kashmiri Muslims, Sharif could not validate them by invasion. Nor could Clinton cover Sharif's retreat. If he did, the Indians would howl against the precedent for rewarding transgression.

Sharif called back with a desperate notice that he was flying to Washington anyway. Protocol flew out the window. U.S. diplomats announced through gritted teeth that Pakistan's prime minister was always welcome, and Clinton canceled his first few events scheduled for July 4th. Declining to receive Sharif at the White House, he met him across the street in the Blair House library. Clinton put his position bluntly. If

Sharif withdrew Pakistani troops from Kashmir, the United States would express relief without praise. If Sharif refused to withdraw, the United States would be forced to shift its historic alliance with Pakistan publicly toward India. For hours, said the president, Sharif's delegation invented trick language to suggest that Clinton somehow blessed a Pakistani withdrawal. Or that Pakistan itself did not need to withdraw, because the fighters in Kashmir were really mujahideen fighters disguised as soldiers rather than vice versa. These arguments in the July heat overwhelmed the Blair House air-conditioning system. "It was hot," the president told me. "They were comfortable in their silks, but I was sweating."

Finally, the president excused the aides on both sides to confront Sharif alone. He said this was far worse than a border skirmish. Kashmir was still the most likely flash point on earth for nuclear war, worse than Cuba in the Missile Crisis of 1962. When the United States and Soviet Union nearly blew up the world, the leaders knew far more about each other's nuclear capabilities than India knows about Pakistan today, or Pakistan about India. You do not have the information or control to minimize the risk of nuclear war, and your brinkmanship can set off nuclear exchanges. Clinton pounded for retreat, and Sharif pounded back. For him, as the elected defender of Pakistan's fragile democracy, surrender was worse than war. In the extreme, he faced a choice between ordering a nuclear attack as a patriot or being overthrown as a traitor by the army's new chief of staff, Gen. Pervez Musharraf. Sharif blamed the whole Kashmir gambit on Musharraf. It was wrong, but the Pakistani people were too aroused now to tolerate withdrawal. Sharif could yield to Clinton only by baring his own neck to Musharraf. The president said so be it. Sharif was the head of government. He did not have to apologize, but he had to withdraw and cover himself however he could. The president called their argument, which consumed Independence Day, his most ferocious encounter in politics—bar none.

On a lighter note, Clinton did manage to get to two Women's World Cup matches around the Sharif crisis. Hillary and Chelsea joined him in Washington for the U.S. quarterfinal victory over Germany, and the president went alone to the Rose Bowl final for the thrilling struggle with China. He said Mia Hamm's husband, Christian, a military pilot stationed in Japan, wept openly through her penalty kick in the tiebreaker finale. It was very moving. On his other side, the actor Edward James Olmos explained the long odds against stopping penalty kicks in world-class soccer, which made it remarkable for U.S. goalkeeper Briana Scurry to manage one save in five tries to win the Cup. The president said he got to congratulate the oldest American player, Michelle Akers. She was beaming, with a bruise on her face.

A week later, Clinton called Chelsea before dawn at her Montana vacation with sad news that John F. Kennedy Jr.'s private plane had crashed near Martha's Vineyard. She cross-examined him about the weather, the search grid, and his chances for survival. When he told her it looked hopeless, she asked to come home in a voice that told him their connection was stronger than he realized. His Kennedy bond, and Hillary's, had been primarily with Jackie, about how to live and raise a family in the White House, but both Caroline and John Jr. had treated Chelsea like a niece. John had invited Chelsea to parties, and looked after her in her early teens.

Shortly after this somber funeral, the president attended state rites for King Hassan of Morocco. He took his mother-in-law, Dorothy, because she loved Morocco enough to move there. Mubarak of Egypt, among many rulers present, confided that Asad of Syria had boycotted because Hassan had befriended Asad's estranged brother. Clinton said he flew forty hours that week, and walked three miles in the blistering sun behind Hassan's cortege. Jimmy Carter and former secretary of state James Baker also made it the whole way through a thick crowd of two million people. The eerie, high-pitched ululations of grief were so unnerving that the Secret Service detail kept trying to abort. Only former president Bush, said Clinton, spoke up for him in a running argument with the agents. Bush told them it meant a lot for all these people to see the American delegation walking like everybody else, paying tribute to their king.

All this past week, he said, Hillary had been "tighter than Dick's hatband about the interview in *Talk* magazine." I didn't understand the phrase, and debated whether to ask. Just today, he said, reporters probed their motives and defenses at a joint campaign stop in Chautauqua County, New York. Then, back here in the Rose Garden, he announced that the Treasury was buying back $87 billion in outstanding government bonds this year—the largest in history—on a pace now to pay off the entire national debt by 2015. A reporter asked him to clarify what Hillary intended by her insinuation that he was emotionally scarred. He repeated that he never considered himself abused as he understood the term, because his mother made him feel always that he was special in her life. He didn't believe the broken family or rough times had a thing to do with his motivation for what happened.

Something welled up. "I think I just cracked," he said, over and over. He felt sorry for himself. When this thing started with Lewinsky in 1995, he had gone through a bad run of people dying at the start—his mother, Vince Foster, Rabin—plus the mean-spirited investigations of him and Hillary and everybody else. Oh, and they ran over him with the "Contract With America" and took the Congress. He had just cracked. He said he could have done worse. He could have blown something up.

The silence was unbearable. Well, I said, the great sadness for me was that he had come so close to proving all the scandals baseless. Now, Lewinsky alone vindicated cynicism. You let them off the hook just when their accounting was finally due, I moaned. That setback was bigger than impeachment or the pain with Hillary. He said he knew all that. He just cracked, more than once. He cracked again in 1997, when he convinced himself reelection would make everything go away and it didn't.

We were briefly a miserable sight. He recovered to discuss his memoirs again on my way out—one volume, two volumes, ways to collect memories from officials who had served the administration. I was still reeling.

CHAPTER THIRTY-FIVE

TO THE MILLENNIUM: PEACEMAKERS AND TREASON

Monday, October 18, 1999

Thursday, November 11, 1999

Thursday, December 16, 1999

O ur taping lapsed through September, while Clinton tackled the annual backlog of deferred activity from his vacation. Congress reconvened in an especially bad mood, anticipating next year's elections, and Chelsea left for her junior year at Stanford. Nancy Hernreich called to commiserate that there were no two-hour windows in a presidential calendar packed nightly with meetings, dinners, and receptions. Christy and I did receive an invitation to one of the black-tie events, at which the Clintons circulated through formal White House rooms on the main floor beneath the residence, shaking hands. We barely saw them before they retired for the evening. As we gathered our coats to leave, social secretary Ann Stock surprised us with notice that we were requested upstairs in the Solarium.

President Clinton was presiding grandly over his card table. We pulled up seats behind George McGovern in a welcome assignment to coach our revered old boss. The game "Oh Hell" was too screwy for him to keep up with at seventy-seven, McGovern kept protesting, but he more than held his own in raucous banter. He turned to chide director Steven Spielberg for neglecting McGovern's World War II flyboys in the film *Saving Private Ryan*. When her ace was trumped, actress Kate Capshaw rebuked the president with merrier abandon than Clinton's guys permitted themselves at Hearts: "You're a big, fat old boogeyman!" Hillary once stood to challenge the scorekeeper, appealing one by one to players and bystanders who vouched unanimously for Clinton's record of her bid on the hand. After a quizzical pause, she slumped from indignation to a smile. "Well, I *thought* that was the way it was," she said. On the side, Hillary joined Clinton and me to exchange gallows humor with McGovern, recalling our Texas encounters during his failed presidential campaign twenty-seven years earlier.

The president greeted me alone at this Solarium table in October. Nancy Hernreich, having despaired of night slots for a while, promised to bottle up the West Wing staff while we chanced an afternoon session to catch up on tape. Among his vacation memories was the discovery that England's Prince Andrew, the Duke of York, had a real career in the British navy as opposed to a royal sinecure. An avid golfer, Andrew played a round with the president on Martha's Vineyard. Clinton loved hearing singer Phoebe Snow. He described the family search for a future New York house within forty minutes of the city—hoping to cut down on the strain of late-night journeys home. They had picked out an 1880 farmhouse near Chappaqua, with all but one acre of its surrounding land sold off for suburban homes. The Secret Service vetoed smaller plots, citing the minimum footprint for a secure perimeter, and Clinton said he could not afford a bigger one. Mostly, he repeated, "I just wanted to find a place where Hillary will be happy when she wakes up in the morning." They had sneaked away for two days last week to celebrate their anniversary at Camp David, watching old movies.

From Martha's Vineyard, he attended the seventh APEC summit in New Zealand. All hell had just broken loose, said Clinton, on the island of East Timor 3,600 miles to the northwest, above Australia. After four hundred years of Portuguese colonial rule, then twenty-four years of bloody repression from the Indonesian army beginning in 1975, the East

Timorese people voted 80 percent for independence in a U.N.-supervised referendum on August 30. Shocked, denouncing ingrates and rebels, Indonesia fomented violent clashes, and 300,000 of East Timor's million people were refugees when the APEC leaders gathered ten days later. On tape, the president described hard diplomacy to secure withdrawal by Indonesia's President B. J. Habibie, followed by international peace-keepers and relief efforts,* in the midst of parallel talks to stop future nuclear tests by North Korea. Quoting Tony Lake, Clinton called the latter effort "a dog that didn't bark," meaning a hard-won success that attracted little attention.

There was a tourist's detour to Queenstown, New Zealand, which he called an even prettier enlargement of Jackson Hole, Wyoming. Some White House staff members jumped off picturesque cliffs, suspended by bungee cords, while others descended into gorgeous caves with all kinds of exotic flowers and animals, including eels. The president said he cherished the rare company of Chelsea, who usually traveled abroad with her mother. They visited with Edmund Hillary, the famed explorer of Mount Everest and Antarctica. Clinton released satellite photographs of the polar ice cap for Hillary's scientific studies of global warming.

Back at APEC, the president met Russia's new prime minister, Vladimir Putin, whom he gave a tepid endorsement. Putin was brisk, reserved, and gravely intent upon stamping out the Chechen rebellion, but Clinton was preoccupied for now with the erratic behavior of his boss, Boris Yeltsin. This was his fourth abrupt switch of prime minister in the past sixteen months. Yeltsin's mental focus was slipping. His heart and lung ailments were a constant intrusion. "I still think we've done the right thing to pursue this relationship for Russia," said the president, "but it's disintegrating in front of us."

He sketched APEC consultations with Jiang Zemin and others about the financial crisis in Asia. Pointedly, his business sessions excluded the newest of APEC's twenty-one member nations, Vietnam. Although they had established full recognition, it remained a politically charged barrier

---

* The APEC nations subsidized peacekeepers and the political transition in the wake of the 1999 upheaval. East Timor gained recognition as an independent country in 2002.

for an American president to bargain directly with an heir of the legendary Ho Chi Minh. Only by quirk of protocol, and proximity in the alphabet, did the U.S. and Vietnamese leaders find themselves next to each other on ceremonial occasions. At one meal, said Clinton, Prime Minister Phan Van Khai turned to him with feeling. "Mr. President," said Khai, "I can't tell you how much it means to me knowing that you opposed the war against our country." He had been born in the old capital of Saigon, and fought French colonialists as a teenager before migrating north to Hanoi for decades of war with the United States. Two of Khai's brothers had been killed. That conflict was the overwhelming legacy of his generation.

"Yes, I did oppose the war," Clinton replied. "I thought it was wrong. But at the same time, Mr. Prime Minister, I want you to know that the people who led us in that war had been fighting Communism a long time." That was their cause. Because of Communism, they could not appreciate the Vietnamese drive for independence, but neither did they have a colonialist or imperialist motive to control Vietnam. "I believe it was an honest mistake," Clinton told him. Freedom is everything for Americans, and they saw it as a war for freedom. "I know they did," Khai replied. The two got choked up trying to understand colliding patriotisms, and the president faltered again at the memory. I asked whether Khai invited him to Vietnam. "Yes, he did," said the president, "and I'm probably going next year."

Returning home, Clinton exhorted the fifty-fourth General Assembly at the United Nations toward three high goals for the millennium ahead: to overcome the "enduring human failures" of extreme global poverty, ethnic hatred, and cataclysmic war. The structure of his speech, I commented, echoed Dr. King's 1964 Nobel Prize lecture commending nonviolent methods against mankind's "triple scourge." King had summoned hope for the world's "barefoot and shirtless people." Clinton said 1.3 billion people, mostly children, still live on less than a dollar per day. The acclaim of the U.N. audience, while strong, did not match the previous year's emotional wave in the face of impeachment, partly because many delegates simmered against the United States for nonpayment of U.N. dues. He lamented this delinquency as the product of a hardened stance by the Republican Congress.

Two days after his U.N. speech, Clinton vetoed a $792 billion tax cut rammed through Congress on a partisan vote. It was skewed to benefit wealthy Americans, he said, and would have forced cuts in spending for education, Medicare reform, and the environment. This tax cut would turn surpluses back toward deficits. Would our baby boom generation reduce—even eliminate—the enormous debt burden to fall upon our descendants, or would we rationalize deficits again to preserve our disposable income? Clinton said Republicans skirted this question with a political reflex: my tax cut is bigger than yours. Democrats sustained his veto for now, but only voters could uphold it for the long run.

Republicans struck next where Congress could do damage on its own. Last week, the Senate voted down the Comprehensive Test Ban Treaty (CTBT) by a partisan phalanx. Not a single Democrat voted nay, and only four Republicans voted in favor. The treaty failed to gain even a simple majority, 48–51, falling nineteen votes short of the two-thirds required for ratification. Clinton called this rejection one of the most significant defeats of his presidency. He and his allies had been snookered on parliamentary procedures, so that they could not even stave off humiliation with a face-saving postponement. Republican leaders, who had been marshaling their fifty-five senators quietly, blocked votes on riders and reservations to help kill the treaty outright. Historians likened it to the Senate's rejection of Woodrow Wilson's Treaty of Versailles after World War I, which doomed the League of Nations and fixed the course of U.S. isolationism until World War II. Observers sensed a sharp departure from decades of bipartisan U.S. leadership to stop the proliferation of nuclear weapons. President Eisenhower had proposed a ban on all nuclear testing in 1958. President Kennedy had achieved the 1963 partial ban against testing in the atmosphere. Twenty-six of the world's forty-four current and potential nuclear powers already had ratified this test ban treaty since 1996. Now, to justify their refusal to join the treaty, wavering nations like China and Russia could invoke the example of the United States.

Three crucial countries—India, Pakistan, and North Korea—had neither ratified the CTBT nor signified general approval of its terms. One of these—Pakistan—had just suffered a military coup, dire news that had reached Clinton during his anniversary getaway at Camp David. As

Prime Minister Nawaz Sharif had predicted in the Blair House show-down, Gen. Pervez Musharraf overthrew the elected government when Sharif defused the nuclear brinkmanship in Kashmir. Sharif lost his job, his constitution, and perhaps his life. "You'll notice that Musharraf is saying a lot of nice things about wanting to restore democracy," said the president with a sigh, "but he never includes any target dates, partners, or interim steps." Instead, Musharraf accused Sharif of spoiling the ar-my's glorious victory over India. This claim was both salve and bombast, but the president said Musharraf did have Pakistani patriotism aroused behind his coup—at least for a while. Our allies must be careful as we prepared to cut off aid to Pakistan. I asked whether he had talked with Sharif or Musharraf. He said no. I asked whether the coup might activate his warning that the United States would downgrade relations with Pak-istan. No, he replied. That was specific to the Kashmir crisis, which had abated. "But I am inclined to think we ought to be more friendly toward India, anyway," he said. Now he had much bigger problems. The instiga-tor of the semi-rogue invasion of Kashmir was in charge of Pakistan's nuclear weapons, and two hostile nuclear powers still menaced each other on the Asian subcontinent.

What was worse was that the Senate had torpedoed four decades of U.S. leadership for international cooperation to stop proliferation. At the last minute, said Clinton, there was such an outcry that Senator Lott scrambled to pull back. With Virginia's John Warner, Indiana's Richard Lugar, and other responsible Republican senators, Lott maneuvered to leave the CTBT un-ratified short of formal rejection. By then, however, they needed unanimous consent to divert the parliamentary train, and their own hotheads adamantly refused. These were the Fortress America Republicans, united behind Jesse Helms, determined to spike the treaty no matter what. They did not care if the controversy ignited a campaign issue against them next year. The president, citing Senator James Inhofe, called them the "tanks, missiles, and concrete" wing of the Republican Party. To them, legitimate government was confined to those three items, and they begrudged every nickel for peace agreements, U.N. dues, and cooperative politics generally, foreign and domestic. Their attitude was basic: we've got more money, taller walls, and bigger nukes than anyone else—so fuck the little people. The president paused. "Oh, gosh," he said. "I shouldn't have used that word on the tapes, should I?" He shrugged. It was probably on there more than once.

The president smiled, grim but feisty. He gave credit for smart politics to Texas governor George W. Bush, who was running ahead of John McCain for the GOP presidential nomination. Lately, he said, Bush was attracting glowing public notice with his admonishment for conservative peers. Too often, Bush declared, fellow Republicans sought to balance budgets on the backs of the poor, and too often they confused limited government with disdain for government itself. Such comments made Bush a fresh voice against cynicism, expanding his appeal, and yet he managed not to alienate the right wing of his party. Clinton, admiring his deft skill, said Bush cultivated a runaway double standard in the press. Reporters wrote about his easygoing swagger rather than gaffes or contradictions. They admired his gift for practical jokes while ignoring a career of business favoritism that would have become endless fodder against Clinton or Gore. Bush pronounced "the gova-mint" sourly, like a cussword, and "War-shington" like an alien implant. Beyond attitude, he supported core conservatives on positions from nuclear hegemony to the biggest imaginable tax cuts. Clinton said Bush marketed himself as "Reagan Lite." Moments later he called the emerging brand "a kinder, gentler Gingrich," in a parody of the slogan used by Bush's father. The president seemed to be experimenting with phrases to expose Bush, which was a form of tribute.

I WALKED INTO several moving subplots before our November session. The president, still sleepy from an evening nap, talked on the phone with Hillary from Israel while sharing fried chicken and CNN news reports with Hugh Rodham in the Solarium. There was a crisis over Suha Arafat, wife of Yasir, who had swooped in from her Paris home to occupied Palestine. In Arabic, standing next to Hillary, she told reporters that the Israelis used too much tear gas and that the Palestinian cancer rate was abnormally high. Hillary confined herself to diplomatic remarks, but sensational interpretations were exploding in the New York senatorial campaign. Did Hillary really condemn a secret, cancer-causing Israeli gas? Clinton edited her written statement out loud, changing one phrase from "I didn't hear it that way" to a conditional "If she said that." Meanwhile, Hugh changed the channel to preseason basketball between Duke and Stanford, swapping forecasts between the president's follow-up phone calls with Sandy Berger, John Podesta, and Harold Ickes. Stanford had a promising set of six-foot-eleven freshman twins. Clinton owed cigars from a bet on last week's Arkansas–Ole Miss football game. Finally hanging up, the president turned winsome. "Because of the Irish and the Jews," he reflected, "I'm going to die before my time." Wearily, he told Hugh it was time to work, then excused us to a table in the third-floor hall where we had taped once before.

Part of me missed the Treaty Room, for its stately calm. Before my first question, the president asked to record an odd story he might not use in his memoirs. Colonel Muammar el-Qaddafi of Libya, after thirty years as an eccentric outcast among world rulers, had been making entreaties to normalize relations. Clinton sketched gestures leading up to Qaddafi's delivery of Libyan suspects for trial in the 1988 terrorist bombing of Pan Am Flight 103 over Lockerbie, Scotland. All channels reported Qaddafi to be sober and responsible, but Clinton could not shake images of a flamboyant, deadly lunatic. When he confided his misgivings to Qaddafi's Egyptian neighbor, President Mubarak waved them aside. "No, he is not crazy," Mubarak insisted. "*All* Libyans are crazy. Compared to most, Qaddafi is quite stable." Clinton had tried to play off the joke until he realized Mubarak intended no humor whatsoever. Even so, he made light of the secret dilemma to a Saudi prince who had known Qaddafi for years. "Mubarak is right," observed the prince. "All Libyans are crazy."

We recorded at length on Middle East negotiations. With Arafat and Barak, Clinton held "last sprint" preparations in Oslo toward the final-status talks in February, with a tribute dinner for Yitzhak Rabin attended by his eloquent widow, Leah. The president adjusted his take on Barak. The prime minister seemed blunt because he meant to be precise. He preferred to promise less now and deliver more later, rather than the reverse. To his own surprise, the president no longer believed the last sticking points would be Israeli settlements or the clashing claims to Jerusalem. These issues could be solved. Barak already had specified illegal settlements to be removed versus manageable ones to stay— numbered at thirty and seventeen, respectively. Clinton described how

Jerusalem could become a joint prize as well as a city for the world. He predicted the last rub would be which West Bank lands must be surrendered to create a viable Palestinian state. Arafat, while bargaining for more, faced a tricky paradox on Palestinian exiles. Officially, he demanded a welcome place for them all, but he wanted most of them to stay abroad, sending home money rather than their troublesome bodies and demands. At Oslo, all parties agreed to make no inflammatory public statements, but Suha Arafat was a loose cannon. She hardly ever saw her husband. Clinton rolled his eyes. He thought she had deliberately ambushed Hillary's campaign with her boutique bombshell.

The Middle East carried over into our December session. Barak had opened a quick parallel track with Syria to gain momentum for a settlement with the Palestinians. This was no slight ambition. President Asad of Syria, his health failing rapidly, had ignored talks for nearly four years, and his foreign minister was recovering from an aneurysm. Nevertheless, Clinton gave Asad urgent notice that a treaty was now or never. Then he got permission from Barak to sweeten the invitation by communicating to Asad a secret "pocket" assurance long reserved by Rabin—that Israel was willing indeed to surrender the Golan Heights on reasonable terms. Asad acted decisively before hearing of the sweetener. Barak was serious, Asad concluded, and so was he. At last, it was time to move. Asad sent Foreign Minister Farouk al-Shara straight from his sickbed to meet Barak at the White House on December 15, which was the day before our session. This breakthrough summit was the highest Israeli-Syrian contact since biblical times.

By this morning, the two sides had agreed to lock themselves away under Clinton's tutelage until they bridged all gaps in their treaty agenda. Their model was the Dayton process on Bosnia. They would assemble within three weeks at a secluded site near Washington, to be selected and prepared by the United States. In the interim, Shara pressed to take home to Syria secret notice of the "pocket" assurance on the Golan Heights, saying it would encourage Asad to approve a comprehensive deal. The president refused. Inevitably, he explained, that concession would leak with terrible repercussions for Barak. No Israeli leader could survive an impression that he would give away this strategic high ground simply for a piece of paper marked "peace." Clinton told me Shara held a degree in English literature. He could switch from rapture about Shakespeare into character for his home audience in Damascus. Privately at the White House, after Shara delivered a long litany of alleged affronts by Israel, Barak replied succinctly. "All that is true," he said. "I am not here to repeal the past, but to build on it." There was no spiral of counterclaims, and the meeting moved forward after a stunned silence. Shara would take *that* news home to Asad, said Clinton. He understood theatrical rules and constraints.

On the presidential race, Clinton was not surprised to see John McCain pulling even with Bush in the New Hampshire polls. Generally speaking, he said, Republicans were a more orderly party than Democrats. They tended to fall in line behind the anointed favorite and wrap up their nominations early. However, New Hampshire was a rare state that favored upstarts and underdogs—even for the GOP. Pat Buchanan had won the primary handily in 1992, and then got clobbered. Warren Rudman, respected nationally as Mr. Rock-ribbed New Hampshire Republican, was unusual in his enthusiasm for McCain. Most senators, said Clinton, bridled against McCain's prickly temper and standoffish, holier-than-thou manner. New Hampshire suited McCain the maverick, but his real test would come in the GOP's establishment states. If his campaign did well in South Carolina, McCain could "get legs" afterward.

Among Democrats, Gore was gaining steadily against former senator Bill Bradley. Clinton called Gore the ultimate nonmaverick. He was growing out of an inevitable gelded image that made it hard for vice presidents to win,[*] and he drew the lion's share of amused scorn in the press. Reporters tended to fawn over Bradley, McCain, and even Bush. If Gore could win New Hampshire, said Clinton, the Democratic contest was over. If Gore could stay within ten points of Bush's current national lead, he would be in good position to win the general election. Clinton thought Gore was adept at jabs at the front-runner. He had blasted Bush's statement that the military coup in Pakistan was "good

---

[*] Only two vice presidents have won elections to succeed a two-term ticket mate: Martin Van Buren after Andrew Jackson in 1836, and George Bush after Ronald Reagan in 1988.

news" for America, but he did not pile on Bush for failing a pop quiz on the names of foreign leaders. The president said voters seemed untroubled so far that Bush did not know anything. If he enjoyed a forgiving presumption from his father's stature, Clinton was unsure how long it would last.

He offered scattered observations on political trends. American reactionaries had excelled at polemics ever since they accused Thomas Jefferson of conspiring to abolish religion, propagate French orgies, and so forth. A year that began with impeachment was ending with sporadic riots converging from left and right against the World Trade Organization meetings in Seattle. Roving bands attacked the WTO as both a socialist cabal and capitalist sweatshop. With order restored, Clinton gave speeches on hard lessons for the future. Progress would not last automatically, he said. It required continuous intelligent choice. As a matter of common sense, the ever more interdependent world needed structured rules for finance and commerce, but trade could not survive on policy wonks and CEOs alone. Broad public confidence was essential.

Clinton praised Gore's unabashed advocacy for interracial coalitions. This, too, was a lifetime transition. Republicans, especially in the South, harvested votes like old segregationists as the presumptive party for white people. Democrats must not be timid. Their new coalitions, while wobbly by historical standards, blazed the path ahead for both parties. Democratic candidates only hurt themselves whenever they mumbled and minimized civil rights, said Clinton. They lost the submerged racial vote anyway.

WE THEN RECORDED stories of his ten-day trip through Mediterranean countries into the Balkans. A complex arrangement to pipe oil from Azerbaijan was finalized. In Turkey, the Clintons slipped away to visit earthquake victims in refugee tents, touching off a cultural seminar with foreign dignitaries who found this American ritual pointless and degrading. He described a televised clash in Istanbul with an irascible Yeltsin. The president joined Chelsea in Athens to view the Parthenon at daybreak. We covered fine points about optics and the tapered Doric columns. He said Greece faced security threats from anarchists, fascists, and the last active Stalinist party in Europe. Cadres still seethed, marveled

Clinton, that Harry Truman had kept Greece from becoming a Soviet satellite, and a much larger segment resented the United States for condoning a 1967 military coup. Other favored moments included the crowd near Alexander Nevsky Cathedral in Sofia, Bulgaria. You came across things so old, he kept saying, such as structures built for Philip of Macedon, father of Alexander the Great. He exchanged bracing salutes with U.S. troops and NATO peacekeepers all the way to bases in Italy.

Notably, from Kosovo, he conveyed the charged atmosphere of one muddy schoolyard packed separately with cheering Albanians, squealing children, sullen Serb politicians, and nervous minority Turks. All went silent the instant a translator relayed his first plea for them to reconcile, and he had plunged ahead to argue why. No one could make them do so, but he had risked many lives to give them the chance. Sadly, they weren't the only spattered people on earth. He told them he had sat on a chair like this to hear fathers and mothers tell of waking amidst whole families hacked to death with machetes. He said that three-quarters of a million Rwandans were killed without any guns in three months' time. In Israel, children had shown him photographs of friends blown up on school buses. In Northern Ireland, a girl sang for him who had been blinded and disfigured by a bomb in the flower market. Ethnic hatred was the world's worst problem, he told them. Its solution was always the same. He was Irish. If his people finally ended the terror among themselves, they would wonder why they hadn't begun the hard work of reconciliation decades before. Looking back, on tape, Clinton was proud of his exhortation, but he conceded that it had earned frowns and only polite applause.

Chelsea popped into the tiny kitchen with two friends, including a Stanford diver, home for the December holiday. She delivered a monologue on the phenomenon of college grogginess. Students under stress stayed up consecutive nights until they entered a giggling zombie zone, illustrated in her case by a habit of burning candles around the computer, which somehow lit one term paper on fire, and her best addled response was to shake the burning document in the air, fanning the flames, igniting her blanket among other things, and this was only the start. Her computer then refused to print the letter "i," which was full of meaning itself, and she had to insert them all manually before sprinting out with her paper to beat the semester deadline, freezing in flip-flops and a purple T-shirt, laughing hysterically when her entry card failed to open the teacher's building because of an overdue library book. Eventually, there was a happy ending, and the president responded with his own memories of a Georgetown religion professor who gave oral exams in twelve different languages.

Back on tape, the president passed lightly over topic thirteen on my list of sixteen for the night. Of the Kennedy Center Honors Gala, he said only that Hillary thought she had died and gone to heaven because she was seated next to Sean Connery. By contrast, he dug into Panama with surprising force. He had declined to attend the recent ceremony restoring local sovereignty over the Panama Canal lands. Stories sniped that Clinton did not want to share glory or blame with the treaty's author, Jimmy Carter, and was angling instead for a "victory lap" in Northern Ireland. None of this was true. He had no qualms about Carter's treaty, nor any spot on the next ballot to worry about. He had reserved the date for a priority trip to Syria, not Ireland, and he was tired from fourteen foreign trips already this year. What upset him was Madeleine Albright. He had instructed the secretary of state to represent the nation in Panama. He said her puzzling refusal, communicated by newspaper, damaged the foreign policy of the United States. The president did not care about the excuses. He had made sure she knew he was furious.

The year closed on spies and terrorism. The Justice Department, after fierce debate among the security agencies, indicted nuclear scientist Wen Ho Lee on fifty-nine counts of copying classified material to his personal computer. Lee was being handled like a radioactive espionage defendant—no bail, lockdown, solitary confinement—even though the long dragnet had produced no evidence that he offered secrets to China or anyone else. The president said experts were telling him the worst spies sometimes stored their treason for a rainy day. This sounded fishy to me. Clinton shrugged. Nothing would please him more than to establish Lee's innocence.

Speaking of treason, he jolted me on Pakistan. "Musharraf wants to kill Sharif," he said. "I believe that's his goal." Just as the prime minister had feared his own army, the ascendant general now plotted revenge. Clinton was mounting a concerted pitch for Musharraf to refrain from testing more nuclear weapons and leave Sharif alive. If he met those two conditions, there were things the United States could do to help Musharraf's government. "I don't know if it will work." He sighed. Off tape, at the end, he told me to put Saudi terrorist Osama bin Laden on my list for next time. Musharraf had arrested a bin Laden lieutenant near the border with Afghanistan, he said, and was shipping him to Jordan for interrogation. There were intelligence warnings that bin Laden planned attacks on American targets in Jordan over the millennium period just ahead, up through Ramadan.

ON TO
NEW HAMPSHIRE

Monday, January 24, 2000

Tuesday, February 15, 2000

Tuesday, March 14, 2000

The president was eating a bowl of bran in January. He said Bob Squier, the campaign consultant, never had a colonoscopy in his life. They diagnosed him six months ago, and he died today at sixty-five. The end comes on quickly if you don't catch it early. "I always eat bran when a friend dies of colon cancer," Clinton said. His mordant tone lasted through a story about the millennium celebration on New Year's Eve. Later, on tape, he would recall its forecasts of cyberspace and the human genome, along with the Y2K networks behind a safe rollover of the world's computers into the year 2000. Now he chortled about being seated at the black-tie dinner between actresses Sophia Loren and Elizabeth Taylor, whom he had never met. He quoted Taylor's first words in response to his standard hello. "Have you looked at her tits yet?" she asked. Startled, he said no. She gave him a withering look of disbelief, probably from her Cleopatra role, until Clinton admitted that he had noticed Loren's low-cut dress previously this evening. "That's better," said Taylor, introducing herself.

We worked again in the upstairs kitchen and a shift quickly emerged in his general outlook. The president pronounced gritty new optimism

for his domestic agenda, but he was frustrated about several of his carefully constructed peace missions. He was especially dismayed about the
Syria-Israel summit talks at Shepherdstown, West Virginia, now in recess. "The political timing did not fit the diplomatic window," he said.
Prime Minister Barak gave a stirring speech on the historic moment,
quoting Rabin, and the Syrian delegation surprised everyone by "showing a little leg," as Clinton put it. Foreign Minister Shara, to display
good faith, offered three significant changes in the notoriously glacial
Syrian position. First, he offered Israel a ten-meter buffer of ownership
around Lake Tiberias (Sea of Galilee). This was less than Israel wanted,
said the president, but never before had Syria ceded claim to the lake
itself, which was crucial to the complex issue of water rights. Second,
Shara raised from six to eighteen months the allotted grace period for
the removal of Israeli settlements from territory reverted to Syria. (Israel
wanted five years.) Third, Shara said Syria would allow U.S. and French
troops to be stationed on the Golan Heights, if agreeable, as a buffer
against surprise attacks by either side.

Prime Minister Barak answered with a reprise of his opening speech.
By his third or fourth cycle, said Clinton, the Syrians were fuming and
the Americans were prowling the corridors to find out what went wrong.
Barak confessed he was in a compulsory stall. Too many Israelis thought
he was "giving away the store." He was eager to engage these Syrian
terms, but first he must shore up the governing coalition. His troubles
were concentrated among Israel's fast-growing religious and immigrant
political parties. Many Jewish émigrés from the vast former Soviet Union
could not imagine how their tiny new country could surrender land,
captured or not. Political leader Natan Sharansky brushed off Sandy
Berger's questions about why he would take lessons from a system that
had jailed him in the Gulag. "I'm still a Russian," said Sharansky, "and
Russians never give back *any* territory. We haven't even returned the
Kuril Islands to Japan." *

Clinton groaned. If we had known of Barak's retreat in advance, he

---

* Since the mid-nineteenth century, Japan and Russia have disputed four of the
tiny Kuril Islands in the Sea of Okhotsk. The Soviet Union seized them during
World War II.

said, we could have prepared the Syrians. As it was, we had misled them. Plus, they could not understand why the Israeli delegates argued among themselves, even about details of Barak's cosmetic stance. The president said Syrians lived in an insulated world. They seldom heard people disagree. Then news leaked that Israel was ignoring friendly overtures from Asad. The Syrians felt burned—trifled with. Asad removed from the Shepherdstown agenda his client state of Lebanon, which upset the Israelis because Hezbollah rockets were fired from Lebanese bases. In recess, presidential phone calls grew strained, including one with Asad from Clinton's new and future home in Chappaqua, New York. The dictator still said he wanted a legacy of peace in order to modernize Syria, but his voice was unsteady. It took longer for him to get beyond his anger. Clinton said he was laboring on two fronts to recover from the lost moment. He and Barak had spoken twice today.

The president surveyed teetering hopes elsewhere in the world. Boris Yeltsin's failing health had compelled him to resign the presidency in favor of his latest prime minister, Vladimir Putin. Yeltsin's shaky plan was for Putin to grow into a capable elected leader from his proven ability to cope in the murky underworld of Russian politics. So far, Putin had elevated his popularity by crushing the Chechen rebellion with few Russian casualties. Clinton said Chechnya's capital city of Grozny looked like bombed-out Stalingrad in World War II. Meanwhile, his friend Helmut Kohl, architect of German reunification and the European Union, had slipped not only from power but into investigation for personal corruption. From Northern Ireland, Gerry Adams had just visited to warn Clinton that the new unity government could come apart over demands from backsliders on all sides. Finally, reminded of his wish to discuss Osama bin Laden, the president connected two ominous events. Our experts, he explained, were convinced that an Algerian recently arrested in Seattle with bomb materials was a bin Laden disciple, indicating that bin Laden was "up to stuff" in the United States. And India asserted that Pakistan was behind a spectacular Christmas Eve hijacking of an Indian jetliner into Kandahar, Afghanistan, where India obtained the safe return of 155 hostages only by giving up three imprisoned Kashmiri fighters to go free with the hijackers into bin Laden's Afghan-based laboratory for terrorist jihad. Blurry clues painted the Musharraf government in Pakistan both for and against bin Laden.

Clinton's spirits rose on topics back home. He confirmed that he had been testing markers for his last State of the Union Address on Thursday—only three days hence. I renewed a plea for him to set forth visionary goals—the equivalent of landing astronauts on the moon. A chipper Clinton said he was on the case. He mentioned curing cancer through genetic research, but he also expressed caution. Reception for bold proposals depended on the public mood as well as quality and presentation. No president, especially in a final year, could match the wallop of JFK's moon speech. We were in a nonreceptive phase. As one illustration, he cited his recent initiative to eliminate the high-emissions preference for SUVs and light trucks by 2009. This presidential announcement, with enormous potential impact for pollution, global warming, and dependence on foreign oil, barely made a back page in the *New York Times*. Similarly, Congressional Gold Medals for the Little Rock Nine—bestowed by the hard-shell Republican Congress, announced by the normally monosyllabic Speaker Dennis Hastert with an ease scarcely imaginable when these school pioneers broke the color line—earned a squib on the *Washington Post*'s society page. Our media culture, said the president, often reversed gossip and news.

He called the political climate a handicap short of disaster. It required adaptation. For one thing, he had learned to bargain with impatient Republicans. That's how he recently squeezed through 100,000 new teachers, doubled the funding for after-school care, and got rid of several obnoxious environmental riders. In his speeches, Clinton often found it wise to break one attention-grabbing goal into smaller constituent parts. Political dividends could justify all the extra effort. The president was amassing sensible, energetic ideas now to render impossible or costly Senator Lott's announcement—already on record—that Congress would pass nothing of significance for the entire 2000 election year. In fact, Clinton cut short our January session to work late on his State of the Union. The speechwriters were revising nonstop, and Tommy Caplan stayed overnight to offer suggestions on phrasing.

•   •   •

WEEKS LATER, ON February 15, my questions rekindled his giddiness. The State of the Union Address was an art form, and this one had been a joy. His text was shorter than several previous ones, but his delivery in the House chamber ran longest by eight minutes. The president had been in no hurry, of course, when declaring so much progress. Crime and teen births down seven years in a row. Jobs up by more than twenty million. Five thousand Soviet nukes disarmed. Welfare cut in half. Adoptions up 30 percent. Active peace initiatives from Bosnia to Belfast, Jerusalem to East Timor. The smallest federal workforce since 1959. Making these declarations, the president said he lingered whenever television monitors showed the assembled Republicans dragged into a standing ovation. Many of them looked surly about the good news. "They just can't help it," he said. Then he blasted notions of a lazy exit by announcing no fewer than *sixty* initiatives—all precise, some controversial, most drawing cheers in sustained rhythm. Extended health coverage for children and seniors. A commonsense gun bill. Tax cuts for college and a tax increase on cigarettes. Research targeting the human genome, stem cells, miniaturization, and five-hundred-mile-per-gallon biofuels. All the public investment was budgeted to preserve and accelerate historic new surpluses. On this extraordinary course, by conservative scoring, the $5 trillion national debt would be paid off by 2013.

As usual, critics reacted more negatively than voters. Bee-sting liberals disparaged his speech as a laundry list of "Calvin Coolidge economics," obsessed with deficits. Conservatives warned Republicans in Congress not to be fooled by the budget surpluses, and conservative columnist Robert Novak nearly shrieked in print that Clinton was more liberal than Lyndon Johnson. The president chuckled that he must be doing something right. He would try to assuage liberals with signposts—pointing out, for instance, that one cluster of his proposals, if aggregated, would go a long way toward eliminating child poverty in the United States. Mostly he would push for smaller openings in Congress, because he was acutely conscious that the election season would overshadow his agenda. To some degree, he was marking time already.

He boasted of his prediction that McCain would upset Bush in the New Hampshire primary. Bush did not spend anywhere near enough time up there, which meant he was taking the wrong people for granted. New Hampshire voters all think they're senators, said Clinton, and everybody expects to be courted. Then Bush had compounded his mistake by sending his mother and father to campaign for him. Papa Bush was a living symbol of New Hampshire's devastation in the recession of 1991–92, and the local voters had long memories. "A lot of them don't like me," said the president, "but they voted for me anyway, because they believed my policies would work." Bush gave himself no chance, but he could recover this weekend in South Carolina. Clinton called it a "herd state" for Republicans, at the opposite end of the spectrum from New Hampshire. Bush would win unless McCain could turn out a record number of independents.

He asked me which Republican would be easier for Gore to beat. I said probably Bush, for admittedly superficial reasons. I thought Bush's smirk may be fatal, but he would have a united party behind him, whereas Republican leaders gnashed their teeth over McCain. Clinton smiled. They gnashed their teeth over Teddy Roosevelt, too, he said, but were glad to run with him. McCain was much less a reformer than TR. He was a right-winger with a little maverick streak.

On the Democratic side, Clinton praised Gore for reconstituting his campaign in Nashville toward the end of 1999. From a big deficit in the polls, Gore had recovered quickly to beat Bill Bradley almost two to one in the Iowa caucuses. Then, when Bradley panicked and started slinging mud in New Hampshire, Gore decided to go lofty and ignore him. This probably cost half his ten-point lead, said Clinton, with a trace of criticism, but Gore still won a state tailored for Bradley. The president thought Gore had the nomination all but sewed up, although Bradley was planning to spend $10 million in California and New York. Since losing New Hampshire on February 1, Bradley seemed aimless and disconnected. He did not even dress well, said Clinton.

Gore, meanwhile, would set his course for the general election with one pitfall on the horizon. Elian González, a six-year-old Cuban boy, had survived his mother's drowning on a swamped boat headed for Miami. His fate was a national soap opera of politics versus family, pitting the determination of Florida relatives to keep Elian against the father's demand that his son be returned home to Cuba. Clinton called the pending case a politician's nightmare. Immigration law, for good reason, favored the claims of a sole surviving parent, but Elian was a political trophy. Both Bush and Gore straddled the issue—playing to Cuban-Americans without quite stating a precedent that would separate families from other countries. Still, Clinton said Gore's position in the government put him at a disadvantage. If the U.S. courts ultimately ordered Elian sent home to his father in Cuba, as Clinton predicted, it would injure Gore with Cuban-American swing voters in the crucial states of New Jersey and Florida.

We were taping in the family parlor, with the Arkansas-Florida basketball game muted on the television, and he yelled at players occasionally for missing layups. The president seemed distracted, with several things on his mind at once. We bounced off topics more than usual. Believe it or not, he said, our unemployment rate was down because we had so many people in prison—two million of them. Tony Blair had been obliged last Friday, February 11, to reassert British control over Northern Ireland, but Clinton was unfazed. They would restore self-government in spite of the birth squabbles, and "nation building" was a Pollyanna term because it took decades or more to forge stable new institutions. At the end, I asked whether he was lonely around the White House these days, with his agenda winding down and Hillary gone so much. No, he replied. He was reading more and was not sad or bored. He was savoring his last year. "My only regret is that I have to sleep so much," said the president. "I'd like to be awake all the time."

While packing up, I told him that his secretaries had been sending me copies of memos and articles anticipating his legacy. Was I supposed to do something with them? Just think about his library and memoirs, he replied. We had been discussing them for months. I told him there was even a story about his fondness for *High Noon,* which must be related to the framed studio picture nearby of Grace Kelly with Gary Cooper. He laughed. That was a treasure from the producer, Stanley Kramer. The president remembered the film from 1952, when he and I were tykes and movies cost a dime. *High Noon* remained his favorite. Film buff Clinton spun yarns about on-the-set romances and Hollywood intrigue, including John Wayne's hostile take on the film's subliminal politics. He jumped to the controversies about *Three Kings,* a contemporary film starring George Clooney. Through actress Katy Jurado, a co-star in common, I connected *High Noon* to one of my own favorites, *One-Eyed Jacks*.

Abruptly, Clinton turned serious. When the current seven-year economic expansion surpassed the previous record from the 1960s, many commentators and some historians said the United States had turned bitter after the Kennedy assassination of 1963. That is not true, he objected. We were heartbroken, but still optimistic. We passed the Civil Rights Act in 1964, and most people believed we were doing the right thing in Vietnam. Two years later, we had race riots at home and 300,000 soldiers in Vietnam. Two years after that, when he was about to graduate from college, we had 500,000 soldiers fighting in Vietnam and Martin Luther King and Bobby Kennedy were murdered. That was 1968. The country was split right down the middle, and we've been split ever since.

He said it has taken us almost thirty-five years to begin healing. We rebuilt the opportunity to address our problems, make investments, and act confidently in the world. "I don't want to throw this chance away," the president declared, "because we barely got there last time when things started going awry."

THE MARCH 14 session was poignant and harried for us both. President Clinton met me hungry in the little kitchen at ten o'clock, late from a meeting on China, anxious about leaving for India this week. I arrived almost straight from Alabama—sunburned, satisfied, and sore from a week-long, fifty-four-mile march from Selma to Montgomery, bearing souvenirs and mementos. The entire front page of the *Montgomery Advertiser* showed Clinton crossing Selma's Edmund Pettus Bridge on the thirty-fifth anniversary of the "Bloody Sunday" demonstration for black voting rights, with a giant headline quoting his remarks—"CLINTON: 'Another Bridge to Cross.' " He had not seen this collector's edition, having already departed on Air Force One. I had waved to him from the crowd and stayed on with a tiny remnant that reenacted the historic march through wilderness and swamp to Montgomery. There were a few hardy survivors from the original trek, plus one white couple from California, several drum-beating Buddhists, and two busloads of energetic students from Spelman College in Atlanta and Renaissance High School in Detroit. We sang, meditated, and held roadside seminars. A rolling phalanx of somber state troopers escorted us. We kidded them as a ceremonial anachronism, but the commander cited threats against us.

This was a career pilgrimage for me. Among its lessons was that fifty miles is a long distance on foot. I was beginning my last King-era book with a narrative account of this 1965 saga—three tries over Pettus Bridge, three martyrs, three weeks to Montgomery, answered by President Johnson's call for the Voting Rights Act—and I spoke to Clinton of some thoughts along my way about his memoirs. In Selma, a citizens movement and national politics achieved a messy synthesis, adding momentum that was obscured by 1968 under a backlash on all sides. Ever since, partisan arguments have concealed a common cynicism from left to right. It was a daunting task to restore a sense of national purpose. Clinton was wise to model himself on a transformational activist like Theodore Roosevelt, who had rescued American politics from the doldrums of the Gilded Age. We discussed parallels and distinctions. How much was Clinton like TR? Not all the comparisons offered him comfort.

On tape, he addressed the presidential nominations. As he had predicted, Bush beat McCain in South Carolina on February 19 by smiling as the anointed while his operatives played rough, dirty politics. They accused McCain of fathering a black baby and betraying fellow POWs in Vietnam. McCain fumbled a response, and messed up his own issues. He reduced his campaign reform issue to boring, academic purity, leaving Bush to run unchallenged. McCain should have warned average South Carolina Republicans that Bush had vacuumed up a corporate war chest by promising the wealthiest Americans a ten-to-one return through his giant tax cut proposal. McCain attacked evangelists Pat Robertson and Jerry Falwell at the last minute. If you're going to do that, said Clinton, do it early, as a matter of principle about where you want to center your party. McCain misfired, coming off instead as a sour grapes whiner over the endorsements for Bush.

McCain committed his worst blunder on the night he lost South Carolina. Instead of writing off a natural Bush state, and learning from what just happened, he pledged piously to shun all negative advertising. And wham, said Clinton, New York's mayor, Rudy Giuliani, and several other Bush henchmen stabbed his bared neck—on breast cancer, no less. Bush ads popped up claiming that McCain opposed breast cancer research, being insensitive to women. This was the grossest distortion. McCain had voted against one bill larded with pork. Clinton knew the bill. Nearly all breast cancer funds were in the National Institutes of Health budget, but the president had tried to funnel extra dollars through the Pentagon. McCain, as a war hero, had the stature to vote against defense appropriations because of immense waste. The tiny smidgen for breast cancer was immaterial. McCain's own sister had breast cancer, and he consistently supported cancer research. Yet McCain, having disarmed himself, let Bush steal his decisive lead among female voters in state after state. Clinton said McCain should have pounced. He should have handed a direct choice back to voters. Here is my record. Can any fair reading justify this dirt? Can you trust a man to govern who makes such claims? "I would have wrapped that around Bush's neck," said the president.

Clinton shook his head, amused. Both Bush and McCain hated him. He did not mean to take up for either one, but he thought the objective performance was clear. These two Republicans were mirror candidates. Bush was unqualified to be president, said Clinton, but he had shrewd campaign instincts. McCain might make a good president, but he had no idea how to run. On the Democratic side, Clinton thought Bradley lasted just long enough to help Gore become a better candidate.

I asked whether he feared mischief from the collapse of both nominating contests so early, five months before the fall campaign. Yes, he did. There was gurgling already around some of the dormant scandals. Ken Starr had resigned at last, after five years, but his successor, Robert Ray, was keeping the scattered Whitewater investigations on hold, unresolved. Did I know Louis Freeh had bestowed an FBI commendation on the special prosecutor from the Henry Cisneros case, which was a travesty of justice? "Don't get me started," said the president. Freeh connived with the various special prosecutors, who in turn functioned as auxiliary crutches for the Republican Party even without Starr. Especially if Gore won the November election, Clinton thought zealous ideologues among those prosecutors might bring criminal charges against him once he was out of office, and Hillary, too, just to gum up any substantive national purpose. It was all politics. He foresaw zero chance of being convicted, but the calculation itself seemed defensive.

We talked about guns. There was sporadic press interest in gun safety this month, approaching the first anniversary of the Columbine High School massacre. A dozen children die of gunfire every day. Two weeks ago, a six-year-old in Michigan shot to death his first-grade classmate, Kayla Rolland. The ensuing uproar enabled Clinton to convene a private summit over gun safety legislation, which had been stalled for eight months between slightly different versions passed by the House and Senate. House Judiciary chair Henry Hyde, Clinton's tormentor during impeachment, proved eager to explore compromise on provisions like commonsense trigger locks. Senator Orrin Hatch refused. Because no bill would survive, the only effect of a legislative conference would be bad publicity for Republicans. Therefore, Hatch was better off not to participate, and he killed the bill by the prerogative of the Senate Judiciary chair. Thus, according to Clinton, Hatch conserved his "real stroke" among Republican senators, which lay in horse trades over the confirmation of judges. Gun control, meanwhile, would recede into a fall campaign issue in districts targeted by the NRA. Its chief lobbyist accused Clinton of welcoming "a certain level of killing to further his political agenda." Clinton said the NRA was on the warpath again.

Hillary called from New York. From his end of the conversation, they exchanged an update on the first month of her official Senate campaign. Her positives were rising in polls he saw today. She could make headway if she stuck with her issues and did not get too tired. Four hours of daily phone calls was probably too much. To schedule herself, she needed to figure out whether a rest break was better in the morning or late afternoon. Yes, he did talk with Chelsea about her paper on Sartre and existentialism, which was hard to sort out. Chelsea was upset about a test. Sometimes they had to remember that beneath all her sophistication, she was still their girl. Yes, overwrought. Of his own day, he reported still pushing the trade bill with China, and his long talk with Tony Blair about Northern Ireland and violence in Kosovo. "Oh, well, it's not that bad," said Clinton. "We came up with some ideas." He told Hillary I had brought this collector's newspaper from Alabama. He beckoned for me to hold it up as he described the photographs and layout. I handed it to him. There he was with Coretta King, and John Lewis, and John's wife, Lillian. They reprinted his whole speech. "You know, that day meant so much to me," he told Hillary. "Sometimes I think it was worth all the shit we've taken for seven years. By itself. That one day in Selma."

We went back to work. The president thought Fed chair Alan Greenspan had "out-tinkered himself" on interest rates. Clinton was trying to drive oil prices down from $34 per barrel. He stopped me halfway through my list. There was something else he wanted to get on the tapes before he gave out. The Secret Service did not want him to visit India, said Clinton, and all the security agencies were adamantly against stops in Pakistan and Bangladesh—"going bananas," he put it. They had intelligence that Osama bin Laden may be moving to Bangladesh, indicating bin Laden had contacts high within the government there, and we knew already that bin Laden cooperated with elements of the Pakistani military. The security people could not insure a reasonable margin of safety for Clinton. He explained why he had overruled them for the first time.

Our foreign policy in South Asia remained unbalanced from the Cold War, when we tilted away from India, toward Pakistan, to offset India's defensive alliance with the Soviet Union against China. This posture made no sense now. India was the largest democracy in the world, with the biggest middle class. Far more urgently, Clinton said his experts still believed India and Pakistan may go to war again over Kashmir. Mutual irrationalities and hatreds, with nuclear weapons on both sides, made it the most dangerous place in the world. The president said he must prevent a war if he could. He must go quickly, to balance our relations before another crisis. He could not visit one of these volatile rivals without the other. One faction in the State Department opposed the Pakistan stop because it may suggest approval for the coup by Musharraf, but Clinton said he rejected the strategy of avoidance. We were heavily involved already. The Pakistanis knew we disapproved of their coup. Clinton was leaning heavily on Musharraf to keep former prime minister Sharif alive in prison. Three mysterious gunmen had assassinated Sharif's lawyer last Friday at his office.

Air Force One had formidable defenses at high altitudes and speeds, said the president, but the plane was a big, fat, slow target on takeoff and landing. Our people would be clearing an evacuation zone on either side of runways in Pakistan and Bangladesh, but that may not be enough to protect from a shoulder-fired missile. We were working on a few additional tricks and surprises. Still, he had to recognize what we do not accept: that politics is a blood sport for leaders in South Asia. In India, both Indira and Rajiv Gandhi were assassinated, among others. In Pakistan, General Zia overthrew and hanged Benazir Bhutto's father, the elected prime minister, before Zia himself was killed in 1988.* They play for keeps over there, said Clinton. Here, he had plunged into crowds without fear even during security alerts, but this is something to think about. He had never worried like this. "I hope I'm sitting here with you again next month," the president concluded.

He was more somber than emotional. While rewinding, I gave him a copy of my two-minute speech in Montgomery at the end of our march a few days ago, given from Dr. King's old Dexter Avenue pulpit. I had not shown it to anyone but Christy. To my surprise, he went through my remarks line by line, with enthusiasm. We had some themes in common about being white Southerners from that era. We hugged, and I walked with him across the hall to stow tonight's tapes in his secret hiding place—the socks drawer of his closet. He was telling me that speechwriter Terry Edmonds came up with most of his good language for Selma, including its "bridge to cross" refrain. I told him Terry used one of my suggested quotations from Dr. King.† Terry was good, but I confessed being unusually blunt with him about the poor quality of the draft for the Advisory Board on Race. I hoped I didn't offend him. This was too important to be bad.

I closed the drawer, having compulsively verified both complete sets

---

* Benazir Bhutto became Pakistan's first female prime minister in 1988. Elected twice, but driven into exile on corruption charges, she returned to Pakistan under an amnesty grant from President Musharraf in October of 2007. She was assassinated two months later during her campaign for prime minister.

† "It is history's wry paradox," said King in 1962, "that when Negroes win their struggle to be free, those who had held them down will themselves be free for the first time."

of tapes in their boxes. The evening had me rattled. Clinton assured me about Terry. Most people agreed the draft report on race relations was a disaster, and Terry had written almost none of it, anyway. The president was taking the document to Asia. He said, "I'm going to work on it myself in Bangladesh."

CHAPTER THIRTY-SEVEN

CAMP DAVID

Thursday, May 4, 2000

Friday, July 14, 2000

A butler delivered me with four Excedrin to President Clinton, who did not feel well after a long hot day promoting charter schools in Minnesota. There had been only one such experiment in the whole country when he took office; now there were nearly two thousand. He was in the Solarium, finishing late dinner and a round of three-dimensional Scrabble with Hugh Rodham. They were also watching the telecast of an NBA playoff between the Indiana Pacers and Milwaukee Bucks, discussing where Arkansas might recruit a high school player taller than six feet eight inches, and occasionally consulting a heavy dictionary about borderline moves for UpWords. As Rodham hunched over its maze board of stacked letters, brooding in his strap T-shirt, the president tossed him suggestions. They played a Zen-like variation, he explained, stressing total score over individual competition. Tonight's combined 1,100 points wound up 200 shy of their record. I warded off invitations to try for the three-way mark, and Clinton excused us to work in the third-floor hall.

Almost immediately, Hugh forwarded an incoming phone call from Hillary. Cardinal John O'Connor of New York had died yesterday, and Monday's funeral at St. Patrick's Cathedral would be a major event in the campaign year, attended by both presidential candidates and U.N. secretary-general Kofi Annan. "I'd rather take a whipping than go," Clinton told Hillary. The cardinal had been vociferous against gay people, and hostile to any form of safe sex except abstinence. It was well known that he disliked Clinton, and had been practically a cheerleader for Hillary's likely opponent, Mayor Giuliani. Still, this was an institutional funeral for the titular head of New York's Catholics. The Clintons hashed over their options. They decided it would look less political if they went together. They could give each other some cover. Clinton sighed. "I'd still rather take a whipping," he said.

The president had survived South Asia in March. On tape he stressed the political wounds and grievances lingering in India from our Cold War policy favoring her mortal enemy, Pakistan. He described labors to initiate a more evenhanded approach with all the tools of a state visit. He had agreed late to cancel one stop in Bangladesh—a helicopter trip to the village of Joypura—because of hard intelligence that Osama bin Laden had lined the route with assassins. They did not announce this threat, of course, which gave leeway for the traveling U.S. press corps to ascribe motives of cavalier indifference toward the poor ("Big Day Spoiled for Bangladesh Villagers"). At one colorful ceremony, Clinton did get to dance with mothers who had opened a cell phone cooperative on loans from Muhammad Yunus, inventor of micro-credit finance. This pioneer system, already of global significance, offered a joyful counterpoint to Bangladeshi national politics, which the president called essentially a blood feud between the camps of two women.[*]

The intelligence reports shifted in mid-trip. Bin Laden was said to have diverted some or all of his assassins from Bangladesh ahead to Pakistan. A covert "snatch team" raided one specific house near the airport runway in Islamabad, but bin Laden's men escaped with a shoulder-fired Stinger missile. Then, said the president, his security team activated its most elaborate precautions. He felt bad for the pilots who flew an

---

[*] Sheikh Hasina Wazed (prime minister, 1996–2001 and 2009–) was the daughter of Bangladesh's founding father and first president, who had been assassinated with most of his family in a 1975 military coup. Khaleda Zia (prime minister, 1991–96 and 2001–06) was the widow of a military president killed in a 1981 countercoup. Like Benazir Bhutto in Pakistan, both charismatic rivals retained mass support despite chronic charges of corruption and vehement opposition from Muslim fundamentalists because of their sex.

empty decoy plane with the markings of Air Force One, but this nerve-racking mission was their job. Clinton landed secretly off-schedule in an unmarked plane, taking with him the smallest functional entourage "consistent with the dignity of the United States." On live television, he addressed the people of Pakistan ("Democracy cannot develop if it is constantly uprooted . . ."), and negotiated privately with General Musharraf about delicate topics from Kashmir and nuclear sanctions to terrorism. Early in April, days after Clinton's departure, Pakistani courts sentenced the deposed prime minister Nawaz Sharif to life imprisonment rather than the gallows.*

On his way home from Pakistan, the president stopped in Geneva to meet President Asad of Syria. This was largely a favor to Israeli prime minister Barak, who hoped to make up for his rebuff of Syrian overtures at Shepherdstown in January. Clinton brokered nonbinding ideas to rekindle Asad's interest. Perhaps Syria could reclaim full sovereignty right up to the northern shore of Lake Tiberias—if Asad would lease back to Canada, or some other nonaligned nation, a negotiable buffer strip of empty land around the lake. This would soothe Israel's concerns about water rights. The president had scarcely begun, he recalled on tape, when Asad declared the whole subject a waste of time. Asad misre-membered or retracted prior positions. He seemed crotchety and weak, yet decisive—to the point that he cut the president short. No need to hear this, he snapped. His curt dismissal was a diplomatic insult, as well as a scalding surprise for dozens of Syrian, Israeli, and U.S. officials who had prepared a different summit. They scrambled to put the best face on the disaster.

Clinton groaned. He remained sure within himself that Asad's desire to make peace, regaining the Golan Heights, had been genuine. Now he speculated that the shrewd but aging president simply lacked the imagination to escape his lifetime of slogans against Israel. Alternatively, Clinton thought Asad's mortal preoccupation may have tilted

---

* Sharif left prison within eight months, when Saudi Arabia accepted him into restricted exile. Nearly seven years later, under pressure to hold national elections late in 2007, General Musharraf allowed both the banished prime ministers, Sharif and Benazir Bhutto, back into Pakistan.

from his own legacy to an uncertain succession for his young son Bashar. If he died soon, a fresh peace with Israel would make it harder for Bashar to control his Syrian military. Right now, Syria's generals enjoyed a perpetual gravy train—a huge budget claim on their economy just to growl at the declared enemy next door, without much danger of an actual fight. Any peace might stir civilian and military discontent before Bashar could establish his own dominance. Asad's people, the president informed me, came from a tiny sect of Shia Muslims confined almost entirely to Syria, the Alawites, comprising only 13 percent of Syria's population. Like Saddam Hussein in Iraq, the Asad family ruled by ruthless coalitions built from a minority base.

Whatever its cause, the slap from Asad seemed to disturb President Clinton more than his personal hazards in South Asia. Perhaps it was the accumulated stress. While reeling off consequences, he crossed his legs in a lotus position on the hall sofa. Alternately, he wrenched one knee and the other upward next to his ear, punctuated by creaks and grimaces, while talking nonstop. I could not bring myself to interrupt. He said Barak was devastated, and Arafat was furious. The prime minister had hoped a Syrian peace would guarantee a cessation of Lebanese rocket attacks from Asad's Hezbollah clients, cushioning the pullback at last of Israeli troops from southern Lebanon after eighteen years of costly, fruitless occupation. Instead of forward momentum on the Palestinian issue, Barak faced political scorn at home and a united wave of machismo from Arab nations, which cheered Asad for defying Israel and the mighty United States.

Arafat seethed. From his point of view, he had labored years to prove himself a worthy peace partner, only to be relegated last behind Syria and then swamped by Palestinian acclaim for Asad, of all people, who had done nothing but sneer and say no. Clinton described April meetings at the White House with Barak, then Arafat. The seven-year window from the Oslo Accords was set to expire in September, when Arafat would face pressure to make an empty declaration of Palestinian statehood. Barak would counter by reinforcing and annexing the occupied West Bank. After all this, Clinton said there may be no peace while he was in office. It was very sad.

I offered leavening jokes, including one in poor taste about whether Billy Graham could unsnarl some religious disputes over Jerusalem. The president continued with a disapproving flinch. His mood did lift when asked about his first starring film role, a four-minute short made with producers from the television comedy *Everybody Loves Raymond*. Clinton played a dysfunctional president who was learning useful chores at last. He demonstrated, for instance, how to elbow a vending machine in the White House basement for free sodas, and he made sack lunches for a busy first lady as "Miss Hillary's Helper." This film was a smash hit at the White House Correspondents Dinner, hosted by Jay Leno, showing off Clinton's ability to laugh at himself in the twilight of an embattled presidency, helping to spike his job performance ratings well above 60 percent and his personal approval back near 60, which, he said, marked recovery from the Lewinsky scandal.

No, he did not think it would rescue his legislative agenda. Congress did not pay much attention unless adverse polls struck members directly, and Clinton said Republicans had decided to make the Senate their obstreperous body this year, given a safe ten-seat margin, letting the House make nice. He was grateful for House passage of his Africa and Caribbean trade bills, which led to a digression on policy distinctions between the Central American big banana and the Caribbean small banana. The Republican strategy, he concluded, was to block all judicial confirmations, defeat his bills, demand enormous tax cuts instead of modest ones, and see what the election would bring.

THE PRESIDENT FRETTED in spurts about Al Gore's campaign to succeed him. He thought Gore had made a basic mistake by letting the August convention get maneuvered into Los Angeles. Democrats might as well quit if they needed a boost to win California, and a Philadelphia convention would have challenged the GOP head-to-head from the rust belt into New England. Less sharply, Clinton said Gore got himself hammered from both sides of the Elian González controversy—first upholding the immigration law, then caving to Cuban-American demands for an "adopt-Elian" bill. He and Gore had clawed to put Florida's electoral votes within reach. They moved the southern military command to

Miami, invested heavily to save the Everglades, and worked to reduce the GOP's pandering advantage among Cuban-Americans, who were 12 percent of the state's crucial electorate.

The soap opera over Elian ruined all this, said Clinton, even though reality defied media stereotype. Florida governor Jeb Bush privately complained that the Miami relatives holding Elian seemed unstable, threatening popular revolt and guerrilla resistance before they would surrender him for a custody hearing. Attorney General Reno's own secretary refused to speak to her, and several of Reno's closest friends knew—or were themselves—children sacrificed by their families to be free outside Cuba. They denounced her legal duty. Two weeks ago, Reno had reported past midnight on tense negotiations toward peaceful compliance, but John Podesta woke Clinton with notice that she was sending in a SWAT team. Something happened to snap her patience, or convince her that further delay risked safety. The extraction raid lasted less than three minutes, without shots fired or blows struck, but hysteria erupted over "Gestapo tactics" to benefit Castro. Clinton predicted, accurately, that the U.S. Supreme Court soon would mandate Elian's return to his father in Cuba. Political fallout would last for years. To his credit, said the president, Gore did not blame him for letting the law take its course.

Gore had drifted for six weeks since his skillful dispatch of Bill Bradley in the Democratic primaries, granting a truce for George W. Bush to overhaul his image after the gutter tactics against John McCain. A new Bush wandered free, scoffed Clinton, posing for photographs with people of color, talking daily about the environment and education reform, promising to extend the current prosperity without its partisan rancor and debilitating scandal. Bush had established a campaign of style over substance, based on the false premise that progress comes easy. You cannot allow that, said Clinton. Even while formulating themes for a general campaign, Gore must dispute his opponent's self-portrait. Bush had no credible record on the environment, nor on race, nor much platform on any tough issue for the future. The president spoke more harshly than before. He called Bush an empty suit, meaner than his dad. Clearly, if elected, Bush would take the country in a sharply different direction—back to deficits through large tax cuts, with environmental standards gutted, more government secrecy, and welcome restored for the NRA and tobacco companies. This choice was submerged in public debate, fumed Clinton, because Gore allowed Bush to get by on shadow puppets and his squinty smile.

Clinton still thought Gore would win. Most people considered him smart, experienced, and motivated. He examined the pitfalls for Gore in a campaign showcasing presidential character over detailed agendas for the country. Reporters called Gore "stiff," but Clinton discounted this liability. He thought Gore's droll sense of humor would wear well over time. Gore also was perceived to be too conventional a Democrat, therefore lacking independence, which called for Gore to emphasize more his own passions and initiatives. Then the president said Gore could have a brooding quality about him, not worrisome or off-putting in itself, but potentially damaging if his serious nature failed to give voters a lift. Clinton isolated the word "sunny." Gore needed more of it. Other things being equal, voters tended to prefer the candidate with a sunnier, more positive disposition. The great exception in our lifetime was Nixon over Humphrey in 1968, for peculiar reasons, but Reagan had been funnier than Carter or Mondale, Bush sunnier than Dukakis in 1988.

Clinton thought Gore could make adjustments in this area. Stress to voters the upside of his policies in their everyday lives. Choose a running mate with a complementary, upbeat nature. Just today, the president said, he had called Warren Christopher, the former secretary of state, who was heading Gore's vice presidential search team, to recommend that Gore consciously include temperament to balance the Democratic ticket. In 1992, critics had faulted Clinton for choosing Gore—another small-state, white Southern moderate—but Gore had balanced Clinton in more important aspects than geography and ideology. Gore was deliberative, as against Clinton's instinctual approach. Gore knew Washington. Believe me, said the president, his administration would have made many more errors in the first two years had it not been for the vice president. Now he was advising Christopher to look for a bright spirit to balance Gore. If the running mate had to come from Washington, he suggested, make it someone with a tonic gift like Senator Richard Durbin of Illinois.

We flashed back to bull sessions with Gore, which the president enjoyed immensely. My dictation was fuzzy about what triggered the recap, but their dynastic dreams and investigations had explored the origins of the Democratic Party with three consecutive two-term presidents: Jefferson, Madison, and Monroe. Clinton and Gore mined lessons from these illustrious forebears. Their personalities varied greatly. Of the three, only Monroe was a naturally gifted politician, and their continuity survived adjustments—even major mistakes. Clinton thought Jefferson, for instance, was on the wrong side of many early disputes with Alexander Hamilton about the necessary institutions for republican government. He saw in Jefferson a slow convert to nationalism for the Louisiana Purchase, negotiated in part by his young envoy James Monroe. From an unstable mix of agrarian fantasy, states' rights for slaveholders, and sympathy for French revolutionaries against British aristocrats, the three party founders forged an abiding political tradition. Their progressive nationalism had established the young country until the crisis over slavery. Modernized, it could guide the Democratic Party out of political retrenchment since the 1960s. Clinton and Gore hoped to build on each other like the triumvirate from Virginia.

I asked a question about the upheavals in Iran. Moderates had won overwhelming victories in recent parliamentary elections, but fundamentalists from the Islamic revolution of 1979 clung to their positions in the courts, military, police, and intelligence agencies. Essentially, said Clinton, Iran had two governments. He paid tribute to those who protested the repression of their representatives. They maintained peaceful demonstrations in the streets, knowing they had a popular majority, but it was hard to know how long they could resist authoritarian control. For the present, he said, diplomatic encouragement tended to backfire against the moderates. Saheed Hajjarian, Iran's leading reform theorist, had been shot in the face and paralyzed in an ambush, and the Islamic courts conducted show trials of Iranian Jews charged with spying for Israel. Not entirely as a joke, he likened Iran's mullahs to the hard-line Republicans who tormented him with a succession of special prosecutors. An ideological faction had converted key government powers into a political weapon, impervious to checks and balances.

Midnight passed. We ran out of major topics, and the president veered into stories of his own. He described an education tour into Owensboro, Kentucky, reading *Charlotte's Web* with children whose test scores had soared since class size was reduced from forty to fifteen. He spoke a few words of Navajo learned on his "digital divide" trip to Shiprock, New Mexico. Myra Jodie, an articulate thirteen-year-old, told Clinton of winning a computer in a contest but being unable to access the Internet because her mother, like 78 percent of Navajos, had no telephone service. The publicity attracted a host of satellite companies to donate Internet connections to the Navajo families, some of whom had occupied the same land for a thousand years. Just before Shiprock, the president volunteered, he had detoured from California fund-raisers and a full presidential schedule to stop by Stanford, where Chelsea took him to a class. Her professor mentioned that the students were reading one of my books, *Parting the Waters,* which gave Clinton a chance to tell them how he and I came to know each other, and why the civil rights era meant so much to us. He said it was very moving.

I purred like a fool but fortunately said nothing as he rushed on to his point, battling emotion. For two years, Chelsea had met him at California sites away from the Stanford campus—usually at the secluded home of a donor. She had been loyal even when angry and hurt, but her true feelings quarantined him from her college friends. He understood why. Since the Lewinsky scandal, Clinton said, he had felt worse for Chelsea and worried more about her than anyone, including Hillary, because she had to endure the searing exposure of her father's sex life at an age when peers meant the whole world. His presence at Stanford had been unbearable for her, which made it such a healing step to bring him again into their bubbling wit and enthusiasm. She seemed happy to have him back. "I can't tell you how good that made me feel," he said. Our session broke off. To transfer the finished tapes, I found him downstairs on the phone with Hillary, talking about the funeral for Cardinal O'Connor.

TWO MONTHS WENT by. Clinton was always out of the country, explained Nancy Hernreich, or raising money every night for Democratic candidates at home. Abruptly, a call about noon in July flipped an emergency switch. Could I drive to Camp David before three o'clock? The president was on the fourth day of negotiations between Arafat and Barak but had secured an afternoon window to preserve an account. Only cell phones made the breakneck journey feasible. Lost on empty back roads in western Maryland, deciphering faxed directions from Washington instead of Baltimore, I found enough patches of cellular service to home in on an inconspicuous gate in the forest, which fed me through a gauntlet of roadside checkpoints—American, Israeli, Palestinian—with the tape recorders drawing attention and long-handled mirrors poked in and under every crevice of my car. A golf cart transported me across a hilly, wooded camp, with off-duty soldiers jogging along paths patrolled by agents with radio earpieces, vigilant but serene like summer counselors. My escort, a new graduate of Duke, pointed out extra counselors around Dogwood Cabin, where Barak was staying, and Palestinians outside Arafat's Birch Cabin, which Vice President Gore normally occupied. I emerged from a final security zone into the rustic sanctum of Aspen Lodge.

President Clinton and Chelsea were finishing a late lunch at the table next to a half-completed jigsaw puzzle. His T-shirt read, "Trust me, I'm a reporter." Hers featured a big deer face with liquid eyes. He rose up from his crossword with a smile and an expansive welcome to Camp David, pointing through glass doors and windows to the pool and the Eisenhower golf hole, which he said you could play from three different tee boxes in the clearings below. He frowned at a golf bag on the patio, getting wet in the rain, and thanked me for coming on short notice. I said I had absorbed very little about the place yet, being rattled by delays and the unfamiliar security for this three-way summit. To my annoyance, he had heard I had gotten lost. It was now three-thirty, and he sent mixed signals. His time was short, but he was no longer sure what, if anything, he wanted to record about the Middle East talks. Regardless, he had to make some political calls before we started. Some nut had called Hillary an anti-Semite in the New York campaign.

I sat down near Chelsea to prepare the notes and recorders, taping Clinton's side of at least one strategy call. She inquired politely about Macy and Franklin, then asked about a book from my briefcase by Patrick O'Brian, who wrote about the British navy during its wars with Napoleon. She mentioned her favorite historical novelist, Dorothy Dunnett, whose tales were set a few centuries earlier in northern Europe. Asked about Stanford, she said all that remained for her senior year was a thesis on literature pertaining to Ireland. We discussed possible topics. She was fascinated by Rudyard Kipling's condescension toward the Irish as an inferior species, fit to be cogs in the British Empire.

I told her my work on the King years had taken me back through pseudoscience from the imperial and colonial eras, when Kipling flourished, and Chelsea picked right up on a virulent strain of "Ivy League racism." She was aware that Long Island's Cold Spring Harbor Laboratory, now famous for DNA discoveries, had been founded in 1900 to sort all humanity beneath superior traits presumed for the Anglo-Saxon breed. She traced its eugenics movement behind our hierarchical immigration law of 1924, which had excluded whole swaths of the globe through Asia and Africa, curtailing legal entry even from "swarthy" European countries such as Greece. We shared an appreciation for Lyndon Johnson's unheralded reform law in 1965, which finally repealed the eugenics-based filter on legal immigration into the United States.

Had the president told Chelsea what we were trying to accomplish with the oral history tapes? When she said yes, I invited her to join us today. Lately, I had been trying to elicit a bit more general reflection, looking back, but the whole process was guesswork. Secrecy precluded any consultation to refine the priorities we carved ad hoc from the president's time. If Chelsea wanted him to address a neglected subject, or felt some particular answer might be valuable on the record years hence, she should speak up. Thank you, she replied, curious enough to stay on and see.

The president summarized Hillary's campaign crisis on tape, and paused to take another political call. Because he seemed distracted, and still hesitant to talk about the Middle East, I asked about June's breakthrough summit in Pyongyang between the two warring Koreas. Clinton beamed. "We've been working on that for a long time," he said. Observers on both sides collapsed in disbelief that civil contact took place. South Korea's president, Kim Dae-jung, deserved enormous credit for his lifetime crusade to break down the lethal hostility between his capitalist showcase and the starkly desperate, nuclear-tinged pariah in the north. Clinton said Kim briefed him afterward by phone, and sent his intelligence chief to report personally at the White House. The South Koreans found "the northern Kim"—North Korea's dictator, Kim

Jong-il–surprisingly well informed and balanced about the outside world. His delusional behavior must be partly calculated. North Korea, facing starvation even for its high-ration soldiers, craved normal trade with the West, especially the United States, and Clinton thought the summit validated his five-year policy of demanding normalization first with South Korea. Until then, by forcing the North Koreans to deal with us through Kim Dae-jung, we would use our leverage to defuse one of the world's ticking bombs.

He said self-government in Northern Ireland was "up and running again," thanks to an elaborate construct of face-saving measures to neutralize the IRA's terrorist weapons without outright surrender. Ulster's Unionist Party narrowly voted to accept an international inspection certifying the weapons "beyond use," which allowed Tony Blair to withdraw England's soldiers again. IRA hotheads wanted to fight on for union with Catholic Ireland, while Protestant foes marched to restore their cherished rule under British protection, but the great mass of citizens steadfastly demanded peace from the unity government. Progress in Northern Ireland came slowly and in fits–maddening and inspirational, silly and mundane–leaving Clinton upbeat but tentative about its long-term miracle.

By contrast, he was melancholy over Cuba. The U.S. courts had sent young Elian González home to his father. Political tension was thick. The president said he was nursing one long-shot scheme to seize a few million dollars of Cuban assets somewhere in the world. Then, applying those funds to the wrongful death claims over the four pilots shot down by Castro in 1996, he could move around that land mine of terrorist debt to dismantle our forty-year-old economic embargo. Far more likely, the embargo would outlast his term in office. Strangely, he remarked, Vietnamese exiles pursued the same goal as Cuban-Americans by the opposite strategy. They agitated constantly to establish U.S. trade with Vietnam, aiming to liberate their Communist homeland through commerce. This idea was anathema to most Cubans, who thought they could strangle Fidel Castro somehow with a cold shoulder.

Six weeks ago, Prime Minister Barak of Israel had intercepted Clinton in Portugal to plead for the Middle East summit being held now at Camp David. The president skipped over the issues and terms to recall his own twenty-one-gun salute from warships and shore batteries on arrival in Lisbon Harbor, with enough pageantry, he laughed, to make him feel like a real president. From meetings of the European Union, he played golf on a gorgeous mountain course with Portuguese prime minister António Guterres, one of the handful of peers—along with Yeltsin, Blair, Kohl, Mandela, Zedillo of Mexico, and a few others—with whom Clinton felt he had established a strong personal connection. He continued to Aachen, Germany, where he received the Charlemagne Prize for European leadership, recording details of the chapel there attended by Charlemagne himself some 1,200 years ago. Clinton saw Chancellor Gerhard Schröder in Berlin, along with his old friend Kohl, whose health was failing badly, and proceeded to Moscow one month after the inauguration of Vladimir Putin as Yeltsin's elected successor.

They had agreed jointly to destroy thirty-four tons of weapons-grade plutonium, which did make news, but the president dwelled on his impressions of Putin. He called him smoothly commanding—an unfinished work. After dinner in an elegant chamber at the Kremlin, Putin presented a private concert of big-band jazz starring Igor Butman. "I never heard Coltrane live," conceded Clinton, listing other immortals on his own chosen instrument, but Butman mesmerized him like no other tenor saxophone player on earth. Putin cut through the music with words of ice. Ten years after the Soviet collapse, he told Clinton, Russia was a carcass. His vows to rebuild evoked the Russian empire, despite careful disclaimers. The president said he was not sure yet about Putin. Certainly, they were on guard at his next stop in Kiev, capital of Ukraine, whose sixty million people felt obscured by Moscow's shadow. I asked what had been needed from the United States to close the poisonous sore at Chernobyl, near the Ukrainian town of Pripyat, fourteen years after the world's worst nuclear disaster. "Money," he replied.

HOME FROM THE long trip, barely touching down to receive the king of Jordan—for advisory preparations toward this Camp David summit on Abdullah's Palestinian flank—he had flown to the funeral of Japanese prime minister Keizo Obuchi. The choice to attend meant a grueling eighteen-hour flight, eight hours on the ground at Tokyo's Budokan arena, and eighteen hours back to the White House for the eleventh bilateral meeting with Mexico's president, Ernesto Zedillo. Well, Clinton kept saying, it was worth the effort many times over. The Japanese are a very sensitive people. Ten years ago, they felt positioned to dominate the global economy, buying up New York and London, but their financial model suffered a bewildering collapse that their government could not repair. Japanese politics had chewed up six prime ministers during his term, said Clinton, of whom Obuchi was by far the most promising until a fatal stroke. Everybody in Japan knew Obuchi had been inspired into public service by a 1963 encounter with Attorney General Robert Kennedy, which made the U.S. partnership poignant.

With national confidence shattered, said Clinton, Japanese culture preserved the bonding ritual of a state funeral built on Shinto tradition. In a gigantic walled backdrop of woven yellow flowers—millions of them—rays of red blossoms fed down to a central burst of the rising sun, where Obuchi's ashes were placed on a platform with six empty chairs for the family of Emperor Akihito. Enraptured, the president described the ceremonial mood and protocol. He quoted poetic eulogies verbatim. He recalled the gestures in a procession up the long ramp—a bow to Mrs. Obuchi, a bow to the ashes, a bow to the sun. Hours later, after his business retreat with the sadly inept new prime minister, Yoshiro Mori, children and ordinary citizens still moved solemnly up the ramp. In Japan, said Clinton, this great occasion lasted so long as anyone wished to place a flower near the departing leader's ashes.

The president took a bathroom break, during which I asked Chelsea if she had heard these stories. She said no. I had found it harder this year to steer him to other subjects, because the newspapers were preserving only the most cursory record of his travel abroad. Did she understand his reluctance to discuss the current summit, which I had thought was a prime purpose for this session? She could only guess that he was skittish about unpredictable demands from so many working groups. She said I had probably not noticed, with my back to the picture window, but a sound crew had been setting up on the covered patio for him to record tomorrow's national radio address.

When the president returned, I made one more stab by asking if President Asad's death on June 10 would influence these talks. Not much, he said. He was very disappointed in Asad, whose son Bashar now was establishing his Arab bona fides by barking at Israel. Then the president recorded roughly fifteen minutes about Camp David. He said Barak had come to Lisbon pleading for this summit in order to leap over the backward drift of his negotiations with the Palestinians. Arafat strongly resisted for the same reason: backward drift. There was not enough progress to justify a summit, which Arafat feared would fail. He said Barak did not even honor previous commitments to release some prisoners and transfer jurisdiction for three Israeli-occupied Palestinian villages in East Jerusalem. Barak had not wished to take the political hit for such steps while he was concentrating on Syria. Now Barak said he was ready to make up for it, but Arafat fumed that Barak had parked him behind Asad, for nothing, and withdrawn Israeli troops from Lebanon, for free, which rendered Arafat a laughingstock among Arabs.

For these first four days at Camp David, said Clinton, the Israeli and Palestinian delegations mostly had sulked. But pressure was building. "This is not a holding pattern," he kept saying. There could be no option to set things aside for later, as everyone believed failure would lead to deterioration of "facts on the ground." He had a whole encyclopedia in mind about the negotiating gaps and strategies, but it should wait. Not enough had happened yet, and he wanted to be able to say he had not discussed the details with another soul. There had been no leaks.

Finally, the president said he had just received an extraordinary briefing. Every now and then, the CIA did something to make you realize that its business did not always pervert the word "intelligence," and this unnamed guy had earned Clinton's respect with a gripping portrayal of mortal fears at Camp David. Both delegations were acutely conscious that predecessors had been killed by their own people—Sadat in Egypt, Rabin in Israel—and the CIA official described their internal suspects and suspicions, down to the triggering issues for various plots, centered on religious and national identity. There was a sharper edge than at Shepherdstown, where Clinton had hoped he could drag a compromise over the finish line. Even subordinates had their necks on the line.

John Podesta popped in with the script for the radio address. Secretary of State Albright stood expectantly at the window. Hurriedly, I asked Chelsea if we had missed anything vital. "Tell him about the Fourth of July," she said, and he described their early rise at Chappaqua for a sail with Hillary down the Hudson River to view a breathtaking armada of tall ships—more than the Bicentennial in 1976—and on to a naturalization ceremony at which Janet Reno swore in new American citizens from all over the world. Yes, and he reprised an unforgettable introduction there by one of them, a naval officer who had immigrated to Brooklyn as a child. She still sent money to her mother back home in Guatemala. No, Chelsea corrected, the Dominican Republic. Clinton nodded. The young officer said her mother lived alone in a village so remote that it took her a day's walk to pick up the mail.

Clinton stepped out to record the radio address: five minutes, without a stumble or hitch, on why he would veto a bill to repeal the estate tax, which would add $750 billion in national debt over ten years, payable to the wealthiest Americans. Podesta asked quietly if we could help the president improve his advisory report on race. Sandy Berger said there were troubles ahead over the comeback election of Aristide in Haiti. The president returned and drew me aside. Could I keep these two tapes for now and return them next time? Of course, and good luck here. I went outside. Aides thought I was instructed to stay overnight. No one knew where my car was parked. While sorting out the logistics, they stowed me in the jammed Shangri-La Bar at Hickory Cabin. A sign there advertised one-dollar haircuts, and a ship's bell, by Navy tradition, obliged anyone caught wearing a hat to buy drinks for the house.

CHAPTER THIRTY-EIGHT

JERUSALEM AND THE THREE Ps

Thursday, August 3, 2000

For the first time in memory, the president stopped by the Usher's Office to pick me up for an evening session. My heart sank when we approached the Solarium to find guests poised around the television for George W. Bush's acceptance speech from the Republican National Convention. Such an event ordinarily beckoned Clinton to glad immersion in his craft, but he was strangely disinterested. He excused the two of us to work in the tiny kitchen, and I decided not to ask if he felt all right, for fear he might change his mind.

From my backlog of notes, we resumed with a victory declaration for the Human Genome Project, which had mapped all three billion components of life's chemical inheritance. Clinton used the word "thrilling" several times to describe its threshold potential to understand and cure disease. He likened the joyful White House ceremony to an 1807 welcome in the same East Room for the famous chart to the Pacific Ocean secured by explorers Meriwether Lewis and William Clark. He savored the participation by satellite feed of national leaders from Germany and Japan, plus Tony Blair, who had called back hours later with news of a dramatic milestone for the new government in Northern Ireland. The same day, with concurrence from Republican budget experts, the president had announced a stunning upward revision of the projected ten-year surplus to $4.2 *trillion* by 2010, including $2.3 trillion that no longer was being filched from Social Security reserves with annual IOUs. On tape, he waved aside for later the numb disbelief in our capacity to become a debtless nation. That freighted subject led into politics, and he was consumed by a personal memory from this crowded calendar on June 26. Diane Blair had died in Arkansas.

She was Hillary's dear friend for twenty-five years. Jointly, Diane and Hillary had battled to reform their recovering male chauvinist mates, and the Blairs became without doubt their closest friends as a couple. The president called this a rare and precious balance over time, sustained by bonds among the four of them in every combination. Her cancer had appeared shortly after a perfect physical exam, moving from a spot in the lining of her lungs through the rib cage to form a lump beneath her shoulder blade. Within two weeks of diagnosis, Jim Blair's obsessive devotion made him an expert nearly on a par with leading specialists. Yet this virulent growth killed her within four months, said Clinton, which is a reminder of how transitory we are. He kindly regretted that our project had sequestered me from much acquaintance with Diane, a gifted professor, saying he thought we would have shared many interests in history. He gave thanks that the Blairs could afford a sophisticated pain management belt around her waist. Its embedded needle, by dripping regulated doses of morphine directly into the spinal column, kept her stable but not woozy almost to the end. He recalled his last visit and their spirited goodbye phone calls. A month after her death, he said, his only consolation in shutting down the Middle East peace talks was that he could rush from Camp David to her memorial service. It shook his composure to reprise several of the eulogies. He and Hillary had gotten through many tough funerals, said the president, but they barely survived this one.

Candidly, but sadly, Clinton recorded the Camp David talks in greater detail than I could recall later for dictation. He named corridors and roadways between isolated West Bank villages in contention, and he profiled personalities of the five or six key subordinates on each side. The younger Palestinians tended to be a little more disposed to peace than Arafat's two older deputies, whereas the younger Israelis favored a harder line. He said very little occurred in the first few days, as of my visit to Camp David three weeks ago. Both principals were sullen. Arafat did not want to be there, and Barak felt that his risky overtures went unappreciated. Barak had been elected on a peace platform that never-theless pledged to keep all of Jerusalem under Israeli control. Tentatively, he tried to kick-start talks on Jerusalem with an offer to concede sover-eignty over specific villages in East Jerusalem. Arafat scoffed. He refused to accept anything less than U.N. resolutions calling for a return to the boundaries before the Six Day War of 1967. This was his cherished map, which clearly implied all of Jerusalem for Palestine. Arafat parried Barak without conceding anything in a proposal of his own. The president said he twice pronounced the negotiations nearly stillborn. Once he stalked out rather than transmit Barak's testy retraction of his offer. Another time, he confided sharply to Arafat that he, Clinton, would shut down their last chance for peace if they could not find creative ways to explore compromise.

They made progress into a second week on the toughest issues: Is-raeli settlements, the boundaries of West Bank territory for Palestine, and the rights of Palestinians displaced since 1948. Barak, with sweat and anxiety, preserved 80 percent of Israeli settlers into fingerlike extensions of Israel, on less than 10 percent of the West Bank, including connector roads. Outside of Jerusalem, this left 90 percent of this occupied terri-tory for the new Palestine, and map wizards worked out an intricate maze of land swaps elsewhere from Israel to make up the difference. For displaced Palestinians, an international consortium would provide gen-erous compensation to families and descendants who elected not to re-patriate under specified deadlines. The incentive formulas promised to lessen the number of returnees, who could be inconvenient, while hon-oring principles important to both sides. On the sly, said Clinton, Barak wanted a buffer strip of Israeli sovereignty along the Jordan River. Jor-dan's government secretly supported this demand because of its own security concerns with Palestinians—but could not afford to say so. The negotiators boiled down what amounted to an Israeli checkpoint zone along a short, vulnerable stretch east of Jerusalem, leaving the Jordan River otherwise a naked international border for 85 percent of its course to the Red Sea.

LAST CAME THE bargaining over Jerusalem. The president said his own pri-vate odds for a peace deal jumped from about 10 percent to even or better. He thought Jerusalem was symbolically difficult but conceptually doable. Unlike the settlement and West Bank issues, the "facts on the ground" were relatively stable. He said the framework was simple: divided sovereignty over greater Jerusalem, allowing both countries room to plant flags for a permanent national capital, with international guarantees as needed to secure universal access to sacred sites of the three Abrahamic faiths. On these details, they all stayed up several nights until dawn at Camp David, with couriers between cabins and bleary-eyed inspection of Jerusalem's street maps down to the gates and portals. There was painful division of neighborhoods in the outlying areas, but the more sensitive controversies were over the walled Old City at the center, which had been divided for centuries into practical quadrants: the Jewish, Muslim, Christian, and Armenian quarters. Here as elsewhere, history supplied both logic and contradiction in deep layers. Armenians were Christians, of course, but they had earned their own quarter with lonely persistence through the Middle Ages. Christians occupied half the Old City by sufferance and custom, despite their abysmal intolerance during rule by the Crusaders.

In hard negotiation, said Clinton, the Palestinians were willing to internationalize the walled Old City, but Barak balked out of distrust of the United Nations. Israelis felt outnumbered and consistently mistreated in most world bodies, especially that one, and Barak floated his own proposal instead. Israel, while retaining formal sovereignty over the Old City, would concede a zone of Palestinian control through its Muslim quarter to the high stone plaza at the heart, known to Muslims as Haram al-Sharif ("Noble Sanctuary") and to Jews as the Temple Mount. In return, Barak proposed a gesture to compensate religious Israelis. On specified occasions, Jews would be permitted to offer prayers on the Temple Mount for the first time in nearly two thousand years, since Rome had destroyed Herod's Temple after a first-century Jewish rebellion.

"Arafat went berserk," said the president, and his fellow Palestinians cried that Jews never before had dared such blasphemy. Even during the military occupation since 1967, Israeli police had prevented Jews from congregating to pray on the Temple Mount, where Muslims had managed continuous religious observance since the year 1187. Arafat's tirade shocked the Israeli negotiators. At first, Barak sputtered that he expected very few Israelis to exercise such a prayer privilege. Orthodox Jews would feel unworthy, and others would be uncomfortable. But why should the occasional Jew not be free to pray like Christians, Buddhists, and others? Why was religion ecumenical for everyone but Jews? Barak got his back up, Clinton recalled. He and Arafat soon were telling each other to go to hell.

The president described two late night intercessions. To Arafat, alone, he pleaded for counterintuitive understanding of a vulnerability that coexisted with Israel's military dominance. Clinton and Arafat belonged to religious cultures fortunate to preserve many ancient shrines. Christians had the Vatican, Bethlehem, and the Church of the Holy Sepulcher, among others. Muslims revered the Kaaba in Mecca and the Tomb of the Prophet in Medina, plus the Dome of the Rock and Al-Aqsa Mosque there on Jerusalem's Haram. Jews, lacking such treasures, centered their faith memories upon a fragment of the Western Wall beneath the destroyed temples of Solomon and Herod. Devout Israelis hoped one day to find their biblical Ark of the Covenant underneath by excavation. Such ruins and relics were all Jews had, but they meant no less than did two of the glorious places sacred to Muslims on that same central spot in the Old City. Surely, the negotiators could figure a way to honor differences born of the same yearning. Clinton said he appealed to Arafat with every wisp of common spirit he could reach.

His crisis message for Barak was different. He stressed deepening admiration for the prime minister as a distinguished scientist, musician, and decorated soldier. Claiming senior status for himself only in politics, the president commended one lesson from the battles he had studied and seen. He said it does no good to consign an enemy to hell if you can't make him go. Barak could cause Arafat all manner of grief, but the grief itself would fester into a greater trouble for Israel than Arafat's potential success. Therefore, Clinton urged patience.

All his ministrations achieved no better than a seething truce, he acknowledged, but Barak and Arafat were chagrined by the summit deadline. Rather than accept failure, they asked to keep talking at Camp David while the president attended G-8 meetings in Japan. This was highly unorthodox, but welcome. On tape, Clinton said the interval allowed him to drum up indirect support from world leaders. Because the Camp David negotiating terms remained deeply secret, he could make only general appeals. To Arab heads of state, he argued that Arafat should spare more than a Jewish slice of Jerusalem for Israel, especially if the real alternative was no Palestine at all, and the feedback revealed an uneven grasp of basic facts. Mubarak did not know, for instance, that the Dome of the Rock, commemorating the stone from which the Prophet Muhammad was said to ascend into heaven, stood on the exact site of Solomon's Temple. Though president of Egypt for nearly twenty years, Mubarak had missed this historical flash point between Muslims and Jews. Appalled, Clinton doubted that his appeals did much good.

He found the stalemate intact, if slightly more civil, on his return from Okinawa, and they suspended the Camp David summit after two more all-night marathons. Now the president assessed diminishing chances for success before he left office. Their timing had been consistently out of phase. Barak missed chances. Also, Arafat romanticized the memory of Yitzhak Rabin into an excuse for inaction—telling himself Rabin would have given him what he asked from Barak. This was never true, said the president. Besides, Barak's political constraints were tighter than Rabin's. Elected as the peace candidate, Barak was delivering neither peace nor security. Clinton clung to optimism. He thought Israelis would vote for a reasonable settlement. He believed the secret negotiations thus far had cracked the most intractable issues, from settlements to borders. Even on Jerusalem, they had created a blueprint for two nations to share the modern city.

Their remaining divide touched the core of identity. Here Clinton drew hope from personal observation—at least for this paired set of negotiators. They all had lived together at Camp David for two weeks, getting to know each other at meals and walks in the woods. They compared customs along with home memories of everything from street signs to mountain vistas. Except for two or three nasty confrontations, they talked often of diets and girlfriends, and such small things could spark imagination for a new world. In Northern Ireland, said the president, Catholics and Protestants had begun to make peace while refusing to shake hands, and the Bosnian factions could barely stay in the same room. At Camp David, by contrast, Israelis and Palestinians learned to swap jokes under pressure. One of Arafat's lieutenants had a sister younger than his own grandchildren, and quick-witted delegates traced every setback to this phenomenon. His family personified stubbornness, misplaced virility, lost generations, a right of perpetual return, and the wondrous fertility of their desert land.

The antagonists were cousins by culture, and Clinton found it a good sign that they could plumb fellowship even into dangerous, historic failure. Jewish humor was a staple of American life, but he and the Israelis were impressed that the Palestinians more than held their own. The same subordinates who quaked before Arafat's fateful decisions also teased him to and about his face. One day, they kept saying, Arafat came into the presence of Allah, who pronounced judgment with a grant of one wish. Arafat beamed. Allah is great, he said. He had dreamed of this moment. Reaching into his military tunic, Arafat pulled out the tattered map of Palestine before the Six Day War in 1967, and submitted a wish for peace in its shape. Allah frowned in reply that some things are too difficult even for the Almighty. Arafat was crushed. He writhed in mourning, but in time, dazzled by holiness, he requested the consolation of an eternal likeness modeled on Tom Cruise. Allah frowned again, stalled, and plaintively asked, "Can I have another look at that map?" Everyone howled, said Clinton. They mined endless fun from Arafat's dream, Allah's limitations, and the beauty of every camel to its kind.

CHELSEA STOPPED BY the kitchen during a break. She wore a T-shirt with a Quaker logo. In a rush, she appraised speeches from the Republican convention so far. Lynne Cheney was so terrible that no one could blame the networks for cutting away to pundits. Laura Bush was strong, said Chelsea, approving her delivery and personal appeal. Governor Bush was about to begin his address. Could she watch with her dad? This question put me in a bind. I told her I would check when he returned, but my impression was that we had come here deliberately to avoid television. Chelsea looked mystified, doubtful that he would skip such a moment. She shrugged and darted away.

The president wanted to keep taping. We covered some of the G-8 summit at Okinawa, plus the complicated antitrust suit against Microsoft and a procedural scrape with Senator Byrd over the Clean Water

Act. Mostly, he expounded on his running battle with Congress over its "tax cut a week" campaign. Since last year, when Clinton had hurt the Republicans badly in the polls by vetoing their gigantic tax cut bill, he said Senator Lott devised a plan to make the idea look less irresponsible by chopping it into little pieces. Simultaneously, Lott orchestrated his majority to block all Clinton's legislative proposals including the trade bill for China, which most Republicans favored. They would delay votes on the trade bill until the last minute before the election, said Clinton, in order to maximize strain between Democratic candidates and labor unions. Otherwise, Republicans were pounding home a single message that they would cut every form of tax, tomorrow if not today. In response, Clinton rehearsed public relations themes to justify his targeted, cautious tax cuts. Republicans, he recited, were peddling a feel-good bonanza like sweepstakes promoter Ed McMahon, who rang doorbells on television with news that awed families may have just won $10 million. Make sure Ed's hype is real, he advised. Citizens should watch out for rosy assumptions that there will be no recessions or emergencies. Pay down some debt first. The projected surplus, Clinton muttered to me, could never survive temptation and misfortune intact.

This was standard politics. The president believed he could win, but he gave credit to the opposition for coherent simplicity. He said congressional Republicans reinforced the emerging Bush strategy against Gore. According to Clinton's best spy down in Texas, who was close to the family, Governor Bush proudly had reduced all the politics and issues to three elementary Ps—personality, prosperity, and partisanship. Stripped to its essence, Bush was framing his campaign on the assumption that whoever prevailed on two of the three Ps would win the White House. On personality, the governor presented himself as a regular guy who was more fun to have a beer with than the hectoring, complex Al Gore. To seek a draw on prosperity—Gore's strong point—Bush would embody the tough, king-sized good life in Texas. On partisanship, which Bush assumed would be the deciding factor, he devised his boldest stroke. He campaigned to define partisan politics as everything bad. It was scandal, personal attacks, chaotic discord, and selfish ambition—in short, "the mess in Washington." Bush was against it. He said he was a problem solver, not a politician.

The president seemed rattled. Bush's strategy denigrated the politics Clinton loved. At the same time, Bush aimed to win votes by doing so, which was politics, and therefore he earned Clinton's grudging admiration. Most brazenly, Bush attributed all the scandal mongering and strife of the past eight years to Democrats by extension from Clinton. He single-mindedly rejected any suggestion that Republicans had pursued vendettas from Whitewater to Chinese spies. That sort of quibbling, Bush insisted, further ensnarled Washington's gridlock. By focusing on his three Ps, the nominee managed to submerge normal debate about public conditions, fidelity to promises, and even the comparative voting records of candidates. Clinton said other Republicans adopted Bush's aggressive defense. Representative Rick Lazio, in New York's race for the U.S. Senate, denounced Hillary for unpardonable personal attacks whenever she pointed out that Lazio had voted twice to shut down the government. Bush's running mate, Dick Cheney, brushed off reminders that he had opposed House resolutions petitioning South Africa to free Nelson Mandela. Cheney called such talk negative politics from the past, and vowed to fix it. His inverted language was straight out of *Alice in Wonderland,* marveled Clinton. These people had spared nothing, including the Constitution, to mesmerize the country with personal attacks on him, and now they blithely called themselves the sunshine reformers.

He expressed fascination with Bush's selection of Cheney, who had supervised the search for a running mate until he wound up choosing himself. Bush did not bother to wait, Clinton had heard, for the usual vetting studies on Cheney, including political analysis of his ten-year voting record in the House of Representatives. It made sense to him that Bush would spurn these fundamentals. Cheney offered traditional balance to the GOP ticket only with his varied government service, which could make up for Bush's relative inexperience. Otherwise, said the president, Cheney reinforced Bush's determination to make the campaign about attitude. Bush and Cheney were political twins. They both projected a cocksure manner with an economy of words. Like gunslingers in movies, they promised to cut through palaver and get things done. While submitting to democratic norms for the election season, they talked down to voters with a disguised autocratic streak. Clinton thought their governing approach would lean heavily to command over partnership.

•   Contrary to news reports, the president said he did not ask Gore to consider Florida senator Bob Graham for the vice presidential slot on the Democratic ticket. Nor did he recommend his able negotiator in Northern Ireland, former Senate majority leader George Mitchell of Maine. Instead, he wanted Gore to shake things up. To my surprise, he mentioned Bill Bradley as a worthy long shot. Bradley would offer Democrats a big fund-raising boost and a favored image in the press. Gore would be magnanimous to pick his rival from the primaries, whereas Bush had passed over John McCain. Clinton said Bradley seemed rejuvenated lately, and complimented him for a spirited endorsement of Gore in Wisconsin. Soon, however, prior misgivings seemed to overtake his strategic enthusiasm. You never knew when Bradley might start moping again. If he did, with his informal wardrobe, Clinton said Bradley tended to look like he had slept in his clothes. The president moved on to another dark horse of whom he had seldom spoken well, Senator Bob Kerrey of Nebraska. Kerrey's weakness was that he popped off independently on volatile issues, like Social Security, but this very maverick quality might spice up the Gore ticket in a national race. Kerrey was a born campaigner with a proven skill for attracting conservative votes.

It was not Gore's style to take big risks, said the president, which ruled out Clinton's favorite wild-card candidate, Senator Barbara Mikulski of Maryland. No one supported or even mentioned her for vice president, but he was not joking. He conceded that my home state senator might produce shockwaves of disbelief at first. Mikulski was well under five feet tall, with a frumpy figure and a beer-hall voice. Still, Clinton predicted that she could rise to folk-hero status above the prepackaged image of a potential president. She was feisty, with an amazing life story in community service. She had done more with her talents than many other women, and the president thought she was wiser than the female running mate on Gore's list, Senator Dianne Feinstein of California. Above all, he praised Mikulski's gift for communication. Her words engaged voters of every stripe. Clinton had commended her often in this regard, but he made special application to the presidential campaign taking shape. He said Mikulski dramatized hard political choices and their consequences for everyday life, inviting citizens to take charge by thoughtful responsibility in the public square. As such, Clinton thought she was an ideal running mate to help Gore cut through the artificial gamesmanship of Bush's three Ps.

Did I know how Mikulski once spiked sinister rumors that she was a lesbian? This drew a clueless shrug from me, and the president smiled. Well, he said, politicians knew. She gave us a great moment in modern campaigns. When her first Senate opponent planted gossip in coded newspaper stories, Mikulski scheduled a speech to prominent business developers in Baltimore. Facing the assembled big shots and deal makers, who had grown up with and around her, she told them she heard their whispers. She knew what they were thinking. Look, she said, here is what's real. I am your maiden aunt. Every family has one of me. I'm the one who takes care of the kids when you go on vacation. You know who I am, and if it bothers you, all I can say is this: Where were you when I needed a date to the prom?

The president heaved with mirth, fighting tears. In his admiring opinion, she had punctured her opposition in less than a minute without uttering a harsh word. "I've always loved Barbara Mikulski," he said. "You want to be in a foxhole with her." Of course, Gore was not likely to make her his running mate, and Clinton was not sure she would be the right choice.

Slowing down, he hoped we could have another session about Camp David if the talks resumed. He said the peace quest was not finished, but I sensed an overriding drift into melancholy. Gore's troubles already shadowed Clinton's legacy. Moreover, the president was dismayed by Bush's early success with the three Ps. Even if there was some miraculous breakthrough for the Middle East, he feared it could be discounted like much of his record. This was the price of Lewinsky, which had rescued seven years of Whitewater propaganda for his enemies. Without it, would Gore be safely and credibly on the offensive? Did Clinton's tawdry lapse spoil a great historical reckoning? As he kept slipping into regret, I wondered to what degree the Lewinsky scandal caused or reflected the political climate.

Rewinding the tapes, I asked how much Gore consulted him about campaign plans with the Democratic convention looming only ten days ahead. The president looked pained. "We used to talk once a week," he replied. "But he hasn't called me for a couple of weeks. I think maybe he's slipped off into a trance or something." It was early in the race, but Gore had enjoyed only two good political weeks since sewing up the nomination in March. Clinton said he could not resist trying to help, feeling restless and neglected on the shelf. Last Friday, at some Democratic function, he had tossed off a spontaneous parody of Bush's stump speech, terse and full of twang: "Well, how bad could I be? I'm a governor. My daddy was president. I owned a baseball team. They *like* me down in Texas." This salvo drew fire from candidate Bush, who said it proved Gore was desperate. Clinton winced like a semi-chastened schoolboy. While pleased to have exposed a sensitive spot in Bush, he faulted himself for lack of restraint. He said partisan attacks from him backfired on every front. They drove down the presidential performance rating, which was the only certain measure of his impact on Gore. They rallied voters to Bush as an underdog victim, and they made Gore look like he needed help from the White House.

The president said he made mistakes in part from fatigue. "I did four fund-raisers just yesterday," he complained of his nonstop role behind the scenes. He stood to leave the kitchen, saying Hillary would be home soon from New York. We guessed the Republican convention must be over by now. I found him a few minutes later in the yellow hallway, quizzing someone on the phone about what Bush had said in his acceptance speech. He took tonight's cassettes along with the two tapes saved from Camp David, nodding in distracted thanks, which signaled it was time for me to go.

CHAPTER THIRTY-NINE

DEADLOCK 2000: "THIS ELECTION IS TIGHT AS A TICK"

Sunday, October 29, 2000

Monday, November 27, 2000

Nearly three months passed, during which I saw President Clinton only at a White House picnic for his fifty-fourth birthday late in August. Among trees behind the Oval Office, we sampled buffet food and cake at tables around a swimming pool that somehow I had never noticed. Christy knew many of the guests from her two years working for Hillary, but my acquaintance was more limited to old friends. Erskine Bowles, up from his home in North Carolina, patiently translated for nonbusiness minds how our daughter, Macy, might begin a career in finance after college. His successor, Chief of Staff John Podesta, sat down with his hand in a cast from surgery to correct a cramping disorder, and National Security Adviser Sandy Berger carried a plate for his wife, Susan, who was recovering from foot ailments. We all lamented the onset of breakdowns from middle age, until Transportation Secretary Rodney Slater joined our table to reminisce about the all-night rehearsals for Clinton's first inaugural address. The president himself spouted the latest poll numbers. Hillary was comfortably ahead in New York, and

Gore was 3–5 points up nationally, holding a big bounce from the Democratic convention.

There was no summer vacation for the Clintons in 2000. What postponed our next session, aside from extra crises, was his unbroken string of campaign dinners and receptions through the autumn fund-raising deadlines. My next summons came when least expected—nine days before the election—amid news reports that Gore's advisers refused to schedule appearances with or by Clinton at rallies, for fear of offending swing voters. The stories braced me for an unhappy president, marooned in the campaign stretch, and unspecified delays parked me downstairs well into the evening.

Skip Allen, the usher on duty, said the permanent staff was frantic already over a moving day less than three months off. An army of employees sorted fifty-six furniture pallets stored on arrival from the Arkansas governor's mansion in 1993, separating items bound for Chappaqua from other destinations. More extensively, eight years of accumulated presidential loot was stacked in the basement, painstakingly appraised and catalogued by Gift Office experts over in the EOB. Unwanted junk was sold periodically at auction. Everything else was property of the government—headed to the Smithsonian or a Little Rock warehouse for the future Clinton library—unless some aide marked them for purchase by the first family. Allen said two-term presidents were an administrative nightmare. Clinton ranked high in art treasures from foreign travel, but he thought Nixon had the record with a veritable emperor's booty from his trip to China alone. Toward nine o'clock, a buzz for Allen sent me upstairs to the family living room.

"This election is tight as a tick," President Clinton announced in what became a refrain for the night. He moved his memos and calculations to make room on the card table for my recording materials. One by one, he listed thirteen or fourteen states for Gore, adding up to 209 electoral votes of the 270 needed to win. Bush had about twenty states with 200 electoral votes. Of the close ones, Clinton glumly assigned Ohio's 21 electors to Bush. He thought Gore would get Pennsylvania, Wisconsin, and Oregon. Six states fell within the margin of error, too close to call. Clinton described closing trends for each one from experience in his two victories. They were all tight as a tick now. Lately, he said, Delaware loosened from Gore toward Bush. That was a bad sign.

He seemed more clinical than angry about being sidelined for the climactic week of the campaign. Gore's people had made many errors, he said, which reminded him of his brash young staff in 1993. Playing to newspapers and television, they were getting across only half the message intended by choosing the straitlaced ticket mate Joe Lieberman from Connecticut, the Democratic senator most overtly scornful of Clinton's personal faults. They should be running essentially for a third term, said the president, but they were afraid the Clinton-Gore record would tarnish them with Clinton's character. Therefore, they seized the disadvantage of uphill competition with Bush-Cheney as agents of change. By trusting pundits more than voters, they made themselves timid even on factual disputes. In the second presidential debate, moaned Clinton, Gore let Bush get away with charges that the United States was suckered unfairly to supply all the peacekeepers in Kosovo. "Here's what I would have said," he recited: "Governor, perhaps you don't know that we're only 15 percent of the troops there. Our European allies, including Russia, already make up 85 percent of the ground forces."

On this answer and several others, the president opined that he would have smiled and tried to be a good fellow while he tore Bush apart. Gore lacked confidence in a light touch. Whenever he tried to be aggressive, said Clinton, Gore could come off ponderous and harsh, like Mussolini, and he adjusted by letting charges slide instead, deferring too much. Even so, the whole national race was teetering within a point or two. Clinton thought marginal voters valued Gore's knowledgeable sincerity despite lampoons in the media. The undecided few tended to like Bush better, he said, but they were not sure he was ready. They knew Gore was ready to be a good president, but they were not sure they liked him. Clinton refined a pragmatic message. Subtly, he would try to tilt opinion in crucial states toward Gore's witty and heartfelt side.

Gore might want him to go to Michigan, which was why the president said he had to take a call from Mayor Dennis Archer of Detroit. Coming back, he said Gore had bared himself in one of their stressful consultations by insisting that he, Gore, was a good politician, elaborating that he meant good on the policy, and also good on the politics, but admitted that he did not instinctively blend the two. Gore said he had to think about it, and Clinton thought this was pretty close to the bone. As a policy person, and a government person, Gore would make wise choices. He had the stuff to be a great president, and this was the message that Clinton must convey somehow without seeming to brag on his own record.

The president took a phone call from Hillary. They discussed strategy for her final weekend, coordinating logistical challenges around next Sunday's New York Marathon. While he talked, pacing, I did my best to decipher and copy his national computations. A wavy line had moved Arizona's 8 electoral votes into the "Leaning Bush" column. Six states with 58 electoral votes remained in his toss-up list: Iowa, Florida, West Virginia, Missouri, New Hampshire, and Arkansas. There were assorted notes, doodles, and a few exclamation points.

When he returned, we recorded on nonelection topics. From a recent trip, he described Nigeria's agonizing trap between immense resources and crippling corruption. Its embattled president, Olusegun Obasanjo, was mobilizing Nigeria against the early stages of an AIDS epidemic, but tribal customs severely inhibited public education about safe sex. He told of wrenching encounters with infected mothers. There was mediation in Burundi, which he said had suffered genocide before Rwanda, followed by an airport stopover in Egypt for breakfast with President Mubarak about reviving the Camp David talks. Back home for the millennium peace summit at the U.N., he said, he literally had bumped into Fidel Castro, and huddled with leaders from Tony Blair to Jiang Zemin, but his memories focused on Arafat and Barak. By the end of September, his confederates had coaxed them back into each other's presence for the first time since July—at Barak's home in Israel, no less—with the lieutenants meeting again and the two leaders calling the White House with updates. Tenacious effort and renewed optimism made it particularly cruel when the Middle East blew up that same week.

All sides, said the president, had intelligence warnings of the surprise visit by Israeli general Ariel Sharon to Jerusalem's Temple Mount on September 28. Barak's government could not dissuade him from going. The Israelis now swore the Palestinians had said they could cope with Sharon on the big plaza, so long as he did not profane either of its two Muslim mosques. Clinton still subscribed, with reservations, to U.S. intelligence that Sharon did not intend to provoke such epochal violence with a cowboy stunt geared toward politics within Israel. Sharon, jockeying with Benjamin Netanyahu in the conservative Likud Party, strikingly advertised his opposition to peace terms that might relinquish Israeli sovereignty anywhere in Jerusalem, including the Muslim holy sites. He was brandishing the prerogatives of war, said the president, but no one expected Sharon to arrive with an escort of nearly a thousand heavily armed Israeli police officers. In a better world, Palestinians and Muslim worshippers would have welcomed Sharon's posse to their sanctuary with disciplined forbearance. In reality, they jostled as word of the massive provocation flashed through the Muslim quarter, touching off street demonstrations. Six Palestinians were killed the next day, and spasms escalated from rock-throwing mobs into roving gun battles with Israeli riot squads. Palestinians went berserk, as though acting out Arafat's rhetorical fit at the mere idea of Jewish visitors on the Haram. We could not be sure how much Sharon knew of this clash during the secret talks at Camp David, or whether it had figured into his plan.

Daily casualties defied truce initiatives. Nearly two hundred people were killed through this month of October, mostly young Palestinians, and Clinton reviewed inevitable claims that atrocities were being fomented by the political antagonists. A mob lynched two stray Israeli reservists on the West Bank. Worldwide television viewers saw a twelve-year-old Palestinian boy shot to death trying to hide in a cross fire. The president described efforts to smother the crisis with international mediators. He was imploring Turkey to join a balanced inquiry for the facts. At one of the feverish conclaves, he said, Arafat approached Clinton with a quiet urgency the president had never seen. Arafat said it was time to make a deal for peace. The president relayed this overture to Prime Minister Barak, who was struggling to keep his government afloat. "If he's serious," Barak replied, "I'm willing."

Strangely, said Clinton, the full range of outcomes was possible in the next few weeks—from comprehensive peace to all-out regional war. On the positive side, Barak and Arafat strived for what Clinton called "some lesser interval of violence" to resume negotiations, but intensified efforts had failed now for ten days. At the ominous extreme, he disclosed that Saddam Hussein was moving two combat divisions westward across Iraq toward Israel, and young Bashar Asad of Syria was trying to goad Egypt and Saudi Arabia into a pan-Arabic war. "We have game-planned every military scenario," the president said gravely. Each country had stockpiled more armaments and firepower since the last major war in 1973, but Israel's relative advantage had increased against any combination of foes. A general war would produce strategic defeat and catastrophic losses for Arabs. At the Pentagon, he said, the principal unknown was how many Israelis might be killed in desperate suicide attacks. It would be very ugly.

HIS WHITE HOUSE team had been working harder than ever. "That's how it should be," he observed. The job came first, and its enormous stakes reminded him to be circumspect about interventions in the Bush-Gore campaign. Mistaken forays, without helping Gore, would only deflect him from vital business. The past two months, for instance, brought the culmination of the long struggle with Slobodan Milosevic. When Yugoslav voters finally revolted over his misguided war in Kosovo ("We didn't buy votes," Clinton said carefully), Milosevic quashed the result, refused to leave, and promulgated military rule. World leaders strengthened the sanctions against his regime, but the president said the decisive pressure came from massive protests for several weeks by Yugoslav citizens themselves, which melted the regime's functionaries from their offices. Milosevic finally yielded on October 7 to his elected successor, Vojislav Kostunica. Clinton analyzed a triumph drawn from restraint, military resolve, and applied democratic principle. Almost forlornly, he said few Americans noticed the end of Milosevic or the lifting of international sanctions—milestones overshadowed by our presidential race and the Middle East conflagration. Rather than a glorious victory lap, Sandy Berger joked to NATO allies that we barely managed a "victory hop."

We started a potential victory hop on North Korea. The president said his secret reports had made Premier Kim Jong-il into a recluse "three bricks shy of a load," interested only in movie stars, and warned that Kim's top general, Jo Myong-rok, was too brainwashed for normal conversation. Much to his surprise, General Jo turned up urbane and well informed some three weeks ago on October 10–the first North Korean official ever to visit the White House–with an outline of Kim's design to join the family of nations. Because of cooperation from South Korea's visionary president, Kim Dae-jung, Clinton explained why he had an outside chance in these last weeks to visit Pyongyang and clinch a deal stopping North Korea's missile program, which would resolve a chronic national security threat.

Abruptly, Clinton excused himself to deal with campaign troubles on the phone. From the president's replies, Senator Breaux seemed to be saying Gore had no chance in Louisiana, which Clinton had carried twice, because Bush was getting 78 percent of the white vote. With Hillary, and pollster Mark Penn, Clinton was upset over shrill charges from her opponent, Representative Lazio, calling her a friend of terrorists. Rebut him sharply, he advised. How dare he? Remind everybody they had tracked down and convicted the terrorists who bombed the World Trade Center in 1993. And we caught the guy in Pakistan who shot up those people outside the CIA.* Was there time to make an ad showing Hillary in Norfolk, stricken at the service for the seventeen sailors killed by terrorists on the USS *Cole*? I gave him space for these conversations by wandering into their bedroom. A pillow sat primly on a chair, embroidered with an Einstein quote that made me chuckle: "Great spirits have always encountered violent opposition from mediocre minds."

Back on tape, we discussed the October 12 suicide attack against the *Cole* in the port of Aden, Yemen, near the juncture of Africa with the Arabian Sea. The president said they thought the instigator was bin Laden. Our people knew where part of the bomb was made. The FBI, leading a strike force of 250 U.S. investigators, was at loggerheads with the government of Yemen. Each side demanded to be in charge, mistrusting the other, and Clinton said we were lucky that so little friction had leaked into the press. This conflict was raw–some petty, some fundamental–and he could only push for results. The president shrugged. "Look," he recalled, "I've had a lot of trouble with the FBI myself."

---

* Mir Aimal Kasi, sentenced in 1998 for two murders and the malicious wounding of three victims with an AK-47, was executed by lethal injection in 2002.

He cited ongoing disputes over the FBI's treatment of Wen Ho Lee, the nuclear scientist of Taiwanese birth who had worked more than twenty years at the prestigious laboratory in Los Alamos. Suddenly arrested last year for espionage, Lee had been denied bail and imprisoned under draconian conditions—without a cell window or reading light, under constant surveillance, confined in solitary for all but one hour per week. The prosecution collapsed in September, with all charges dropped except a minor count of mishandling classified information on a laptop computer. U.S. district judge James Parker rebuked federal officials for gross misconduct, and President Clinton declared his regret. For some time now, he had scribbled my initials on selected papers to have me sent duplicates, and I had just compiled for him a two-year summary of this Chinese spy scandal. It felt bogus, I wrote. To me, the pattern was "almost a copy of Whitewater: prolonged hysteria and then convenient amnesia."

Clinton parsed his comments. He agreed there had been shameless hype from partisan politicians and especially from the press. Like Whitewater, he said, the stampede against Wen Ho Lee bore the imprimatur of the *New York Times*—ginned up by the same reporter, Jeff Gerth, and cheered on by the editorial page. Also, FBI officials clearly exaggerated evidence. (There were reports that agents had waved Gerth's first story about nuclear treason at Wen Ho Lee, demanding his confession to avoid the death penalty.) Nevertheless, the president hedged about his government's stance. He was not prepared to call it wholly fraudulent, like the 1996 rush to convict Richard Jewell for bombing the Atlanta Olympics. This was a spy case. The evidence was secret, and politics often trumped the elusive facts. Whether Lee was guilty or not, many security agencies had a stake in the emergency powers used to investigate him. From Justice, Energy, CIA, the Pentagon, and elsewhere, cabinet officers gamely defended the FBI's suspicions even now. Lee, supported by many colleagues at Los Alamos, was trying to establish his innocence in a defamation suit, and Clinton sidestepped that fight.*

---

* In June of 2006, Wen Ho Lee settled for $1.6 million from assorted defendants: the U.S. government, ABC News, the Associated Press, the *Los Angeles Times,* the *New York Times,* and the *Washington Post.*

Clinton did agree with Judge Parker that the prosecution's erratic course had been a travesty. You cannot declare someone so dangerous to the nation that he cannot be allowed to see daylight, or talk to his wife, and then turn around and make a deal to set him free.

Clinton closed with a confession. During this review, officials had disclosed worse cases to make Lee's treatment seem comparatively benign. At least Lee was indicted, said the president, but others were being held in secret, uncharged and untried, under a strained interpretation of anti-terrorist provisions in his crime bill. He was embarrassed now to have sponsored this measure into law without foreseeing such arbitrary detentions. You cannot deny a hearing, he said. Under the terrorist act, any prosecutor should decide within the legal limit—thirty days, or sixty days—whether to bring charges on the testimony of a secret informant or otherwise. To his dismay, Clinton had learned of defendants held incommunicado for more than six months. One extreme detention had lasted three years. "I think it's wrong," he said. "It's not American. We accept guilty people on the streets to enjoy and protect our freedom."

Skip Allen stepped in with apologies. He had found tomorrow's continuing resolution that President Clinton must sign to keep the government from shutting down at midnight. We were in a showpiece reprise of the big collisions in 1995. Republican leaders could not adjourn Congress without passing the required appropriations bills, which were overdue. In ritual standoff, they called for Clinton to sign their big tax cut first, but they also yearned to go home and campaign. The president grinned. "They're madder than hornets that I won't sign a resolution for more than one day at a time," he said, mulling his final campaign remarks on the way to the elevator.

What was my gut feeling on the election? My gut feelings were churning elsewhere. I said I was sorry to see the contest so close. Clinton was, too. "I think we have more shots to win it than Bush does," he concluded.

LATE IN NOVEMBER, the cell phone rang in my pocket while I was rushing to plant a batch of daffodils before dark. A scrambling journey cleared me through the Southwest Gate for once, not the Southeast, and up to the Treaty Room by nine o'clock. The president stood in blue jeans amid books stacked on the rug. I told him I had been startled to see packing boxes already in doorways. Yes, they were getting a head start. He had crated up a thousand books, given away that many, and had six thousand left to sort. Boxes were strewn about by categories. He asked the usher on duty to send up a bottle of water and a handful of Tylenol, along with our usual Diet Cokes.

His words gushed before I could open my briefcase. He did not feel well. Advisers were split over whether he should go to North Korea. He might need to go to Northern Ireland or Jerusalem instead. So much was in play. He was working like crazy to salvage this Hague Convention on global warming. There was Putin on the Middle East, where the two months of violence spiked political retribution from every quarter— Arafat branded both sinister and weak, Barak an ineffective peacenik now giving in to demands for early elections. Clinton was heartbroken to fall short. You could only push so hard, but long-range instability was driving him to cajole Putin toward Russia's first positive engagement with the Israeli-Muslim tinderbox.

My hands jumped back and forth—rushing to set up the equipment, beckoning him to save this material for the tapes. With the red lights finally lit, he interrupted my standard introduction to ask if this could really be our seventy-seventh session. Yes, since a late start in his first year, we had averaged close to one taping per month. The president smiled mischievously. "If I just sold these things raw," he quipped, "I could make a lot of money, couldn't I? It would probably ruin my reputation." He waved to assure me he had more dignified purposes in mind. I laughed. "Well, Mr. President," I replied, "you control when they'll be opened for research. Maybe Chelsea could sell soundtracks in a few years, once your opinions don't matter so much."

We recovered due gravity. Here we were, twenty days after the Bush-Gore election and still no winner. Gore reliably had won 266 electoral votes, 4 short of victory, but Florida's 25 electoral votes were being disputed out to the fifth or sixth decimal point. Like impeachment, we were engulfed in a political rarity not seen since Reconstruction, when a congressional deal had resolved the Hayes-Tilden deadlock of 1876. Clinton's term once again became objectively but uncomfortably historic, and he dissected the controversies for nearly an hour. He was talking to

Gore and Gore's people every day. He believed Gore had won Florida by as many as twenty thousand votes, but most of that margin was beyond practical recovery. There was no legal remedy for several thousand African-American voters disenfranchised in Duval County, or for the nineteen thousand votes discarded because defective butterfly ballots recorded dual preferences for president. Similarly, outrage could not rescue accurate votes for the three thousand Jewish voters whose ballots were counted for Pat Buchanan, even though statisticians showed by sampling and consistent polls that this tally was almost certainly wrong. He reviewed the high-profile suits and countersuits, including several "out-of-the-box" cases filed by advocacy groups other than the opposing campaigns. Election law was messy. "I used to teach this stuff," said the president. You cannot mandate a "do-over" even if you prove fraud, because the election date is fixed by the Constitution.

Chelsea burst in to ask whether we had seen Gore's speech on television. Calling him the vice president, she gave us a more or less verbatim reprise. Gore was officially contesting yesterday's certification of a Bush victory in Florida by state officials. In an election this close, he said, we should all cherish the legal redress to make sure every vote was counted fairly. If we overlooked or suppressed someone else's vote in Florida now, no one's ballot would be secure in the future. She called it his most presidential performance in the standoff thus far. He had made only one accurate, but partisan-sounding, allusion—to the orchestrated near-riot last week that stopped the physical inspection of ten thousand uncounted ballots in Miami-Dade County. Otherwise, Gore said simply count all the votes and he would abide by the result either way. The vice president did well, but she thought not enough Democrats were on his message to counter a unified GOP voice, out there in force, saying the same thing on every channel.

Clinton agreed with her on public relations. The Bush refrain had been consistent: Florida had been counted to death, and Gore was trying to steal the election. Legally, said Clinton, Gore was correct that the proper time to contest a close election only begins with certification, but tension and impatience ran heavily against him. Gore had made mistakes early in the duel of words over Florida, when his people seemed to cherry-pick jurisdictions for recount. The press generally fell in behind the Bush clamor for him to concede. When Gore himself had talked more than once about quitting, Clinton advised him privately to push on instead for examination of all the disputed or uncounted votes. As president, however, he stayed neutral in public. Nothing he said or did could help Gore anyway, and it could injure the country if the crisis turned worse.

He brightened when Chelsea left. She and her mother had been out all day with a real-estate agent, bringing back news it would be very expensive for him to house and support a United States senator in Washington. Not that he minded. He was so proud of her campaign. Most of the polls had her up 2 or 3 points at the end, but she won by 12. Having passed this test, he figured, she would never face another tough race in New York.

We sprinted through some presidential stories. With the election hanging, he had attended the APEC summit in the Pacific island kingdom of Brunei, near Indonesia, at a fantasyland resort built by its sultan. There he inveigled Putin on the Middle East and congratulated Kim Dae-jung of South Korea on his Nobel Peace Prize, brainstorming with them both about North Korea. He went on to describe three glorious days in Vietnam, where he rang the scholars' gong in Hanoi's Temple of Literature, nearly a thousand years old. He met a mix of old Stalinists, technocrats, entrepreneurs, and eager students, drawing enormous crowds everywhere. The mayor of Ho Chi Minh City—old Saigon—was a fountain of boosterish facts and introductions, like a rising pol in Ohio or Rhode Island, while an excavation site for the remains of U.S. soldiers was a display of reverence so painstaking that he was sure something good would grow eventually from the invisible cooperation. On the Hague Convention, which had collapsed two days ago, his solace was that every nation knew we did not pull the plug. What killed this global warming initiative was a bizarre mix of European Green Party politics, centered in France and Germany, which revolted against emissions caps as a compromise with the devil, and inexplicable opposition from Brazil on measures to preserve the rain forest. Most assuredly this quest would return. Even Bush, he noted, recognized the gathering threat of global warming in his campaign.

He explained why he had vetoed a bill to punish government employees who leaked information to the press. He described yet another anti-smoking initiative, the Great American Smokeout Day, and disputed predictions of a recession. Maybe the stock market was overvalued, he admitted, because the run-up had been so steep and prolonged. The Dow had more than tripled during his administration. A current drop in high-tech stocks was an inevitable corrective, he said. Yes, the unprecedented climb in GNP probably had to end sometime, but he insisted that the economic fundamentals were still sound. Wearily, he saw no downturn on the horizon.

The two hundredth birthday for the White House was more fun. He said George and Barbara Bush attended in good spirits, even though their son's bid for the presidency hung in limbo. The Carters came, too, along with Gerald Ford and even Lady Bird Johnson, to celebrate the bicentennial of the day President John Adams and his wife, Abigail, moved into the brand-new White House in 1800. Adams was already a lame duck then, defeated by Thomas Jefferson. Yes, Gerald Ford did steal the show that night with toasts about hosting Queen Elizabeth. Did I see him on C-SPAN, or the news? No, I had been there in person, several tables from him in the crowded East Room. Nancy Hernreich or somebody must have put me on a guest list for farewell events, seated memorably next to opera star Jessye Norman. Her voice lifted me off the floor when we all sang "God Bless America," and we bonded in stories about her brother Silas, who had been a civil rights leader in Selma. Good, said the president. He was glad I could be there, and Ford was funny indeed. "I only wish I could be in such good shape when I'm eighty-seven," he said with a whimsical smile. "Of course, I don't think I'll ever see eighty-seven."

We closed on tangents and leaps. Periodically in our sessions, I had tried to imagine questions off the beaten track of events, hoping to elicit something new or unusual for the record. This time I embarrassed myself. Did the president ever think about a comeback? He was only fifty-four. The Twenty-second Amendment barred more than two consecutive terms, but was it conceivable that he might sit out a term and run again in 2004 or later? Well, he replied gently, I had misread the Constitution. The Twenty-second Amendment was a lifetime ban on more than two terms, specifying that no person shall be elected more than twice. Then he smiled. Believe me, he said, he had studied it. There was a tortured construction under which he might succeed again to office from the vice presidency, but it was utterly impractical. He wished the wording were different. The amendment could fulfill its purpose to prevent dynasties and yet allow return tries after an interval. "I love this job," he said. "I think I'm getting better at it. I'd run again in a heartbeat if I could."

I tried a few neglected themes, such as agriculture policy and housing. Gamely, he also discussed streamlined government and trends for global institutions such as the WTO, APEC, and G-8. But he was tired, soon reaching again for the Tylenol. Was there a chance the Bush-Gore impasse could degenerate into a full-fledged constitutional crisis? God forbid, he replied, but yes. First, if the Florida Supreme Court mandated a review of the disputed ballots on Gore's petition, as was likely and legal, the president had very little doubt that Florida's Republican secretary of state would refuse to certify any result making Gore the victor. Furthermore, if the Florida Supreme Court then mandated certification of its recount, which could hand the White House to Gore, Clinton said the Republican legislature in Florida might refuse to validate the state's 25 electors. In that case, Gore would be stuck at 267 electors and Bush with 246—beneath the 270 required to become president. This would pitch the contest into the House of Representatives. Gore would have won the popular vote nationally, as well as a majority of the electors, but Bush would have a majority in the Republican House, voting by state. Each side would have powerful claims, and the potential clash could erode respect for the vote itself.

Finally, and prophetically, the president said he thought the U.S. Supreme Court would do anything it could to help Bush. He wasn't sure how the justices could get a legal foothold, but he said they were political enough to engineer a conservative president in order to perpetuate justices like themselves on a conservative Court. Justice Clarence Thomas, he added, would be driven to repay Bush's father for his own nomination. In summary, President Clinton said all the major institutional forces were lined up behind Bush, except for the Florida Supreme Court. He specifically included the media. Therefore, it would be very difficult for Gore to win. Sadly, this was true even though Clinton believed to a moral certainty that Gore would prevail in a fair, supervised count of Florida's legal votes, let alone the intended ones. He said he still urged Gore to fight on for now. Even if he could not win, he could isolate the record of fraud, reducing the chance for recurrence.

We stopped on a somber note, hoping for the best. Off the tapes, President Clinton said he hoped to finish with one or two more sessions, possibly ending on his last day. We reviewed ways to preserve and transcribe his tapes afterward, along with options for the structure of his memoirs. He asked whether I had spoken with his former speechwriter, the historian Ted Widmer, about plans to collect a rich trove of oral histories for his future presidential library. Yes, Widmer and others were pretty far along.

I begged a parting favor when I handed him the tapes. My camera was in the briefcase tonight. Could I take some photographs of the residence? I would sorely miss this place. He said, "Take all the pictures you want."

CHAPTER FORTY

FAREWELL

Monday, January 8, 2001

Tuesday, March 6, 2001

Friday, February 27, 2004

Tuesday, July 6, 2004

We drove down on December 11 for one of the holiday receptions at the White House. I ducked into the Usher's Office to say good-bye to familiar guides and escorts, but Daniel Shanks was frantically busy. The night shift had not yet arrived. In the State Dining Room, where kitchen aides tended hors d'oeuvres for a thousand guests or more, Buddy Carter and several other butlers came over to shake hands. Protocol relaxed in a transition, they said warmly, seeming to remember things they had pretended not to notice. One asked if President Aristide could help him go home safely to visit his grandmother's grave in Haiti. Two stewards recognized Christy from her stint with the first lady. She said she came down just to see the place again.

After wandering, and gazing our fill, we tried to slip away past vigilant staff who kept funneling us into a photograph line. Everybody was supposed to have a presidential photo made. They said it was less trouble to submit than to attempt leaving without a picture receipt. So we inched past exquisite decorations into the Green Room, receiving our instructions in turn, filling out the form handed to the officer with gloves as he swung us into camera position.

"Isn't Scalia amazing?" asked President Clinton. For the Court's 5–4 majority, to halt the Florida recount, Justice Antonin Scalia had just written that considering the uncounted ballots would undermine the legitimacy of the national election. It was blatantly political, said the president. Scalia confessed outright that they were afraid of the votes. By then, after the flashbulb, another military escort had a hand at my ribs to move us along, and I wished Clinton good luck on his trip tonight. Christy was congratulating "Senator-elect" Hillary, who slowed traffic enough to fret about contract negotiations for her autobiography.

Two days later, a voice announced the first lady on the line from Belfast, Northern Ireland. The Clintons were rushing to watch Gore's concession speech tonight in England with Prime Minister Blair, and Hillary remarked that today's decisive ruling on the election would rank with the infamous *Dred Scott* case among the Supreme Court's worst contraventions of democratic principle, in this case the right to vote. Her question for me was about her negotiations with several publishers, partly over the danger of getting stuck with an unsuitable ghostwriter. I advised her to reject any company that demanded exclusive control, saying it was perfectly legitimate—even desirable—to build in provisions for mutual confidence. She quizzed me about potential editors, but I lamented that a hermit's profession gave me acquaintance with very few. In jest, Hillary groused that Bill would have the help of our voluminous tapes to write his memoirs. She had never thought we could keep them secret all these years, and complimented David Kendall for legal wizardry in that feat.

A summons in January proved Clinton not quite done with our history project. Upstairs, in his living room, the president sorted piles of musical CDs into boxes—more than two thousand of them, including what he said may be an unmatched saxophone collection. The ushers had given him a strict packing schedule by the day, and their workers simply boxed everything en masse if the Clintons missed a deadline. With his authority ebbing, the president noted on tape that the country had survived bigger trials and bumps. Life went on. He vented only briefly about the election, insisting that every politician in the country knew Gore would have won if all the votes were counted. Bush's people had to freeze the tally short of the review prescribed under state law. He said they out-talked and "out-thugged" Gore's people. Scalia, who engineered the Supreme Court's intervention, knew it would serve Bush well to be validated by the Court rather than by a nasty scrum in Florida, where Bush's brother was governor. Cosmetically, Scalia's naked version of the miscarriage was probably better for the country.

Clinton described a cordial transition meeting with President-elect Bush, who had surprised him several times with a strong sense of political timing and maneuver. They were both free traders, said the president, and Bush was well aware that he had extra room for deals because he had never promised labor or environmental protections. Bush expressed a coherent sequence for his early initiatives. The most objectionable one was his determination to restore deficits with a big tax cut, and Clinton's hunch was that Bush the father would not have done so. On the other hand, President-elect Bush instinctively welcomed Clinton's plans to break the color line on the Fourth Circuit Court of Appeals with a temporary recess appointment for Judge Roger Gregory. Recalcitrant Republican senators had blocked confirmation for that seat through most of the 1990s, keeping an antiquated all-white bench in the judicial circuit covering Virginia and the Carolinas, with its large black population. Bush was more than relieved to let Clinton take the lead. The president sensed, correctly, that Bush may be shrewd enough to nominate Judge Gregory to stay on in a lifetime position, packaging his Senate confirmation with one or two of Jesse Helms's right-wingers whom Clinton had refused to appoint.

Bush had listened without comment to most of Clinton's extensive briefing on foreign affairs. Unexpectedly, when asked, he encouraged Clinton to seize any opening to stop the North Korean missile program. Bush said he could not imagine going there for at least the first year of his presidency, and if it took a presidential trip to complete the deal, he would hold no ill will toward Clinton for stealing the limelight or boxing in the new administration. "Go ahead, Mr. President," Bush told him. "It sounds like a good idea to me." The president, while appreciative, had decided since against the trip. His time was so short, and the political logistics were cruel. If he went to Pyongyang, he must go also to South Korea, then Japan, and these distant commitments might keep him away from a sudden opportunity in the Middle East. "If something went wrong there because of me," said Clinton, "I'd never forgive my-self." Reluctantly, he had decided to leave the North Korean missile deal "on the table," all but completed for Bush and his incoming secretary of state, Colin Powell.

On the Middle East, a comprehensive settlement was impossible within his remaining twelve days. He had said so privately last Tuesday, when Yasir Arafat could not accept the mediator's blueprint laid out by Clinton to Barak and Arafat in the Cabinet Room on December 23. For sensitive reasons, said the president, he had jiggled these last-gasp terms to the Israeli breaking point—raising the Palestinian share from 90 per-cent up to 94–96 percent of the West Bank territory, with additional land swaps from Israel to include a highway connector to isolated Gaza. All the intricate boundaries were specified for divided sovereignty of Jerusalem right into the Old City's holy places. Barak nevertheless ham-mered a yes from his government, while Arafat still begged more time in the Oval Office. Could Clinton extend his term? Could Bush make him a special envoy? Arafat said Clinton was the indispensable great man. "I told him no, Mr. Chairman," he recalled. "I'm a miserable failure here, largely because you made me one."

He went on at length about the bitter standoff ending seven years' labor toward this peace. Something less may be possible yet, he said doggedly—some sort of Statement of Principles—short of the compre-hensive peace. The president listed three reasons to pursue this consola-tion until his last hours in office. First, it would make peace more likely in the long run. Second, it would give Barak something to run on in Is-rael's election next month. Right now, Ariel Sharon was clobbering Barak for giving away so much without result. Third, if Sharon won the election anyway, a Statement of Principles would make it harder for him to carry through his stated repudiation of the entire Oslo peace process.

Clinton said he had been thinking about this so much. The image was not pretty, but he decided peacemaking quests came in two kinds: scabs and abscesses. A scab is a sore with a protective crust, which may heal with time and simple care. In fact, if you bother it too much, you can reopen the wound and cause infection. An abscess, on the other hand, inevitably gets worse without painful but cleansing intervention.

"The Middle East is an abscess," he concluded. "Northern Ireland is a scab." If Sharon came to power, the abscess of hatred would spread on political inertia and demographics. In Northern Ireland, where cultural estrangement remained a vivid bruise, the economy was getting better and hope was slowly institutionalized. Therefore, he said, the rewards of peace were becoming tangible. On this last trip to Belfast, his conscious theme was not so much to address current disputes over power sharing, nor the hidden arms caches and sporadic street violence, but to underscore the value of the peace process itself. He tried to remind everyone how far they had come. The people themselves were becoming a knitted constituency, able to marginalize and repulse those who made mischief.

I asked the president about reports that Protestant die-hards had accosted him in a corridor of the Stormont Parliament Building. "Absolutely, they did," he replied. "And I would hate to run into any of them in a dark alley. They hate my guts." But it was all right, he grinned, once he got out of there. Those people were enraged because their whole identity and livelihood rested on tribal privilege for Northern Ireland's Protestants, backed by the military sanction of England. Their platform was dying, said Clinton, or at least no longer respectable. They were like the once universal segregationists who ran the South of our childhood.

HE VOLUNTEERED ONE topic not on my list: a two-hour meeting with Gore about the election, alone and off the public schedule. At first, the president said he was unsure about recording details, but he circled back repeatedly until his stories gathered momentum. They were both conscious of the charged moment between them, and Gore tried to begin on a conciliatory note. Surely, it was no secret to the president that people in Gore's camp, especially pollster Stan Greenberg, believed Gore lost the election because of anti-Clinton sentiment in undecided voters. They had feared it from the start. Before the election, Greenberg and other advisers argued strenuously that Gore could not run on the Clinton-Gore record because it reminded people of Clinton. To swing voters, they said, his eight years were inextricable with scandal and discord. Neither could Gore afford to deploy the president in his campaign. Gore had heard Clinton was angry about that, and he wanted to clear the air.

For his own part, Gore was not angry, nor did he blame Clinton for his defeat, but he wanted to acknowledge forthrightly that some people around him did.

The president rumbled softly at first. "I said Al, I'll be straight with you," he recalled. Clinton had not put out any stories complaining of being underutilized in the campaign. Nearly all of them, he told Gore, came from candidates in tight races who were upset that Clinton was not allowed to help them. New Jersey's Jon Corzine, for instance, was furious that Gore strategist Bob Shrum blocked invitations for Clinton to make joint appearances in his bid for the U.S. Senate. There was no way Gore was going to lose New Jersey, and plenty of candidates felt victimized by his campaign. Helping Gore was another matter. The president himself still believed Gore had campaigned rightly on his own. Clinton's useful role was to work diligently at the White House, and it would hurt both of them for him to be on the political stump, for or with Gore—right up to the final ten days. After that, he confessed to Gore, some complaints may have leaked from the White House, because Clinton had chafed to be used in a few strategic states, if only by himself.

He recited four of them to Gore. Clinton believed he could have tilted his home state of Arkansas with a whistlestop tour of two days. It was not far-fetched to think so, anyway. Gore's losing margin there was less than 5 percent. In New Hampshire, where Clinton's ratings were unusually high, well above 60, Bush won by only one percent. Clinton would have arranged his own trips had the Gore-Lieberman schedulers permitted, and either of these small states would have put Gore in the White House regardless of the outcome in Florida. Moving on, the president cited two other socially conservative states—Tennessee and Missouri—where Gore came close (47 percent) despite an avalanche of hostile advertising by the NRA. Clinton would have addressed neglected rural audiences on Gore's behalf. Who among you, he would ask, has missed a single day's hunting on account of our measures to keep guns from criminals and kids? Straight talk works, but you have to challenge the NRA's shameless lies. Gore simply conceded the gun vote to Bush.

"I think you made a mistake not to use me more in the last ten days," Clinton told Gore, "but otherwise that was not a big deal. I was much more upset about your message, now that we're being honest."

His quarrel was that Gore's message was not suited to win. He said Gore won all the little issues and none of the big ones. You did not rise to any themes, he said. You did not run on the environment or the future. You let Bush get away with saying we had squandered our eight years. Your populist attacks on privilege were negative. They implied disingenuously that a sitting vice president was a stranger to power, and they played into Bush's claim that the administration caused all this terrible division. Above all, Gore's message did not work. The president cared less how he was portrayed. To gain votes, he would let Gore cut off his ear and mail it to reporter Michael Isikoff of *Newsweek,* the Monica Lewinsky expert.

Gore fought back. He said Clinton's drag plagued every direction. Consistently, if Gore envisioned the future, the voters in Greenberg's focus groups objected that he was trying to escape from Clinton. If he touted the Clinton-Gore achievements, they recoiled from Clinton's scandalous shadow. The populist theme was Gore's best independent option. Nonsense, Clinton told him. Good candidates connect their record with a prescription for the future. They present choices to the electorate, and voters knew how to separate Gore from Clinton personally. Gore had a record that inclined nearly 60 percent of the electorate to be for him at the start, but he ran away from it. The president became exercised over the recollection of his summary. Gore was an unparalleled vice president, he told him. Gore was better at governance than Clinton, and Gore would have been better for the country than Bush. But he had blind spots in politics. If he could not run his own campaign, he would have done better to heed Clinton's advice. The president kept telling me their confrontation was surreal. The whole world thinks Gore ran a poor campaign from a strong hand. Yet Gore thinks he had a weak hand because of Clinton, and ran a valiant campaign against impossible odds.

The president took a breath and told me he expected everything to settle. He and Gore still agreed on most things. Then he said Gore had raised a fresh grievance. As long as they were at it, he wanted Clinton to know that the Buddhist temple fund-raising scandal had been the worst experience of his life. No one had ever questioned his personal integrity, but corrosive publicity and whispers had tormented him now for over four years. Gore said he had not been disposed to blame Clinton. However, he remembered telling the president that he found himself the only English-speaking person at one of those Asian fund-raisers. And the president was in charge of the party apparatus that was supposed to screen all the donations for trouble. So he did blame Clinton in a way.

The president told me he could scarcely believe the ensuing tales of suspicion. Gore must still be in shock from the election, or unhinged. "I thought he was in Neverland," he said. For a moment, he reviewed with Gore his own outrage over the screening lapses, but he confined himself more to the political ramifications. ("Taylor, I know you care about campaign reform," he remarked, "and that's okay, but it is not a winning issue at the polls.") Relatively few voters consider election finance a burning question, he observed. The media do not report honestly on political revenue—perhaps because of their stake as recipients—to the point of stubbornly obscuring the sharp legislative differences between the two political parties. Therefore, Gore should have left his reform position on the shelf. Instead, he "wore the hair shirt for a week" about how persecution might impede his standing to pass the McCain-Feingold bill, and then he prudently dropped the subject. As a result he got bad publicity both ways, limited mercifully by public boredom. I could not be sure how much of this lecture the president gave Gore, or just to me, but things sounded raw between them.

The vice president asked Clinton about Monica Lewinsky. He had supported Clinton all through the impeachment, publicly and privately, while declaring himself disappointed. Yes, said the president. He appreciated that. However, persisted Gore, Clinton did not confide any personal feelings. He never explained exactly what happened.

There was little to say, Clinton replied, beyond failure and regret. He was humiliated and angry, had made mistakes. He had misled the American people, and he was sorry.

Gore closed his point with emphasis. Well, he said, this is the first time you have apologized to me personally.

Clinton said he did a double take. He had been repeating his public stance, which he meant, but Gore treated the confession as a watershed. Their colliding perspectives made both of them angry. Clinton exploded that Gore's reaction was phony. What was so significant here? Gore was merely revealing himself a creature of Washington and the press, soaked in spin-cycle indignation that Clinton could never apologize earnestly or completely enough. This attitude distorted everything. It probably infected what Gore heard from those focus groups. It skewed politics, demeaned voters, and ignored the public's business. By God, Hillary had a helluva lot more reason to resent Clinton than Gore did, and yet she ran unabashedly on the Clinton-Gore record. With that clarity, she came from 30 points down to win by double digits.

Gore exploded back. He was feeling a stubborn repeat of the defensiveness and delayed honesty that somehow cost the election. Clinton's character was at the root of it. The president admitted shrinking from confessing to the people he knew, but he told Gore he was also glad. If he had talked more, the gossipy spectacle would have become even worse. Democrats would have folded, running Clinton out of office, and Gore would have lost the election anyway.

CLINTON BOUNCED INTO fresh questions, leaving this tension behind. He recalled sitting with Chelsea in the Senate gallery on January 3 to watch Vice President Gore swear Hillary in to office for the 107th Congress. He called it the happiest day of his life except the one when their daughter was born. "Words cannot describe how thrilled I was for her," he said, predicting growth from her stable base, representing New York, to be a catalyst for new ideas and leadership in the Democratic Party. Abruptly, the president turned clinical about the release of Nawaz Sharif in Pakistan. Clinton's pleas for clemency had very little effect, he thought. More likely the general, Pervez Musharraf, found it too much of a headache to have the elected prime minister in jail, and Sharif preferred exile to constant anxiety about whether Musharraf might order him killed. On the U.S. economy, the president conceded a downturn in the major indicators. He said 5 percent growth could not continue forever. The Dow had slipped down toward 10,000, and Greenspan wisely lowered interest rates. He hoped the Bush people would stop talking up a recession. Whether their purpose was to inoculate themselves from responsibility, or to justify their big tax cut, he said they were playing a dangerous game.

When the topics slowed down, I ventured a defense to his passing barb on campaign finance. To me, our sporadic national debate featured ample sanctimony for and against money in politics, but work was scarce on the hard questions of fairness in free elections. My thought came out garbled, and President Clinton tacked elsewhere. He yearned for a competitive system that would restore sanity and normalcy for politicians. Candidates from both parties spent all their waking hours chasing money. They had no choice. Last year, though not on any ballot, Clinton said he attended 180 events "to get up the money" for others. This was grueling enough with a big staff and the convenience of living "right over the store" in the White House. Other incumbent officials, while nominally responsible for the country, traveled constantly in search of campaign funds, and challengers seldom had a political conversation that did not involve money. It was a sacrifice for them to read a book, and almost impossible for them to sit still. Clinton said you can feel the harmful effects. Human nature drove candidates to seek efficiencies and shortcuts by catering to big money. This required callousness over time, even meanness. It was difficult enough to survive. It was hard to keep sight of public purpose, although he insisted that most politicians tried. His voice caught. And it was so very hard to be progressive and win.

I asked what the president planned to do on inauguration day, a week from Saturday. Well, he was going to ride up there with Bush, listen to his speech, take his last flight on Air Force One to JFK Airport, greet whoever met him there with Hillary, drive to Chappaqua, and start puttering and putting things away. The next Monday, he was scheduled to sign with a lecture agency, and he would start working on his book contract. For the next three years, he would divide his time in half between moneymaking projects and the start-up for his library and foundation. He had roughly $14 million in Whitewater debts, counting the legal bills for all his aides subpoenaed by Ken Starr. After that, once Hillary and Chelsea were provided for, he wanted to spend whatever years he had left in public service—concentrating overseas. Jimmy Carter had been a model ex-president, working mostly on election monitoring and human rights, plus the eradication of strategically chosen diseases. He gave a capsule summary of Carter's success against river blindness, a parasitic affliction transmitted by tiny blackflies in Africa and South America. Clinton believed he could do such things on a global scale, too, being a two-term president with connections to find the money.

Already, he tried out one name: the Global Anti-Poverty Initiative. He imagined painstaking collaborations in governance and development. He wanted to begin institutions. Whatever he did, said the president, he would do it intensely because the men in his family were not long-lived.

That would be a start, I teased, rewinding the tapes. He pulled more CDs from boxes to sort them by categories on the floor, and occasionally tried to palm off extras on me. I was grateful for one collector's item of songs written by a fabled team from the 1950s: *Elvis Presley Sings Leiber & Stoller*. Standing to leave, I took a breath to raise a personal regret, or misgiving, at the end of our long effort. Especially in these last few years, I said, I had never offered reaction or counsel about his dealings with Lewinsky, or even his relations with Hillary. I was squeamish about prying, and on tenterhooks about getting such conversations tangled up with his secret project. Still, I debated whether a friend should offer to listen. He was holding so much inside.

"No," he said firmly. "You did fine. You did what was right and what was necessary." After choking off this approach, he lingered beside me down the hall on my departure to stand sentry at his elevator door. Maybe we would have one more session, he said. I was running through a checklist. Did he have a trustworthy technician who could digitize and preserve all his tapes before they began to deteriorate? Transcription would take months, and he could get somebody started on that while he made arrangements to begin his memoirs. We touched again on choices for structure and theme. On his library, I reported a good bit of early infighting about who would collect oral histories about his life and administration. This was important. The Nixon and Reagan libraries had waited too long. Carter and Bush were trying to catch up after many important officials were dead. He perked up to hear charges of dereliction at other libraries. I recommended a dual collection team: one from the University of Arkansas, another from the Miller Center at the University of Virginia. The former specialized in anecdotal interviews with Arkansas contacts, the latter in policy reviews with cabinet types. He needed both. There could be competitive synergy if neither won an exclusive.

He was nodding when he summoned the elevator. I sensed resolve on the library and a filter on the other housekeeping. We blubbered a bit in hugs. He called our sessions a great service. They had allowed him to blow off steam and reflect beyond the present. I thanked him for a treasured experience. He said these eight years had been wonderful, and wished they could have been even better. There was an undertone of finality mixed with regret. I told him he had laid more groundwork than we could see—for positive national purpose, restored belief in public service, and democratic miracles. This would become evident as the history was digested and understood. The president laughed. "God, I hope so," he said.

I SAW HIM once more in office, on Sunday, January 14, when Christy and I stayed overnight for one of the farewell parties at Camp David. Our guestbook in Dogwood Cabin registered prior thank-you notes from Prime Minister Barak last summer on back to Anwar Sadat during the Carter years, along with plenty of signatures by Henry Kissinger and President Nixon's eccentric friend Bebe Rebozo. We bowled with some of the forty staff and friends at Shangri-La Lanes, joining everyone upstairs before supper in the commons. The president and Hillary strolled around, literally taking pictures down from the walls. He drew me aside to express sympathy for a beating I had taken that morning on NBC's *Meet the Press*. My panel about Clinton's legacy looked pretty rough to him. Every time I mentioned public policy, somebody flew into derision about Lewinsky, impeachment, or sordid variations of Whitewater.

Well, I confided, the edge was sharper during commercial breaks. Moderator Tim Russert and other guests traded chatter that Clinton was "off the reservation" already with new girlfriends. "Did they really say that?" he asked. Yes, and when pressed for names and sources, they instead broke out into choruses of a new Clinton theme song, evidently by common knowledge—the pop hit "Who Let the Dogs Out?"—complete with rhythmic pencil taps until the cameras rolled. They shared a casual solidarity of inside secrets, like fist bumpers at a street dance. Clinton shook his head, but I tried to convey a solemn warning along with astonishment. The president said zero on women, making a circle, but he had heard a thing or two about the panelists.

John Podesta drew a standing ovation with his toast after dinner, and Senator Clinton worried out loud that tributes could turn maudlin in a hurry. She touted the camp-style menu of entertainments, ending with a supervised plebiscite on which of two Hollywood films to watch in the Camp David theater. The result came up a tie, naturally, and a "Florida recount" erupted. Lawyers spouted challenges as contestants bartered satirical votes. Above the chaos, with wags begging to take the helicopters up for a ride, Hillary shouted an edict to begin with *Finding Forrester* because it starred Sean Connery. Levity dispelled any mood for further toasts.

CHAPPAQUA WAS THE first stop past Pleasantville, an hour by train from Grand Central Terminal in New York. A suburban village had grown up around the Clintons' old farmhouse, secluded behind trees at a dead end. Secret Service agents bunked downstairs in the small barn, pending renovations of its unfinished second floor. Inside the main house, where a country kitchen opened to a broad living area that reminded me of Camp David's Aspen Lodge, the ex-president introduced me to his naval aide, Oscar Flores. He excused packing boxes here and there. Almost seven weeks after leaving the White House, Clinton padded around these days with Oscar and Buddy the Labrador, still putting things in order.

Familiar photographs lined the way upstairs. One turn at the landing led to my guest room, next to an empty one stacked with Chelsea's things. The opposite way passed Hillary's little office—with the only computer in the house—and a room for her mother. Another picture-filled corridor resembled the passageway up to the Solarium, angling toward the master bathroom. Clinton savored this detail, but he said their clincher for the house was a bedroom on the other side, newly built above the living room, with a ceiling that soared nearly three stories to tilted skylights and views of treetops. New yellow wallpaper matched their pattern from the White House, airy with flowers and boughs. Hillary did like to wake up here, he declared, but the Senate schedule made it rare to have her more than one or two nights a week.

He pointed out several oddities downstairs. There was no fireplace in the main area. The powder room, with a giant shower twelve feet square, would become the makeshift summer clubhouse for a swimming pool in the small yard. It was covered now with canvas and a March snowfall. There was more, but he activated a two-car convoy for dinner in Chappaqua. While boasting of his new driver's license, right there in his pocket, the president admitted no chance yet to take the wheel. Our Secret Service escort shuddered when asked about the prospect. He guessed dryly how much paperwork a solo spin by Clinton would generate. The president was philosophical about his restrictions so far. He said the Secret Service refused to let him ride the train to his office in Harlem, which was not yet ready, because the track would make him too captive and predictable a target. Still, his protective detail was discreet. Once we stepped from the car, he and I walked without a reservation into a little French bistro, and my untrained eye saw no one behind us. We were seated without fuss. Much to my surprise, the only visitor to our table ignored the president and welcomed me briskly to Chappaqua. Could this be normal?

The president, looking around, said he knew a lot of the people here, and they were pretty good about giving him space. Some of them may talk to him after dinner. He leaned forward in confidence. The woman who just greeted me had propositioned him almost his first day here. She also propositioned Hillary, and Chelsea, saying she liked girls, too. She wrote them all a disturbed, pornographic letter about family massage as the key to life. He gave the letter to the Secret Service, and the experts who interviewed her confirmed signs that she had been severely abused. She was volatile but doing better. I leaned back, nonplussed. It felt really exposed out here. My reaction amused Clinton. During our times together, he said, I had been more cooped up in the White House than he was. I was too sheltered.

What changes surprised him out of office? He had expected to play golf all the time, but found himself not wanting to. Golf, he realized, had been a relief from the presidential schedule. Now he needed more mental input, not less, so he read extra books. This week he was going beyond histories and mysteries to try some American Indian spiritual wisdom, *The Four Agreements*, by Don Miguel Ruiz. Another thing new was money. He had earned more in the last month than previously in his entire life. They were throwing it at him from everywhere, and he would pay off his debts soon. A bigger surprise was politics. He always assumed he would miss the White House like a constant toothache, but he did not. He was weary of its problems and glad to be liberated, with one exception. He had been studying these massive power outages in California. They were very complex, but it was basically a case of deregulation wretchedly done. "I could fix that," he said, slipping into talk of interlocking grids and overtaxed spot markets until I asked him to save the politics for our taping session. He paid our dinner bill with cash. I said I could not remember seeing him with a wallet.

Incoming phone calls interrupted our start back on his kitchen table. I let the recorders preserve his end of several conversations. Hillary had done well in a legislative markup meeting today, Senator Chris Dodd reported, but the Republicans were trying to cheat her on office space. She had taken Pat Moynihan's old suite, which nobody wanted, and now Majority Leader Lott was maneuvering to detach from Hillary several of the extra rooms Moynihan had commandeered over his four terms. Annoyed, the president reviewed her tactical options with Dodd. Clearly, Lott had the upper hand. Clinton told me the Senate was famous for its titanic struggles over staff budgets, cubbyholes, and even the spare furniture. It was petty in the extreme but thankfully hidden from sight. His exit from the presidency, by contrast, had spawned an orgy of public pettiness.

Clinton's account was spirited and brief. He had stayed up most of his final night in the White House. After the ceremony for Bush, somebody broke a champagne glass aboard Air Force One, scattering shards that made the goodbye cake inedible, which was just as well because he was so tired that he dozed on the short flight to New York. An overnight news storm alleged that the administration had stooped to unbridled mischief on its way out the door. His people had vandalized the White House and torn up Air Force One. The Clintons made off with stolen treasure, and Clinton was refusing to surrender the spotlight out of peevish disrespect for President Bush. Lastly, he had pardoned unpardonable criminals in corrupt deals. The Bush people planted every one of these stories, he said. "And the press just wolfed them down."

A few weeks later, President Bush himself retracted the vandalism and theft charges, telling reporters his people may have gotten carried away. With a trace of admiration, Clinton said Bush passed off a good-natured prank as though he deserved credit for admitting it forthrightly. By then the scandalized uproar had served a purpose that left Clinton stewing.

He compared the bookend ambushes of his presidency. That first White House morning had yanked him into front-page uproar over gays in the military, and the first day at Chappaqua branded him a scofflaw ex-president. What could this extraordinary recurrence mean? My pet theories were drawn to the path-setting tempest from 1993, in part because of its nuances for journalism. Clinton always attributed the original gays-in-the-military leak to one of his young, inexperienced staff aides. To me, the story was more likely engineered by a reporter who picked the most explosive campaign promise among hundreds, then shopped for a sucker to confirm that the president intended to fulfill them all. This interpretation raised the question why Clinton had allowed the press to set his agenda. Had he failed a test of will at the start? Could he have ordered his own priorities? Did he lack an authoritarian streak to control the press?

Clinton deflected these questions. He was fixated on the pardons from his last day in office. The press had gone ballistic. Stories went so far as to raise arguments for a retroactive impeachment. Admitting self-pity, Clinton described his decision to commute the sentences of four Hasidic rabbis convicted for stealing school funds in New York. He discussed in greater detail his pardon for Marc Rich, a billionaire fugitive indicted for tax schemes to route oil imports illegally through foreign countries, including Iran. The president mentioned at least twenty people involved. Prime Minister Barak of Israel lobbied for the pardon three times, along with Miles Lerman from the Holocaust Museum. Many prosecutors and half his advisers weighed in on the other side. He said his biggest mistake was failing to get key Republicans to put their balanced assessments in writing. Rich had lived luxuriously for two decades in Switzerland, beyond reach of extradition. The racketeering statute used for his criminal indictment had been discredited and abandoned for such cases. Other oil importers contested similar civil tax disputes with mixed results. In the end, Clinton said he decided to make a criminal pardon conditional on a signed waiver by Rich of procedural defenses that might otherwise be interposed against civil prosecution for tax fraud. This route gave the government at least a chance to make the taxpayers whole.

He lamented that no one paid the slightest attention to his reasoning. They simply ascribed corrupt motives and shaped facts to their outrage. They said you don't pardon fugitives, ignoring all the draft evaders spared under Carter's amnesty. They said you don't pardon unfinished cases, forgetting Ford's preemptive pardon for Nixon in Watergate, among others. They said Rich was a bad guy, as was nearly every applicant. They said Clinton had a conflict because Rich's ex-wife was a donor to his library. Lord have mercy, he cried, Papa Bush pardoned Caspar Weinberger and others before the Iran-contra prosecutions may have targeted Bush himself. Nobody fussed. They said Clinton failed to follow established precedents for review, but the pardon belongs exclusively to the president. It is the most arbitrary power in the Constitution, without checks or balances. Yet here poured the passion so woefully absent for the vital processes of government, where public information could make a difference.

It was an unchecked stampede, he said, and Democrats piled on. Helpless in Chappaqua, Clinton sent a private letter to his former commerce secretary, Bill Daley of Chicago, rebuking him for public statements that the president had sold the Rich pardon. You know me better than that, he wrote. Clinton had never cared about money, and it was the last thing he had to worry about now. What a slander to presume he would turn crook in a fishbowl, with Hillary going into the Senate, and shame on Daley for fostering the lie.

In light of these troubles, did he regret the closing statement in his farewell address to the nation—that he was leaving office more idealistic than ever? He answered without pause. "Absolutely not," said Clinton. "I still believe that." That was a judgment about the country as a whole. Look at the symptoms. Six weeks of unremitting character assassination had dented his approval rating only slightly with citizens at large. People still responded to substance. Often they could frame responsible alternatives to cynicism and fear on their own. In that sense, he remained more optimistic than when he took office. The voters could address situations that might seem hopeless, and accomplish very difficult tasks.

·   ·   ·

IT WAS LATE. He was drinking hot tea for a cold, and we trotted to the end. In Congo, President Laurent Kabila's murder by bodyguards came so close to the inauguration that the president's information was sketchy. Had I read *King Leopold's Ghost,* by Adam Hochschild? Its compelling account made you wonder how that region in Africa could repair the damage done by Leopold of Belgium long ago.

Yes, there had been considerable infighting over his farewell speech. Aides pressured him to boil down his parting recommendations from three to one. They said the most memorable admonitions were singular, like Eisenhower's warning about the military-industrial complex, but Clinton said he insisted on three. They were distinct to him, and almost equally important in the cause of freedom. The address was very short. First, keep paying down the national debt for discipline and relief. Second, maintain global involvement for peace and prosperity. Third, pursue the more perfect union of race and culture.

Robert Ray, the Whitewater special prosecutor, came to the White House on Clinton's last full day in office. The president said he received him in the Map Room downstairs and listened, per instructions from David Kendall, without saying a word. He found Ray not nearly as unpleasant and partisan as his predecessor, Ken Starr, yet clearly hoping "to get something out of my hide" before Clinton left town. The president was eager to finish things, too. Ray proposed sanctions only as an intermediary for the Arkansas Bar Association, whose disciplinary board wanted Clinton to accept the suspension of his law privileges for five years. On Whitewater, after more than seven years, Ray brought no charges, required no admissions, made no adverse findings, and alleged no misstatements by Clinton in any sworn testimony, which had been the whole basis for impeachment. The president called it irksome that no major news outlets bothered to note this glaring result, but he was happy to sign Ray's final settlement.

My efforts failed to elicit much about the inauguration day itself. He said Gore was miserable, of course, and the Bushes were perfectly civil. With some prodding, he added that President-elect Bush was upset to see demonstrators outside their limo on the drive to Capitol Hill. From the aftermath, nothing engaged Clinton until I asked whether he hoped to speak at Oxford University in May. Yes, he did, especially because

Chelsea may be going there for graduate school next fall, which reminded him that she had been one of twelve Stanford students recommended for a Rhodes Scholarship. That saga put him and Hillary
through a wringer. Chelsea dashed their joy with firm but reticent notice
that she did not intend to apply. They were mystified and disturbed
until the three of them could meet. Was there something wrong? No.
Was she afraid she might be turned down? No. Was she afraid she might
be presumed to win because of her parents? No. Did she want to go to
Oxford? Yes. Then why not apply for the Rhodes? Well, the scholarship
had changed his life forever, and theirs indirectly, but Chelsea already
had lived in the White House and traveled the world. She decided to
leave such possibility for someone else. Her parents were touched but
chagrined. "I underestimated my daughter," said the president.

It was quite a leap from there to Ariel Sharon, but the president had
underestimated him, too. Only in Israel, he said, could a major politician precipitate a riot in the middle of peace negotiations, touch off four
months of deadly violence, undermine his government, and wind up
causing voters to elect the man who started the trouble. Clinton called
to congratulate Prime Minister Sharon for his victory. He said Sharon
bluntly acknowledged their fierce differences over the years, but kindly
observed that no U.S. leader had immersed himself so completely in the
details of Israeli security, which Sharon appreciated, and therefore he
asked Clinton's advice about what to do now with the Palestinians.

There was not much to say. Sharon already knew Clinton was angry
with Arafat. He could tell Arafat that he would never get a better deal
than the one he turned down, but Sharon had no desire to go near such
terms again. The best Clinton could recommend was for Sharon to consider a partial, experimental settlement, to see if the benefits of state institutions might grow in the cross fire of Palestinian politics.

The Sharon call was pro forma. Clinton was thinking constantly
about the defeated prime minister, Ehud Barak. He was a good man, still
potentially historic or tragic for the Middle East. The president still
ached from all the imagination bottled up and stowed since that last
agonizing failure in December. He thought Barak misplayed it. Who
could say for sure, because the signals were so coded and circumscribed
on all three sides? Still, those last terms presented by Clinton should

have made Barak say no. They were too hard for Israel. They went too far on the territories and Jerusalem. Then perhaps Arafat could say yes to the terms that had made Israel balk. Only then might Barak have closed the deal by changing his mind. The shift would have exposed him politically in Israel as a waffler on top of everything else. And maybe Israeli voters would have rejected both the peace treaty and Barak in favor of Sharon. But what a race to have run. There had never been a campaign that weighed the possible reverberations of an actual peace.

Barak said yes too fast, Clinton feared. He had nothing left to give, and Arafat's instinct when offered 100 percent was to demand 120. Otherwise, Arafat feared ridicule or worse among Arabs as a "me, too" convert to the Israeli position. Beware the stateless exile, with an extra layer of insecurity. The president said this was the lesson still eating at him. In all their pirouettes, they should have found a way to let the head of a functioning state make the last concession, or look like it, anyway. He was still thinking of Barak.

Hillary called from their new home in Washington. He mentioned the markup session with Senator Dodd but not the skirmish over office space. They discussed arrangements for the weekend and whether they could stay together at the Waldorf. Apparently, there was a story in today's *Times* about her brother Hugh Rodham.

We went upstairs to Hillary's little office. The president dropped tonight's cassettes into two large boxes with all the others. I advised him to store one set in a safe-deposit box, in case of fire or theft. As requested, I delivered a computer disk and printouts of all the daily chronologies compiled for our sessions. He said they would be handy for his memoirs. You would not believe the offers coming in. Here was a letter from a presidential ghostwriter who lived by coincidence in Chappaqua. Clinton was still at sea about structure, editors, ghostwriters, and researchers. I thought he should assemble researchers first. They could gather presidential files he may need while supervising the transcription of these tapes, which was a massive chore. He asked separately about his library. Well, Bruce Lindsey had assembled the rival historians from Arkansas and Virginia, who were excellent in different ways. I thought they would cooperate. Good, said the president. He wished they were recording oral histories already. Old-timers with wonderful stories were dying off in Arkansas. They should interview older cabinet members first, such as Lloyd Bentsen. Of the foreigners, he might help with quick access to Helmut Kohl, Kim Dae-jung, and Nelson Mandela.

The kitchen bustled in the morning. Traveling aides had arrived with today's speech draft for Atlantic City, and a small motorcade idled in the driveway. The president, dressed to perform, swallowed a handful of vitamins laid out by Oscar Flores on a napkin. He said he had not felt well even before the early calls. Four or five newspapers were spread across the countertop, all with headlines about a White House summit. South Korea's president, Kim Dae-jung, was in shock, said Clinton. Bush treated him like a novice and a meddler. He did more than rebuff Kim's pleas for the next agreement to bring North Korea out of prickly isolation. He rejected the whole premise of the marathon negotiations. He told Kim that North Korea could not be trusted. It was a primitive dictatorship. Maybe they had not double-crossed us yet, but any pending deals would prove worthless. You had to be firm with these people.

Clinton said this was much worse than expected. Along with the proposal for a massive tax cut, President Bush already had thumbed his nose at two of Clinton's three parting wishes for the country. I asked a leading question. Did he think the new president aimed merely to distinguish himself from Clinton's foreign policy? Or was Bush bad enough to scuttle the whole Korea program in order to justify the missile defense system he had advocated in the campaign? The president shook his head slowly. "I'm afraid he's that bad," he said slowly. Then he qualified himself. He was not sure about the missile system. But he felt sure of Bush's strong preference to rally against a villain. Bush was uncomfortable with foraging, creative, institutional leadership. He wanted to point out the bad guys and lead a charge. "There are not many places in the world where that kind of leadership is going to work," said Clinton. "Including Iraq, where I know he wants to take on Saddam Hussein."

He was late for the plane. Aides pulled him out the door.

NEARLY THREE YEARS later, the president invited me back to Chappaqua on a confidential mission. He sequestered me to evaluate the first seven hundred pages of his book manuscript, and I read through the night in a changed world. A smoldering insurgency pinned down 120,000 U.S.

troops after the victorious invasion of Iraq. The overthrown dictator, Saddam Hussein, was headed for the gallows after recent capture in a "spider hole," and the terrorist attacks of September 2001 had rattled even my meetings with presidential archivists and historians. President Bush had effectively revoked the Presidential Records Act of 1978, declaring its provisions for disclosure an infringement of his inherent powers as commander in chief. Henceforth, by executive order, no presidential documents from any era could be released without his explicit consent. Historians bemoaned an indifference to constitutional questions. Did the Supreme Court not care that Bush plainly usurped its role? Did Congress notice that he repealed a statute by fiat? What could we do?

Long after midnight at Chappaqua, when I came to the end of page seven hundred, Clinton was finishing the 1992 presidential campaign. The White House memoir had not yet begun. What happened? Highly agitated, I could barely sleep, but the president was up ahead of me at dawn. I blurted my summary. All I read of his early life was compelling. The voice was clearly his. There was abundant wisdom and humor without a ponderous moment. I had notes of minor suggestions and questions, but this was an achievement so far. Where was the rest?

Well, he was working on the next chapter. My heart sank. Mr. President, they have announced your book for Father's Day in June. This is the end of February. You can't write your whole presidency in a month or two. That's impossible. Well, he would try. He had worked all night in the barn, in fact, and he would get back out there after a nap. I stared in disbelief. He looked dead serious. I saw only two rational choices. He could demand more time, or he could split his book into two volumes.

He said the publisher wouldn't let him. He had a deadline, and they would sue him. No, they won't, I said. They could make more money on two books. And to hell with them if they did sue. You are President of the United States. Say what you want and let the business people adjust. To rush your worldwide chance for these memoirs is insane. It's a waste. I went on for some time in spasms of desperation.

Clinton stared at me, commanding a pause. "Would you say all that to Hillary?" he asked. I laughed in spite of my state. Of course I would. She would be home soon. Perhaps to calm me down, he showed me the barn where a haggard aide, Justin Cooper, was typing Clinton's hand-written overnight draft from a legal pad. The transcripts from our White House interviews filled a whole shelf in neatly bound volumes. He said they were amazing. I contemplated their girth numbly, having never seen them before. To accomplish his goal, Clinton needed to digest and cover about six months a week.

This thought subdued me. Clinton seemed determined to carry a staggering burden. He was mysteriously resigned. Should I make it any harder? We went over his manuscript for a breather, making little changes. Strangely, I became more careful with him. It would be wonderful, I said, if he could sustain this quality of thought and observation through the White House years. Sympathy and frustration haunted my train ride home. There was lost opportunity in those tapes, but whose loss would it be?

IN JULY, THE president invited me to celebrate the publication of his book at their home in Washington. I found him alone in the dining room, signing copies of *My Life* on the dining room table. He asked me to sit down and spoke to me quite sternly. "I have something for you," he said, "and you'll really hurt my feelings if you don't take it." He handed me an envelope with a check for $50,000. I was speechless. Clinton continued like a runaway train. "Now, I'm giving out bonuses to everybody who was involved in the book, and there couldn't have been a book without you. I couldn't get you to ghostwrite for me. You've turned down money, but I want you to have this. I'm the same person I was when you and I were in Texas together and neither one of us had a pot to piss in. And you've spent all this time writing about Martin Luther King, and sometimes I wish I had done that myself. But you *still* don't have a pot to piss in. I've never had any money, and now I do, and frankly the only reason I want some is to share it with people who are my friends and are doing good."

I said I was overwhelmed. My only hesitation was that I had gotten all wrapped up in this project as a public service, keeping it secret, and being a friend to a president. I did need the money, thank you, but this made my present for him look piddly.

He took a music CD. "What's this?" he asked. It was a custom mix of two singers I liked, Eva Cassidy and Keb' Mo', marked "Engineer: Franklin," because I did not know how to burn a disk. Clinton smiled. He wanted to give Franklin a putter.

The president turned serious again. He said he knew I wanted to write about the taping sessions from my own memories and notes. He hoped I would one day. But this was already three and a half years later. There had never been any expectation of payment, he said, and this bonus would not affect the integrity of anything I wrote.

This moment hung. He had lived the politics. How we wrestled with the history was up to the rest of us.

AFTERWORD

This book sits somewhere between politics, journalism, and history. It consists mostly of paraphrase resting on memory—paraphrases of President Clinton's contemporary voice on countless subjects, drawn from memories dictated on my drives home to Baltimore. The verbatim quotations indicate confidence in my notes about striking presidential phrases and expressions from each session. They are roughly equivalent to the quotations a reporter might use in a story written after an interview. I could not verify the quotations against his actual words, of course, because Bill Clinton alone possesses the tapes and transcripts of our interviews. Whenever he decides to open them for public research, I will be exceedingly curious about my own accuracy, being accountable for a faithful record.

In the final chapter, I quote Clinton telling me with passion that he sometimes wished he had pursued a career like mine, writing books. Surely, this was rhetorical. He loves politics, and few people have been more suited to the profession. Yet I believe his comment was sincere. Clinton is devoted to history as well. He initiated what became our project with astonishing foresight, before taking office. He endured hardships to compile a record for posterity, and we talked often of plans to incorporate them in his autobiography. Indeed, Clinton had been so steadfastly eager to enter the published reckoning that his sudden switch flabbergasted me at Chappaqua. I could scarcely believe his intention to address an entire two-term presidency within a writing span of three months. He seemed strangely passive in the face of my pleadings that this schedule would shortchange his own skills and preparations.

Not for months did it occur to me that President Clinton may have

constrained himself deliberately, leaving just enough time for a cursory
sprint through a White House past that still consumed his active mind.
To open the interpretive fray would refight all his battles on different,
adverse ground. He moved on to a new life ahead. I did not fully understand his motives. He never said he was entrusting the secrets and sub-
texts of his tapes to me, or to other writers, but that may have been the
import of the rare, uncomfortable silences in our argument.

I wanted to introduce these tapes into public debate for special reasons, and often reminded him in the White House why we had parted
ways after the 1972 presidential campaign. Elective politics disillusioned
me after our youthful awakening in the early 1960s. The country sank
into recrimination through many years of the Vietnam War, until, with
great issues at stake, our latest candidate was trounced while we refereed
petty squabbles among Texas politicians. I swore off political work in
favor of journalism, seeking greater integrity and potential in the written
word. Not surprisingly, Clinton remembered not only my old pronouncements but also his defense of politics: "If you want to solve the
world's big problems, you have to start with fights over who rides first in
the motorcade." He said your purpose must be strong enough to work
through human nature, not around it. In Texas, I thought he was ratio-
nalizing his ambition to run for Congress. In the White House, to my
mortification, I found him consistently more candid and idealistic than
my colleagues covering him for the press.

Whose poses were cheap and self-serving? There is ample grist for
that question in these pages, but here is not the place to explain or resolve the gulf between President Clinton and the political culture of his
eight years. Permit me instead a note for the future. The landscape of
information has shifted since he left office. Almost certainly, electronic
audiences will fragment as they multiply, and more shrunken newspapers will disappear. As news sources evolve, each person faces a greater
challenge to acquire reliable information to function properly in the
world. Free government was a test of public education from the beginning, considered impossible for many centuries, and political economy
has become far more complicated since the founders designed our experiment. Hard civic questions abound for professors and everyone else.
Democratic norms cannot be taken for granted. Facile slogans of con-

sumer politics will fall short, and the burden of good citizenship will grow. In this context, American history is a vital foundation.

Clinton's tapes are a resource yet to be measured, like the telephone recordings still being released from his Cold War predecessors. Future scholars and specialists will find useful—often essential—the president's exact words on many details that escaped my summary dictation. This book is a preview in close witness. Its format is distinct from a history, which strives to base compelling narrative and balanced judgment on evidence from wide-ranging, comprehensive sources. I did not try to evaluate Clinton's version of complex events, and this first-person presentation makes me a participant in a memoir, not a history, gathering testimony from one central actor in American politics—Bill Clinton. His stories enjoy the benefits of privacy, immediacy, and control, but not hindsight. They are revealing but not conclusive. If they jar perceptions of Clinton or his presidency, healthy debate among citizens can repair mistakes and dispel even durable myths.

ACKNOWLEDGMENTS

I began with a bucketful of microcassettes, each one marked "Clinton Contacts" by number and stored in a safe-deposit box at our Baltimore bank. These dictation tapes were born of compulsive respect for firsthand presidential memories, which became ingrained over several decades of research on presidents from the 1950s and 1960s. The earliest cassettes described my reacquaintance with President-elect Clinton in 1992, but most of them contained notes dictated after the seventy-nine oral histories taped through the Clinton presidency, 1993 to 2001.

Each of these sessions started with an invitation by phone from Nancy Hernreich, director of Oval Office Operations, or from her assistant, Kelly Crawford, who was succeeded by Rebecca Cameron and Mary Morrison. The four of them guided me through the clearance procedures into the White House residence, which could be unnerving. Over time, Nancy's efficient service to President Clinton felt to me like a sponsoring shield for the confidential interviews. I am grateful also to employees from the household staff—chiefly the ushers, doormen, and butlers—who tended our meetings at the president's direction. Many are named in the text, but I thank others who served anonymously.

After President Clinton left office, archivists at the University of North Carolina–Chapel Hill transferred my aging cassette tapes onto digital CDs for protection and preservation. Steve Weiss and Abbey Thompson completed the job skillfully. Tim West, director of the Southern Historical Collection at UNC's Wilson Library, also supervised the receipt and processing of papers gathered since 1982 for my civil rights trilogy. That larger collection was opened to researchers in 2006. By mutual agreement, beginning in January 2010, the Southern Historical Collection at Chapel Hill will make available all sources used for *The Clinton Tapes*. These additions will include my dictation tapes and transcripts, plus memos, files, clippings, and related documents. I am indebted to Tim West, his staff, and the leadership of my alma mater for preserving access to these materials.

In 2006, editor Alice Mayhew helped turn my experience with President Clinton into the conceptual design for a book. For more than thirty years now, my literary efforts have begun and ended with Alice. She is rightly a legend among nonfiction editors in her time, and, if pressed, she does not deny involvement with my lone work of fiction in 1981. I will always treasure her as a friend and professional anchor.

My literary agent, Liz Darhansoff, endured many crises with her usual aplomb, but for once she did not have to negotiate a contract extension. I am pleased to wear a hat from her Maine golf club in the photo section. Her partner, Chuck Verrill, helped us reach a new business agreement with Alice and the principal executives at Simon & Schuster, Carolyn Reidy and David Rosenthal. We have worked together in the past. I value their judgment, and try hard to justify their confidence.

Once under way, this book project relied heavily on Martha Healy to transcribe the voluminous dictation tapes. We had met years ago at the University of Virginia's Presidential Recordings Project, and she came to transcribe many of President Lyndon Johnson's White House telephone conversations for my research toward *At Canaan's Edge*. An avid believer in presidential recordings, Martha again proved a cheerful whirlwind with her earphones, foot pedal, and keyboard, making my Clinton tapes usable on paper.

For technical support in the computer age, I have been heavily dependent on Dan Hartman and his staff at Discount Computer Service in Baltimore. To check President Clinton's references to public statements and events, I relied on the American Presidency Project Web site from the University of California at Santa Barbara, www.presidency .ucsb.edu, a valuable public resource created by John Woolley and Gerhard Peters. As the manuscript progressed, I received courteous help with identifications and illustrations from the following people at the Clinton Library and foundation in Little Rock: Racheal Carter, John Keller, Bruce Lindsey, and Stephanie Streett.

Alice Mayhew guided the book to completion at Simon & Schuster. I am thankful to her colleague Roger Labrie for his productive grace under pressure. Two dedicated professionals, Fred Chase and Jonathan Evans, actually went on the road to refine my language in these pages, and I appreciate them for turning labor into fellowship. My thanks go in mass to many unseen publishing employees and contractors who helped make this book a reality, but I want to acknowledge the able contributions of several I have come to know: Marcella Berger, Joshua Cohen, Marie Florio, Douglas Johnson, Irene Kheradi, Victoria Meyer, Julia Prosser, Elisa Rivlin, Jackie Seow, Elisha Shokoff, Gypsy da Silva, Karen Thompson, and Alexis Welby.

Two Baltimore friends, Lisa Moore and Mary Jane Williams, gamely read the manuscript for clunkers. They offered all too many helpful warnings, despite tight deadlines, leaving me indebted to them for repairs.

In Washington, former deputy secretary of state Strobe Talbott read the finished proofs. Under restrictions of confidentiality, in the most difficult personal circumstances, Strobe evaluated potential dangers across the board, from hazards of state to injurious mistakes between two longtime friends, Bill Clinton and myself. His mission was to warn of hidden land mines, but he advanced many other ideas to improve the book. I am very grateful. Because of our respective roles and associations, the author's cliché on responsibility applies with extra force. Strobe deserves credit, but any errors and impropriety belong wholly to me.

While President Clinton held office, the secrecy required for his tapes project affected my immediate family. I was often called away on short notice. Our children, Macy and Franklin, watched me struggle to be discreet around friends and neighbors without telling lies. I am grateful to them for understanding and love. To Christy, who endured also the later torment of being around me through a hard writing schedule, I give public thanks in addition to all the bonds between us.

Finally, I want to thank the three Clintons. They treated me like family when the White House was their home. Now, after an interval of some years, I am presenting glimpses of their family life as indispensable to an accurate portrait of the presidency. That office is a crucible occupied by real people. My goal is to portray a U.S. president candidly in texture. I hope this approach improves public appreciation for the rich history of our politics, which in turn can serve the country. President Clinton certainly believed so. His foresight initiated this project, and he sustained it through many trials. I will always be grateful to him for letting me help.

Baltimore
June 2009

INDEX